A History of Wine
in America

A HISTORY OF WINE IN AMERICA

From the Beginnings to Prohibition

Thomas Pinney

UNIVERSITY
OF
CALIFORNIA
PRESS

Berkeley
Los Angeles
London

University of California Press
Berkeley and Los Angeles, California

University of California Press, Ltd.
London, England

First paperback printing 2007
© 1989 by The Regents of the University of California

LIBRARY OF CONGRESS CATALOGING-IN-PUBLICATION DATA

Pinney, Thomas.
    A history of wine in America from the beginnings to Prohibition.

    Includes index.
    1. Wine and wine making—United States—History.
I. Title.
TP557.P56   1989   663'.2'00973   88-10798
ISBN 978-0-520-25429-9 (pbk : alk.)

Printed in the United States of America
15   14   13   12   11   10   09   08   07
9   8   7   6   5   4   3   2   1

Natures Book contains 50% post-consumer waste and meets the minimum
requirements of ANSI/NISO Z39.48-1992 (R 1997) (*Permanence of Paper*). ∞

To my wife,
Sherrill Ohman Pinney

olim legendum

Contents

PART II. THE ESTABLISHMENT OF AN INDUSTRY

5

6

7

8

PART III. THE DEVELOPMENT OF CALIFORNIA

9

10

Illustrations

Figures

Graphs

Preface

This history is a first attempt to tell the story of grape growing and winemaking in the United States from the beginning and in detail. Now that winegrowing in the United States has succeeded so brilliantly after long years of frustration, and now that it is beginning once again to spread to nearly every state in the union, it seems to me particularly fitting that the many obscure and forgotten people and their work lying behind that success should be brought out into the light. It is also instructive to see how many names celebrated in other connections also belong to the story of American winegrowing, from Captain John Smith onwards. Even more important, a knowledge of the difficulties they faced and of the work they did will help us to understand better the success that has at last been achieved. At any rate, that is the conviction from which this history has been written.

The struggle to make the New World yield wine such as they had known in Europe was begun by the earliest settlers and was persisted in for generations, only to end in defeat over and over again. Few things can have been more eagerly tried and more thoroughly frustrated in American history than the enterprise of growing European varieties of grapes for the making of wine. Not until it was recognized that only the native grape varieties could succeed against the endemic diseases and harsh climate of North America did winemaking have a chance in the eastern part of the country. That recognition came slowly and was made reluctantly. Then, midway through the nineteenth century, the colonization and development of California transformed the situation. In California the European grape flourished, and the state quickly became a bountiful source of wines resembling the familiar European types. At the same time, the development of new hybrid grapes and an accumulating experience in winemaking produced a variety of wines in the diverse conditions of the country outside of California. By the beginning of the twentieth century the growing of grapes and the making of wine across the United States was a proven and important economic activity. The hopes of the first settlers, after nearly three centuries of trial, defeat, and renewed effort, were at last realized. Then came national Prohibition, apparently putting an end to the story at one stroke. Such, in barest outline, is the story that this history fills out in detail.

The choice of the era of national Prohibition as the stopping point of the story was not my original intention, but it came to seem inevitable as I learned more about the subject. There are deep continuities that hold together the history of

American winegrowing before and after Prohibition. But the story since Repeal is distinctly different. The industry faced different problems, had different opportunities, and developed along lines that could not have been foreseen in the pre-Prohibition era. More to the point, the very recentness of the period means that its story could not be told on the same scale that was possible for the years before Prohibition: we know too much about it, and any adequate account of the past fifty years would simply overwhelm the narrative of the beginnings. So the story of American winegrowing since Prohibition will have to be another book.

Perhaps the most striking fact that I have learned in writing this book is how little is known about the subject. There is a history of winegrowing to be written for almost every state in the nation, and frequently there is room for more localized histories as well. For the most part, the work remains undone. I have therefore had to depend all too frequently on my own resources. I sincerely hope that one effect of this book—perhaps the most important one that it can have—is to stimulate others to take up the historical inquiry. The gaps, distortions, misunderstandings, and mistakes of my own work will then be revealed, but the history of an important and fascinating subject will be much better served.

I have not been without the invaluable help of predecessors, however. First among them I would name two distinguished botanists and writers, Liberty Hyde Bailey and Ulysses Prentiss Hedrick. Bailey's *Sketch of the Evolution of Our Native Fruits* (1898) is only a modest item in the vast production of its author, and the section devoted to grapes is only a part of the *Sketch*. Nevertheless, it remains an original and valuable work. It is continued and expanded in Hedrick's misleadingly titled *The Grapes of New York* (1908), a monumental work that takes the whole subject of viticulture in the eastern United States for its province. For California there are far more authorities than for the eastern states, but just for that reason there is no one outstanding figure. The many publications sponsored since Repeal by the Wine Institute are together the single most important source of historical information; they include a long series of detailed and informative articles by Irving McKee, published in the 1940s and 1950s.

Three recent articles of remarkable importance illustrate the kind of fresh and original inquiry that the history of winegrowing in this country so badly needs. All three of them challenge received opinions on key points of that history, and all three demonstrate—conclusively to me—that received opinion has been utterly uninformed and utterly untrustworthy. They are Roy Brady's "The Swallow That Came from Capistrano" (*New West*, 24 September 1979), dating the origin of winegrowing in California; Charles Sullivan's "A Viticultural Mystery Solved" (*California History*, Summer 1978), demolishing the myth of Haraszthy's introduction of the Zinfandel to California; and Francisco Watlington-Linares' "The First American Wine" (*Eastern Grape Grower and Winery News*, October–November 1983), demonstrating the hitherto unrecognized claim of the Spanish on Santa Elena Island to be the first to plant vines in what is now the United States. It is exciting to think of how many comparable points remain to be investigated critically for the first time; the three articles in question set an admirable standard for further such work.

I have been fortunate in having two notable experts read the larger part of this history in draft: Dr. John McGrew, formerly research scientist with the Department of Agriculture and the final authority on eastern American viticulture, and Leon Adams, whose comprehensive *Wines of America* does not begin to exhaust the knowledge of American winegrowing that he has acquired in a lifetime of association with the industry. It goes without saying that they have to do only with such virtues as my book may have and not with its defects.

It would be wrong to conclude the many years of pleasant work that I have spent on this history without at least a summary acknowledgment of the libraries upon whose resources I have largely depended. In England, for the colonial period, the British Library and the Royal Society of Arts yielded a number of interesting finds; as in this country, for the national period, did the American Philosophical Society, the Library of Congress, the National Agricultural Library, and the Kansas State Historical Society. In California, the Bancroft Library of the University of California and the Special Collections of the Library of the California State University, Fresno, were of particular value; I would like to single out Ron Mahoney of Fresno State for the freedom he generously allowed me to ransack the shelves of the library's rich collection, originally formed by Roy Brady and greatly extended under Mahoney's direction.

Beyond all of these excellent libraries, I have depended on the Huntington Library's splendid collection of American history to provide the information out of which this narrative has been constructed. It is people rather than institutions who ought to receive dedications, but if this book were to be dedicated to an institution, it would have to be to the Huntington.

Finally, I should like to make grateful acknowledgment to a writer personally unknown to me, Philip Wagner. For more than fifty years he has been writing gracefully, originally, and authoritatively about American wines and vines, and no one else now living can have done so much through his writings to foster an intelligent interest in wine among Americans.

FROM THE DISCOVERY
TO THE REVOLUTION

1

The Beginnings, 1000-1700

The history of the vine in America begins, symbolically at least, in the fogs that shroud the medieval Norsemen's explorations. Every American knows the story of Leif Ericsson, and how, in A.D. 1001, he sailed from Greenland to the unknown country to the west. The story, however, is not at all clear. Historians disagree as to what the records of this voyage actually tell us, since they are saga narratives; they come from a remote era, from a strange language, and are uncritical, indistinct, and contradictory. Most experts, however, will agree that Leif—or someone—reached the new land. There, at least according to one saga, while Leif and his men went exploring in one direction, another member of the company, a German named Tyrker, went off by himself and made the discovery of what he called wineberries—*vinber* in the original Old Norse, translated into English as "grapes."[1] The Norsemen made Tyrker's "grapes" a part of their cargo when they sailed away, and Leif, in honor of this notable part of the country's produce, called the land "Wineland."

As a German, Tyrker claimed to know what he was talking about: "I was born where there is no lack of either grapes or vines," he told Leif. But the latest opinion inclines to the belief that the vines of Leif Ericsson's "Wineland"—most probably the northern coast of Newfoundland[2]—were in fact not grapes at all but the plants of the wild cranberry.[3] Another guess is that what the Vikings named the land for was meadow grass, called archaically *vin* or *vinber,* and misinterpreted by later tellers of the saga.[4] No wild grapes grow in so high a latitude. Though it is powerfully

3

I   A modern rendering of the joyous moment at which Tyrker the German found grapes growing in Vinland. The episode begins the history of wine in America; the questions surrounding it will probably never be satisfactorily answered. (Drawing by Frederick Trench Chapman in Einer Haugen, *Voyages to Vinland* [1942])

tempting to believe that the Vikings really did discover grapes in their Vinland, the evidence is all against them unless we suppose that the climate of the region was significantly warmer then than now. Their name of "Wineland," however, was excellent prophecy. For the continent that they had discovered was in fact a great natural vineyard, where, farther to the south, and from coast to coast, the grape rioted in profusion and variety.

Grapes grow abundantly in many parts of the world: besides the grapes of the classic sites in the Near East and in Europe, there are Chinese grapes, Sudanese grapes, Caribbean grapes. But, though the grape vine is widely tolerant and readily adaptable, it will not grow everywhere, and in some places where it grows vigorously, it still does not grow well for the winemaker's purposes. The main restrictions are the need for sufficient sun to bring the clusters of fruit to full ripeness, yet sufficient winter chill to allow the vine to go dormant. There is another consideration. The so-called "balance" of a wine requires that the sugar content of the grape—essentially the product of heat—not overwhelm the acid content. Too much heat leads to too much sugar and reduction of flavor. Too little, to too much acid. Either extreme destroys the balance of elements. Since the continental United States lies within the temperate zone of the Northern Hemisphere, it is, most of it, potential vineyard area—though not necessarily good vineyard area. In fact, more species of native vines are found in North America than anywhere else in the world. The number of its native species varies according to the system of classification followed, but it is on the order of thirty, or about half of the number found throughout the entire world.[5]

One must emphasize the word *native*. The vine of European winemaking, the vine that Noah planted after the Flood, is the species *vinifera*—"the wine bearer," in Linnaeus's Latin—of the genus *Vitis,* the vine. *Vitis vinifera* is the vine whose history is identical with the history of wine itself: the leaves of vinifera bind the brows of Dionysus in his triumph; the seeds of vinifera are found with the mummies of the pharaohs in the pyramids. It was the juice of vinifera, mysteriously alive with the powers of fermentation, that led the ancients to connect wine with the spiritual realm and to make it an intimate part of religious ceremony. In the thousands of years during which vinifera has been under cultivation, it has produced thousands of varieties—4,000 by one count, 5,000 by another, 8,000 by yet another, though there is no realistic way to arrive at a figure.[6] The grape is constantly in process of variation through the seedlings it produces, and the recognized varieties are only the tiny fraction selected by man for his purposes from among the uncounted millions that have grown wherever the seeds of the grape have been dropped.

The grapes that vinifera yields for the most part have thin skins, tender, sweet flesh, delicate flavors, and high sugar, suitable for the production of sound, well-balanced, attractive wine. The wines that are pressed from them cover the whole gamut of recognized types, from the coarse hot-country reds to the crisp, flowery whites of the north. Among the great number of excellent and useful varieties of vinifera, a tiny handful have been singled out as "noble" vines: the Cabernet Sauvignon of Bordeaux and the Pinot Noir of Burgundy among the reds; the Riesling of the Rhine and the Chardonnay of Champagne and Burgundy among the whites; the Semillon of Sauternes for sweet wine. A few other essential names might be added, and a great many other excellent and honorable names, but the point is that after centuries of experience, and from thousands of available varieties, a few, very few, vinifera vines have been identified and internationally recognized as best for the production of superior wines in the regions to which they are adapted.

No such grape is native to North America. The natives are, instead, tough, wild grapes, usually small and sour, and more notable for the vigor of their vines than for the quality of the wine made from their fruit. They grew and adapted to their circumstances largely unregarded by man, and while the development of *Vitis vinifera* was guided to satisfy the thirst of ancient civilizations, the North American vines had only survival to attend to. The natives are true grapes, no doubt sharing with vinifera the same ancestor far back along the evolutionary scale. But in the incalculably long process of dispersion and adaptation from their conjectured point of origin in Asia, the native grapes have followed widely different patterns of adaptation. That is one of the most striking facts about the numerous wild American grapes—how remarkably well adapted they are to the regions in which they grow, and how various are the forms they take.[7] There are dwarf, shrubby species growing in dry sand or on rocky hills; there are long-lived species growing to enormous size, with stems more than a foot in diameter and climbing over one hundred feet high on the forest trees that support them; some kinds flourish in warm humidity, others on dry and chill northern slopes; some grow in forests, some along river banks, some on coastal plains. As the great viticultural authority U. P. Hedrick observed early in this century, so many varieties of native grape are distributed over so wide an area that "no one can say where the grape is most at home in America."[8] But the fruit that they produce is often deficient in sugar, or high in acid, and sometimes full of strange flavors, so that the wine pressed from it is thin, unstable, sharp, and unpleasing—if drinkable at all. Wine from the unadulterated native grape is not wine at all by the standards of *Vitis vinifera*.

Early Explorers and Native Grapes

All of the explorers and early settlers made note of the abundant and vigorous wild grape vines—they could hardly help doing so, since they were obviously and everywhere to be seen along the coast of eastern North America. Within two years of Columbus's discovery, for example, the Spaniards reported vines growing in the Caribbean islands.[9] The Pilgrims in New England found the species now called *Vitis labrusca* growing profusely in the woods around their settlements.[10] The labrusca, or northern fox grape, is the best looking of the natives, with large berries that may come in black, white, or red. It is the only native grape that exhibits this range of colors. Labrusca is still the best known of the native species because the ubiquitous Concord, the grape that most Americans take to be the standard of "grapeyness" in juice and jellies, is a pure example of it.

The name "fox grape" often given to labrusca yields the adjective *foxy*, a word unpleasant to the ears of eastern growers and winemakers as an unflattering description of the distinctive flavor of their labrusca grapes and wines, a flavor unique to eastern America and, once encountered, never forgotten. One of the dominant elements in that flavor, the chemists say, is the compound methyl anthranilate;[11] it can be synthesized artificially to produce the flavor of American grapeyness wherever it may be wanted. But why this flavor (which, like all flavors, is largely aroma) should be called "foxy" has been, and remains, a puzzle (see Appendix 1).

Hundreds of miles to the south of the Pilgrim settlements, and even before the Pilgrims landed, the gentlemen of the Virginia Company at Jamestown encountered a number of native grape species, among them the very distinctive one called *Vitis rotundifolia*—round leaf grape—that grows on bottom lands, on river banks, and in swamps, often covering hundreds of square feet with a single vine. The rotundifolia grape, commonly called muscadine, differs sharply from other grapes; so different is it, in fact, that it is often distinguished as a class separate from "true grapes." The vine is low and spreading, and the large, tough-skinned, round fruit grows not in the usual tight bunches but in loose clusters containing only a few berries each: hence the variant name of bullet grape. The fruit is sweet, but like that of almost all natives, its juice usually needs to have sugar added to it in order to produce a sound wine. The fruit has also a strong, musky odor based on phenylethyl alcohol that carries over into its wine.[12] Scuppernong is the best-known variety of rotundifolia, and the name is sometimes loosely used to stand for the whole species.

Both Pilgrims in the north and Virginians in the south would have known the small-berried and harsh-tasting *Vitis riparia*—the riverbank grape—which is the most widely distributed of all native American grapes (difficulties in classification have produced some variant names for this species, of which *Vitis vulpina* is the most common). Riparia ranges from Canada to the Gulf, and west, with diminishing frequency, to the Great Salt Lake. As its name indicates, riparia chooses river banks or islands. As its range suggests, it has a tough and hardy character that allows it to survive under a great variety of conditions. It is currently, for example, being used as a basis for hybridizing wine grapes for the cold climates of Minnesota and Wisconsin.[13]

Another grape widespread throughout the eastern United States is *Vitis aestivalis,* the summer grape, the best adapted to the making of wine of all the North American natives, though not the most widely used. Unlike the rotundifolia and others, it has adequate sugar in its large clusters of small berries; and it is free of the powerful "foxy" odor of the labrusca. Aestivalis fills in the gaps left by riparia and labrusca, for unlike the former it avoids the streams, and, unlike the latter, it prefers the open uplands to the thick woods. Another grape common in the East, *Vitis cordifolia,* the winter grape, has a taste so harshly herbaceous that only under the most desperate necessity has it ever been used for wine.

As settlement moved beyond the eastern seaboard and made its way west, a new range of species and varieties was encountered, though none of such importance as those just named. The best known is *Vitis rupestris,* the sand grape, which favors gravelly banks and dry water courses and is distributed through the region around southern Missouri and Illinois down into Texas. Since it is not a tree climber, it has been very vulnerable to grazing stock and is now almost extinct in many areas.

There are many other species and subspecies that might be named among the

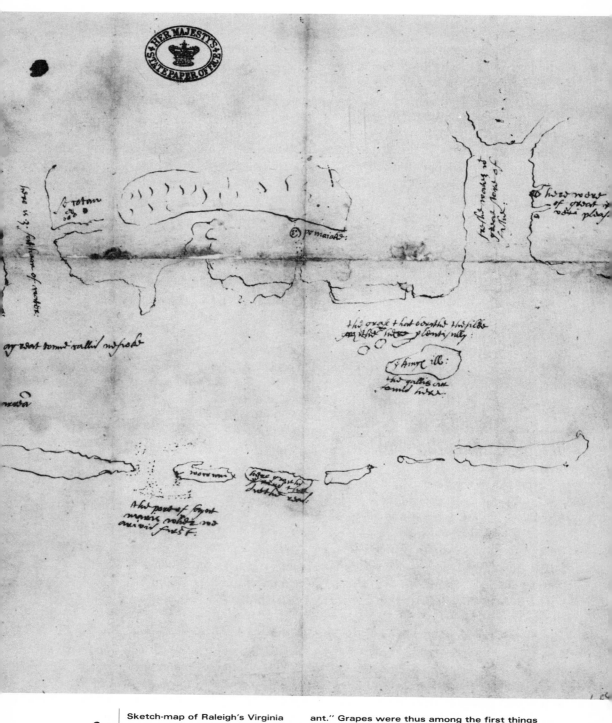

2 Sketch-map of Raleigh's Virginia (that is, the North Carolina coast), September 1585. The note at the far right of the sketch reads: "Here were great store of great red grapis veri pleasant." Grapes were thus among the first things to greet the English in the New World. (From D. B. Quinn, ed., *The Roanoke Voyages, 1584–1590* [1955]; original in the Public Record Office, London)

3 "The arriual of the Englishemen in Virginia": drawing by John White, engraved by Theodor de Bry, based on the sketch-map shown in Fig. 2. The drawing represents grapes under the word "Weapemeoc" in a position corresponding to that indicated on the sketch-map. (Theodor de Bry, *America*, part 1 [Frankfurt am Main, 1590]; Huntington Library)

native vines, but those already given include most of the varieties that formed the stock available to the early settlers and that have since had any significance in the development of hybrid vines.[14] Two things may be said generally about the natives by way of summarizing their importance both to the American industry and to the world of wine at large. First, except for the muscadine, they enter readily into combination with other species, so that by judicious hybridizing their defects have been diminished and their virtues enhanced in combination with one another and with *Vitis vinifera*. Such improvement through breeding began in the nineteenth century (though some very important accidental crosses had occurred earlier) and has been continued without intermission since: had it been begun earlier in a deliberate way, the whole face of winemaking in the United States might have been changed beyond recognition. Second, the native vines have, or some of them at any rate have, an inherited resistance to the major enemies of the vine in North America: the endemic fungus diseases that destroy leaves and fruit; and the plant louse called *Phylloxera vastatrix*, a scourge native to North America and introduced with catastrophic effect into Europe in the latter half of the nineteenth century. By

4 | The characteristic native grape of the American South, *Vitis rotundifolia,* the muscadine, often loosely referred to as "Scuppernong." Flourishing especially in the Carolinas, it was probably the source of the first American wine and was the basis of Virginia Dare, once the most popular wine in America. (From Liberty Hyde Bailey, *Sketch of the Evolution of Our Native Fruits* [1898])

grafting *V. vinifera* to American roots, the winegrowers of Europe were able to save their industry at a time when it seemed likely that the ancient European civilization of the vine was about to become a thing of the past.

The summary just given is based on information laboriously accumulated by professional botanists and field workers over the course of many years, people whose devoted labors have made it possible to state clearly and confidently what grapes belong to what species and where they may be found. It was all very different, of course, when the first explorers and colonists looked about them and attempted to identify what they saw. The early accounts all have in common a certain indistinctness combined with an excited hopefulness, the one probably being the condition of the other.

Take, for example, the earliest reference on record to the grapes growing in what is now the United States. In 1524, only a generation after Columbus, the Italian explorer Giovanni da Verrazzano, coasting north along the Atlantic seaboard, encountered a region so lovely in his eyes that he called it Arcadia.[15] Admiral Samuel Eliot Morison, the latest student of the subject, is of the opinion that Verrazzano meant Kitty Hawk, of Wright brothers fame, off the North Carolina mainland—a region that no one would identify as Arcadian now.[16] But there Verrazzano found "many vines growing naturally, which growing up, tooke hold of the trees as they doe in Lombardie, which if by husbandmen they were dressed in good order, without all doubt they would yield excellent wines."[17] Verrazzano's association of wild coastal North Carolina with the carefully gardened landscape of Lombardy was a combination of impossible contrasts, yet it was evidently quite possible to hold it in imagination. Only a decade later, far to the north of the land that Verrazzano saw, Jacques Cartier described how, in the St. Lawrence, he and his men came across an island where "we saw many goodly vines, a thing not before of us seene in those countries, and therefore we named it Bacchus Iland."[18] It was natural for both Verrazzano and Cartier to conclude that the grapes that they saw must yield wine, but neither had the time to make the experiment and neither could guess what labor and what frustration were in store over hundreds of years before Bacchus could be coaxed to live among us. They might have suspected some difficulty from the fact that none of the Indians they saw had any knowledge of wine; in fact, no eastern Indians had any fermented drinks of any sort, though this fact tells us more about the accidents of culture than about natural possibilities.[19]

The first reference to the actual making of wine in what is now the United States is in the report of his voyage to Florida in 1565 by the rich and respectable pirate Captain John Hawkins, afterwards Sir John. In 1564 the French Protestant Admiral Gaspard de Coligny had sent out a colony of Huguenots to the mouth of the St. John's River in Florida, and there, at Fort Caroline, Hawkins found the wretched survivors a year later on the verge of starvation. Hawkins sold them a ship and left them food, noting with some disapproval that, though they had failed to grow food for themselves, yet "in the time that the Frenchmen were there, they made 20 hogsheads of wine."[20] It must, one supposes, have been made from rotundifolia grapes—that is, from the muscadine.

Recent inquiry into this story, which has long been received without question, shows strong reason to doubt it. The testimony of the French themselves is that they had no wine at all except for what they got from external sources.[21] After the French had been driven away from the Florida coast, the Spaniards made a settlement on nearby Santa Elena Island—now Parris Island, South Carolina—and a vineyard was reported as planted there by 1568. There is some evidence that the vines planted were vinifera, and, if so, the odds are overwhelming that no wine was produced from them.[22] But of course the Spanish colonists were surrounded by abundant wild grapes and so could easily have made the experiment of trying them for wine: in all probability they did. In any case, Parris Island may claim to be the place where the first attempt at winegrowing in America was made.

In 1584 the first expedition of Sir Walter Raleigh's ill-fated colonial enterprise landed on the low coast of Hatarask Island, North Carolina (though they called it Virginia then), the "Arcadia" of Verrazzano sixty years earlier. What the English found on first setting foot on the land was a carpet of grapes, growing so close to the water's edge that "the very beating and surge of the Sea overflowed them." The report goes on in language that was doubtless heightened to attract settlers to the colony, but that also seems genuinely excited by the vision of plenty in a new land. The grapes spread beyond the shore, the chronicler says:

> We found such plentie, as well there as in all places else, both on the sand and on the greene soile on the hils, as in the plaines, as well on every little shrubbe, as also climing towards the tops of high Cedars, that I thinke in all the world the like abundance is not to be found: and my selfe having seene those parts of Europe that most abound, find such difference as were incredible to be written.[23]

The likelihood is that the grapes in question were muscadines, though they would not have been ripe in July, when the expedition landed.

Raleigh's unfortunate Roanoke colony, the one founded by the third expedition in 1587, vanished without trace, so that if the colonists attempted winemaking, we do not know with what results. There is still an immense Scuppernong vine on Roanoke Island, which people please themselves by calling the "Mother Vine," though it can hardly be anything other than a very great granddaughter of the generation of vines that the Roanoke people saw. But it is not at all unreasonable to think that they did try to make wine and so began the long chapter of hopes and failures written in the English colonies down to the Revolution.

The Promise of Virginia Wine

For the next determined effort at English colonization in the American south, the information is much fuller. Like all observers before them, the settlers of Jamestown, Virginia, in 1607, the first permanent colony, were struck by the rich profusion of grapes that adorned the woods of their colony. Indeed, by this time, they expected to see them, for the ability of the New World to grow grapes "naturally"—that is, wild—is one of the details constantly and optimistically noted in the accounts published by Hakluyt and other promoters of exploration and settlement.[24] This attractive gift of nature helped to inspire a vision that persisted for many years in the English imagination. In this vision, the myth of Eden mingles with legends of fabulous wealth in the New World, legends supported by the actual example of Spanish successes in Mexico and South America. The vision was supported, too, by an orthodox economic argument. In order to obtain such products as silk, wine, and olive oil, England had to pay cash to Spain and France, its rivals and enemies. One of the persistent objects of early English colonization was therefore to provide England herself with silk, wine, oil, and other such commodities. With her own source for these things, England might laugh at the French king and defy the Spanish, a heady prospect that powerfully influenced the English vision of America. For years, the French had insulted the English in both act and word, as in this old song:

> Bon Français, quand je bois mon verre
> Plein de ce vin couleur de feu,
> Je songe, en remerciant Dieu,
> Qu'ils n'en ont pas en Angleterre.[25]

Such taunts as these would cease if English colonies could be made to yield wine.

Wine and silk, those two luxurious commodities, were constantly linked in the English imagination as the most desirable products (other than gold) that America could yield; as one writer has said, the duet of the vine and silk formed from the beginning "one of the major themes in the vast symphony of colonial hopes that enchanted, for half a century, the England of Elizabeth and James the First."[26] Indeed, the enchantment lasted far longer than that, for one regularly finds silk producing and winegrowing (with the olive sometimes taking a third part, or replacing silk in the pattern) linked together by hopeful speculators well into the nineteenth century. For its persistence and ubiquity, the dream of wine and silk (and oil) to be poured out copiously and carelessly from the warm and fertile New World has some claim to be identified as genuine myth.

Even before they left England the Jamestown adventurers were promised, in an "Ode to the Virginian Voyage" by the poet Michael Drayton (who had obviously been reading Hakluyt for his details) that they would find a place where

> The ambitious vine
> Crownes with his purple masse
> The Cedar reaching hie
> To kisse the sky.[27]

Nor were they disappointed. On reaching the James River they at once saw "great store of Vines in bignesse of a man's thigh, running up to the tops of the Trees in Great abundance."[28]

The Virginia settlers tried a little experimental winemaking at once. A report by an Irish sailor who made the first voyage to Jamestown says that he sampled one or two of the wines produced and found them very similar to the Spanish Alicante, but this is probably an Irish fantasy rather than a sober report.[29] A more modest statement was made by one of the promoters of the Virginia Company, who wrote in 1609 that "we doubt not but to make there in few years store of good wines, as any from the Canaries."[30] Not much wine can have been made by that early date, and even less can have been tried in England, though the same authority, Robert Johnson, who foresaw Virginia as a rival to the Canaries, wrote that the Jamestown settlers had sent some of their wine to London before 1609.[31] Johnson's prophecy of Virginia's winemaking promise is particularly interesting for its idea of how that promise was to be realized—that is, "by replanting and making tame the vines that naturally grow there in great abundance."[32] Johnson was writing in ignorance and can claim no credit for prophetic authority, but he did thus predict by accident what, after long years, turned out to be the method—approximately—that made viticulture possible in the eastern United States: the use of improved native varieties. But the process of "taming" vines merely by cultivating them, an idea that long persisted, is fallacious.

Captain John Smith is authority for the statement that the colonists of the first Virginia Voyage made "near 20 gallons of wine" from "hedge grapes";[33] but Smith was writing some years after the event and is not distinct as to dates. More circumstantial, but still doubtful in some points, is the statement by William Strachey, who spent the year 1610–11 in Jamestown, that there he had "drunk often of the rath [young] wine, which Doctor Bohoune and other of our people have made full as good as your French-British wine, 20 gallons at a time have been sometimes made without any other help than by crushing the grape with the hand, which letting to settle 5 or 6 days hath in the drawing forth proved strong and heady."[34] "Rath wine" indeed! The statement about making twenty gallons of wine as good as "French-British" wine—perhaps French wine for the British market is meant—was copied by Strachey from the book that Captain Smith published in 1612, an easy sort of plagiarism common enough at the time. But the particulars about Dr. Bohune and his winemaking technique seem to be from Strachey's own observation. It certainly makes sense to drink at once such a wine as he describes: the yeasty headiness of a wine still fermenting would probably be the main virtue of the highly acid juice.

Dr. Laurence Bohune (or Boone), whose wine Strachey drank, has the distinction of being the first winemaker in America whose name we know. He came out to Jamestown in 1610, later became physician general to the colony, and was killed in a sea battle with the Spanish on a voyage from England back to Virginia: an omen, perhaps, of the ill-luck that the winemaking enterprise was destined to encounter.

Word about the actual quality of Virginia wine had already reached England by 1610. When Lord De La Warr was appointed governor of the colony in that year, he sent instructions in advance of his arrival that a hogshead or two of the native wine, "sour as it is," should be sent for a sample to England.[35] Probably he hoped to stimulate the interest of trained winegrowers, for whom the Virginia Company was already searching. Indeed, De La Warr seems to have taken some French vine dressers with him on his voyage to Virginia in 1610, though the information is tantalizingly indistinct. In the official—and therefore not wholly reliable—"True Declaration of the Estate of the Colony in Virginia" (1610), a tract written to raise fresh funds for the company after the disastrous "starving time" in the winter of 1609–10, we hear of "Frenchmen" with Lord De La Warr "preparing to plant vines," who "confidently promise that within two years we may expect a plentiful vintage."[36] This sounds most promising, but nothing more is heard of the matter, and De La Warr himself writes at the same time as though no provision had yet been made for cultivating the vine:

... In every bosk and common hedge, and not far from our pallisado gates, we have thousands of goodly vines running along and leaning to every tree, which yield a plentiful grape in their kind; let me appeal, then, to knowledge, if these natural vines were planted, dressed, and ordered by skilfull vinearoones, whether we might not make a perfect grape and fruitful vintage in short time?[37]

On his return to England in 1611, De La Warr was able to state in his official report that "there are many vines planted in divers places, and do prosper well."[38] One of these vineyards was perhaps that mentioned by Ralph Hamor, who was in the colony from 1610 to 1614, and who wrote that there they had planted wild grapes in "a vineyard near Henrico" of three or four acres (Henrico was founded in 1611).[39] The *Laws Divine, Moral and Martial,* the stern Virginian code drawn up in 1611, forbade the settlers to "rob any vineyards or gather up the grapes" on pain of death.[40] But this must have been merely an anticipation of the future, not a present necessity.

Despite the company's advertisements and the governor's plea for skilled "vinearoones," none seems to have ventured forth until a long eight years later.[41] By that time the company, alarmed by the rapid establishment of tobacco as the sole economic dependence of the colony, determined to encourage a diversity of manufactures and commodities, wine among them. In this it had the eager support of King James I, who abominated tobacco (see his "A Counterblast to Tobacco," 1604) and was entranced by the vision of silk and wine. He urged on the company the importance of developing these commodities at the expense of tobacco, but the royal attempt to put down the weed proved just as futile as any other, then or now.

The company began its new policy by causing a law to be enacted in 1619 requiring "every householder" to "yearly plant and maintain ten vines until they have attained to the art and experience of dressing a vineyard either by their own industry or by the instruction of some vigneron."[42] The instruction was to be provided by the "divers skilfull vignerons" who, the company reported, had been sent out in 1619, "with store also from hence of vineplants of the best sort."[43] The last item deserves special note: it is the earliest record of the effort to transplant the European vine to eastern America. The event may be said to mark the beginning of the second phase of viticultural experiment in America, the first being that period of brief and unsatisfactory trial of the native grape.

There were, we know, eight *vignerons* sent to Virginia in 1619, Frenchmen from Languedoc—Elias La Garde, David Poule, Jacques Bonnall are among the names preserved of this group. We know also that they were settled at Kecoughton, Elizabeth City County, near the coast and therefore relatively secure from Indian attack.[44] This region had been recommended as early as 1611 by Sir Thomas Dale, who observed that the two or three thousand acres of clear ground there would do for vineyards and that "vines grow naturally there, in great abundance."[45] Indeed, the suitability of the region had been remarked even earlier, in 1572, by the Jesuit Father Juan de la Carrera. Carrera, with what his editors describe as "typical pious exaggeration," wrote that the Spanish found at Kecoughton (which he called "the Bay of the Mother of God") "a very beautiful vineyard, as well laid out and ordered as the vineyards of Spain. It was located on sandy soil and the vines were laden with fine white grapes, large and ripe."[46] No such vineyard as Father Carrera describes could possibly have existed. No doubt he saw grapes growing, and perhaps the vineyards of sixteenth-century Spain were somewhat unkempt, but much imagination would still be required to make untouched Virginia exactly resemble long-settled Spain. Such transformations of the unfamiliar wild scenes of the New World into images drawn from the familiar forms of the Old are common enough in the literature of exploration.

The official company statement says that the French *vignerons* went out in 1619, but they must have arrived too late to do any planting that year—indeed, a letter from Virginia as late as January 1620 pleads for both vines and *vignerons* from Europe, a fact that suggests the company was slower to carry out its claims than to publicize them.[47] The same letter, however, mentions that vines brought by the governor, Sir George Yeardley (presumably on his return from England in 1619) "do prosper passing well," but his *Vigneron*— "a fretful old man"—was dead: no doubt this was one of the Languedociens. Despite that setback, the signs at first were prosperous, or at least the reports were enthusiastic. It was affirmed that the vines planted in the fall bore grapes the following spring, "a thing they suppose not heard of in any other country."[48] Just when the Frenchmen planted their vines is not clear. Those that Sir George Yeardley brought were planted in 1619; another source refers to the Frenchmen as having planted their cuttings at "Michaelmas last"—that is, around October 1620.[49] These were probably the vines that marvelously fruited the next spring.

In 1620 the company, encouraged by the early reports, announced that it was looking for more vineyardists from France and from Germany, and that it was trying to procure "plants of the best kinds" from France, Germany, and elsewhere.[50] Whether this was done is not recorded; probably it was not. A year later, in 1621, we hear that on one site, at least, some 10,000 vines had been set out, though not whether they were native or vinifera.[51] In the next year, at the king's command,[52] the company sent to every householder in Virginia a manual on the cultivation of the vine and silk by the Master of the King's Silkworms, a Frenchman named John Bonoeil, the same Frenchman who had recruited the Languedoc *vignerons* in 1619 (probably the *vigneron* named in English spelling as Bonnall was a relative). Bonoeil's treatise, with its "instructions how to plant and dress vines, and to make wine," is not the first American manual on viniculture, since it was written by a Frenchman in England; but it may fairly claim to be the first manual *for* American winemakers.[53] With this book in their hands, and the king's command to spur them, the Virginia colonists, so the company admonished them, could have no more excuse for failure.[54]

Bonoeil could not have had any direct knowledge of American conditions, but he at least tried to imagine and prescribe for them. After recommending that the

5 The royal seal of King James I, from John Bonoeil's *His Maiesties Gracious Letter to the Earle of South-Hampton* . . . (London, 1622). Written at the tobacco-hating, wine-loving king's command, this work offered instruction in wine-making to all the Virginia settlers. It begins the literature of wine in America. (Huntington Library)

native grapes be used for immediate results, he provides general instructions for winemaking, beginning with the treading of the grapes "with bare legs and feet" and going on to a recipe expressly devised for the wild native grapes. If, he says, men would trouble to gather such grapes when they are ripe, and tread them, and ferment them, the juice

> would purge itself as well as good wine doth; and if the grapes be too hard, they may boil them with some water; . . . and then let them work thus together five or six days. . . . After that, you may draw it, and barrel it, as we have said, and use it when you need. I have oftentimes seen such wine made reasonable good for the household. And by this means every man may presently have wine in *Virginia* to drink.[55]

We do not know if this recipe was followed. The colony was liberally supplied with the book containing it, but one witness in that year reported that the colonists "laughed to scorn" such instructions, for "tobacco was the only business."[56] And heaven only knows what result Bonoeil's process yielded. The boiling would have extracted an intense color, but the water would have diluted the already inadequate proportion of sugar in the native grapes. Wine that puts the teeth on edge and the stomach in revolt was the likeliest result. Nevertheless, it is notable that Bonoeil, like a good Frenchman, was not so much thinking of making a profit for the company's shareholders through the export of Virginia wine as he was charitably wishing that every man in Virginia should have "reasonable good" wine to drink.

The sequel to all this preparation was disappointment. How could it have been anything else, given the practical difficulties? A little wine was made from native grapes, but it proved unsatisfactory. And the failure to make anything out of wine-growing in the face of a prosperous tobacco industry soon led men to give up a losing game. Besides that, the get-rich-quick mentality that dominated in early Vir-

vp the Barrels euery day, according as it dimi-
nisheth with working, otherwise the Lees and
other corruptions will goe downe into the Barrels, and when hot weather commeth, will spoile
the Wine. You may do so with the Claret, when
you will not haue it too red, but cleere, and name-
ly in hot countries.

9. *Obseruations touching the wild Vine, that groweth in* Virginia, *and how to make Wine of the same.*

I Haue been informed by such as haue bin in
Virginia, that there grow infinite number of
wilde Vines there, and of seuerall sorts; some
climbe vp to the top of trees in the woods, and
they bring forth great quantities of small blacke
Grapes, which are the plainer to be seene, when
the leaues are falne off from the trees. Another
sort of Grapes there is, that runne vpon the
ground, almost as big as a Damson, very sweet,
and maketh deepe red Wine, which they call a
Fox-Grape. A third sort there is, which is a
white Grape, but that is but rare, which are all
deuoured by the birds and beasts.

Now if such men as dwell there, would take
the paines to gather some of them, when they be
ripe, and tread them as aforesaid, and make the
Wine worke with water, putting it in Vats or
Tubs, as we said, it would purge it selfe as well as
good Wine doth; and if the Grapes bee too
hard, they may boyle them with some water;

H   and

6 The beginning of Bonoeil's instructions to Virginia winemakers. The book, we are told,
was "laughed to scorn" by the Virginians, who
were too busy growing tobacco to trouble
themselves with the uncertainties of winemaking. Note the very early reference to the "Fox-
Grape." (Huntington Library)

ginia—one writer describes Jamestown in the 1620s as a model of the boomtown economy[57]—was ill-suited to the patient labor and modest expectations of wine-growing. In 1622 some Virginia wine was sent to London; it must have been wine from native grapes, since the vinifera vines brought over in 1619 could not have yielded a significant crop so soon, even supposing that they were still alive. The wine, whatever it may have been to begin with, was spoiled by the combination of a musty cask and the long voyage, and the company in London, desperately eager to make good its claims about Virginia's fruitfulness, was forced to swallow another disappointment. Such wine, it wrote to the colonists, "hath been rather of scandal than credit to us."[58]

So far from being able to supply an export market with acceptable wine, Virginia was quite unable to provide for its own needs. This was partly owing to the difficulties in growing wine, no doubt, but also partly to the fact that tobacco cultivation left no time for anything else, and yet was the only profitable activity. Under the circumstances, the company in London was willing to listen to such wild propositions as one made in 1620 to supply the colony with an "artificial wine" that would cost nearly nothing, would never go flat or sour, and was ready to drink on the day that it was made. This remarkable fluid, it appears, was made of sassafras and licorice boiled in water, but whether it was successfully imposed on the poor colonists may be doubted.[59]

The Virginians were so eager for wine that in 1623 the governor was obliged to proclaim price controls on "Sherry Sack, Canary and Malaga, Allegant [Alicante] and Tent, Muskadell and Bastard" ("Tent" was red wine—Spanish *tinto*—and "Bastard" was a sweet blended wine from the Iberian peninsula).[60] Shortly after, the governor complained officially to the company in London that the shippers were exploiting the Virginians with "rotten wines which destroy our bodies and empty our purses."[61]

Things were made more difficult than ever by disasters in Virginia and by dissension among the directors in London. The great Indian massacre of 1622, which cost the lives of nearly a third of the colonists, did severe material damage as well. In London, stockholders were exasperated when the profits that had seemed so near in 1607 repeatedly failed to materialize, and disagreement over general policy led to strife at headquarters. Company officials defended themselves as best they could, claiming that, even despite the massacre, vineyards had been planted, "whereof some contained ten thousand plants."[62] At the same time, the company wrote anxiously to Governor Sir Francis Wyatt: "We hope you have got a good entrance into Silk and Vines, and we expect some returns—or it will be a discredit to us and to you and give room to the maligners of the Plantation. Encourage the Frenchmen to stay, if not forever, at least 'till they have taught our people their skill in silk and vines."[63] The company was disappointed: no wine was sent in 1623, and the "maligners of the Plantation" seized their opportunity. They denied that any promising work had been accomplished: the claim that the company had sent out a supply of the best vines was false, they said, for though vines had been

7 | Glass wine bottles from the seventeenth century found at Jamestown, Virginia. Thousands of such bottles have been found, but they can only occasionally have contained Virginia wine. Most of what the Virginians drank had to be imported, and much of that was bad. (From John L. Cotter and J. Paul Hudson, *New Discoveries at Jamestown* [1967])

brought from Malaga they were never forwarded across the Atlantic; as for the much-touted French *vignerons,* some were dead, and the survivors were being given no assistance in the colony. The claim to have established a large vineyard was also hollow, so the company's enemies said, for it was only a nursery planting and the vines were native rather than European.[64]

What the truth in all this was is not clear from the evidence. No doubt the company's enemies, hoping to bring the colony under royal authority, exaggerated the failure to get anything done. But the report of well-affected observers on the spot shows that little had been accomplished. George Sandys, the poet who had gone out to Virginia with Governor Wyatt, reported to London in 1623 that though many vines had been planted the year before, they "came to nothing." The massacre was but a part of the reason. "Want of art and perhaps the badness of the cuttings" were also responsible, but the most important of all the causes was simple neglect:

Wherefore now we have taken an order that every plantation . . . shall impale [fence] two acres of ground, and employ the sole labor of 2 men in that business [planting grape vines] for the term of 7 years, enlarging the same two acres more, with a like increase of labor. . . . By this means I hope this work will go really forward, and the better if good store of Spanish or French vines may be sent us.[65]

Sandys himself hastened to obey the law, for the census made early in 1625 records that he had a vineyard of two acres on his plantation on the south bank of the James.[66] But how ineffective the measure was in general may be guessed from the fact that in the year after it was enacted, at the very moment when the Virginia

8   The poet George Sandys (1578–1644), who went out to Virginia as treasurer of the colony in 1621, was responsible for encouraging the agriculture and manufactures of the struggling settlement. He planted a vineyard of his own and reported optimistically about the prospects of winegrowing. (From Richard Beale Davis, *George Sandys* [1955])

Company was expiring, the General Assembly passed a law requiring twenty vines to be planted for every male over twenty years of age.[67] This new law, the last in a series of attempts to legislate an industry, was quietly repealed in 1641. But even then it does not seem that there was any willingness to admit that the obstacle was in the natural difficulties of the situation. Instead, excuses were found, and accusations of bad faith, idleness, and ignorance prevented a clear understanding of the problems that were in fact created by the unfamiliar climate, soils, diseases, pests, and materials. Men continued to think that if they simply persisted along the usual path the thing must succeed.[68]

The unlucky French "vinearoones" were a principal scapegoat. As early as 1621 the government was instructed from London to take care that the French were not allowed to forsake vine growing for tobacco, "or any other useless commodity."[69]

Seven years later, by which time all of the original hopes to produce a large "commodity" of wine had been falsified, the colonial council complained to England that "the vignerons sent here either did not understand the business, or concealed their skill; for they spent their time to little purpose."[70] Four years later, an act of the assembly directed that all the French *vignerons* and their families be forbidden to plant tobacco as a punishment for their crimes: they had, it was asserted, wilfully concealed their skill, neglected to plant any vines themselves, and had also "spoiled and ruinated that vineyard, which was with great cost, planted by the charge of the late company."[71]

What basis could so strange a charge have? Perhaps some light is thrown on the question by a passage in a tract of 1650, Edward Williams' *Virginia Richly and Truly Valued*. Williams says (his information is supposed to be derived from John Ferrar, who had been in the colony) that the colonists did not live up to their agreement with the French: "Those contracted with as hired servants for that employment [vine growing], by what miscarriage I know not, having promise broken with them, and compelled to labour in the quality of slaves, could not but express their resentment of it, and had a good colour of justice to conceal their knowledge, in recompence of the hard measure offered them."[72] If only that had not happened, Williams laments, Virginia would already be a great winegrowing land, blessed with "happiness and wealth" and fulfilling the biblical ideal of prosperous life, with every man at peace under his own vine.

If only it were so simple. But the failure of the first French *vignerons* was just what would have happened to anyone in the circumstances. Another group of Frenchmen, for example, went out to Virginia in 1630 "to plant vines, olives, and make silk and salt" under the direction of Baron de Sance.[73] Their settlement on the lower James may well have yielded salt, but certainly not the other, more elegant, products, even though they were working for themselves and not for the profit of some unjust taskmaster.

By midcentury it had long been evident that Virginia was not easily going to become a source of abundant wine. No records of actual production exist, but if there was any at all, it was on a purely local and domestic scale, and entirely based on native grapes, either wild or cultivated. Yet the dream persisted, and was likely to be acted on during those frequent seasons when tobacco was a drug on the market. In 1649 William Bullock (who had never been to Virginia) wrote that wine was made there from "three sorts of grapes" and repeated the familiar hope that in time a winemaking industry might arise to balance the colony's dependence on tobacco.[74] In the same year it was reported that one gentleman, a Captain William Brocas by name, had made "most excellent wine" from his own vineyard in Lancaster County along the banks of the Rappahannock.[75] It is also said that Sir William Berkeley, who governed Virginia from 1642 to 1652 and again from 1662 to 1677, successfully planted a vineyard of native grapes: "I have been assured," so the Reverend John Clayton wrote some years after Berkeley's death, "that he cultivated and made the wild sour grapes become pleasant, and large, and thereof made good wine."[76] Robert Beverley, the early historian of Virginia and a pioneer wine-grower of importance, tells a different story of Berkeley's efforts: "To save labour, he planted trees for the vines to run upon. But as he was full of projects, so he was always very fickle, and set them on foot, only to shew us what might be done, and not out of hopes of any gain to himself; so never minded to bring them to perfection."[77] Though Berkeley and Brocas are stated to have had regular vineyards, their methods were probably not much different from those implied in this description of Virginia in about 1670, written by the English physician Thomas Glover:

> In the woods there are abundance of *Vines,* which twine about the Oaks and Poplars, and run up to the top of them; these bear a kind of *Claret-grapes,* of which some few of the Planters do make Wine; whereof I have tasted; it is somewhat smaller than *French* Claret; but I suppose, if some of these Vines were planted in convenient vine-yards, where the Sun might have a more kindly influence on them, and kept with diligence and seasonable pruning, they might afford as good grapes as the Claret-Grapes of France.[78]

In 1650 another enthusiast, fired by the old vision of wine and silk, published a rhapsodic prospectus of what still might be done with those things in Virginia. Edward Williams (who, like Bullock, had never been to Virginia), observing that the poor Virginia planter "usually spends all the profits of his labour on foreign wines," urged the colonists to try again the experiment that had failed thirty years before by importing European vines and winemakers. This time, however, he advised that Greek vines and winegrowers be imported in place of French, since Virginia lay on a Mediterranean latitude (Athens and Jamestown are on nearly the same parallel). Williams also believed, as so many others did then, in the notion that the Pacific Ocean lay only a few miles to the west of the Virginia settlement,[79] so that the colony might reasonably hope to have the vast market of China laid open to them. And the Chinese, he says, "that voluptuous and gluttonous nation," were well known to "wanton away their wealth in banquets" and would be eager to buy Virginia's wine—if there were any.[80]

To give practical meaning to his argument, Williams published a guide to silk manufacture and winegrowing under the title *Virginia's Discovery of Silk-Worms. . . . Also the Dressing and Keeping of Vines, for the Rich Trade of Making Wines There* (1650). The thirty pages of this given over to a "Treatise of the Vine" are drawn exclusively from European sources and have no authentic reference to Virginian conditions. But the treatise may take rank as the second, after Bonoeil's (which Williams had evidently read), of the books written for American grape growing. Williams' geography and his economic advice were equally unreal, and we hear of no response to his call to grow the "Greek, Cyprian, Candian, or Calabrian grape" in Virginia. His argument that the grapes from one latitude in Europe should grow on the same latitude in North America is one that occurred to other writers later and is frequently met with in the speculation on this subject in the next two centuries: indeed, one still sees it as an advertising claim today. It is, in simple fact, quite fallacious. Labrador and London are on the same parallel, but does anyone seriously think that the same botany will be found in both places?

The last official encouragement of winegrowing in seventeenth-century Virginia was an Act of Assembly in 1658 offering ten thousand pounds of tobacco to whoever "shall first make two tunne of wine raised out of a vineyard made in this colony."[81] After that—presumably no one ever gained the prize—the official record is silent, though the instructions to each succeeding governor continued to include the charge to encourage the production of wine in the colony. Even this was, at last, quietly dropped in 1685, in tacit acknowledgment that, officially at least, the hope of winegrowing was dead.[82] Two years later a writer describing the state of Virginia to the eminent scientist Robert Boyle reported succinctly that, though several sorts of grapes grew wild, "there be no vineyards in the country."[83]

With every inducement, both real and imaginary, to develop a native industry—official policy and public wish agreeing on the desirability of the work—the early Virginians nevertheless failed to achieve even the beginnings of a basis. Why? The Jamestown experience is worth telling in detail just because it is so exact a pattern of experiments in American winegrowing that were to be repeated over and over again in different regions and by different generations. First comes the observation that the country yields abundant wild grapes, followed by trials of the winemaking from them, with unsatisfactory results. Then the European grape is imported and tended according to European experience; the early signs are hopeful, but the promise is unfulfilled: the vines languish, and no vintage is gathered. No amount of official encouragement, no government edict, can overcome the failure of the repeated trials, and after a time men become resigned to the paradox of living in a great natural vineyard that yields no wine, though an enthusiast here and there in succeeding generations takes up the challenge again, and again fails.

One French commentator has made the interesting suggestion that the colonial English were inclined to think that winegrowing was far easier than it is in reality: they knew and liked good wine from France but were content to drink it without ever learning what pains it cost the Bordelais to grow it. "Neither Lord Delaware nor the rich merchants of the Company in London could know that the winegrower's metier is one that is learned slowly, if one has not been early initiated to its patient disciplines, and, especially, if one is not a countryman, in unreflecting, genuine communion with the soil."[84] On this view, the combination of optimistic ignorance with unforeseen new difficulties, was quickly fatal to the effort at winegrowing by Englishmen who had no traditional feel for the task. The notion that winegrowing is a craft requiring much time and experiment to learn is no doubt true, but it is distinctly unfair to the English to say that they failed because they lacked tradition. They failed because the European vine could not grow here. It is amusing to speculate about what might have been if the French rather than the English had made the earliest settlements along the Atlantic coast. Would they have turned to the native grapes when all others failed? And would they have persisted until they had tamed them? One may doubt it.

One must also emphasize the fact that the early settlers of whatever nationality had every sort of natural disadvantage to contend with in seeking to adapt the European vine to a new scene. Agriculture generally was difficult, for the soil was poor. As a modern scientist puts it:

> The sandy soil of the Atlantic Coastal Plain, which is all that the colonists had to farm, is really terrible. In New Jersey it forms what we call the Pine Barrens, and in Virginia it is little better. It had been forested for some thirty thousand years, and thus it had acquired a little pseudo-fertility—it could bear crops for two or three years. Then it was finished. Only the strenuous efforts of the settlers kept it going longer. It was not until the chemist Justus von Liebig discovered the role of mineral fertilizers that this land could be farmed successfully and continuously.[85]

From the point of view of the tender *Vitis vinifera,* the New World was no Garden of Eden but a fallen world where the wrath of God was expressed in a formidable array of dangers and pestilences. First, the American extremes of climate, so different from what prevails in the winegrowing regions of Europe, alternately blasted and froze the vines. The summer humidity steamed them and provided a medium for fungus infections like powdery mildew, downy mildew, and black rot, diseases unknown in Europe until the latter half of the nineteenth century. Among the many destructive insect pests were the grape-leaf hopper, which sucks the juices of the foliage, and the grape berry moth, whose larvae feed on the fruit.

Other European fruits, such as apples, pears, and peaches, succeeded at once in the New World, but not the grape. The reason is probably that there were no native plants resembling the apple, pear, and peach, so that no native pests had evolved to prey upon them. There *were* native grapes, though, and a complete array of native pests established in association with them. Thus the very fact that America had native vines, which so excited the early settlers with the promise of winemaking, was the cause of the European vine's failure there.

The fungus diseases were the most immediately and comprehensively destructive enemies; all vinifera vines are extremely susceptible to them, and without control they will make the growing of such vines practically impossible. Powdery mildew (*Uncinula necator*) is endemic in the East but seldom does severe damage to the native vines. It lay in wait there for its opportunity against the untried vinifera. In the 1840s powdery mildew reached Europe, where it did great damage before the discovery that dusting with sulphur controlled it. In Madeira, where it was particularly virulent, it all but extinguished viticulture. The island has not, to this day, fully recovered the position in winegrowing that it once held before it received the setback dealt by this disease.

Downy mildew (*Plasmopara viticola*) flourishes in humidity, and is therefore a much more destructive disease in the East than in the arid West. It concentrates on the leaves of the vine, and by killing them defoliates the vine and brings about its starvation. Black rot (*Guignardia bidwellii*), the most troublesome of the fungus diseases, with a long history of destruction in eastern American vineyards, is particu-

9 | The effects of black rot (*Guig-nardia bidwellii*), the most wide-spread and destructive of the fungus diseases that plague the grape east of the Rocky Mountains. (From U.S. Department of Agriculture, *Report, 1885*)

larly damaging to the fruit itself, which it leaves hard, shrivelled, and useless for any purpose. It is, in the words of the authority A. J. Winkler, "probably the most destructive disease in vineyards of the United States east of the Rocky Mountains, where it virtually prevents success in growing *vinifera* varieties."[86] Even today it is a constant threat, ominously hovering over every hopeful planting in the East. "Sooner or later," as one contemporary expert resignedly remarks, "it will move into a vineyard and become a perennial problem for the grower."[87]

No clear reference to these diseases occurs in early colonial literature, and it was not until the nineteenth century that the connection between fungi and plant diseases was worked out. But the diseases were certainly there, and, after destroying the burgeoning industry along the Ohio River in the mid nineteenth century, they remain threats against which every eastern vineyardist must guard today. They have also been exported to Europe, where they require a constant and burdensome program of preventive spraying—a legacy from the New World that the Old would gladly do without.

In the regions south of Virginia, if a vine somehow escaped its trial by fungus, it had another ordeal by disease to endure; probably no vinifera among those planted in the East in colonial times ever reached this stage, and therefore the disease in question was not described until late in the nineteenth century, and then in California, where it is not native. Pierce's Disease (named for the expert who first studied it effectively), a bacterial infection that is fatal to the vine, was first brought to public attention in the 1880s, when it devastated the vineyards of southern California. It was for a time known as the Anaheim disease, after its destruction of the once flourishing vineyards there. Pierce's Disease has not had the catastrophic international effect that phylloxera did, but it is a dangerous thing to the grower: its mechanism is not understood, it kills what it affects, and there is no cure. Only very recently has it come to be suspected that its native place is in the southeastern United States, where the local species of grape show some tolerance for it. Any of those doomed colonial vineyards in the south, then, supposing that they had weathered climate, insects, and fungus, would surely have given up in weariness before Pierce's Disease.

Now suppose that, by some freak, the vines survived the onslaughts of mildew, rot, flying insects, bacterial infection, and extremes of weather. They would then have met another scourge, one which was not then recognized, and which, more than two centuries later, was to infest the vineyards of the world with disastrous results. This was the *Phylloxera vastatrix,* or "devastating dry leaf creature," a microscopic aphid, or plant louse, native to America east of the Rocky Mountains. One form of the insect—which has a most complex life-cycle generating a bewildering sequence of stages—lives on the leaves of the vine and is relatively innocuous. Another form lives its destructive life underground, sucking the roots of the vine, and killing the plant both by forming root galls, which then rot, and by injecting poison spittle into the roots. It was not until the mid nineteenth century, when the insect had been introduced into Europe, that it was identified and studied. But it no doubt did its bit to hasten the repeated and comprehensive failures of *Vitis vinifera* in America. By long adaptation, some of the tough-rooted native varieties have acquired greater or lesser resistance to the attack of phylloxera, as well as to the fungus and bacterial diseases endemic in North America.[88] But vinifera has fleshy, succulent roots that are just to phylloxera's taste and are wholly unable to resist its attack. It is a mistake, however, to suppose, as many writers have done, that the early trials of vinifera were ended by phylloxera. The fungus diseases were much more immediate, and in most places were probably supplemented by winter kill. Moreover, the sandy soils of the East Coast discourage the insect, which prefers clay and loam. Phylloxera as the special enemy of vinifera was not recognized until the mid-nineteenth century, for the good reason that it had little chance to operate as the sole destroyer of vines in this country: they had already been blasted and blighted. In Europe, it was different.

There is no "cure" for phylloxera to this day. Measures may be taken to prevent its spread. But where it is already present, the only practical means to continue the culture of vinifera is by grafting to resistant American root stocks, a method devised during the great phylloxera crisis of the nineteenth century and still standard practice today in both New World and Old World vineyards.

We can begin to see now what must have happened to the European vines in Virginia. Most vineyards were probably just abandoned; their cultivators took up tobacco growing instead. But some vineyardists must have tended their plantings carefully, hoping to obtain the blessing of good wine. And what was their reward? At first, as we have seen, the plants made good growth. Then fungus infestation would have begun, though not at first sufficient to put an end to hope. It takes at least three years, and more often four or five, before a vine produces a significant crop, and the intensity of fungus infection might vary from year to year according to the character of the season. Downy mildew might overrun the leaves and fruit. More likely, black rot would shrivel the berries and dessicate the leaves. Some fruit would survive, but the losses would be severe.

In sandy soils, such as are the rule along the eastern seaboard, the phylloxera does little damage, which makes it seem almost certain that the early failures of vinifera in this country were not attributable to that pest. But since phylloxera is so important an enemy in other sorts of soils wherever vinifera may be grown, and since it had such a devastating effect later in Europe and California, one may briefly describe its work here. The effects of phylloxera do not appear until the second year of infestation, when the vine growth slows and sickly yellow leaves appear, showing galls on the underside. In the third year, the signs of decay and disease intensify, and either then or in the next year the vine dies. If it is then dug up, the vine shows gnarled roots already decaying from the action of saprophytic fungi, but the insects themselves will have migrated to the next living plant. Even though the tiny insects are microscopic, they cluster so thickly upon a fatally infected vine that they are visible to the unaided eye. But a man is not likely to dig up a vine not yet dead, and until he did he would have no chance to see the cause of his vines' distress. Phylloxera thus went long undetected in this country, where it is at home. There were plenty of visible afflictions to be seen, so that one did not need to search for any hidden causes.

The idea of grafting the European vine onto American roots, the practice that was to save the vineyards of Europe and California from annihilation in the nineteenth century, occurred to many early American growers. But in the conditions of eastern America, such combinations, though they might have been effective against the unrecognized phylloxera, were futile without the support of modern fungicides. Mildew and black rot would have destroyed leaves and fruit as usual. And the hot, humid summers and the sub-zero winters would not have been any kinder.

Because this was a new land, where everything had yet to be learned, and because it was long before the time of scientific plant pathology, the causes of the failure of grape growing were not discovered—could not be discovered. The early colonists, then, naturally chose to blame as the source of their difficulties what was visible and familiar—bad soil, bad stock, bad methods, laziness. So American winegrowing continued up a dead end for many years to come.

The Other Colonies in the Seventeenth Century

The experience of the English in Virginia was a model, repeated more or less fully and persistently, in all the other colonies of seventeenth-century America. If we disregard exact chronology and simply follow the map of the coastline from north to south, each separate region presents its brief chronicle of experiment and failure. To begin with Maine, in the far north: in 1620 a speculator named Ambrose Gibbons proposed to found a plantation at the mouth of the Piscataqua River, on what is now the Maine–New Hampshire border, and there, in that bitter northern climate, to "cultivate the vine, discover mines . . . and trade with natives."[89] The latter two objects he might hope to realize; the first one, in the then state of botanical knowledge, could only be a wish rather than a practical possibility.

To the south, in Massachusetts, there is a pleasant fiction that wine from native grapes figured in the first Thanksgiving, in November 1621.[90] The Pilgrims of course saw "vines everywhere" at Plymouth Bay, as William Bradford wrote,[91] but the unique source from which our notion of the original Thanksgiving is derived, Edward Winslow's letter of 11 December 1621, makes no reference to wine at that meal. Winslow does describe the "grapes, white and red, and very sweet and strong also"[92] to be found growing in the local woods, but that is another matter. Perhaps the Plymouth Pilgrims had made wine from those grapes, but if so Winslow does not tell us.

In the Massachusetts Bay Colony, wine was made from native grapes in the first summer of settlement in 1630.[93] The result was doubtless one of the reasons why the colonists petitioned the Massachusetts Bay Company back in London to have Frenchmen experienced in "planting of vines" sent out to them. Unluckily, the company could not find any, though "vine-planters" were on the list of those things "to provide to send for New-England" that it noted in its preparations for 1629.[94]

The example of winegrowing was set at the top of the hierarchy in Boston. Governor John Winthrop, in 1632, secured the grant of Conant's Island in Boston Harbor, on condition that he plant a vineyard there. Three years later his rent for the place, then called Governor's Garden, was set at "a hogshead of the best wine that shall grow there to be paid yearly." In 1640 this was changed to two bushels of apples—evidence that winegrowing had not succeeded.[95] Despite this result, the intelligent and experienced Dr. Robert Child, preparing in 1641 to emigrate from

England to Massachusetts, proposed to establish a vineyard in the colony, and visited France during the vintage season to learn how the French made wine. "Already in imagination," as Samuel Eliot Morison writes, "he saw the hills of New England lined with terraced vineyards, becoming the Beaune or the Chablis of the New World." Child at last arrived in Massachusetts in 1645, having sent several varieties of vines before him and intending to establish his vineyard in the Nashua Valley. Despite his confidence that "in three years wine may be made as good as any in France," nothing came of his intentions; he was soon embroiled in quarrels with the Puritan magistrates and returned to England before success or failure with his vines could be determined.[96]

The discouraging experiences of Winthrop and Child were the familiar story in Massachusetts, but travellers and local historians continued for decades to comment on the abundance of native grapes in the region. No further effort to develop winegrowing seems to have been made until late in the seventeenth century, when Huguenot settlers planted vineyards in western Massachusetts;[97] vines of their planting still grew there as late as the 1820s, sufficient evidence for the fact that they must have been using one of the native species.[98] At the same time, another group of Huguenots planted vines in Rhode Island, from which they succeeded in making wine that was well received in Boston.[99] Both settlements soon came to an end, however: Indian attack drove the Huguenots from western Massachusetts, and legal difficulties over land title those in Rhode Island. The once-celebrated nineteenth-century American poetess Lydia Sigourney—"the Sweet Singer of Hartford"—was married to a descendant of one of the Massachusetts Huguenots. After paying a visit of piety to the remains of their settlement in 1822 she produced a poem addressed to one of the vines still growing there:

> Not by rash, thoughtless hands
> Who sacrifice to Bacchus, pouring forth
> Libations at his altar, with wild songs
> Hailing his madden'd orgies, wert thou borne
> To foreign climes,—but with the suffering band
> Of pious Huguenots didst dare the wave
> When they essay'd to plant Salvation's vines
> In the drear wilderness. . . .[100]

The rest of the poem is in the same style. It is pleasing to think that this decorous vine, turning from Bacchic orgies, adapted itself so well to the austere style of Huguenot Massachusetts. But as it was certainly an American native, it had never known anything about Bacchic orgies, though the fact would probably not have disturbed the lady's muse.

As for Rhode Island, viticulture did not persist after the retreat of the Huguenots, dispossessed in 1692 from their settlement at Frenchtown. The charter of Rhode Island, granted by King Charles II in 1663, contains the expression of the royal intention to "give all fitting encouragement to the planting of vineyards (with which the soil and climate seem to concur)."[101] The judgment is correct: Rhode Island ought to be a winegrowing region, but the social and economic conditions were evidently wrong, despite the example set briefly by the Huguenots.

The state of things in New England generally was summed up in 1680 by the early historian William Hubbard:

> Many places do naturally abound with grapes, which gave great hopes of fruitful vineyards in after time: but as yet either skill is wanting to cultivate and order the roots of those wild vines, and reduce them to a pleasant sweetness, or time is not yet to be spared to look after the culture of such fruits as rather tend to the *bene,* or *melius esse,* of a place, than to the bare *esse,* and subsistence thereof.[102]

Even the growing of grapes in farm gardens never caught on in New England. The Yankee tradition was simply to make use of the wild grapes growing freely in every wood, so that the work of selection and cultivation to improve the native varieties never really got started. Massachusetts was highly important at a later stage of American viticultural history for what it did do at last towards improving the natives—the Concord grape is its best known, but by no means its only, contribution; meantime, the settlers turned to rum and Madeira.

Further down the coast, in the New Netherland of the Dutch settlers, a vineyard was planted as early as 1642, but was destroyed by the severe winter temperatures; though we do not know, this fact suggests that they were vinifera vines.[103] Immediately after the English took over the colony from the Dutch in 1669, the new governor granted a monopoly of grape growing on Long Island to one Paul Richards, who also received the privilege of selling his wine tax-free.[104] Whether he ever had any to sell the records do not tell us, but such silence is significant. A Dutch traveller visiting Coney Island in 1679 found abundant grapes growing wild and noted that the settlers had several times planted vineyards without success. "Nevertheless," he added, "they have not abandoned the hope of doing so by and by, for there is always some encouragement, although they have not, as yet, discovered the cause of the failure."[105] This could hardly be bettered as a summary of the colonial experience: repeated effort, repeated failure, persistent hope, and the tantalizing fact of flourishing wild grapes. How many trials may have been made in the promising terrain of the settlements around New York harbor, and along the Hudson River, there is no means of knowing.

The Swedes along the Delaware in what is now New Jersey and Delaware were just as eager as the English and the Dutch to turn their place in the New World into a fountain of wine. The official instructions given to the Swedish governor, Colonel John Printz, in 1642 included viticulture among the objects of the colony,[106] but it was not long before the Jersey farmers turned to apple growing instead and began to produce the cider for which they were famous throughout the colonial period and after.

Across the river in Pennsylvania, William Penn hoped to make viticulture flourish in his American woods. In 1683, within a year of his arrival in the new

IO   William Penn took French vines with him to Pennsylvania in 1682, his first trip to the colony he had founded, and in the next year had his French *vignerons* lay out vineyards. The portrait shows him as he appeared around 1696. (Drawing by Francis Place; Historical Society of Pennsylvania)

colony, Penn recorded that he had drunk a "good claret" made of native grapes by a French Huguenot refugee, Captain Gabriel Rappel.[107] He wondered then whether the future of American winegrowing might not lie with the native varieties rather than with the European vinifera:

> 'Tis disputable with me, whether it be best to fall to fining the fruits of the country, especially the grape, by the care and skill of art, or send for foreign stems and sets, already good and approved. It seems most reasonable to believe, that not only a thing groweth best, where it naturally grows; but will hardly be equalled by another species of the same kind, that doth not naturally grow there. But to solve the doubt, I intend, if God give me life, to try both, and hope the consequence will be as good wine as any European countries of the same latitude do yield.[108]

The idea of developing the native grape of course occurred to others too. Around 1688 Dr. Daniel Coxe, a large New Jersey proprietor resident in London, describing the wealth of his lands, wrote that they abounded in grapes, from the best of which was made "very good wine" and, from the less good, brandy. "It is believed by judicious persons, French vignerons and others, that some sorts of them improved by cultivating would produce as good wine as any in the world."[109]

Possibly, if Penn had in fact turned to the "fining" of the native vine, he would have developed a successful viticulture. But he seems to have concentrated on vinifera instead. Before he left England on his first voyage to Pennsylvania, Penn had sent for vines from Bordeaux to be taken with him.[110] These he had had planted for him by a Huguenot refugee named Andrew Doz on a spot now a part of Fairmount Park in Philadelphia, along the banks of the Schuylkill.[111] Like all other such trials, this one had no immediate success, though it had later results not dreamed of at the time.

Penn also took an interest in the work of Francis Pastorius, leader of the Pietist German settlers at Germantown, who in 1691 chose for their town seal a device showing a grapevine, a flax blossom, and a weaver's spool. The meaning of the seal, Pastorius wrote, was to show that "the people of this place live from grapes, flax, and trade" (that is, the weaving trade).[112] Though the community flourished, the grapes did not. And Penn, who kept a cellar in his Philadelphia house, had to furnish it, not with the vintages of Germantown or the Schuylkill, but with the produce of Europe. Perhaps he was not sorry to do so, despite that "good claret" he once drank from his own woods. The favorite wines of the Penn household, we are told, were "canary, claret, sack and madeira."[113] Pennsylvania was in no way ready to yield such wines.

Many miles south of Penn's woods, some twenty years before Philadelphia was laid out, Lord Baltimore, the proprietor of Maryland, in 1662 instructed his son the governor, Charles Calvert, to plant a vineyard and to make wine. To the original 240 acres of vineyard on the St. Mary's River (in the far south of the colony, just across the Potomac from Virginia) another hundred acres were added in 1665.[114] Wine made from this is reported, with the uncritical optimism of all such early responses, to have been "as good as the best burgundy."[115] In 1672 Lord Baltimore sent over a hogshead of vines to the colony, but his son reported in the next year that every one had perished, frustrating his hope to be able, in a few years, "to have sent your Lordship a glass of wine of the growth of this Province."[116] Tobacco established itself so quickly and overwhelmingly as the dominant crop in seventeenth-century Maryland that viticulture, whether as good as the best in Burgundy or not, had no chance.

Passing by Virginia, whose struggles with the grape we have already seen, we arrive at the Carolinas, which offer the most striking illustration of what we may call the Virginia syndrome in seventeenth-century America. Raleigh's expedition in 1584, we remember, took note of the promise made by the abundant wild grapes growing thickly along the Carolina coast. Some eighty years later, in 1663, the proprietors of Carolina, newly chartered by Charles II, drew up proposals for a colony that would concentrate—despite the experience of Jamestown—on just

I I   Seal of Germantown, Pennsylvania: the three leaves of the clover bear a weaver's spool, a flax blossom, and, on the right, a grape vine, to show that the German Pietists who founded the town in 1683 meant to live from winegrowing and weaving. (Masthead ornament from the *Germantown Crier* [Germantown Historical Society], Fall 1986)

those "three rich commodities," wine, silk, and oil, that Hakluyt and others had dreamed of producing in an English Mediterranean invented along the Atlantic coast. Sir William Berkeley, one of the distinguished proprietors of the Carolina colony (together with such eminent figures of Restoration England as Anthony Ashley Cooper, later Lord Shaftesbury; Lord Clarendon, the lord chancellor of England; and the duke of Albemarle) was commissioned to appoint a government for Carolina. His instructions included a proviso for setting aside 20,000 acres of land for the proprietors, taking care that some be "on sides of hills that look to the southward which will be best for vineyards";[117] such land would be highly profitable, it was argued, for an "acre in the Canaries" then produced £60 per annum,[118] and what might not be expected from virgin land? One wonders what Berkeley, who had been in Virginia for more than twenty years and had seen the vinegrowing plan fail again and again, thought of all this? He was interested in the possibility of viticulture, and, as has already been mentioned, had planted a vineyard of native vines to set an example to the colonists. Certainly the production of the longed-for "rich commodities" had not had fair trial yet, and who could say what might not be done in a different, untested place?

In the way of so many New World projects and speculations, this grandiose official scheme for viticulture does not seem even to have been begun, much less carried out, though the evidence, as usual, is exceedingly indistinct. The economic development of North Carolina was generally slow: the northern coast was largely without good harbors, settlement there advanced gradually and irregularly, and such trade as there was was mostly carried on through the ships and merchants of other colonies. All this, as one historian writes, "produced a type of small-scale farm economy primarily self-sufficing and essentially local and isolated."[119] Some traffic in tobacco grew up, but the main resource came from the great pine forests and their yield of tar, pitch, turpentine, and lumber of all kinds. Grape growing and winemaking do not seem to have gotten started at all in the earliest settlements of what is now North Carolina (the separation between the two Carolinas did not officially exist until 1712). The surveyor appointed by the proprietors wrote in 1665 that he did "most highly applaud" their "design of making wine in this country";[120] but we hear nothing afterwards of the result of that design in the first settlement in this colony.

A second settlement in North Carolina, along the Cape Fear River farther south, was publicized by a prospectus setting forth the inducement of seven years' exemption from customs duty on all wine produced locally;[121] once again, no evidence exists to show that anybody managed to enjoy the privilege.

In what was to become South Carolina, the first settlement was directed by the Lords Proprietors of the Carolinas themselves from their headquarters in London. So far, their hopes of generating those "precious commodities" wine, oil, and silk in the huge territory granted to them by royal charter had been entirely frustrated: the settlements in the northern parts of the colony were not commercially productive; the attempt to settle on the Cape Fear River to the south had quickly failed. Now they would try again, yet farther to the south, to make the land yield wine. Accordingly, the leader of the expedition, Joseph West, was instructed to take vines with him when he sailed in 1669.[122] The colonists established themselves around what is now Charleston, South Carolina, on the Ashley River, and reported in their first summer that "there is nothing that we plant but it thrives very well"; "the land," they concluded, would bear "good wine."[123] At first the need to provide food delayed the experiment with vines. By early 1672, however, Joseph Dalton, a member of the colony's council, wrote to Lord Ashley that he hoped the new crop would set them free to begin on

> the husbandry of vines and olive trees. . . . We have indeed plenty of diverse sorts of grapes here, some very pleasant and large but being pressed the thickness of their outward skin yields a kind of harshness which gives us reason to fear (though we intend to make trial of them) that they will hardly ever be reclaimed or with very great difficulty. We must therefore recommend to your Lordship to furnish us with the plants of good vines and olives with some persons who know the true husbandry of them; herein your Lordship need not doubt the diversities of vines, for I do verily believe we have ground suitable to all their variety.[124]

In the same year a Spaniard sent to spy out the land where the English had settled reported to the authorities that each house in Charleston had a trellis "for grape vines of different sorts."[125] Were the colonists trying out the native vines on these trellises? It seems likely.

Ashley was evidently strongly attached to the hope of profit through the trinity of wine, oil, and silk, for in 1674 (he was by then the earl of Shaftesbury) he wrote to his kinsman Andrew Percevall, then about to sail for Carolina, that the proprietors were determined to "lay out their money in procuring skilfull men and fit materials for the improvement of the country in wine, silk, oil etc.," and that a plantation of 12,000 acres was to be set aside for experiment in these things.[126]

Three years later the proprietors wrote to the colony that they were "laying out in several places of the world" for both plants and for "persons that are skilled in planting and producing vines, Mulberry trees, rice, oils and wines and such other commodities that enrich those other countries that enjoy not so good a climate as you."[127] That something, at least, towards recruiting skilled winegrowers was done is attested by the evidence of a Savoyard who fled from English Carolina to Spanish St. Augustine in 1683; he told the Spaniards that he had come to Carolina under a four-year indenture to plant vines.[128] That he had later felt compelled to escape the colony might mean any of a number of things. It is not, however, very likely evidence of flourishing vineyards.

A new turn was taken in 1680, when the first organized company of Huguenots landed in South Carolina expressly to undertake the manufacture of silk, oil, and wine.[129] The religious persecution of the French Protestants called Huguenots—persecution that went on despite the legal protection of the Edict of Nantes—drove these people in large numbers out of France to places all over the world, especially to England and to those spots on the globe where English colonies had been planted. Huguenots helped, in this decade, to establish the great winegrowing enterprise of South Africa around Cape Town; and, though they did not fully succeed in winegrowing on the American continent, they certainly had a large share, in their settlements and in the work of individuals scattered here and there in the colonies, in keeping the effort alive. As we have heard of them already in Massachusetts, Rhode Island, and Pennsylvania, so we shall hear of them repeatedly in the sequel. These early Huguenots of South Carolina, though not the first of their kind to arrive in America, have the distinction of having founded one of the most successful and important centers of French influence in British America.

In the report of Thomas Ashe, a gentleman who went out on the same ship that was, at the expense of King Charles himself, carrying the Huguenots to South Carolina, we hear the familiar hopeful note, the conviction of quick success just round the corner:

> 't is not doubted, if the Planters as industriously prosecute the Propagation of Vineyards as they have begun; but Carolina will in a little time prove a magazine and staple for wines to the whole West Indies; and to enrich their variety, some of the Proprietors and Planters have sent them the noblest and excellentest vines of Europe, viz. the Rhenish, Clarret, the Muscadel and Canary, etc. His Majesty, to improve so hopeful a design, gave those French we carried over their passage free for themselves, wives, children, goods, and servants, they being most of them well experienced in the nature of the vine, from whose directions doubtless the English have received and made considerable advantages in their improvements.[130]

Ashe also tells us that some Carolina wine had already been sent to England and that it was "well approved of" by the "best palates." In the same year as Ashe's report, 1682, an employee of one of the proprietors, Samuel Wilson, published in London an *Account of Carolina* with an encouraging report on the success of the

Huguenots. They had planted vineyards of the European varieties sent over with them and also had hopes of making good wine from some, at least, of the native varieties. Meanwhile they had succeeded in making a little wine "very good both in colour and taste"[131]—no doubt this is the wine that Ashe refers to, and no doubt it was from native grapes, muscadine especially.

It was a hopeful time: another observer in the year 1682, writing from Charleston, says that the colonists had "great hopes" of making good wine, and that "this year will be the time of trial, which, if it hits, no doubt but the place will flourish exceedingly, but if the vines do not prosper I question whether it will ever be any great place of trade."[132] In the next year, one of the Huguenots, Frances de Rousserie, a native of Montpellier, was awarded a grant of 800 acres by the proprietors "because he had with great industry applied himself to the propagation of wine and other things in Carolina."[133] But by that time it was no doubt becoming evident that, despite the great hopes, the vines did not prosper. De Rousserie, if he succeeded, presumably did so with native vines.

Thus the impulse that the Huguenots gave to winegrowing could not have lasted long. A decade later, in 1694, the assembly passed an act to "encourage the making of wine, indigo and salt"[134]—a sure sign, as such acts had earlier been in Virginia, that wine was not being made. In the same year, one James Boyd was granted 3,000 acres as a bounty for his labors in "endeavoring the establishment of a vintage";[135] but this exception merely confirms the general fact. As Robert Beverley wrote in 1705, the Frenchmen sent to Carolina on purpose to make wine "could not succeed in it, but miscarried in all their Attempts."[136]

The early hopes of winegrowing in South Carolina petered out in the efforts of Sir Nathaniel Johnson. Johnson, who lived in South Carolina from 1690 until his death in 1713, served as governor of the colony for six of those years. He was an energetic experimenter with plants and crops, especially keen on succeeding in the manufacture of silk—he named his plantation on the Cooper River, near Charleston, "Silk Hope." He tried to promote winegrowing, too. According to the Quaker John Archdale's account, Johnson planted a "considerable vineyard";[137] another contemporary, John Lawson, tells us that Johnson had "rejected all exotic vines, and makes his wine from the natural black grape of Carolina."[138] But at the same time, Lawson makes it clear that Johnson's experiments created no general response. There was not experience enough to solve the questions of winemaking in a strange world where the old practices simply would not work and where men knew not what to do. On Johnson's death, his estate went to a daughter, and, according to a later eighteenth-century writer, "she married; and her husband destroyed the vineyard and orchard to apply the soil to Turky-corn."[139]

Visionary forms of viticulture were still available, however. In 1717 the projector Sir Robert Montgomery put forth in London proposals for a model colony, to be founded in the territory of South Carolina (the region in question is now part of Georgia and Alabama) and to be called Azilia. As Montgomery correctly noted, there were in the destined regions of settlement vines flourishing upon the hills and bearing grapes in the "most luxuriant plenty."[140] The neatly schematic map of the proposed margravate of Azilia published by Montgomery shows stylized vineyards as part of the picture, but the entire project remained a dream. The scheme is a slight added testimony to the stubborn persistence of the idea that wine *could* be grown despite all the discouragements.

The last word on the enterprise of winemaking in seventeenth-century South Carolina may be spoken by the English writer John Oldmixon in his *History of the British Empire in America* (1708). After quoting various enthusiastic reports on the produce—actual or fancied—of the colony, Oldmixon naturally asks: "Since the climate is so proper, since the grapes are so plentiful, and the wine they make so good, why is there not more of it? Why do we not see some of it?" He answers his own question thus: "The inhabitants either think they can turn their hands to a more profitable culture, or impose upon us in their reports; for I would not think them so weak, as to neglect making good wine, and enough of it, if they could, and thought it worth their while."[141] Oldmixon has put it very clearly. The colonists could not make the European vine grow, nor was it yet worth their while to develop the native vine. About the time that Oldmixon was putting his skeptical questions, John Lawson in North Carolina was explaining the difficulties from the settler's point of view: "New planted colonies are generally attended with a force and necessity of planting the known and approved staple and product of the country," Lawson wrote. Because the planter's time was thus taken up, the country would have to wait first until skillful *vignerons* should set to work and make it their chief business. Then, Lawson continues, "when it becomes a general undertaking, every one will be capable to add something to the common stock, of that which he has gain'd by his own experience. This way would soon make the burden light, and a great many shorter and exacter curiosities and real truths would be found out in a short time."[142]

It must be admitted that nothing like this has happened yet: viticulture and winemaking have never become enterprises general throughout the United States, and even now no genuinely national means of coordinating experiment and of disseminating information exists. Nor is there any national policy designed to encourage the production of wine. It is an innocent recreation to imagine what might have been, however, had the colonists somehow managed to make winegrowing with native grapes a staple activity up and down the Atlantic seaboard and so have given us a tradition of wine. We would by now, for sure, have a wealth of regional and local varieties and styles, complex enough to challenge the interest of connoisseurs through a lifetime. The vision of what might have been if things had gone that way has been gracefully sketched by Frank Schoonmaker and Tom Marvel in their now classic *American Wines*. Their catalog of wines that might have been but never were realized begins in Maine, "where there is a little wine grown north of Bath . . . it is pale and thin and possesses a peculiar bitterness which the inhabitants say is due to the vines being grown near brackish waters." Massachusetts, in this imaginary review, presents an array running from the "spicy pink Chicopee" of the Connecticut Valley to the white wines of Cape Cod, "without which no loyal Bay State son or daughter would think of eating Cape Cod oysters." Connecticut boasts of its Housatonic wines, "the best reds east of the Hudson"; the Delaware Valley yields "full-bodied and generous vintages" both red and white; New Jersey produces a wine savoring of cranberries, much esteemed by the oenophiles of Philadelphia; and so on down along the coast, to the red Pocomokes and white Choptanks of Maryland's Eastern Shore. It is a charming fancy, still worth pursuing.[143]

2

The Georgia Experiment

A t the beginning of the eighteenth century, the prospect of winegrowing in America was hardly any clearer than it had been a century earlier. The Virginians had tried, through many years of the century preceding, to lay the basis of an industry. The secret eluded them as it did the colonists of the Carolinas, who also made an officially sponsored effort, less prolonged and less intense than in Virginia. Alongside of these publicly encouraged trials, dozens, scores, no doubt hundreds of local, individual, and amateur experiments in vinegrowing and in winemaking had been attempted from the beginning to the end of the century up and down the entire length of the Atlantic coast. The scale of all this, however, was so small as to be hardly visible even on the narrow strip of early colonial America. The work, frustrated after a few years wherever it began, established no tradition; nor was there any possible coordination of effort and experience among the small, isolated, and widely separated colonial communities. For practical purposes, each hopeful projector of winegrowing in 1700 was just where his fellow-spirit of 1600 had been, except that the lapse of a century without effective good results in this business was bound to suggest doubts and difficulties to him such as the first settlers could not at once suspect.

Nevertheless, the prevailing ignorance meant that hope remained alive. For who could say that the next optimist might not succeed? True, European grapes *had not* grown well; but since no one knew any reason why, no one could say that the wine grape *could not* flourish here. And, indeed, on this question, perhaps the most interesting one still for the future of American viticulture, the answers, four centuries after the beginnings of settlement, are not yet in. Whatever the truth may finally appear to be as to *Vitis vinifera* in the eastern United States, the colonist at the beginning of the 1700s knew simply that the wild vine, as it always had, still flourished powerfully, that it must therefore be possible to grow some sort of grape for making wine, and that the enterprise was worth a try. Hope could thus persist, and the persistence, at the level of official policy, is best shown in the eighteenth century by the early history of Georgia, last of the original thirteen colonies.

Georgia, as every schoolboy knows, was to be a place where the potential of a virgin land was to be put at the service of philanthropy. In the idea of Georgia's chief founder, General James Oglethorpe, men who had no place and no hope under the system of the Old World might become prosperous and upright in the spacious system of the New. This was very unlike Massachusetts, a colony founded by stern sectarians who sought a place apart for the exercise of their exclusive religion; or Virginia, where the simple prospect of gain was a sufficient motive. There were, to be sure, other considerations in the founding of Georgia. Providing a bulwark for the English colonies against the Spanish to the south and the French to the west was one. Another was the familiar commercial policy of providing Britain with those commodities for which it depended on foreign suppliers—notably that familiar trio, silk, oil, and wine. But the philanthropic motive was the strongest in the public imagination.

To make sure that the refugees from old England should not be corrupted in their new Eden, there were to be no slaves and no rum in Georgia. The economic basis of the colony, so its philanthropic projectors imagined, was to be those two commodities whose charm, a hundred and fifty years after Hakluyt, was still irresistible—silk and wine. By producing these from land "at present waste and desolate" the paupers of England might—so the royal charter ran—"not only gain a comfortable subsistence for themselves and families, but also strengthen our colonies and increase the trade, navigation, and wealth of these our realms."[1] Silk was the principal object, but wine came right after it. An early propagandist for the colony, appealing to the ideal "Man of Benevolence" whose pleasure was to relieve the distressed, exhorted him to imagine what Georgia might quickly become:

> Let him see those, who are now a Prey to all the Calamities of Want, who are starving with Hunger, and seeing their Wives and Children in the same Distress; expecting likewise every Moment to be thrown into a Dungeon, with the cutting Anguish that they leave their Families exposed to the utmost Necessity and Despair: Let him, I say, see these living under a sober and orderly Government, settled in Towns, which are rising at Distances along navigable rivers: Flocks and Herds in the neighbouring Pastures, and adjoining to them Plantations of regular Rows of Mulberry-Trees, entwined with Vines, the Branches of which are loaded with Grapes.[2]

The effort to realize this animating vision (the vine wedded to the mulberry suggests a specifically Italian model) began in February 1733, when the first settlers landed at the site of Savannah and set about laying out the town. One of

I 2 General James Edward Oglethorpe (1696—1785) founded Georgia as a place where neither slavery nor strong drink was to be allowed, but where winegrowing was to be a basic economic activity. "We shall certainly succeed," he affirmed; but the best intentions were not good enough. (Artist unknown; Oglethorpe University)

their immediate undertakings was to establish a public garden, or nursery, where they could grow and propagate the mulberries, vines, olives, oranges, and other plants upon which the Mediterranean culture that they dreamed of was to be founded. This public garden, or Trustees' Garden, as it was called, was planted on ten acres of land between the town site and the river, to the east of the town in a spot still known in Savannah as Trustees' Garden.[3] Less than a year after its establishment, one traveller described it as a "beautiful garden . . . where are a great many white mulberry trees, vines, and orange trees raised."[4] But the repeated assertions made through the troubled years of the garden's life that it was badly sited on barren ground seem closer to the mark: it stood, said one critic, on "a large hill of dry sand."[5]

Even before any colonists had arrived in Georgia, the trustees of the colony,

13 The Trustees' Garden, Savannah, Georgia, from a print published in London in 1733. Called "the first agricultural experiment station in America," the garden was intended as a source of grapes, mulberry trees, oranges, olives, and other plants for the new colony. (University of Georgia Library)

eager to promote their plans for agriculture, had hired Dr. William Houston, a botanist of some distinction, one of the many correspondents of the great Linnaeus, to collect plants for trial in Georgia. Houston at once began his explorations by way of Madeira in 1732; from there he sent on "two tubs of the cuttings of Malmsey and other vines" to Charleston, to await the arrival of Oglethorpe's first band of settlers.[6] An agent was already in Charleston to supervise a nursery from which, in turn, the Savannah garden was to be supplied. The choice of Madeira as the source of vines for Georgia makes clear that the familiar logic of the argument from latitude was being applied. Savannah and the Western Islands lie within a degree of each other, and what more reasonable in theory—though false in fact—than that regions in the same latitude should yield the same produce? Dr. Houston intended to study the methods of vine cultivation and winemaking at Madeira too, in preparation for his arrival in Georgia. Unluckily, he fell ill at Jamaica and died there in 1733 without ever reaching the new colony to whose future he had hoped to contribute.[7]

Friends of the colony in England also helped: the famous gardener Philip Miller, in charge of the Botanical Gardens at Chelsea, sent a tub of "burgundy vines" late in 1733[8] (what the measure of a "tub" was I have not found, for it varied with the thing to be packed). A Mr. Charles King, of Brompton, who owned a vineyard there, sent not only three tubs of vines but ten dozen bottles of "Burgundy Wine" of his own manufacture—probably no Burgundian *éleveur* was aware of this suburban London rival—as a present to Tomochichi, chief of the local

Yamacraw Indians at Savannah.[9] King seems to have been the most persistent of the sponsors of winegrowing among the English friends of Georgia; from the trustees' records we learn that he sent another two tubs of vines in 1737 and, in the next year, a thousand vine plants. And there were other such gifts from other sources.

Such of them as survived the Atlantic voyage were set out in the Trustees' Garden, which seemed at first to flourish. The trustees were told in 1737 that the vines in the garden had succeeded extremely well, so that people "did not doubt of making good wines."[10] Two years later Oglethorpe reported that there was a half acre of vines in the garden, where they "have begun to shoot and promise well."[11] But that is the last hopeful note inspired by the garden: shortly afterwards a severe frost did grave damage, and that setback seems to have confirmed latent doubts about the garden's future.[12]

The garden was unlucky, in the way that the colony as a whole was unlucky. We have already seen that the first botanist appointed to advance the horticulture of the colony, Dr. Houston, died in Jamaica without ever reaching Georgia. His successor, Robert Millar, while collecting specimens of tropical flora in Mexico, was imprisoned by the Spanish on two successive voyages, his materials were confiscated, and he himself was finally returned to England empty-handed and without contributing anything directly to Georgia.[13] The first gardener actually to work in the garden, Joseph Fitzwalter, began enthusiastically, but then fell out with Paul Amatis, a Savoyard brought over by the trustees to develop the culture of silk. Amatis and Fitzwalter clashed over who was to be master of the garden. Amatis seems to have been a quarrelsome man, and at one time he grew so angry that he threatened to shoot Fitzwalter should he ever enter the garden again.[14] Early in 1735 Amatis had sent some 2,000 vines to the Savannah garden from the stock accumulated at Charleston. By July, he claimed, Fitzwalter had given some away as presents, to "I know not who," and had let the rest die.[15] Furthermore, the public character of the garden made things difficult: people stole the plants and stripped the fruit, to the despair of the gardener. "Fruits, grapes and whatever else grows is pulled and destroyed before maturity."[16] Amatis finally succeeded in establishing his authority over Fitzwalter, who left the colony for Carolina. Amatis himself died late in 1736, and in the decade or so of its remaining life, the garden saw several different gardeners come and go.

One of them, an educated Scotsman named Hugh Anderson, left a good description of the state and character of the garden and a plan for improving it. The soil was poor, he wrote to the trustees, and the site exposed to wind and sun. It would do very well as a nursery for mulberry trees, but if the trustees seriously wished to encourage "vines, olive trees, plant [sic], drugs, etc.," they must create windbreaks, raise hedges to divide and protect the garden, drain the swampy land, build a greenhouse, dig a well, and set up a laboratory and a library.[17] The trustees must have wondered at what so simple an idea as a garden required in a strange new land.

By 1740 the garden was productive only as a nursery of mulberry trees, and it was clear that the main part of the tract was too sterile to suit horticulture. A rich, swampy section of the grounds was cleared and drained in 1742 to serve as a nursery for the vine cuttings that the trustees continued to send over to the colony,[18] and some rooted vines were distributed from this source in the years following. But the garden—"that barren place, where all labour was ill bestowed," as it was described in 1745—did not prosper.[19] Later in that year the gardener was fired for neglecting his charge, though he must have had a thankless task of it even had he been irreproachably conscientious. In 1755 the land, which had apparently long ceased to be employed as a garden, was, on his petition, granted to the first royal governor, John Reynolds.[20] Nearly two hundred years later an effort was made to reestablish a part of the original site as a museum and memorial garden, but its bad luck seems to have continued to pursue the spot, and the effort failed.[21]

The Trustees' Garden has been called "the first organized experiment station ever,"[22] and is thus the prototype of an excellent institution. As a practical encouragement to winegrowing, however, it was no more successful than the Georgia trustees' hopeful prohibitions against slaves and spirits, both of which hopes expired in the same decade as the garden.

"All the vine kinds seem natural to the country" wrote one Georgia traveller in 1736;[23] it is the familiar observation of all early American travellers. There is a special pathos in this instance, though, since the writer, Francis Moore, is describing the vines of St. Simon's Island, only a few miles north of the Huguenot outpost in Florida where, it was alleged, the earliest American wine on record had been made in 1564. Now, nearly two centuries later, not much had changed: the Spaniards were still a threat, the vines still flourished mockingly, and the production of wine remained a dream.

At the same time that Moore was remarking the abundance of vines along the coastal islands, a more celebrated observer was taking notes on the grapes of Georgia: "The common Wild-Grapes are of two sorts, both red: the fox-grape grows two or three only on a stalk, is thick-skinn'd, large-ston'd, of a harsh taste, and of the size of a small Kentish Cherry. The cluster-grape is of a harsh taste too, and about the size of a white currant."[24] This is from the journal of John Wesley, whose labors at soul-saving in Georgia, where he had gone in the earliest days of that colony, were as troubled and unsatisfactory as the struggles of any Georgia vineyardist to grow wine. Back in England, John Wesley's brother Samuel had hailed the Georgia enterprise in a poem entitled "Georgia, and Verses upon Mr. Oglethorpe's Second Voyage to Georgia" (1736), in which the imagined vintages of Georgia are presented in glowing terms:

> With nobler Products see thy GEORGIA teems,
> Chear'd with the genial Sun's director Beams
> There the wild Vine to Culture learns to yield,
> And purple Clusters ripen through the Field.

Now bid thy Merchants bring thee Wine no more
Or from the *Iberian* or the *Tuscan* Shore;
No more they need th' *Hungarian* Vineyards drain,
And *France* herself may drink her best *Champain.*
Behold! at last, and in a subject Land,
Nectar sufficient for thy large Demand:
Delicious Nectar, powerful to improve
Our hospitable Mirth and social Love.[25]

This outburst is a valuable expression of the attractive power that the vision of what may be called imperial winemaking had upon the sober English imagination, but it was a vision evidently much easier to sustain in the fields of Devonshire than in the woods of Georgia, where John Wesley encountered the "thick-skinn'd, large-ston'd" grape of "harsh taste" (evidently rotundifolia).

The hopes of Oglethorpe, the founder of Georgia, were not easy to defeat. He had supervised the laying out of the Trustees' Garden, and, despite the evidence to the contrary, persisted in his optimism. "We shall certainly succeed in Silk and Wine," he wrote to the trustees in 1738, and again, "there is great hope, nay, I may say, no doubt, that both Silk and Wine will in a very short time come to perfection." He was repeating the same confident assurances as late as 1743.[26] What reason did he have to make them? Probably none. But it is at least understandable that the founder of a colony in desperate straits, as Georgia was then, might feel himself bound to take a view opposed to all the plain evidence before him.

We learn hardly anything distinct from contemporary reports about the fate of the European vines that were actually planted in Georgia. Some say that those planted in the Trustees' Garden did well; others affirm that the vines were neglected or abused. Whether any were actually tended long enough to make it clear how they would do does not appear, but such information as exists makes that seem doubtful. As for winemaking in the colony, the few accounts make it plain that native grapes were always the source. Early in 1739, for example, a Mr. Cooksey told the trustees, who were naturally anxious to know something about the Georgia wines and vines that they hoped to promote, that he had himself "made wine of the wild grape of the country . . . but it grew sour, and would not keep, tho' very pleasant to drink when new, and of a fine colour."[27] Later in that year the trustees heard from Mr. Auspurger, their engineer and surveyor, just returned from the colony, that "he eat some grapes at Savannah in July as fine as can be seen, and he believed they would make the best Vidonia wine"[28] (Vidonia wine was the most highly regarded wine of the Canary Islands, a dry white wine exported to the English colonies as a minor competitor to Madeira).

Many miles to the south of Savannah, on St. Simon's Island, Colonel William Cooke, who had sent out sixteen different sorts of vine cuttings from France in 1737, had begun to make wine from native grapes (his French grapes would not yet have been bearing—or, more likely, they had died). The result of Cooke's experiments was described to the trustees in 1740 by a Lieutenant Horton, one of Cooke's neighbors, as having "a pleasant sweet flavour and taste, and he believed would keep near a year." Cooke's experiments, Horton added, made many in the southern part of the colony "determined to push on the plantation of vines."[29] Only a year later the trustees heard from a different witness that the impulse had come to nothing, "that some had planted grapes but left off, finding the grape small and unprofitable."[30] Still, where all was yet uncertain, one might hope to hear a very different story. Horton, for one, was still optimistic, for he was, in 1744, among those who received the 3,000 cuttings sent to the settlement of Frederica by William Stephens (of whom more in a moment).[31] Yet another colonist in 1741 told Lord Egmont, one of the trustees most interested in the fortunes of Georgia winemaking:

> That the wine for export will certainly succeed in Georgia: that himself had made some even of the Wild grape cut down, which had as strong a body as Burgundy, and as fine a flavour: that by cutting the thick coat of the grape grew thinner, and if the cuttings were transplanted into vinyards or gardens, the Vine will every way answer still better.[32]

If the growing of good wine had any real chance in the conditions of early colonial Georgia, it would certainly have been found out by a gentleman sent over by the trustees as secretary to the colony in 1737. This was Colonel William Stephens (colonel of the militia, like so many colonels, English and American), a man already of advanced age for pioneering enterprise (he was sixty-six when he went to Georgia) and of rather tarnished fame.[33] Though he had represented the Isle of Wight in Parliament for twenty years, he was unlucky in business and had twice had to abandon home and position in order to flee from his creditors. Sent to Georgia by the trustees primarily to provide full reports on the colony, he became there an enthusiast of pure and holy fervor in the cause of the grape. He was always disappointed, but he deserves some memorial as the first official residing in the colonies to make a sustained attempt to realize the vision of winemaking so easily indulged at home in England but so heartbreaking to pursue in the wilderness.

Stephens also had the merit of keeping a journal—it was this habit that decided the trustees that he was the man to write the full and current reports they badly wanted—and from this journal we can learn in some detail of the hopes raised and the disappointments suffered in the struggle to make Georgian wine.

When Stephens arrived in November of 1737, he found both good news and bad news. The bad was that the vines in the Trustees' Garden were not doing well, and nobody could tell whether that was because the conditions in Georgia were wrong, or, as Stephens himself suspected, because of the "unskillfulness or negligence" of the gardeners.[34] The good news was that one grape grower, at least, was doing well. Stephens' journal for 6 December 1737 records the hopeful evidence:

> After dinner walked out to see what improvements of vines were made by one Mr. Lyon, a Portuguese Jew, which I had heard some talk of; and indeed nothing had given me so much pleasure since my arrival, as what I found here; though it was yet (if I say it properly) only in Miniature, for he had cultivated only for two or three years past about half a score of them which he received from Portugal for an experiment; and by his skill and management in pruning, etc. they all bore this year very plentifully.[35]

The man Stephens calls Mr. Lyon was Abraham De Lyon, one of a number of Portuguese Jews, who, somewhat to the annoyance of the trustees, had been among the very first settlers in the colony.[36] Another member of this group, Senhor Dias, is said to have imported some vines in 1735, and when Dias died these vines came into the hands of De Lyon, with others that De Lyon had provided for himself.[37] By 1737, to judge from Stephens' enthusiastic report, the vineyard was flourishing and De Lyon committed to a serious effort at winegrowing.

So were other members of the Savannah Jewish colony; it was reported to the trustees in June 1737 that the Nunez family, to whom De Lyon was connected by marriage, wished to exchange their swampland holdings for dry land in order to plant vines (though one would suppose that they needed no special reason for wishing to make such a trade). One Isaac Nunez Henriques was most active in this business; "but all the family," the report went on, "are equally desirous with him to plant vineyards and each has made preparations for it, having vines ready to transplant and some in great forwardness."[38]

Perhaps it was the encouragement of Stephens that led De Lyon to petition the trustees for a loan of £200, claiming that he had already expended "the sum of four hundred Pounds in the Improvement of his Lot, and the cultivation of the Vines which he carried with him from Portugal, which he hath brought to great Perfection."[39] On 17 May 1738 the trustees ordered the money to be paid to De Lyon for repayment in six years' time. Less than a year later, in March 1739, Oglethorpe reported from Georgia that De Lyon had by then planted three-quarters of an acre of vineyard, "which thrives well," and that he had twenty acres cleared for fall planting.[40]

At this point something went wrong between De Lyon and Oglethorpe, and the encouraging beginning was stalled. In his letter to the trustees' accountant of 22 November 1738, Oglethorpe stated that he had, as directed, paid the £200 that had been authorized as a loan to De Lyon.[41] But evidently the transaction was not straightforward. A pamphlet published in Charleston in 1741 by a group of disgruntled Georgians alleged, among many other angry charges against Oglethorpe, that he had sabotaged the efforts of De Lyon. Just when De Lyon, they said, was ready to bring in both vines and *vignerons* from Portugal, Oglethorpe refused to hand over the money the trustees had authorized, and so the scheme failed.[42]

This cannot be the whole story, since De Lyon in fact gave his receipt for £100 of the money.[43] A more temperate explanation of what happened is given by Thomas Causton, the chief magistrate of Savannah, who informed the trustees that Oglethorpe had given directions for the loan to be paid, but that his agent had instead deducted from the sum a debt that De Lyon owed to the community store, and so De Lyon "was not able to perform his contract."[44]

Yet another, and anti-Semitic account, is given by the earl of Egmont, a trustee of the Georgia colony, who states that Oglethorpe determined to dole out the second £100 in small sums, "being desirous first to see how faithfully that jew would perform his covenants."[45] Whatever the reason, De Lyon literally wanted out. As

Stephens wrote in his Journal for April 1741, De Lyon had neglected his vines and had attempted to send some of his goods out of Georgia in preparation for leaving the colony. "I cannot," Stephens concluded, "any longer look on him as a person to be confided in."[46]

The Nunez family, one of whose daughters De Lyon had taken to wife, had all left Georgia for Carolina by September 1740 "for fear of the Spaniards" according to a contemporary chronicler,[47] and perhaps De Lyon, in wishing to follow them, had no more sinister motive than they had. The Portuguese and Spanish Jews in Georgia had known the persecution of the Inquisition in their native lands and had therefore a special reason to be frightened by a threat from Spanish forces. But another reason—one more ominous for the future of the colony—is given in the record kept by Lord Egmont of a conversation with a gentleman newly returned from Georgia in February 1741. His witness gave Egmont this sorry news:

> That every one of the Jews were gone, and that industrious man Abrm. Delyon, on whom were founded all our expectations for cultivating vines and making wine.
>
> I asked him the reason: he reply'd, want of Negroes, which cost but 6 pence a week to keep; whereas his white servants cost him more than he was able to afford.[48]

Since Stephens, writing two months after the date of Egmont's note, implies that De Lyon had not yet left Georgia, the statement that he had already done so is premature. But it was not long before De Lyon departed in fact, for we learn from the proceedings of the Savannah town council in October 1741 that De Lyon had by then been gone for several months, that he was not likely to return, and that his vines were "wholly neglected." The magistrates gave orders to "find out a proper person amongst the German servants to watch and look carefully after the said vines for the benefit of the Trust," but it is doubtful whether anything was actually done.[49] As for De Lyon, he took his family northwards and is afterwards heard of in Pennsylvania and in New York. A son of his returned to the South later, took a wife, and settled in Savannah, not as a vine grower but as a lawyer.[50]

One of the most frequently complained about difficulties in Georgia was that of getting good cuttings for planting. As early as February 1735 one colonist was begging the trustees that a "sufficient quantity of slips, etc. of vines may be delivered as against the next season. Had I enough ready I would plant now at least two acres." Two years later, the same writer repeated his request.[51] In December 1738, the trustees' records report, a parcel of vine cuttings, "mostly of the Burgundy kind," went out to Georgia by the ship *America*.[52] Stephens' journal tells us how they looked when they got there:

> Among other things sent from the Trust by the ship America, lately arrived, was a parcel of vine-cuttings, which with proper care in packing would have been extreamly valuable, and are much coveted. But unhappily they came naked, without any covering, and only bound up like a common faggot; so that being in that manner exposed, and possibly thrown carelessly up and down in the voyage, they had the appearance of no other than a bundle of dry sticks.[53]

Despite this and other setbacks—successive shipments of cuttings from England all seemed to arrive dead or dying—Stephens remained sanguine. Early in 1740 his journal describes some very hopeful signs appropriate to the spring season: "One thing here I cannot but take notice of with some pleasure, which is, that I find an uncommon tendency lately sprung up among our people of all ranks, towards planting vines; wherein they shew an emulation, if they get but a few, of outdoing one another."[54]

By the end of the year, Stephens is even more emphatic. In his vindication of the colony, "attested upon oath in the court of Savannah, November 10, 1740," and intended to silence the critics of the government, he declared: "The staple of the country of Georgia being presumed, and intended to be principally silk and wine, every year confirms more our hopes of succeeding in those two, from the great increase (as has been before observed) of the vines and mulberry-trees, wherein perseverance only can bring it to perfection."[55] Still, seven years after the first settlement, hardly any wine seems to have been made, and the critics were growing loud. In a debate on supply in the House of Commons in February 1740, John Mordaunt, member for Whitechurch, sarcastically opposed a grant to the Georgia trustees on the grounds that their promises generally, and that about wine in particular, had not been made good: "As to wine, he believed it would be well to give it to the inhabitants for their own drinking, and wished them good luck with it, for it would be all would ever be seen of their wine, and if the people of the place drank no other, they would be the soberest subjects in the world."[56] Since the mercantilist argument of making England self-sufficient in wine was one of the most powerful appeals that the trustees had for coaxing money from Parliament, the inability to perform the promise was a serious matter.

A petition of December 1740, addressed to the king by a group of Georgians hoping to get slaves admitted to the colony, argues that the projected commodities of wine and silk would never be produced without slave labor. In all the history of the colony hardly any silk had been made, the petitioners affirm, and of wine, "not ten gallons."[57] Perhaps there had been a good deal more than that made, but not enough, certainly, to be anything more than a promising curiosity. We have already mentioned the vintages of Mr. Cooksey and of Colonel Cooke. In 1740, when Stephens was repeatedly assuring London that things were beginning to flourish, he was actually able to produce a bottle of wine for official tasting. In September of that year, Stephens left Savannah for Frederica, where Oglethorpe, whose time was more absorbed in fighting the Spanish of St. Augustine than in presiding over his colony, lay ill of fever. In his baggage, Stephens writes, "I had a bottle of Savannah wine at his service, made there, which I had brought with me, to present it with my own hand from the maker."[58] Next day the bottle—"a large stone bottle"—was presented to the ailing general for his judgment. He tasted it before the anxious Stephens and pronounced it to be "something of the nature of a small French white wine, with an agreeable flavor." Stephens adds, for our further assurance, that "all young vines produce small wines at first, and the strength and goodness of it increases as the vines grow older."[59] Not everyone was so hopeful as Stephens, or so tactful as Oglethorpe. Major James Carteret, who was also at Frederica when Stephens presented his Savannah wine, later told the trustees that "he had tasted the wine made at Savannah which Col. Stephens carry'd from thence to Col. Oglethorpe, which was sad stuff, and bitter, rather the juice of the stalk than of the grape."[60]

By the next year Stephens saw even more reason for encouragement. People were actually competing with each other in establishing vineyards, he told the trustees in January 1741.[61] By May he was exulting in the flourishing condition of his own vineyard, in which "many of my vines, that had been of one or two years standing at most, made an agreeable prospect, by putting forth clusters of grapes in pretty good plenty, that had the appearance of coming to perfection."[62] The yield from the new vineyards was not yet enough to produce any substantial measure of wine, so Stephens suggested that three or four growers might pool their grapes, "whereby they might probably attain to a cask of wine, more or less sufficient to make some judgment of what they might expect in time coming."[63] By July, Stephens' eyes were gladdened by the sight of an actual vintage. James Balleu, a Frenchman from near Bordeaux, had had vines growing for the past three years at Savannah and was about to make wine from the crop. Stephens attended the occasion as an observer, and, he tells us, "had the satisfaction of seeing upwards of thirteen gallons press'd, and put into a cask for working; which from the richness of the juice, I should expect will become a wine of a good body, at a due age."[64]

That there really was visible activity in Savannah winegrowing, not just a fantasy of Stephens' hopefulness, is confirmed by Thomas Causton, whose survey of the "products of the colony of Georgia" made at the end of 1741, after noting the dereliction of De Lyon and the general difficulty of obtaining suitable cuttings, says that nevertheless "great progress has been made within this 3 years past." Winegrowing only needed "encouragement" in order to be established, and to this end he suggested a bounty of £100 "for the first pipe of wine which should be made in Georgia."[65] At the same time, Stephens was writing to the trustees' accountant in London that he would soon send a full statistical survey of the wine industry in Georgia, which would show how reasonable it was to expect success in winegrowing and would "convince every body, that all we have said, is not an empty Chimera."[66] The emphasis of the assertion suggests that Stephens had had to listen to loud and frequent doubts; and the skeptics were of course right. If Stephens ever prepared his promised statistical account, I have not found it. It could not have communicated much optimism to the trustees, for in the official defense of the colony prepared by their secretary in 1741, though it is said that the venture in winegrowing "shows a great probability of succeeding," it is prudently added that "this produce must be a work of time, and must depend upon an increase of the people."[67]

We know something of Stephens' own efforts as a viticulturist at this time; he, at any rate, was working in good faith and with good hope. As part of his compensation from the trustees, Stephens had been granted a plantation of 500 acres (the maximum allowable under the rule for Georgia), some thirteen miles south of Savannah at the mouth of the Vernon River, which he named Bewlie, after an estate in England to which he fancied he saw a resemblance.[68] He seems to have planted grapes as soon as ground could be cleared, and his pleasures and troubles growing out of his vineyard at Bewlie make a major theme running through Stephens' journal. Early in 1742 Stephens, using cuttings taken from the Trustees' Garden in Savannah, made an extensive planting of vines under the direction of a man from the Swiss settlement at Purrysburgh (perhaps he was the Monsieur Rinck whom Stephens later called the most skillful *vigneron* in the colony).[69]

In April of 1742 Stephens was pleased to see that of the 900 vines he had planted that spring only a few had failed to grow. By 1743 he had 2,000 vines growing at Bewlie.[70] Despite the chronic difficulty of getting labor sufficient to keep up the plantation, let alone expand it, Stephens was able to look forward to a vintage in but a short time. The vines bore in their second year, but, on the advice of the unnamed *vigneron* whom he employed, the fruit was thinned so that the vines themselves would make better growth. James Balleu, of whom we have already heard, expected to make thirty gallons in 1743, and Stephens himself ordered a small experimental batch of wine made from his own grapes so that he might have some of the 1743 vintage to compare against the next year's promised production. "I found it of a stronger body than any I had yet met with," Stephens writes of his first wine, "a little rough upon the palate, and with a bitterish flavour, somewhat like the taste of an almond. The colour was of a pale red."[71]

By this time, the encouraging state of vine growing in Georgia began to attract the attention of neighboring South Carolina, where the thought of producing wine had never been entirely forgotten since the founding of the colony. In April 1743 Stephens reported a conversation that he had had with two Carolina men, who had told him that, if Georgia succeeded in growing vines, they would plant vines and encourage the industry in Carolina. Stephens was pleased by their interest, but then reflected sadly that Georgia, despite its head start, might be quickly overtaken since labor was so hard to get—Carolina, of course, had plenty of slaves for its rice and indigo plantations, and they might easily be made vine dressers as well.[72]

In January 1745, at a time when Carolina rice was glutting the market, Stephens heard rumors that the Carolinians were planning to go ahead with vineyard planting. Worse still, they had "seduced one of the most skilfull vignerons among the foreign settlers in Georgia to go and instruct them in their first planting."[73] Worst of all, certain Georgians, Stephens was told, had agreed to furnish vine cuttings from the stock available in Georgia. The stories were only too true. James Habersham and William Grant, prominent settlers both, sailed in February with 15,000 cuttings and an unnamed *vigneron* for South Carolina, where they were to deliver their goods to a Port Royal planter. "But can such be looked on as good Georgian men?" Stephens asked his journal.[74] For himself, he was certain that he would never raise up competition against Georgia. The fate of the Carolina vines does not appear, but Stephens probably need not have worried about them to judge from his own experience.

The crisis of Stephens' expectations came in 1744. He was able to distribute 9,000 cuttings from the pruning of his vineyard that spring, and had good reason to tell the trustees that "the propagation of vines seems to promise as one would wish." In the same letter he revealed his hopes, at the time of the vintage, "to press such plenty of grapes, as will give some specimen of what we may expect hereafter, both in quantity and quality."[75] The grapes ripened rapidly under the Georgia sun, and by the end of June Stephens was happy in the contemplation of a heavily laden vineyard. Called away to Savannah and kept there by his official business, he was thunderstruck to learn, just when he expected to hear news of a prosperous vintage, that his crop was ruined. His son and plantation manager, Newdigate Stephens, rode in to Savannah to give him the incredible news: "that plenty of clusters which hung so delightfully within a week past . . . now lay dropt off, and almost covered the face of the whole vineyard, half buried in dirt, and utterly lost."[76] There had been a storm of wind and rain in the week, though whether that would account for so catastrophic a destruction I do not know. Stephens responded with his indomitable optimism—he certainly had the true pioneer spirit and it is impossible not to wish that he had had better success: "If I live I'll persever and leave nothing in my power undone, that I think will conduce to the produce of wine in good perfection. The trifling quantity that is now fermenting, convinces me twill not want a reasonable share of those qualities most likely to recommend it."[77]

Some modest success was had by others that year, since Patrick Houston, early in 1745, was able to send to Oglethorpe a cask of what Houston described as "a pretty good Rhenish" made from vines growing at Frederica.[78] Probably they were native vines, though we are not told.

The next year, 1745, produced the same cycle of high expectation and crushing failure for Stephens. Once again the grapes at Bewlie grew promisingly. From the "pleasant show of plenty we now see on the vines," Stephens wrote, "I can do no less than entertain once more good hopes of what's to come."[79] But what came was utter failure, this time owing to the intense heats that scorched the grapes ripening in a Georgia midsummer; some, says Stephens, were "coddled" by the sun, while other parts of the bunch remained green and stopped growing. The affliction was general throughout the young vineyards of the colony, so that the year produced no vintage at all.[80]

Stephens' extant journal ends in 1745, though he remained as governor until 1751 and did not die until 1753. We do not know in detail what success he may have had in those later years, but it is not hard to guess. It does not appear that any wine worth sending to the trustees ever materialized, for their records mention no such thing. Wine was always something about to be, and all hope that the trustees entertained for a Georgian wine ended with the passage of the colony from their hands to the royal government at the end of 1751. By that time there were slaves and rum in Georgia too, so that the original plans for a free, temperate, winegrowing plantation in the New World seemed to have been negated entirely. In the same year, 1751, the leader of the German colonists settled at Ebenezer, above Savannah on the Savannah River, wrote in response to a European gentleman's query "whether there are vineyards, or if there are none, whether it is considered possible to start any there?" that there were in Georgia "no vineyards": "The attempt has been made in Carolina and Georgia (I, too, tried in a ditch) to start wine gardens, and they did bear plenty of white wine after two or three years (the red wine was less successful) but died again [*sic*] by and by. I assume that we do not know the way to plant and prune."[81]

The repeated failures between the establishment of the Trustees' Garden in 1733 and the disaster to Stephens' vineyard in 1745 had their inevitable effect. The hope of successful viticulture did not absolutely perish—it never did anywhere in the United States—and we hear, for example, in 1766, of two gentlemen named Wright who had begun a vineyard of twenty acres on the St. Mary's River.[82] But by 1771, John William De Brahm, who had earlier brought over a group of Germans to Georgia, reported that no one there, not even the Germans, showed any interest in working with the native vines that grew so vigorously all around them.[83] A final glimpse of the scene in Georgia is provided by the naturalist William Bartram, who, riding from Augusta to Savannah in January 1776, met an Irishman "lately arrived" on his way to cultivate wine grapes, grapes for currants and for raisins, and such items as olives, figs, and silk in the backwoods of the colony.[84] Whether this poor Irishman ever began his experiment, and if he did, how long he may have persisted, we do not know. The Irish are a hopeful race, but it was clear by 1776 to those not "lately arrived" that something more than hope was required.

3

Virginia and the South in the Eighteenth Century

South Carolina; Florida; North Carolina

The Georgia experiment was an exception to the rule, for by the eighteenth century the home government no longer believed that the development of a colonial wine industry could be an item of official policy. Throughout the century, however, sporadic outbursts of encouragement persisted among officials. In South Carolina, for example, Governor Robert Johnson reported to the Board of Trade in London as late as 1734 that the thing could be done if the government would only make it worthwhile: "If a considerable premium was to be given to the first person that made the first tun of good wine" in South Carolina, he wrote, that would overcome the greatest single obstacle, which was the labor and expense and time required for establishing the work "before any profit arises."[1] No evidence exists that the London officials responded—the appeal was one they had certainly heard often before. A decade later, according to the rather indistinct report of the German traveller Johann David Schoepf, the authorities in the colony provided a prize of £60 "to any one exhibiting a pipe of good, drinkable wine made in the country." This, says Schoepf, was responded to by a Frenchman near Orangeburg, who took the premium for several years in succession. "But so soon as the premiums were discontinued, he gave up vine-culture, saying that he could find a better use for his land."[2]

Schoepf's information may not be exact, but it is a matter of record that the Commons of South Carolina in 1744 resolved in favor of a bill offering £100 "to the first person who shall make the first pipe of good, strong-bodied merchantable wine of the growth and culture of his own plantation."[3] A few years later the ante

14 Before his career as a distinguished revolutionary patriot, the Charleston merchant Henry Laurens (1724—92) imported Madeira wines, encouraged the winegrowing efforts of the French in New Bordeaux, South Carolina, and dreamed of a time when Charleston would export the wines of South Carolina rather than import those of Europe. The portrait, by John Singleton Copley, shows Laurens as president of the Continental Congress in 1782. (National Portrait Gallery, Smithsonian Institution)

had been raised tremendously, for in 1748, one Robert Thorpe, Esq., laid his claim before the Commons in respect of his having produced "four casks of wine, each containing 30 gallons"; on investigation, the claim was honored and Thorpe was paid "the sum of five hundred pounds, being the bounty on a pipe of wine."[4] In terms of the purchasing power of money in the mid eighteenth century, this was an astonishing sum.

Thorpe's success must have helped to intensify the interest in winegrowing in South Carolina, an interest that was, indeed, growing generally throughout the colonies in the years down to the Revolution. In 1756 Alexander Garden, a distinguished physician and horticulturist of Charleston, informed the Society of Arts in London that grapes could be much better grown in South Carolina than they had so far been.[5] The society obliged by sending him slips of the Zante and Tokay varieties for trial, accompanied by the reflection that Bacchus had been deified by the people of the early ages for teaching "the Making of Wine, and among some of our Colonies there is Room at this Day for the doing almost as much Good."[6] A few years later the society was informed that another amateur, Colonel Colleton, had found a good wine grape growing in South Carolina;[7] this is interesting especially in light of South Carolina's role later as the fountain of new American hybrid grapes. Evidently the frequency of trials made with European grapes and the abundance of native grapes in the colony made it the preeminent place from which chance hybrids of commercial value originated. What Colonel Colleton had chanced upon we do not know, but it may well have been a native improved with vinifera blood. Such hybrids were later to become the basis of eastern viticulture.

One notable South Carolinian who hoped to see his state produce wine was the Charleston merchant and revolutionary patriot Henry Laurens, a commercial importer on an extensive scale of wines, including the fine Madeiras for which South Carolinians had a notable taste. Notwithstanding his interest in this part of the wine trade, Laurens did all he could to encourage the development of winegrowing in South Carolina itself. He assured one English investor who thought of planting vines in the Carolina back country in 1764 that all that was wanted was "time enough for experiments and perseverance . . . I am quite sure that good Grapes may be produced and kept up *even in the Lower parts of Carolina.*"[8] For evidence, he could point to a splendid vine in his own Charleston garden, which yielded, he said, some three to four hundred pounds of white grapes each year. "This vine of mine has given Spirits to our New French incomers; 'tis said by many Gentlemen to be as fine as any they have seen in Lisbon or Spain and the French cry out; *C'est beau et bon.*" A later writer identified Laurens's vine as a Chasselas Blanc, a true vinifera;[9] but despite his success with a European vine, Laurens himself seems to have thought a native industry would be based on native vines. Laurens, of Huguenot origin himself, took a special interest in the Huguenot settlement of New Bordeaux, where winegrowing was the main purpose of the community. On a trip through France in 1772, while he drifted on a canal boat through the vineyards of Burgundy, he could not help imagining, as he wrote to his family, a

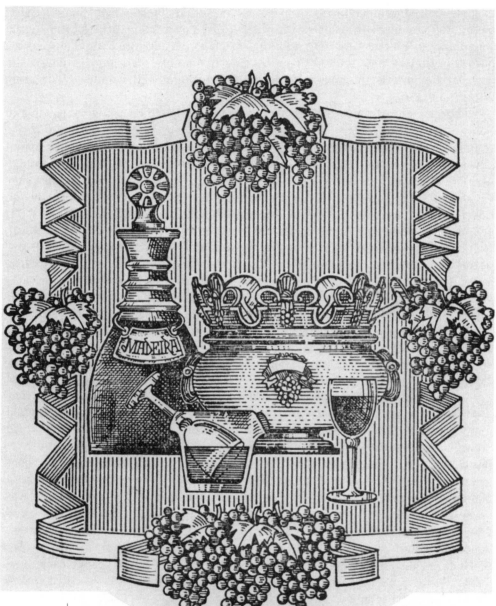

15 The wines of Madeira, privileged by the commercial agreement between England and Portugal, became the overwhelming favorite of the American colonies. The choice and rare madeiras sought out by American connoisseurs, especially in such port cities as Philadelphia, Baltimore, and Charleston, were drunk according to cherished rituals. Here the decanter for holding the wine, the rinser for cleaning the glass, and the "monteith" for cooling the glasses, are shown. (From S. Weir Mitchell, *A Madeira Party*, with introduction by William J. Dickerson, M.D., and appendices on Madeira wine by Roy Brady [1975])

vision of South Carolina's future in which he saw "my grand children receiving, exporting, and drinking wine made at Long Canes and Keowee, convey'd by the Savanna, Edisto, Ponpon, Santee, and Cowper Rivers to Charles Town."[10]

In 1773 the young Bostonian Josiah Quincy, on a tour through the South, was greatly smitten with the luscious Madeiras provided by his South Carolinian hosts; he noted that Joseph Allston, one of these hospitable gentlemen, had "propagated the Lisbon and Wine-Island grapes with great success."[11] South Carolina was not destined to rival the Wine Islands in the matter of sweet wines; indeed, no major commercial winemaking has ever been established there. Yet it has continued to be the scene of experiments and has an unbroken, and sometimes significant, history of viticulture down to the present day. Its most important episodes in the eighteenth century belong to the continental emigré communities, to be described later.

To the south of the Carolinas, in the inhospitable humidity of Florida, it yet seemed possible to produce wine. The settlers in the country probably knew nothing about the unhappy Huguenot colony of 1564 on the St. Johns River in Florida or the Spaniards on Santa Elena. But they could see wild grapes such as those described by the early American naturalist William Bartram on his travels in Florida, where he found the soil "peculiarly adapted for the cultivation of vines." Here Bartram saw vines "astonishing" for their bulk and strength: "they are frequently nine, ten, and twelve inches in diameter, and twine round the trunks of the trees, climb to their very tops, and then spread along their limbs, from tree to tree, throughout the forest."[12] In the twenty-year interval (1763–83) of British possession of Florida, the home authorities offered bounties for the production of certain commodities, wine among them, and the records show that there were actually exports in 1774–79.[13] Florida claret could only have been a rare, exotic, and dubious beverage, however.

Perhaps some of it was made by the colonists brought over to the settlement promoted by Dr. Andrew Turnbull. The acquisition of Florida, most southerly of American colonies, at once stimulated the imaginations of colonial planners along the familiar lines: here would be a place to grow wine, oil, and silk! It occurred to at least three of these speculators that the people to do the work should be Greeks, real Mediterranean people. William Knox, agent in London for Georgia and East Florida, formally proposed such a move to the Board of Trade in 1763; Archibald Menzies, a Scot who had travelled in the Levant, published a pamphlet in the same year to the same purpose; and in 1766 Dr. Turnbull, another Scot, actually set out to make the experiment.[14]

Turnbull, who had served as British consul in Smyrna and who had married a Smyrna Greek, thought he knew how the plan could be worked. Forming a company with certain highly placed Englishmen, including George Grenville, the prime minister, Turnbull succeeded in acquiring grants of land that ultimately totaled 101,000 acres.[15] He at once took his family to Florida to settle them there and to choose a site. This he found some seventy miles south of St. Augustine (then the only settlement of any consequence along the coast), at the mouth of the Indian

River. Turnbull then sailed back to Europe to recruit his colony, which he was enabled to do by a bounty paid by the Board of Trade for every hand that he could sign on. Hearing that Italian laborers might be available, he called with his ship at Leghorn and managed to enlist a number of *paisanos*. But in Greece he ran into trouble. The Turks, who then ruled the country, made it difficult for him everywhere he went, and at last he was forced to restrict his efforts to a wild region of the Morea, where the mountaineers had been fiercely holding off the Turks for years. Turnbull collected almost 400 of them, starved and desperate as they were. He then sailed back to the west, and set up his recruiting station on the island of Minorca, off Spain, whose impoverished inhabitants, Spanish-speaking and Catholic, were added in large numbers to the Italians and Greeks already assembled.

When Turnbull set sail again for Florida late in 1767, he took a fleet of eight ships loaded with grape cuttings and with 1,500 emigrants—some miscellaneous French and Corsicans included with the Minorcans, Italians, and Greeks. This was the largest single group ever to begin a settlement in the New World, and of course its size did nothing to ease the tensions already generated by its mixed and incongruous elements. Revolt and disease broke out almost as soon as this bewildered and ill-sorted group found itself on Florida soil, struggling to clear land of its tropical vegetation and to impose upon it the Mediterranean order of vines, olives, and mulberries.

Turnbull did his best. He resided with his family on the huge property, called New Smyrna after his wife's native city; he personally directed the large-scale operations of land clearing, building, canal digging, and planting that were in fact carried out with some success. But the whole thing was too unwieldy to prosper long. Expenses mounted far beyond what had been foreseen. Serious quarrels with the colonial governor arose, further dividing the colonists. And, finally, the outbreak of the Revolution dissolved what was already beginning to fall apart. In 1781, disgusted and heavily out of pocket, Turnbull retired to Charleston and returned to the practice of medicine.

We know that grapes were planted at New Smyrna, but not much more than that. The German traveller Johann Schoepf, who knew Dr. Turnbull in Charleston after the collapse of New Smyrna, learned from him that the vines planted had "thrived tremendously" and that Turnbull had developed a method of training them on high stakes "as is customary in Madeira."[16] Any further resemblance between the viticulture of New Smyrna and Madeira must have been illusory.

In North Carolina, the failure of the original grape-growing scheme to come to anything had not changed the fact that the region abounded in native grapes. The explorer and surveyor-general of the colony, John Lawson, writing in the first decade of the century, calls the grape the most important of the native fruits and describes six varieties. First are the "black bunch-grapes, which yield a crimson juice." "Bunch-grape" is a southern term, used to identify the standard sort of cluster-yielding vine as opposed to the familiar rotundifolia vines of the southeastern states with their separate large round berries. Another sort of bunch grape in North Carolina, Lawson says, is notable for its yield of light, almost white, juice. The remaining four varieties Lawson calls "Fox-Grapes": black and white "summer" varieties, ripening in July, and black and white "winter" varieties, ripening in October or November. These were, evidently, rotundifolia, for they did not set fruit in clusters (to the general confusion of things, "fox grape" in the South usually means rotundifolia; elsewhere, it usually indicates labrusca). The vines of the summer grapes "always grow in swamps, and low moist lands. . . . They afford the largest leaf I ever saw, to my remembrance, the back of which is of a white horse-flesh colour." Winter fox grapes grew on all soils and were "great bearers. I have seen near twelve bushels upon one vine of the black sort." Both red and white varieties of bunch grapes and the four varieties of rotundifolia "grow common, and bear plentifully."[17] The account makes clear how tantalizingly close the vision of winemaking was to all the early settlers and how baffling the withdrawn promise must have been.

Lawson tells of transplanting native varieties to his garden, where they flourished, and he had also made the experiment of planting *Vitis vinifera* from seed, with hopeful results. Lawson was captured, tortured, and killed by the Tuscaroras two years after his book appeared, and his grape growing died with him. He makes clear in what he published how utterly without guidance the aspiring vine grower was in the New World, even though he stood surrounded by vines. Lawson had a number of ideas about what might be done, all of them wrong. For example, he thought that the "deep, rich, black mould" of the river valleys was the most suitable soil, since there the native rotundifolia grew in such luxuriance that it was sometimes impossible for a man to force a path through them. He thought, too, that the European vine in America should, like the American vine, be allowed to grow unpruned, and encouraged to "run up trees, as some do, in Lombardy, upon elms." Whether the native varieties could be improved by grafting he was not sure, but he did not doubt that "that noble vegetable the vine" could quickly be brought to perfection in Carolina.[18]

There were optimists among public officials as well as among private individuals in North Carolina. Governor Gabriel Johnston informed the Board of Trade in London in 1734 that experiments in vine planting were then going on along the Cape Fear River. Using the familiar and still persuasive appeal to mercantilist theory, Johnston urged that the commissioners grant some official "encouragement"—that is, a subsidy—so that England might get its wine from its own colony rather than pay "ready money to foreigners" for wine, and, at the same time, avoid forcing the colonists to turn to manufactures in competition with those of the mother country. The commissioners, no doubt wary after long experience of disappointment, replied drily that they would be glad to encourage winemaking, but that they would like to have some wine from the colony first.[19] Johnston persisted, or at least he claimed to have persisted, in turning the thoughts of the Carolinians to winegrowing; in 1749 he wrote to the duke of Bedford that his efforts, prolonged through fifteen years, "have brought wine and silk to a good degree of perfection."[20] What that meant, if anything, is not explained by any other record.

Johnston was an exceedingly unpopular and ineffective governor, and his claims to have persuaded the settlers to carry out any of his policies must be doubted, however attractive those policies might have been in themselves. Governor Arthur Dobbs, Johnston's successor, reported early in 1755, shortly after his arrival in Carolina, that the native grapes of the colony yielded "rich wines," but he adds that the vines "want proper vine dressers to improve them."[21] Things were in much the same condition that they had been in a century earlier when the colony was founded in the hope of producing a "rich commodity" of wine.

An exception might be made for the Moravians who settled at various communities in North Carolina in the mid eighteenth century: they made there—as they did also at their settlements in Pennsylvania—some trials at cultivating vineyards. Their object, however, was not to develop an industry, but rather to supply their own simple needs, especially that for communion wine. When European grapes failed, they cheerfully accepted the alternative of making what they needed from the vines growing wild in the woods around them. Thus we hear of their making nineteen hogsheads from wild grapes in 1769, presumably a regular practice.[22]

Domestic Winemaking in Virginia

In Virginia, after an even longer history of settlement, and a greater effort to encourage winegrowing, things were pretty much as they had been. The story there continues to be mostly one of failure, yet down to the Revolution public interest in winegrowing in Virginia not merely persisted but steadily gained in strength. There were even some moments of encouraging achievement, and one has the feeling that had it not been for the Revolution, the Virginians whose names now figure on the roll of Fathers of Their Country might have managed to be Fathers of Native American Wine as well.

In no colony in the years before the Revolution did the actual enterprise of systematically growing and harvesting grapes, and then of crushing them for wine, extend to more than a very few individuals, despite subsidies, premiums, special prerogatives, exhortations, legislation, and penalties. Doubtless thousands of small farmers and town-dwellers ventured to try how a few gallons of native grape juice might turn out after fermenting; of these, in the nature of things, no record exists. But it is possible to identify a considerable number of proprietors who grew grapes and made wine, with varied success, either on their own initiative, or with public encouragement, or both. Hardly anyone in those days undertook the experiment without a surge of patriotic enthusiasm and a hope that the glory of bringing sound, cheap, American wine to his countrymen might be his.

The Virginians are much the most prominent in the account of purely domestic

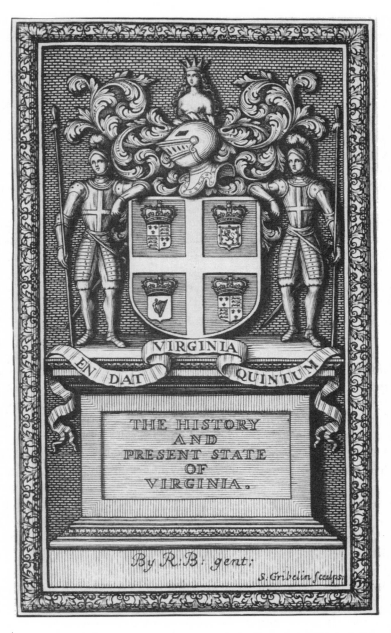

VIRGINIA

EN DAT QUINTUM

THE HISTORY
AND
PRESENT STATE
OF
VIRGINIA.

By R: B: gent;

S. Gribelin sculps.

16 The engraved title of Robert Beverley's *History and Present State of Virginia* (London, 1705). Beverley not only provided an account of the grapes of Virginia and of hopes for winemaking but went on to make wine successfully at his estate, Beverley Park. (Huntington Library)

winemaking, and most prominent among them in the early eighteenth century was Robert Beverley (c. 1673–1722), author, in 1705, of the first comprehensive history of Virginia, and a planter at his estate of Beverley Park. This lay in King and Queen County, at the headwaters of the Mattapony, about thirty miles north of modern Richmond, in what was then the wilderness of the Middle Neck. Beverley was an enthusiastic champion of Virginia and its resources. As one of the largest of Virginia landowners, he was interested in promoting settlement, especially Huguenot settlement, on his property, and he was therefore liable to exaggerate the winegrowing potential of his country. But even after allowing for the excesses of mingled commercial and patriotic interest, we find in Beverley's *History* what, in the authoritative opinion of U. P. Hedrick, is the "best account of the grapes of Virginia . . . in the later colonial times."[23] There are six native sorts, Beverley writes: red and white sand grapes; a "Fox-grape," so called for its smell "resembling the smell of a fox"; an early-ripe black or blue grape; a late-ripe black or blue grape; and a grape growing on small vines along the headwaters of streams—"far more palatable than the rest."[24] Compare this list with that of Robert Lawson, written about the same time not very many miles farther to the south, and one sees why it is that such early accounts are the despair of later classifiers.

Beverley thought that good wine could be made from these natives, believing that earlier failures were all caused by the malignant influences of the pine lands and salt water that affected all the early, lowland vineyard sites. The grape, he correctly thought, wanted well-drained hillside slopes. Beverley complained that so long as the Virginians made no serious effort to domesticate their wild grapes, they could hardly attempt making wine and brandy; but he also seems to have thought that the European vine would flourish in Virginia—if suitably removed from the malignant influences already named.[25]

Within a few years of publishing his *History*, Beverley put his own recommendations into practice, planting a vineyard of native vines upon the side of a hill and producing from it a wine of more than local celebrity. News of it travelled even to London, where the Council of Trade and Plantations was informed in December 1709 that Beverley's vineyards and wines were the talk of all Virginia.[26] A visit to Beverley at Beverley Park in November 1715 is reported in some detail in the journal of John Fontaine, an Irish-born Huguenot then travelling in Virginia. Fontaine, who had been in Spain and had some knowledge of Spanish winemaking practice, observed that Beverley neither managed his vineyard nor made his wine correctly according to Spanish methods, though he does not explain what he means, or why he thought that Beverley should have known how to follow the Spanish way. Beverley could hardly be expected to duplicate, in his pioneering situation, the procedures of an ancient winemaking tradition. For the rest, Fontaine was pleased by Beverley's arrangements on the frontiers of settlement: he had three acres of vines, he had built caves for storage, and had installed a press; by these means he had produced 400 gallons in the year of Fontaine's visit (if all three of Beverley's acres were producing, that figure implies that his vines were yielding about one ton an acre, an extremely low, but not surprising, yield considering that he was growing the unimproved natives). The origin of the vineyard, so Beverley told Fontaine, was in a bet that he made with his skeptical neighbors, who wagered ten to one that Beverley could not, within seven years, produce at one vintage seven hundred gallons of wine: "Mr. Beverley gave a hundred guineas upon the above mentioned terms and I do not in the least doubt but the next year he will make the seven hundred gallons and win the thousand guineas. We were very merry with the wine of his own making and drunk prosperity to his vineyard."[27] Fontaine seems to say that Beverley actually began his vineyard for a wager, but that cannot be so. As we have seen already, his experiment was the talk of all Virginia as early as 1709, six years before Fontaine's visit. And, as another witness reports, it was Beverley's constant bragging about the prospects of the small vineyard he had already planted that provoked his neighbors to make the bet.[28]

Fontaine, incidentally, has left us another reference to Virginian wine in the next year, in a well-known passage describing the luxurious style kept by the gentlemen of Governor Alexander Spotswood's expedition of exploration to the Shenandoah Valley. On 6 September 1716 the company celebrated its crossing of the Blue Ridge thus:

> We had a good dinner. After dinner we got the men all together and loaded all their arms and we drunk the King's health in Champagne, and fired a volley; the Prince's health in Burgundy, and fired a volley; and all the rest of the Royal Family in Claret, and a volley. We drunk the Governor's health and fired another volley. We had several sorts of liquors, namely Virginia Red Wine and White Wine, Irish Usquebaugh, Brandy, Shrub, two sorts of Rum, Champagne, Canary, Cherry punch, Cider, Water etc.[29]

What can the "etc." after "water" possibly stand for? Fontaine does not describe the Virginia red and white wines, but it is highly interesting to know that Robert Beverley was one of this merry party; he might well have been the source of the wine. But so, too, could the expedition's leader, Governor Spotswood, for in 1714 he had sponsored a settlement of Germans at a place called Germanna. We know that this group was making wine a few years later, and it is possible that they had experimented with wild grapes before 1716.[30] If both Spotswood and Beverley had provided samples of their wine, the gentlemen of the expedition may have carried out what would have been a very early comparative tasting of native wines. One doubts that they were in a condition to make very discriminating judgments on the day Fontaine describes.

Beverley won his bet. In the second edition of his *History* (1722), he wrote that since the book had first appeared "some vineyards have been attempted, and one"—evidently his own—"is brought to perfection, of seven hundred and fifty gallons a year."[31] Such was the flow of wine at Beverley Park, so the Reverend Hugh Jones stated, that Beverley's "whole family, even his negroes drank scarce any thing but the small wines." As for Beverley's "strong wines," which Jones says he often drank, they were of good body and flavor, the red reminding him of the

17 An eager promoter of his Virginia lands, William Byrd (1674–1744) planted many different sorts of vines at Westover and hoped that Swiss immigrants would turn his "Land of Eden" property near Roanoke into a country of vines and wines. (Portrait by Sir Godfrey Kneller; Virginia Historical Society)

taste of claret and the strength of port. As the allusion to port suggests, "strong wine" must have meant wine fortified with brandy or other spirit. Jones adds that European grapes were flourishing in Beverley's vineyard, though we cannot know what the truth of this assertion was.[32]

As did almost every eighteenth-century gentleman who experimented with winemaking, Beverley took it as his patriotic duty to sponsor the development of a national viticultural industry. Though I have found no other record of the fact, according to the statement of a later Virginia winegrower, Beverley unsuccessfully urged the Virginia Assembly to pass an act "for the Education of certain Viners and Oil Pressers."[33] Beverley is also said to have put the thousand guineas that he had won on his wager over his vineyard into "planting more and greater vineyards, from which he made good quantities of wine, and would have brought it to very high perfection, had he lived some years longer."[34] But he was dead by 1722, and though his only son, William, survived him and prospered greatly, building a notable mansion called Blandfield, we do not hear that he carried on his father's work as a viticulturist.

Beverley's example probably inspired his brother-in-law, William Byrd of Westover, the best known today of early eighteenth-century Virginians, to experiment with vine growing on his Tidewater estate. Some time in the late 1720s, Byrd collected all the kinds of grape vines he could get and planted a vineyard of more than twenty European varieties "to show my indolent country folks that we may employ our industry upon other things besides tobacco."[35] Byrd also proposed to graft European scions on native roots, a prophetic idea. He corresponded with the London merchant and horticulturist Peter Collinson, who advised him on viticulture and encouraged the trial of native grapes. Among Byrd's manuscripts is a treatise on "The Method of Planting Vineyards and Making Wine" from some unidentified source, perhaps compiled for Byrd at his request.[36]

By 1736 his example had had some effect, for his neighbor Colonel Henry Armistead had determined to try his hand. Both the colonel and his son, Byrd wrote, were "very sanguine, and I hope their faith, which brings mighty things to pass, will crown their generous endeavors."[37] But Byrd's hopes were chilled when spring frosts destroyed his crop that year, and a year later he wrote to his correspondent Sir Hans Sloane, president of the Royal Society, that "our seasons are so uncertain, and our insects so numerous,that it will be difficult to succeed." Perhaps, he added, the Swiss whom he hoped to settle in the mountains around Roanoke—Byrd's "Land of Eden"—would succeed better; but that dream never materialized.[38] But if Byrd himself did not succeed, he never doubted that others would in time. He wrote to the English naturalist Mark Catesby in 1737:

> I cannot be of your opinion, that wine may not be made in this country. All the parts of the earth of our latitude produce good wine—and tho' it may be more difficult in one place than another, yet those difficulties may be overcome by good management, as they were at the Cape of Good Hope, where many years pass'd before they could bring it to bear.[39]

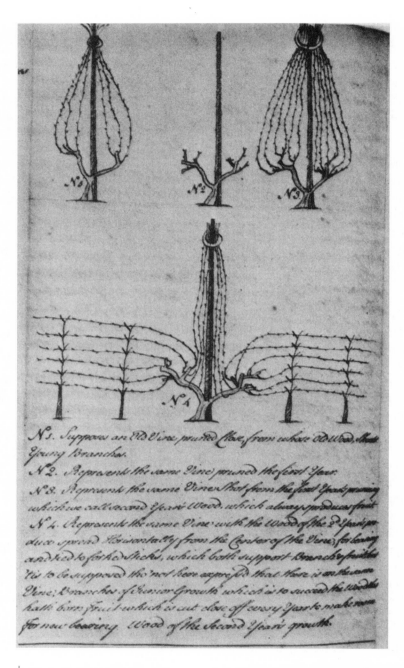

The London merchant Peter Collinson, a distinguished amateur naturalist, corresponded at length with William Byrd on the subject of grapes; the drawing shown is from a letter of instruction from Collinson to Byrd about 1730. Collinson had the interesting idea that native grapes might be the right choice for Virginia: "Being natives perhaps they may be better adapted to your seasons, than foreigners." (Virginia Historical Society)

Public Interest and Public Support

The work of Beverley and Byrd had no direct successors, yet interest in wine-growing began to stir again in the late 1750s, partly because the colony was in an economic decline brought on by excessive dependence upon tobacco. In the twenty years from the middle 1750s to the outbreak of the Revolution in 1776, there was an active, continuous discussion of, propagandizing for, and experimenting with grape growing and winemaking in Virginia that must, but for the interruption of the war, have led to practical results.

One sort of experiment was already familiar—that is, to import vineyardists from the wine regions of Europe and encourage them to develop their trade in a new land; the logic of this was irresistible, and the attempt to act on it, going back perhaps as early as Lord De La Warr's Frenchmen in 1610, was persisted in until well into the nineteenth century. Byrd, as we have just seen, had hoped to do it with Swiss settlers; in the mid eighteenth century another form of this method is recorded in a prospectus circulated by the Virginia planter and statesman George Mason. Dated October 1759, this invited subscribers to a loan for a German named Maurice Pound, settled on property belonging to Mason on the Potomac, where Pound for the past three years had been cultivating German vines. He now needed capital for a press and other facilities to continue the work. Some money was raised by this appeal. George Washington, like most of his neighbors perennially hopeful about grape growing in Virginia, was one of the subscribers to the loan. But though money was raised, wine was not. By 1772 Washington had written off his part of the loan as a bad debt. As for Pound, he is reported to have moved on to the semi-wilderness of the Shenandoah Valley to try winegrowing there.[40] The rest is silence.

Meantime, other experiments were encouraged by public measures, both official and unofficial. In Williamsburg in 1759 a group of local gentlemen calling themselves the Society for the Promotion of Manufactures offered a premium of £500—thus matching the munificence of the South Carolina Assembly twelve years earlier—to any person who should, in the next eight years, make, in any one year, the ten best hogsheads of wine. A large second prize, of £100, was offered as well to stimulate wide competition. These prizes were to be paid by subscription of the members, and the size of the award is good evidence of the keenness of interest in the object.[41] Two years later, the Virginia assembly endorsed the plan of the society and officially joined it by promising to make good any deficiency in the subscription.[42] The list of subscribers is rich in old Virginia names; Washington, responsive as usual, is down for an annual subscription of £2 to the cause.[43]

The Virginia prize scheme was an imitation of that set up a few years earlier by the London Society for the Encouragement of Arts, Manufactures, and Commerce, which offered prizes for various desirable enterprises in the colonies, among them vine growing and winemaking (1758: see discussion, pp. 89–93 below). The Virginians may also have been stimulated by the publication in the *Annual Register* for

1759 of a summary from the papers of the slightly fraudulent polymath and promoter, Aaron Hill, exhibiting "directions for cultivating vines in America." The colonists of Virginia and Carolina, Hill affirms in this, had bungled their opportunities because they lacked "skill and philosophy" in their work as winemakers. The virgin American soil was too vigorous, wrote Hill, and the grape was accordingly thick, pulpy, oily, and strong, producing violent fermentations that concluded in unbalanced wines. Hill recommends that the grapes be kept cool for five days in special cellars, then pressed, and the juice fermented by itself. This, he says, would certainly yield a wine "rich, lively and durable." How Hill could have known all this is a question, since he had never been to America. But where no one has any real knowledge, anyone can set up as an authority. It may well be that the Virginia gentlemen, on reading so confident an assertion of what could be done and how, thought that their £500 would soon be claimed, to the satisfaction of all parties. The premium, however, seems to have remained unclaimed, so that Washington, Randolph, and the rest, had the credit of their good intentions without having to pay for them.

Almost at the same time that the Williamsburg society was announcing its prizes, a committee of the Virginia assembly was formed and charged with the question of economic diversification, a question made urgent by the depression in the tobacco trade.[44] Its chairman, Charles Carter, of the distinguished Virginia family of Carter, entered into a correspondence with the London Society for the Encouragement of the Arts, a correspondence in which the prospects and methods for the cultivation of the grape in Virginia are an important subject. Carter had already begun grape growing at his estate of Cleve, in King George County, on the Rappahannock, where he made wines from both native and European grapes (it is said), and it was natural that he should have chosen commercial winemaking as one of his proposals for economic reform in Virginia. The London society took a sympathetic view of Carter's proposals and recommended various vines and practices, including the trial of distilling brandy from the native grapes; it was well known that the French used their inferior grapes for distillation into brandy.[45] In 1762 Carter, who by then had 1,800 vines growing at Cleve, sent to the London society a dozen bottles of his wine, made from the American winter grape ("a grape so nauseous till a frost that the fowls of the air will not touch it": probably *Vitis cordifolia* is meant) and from a vineyard of "white Portugal summer grapes."[46] These samples were so pleasing a taste—"they were both approved as good wines," the society's secretary wrote—that the society awarded Carter a gold medal as the first person to make a "spirited attempt towards the accomplishment of their views, respecting wine in America."[47]

In 1768, according to one source, Virginia actually exported "13 tons [tuns?] and 135 gallons of wine" to Great Britain;[48] it is not likely that much more was sent either before or after that date, or that the wine could have had a very eager market. Nevertheless, the record does exist, and the trade that it records may have had as its immediate stimulus the work of Carter's committee and the London society.

Charles Carter's interest in winemaking was shared by his brother, Colonel Landon Carter, of Sabine Hall (still standing on the banks of the Rappahannock). Landon Carter kept a journal in which, among other things, he recorded his methods of making wine from native grapes gathered in the woods. He devised an elaborate and tedious process, boiling some of the grapes in order to fix the color, adding honey to increase the sugar content of the juice, and adding brandy to increase the alcoholic content. By such means, Carter wrote, he hoped to obtain a "pleasant liquor," and perhaps he did. What is painfully clear from his description is the ingenious labor that would-be winemakers had to go through in order to make a facsimile of a potable wine from the native grapes that they had in such abundant supply.[49]

In 1769 an ambitious scheme began whose eventual collapse finally put an end to official participation in Virginia winegrowing; not, however, before it had clearly focused the classic question: native grapes or foreign? The episode starts with a Frenchman named André (or Andrew) Estave, who successfully petitioned the House of Burgesses for support of his proposal to establish a vineyard and make from it "good merchantable wine." Estave, according to his petition, had "a perfect knowledge of the culture of vines, and the most approved method of making wine"; he had, moreover, during the two years that he had resided in Virginia, made a special study of the native grape and was confident that it would, if properly managed, "produce very fine wine."[50] Estave was supported by such influential politicians as Severn Eyre, speaker of the House, and George Wythe, Jefferson's law teacher and later a signer of the Declaration of Independence.[51] In November 1769, in response to their lead, the assembly passed an act "for the Encouraging the Making of Wine," whose preamble declared that "the climate, soil, and natural productions of this colony make it very probable that the most delicious wines might be made here." The act appointed trustees, who were authorized to purchase land and slaves, to hire apprentices, to build a house, and otherwise to provide for Estave's necessities; £450 was appropriated for the purpose. If, so the act ran, Estave should succeed in making ten hogsheads of good commercial wine in the six years from November 1770 to 1776, he would gain title to the whole establishment—land, house, and slaves.[52] Land was chosen east of Williamsburg,[53] three slaves were bought, and Estave set to work. By early 1772 he was able to inform the House of Burgesses that his vines were in a "thriving state" and that he was convinced of the "practicability of the scheme." Unluckily, he had had to put his slaves to work growing food; then he had been forced to sell one slave as "unprofitable"; in short, he needed money.[54] The Burgesses obliged by voting a sum to recompense Estave for money already expended and to provide him with £50 per annum for the next two years;[55] evidently they had confidence in their man and his work. Estave continued to have bad luck with his slaves, however, or else he was a bad master, for the Virginia papers between 1771 and 1776 contain no less than six notices of slaves—Quomony, Cuffy, Jack, Saundy, were some of their unhappy names—who had run away from Estave at The Vineyard, as his place was called.[56]

For SALE, at Mr. JOHN PRENTIS's store in Williamsburg,

AN exceeding elegant SPINNET, in a genteel mahogany case, with a music desk, spare wires, quills, &c. This instrument is entirely new, and was lately imported in the Virginia, Capt. Estem The lowest price is TWENTY TWO POUNDS current money.

THE trustees appointed by an act of Assembly, for encouraging the making WINE in this colony, give notice that they, according to the directions of the said act, are ready to receive THREE POOR BOYS, to be bound apprentices to Andrew Estave, who is to teach them the art of cultivating vines, and making wine.

19   By an act of 1769 the Virginia Assembly subsidized the work of Andrew Estave, a Frenchman who vowed that he could successfully grow grapes and make wine near Williamsburg. In this notice from the *Virginia Gazette* in May 1773, the call for apprentices might be taken as a hopeful sign; three years later, however, the enterprise ended in failure. (Huntington Library)

The vines that Estave was tending were both native and European, though there is no information about the specific varieties. By 1773 it was clear to him that the European vines would not prosper. As Estave admitted in a letter to the *Virginia Gazette* (18 March 1773), the European grape was subject to a sad list of afflictions: insects and worms injured it; the Virginia sun ripened it when the heat of the summer was most intense; and the rains fell just at the time of harvest. The native grapes, however, were promising; "it is my humble opinion," Estave wrote, "that the native vines of the country can alone be cultivated with success." When properly cultivated and the juice of their grapes skillfully vinified, they would yield, Estave now affirmed in print, as he had earlier done before the House of Burgesses, a "wine of the best quality." This is not the first recommendation of native grapes as a basis for American wine, but it is perhaps the first made by a man who had direct experience of growing both native and European vines experimentally.

Things were still promising enough for the trustees to advertise in May 1773 for three "poor boys . . . to be bound apprentices to Andrew Estave, who is to teach them the art of cultivating vines and making wine."[57] It is doubtful, if any poor boys applied, that they could have learned much from Estave, whose luck now ran out. A remarkably severe frost in early May 1774[58] sent him back to the House of Burgesses, with a memorial explaining that he had lost his crop and needed yet more money for a cellar and a press; could he have another £50?[59] Whether the Burgesses assented I do not know; probably not, since I have found no record of their action. In the next year we learn that Estave's vines had suffered again, this time by hail, but that he nevertheless had "a prospect of making three or four hogsheads of wine in the fall."[60] It is not reassuring to learn from the same source that Estave had now taken up silk-raising—apparently he had begun to hedge his bets. The end came the next year, when the Burgesses passed an act to dispose of the winegrowing estate, since the land and slaves "are become useless, and of no advantage to the publick."[61] The land—about 200 acres—and slaves were advertised for sale in March 1777,[62] but even in this the property was unfortunate. It seems to have remained on the hands of the trustees until 1784, when the House of Burgesses at last gave it to the College of William and Mary. The college succeeded in promptly selling the land at public auction, and so ended the colony's last official attempt to set up a winegrowing industry.[63]

Even before his failure was certain, Estave had had to face the public criticism of a rival vineyardist, and rival theorist, who opposed Estave's belief in the future of native vines with a fervent belief in the possibilities of vinifera in Virginia. This was Colonel Robert Bolling, Jr. (1738–75), of Chellow, in Buckingham County; there, in 1767, he had made wine from the native summer grapes and had, he said, found it too "acid."[64] Bolling was an interesting, perhaps slightly affected, specimen of Virginia planter and dilettante; he had been educated in England, was fond of reading and of playing the violin, was a student of Latin, Greek, French, and Italian (he wrote a family memoir in French that survives), and he trifled in verse as well. Before his early death in 1775, he also served in the Virginia House of Burgesses.

The challenge of his unsatisfactory wine from native grapes evidently called out the latent determination in the gentleman, for Bolling set off on a sustained effort to learn the principles of viticulture and to apply them to vine growing on his own estate. One result of his labor was the production of a treatise on viticulture, never published but still extant in MS, that ranks as one of the very earliest treatments of the subject addressed to Americans by an American (it is perhaps the second such work; the earliest known is that of Edward Antill: see p. 91).[65] "A Sketch of Vine Culture for Pennsylvania, Maryland, Virginia and the Carolinas" was written around 1773–74 and was designed, so its author states in the high public-minded style almost invariable among early American promoters of the grape, for "the increase of happiness, of numbers, of industry, of opulence." It is, inevitably, for the most part a compilation from standard European sources, both ancient and modern: Columella and Virgil at one extreme and such contemporaries as Nicolas Bidet and John Mills at the other are among his sources. But Bolling also says that by the time he set to work on his book, "there were a few bearing vines at

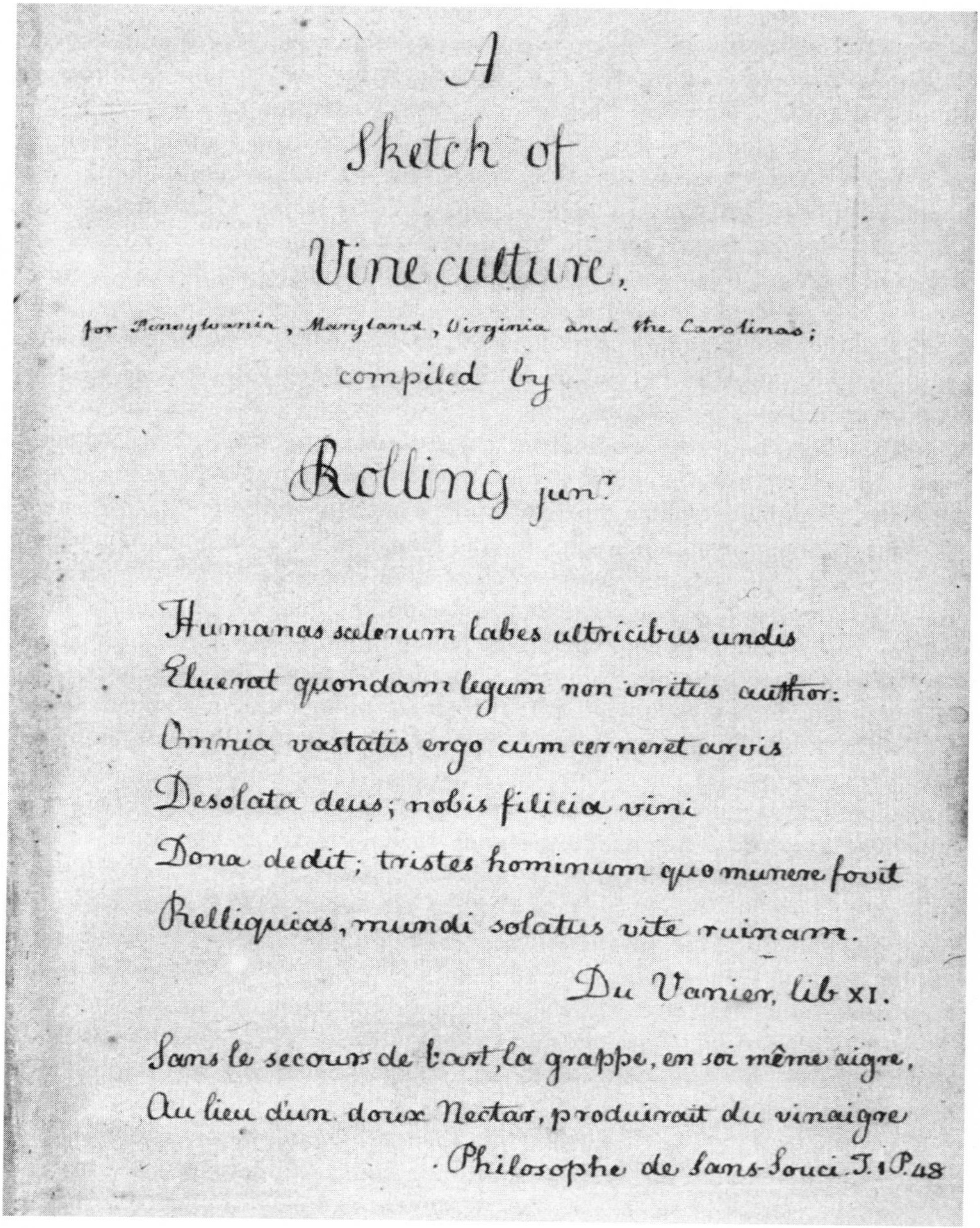

A

Sketch of

Vine culture,

for Pensylvania, Maryland, Virginia and the Carolinas;

compiled by

Bolling jun.ʳ

Humanas scelerum labes ultricibus undis
Eluerat quondam legum non irritus author:
Omnia vastatis ergo cum cerneret arvis
Desolata deus; nobis filicia vini
Dona dedit; tristes hominum quo munere fovit
Relliquias, mundi solatus vite ruinam.

Du Vanier, lib XI.

Sans le secours de l'art, la grappe, en soi même aigre,
Au lieu d'un doux Nectar, produirait du vinaigre
Philosophe de Sans-Souci. T. 1 P. 48

20 | Title page of Robert Bolling's MS treatise on viticulture for the colonies, c. 1773–74. Most of Bolling's information was derived from European sources, but he also drew on his experience with a vineyard at Chellow, Buckingham County, Virginia. (Huntington Library)

Chellow whose progress was carefully observed";[66] he gives instructions about planting and pruning drawn from his own experience, and, indeed, as one recent author has noted, Bolling anticipates by more than a century the standard modern pruning system called umbrella-Kniffen.[67] Bolling was also attentive to what little information he could get from other American sources of vine-growing experience; he made use of Antill's pioneer work, and he preserves the (mistaken) information that the very early American hybrid called Bland's Grape grew from raisin seed. Bolling also describes his own vineyard at Chellow, set out, he tells us, along the crest of a north-south ridge and hedged about with red hawthorn.[68]

By 1773 Bolling felt ready to carry on a campaign of opposition to Estave, beginning with a letter to the *Virginia Gazette* of 25 February entitled "Essay on the Utility of Vine Planting in Virginia," which Bolling had written two years earlier. In this, the author lays out his public-spirited reasons for promoting the subject: he wishes, he says, to provide an alternative to the excessive dependence upon tobacco culture and a means of employing unprofitable hill country; besides this, he wishes to provide a source of good drink for the common people, who need that quite as much as they need employment. The cultivation of the grape might supply both. Bolling meant the European grape. The experiment then being conducted by Estave was, in Bolling's judgment, misconceived and not terribly relevant to the problem of American winegrowing. It proposed merely to answer "whether Andre Estave can raise a vineyard . . . which shall furnish a sufficient quantity of native grapes" and "whether from these he can produce a wine wholesome and potable." But the real question, in Bolling's view, was whether traditional wine grapes— vinifera—would flourish in Virginia? And to answer that question, he argued, widespread trials must be made.

In February 1773 Bolling successfully memorialized the House of Burgesses to subsidize his experiments in vine growing. The House agreed to the extent of authorizing a grant of £50 per annum to Bolling for a term of five years.[69] To assist him in the work, the local paper reported, Bolling had "engaged a Foreigner, thoroughly acquainted with the business, in all its branches."[70] Who the nameless "Foreigner" was I have not discovered; but he was one of a long line of hopefully imported experts, most of whom had to suffer the mortification of seeing their knowledge baffled and defeated. But Bolling now had official recognition of his work, and turned again to the matter of Estave, sending the *Virginia Gazette* an "Address to the Friends of Vine Planting" in which he enthusiastically recommended the vines of warm countries—of Italy especially—for trial in Virginia.[71] The native grapes, Bolling reluctantly conceded, should not be entirely rejected if they showed any promise, but he knew from experience that they were not proper for wine.

Bolling was particularly emphatic on the point that the success or failure of vinifera in Estave's vineyard would settle nothing; the experiment was too limited, and the prejudice of the colonists against European vines had denied them fair trial—at least so Bolling said. He also says that the colony "has unhappily a great partiality for native vines, the only native production to which it was ever partial."[72] The assertion, if true, is surprising; it suggests that local winemaking from native grapes was widespread and that the result was well received. But probably Bolling exaggerates the strength of the tendency to which he was opposed.

Estave was provoked by this latest sally of Bolling's to make a mild response, in which he politely affirmed that his native grapes were doing well and politely doubted that Bolling's imports had much chance of succeeding.[73] Bolling, who had a knack for light verse, was meantime diverting himself at Estave's expense by writing a group of poems called "The Vintage of Parnassus," in which the Virginia planters are exhorted to join the ranks of grape growers, and in which poor Estave is pleasantly derided. For example:

> Let Estave, to end the quarrel,
> Let Estave produce a barrel!
> Here's a goblet, here's a borer:
> Drink to Bacchus peace-restorer.
> Let us drink of our own pressing
> Why postpone so great a blessing?

And again:

> Estave, if I must celebrate
> The wonders of your art
> My thirsty soul first recreate. . . .
> The purple juice impart.[74]

These and other such verses, which survive in MS, were never published, but one can well imagine that Bolling was not reluctant to recite them to any likely listener.

What reason could Bolling have had for his confidence that European grapes, especially those from Italy, would do well in Virginia? None, really, or no more than any other interested observer could have, chiefly the familiar observation of an analogy between Mediterranean warmth and Virginian warmth, elaborated in semiscientific jargon. Bolling was particularly excited by the possibility of adapting the Lachryma grape to Virginia—that is, the grape called Greco della Torre, from which the Lachrima Christi wine is produced on the slopes of Mount Vesuvius. His reasons, as set forth in the MS "Sketch," show how fanciful an argument he depended on. The Lachryma grape, Bolling observes, rarely ripens even in Naples, and yet makes good wine; probably, he thinks, it would ripen in Virginia and so make even better wine. Why? Well, because the "solar rays" of Italy darting on the "sulphureous" soil of the slopes of Vesuvius retard the growth of the vine. Virginia, being less sulphureous, yet quite as warm, ought to be a better place.[75]

"Solar rays" operating on a "sulphureous" soil are not likely to retard the maturity of grapes. But of course the problem in Virginia was not one of maturity but of hostile climate and endemic disease, though Bolling could not know that. He remained energetically and optimistically active to the end. On 26 February 1775 he wrote to the Virginia Quaker and merchant Robert Pleasants, who acted as Bolling's agent in obtaining Portuguese vines, about his vine-growing efforts. Bolling thanks Pleasants for a box of cuttings received in good condition, adds that he has received others both good and bad from other sources, and that he is expecting yet more:

> You cannot imagine how much I am revived under the vexation such miserable and hard-earned collections give me by the interest you take in the affair. The man, who attempts to serve his Country, is generally checked as an arrogant, unacquainted with his insufficiency; and I can assure you, some of the little Heroes around me make one fully sensible that such are their sentiments.[76]

In July of that year Bolling suddenly died at Richmond, the new colonial capital, where he had gone to represent his county at the constitutional convention. An unsigned note in the *Virginia Gazette* of 9 September 1775 hints that something might yet be saved from Bolling's abruptly ended labors:

> The vines planted by Mr. Bolling in the County of Buckingham, although managed according to the directions of the French writers of the 48th and 49th degrees of latitude, are in a condition to yield wine the ensuing year, if well attended to. The slips planted by that gentleman the last year, after the method of the vignerons of Europe inhabiting a climate similar to our own, have now the appearance of vines 3 or 4 years old. A slip planted by him in the spring of the present year has produced two bunches of grapes; a fact which would not be believed in the wine countries of the old world.

The vineyard did not survive its owner long. Years later it was reported that the ignorance of Bolling's heirs and the confusions created by the outbreak of the Revolution in 1776 had as their consequence that "this promising and flourishing little vineyard was totally neglected and finally perished."[77]

The quarrel between Estave and Bolling was left unresolved by the failure of the one and the death of the other.[78] Before that inconclusive conclusion was reached, however, a third vigorous presence was added to the list of publicly supported experimental winegrowers in Virginia in the person of the Italian Philip Mazzei (1730–1816).[79] Mazzei, who was born in Tuscany, had already lived a varied and unconventional life; he had studied medicine in Italy, had spent some years in Turkey, where he successfully practiced as a physician, and had then gone to London, where he operated a prosperous firm importing champagne, burgundy, Italian oil, and Italian cheese. Mazzei was a man of quick curiosity and great confidence, attentive to all sorts of practical, commercial, and political matters, and he seems to have picked up a good deal of information about wine, for which his importing business placed him well. He was also gifted with a remarkable power to charm, so that he attracted acquaintances everywhere he went.

Two among his many friends in London were Americans: Benjamin Franklin, then agent in England for the colony of Pennsylvania, and the Virginia merchant Thomas Adams. Their talk of American freedom and American opportunity inter-

21   Physician, merchant, and colonial agent, the Florentine Philip Mazzei (1730–1816) brought Italian vines and Italian vineyard workers to Virginia in 1773; the Revolution put an end to the scheme, among the most promising in colonial America. (From *Philip Mazzei: Jefferson's "Zealous Whig,"* trans. Margherita Marchione [1975])

ested Mazzei, who, by 1771, had devised a scheme for an ambitious importation of Mediterranean plants and farmers into Virginia: 10,000 French, Italian, Spanish, and Portuguese vines, with a comparable quantity of olive trees and other plants, were to be brought over, together with fifty peasants to attend them, the whole convoy to be sent to the back country and the costs to be paid by Virginia subscribers.[80] Nothing quite on this scale actually came to pass, but Mazzei was encouraged enough by the response to his plan to return to Italy and begin preparations for his American expedition. His arrangements there were protracted through 1772 and into 1773; by that time he had secured the permission of the grand duke of Tuscany to take vines and workers out of the duchy, and at the end of November 1773 Mazzei and ten young Tuscan *viticultores* arrived in Virginia on a ship hopefully named the *Triumph*.[81]

The plan was still to take up land in the unsettled western highlands, but that plan was changed by the intervention of Thomas Jefferson, always on the lookout for interesting company and for agricultural improvements, both of which Mazzei could provide. On his way to inspect the hinterlands of the Shenandoah Valley in company with his friend from London days, Thomas Adams, one of his original sponsors and a landholder in the valley, Mazzei stopped in his journey to meet Jefferson at Monticello. As the story told by Mazzei goes, the two men went for an early morning walk the next day before breakfast; on their return they were met by Adams, who looked at them and at once said to Jefferson, "I can see it on your face that you've taken him away from me; why, I expected as much."[82]

Jefferson had in fact offered some 2,000 acres to Mazzei in the neighborhood of Monticello, and there Mazzei settled his workers and built a house he called Colle (Italian "hill"), perhaps in allusion to Jefferson's Monticello ("little mountain").[83] Whether he planted vines in the winter of 1773–74, the earliest date at which he could do so, is not apparent, but the chances are that he did not. Mazzei was very quickly associated with the political leaders of Virginia and proved himself a ready friend to the cause of American independence from Britain—indeed, he had been predicting it while still in Europe, and was glad to help it come about. The Revolution followed so soon on his arrival, and his interest in its development was so great, that his vine-growing efforts seem never to have had his full attention. Still, he did some definite things. He brought in six more Tuscan *viticultores* in the summer of 1774 (these were all from Lucca).[84] In November 1774 he published detailed proposals for a "Company or Partnership, for the purpose of raising and making Wine, Oil, agruminious [i.e., citrus] Plants and Silk," inviting subscriptions in shares of £50 each.[85] According to Jefferson, £2,000 was provided to Mazzei by this means,[86] and the list of subscribers, like the earlier list of the supporters of the Williamsburg society's prize offers, is a roll of all the influential and wealthy gentlemen of the colony, including the governor, Lord Dunmore (soon to be occupied in raiding and devastating the coasts of the colony he now governed), Washington, Jefferson, and assorted Masons, Pages, Randolphs, Custises, Blands, and Carters.[87]

The *Triumph*, which had brought Mazzei over in 1773, returned laden with seeds and cuttings from Tuscany in the summer of 1774, too late for vine planting that year.[88] Anything that Mazzei might have set out before was killed in the great frost of 4 May 1774. It does not seem, then, that Mazzei actually succeeded in beginning a vinifera vineyard until 1775, when he made a late June planting of 1,500 vines whose shipment from Italy had been delayed.[89] The date of 1775 would agree with Jefferson's later recollection that Mazzei had tended his vines for three years before he left Virginia early in 1779.[90] Of the Tuscan vines that Mazzei planted late in 1775, about half were successfully rooted, and they, according to Mazzei, "produced grapes with more flavor and substance than those grown in Italy."[91] This is a very rare testimony that European vines in colonial America ever actually fruited. Jefferson remembered that the land that Mazzei chose for his site had a southeastern exposure and a stony red soil, "resembling extremely the Cote of Burgundy from Chambertin to Montrachet where the famous wines of Burgundy are made."[92] What marvelous visions of great Virginian vintages Jefferson must have had!

Mazzei was too slow to begin and too quick to leave his plantation at Colle to produce a vinifera vintage; the native vines, however, caught his attention at once. "Especially in Virginia," he wrote, "nature seems to favor vineyards. I have never seen such perfect, varied, and abundant wild grapes."[93] His workmen, he says, saw no fewer than two hundred varieties of wild grape in the woods, and he himself examined thirty-six varieties on his own estate—incredible numbers both.[94] Mazzei made wine from these grapes in 1775 and 1776, describing it as "far better than ordinary Italian wine or what is produced near Paris"; the praise is highly restricted, since ordinary Italian wine and the wine of Paris were both bywords for badness in wine. Mazzei's workers were each given a cask of this native wine, and they were, Mazzei reports, successful in selling it at a shilling a bottle to thirsty Virginians.[95]

To continue the experiment, Mazzei planted 2,000 native vines in the spring of 1776, but with exceedingly poor results; two years later only 87 remained alive. This, however, he attributed entirely to the poor state of the cuttings that he had used.[96] The future lay with the cultivated native vines, Mazzei thought, though he seems never to have doubted that vinifera would grow in America as well; in this choice of the native varieties over the European, Mazzei forms a solitary exception to the rule. Nor did he think that viticulture, so long as land was cheap and labor dear, would develop rapidly in America; it would be a work of time, requiring that the country first be populated. When that time came, then "I am of opinion," he wrote in his *Memoirs* many years after his American experience, "that . . . the best wines in the world will be made there."[97] Mazzei was clearly a man who could see for himself and speak accordingly—not easy things to do when one is confronting new situations.

In 1778 Mazzei was put forward by Jefferson as a man capable of serving the Revolution as Virginia's agent—that is, fund-raiser—in Europe. The suggestion was accepted, and Mazzei left for Europe in 1779. Though he returned to America in 1783 and remained here for two years, his days as a vineyardist were over. He afterwards served as agent to the king of Poland in revolutionary Paris and ended his days in his native Tuscany. Mazzei kept in touch with his American friends, and the Department of State Archives record his sending many items of horticultural information and many new plants to the United States through the consul in Leghorn.[98] But after his departure from it, his Virginia vineyard quickly dissolved. The Tuscan vineyardists drifted away; the house was rented to a German general captured at the Battle of Saratoga and kept prisoner in Virginia while awaiting exchange. The general's horses, so Jefferson wrote in 1793, "in one week destroyed the whole labor of three or four years."[99]

The visible marks of Mazzei's experiment lasted only briefly, but the invisible effects had their importance, not least through their operation on Jefferson, the most enthusiastic of all public men in American history for the attractions of a flourishing viticultural economy. His belief in Mazzei and in Mazzei's view of the possibilities of American winegrowing never faltered. Something must be said about Jefferson's role in the history of this subject later; here it is enough to observe that Virginia in the years just before the Revolution was the right place to be for anyone interested in the hopes of American winegrowing. The Frenchman Estave in Williamsburg, the Italian Mazzei in Charlottesville, and the Virginia gentleman Bolling at Chellow were all busy with their experiments at the same time and to a large extent with the backing of the same interested people. Talk of the imminent, the tantalizingly near, success of one or the other of these men must have been common enough; and many Virginians, in a private way, were hoping to achieve that success for themselves. Charles Carter of Cleve and his brother, Colonel Landon Carter, have already been mentioned as winemakers; Jefferson, of course, was an experimental vineyardist, setting out his first vines with the aid of Mazzei's Italian vineyardists in the spring of 1774.[100] George Washington was already in the field, having begun to plant grapes at Mount Vernon in April 1768.[101]

Washington was skeptical about vinifera for Virginia. As he explained in a letter written while he was commanding the revolutionary army, he had observed the efforts of his neighbors to cultivate the foreign grape, had noted the failure of their vines, had tasted the badness of their wines, and, concluding that Virginia was too hot for vinifera, resolved, as he said, "to try the wild grape of the country." Accordingly, "a year or two before hostilities commenced I selected about two thousand cuttings of a kind which does not ripen with us (in Virginia) 'till repeated frosts in the Autumn meliorate the grape and deprive the vines of their leaves."[102] From this description it appears that Washington had chosen some variety of cordifolia, one of the so-called winter grapes, as his neighbor Charles Carter of Cleve had done ten years before. Washington's diary for 20 November 1771 reports that he began that day to plant cuttings of the "Winter Grape" in the "inclosure below the garden." He finished in December, having planted twenty-nine rows of winter grapes as well as five of the summer grape (perhaps aestivalis).[103] The experiment, however, like those of Bolling and Mazzei, was never carried through, Washington being called to his public destiny before he could see the results of what he had begun. The scattered remarks in his writings show that he never lost interest in the possibility of grape growing at Mount Vernon; they also show that, despite the logic of his view of the native grape, he could not resist the temptation to make repeated trials of the European.

The names of other Virginians who ventured into grape growing about this time frequently occur in the brief contemporary references that are the only record of this sort of private activity; Anthony Winston, who made wine in substantial quantities at his place in Buckingham County, for instance; or the Colonel Baker of Smithfield who made collections of both native and foreign vines for experiment;[104] or Francis Eppes, Jefferson's brother-in-law, who sent cuttings to Bolling at Chellowe,[105] may stand for an indefinite number of interested Virginians who contributed something to the persistent efforts at winegrowing in the last years before the Revolution, though we do not have the means of knowing anything distinct about their work.

The history of winegrowing in Virginia in the more than two hundred years that have elapsed since Washington reluctantly left his vineyard for the command of the army of the Continental Congress shows that the question at issue between Estave and Bolling, and between Washington and his neighbors, of whether to favor the native or the foreign grape, is still not resolved. In the nineteenth century, Virginia made an outstanding contribution to American viticulture through Dr. D. N. Norton's "Virginia Seedling," best known as the Norton grape and still recognized as the best of all native hybrids so far for the making of red wine (this is not high praise, but indicates at least a relative judgment). The Norton, a hybrid of aestivalis and labrusca varieties, came into general cultivation in the 1850s. After the Civil War a wine boom based on the Norton grape developed around Charlottesville, where Mazzei and Jefferson had worked in vain a hundred years before; in the 1870s Charlottesville was grandly called the capital of the "Wine Belt of Virginia."[106] Unchecked diseases, the growing competition of California, and the growing pressure of Dry sentiment dampened the boom; only a vestige of an industry remained for Prohibition to extinguish.

Immediately after Repeal, an attempt was made to revive the Norton-based industry around Charlottesville, but that did not survive the 1941–45 war.[107] Now Virginia is the scene of a revived and growing wine industry, based not only on the old native varieties but on the newer French-American hybrids, and, most interestingly, on vinifera: thus in our time the circle that the original settlers of Jamestown began to trace has been closed. It is one of the fascinations of the subject of winegrowing in the United States, as illustrated by the complicated history of experiment in Virginia, that we still do not know what the necessary, certain basis of viticulture is in most parts of the country: natives? vinifera? some *tertium quid?* Temperaments that are hot for certainty will be distressed by such indefiniteness: but those who take pleasure in speculation will find much to intrigue them in the past and the present of the scene.

4

Other Colonies
and Communities
before the Revolution

Maryland and Pennsylvania:
The Discovery of the Alexander Grape

T he sort of experimental winegrowing illustrated by the Virginia planters just before the Revolution may be taken as general throughout those parts of the colonies where there was any tradition at all of hopeful attempt. Nor were such trials limited to the familiar places. In the exotic territory of Louisiana an Englishman, Colonel Ball, who settled some miles north of New Orleans on the banks of the Mississippi, managed to produce enough wine to send a sample of Louisiana claret or burgundy to King George III in 1775. The Indians put an end to this enterprise by massacring the colonel and his family.[1]

Back in the more settled regions of tidewater, Governor Horatio Sharpe informed Lord Baltimore in 1767 that he was hoping to improve and soften the native grape by cultivation.[2] He evidently favored the European grape, though, and other Marylanders agreed: Charles Carroll of Annapolis planted a vineyard in Howard County in 1770 with four sorts of vines that he called "Rhenish, Virginia grape, Claret and Burgundy."[3] After his death the vineyard was kept up by his son, the famous Charles Carroll of Carrollton, and it was still extant in 1796, making it the longest-lived of recorded colonial vineyards.[4] By that time, however, all but the native vines were reported to be dead. Growers nevertheless continued to try vinifera, as is shown by the newspaper advertisements of Maryland nurserymen

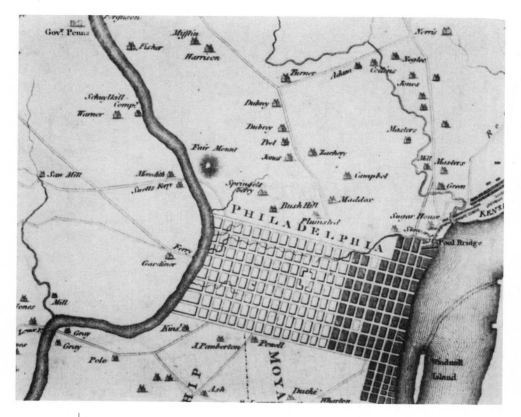

22 | The Alexander grape, a spontaneous hybrid of vinifera and labrusca vines from which the first commercial wines in America were made, was discovered around 1740 by James Alexander in the neighborhood of Springettsbury, just above the northwest corner of Philadelphia, as shown in this map of 1777. This was where William Penn's gardener had planted cuttings of vinifera in 1683. It is probable, then, that Penn's imported European vines had entered into the formation of America's first wine grape by pollinating a native vine. (Detail of William Faden's map of Philadelphia and environs; Map Division, Library of Congress)

right down to the Revolution offering European vines to be sold and planted in Maryland.[5]

Some time before the experiments of Carroll and Sharpe, an event of crucial significance had already occurred in Maryland when, in 1755 or 1756 (the second date is the more likely), Colonel Benjamin Tasker, Jr., a famous horseman and secretary to the province of Maryland, planted a two-acre vineyard at his sister's estate of Belair, in Prince Georges County, about twelve miles from Annapolis.[6] What was of immense, if unrecognized, significance in the colonel's modest enterprise was the grape he planted, called the Alexander. This, a cross between an unidentified native and a vinifera vine, is the earliest named hybrid of which we have record. According to the account given by William Bartram, the vine was discovered around 1740 by James Alexander, then gardener to Thomas Penn, a son of William Penn. Alexander found the vine growing in the woods along the Schuylkill near the old vineyard established in 1683 by Andrew Doz for William Penn.[7] It is thus almost certainly a hybrid of one of Penn's European vines, and so Penn's ideas about refining the native grape were in fact realized, though by pure accident and long after his death.

Colonel Tasker succeeded in making wine of his grape, wine that quickly acquired some celebrity. On his travels through the colonies, the Reverend Andrew Burnaby had it served to him at the table of the governor of Pennsylvania in Philadelphia and approved it as "not bad."[8] A more damaging description than Burnaby's faint praise is given by Governor Horatio Sharpe of Maryland, who, in response to the contemporary Lord Baltimore's request for some Maryland "Burgundy" to be shipped to him, had to reply that

> There hath been no Burgundy made in Maryland since my arrival except two or three hogsheads which Col. Tasker made in 1759; this was much admired by all that tasted it in the months of February and March following, but in a week or two afterwards it lost both its colour and flavour so that no person would touch it and the ensuing winter being a severe one destroyed almost all the vines.[9]

Sad to say, the death of Colonel Tasker's vines in 1760 was followed, in the same year, by the death of the colonel himself at the early age of forty; like every other hopeful beginning of the sort of which we know anything, Tasker's flickered out quickly. In this case, though, there was a crucial difference: the hybrid grape had appeared, though how it travelled from Philadelphia to Maryland remains a subject for pure guessing.[10] The Alexander itself would persist well after Tasker, and, more important, was but the first of a list of American hybrids now grown to thousands and thousands.

Across the newly surveyed Mason-Dixon line to the north of Maryland, the scene in Pennsylvania and New Jersey in the years just before the Revolution resembled that in Virginia. The persistence of indomitably optimistic men had begun to have its effect: there was growing interest in, growing discussion of, and growing experiment with the wine vine that would in all probability have led to substantial results but for the interruption made by the Revolution.

One reason to think so was the presence in Pennsylvania of a great number of Germans who sorely missed the vine they had left behind. As the traveller Gottlieb Mittelberger reported in the 1750s, the Germans in America, especially the Württembergers and the Rhinelanders, missed "the noble juice of the grape." Mittelberger saw that the conditions of sparse settlement, difficult transportation, and undeveloped markets would not soon be overcome; successful cultivation of the grape would not come all at once or soon, but, he wrote, "I have no doubt that in time, this too will come."[11]

In Pennsylvania it is, predictably, Ben Franklin who stands out among the proponents of winegrowing. No man has expressed the beneficent character of wine better than Franklin did in his well-known affirmation that "God loves to see us happy, and therefore He gave us wine."[12] From the earliest moment at which he had access to the public ear, Franklin began giving instruction to his fellow-colonists about winemaking. *Poor Richard's Almanack* for 1743 contains directions for making wine offered to the "Friendly Reader" because, Poor Richard says, "I would have every Man take Advantage of the Blessings of Providence and few are acquainted with the Method of making Wine of the Grapes which grow wild in our Woods." Franklin's methods required the grapes to be trodden by foot—"get into the Hogshead bare-leg'd"—and specify a long cool fermentation lasting until Christmas. The casual freedom of those unregulated days appears strikingly in this word of advice: "If you make Wine for Sale, or to go beyond Sea, one quarter part must be distill'd, and the Brandy put into the three Quarters remaining." But of course where no industry existed, the tax-gatherer was not interested; and so one might distill and sell at retail without licenses, fears, or fees. As his last word, Franklin adds a modest disclaimer: "These Directions are not design'd for those who are skill'd in making Wine, but for those who have hitherto had no Acquaintance with that Art."[13]

In 1765, long after he had ceased to edit *Poor Richard,* and while he was acting as Pennsylvania's agent in London, Franklin took the trouble to adapt and publish for American readers of *Poor Richard* the directions drawn up by Aaron Hill for producing native wine;[14] not very authentic directions, perhaps, but who could know that? The immediate impulse behind Franklin's instructing the Americans in winemaking was probably the Sugar Act of 1764; this laid a duty for the first time on the Portuguese wines—Madeira included—that the colonists by long habit had regarded as immune from all duties. As one of Franklin's friends said on that melancholy occasion, "We must then drink wine of our own making or none at all."[15]

But Franklin did not need so drastic a reason to be active in favor of American wine. In the years before and after 1765 he had been busily encouraging the development of native wines. One anecdote told by the Boston merchant and judge Edmund Quincy is illustrative. Sometime—perhaps in the 1750s—Quincy met Franklin when the latter was on a visit to Boston, and heard Franklin say that the "Rhenish grape Vines" had lately been planted in Philadelphia with good success. Quincy remarked that he would like to have some for his Massachusetts garden, and thought nothing more of the matter until, some weeks later, he received cuttings of such vines in two parcels, one sent by water and one by land. On later meeting Franklin, Quincy learned that Franklin had not only taken the unasked trouble and expense of sending the vines but had had to obtain them some seventy miles from Philadelphia, his information about their growing in the city being mistaken. The young John Adams, who records the story, sums it up as an instance of Franklin's benevolence: all his trouble was "purely for the sake of doing good in the world by propagating the Rhenish wines thro these provinces. And Mr. Quincy has some of them now growing in his garden."[16] In 1761 Franklin wrote to Quincy wishing him "success in your attempts to make wine from American grapes," but whether "American grapes" means simply any grapes grown in America, or that Quincy had abandoned his Rhenish grapes for natives we cannot know.[17] Terminology was so loose in those days that one can never be sure.

A rising expectation that wine could be grown in America characterized the last few years before the Revolution; it has an interesting echo in a proposal made to Franklin in 1772. He was then in London, representing not only Pennsylvania but Georgia, New Jersey, and Massachusetts as well; he was thus the man of preeminent authority and influence in all matters affecting the political and economic life of the colonies. If a projector or speculator had a notion for getting rich in the colonies, Franklin was obviously the man he would want to make sure of. One such ambitious person was the flamboyant Thomas O'Gorman, an Irish adventurer turned respectable Burgundian winegrower (as the fortunes of the Hennessys, Bartons, Lynches, and others suggest, there seems to be some secret affinity between the Irish and the French wine trade—some maintain that even Haut Brion is really O'Brien frenchified). O'Gorman, after serving with the French armies against the English, was made a chevalier, and, thanks to his Irish good looks, married a sister of that strange Chevalier D'Eon who lived sometimes as a man and sometimes as a woman. The marriage brought O'Gorman a large dowry in the form of Burgundian vineyards, which supported him until the French Revolution at last sent him back to Ireland. Long before that, however, in 1772, the rumors of the prospects of winegrowing in the colonies had somehow reached the chevalier, and he came forward with the plan of a winegrowing scheme in the colonies for which he tried to get Franklin's support. The key question was obtaining a parliamentary subsidy; in the vexed state of relations between England and her colonies that, however, was out of the question. Franklin recommended the chevalier to apply to the promoters of a new American colony in the Ohio lands, but their scheme soon collapsed, though not before Franklin had received a gift of wine from O'Gorman's Burgundian estate, vintage 1772: "a Hogshead of the right sort for you," as the chevalier described it.[18]

An even more interesting gift of wine was received by Franklin from a Pennsylvania Quaker named Thomas Livezey, who operated a mill on the Wissahickon near Philadelphia. In June 1767 Livezey sent to England a dozen bottles of American wine that he had made "from our small wild grape, which grows in great plenty in our woodland"; another dozen followed later in the year. "I heartily wish it may arrive safe," Livezey wrote, "and warm the hearts of everyone who tastes it, with a love for America."[19] It may only have been Franklin's diplomatic tact, but in thanking Livezey he affirmed that the wine "has been found excellent by many good judges," and in particular by Franklin's London wine merchant, who was "very desirous of knowing what quantity of it might be had and at what price."[20] One wonders whether Philip Mazzei was one of the judges to whom this American wine was submitted, and whether it had anything to do with his decision to try winegrowing in America? Livezey continued to make wine along the banks of the Wissahickon; tradition says that he sank several barrels of it in the stream to keep

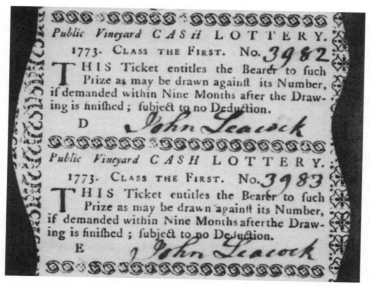

23 Lottery tickets for John Leacock's scheme of a "public vineyard" in Philadelphia, 1773. The lottery did not succeed, but a "public vine-yard" was at last established by the federal government at Washington, D.C., in 1858. (Historical Society of Pennsylvania)

it safe during the Revolution, and that one or two bottles of the wine thus preserved were still extant in the twentieth century.[21]

Another Philadelphian, the naturalist and traveller John Bartram, was thinking about winemaking in this decade. After his journey of botanical exploration through the South in 1765, Bartram wrote to the Reverend Jared Eliot, the pioneer American agricultural writer, that he had found a promising grape (probably a muscadine) in Carolina and hoped to be able to propagate it and others in sufficient quantity to furnish a winemaking industry. Bartram's motive was the cause of temperance: most Americans being "eager after strong liquors and spirits," wine was a highly desirable alternative.[22] The argument is so familiar in the history of this subject that one is compelled to accept the conclusion that Americans, especially in the eighteenth and nineteenth centuries, were formidable drinkers. What success Bartram had we do not know. About twenty years later, Johann Schoepf wrote that many sorts of American vines, collected by the elder Bartram, could be seen in Bartram's Gardens in Philadelphia, then conducted by William, the son. Schoepf reported that the grapes improved under cultivation, a frequently met assertion much easier to make than to prove.[23]

Winegrowing was evidently much in the air around Philadelphia at the end of the 1760s. Samples of wine from native grapes, produced by R. S. Jones, by Dr. Francis Alison, and by Dr. Philip Syng, were exhibited at the American Philosophical Society in 1768.[24] In the same year John Leacock, a retired Philadelphia silversmith, and later the author of patriotic dramas, began planting for himself and other interested experimenters at his farm in Lower Merion Township "white, blue, and purple grapes, as well as Lisbon and Muscadine vines."[25] Some of these Leacock received from other local growers, some were from foreign sources. At the end of 1772 he was encouraged enough to inform the American Philosophical Society that he meant to undertake a public vineyard "for the good of all the Provinces, from which might be drawn such vines or cuttings free of all expence, as might best suit each province."[26] To finance this philanthropic project, Leacock proposed a public lottery—then a popular and legal form of money-raising in Pennsylvania—and actually issued tickets in 1773 for his "Public Vineyard Cash Lottery." By 1775 Leacock had experience enough of the afflictions that ravaged his vinifera vines—rot, insects, and weather—to wonder whether native vines might not be the answer.[27] But, as with so many other efforts at this time, the Revolution put an end to Leacock's work. He left his farm in 1777 in advance of the British occupation of Philadelphia, and does not seem ever to have returned to it.[28]

The Royal Society of Arts Competition

Across the river from Philadelphia, in the province of New Jersey, two other notable efforts at winegrowing were also begun before the Revolution. In 1758 the then newly founded London Society for the Encouragement of the Arts, Manufactures, and Commerce offered a premium of £100 to the first colonist to produce five tuns of red or white wine of acceptable quality from grapes grown in the colonies (a tun equals 252 gallons). The prize offer was renewed until 1765, but no winner appeared, and it was then dropped.[29] Meantime, the gentlemen of the society had reconsidered the question and had sensibly concluded that good vineyards must precede good wine. It is possible that Franklin had something to do with this commonsense conclusion: he had become a member of the society in 1759, shortly after his arrival in London, and he was active in it thereafter.[30] He presided, for example, over the meeting of the society in 1761 at which it was resolved to commission the famous Philip Miller, of the Chelsea Botanical Garden, to write a treatise on viticulture expressly for the American colonies (just the sort of thing that Franklin would encourage), though Miller did not in fact produce one.[31]

In any case, in 1762 the society offered a premium of £200 for the largest vineyard of wine grapes, of no fewer than 500 vines, to be planted by 1767 in the colonies north of the Delaware, and another of equal value for one in the colonies south of the river. Second prizes of £50 each were also assigned to each region. This challenge called forth a successful response, the first prize being awarded to Edward Antill (1701–70), a country gentleman then living at Raritan Landing, near New Brunswick, New Jersey.[32] Like other experimental vineyardists in America, then and now, Antill was animated not merely by the hope of financial gain but by the enthusiast's wish to make the country abound in vines and wine. People laughed at

24 | The Adam brothers' building for the Royal Society of Arts, John Street, London. Through its competitions for colonial American vineyards from 1758 to the Revolution, the society did much to establish the idea that American viticulture would be based on native American grapes. (From London County Council, *Survey of London,* vol. 18 [1937])

his vineyard, Antill wrote in 1765 ("I have been thought by some Gentlemen as well as by Farmers, very whimsical in attempting a Vineyard"),[33] but he could not believe that nature could be opposed to it—"as if America alone was to be denied those cheering comforts which Nature with bountiful hand stretches forth to the rest of the world."[34]

The records of the society (now the Royal Society of Arts) preserve Antill's correspondence and allow us to see his vineyard in greater detail than any other in early America. He began planting French and Italian vines in 1764, on the south side of a hill facing a public road so that his experiment could be advertised to the skeptics. He also offered cuttings and instruction to those who showed an interest; it was the same missionary zeal that led him to compose what is now identified as the first specifically American treatise on viticulture. This work entitled "An Essay on the Cultivation of the Vine, and the Making of Wine, Suited to the Different Climates in North-America," was submitted to the American Philosophical Society in June of 1769 but not published until 1771, the year after Antill's death, when it was published in the *Transactions* of the society, whose original purpose, as expressed by Ben Franklin in 1743, included the "improvements of vegetable juices, as ciders, wines, etc."[35] The American spirit of improvement with which Antill wrote is nicely expressed at the beginning of his "Essay":

> I know full well that this undertaking being new to my countrymen, the people of America, will meet many discouraging fears and apprehensions, lest it may not succeed. The fear of being pointed at or ridiculed, will hinder many: The apprehension of being at a certain expence, without the experience of a certain return, will hinder more from making the attempt; but let not these thoughts trouble you, nor make you afraid.[36]

Antill's knowledge that anyone trying to grow European grapes would be laughed at—we recall that Bolling in Virginia complained of the "little Heroes" who ridiculed his activity—shows that by this time in colonial history the question was firmly settled in the popular mind: European grapes would not grow here.

Antill heavily favored the European vine, and though he was keenly aware of the ignorance that hedged in all his experiments, he writes as though he already had a clear idea of the qualities of the available European varieties in this country. For a "fine rhenish," he wrote a correspondent in 1768, there were the white muscadine and others; some of the "best white wine" came from the Melie blanc; the "black Orleans" and the "blue Cluster" were the "best and true burgundy," and so on.[37] Despite the very positive recommendations, these were necessarily the expressions of hope rather than the record of experience. Antill did not wholly disregard the native grape: indeed, he said that he had collected "the best sort of native vines of America by way of trial."[38] But he did not live long enough to carry out extended trials of his native grapes, and he expressed doubt about them in his "Essay on the Cultivation of the Vine": "They will," he thought, "undergo a hard struggle indeed, before they will submit to a low and humble state."[39]

By 1765 Antill had 800 vines and a nursery. According to the certificate attesting his claim to the Society of Arts' £200 premium, the vines were planted six feet apart in the rows and the rows separated by five feet; the whole was fenced and well cultivated.[40] No one knew better than Antill how much had yet to be learned, and he clearly saw the need for systematic and cooperative work if the colonies were to achieve a successful viticulture; he wrote his "Essay" partly to stimulate such response. He urged the Society of Arts to publish a cheap guide to viticulture for use in America, where experience was lacking and where books were few and expensive.[41] He also proposed in 1768 that the colonies establish a public vineyard by subscription[42]—indeed, Leacock's plan for such a vineyard in 1773 was in acknowledged imitation of Antill's earlier plan: neither came to anything, though in the middle of the nineteenth century there was a public vineyard in Washington, D.C., a belated realization of an early idea.

Though Antill took the prize for a colonial vineyard, he had close competition from William Alexander (1726–83), commonly styled Lord Stirling on account of his claim (never officially allowed) to the lapsed earldom of Stirling. Alexander had imported vines and planted them in vineyards in New York and New Jersey as early as 1763;[43] he did so with a keen sense of the uncertainties of the enterprise: "Of all the vines of Europe, we do not yet know which of them will suit this climate; and until that is ascertained by experiment, our people will not plant vineyards; few of us are able, and a much less number willing, to make the experiment."[44] By 1767 Alexander had 2,100 vines planted at his estate of Basking Ridge, Somerset County, New Jersey, and claimed the society's premium of £200; according to the document presented to the society, the vines were "chiefly Burgundy, Orleans, Black, White and Red Frontiniac, Muscadine, Portugals and Tokays."[45] The rival claims of Alexander and of Antill evidently caused a quarrel within the society, for though the responsible committee adjudged the prize to Alexander, the society as a whole disagreed: the first prize went to Antill for his smaller vineyard; the second prize was not awarded; and a special gold medal went to Alexander.[46]

Antill's original vineyard cannot have survived very long, for Antill seems to have sold his place in 1768, a year after he had won his prize for his work. By 1783, according to the report of the German traveller Johann David Schoepf, Antill's negligent heirs had let the vineyard "fall into decay, because it demanded too much work";[47] it does not figure in the list of vineyards systematically visited in 1796 by John James Dufour. Yet Antill's experiments succeeded in stirring up some interest in viticulture among his neighbors. In 1806, long after Antill's death, S. W. Johnson of New Brunswick published a treatise on the cultivation of the vine in which he shows himself familiar with Antill's example. From it we learn that the vineyard planted by Antill had been restored by the current owner of the estate, Miles Smith, who cultivated there a number of vinifera varieties. Johnson named two or three other vineyardists in New Jersey, who "do honour to the state" and who may also be counted as heirs to Antill's work.[48]

As for Alexander's vineyard, it is not likely to have survived the death of its proprietor in 1783. On the outbreak of the Revolution, Alexander went on active service in the patriot cause and served with distinction as a general officer until his death at Albany. Like Washington, he had no time to pursue the planter's activities that he preferred, and he did not again reside at Basking Ridge; within a few years of his death the estate was described as derelict.[49]

The London society did not score any obvious triumph in the colonies, but it did contribute to a development of lasting importance to American winegrowing by helping to turn attention to the native grape varieties. Taking a retrospective view of the New Jersey experiments of Alexander and Antill, the secretary of the society concluded that the chances of vinifera were doubtful: "but the society's measures," he added, "have occasioned trials of the native vines of America, which were before only considered as wild useless plants, that promise much better success."[50] In consequence, the society offered a new gold medal in 1768, this time for a vineyard of no fewer than 2,000 plants of the "indiginous native vines."[51] The medal was still among the society's list of awards in 1775, and, although in the next year the Revolution put an end to such encouragements from mother country to colony, the public announcement in favor of native vines perhaps had some effect—the society's offers and the policy behind them were evidently carefully watched by influential colonists. By this point in the baffling search for an American wine, the conviction at last seemed to be growing that a practical basis could be found only in the native plant.

The observation that American viticulture would be based on American varieties was, of course, as old as the attempt to grow grapes in the New World, or, more precisely, as old as the discovery that native grapes grew in North America. Thomas Harriot's *Briefe and True Report* of 1588 had prophesied that when the native grapes were "planted and husbanded as they should be, an important commodity in wines can be established."[52] Robert Johnson, in his *Nova Britannia* of 1609, affirmed that the colonists of Virginia, "by replanting and making tame the vines that naturally grow there" would soon make good wine;[53] Lord De La Warr in 1610 was confident that the "naturall vines" would, once they had been tamed and trained, yield "a perfect grape and fruitfull vintage."[54] The same vision had appeared to many another speculative pioneer on looking at the abundant and rudely flourishing vines of the uncleared woods. Sir William Berkeley is reported to have successfully cultivated the wild grapes of Virginia for winemaking before his death in 1677. William Penn, in 1683, had thoughts of domesticating the native grape; Sir Nathaniel Johnson had evidently made the effort in South Carolina in the first decade of the eighteenth century, as did Robert Beverley in Virginia.[55] Other instances of such early interest in sticking to the native varieties might be named, and I dwell on the point at such length because it is often said in print that nobody gave any thought to the native varieties until many, many years after the original settlements had been made. That is clearly not true. Yet it *is* true that nobody had the patience, or the good luck, or the faith, to carry out the necessary labor, or to hit the right conditions, or to endure the uncertain waiting. More to the point, no one knew what to do. The science of controlled plant hybridizing was still in the future, and though hybrids were no doubt naturally generated, they were random and unnoticed. It was only a stroke of luck that, at last, brought the Alexander to notice and pointed a way to the future; for many years to come all hybrids introduced for winegrowing were to be equally accidental and equally misunderstood, more often than not being identified as vinifera.

Under the circumstances, one need not wonder at the long time it took for the Americans to give up on vinifera after repeated, unvarying failure, decade after decade, in place after place. They had nothing else to turn to, really. Hardly any unameliorated variety of the native grape makes a tolerable, let alone satisfactory, wine by itself; the causes of the failure of vinifera were not understood and so could be denied by wishful thinking; and the qualities of the European vine were known. The wine from its grapes was familiar and good. For all these reasons it was inevitable that the fruitless experiment of growing vinifera should be stubbornly persisted in. By the end of the eighteenth century, however, the wish to have such wine as one gets from vinifera seems finally to have been yielding to the perception that Americans, if they were to make any wine of their own at all, would perforce have to invent their own grapes. That was the turning point, going back to the accidental discovery of the Alexander. One authority has observed that the eighteenth century in America was, in agricultural matters, a period of "singular lethargy," so that the "agricultural legacy of the colonies to the states was scant and of little worth."[56] But the introduction of the native hybrid grape makes a significant exception to that general proposition. After the Revolution, the important history of American wine in the eastern settlements is the history of experiment with native grapes.

The Contribution of Continental Emigrants: The Huguenots and St. Pierre

Many individuals of all European nations made their way to the English colonies of North America from the earliest days. In addition, there were many organized efforts—often for speculative rather than philanthropic purposes—to settle whole groups of non-English Protestant peoples to help develop the colonial economy. France, Switzerland, and the German-speaking territories were the prime sources, and more often than not it was winemaking, a work no Englishman was born to, that furnished the main object of such settlements. In this history, the French Huguenots come first.

The earliest group of Huguenot emigrés has already been mentioned, the group that was sent at the expense of King Charles II to South Carolina in 1680 to undertake "ye manufacture of silkes, oyles, wines, etc."[57] The forty-five persons who came for that purpose seem to have been diverted to other work very quickly, and, as we know, no winegrowing tradition was ever established in Carolina. The idea always persisted, though, and in the promotional literature attending any effort to bring over continental emigrés, the prospect of a flourishing viticulture was inevitably made one of the leading attractions. The settlement arranged by the Swiss promoter Jean Pierre Purry at Purrysburgh in South Carolina is an example. Beginning in 1724 Purry proposed various schemes to the British authorities to bring over large numbers of Swiss, including exiled Huguenots living in Switzerland. After some false starts, he succeeded in 1731 in bringing over a contingent of mixed French and Swiss Protestants, who were settled on land granted to Purry on the banks of the Savannah, not very many miles up the river from the spot that was to be the site of Oglethorpe's Savannah in 1733. The kind of blandishment by which Purry attracted his colonists appears in his tract entitled *Proposals of Mr. Peter Purry, of Newfchatel, For Encouragement of Such Swiss Protestants as Should Agree to Accompany him to Carolina,* published in 1731. "The woods are full of wild vines, bearing 5 or 6 sorts of grapes naturally," Purry wrote; for want of vine dressers, no wine but Madeira was drunk in South Carolina, and there, he suggested, lay the opportunity for the French and Swiss. They could take over from the Portuguese the lucrative task of supplying wine to the colony.[58] Purry's project was assisted by Governor Robert Johnson, who was interested in winegrowing for South Carolina (see above, p. 55). The contemporary reports of Purrysburgh make no mention of viticulture, however, and it seems safe to conclude that it was not even seriously begun, despite the expectations and the traditions of the Huguenots.

A third organized migration of Huguenots to South Carolina did make a determined effort to establish vineyards there. This was the community called New Bordeaux, whose origins may be traced to 1763, when some of the many Huguenots still living in London petitioned the Board of Trade for lands along the Savannah River, where they proposed "to apply themselves principally to the cultivation of vines and of silk."[59] The petition was favorably received, and in 1764 some 132 French Protestants were sent to land lying near the Savannah River on Long Cane Creek, many miles above the Purrysburgh settlement. There, amidst the 26,000 acres of their grant, the French laid out their town of New Bordeaux; as the still-surviving map of the original survey shows, of the 800 acres of the town tract, 175 acres were reserved, "to be divided into 4-acre lots for vineyards and olive gardens."[60] It may have been of these settlers' early efforts at winemaking that William Stork spoke in his *Description of East Florida* (1769), saying: "I have drank a red of the growth of that province [South Carolina] little inferior to Burgundy."[61]

Whatever effort they made towards developing their vineyards was powerfully reinforced in 1768, when the community was joined by another migration of French Protestants under the leadership of Louis de Mesnil de St. Pierre.[62] St. Pierre's original intention had been to take his people to Nova Scotia, but accident brought them to South Carolina instead. They could not have had viticulture in mind from the beginning: Nova Scotia was no place for the vine (though there are now vineyards and several small wineries there), and St. Pierre, a Norman, did not belong to the wine regions of France. Once in New Bordeaux, however, he devoted himself to viticulture with a determined zeal. The land, he wrote enthusiastically, "rose into gentle declivities, interspersed with delightful vales of small extent": soil, water, climate, all were perfect for growing wine grapes, so that—the conclusion is painfully familiar—"we may venture to pronounce the success infallible."[63]

The immediate effect of St. Pierre's work was evident in the next year, when the colonists of New Bordeaux petitioned the colonial assembly for new vines and were granted £700 for their purchase.[64] By 1771 St. Pierre had formed a plan to promote the cultivation of vines at New Bordeaux through an ambitious scheme of importing both cuttings and professional *vignerons* from Europe. St. Pierre first took his proposals to the governor and assembly of South Carolina for the necessary appropriation, and though a committee reported favorably and the assembly was sympathetic, he did not get his money. Nevertheless, he was already importing vines from Europe and planting them at New Bordeaux.[65]

His next step was to go to England to press his ideas upon the home authorities. According to his own report, St. Pierre took wine from South Carolina with him to London and submitted it to Lord Hillsborough, then secretary for the American colonies, but received no encouragement.[66] It was later said that Hillsborough was paid £250,000 by the French to dampen the enterprise, since the French were terrified lest South Carolina take away the American wine trade! How likely a story this is need not be argued.[67] St. Pierre had better success with the Society for the Encouragement of the Arts, for those gentlemen in January 1772 awarded him a gold medal in recognition of his samples of wines, indigo, and silk.[68]

Though disappointed in his first effort to gain official support, St. Pierre was not a man to give up without a struggle; from the offices of the minister he appealed directly to the public by attempting to float a public subscription of £4,000 for the "Society for the Encouragement of the Culture of Vine Yards at New Bordeaux," which would undertake to plant not less than fifty acres of vines within three years.[69] A fellow South Carolinian, the retired merchant and statesman Henry Laurens, was then in London and had at first acted as St. Pierre's patron. When St. Pierre determined on his scheme of a public subscription, however, he and Laurens differed: Laurens refused to "subscribe Money in order to induce and lead on other People," and St. Pierre turned from him in anger.[70] Since Laurens, as we have seen, dreamed of a time when South Carolina's wines would float down its rivers to the markets of the world, his refusal to assist St. Pierre's speculation was obviously not that of a man ill-disposed to winegrowing. St. Pierre's enthusiasm evidently could not persuade the more experienced Laurens.

The public subscription failed, but St. Pierre kept up the fight. Some weeks afterwards he published a second proposal under the emphatic heading of *The Great Utility of establishing the Culture of Vines . . . And the absolute Necessity of Supporting the Infant Colony of French Protestants settled at New Bordeaux in South Carolina, who have brought the Culture of Vines, and the Art of raising Silk to Perfection.*[71] This appeal assured the British public that it need not fear the same failure that had overtaken all other such ventures: the difference at New Bordeaux lay in the French—"At

THE
A R T
OF
PLANTING and CULTIVATING
THE
V I N E;

AS ALSO,

OF MAKING, FINING, and PRESERVING
W I N E S, &c.

ACCORDING TO

THE MOST APPROVED METHODS

IN THE

Moſt celebrated WINE-COUNTRIES in FRANCE.

Compiled for the Uſe of ſuch as intend to proſecute that bene-
ficial and national Branch of Commerce and Agriculture in
A M E R I C A, and particularly for that of the Colony at
NEW BOURDEAUX ;

By LOUIS DE SAINT PIERRE, Eſq;

One of His Majeſty's Juſtices of the Peace for *Granville*
County, and Captain of the Company of Militia, conſiſting
of the *French* Vine-Dreſſers, eſtabliſhed at *New Bourdeaux,*
in *South Carolina.*

L O N D O N, Printed:
And ſold by J. WILKIE, Nº 71, St. Paul's Church-Yard;
and J. WALTER, Charing-Croſs.
M.DCC.LXXII.

---

25 | Title page of Louis de Mesnil de St. Pierre's *Art of Planting and Cultivating the Vine* (London, 1772). Published when St. Pierre was desperately working to secure English support for the winegrowing colony of New Bordeaux, South Carolina, the book assured the English that winegrowing was bound to succeed in Carolina and that it could bring nothing but good to England. (California State University, Fresno, Library)

New Bordeaux the Vine is taken care of, and properly cultivated, by Persons bred from their Cradles in Vineyards." He had sent 60,000 Burgundian vines to South Carolina since his first proposals were made, St. Pierre said, and had another 100,000 at his disposal, as well as a number of *vigneron* families ready to go.[72]

When the response to this offer was again unsatisfactory, St. Pierre turned back to the government, this time appealing to Parliament for a grant to pay for the expenses of shipping out his 100,000 plants and 150 new settlers, "all vignerons to a man." What he asked from Parliament was £4,200 at 5 percent interest for ten years, and that was but a part of the expense that he envisaged.[73] At the same time he addressed the Treasury, praying for "encouragement upon him and his infant colony." The Board of Trade endorsed St. Pierre's claim, saying that it "could not fail of being usefull to this kingdom," but these good words were all that St. Pierre got for his pains.[74] Or rather, almost all: he did receive a grant of 5,000 acres, an extraordinary grant to an individual at that time.

His energetic campaign against English pockets kept St. Pierre busy with his pen. Besides his two appeals to the public at large, his petition to Parliament, and various other supporting memorials and petitions to the Treasury and the Board of Trade, he produced for potential subscribers and emigrants alike an apology and a treatise combined, entitled *The Art of Planting and Cultivating the Vine, as also of Making, Fining, and Preserving Wines, etc.* (London, 1772). His strategy in the book is to stress the good that winegrowing in Carolina will create for England: it will divert the colonists away from competition with England's manufactures; it will improve the breed and increase the population—for "whence is France so fruitful in men, but by the use of the juice of the grape?"; by the trade in wine, British seamen and shipbuilders will gain employment, thereby improving the national defense as well; so, too, the employment created will prevent British workers from being lost to foreign parts. With all this to follow from planting vines at New Bordeaux, how could one hesitate? Especially when the flourishing of native vines gave "sure proof of the success of the present enterprise"?[75]

The part of St. Pierre's book given over to viticultural instruction follows European practices. Though St. Pierre says that he visited France for the purpose, and though he seems to have done a conscientious piece of homework, he is not aware of any inadequacy in stating, as he does, that "I have confined my researches to the three wine countries of Orleans, Champagne, and Burgundy."[76] The convergence of dates for the first three treatises by American winegrowers on viticulture— Antill's essay in 1771, St. Pierre's book in 1772, and Bolling's MS in 1774—is striking evidence of how interest in the subject was intensifying immediately before the Revolution. But it is also notable that all three of these take for granted that American viticulture will be founded on the European grape, and that no special reference to American conditions is therefore necessary. St. Pierre's book is now chiefly interesting for its expression of the author's entire confidence in what he is doing: winegrowing *must* succeed in America, St. Pierre insists, even though he cannot put much wine of his own making into evidence.

Neither the English government nor the English public came through for St.

Pierre, though it was said that King George requested him to carry on under the king's private patronage.[77] Somehow he managed to complete a part of his scheme. He returned to South Carolina at the end of 1772 with a group of *vignerons* recruited for his project. They had travelled by way of Madeira, where St. Pierre had acquired another large collection of vines. And at New Bordeaux they would have found things in flourishing condition, for we learn from a report written in June of 1772 that the vineyards already planted there were doing extremely well, so well that no one doubted of ultimate success. A shipment of European vines had also arrived in Charleston, the correspondent noted, where they had been set out to root and where, he added, people were stealing them, so popular was the idea of winegrowing.[78]

"My vineyard is thriving," St. Pierre wrote after his return to New Bordeaux: "Others beside mine are in perfect good order, and next year we shall have a good deal of wine as well as silk made here. . . . of all the vines planted last March, some of which I brought from Madeira, none have miscarried but are now in full growth."[79] Two, at least, of the "others" who were cultivating the vine at New Bordeaux may be identified. One was not a Frenchman but a neighboring German named Christopher Sherb, a native of the valley of the Neckar in Württemberg, who had planted a vineyard on his farm at Broad River, not far from New Bordeaux. Starting with a few cuttings of German vines obtained from settlers in Orangeburg, by 1770 he had a vineyard of 1,539 vines, including both vinifera and natives. The yield was tiny—25 gallons in 1768 and 80 gallons of "tolerable white wine" in 1769, good enough to be sold at a dollar a gallon and to win a £50 bounty from the always attentive London Society for the Encouragement of the Arts in 1770.[80] Sherb's example helped to confirm St. Pierre in his belief that South Carolina was a region destined for winemaking.

The other identifiable grower from the region of New Bordeaux was John Lewis Gervais (1741–95), a Frenchman of Huguenot origin who came to South Carolina in 1764. There he was befriended by Henry Laurens, always interested in viticulture in Carolina, who gave him land at New Bordeaux.[81] Gervais seems to have made vine plantings there for Laurens as well as for himself. When he was visited by the official surveyor to the English Board of Trade, John De Brahm, Gervais had his vines trained according to a method that De Brahm thought admirably adapted to the conditions of the South. The growers of New Bordeaux, De Brahm says, had discovered that

> the grape vine needs no support, neither of sticks or frames, but prospers by being winded on the ground, and piled up in a manner, that the vine itself forms a kind of close bower, (or as the French call it a chapele) where, under it shades its own ground to retain all moisture, which also covers and preserves the blossom of the grapes against vernal Frost, and the grapes themselves against the violent scorching summer heat.[82]

Writing about 1771, De Brahm was not able to say anything about the wine of New Bordeaux. As usual in the colonial story, it was just around the corner: "As for the goodness of the wine itself, its decovery [the discovery of its qualities?] may, without doubt be very shortly expected." So wrote De Brahm, who visited New Bordeaux and believed in its future; he thought that since South Carolina lay between 30 and 35 degrees of latitude, and since the Jesuit fathers were known to have produced wine in Mexico between 25 and 30 degrees of latitude for the refreshment of the Acapulco galleons, winegrowing must succeed in South Carolina.[83]

When William Bartram travelled through South Carolina in June 1775, he was entertained at St. Pierre's residence, Orange Hill, which stood on a hill looking out over the Savannah River and into Georgia, where winegrowing had been tried years before; Bartram found St. Pierre tending "a very thriving vineyard consisting of about five acres" at New Bordeaux.[84] Since St. Pierre had been there since 1768, he was one of the very few of colonial vineyardists who actually persisted long enough to have produced anything (Robert Beverley in Virginia and the Carrolls in Maryland were others). Whether he was as hopeful in 1775 as he had been at the beginning of the decade we do not know. Bartram says nothing about St. Pierre's wine, if there was any. In any case, the Revolution put an end to the enterprise. St. Pierre joined the South Carolinian patriots in the war and was, according to a contemporary note, made "Lieutenant to a Small Fort in the back Country where he lives upon his pay of £30-a year."[85] St. Pierre was killed on an expedition against the Indians, and that "untimely end," as a later memorialist wrote, "overturned the establishment in its infancy."[86] New Bordeaux itself, never very flourishing, dwindled to the crossroads that it now is, where a marker records the site of the old Huguenot church.

Other Huguenot Communities

To go back almost a hundred years, in 1685 a large migration of Protestants from France had taken place in response to the Revocation of the Edict of Nantes, whereby Louis XIV suddenly withdrew from the Huguenots the legal protection that they had secured a century earlier. Though the French government tried to prevent a Huguenot emigration, thousands left the country. There was a general scramble among the proprietors and promoters of American colonies to attract these unlucky people, for they were intelligent, industrious, skilled, well-behaved, and right-thinking—the ideal colonists, in short, and very unlike the average of the marginal types who could be lured into the American backwoods. Landlords in Virginia, the Carolinas, Pennsylvania, and Massachusetts all tried to put their attractions before various Huguenot communities. Virginia managed to secure some: as early as 1686 one Virginia promoter, with an eye upon the Huguenots, advertised his property in Stafford County as "naturally inclined to vines."[87] A Huguenot traveller, Durand de Dauphiné, visiting Stafford County the next year, was much struck by the promising terrain and by the wild vines there; he made, he says, some "good" wine from the grapes, and recommended them for cultivation.[88] His account was published in Europe in 1687, but it apparently did not succeed in attracting any Huguenots and did not lead to any winegrowing development in Stafford County.

In 1700 a large body of Huguenots arrived in Virginia under the special auspices of King William and settled on a 10,000-acre tract along the James River donated by the colony. Here, at Manakin Town (near present-day Richmond) they had succeeded by 1702 in making a "claret" from native grapes that was reported to be "pleasant, strong, and full body'd wine."[89] The information, recorded by the historian and viticulturist Robert Beverley, was evidence to him that the native vines needed only to be properly cultivated to become the source of excellent wine and evidently had much to do in starting him on his own experiments. The opinion of Beverley is confirmed by the Swiss traveller Louis Michel, who visited Manakin Town in 1702 and was impressed by the incredibly large vines growing there, from which, he wrote, the French "make fairly good wine, a beginning has been made to graft them, the prospects are fine."[90] The prospects soon changed for the worse: according to the Carolina historian John Lawson, the French at Manakin Town found themselves hemmed in by other colonists, who took up all the land around them, and so most of them departed for Carolina, where their minister assured Lawson that "their intent was to propagate vines, as far as their present circumstances would permit, provided they could get any slips of vines, that would do."[91]

In Florida, at the same time that New Smyrna was being built in East Florida, the home government attempted to do something for unpopulated and unremunerative West Florida by sending over, in 1766, a band of forty-six French Protestants to pursue their arts of winemaking and silk producing. They were settled at a place called Campbell Town, east of Pensacola, but conditions there were so wild and unpromising that failure was quick and complete. The group was badly led, the incidence of disease was very high, and within four years all the French were either dead or had left the province.[92] This was, I think, the last instance in which London officials tried to create a colonial enterprise by the expedient of simply dumping a band of Huguenots upon the land, with most dire results for the poor Huguenots themselves.

Beyond the South, there were other, isolated Huguenot communities that attempted winegrowing. Those in Massachusetts and in Rhode Island have already been mentioned. In Pennsylvania, the first winemaker whose name we know was the Huguenot Gabriel Rappel, whose "good claret" pleased William Penn in 1683; another of the earliest was Jacob Pellison, also a Huguenot, as was Andrew Doz, who planted and tended William Penn's vineyard of French vines at Lemon Hill on the Schuylkill.[93] Doz, naturalized in England in 1682, came over to Pennsylvania in that same year; Penn called him a "hot" man but honest.[94] The vineyard, which was begun in 1683, stood on 200 acres of land and was described in 1684 by the German Pastorius as a "fine vineyard of French vines." "Its growth," Pastorius added, "is a pleasure to behold and brought into my reflections, as I looked upon it, the fifteenth chapter of John."[95]

Two years later, another witness reported that "the Governours Vineyard goes on very well."[96] In 1690 the property was patented to Doz himself for a rental of 100 vine cuttings payable annually to Penn as proprietor.[97] From that arrangement it seems clear that the experiment of vine growing was still in process after its beginning seven years earlier. It would be interesting to know whether any of the European vines survived as late as that.

William Penn himself was particularly active in seeking to attract Huguenot emigrants to Pennsylvania, and used the prospect of viticulture as a recruiting inducement. His promotional tract of 1683, *A Letter from William Penn . . . Containing a General Description of the Said Province,* was translated into French and published at The Hague in order to reach the French Protestant community exiled in the Low Countries. In his new province, Penn wrote, were "grapes of diverse sorts" that "only want skilful Vinerons to make good use of them."[98] Penn's pamphlet, though written with an eye on prospective French colonists, is ostensibly addressed to the Free Society of Traders in Pennsylvania, incorporated by Penn in London; he concludes by telling this body that the great objects of the colony, the "Promotion of Wine" and the manufacture of linen, are likely to be best served by Frenchmen: "To that end, I would advise you to send for some thousands of plants out of France, with some Vinerons, and People of the other vocation."[99] Penn's efforts at recruiting had good results. Many religious refugees made their way to the colony, Huguenots among them; but the French were soon assimilated into the general community rather than maintaining a separate identity. They may have undertaken viticulture at first, but their dispersal through the community meant that those who persisted at it did so as individuals. As Penn told the Board of Trade in 1697, in Pennsylvania "both Germans and French make wine yearly, white and red, but not in quantity for export."[100]

The best known of Huguenot settlements in America are those of New York State, at New Paltz and New Rochelle, the one going back to the mid seventeenth century, the other founded towards the end of it. In neither does there seem to have been any attempt at winegrowing, despite the likelihood of their sites and the practice of the neighboring colonies in Massachusetts and Rhode Island.

The Contribution of Continental Emigrants: The Germans

After the Huguenots, the continental emigrants most often associated with experimental viticulture in America were German-speaking Protestants of the many varieties native to Switzerland, Austria, and the different German states. Some had been uprooted by the wars of Louis XIV, whose national aims were mixed with the cause of Catholicism against Protestantism. Others were put in motion simply by the attractions of the New World, often compounded by persecution at home. Pietists, Palatines, Mennonites, Mystics, Moravians, Salzburgers, and others came to the English colonies in such numbers that by the Revolution, it has been estimated, there were some quarter of a million inhabitants of German blood in the colonies.[101]

The first settlement of German Protestants, in this case the people then called Pietists, was made under the auspices of William Penn at Germantown in Pennsylvania in 1683. Winemaking was part of the original intention of the settlers; Francis Pastorius, the leader of the colony, brought vines with him, but they were accidentally spoiled by sea water after they had already arrived in Delaware Bay.[102] No doubt some experiments were made; as late as 1700 Pastorius wrote that the people of Germantown were "especially anxious to advance the cultivation of the vine."[103] But the promise of the town seal, showing a grapevine, a flax blossom, and a weaver's shuttle, was not fully realized: Germantown's weaving prospered, but its wine industry did not.

A second German community was established in 1709 by Protestant refugees from the Rhenish Palatinate (the Rheinpfalz as it is now called), devastated by the War of the Spanish Succession. Thousands of these Germans, from one of the most famous viticultural regions of Europe, had made their way to England, where the English were sympathetic but sorely perplexed to know what to do with them. One answer was to export them to the colonies, usually with the thought of putting to work their talents as winegrowers: had they not come from the very heart of the German wine country? So it was with the group sent over in 1709 under Pastor Joshua von Kocherthal. The gentlemen of the Board of Trade and Plantations proposed that the Palatines, as they were called, should be sent to Virginia or other regions of the continent (they were evidently not very particular) "where the air is clear and healthful" in order to make wine.[104] Kocherthal reported to the board from America that the country was certainly fit for winemaking and that the long history of failure was owing only to "inexperience and want of skill." He mentions Beverley's work in Virginia, which was attracting much notice, and he adds the interesting detail that the Pennsylvania Germans had devised methods for grape growing better suited to American conditions than those of the French.[105] The first contingent of Palatines—more than 2,000 of them—was, however, settled on the Hudson River at Newburgh rather than in Virginia or Pennsylvania. They had a hard struggle to get established, and the official instructions were for them to produce supplies for the English navy rather than wine. Under the circumstances viticulture does not seem to have been seriously tried, though the region is one that must have reminded many of the Palatines of their native Rhineland.[106]

A second contingent of Palatines was sent to the North Carolina coast in company with a number of Swiss emigrants under the charge of Baron Christopher de Graffenried of Bern and of the Swiss traveller Louis Michel: the interests of both men seem to have been largely speculative.[107] The possibility of growing wine was one of the inducements held out to the members of this group, who founded the settlement of New Bern in 1710. Probably some experiments were made, without enough promise to encourage sustained work. New Bern thus provides the model for two later German-speaking colonies in the South already noticed, that of the

Swiss and French at Purrysburgh in South Carolina in 1732 and that of the Salzburgers just across the Savannah River from Purrysburgh, at Ebenezer in Georgia. In both places the manufacture of silk and the production of wine had been part of the original intention, but in both winegrowing was quickly dropped.

One might conclude from this summary account of French and German contributions to early colonial winegrowing that they failed quite as emphatically as the English. Practically speaking, no doubt they did. No continuing, substantial production of wine developed out of any of the trials made by French, German, or Swiss—not to mention those of the Italian Mazzei or the Portuguese Jew De Lyon. But their participation in the early efforts to grow wine in this country helps to make it clear that the consistent failure was not owing to ignorance of established methods. The English may not have known what they were about, but the others brought with them a long tradition. Another, more positive point, is that despite the uniform failure of all who tried winegrowing in the American colonies, it was especially the continental immigrants rather than the English who kept on trying. Their matter-of-course relation to wine as a daily necessity of diet was of incalculable importance in finally establishing an industry. The best-known names in the winegrowing trade that did eventually develop in this country are the names of non-English families, who fulfilled a promise that their ancestors could not, but whose ancestors gave the example. The Germans seem to predominate—Kohler, Frohling, Muench, Husmann, Krug, Gundlach, and Dreyfus come to mind at once. But then, in this country, the Germans always outnumbered the French, who were never enthusiastic about emigration without the stimulus of religious persecution. However, the French are part of it too: Pellier, Lefranc, Vignes, and Champlin are only a few of the French names on the list of successful pioneers. The Italians now seem to be almost synonymous with winemaking in America, especially in California, but theirs is really a later story. Enough to say now that without the diffusive influence of Germans and French, the idea of winegrowing in America would not have persisted as it did, nor would the actual achievement have taken the form that it has now.

THE ESTABLISHMENT
OF AN INDUSTRY

5

From the Revolution to the Beginnings of a Native Industry

A fter independence much of the winegrowing in this country in many ways resembled what had been done before the Revolution: companies for developing vineyards were founded, as they had been earlier in Virginia in the seventies; communities of foreign viticulturists were subsidized, as they had been before in the Carolinas and elsewhere; religious communities tried to make winegrowing a part of their economy, as they had tried before in Pennsylvania and New England. In general, the typical American winegrower was likely to be a German or a Frenchman, as he had been before the Revolution. Yet the long-sought success was at last a native affair, brought about by a Pennsylvanian growing a North Carolinian grape in, with symbolic fitness, the nation's new capital, Washington, D.C.

Peter Legaux and the Pennsylvania Vine Company

The first notable postrevolutionary attempt to establish a successful viticulture was carried out near Philadelphia, where Penn had planted his vines a hundred years before. In 1786 a Frenchman of an adventurous, but rather dubious, past named Peter Legaux (1748–1827) bought an estate of 206 acres at Spring Mill, on

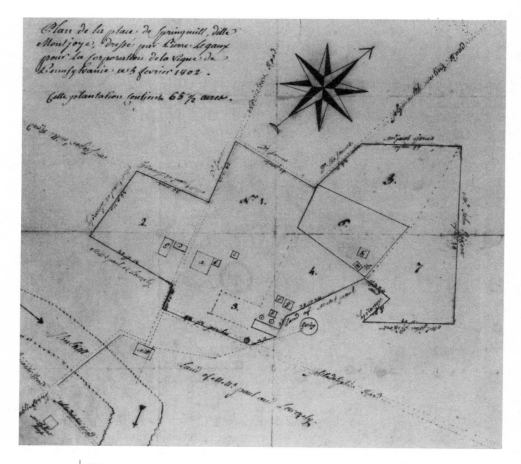

26 "Plan de la place de Springmill, ditte Montjoye, dressé par Pierre Legaux pour La Corporation de la Vigne de Pennsylvanie le 5 fevrier 1802" ("Plan of the site of Springmill, called Mountjoy, prepared by Pierre Legaux for the Pennsylvania Vine Company, 5 February 1802"). This plan of Legaux's vineyards was made immediately after the Pennsylvania Vine Company had at last succeeded in achieving legal incorporation—nine years after the project had been begun—and no doubt expresses the renewed hopes to which the event gave rise. They were doomed to disappointment. (Historical Society of Pennsylvania)

the east bank of the Schuylkill, two miles below Conshohocken in Montgomery County;[1] there he began planting European vines on the slopes of his property and building vaults for wine storage. Legaux's farm has been described for us in unusual detail at an early stage of its development by the French publicist and politician Jacques Pierre Brissot de Warville, who devoted several pages of his *New Travels in the United States of America* (1788) to Legaux as a bright instance of what Frenchmen might hope to achieve in America. Brissot found Legaux in a well-built, solid stone house, enjoying a superb view, and surrounded by all the emblems of plenty: six servants, horses and cattle, fields of grain and meadows of grass, beehives and gardens, and a new vineyard, standing on a southeastern slope and planted with vines from the Médoc.[2] Despite this idyllic presentation, not all was smooth going for Legaux. He lived without his family, who had remained in France; he did not know English well; his servants were often lazy and unruly; and there were quarrels with his neighbors, even though they were all peaceable Quakers.[3]

Legaux, who began life as a lawyer in Metz, was in fact a remarkably difficult and litigious neighbor. When another and later French traveller, the duc de la Rochefoucauld-Liancourt, was directed to Legaux's vineyard as one of the sights of the Philadelphia region in 1795, he took an instant dislike to Legaux—a man, he wrote, whose "whole physiognomy indicates cunning rather than goodness of heart." The duc was scandalized to learn that Legaux, in the nine years of his residence in Pennsylvania, had engaged in two hundred lawsuits, all of them unsuccessful![4] Despite this, or in part because of it, Legaux was widely known and well thought of in Pennsylvania. He seems, in fact, to have had a genius for self-promotion. In 1789, only two years after he set out his first vines, he was elected to the American Philosophical Society, a badge of unquestioned acceptance in the City of Brotherly Love. As so many others before it had done, the experiment that he was making in vine growing at once aroused hopeful curiosity, and, no doubt, as much or more amused skepticism. It was, at any rate, the object of much attention. When, for example, the Constitutional Convention met in Philadelphia in 1792, Washington and other notables journeyed the thirteen miles from town to see the promising new vineyard.[5] There was even an absurd rumor that the republican French, alerted by the favorable description given by Brissot, and anxious as always for the security of their wine trade, had secretly instructed their American minister to pay Legaux to pull up his vines.[6]

After he had had some experience with growing vines and had learned how hard it is to keep an experiment going without financial backing, Legaux decided to obtain public support. To do this he secured an act of the legislature forming a "company for the purpose of promoting the cultivation of vines," usually called the Pennsylvania Vine Company. The enabling legislation was passed in March 1793, when commissioners were appointed to receive subscriptions for the company's stock of 1,000 shares at $20 each.[7] Despite the respectable auspices of the enterprise, money came in slowly. Only 139 shares were sold in a year, and Legaux soon found himself in difficulties. He wrote to General Washington offering to sell his house as a country residence for the president during congressional sessions (then still held in Philadelphia) on condition that he be allowed to continue his "improvements in the cultivation of the vine"—a work that would be lost were Legaux to be, as he feared, sold up for debt.[8] Though his property was, nominally at least, seized in execution of a writ of sale in 1792, by one means or another Legaux yet managed to hang on to it. On 16 August 1793 the Philadelphia *Daily Advertiser* proclaimed that

> the first vintage ever held in America would begin at the vineyard, near Spring Mill, and in a few weeks Mr. Legaux will begin to produce American wine, made upon prin-

ciples hitherto unknown, or at least unpracticed here. This will form a new era in the history of American agriculture. . . . succeeding generations will bless the memory of the man who first taught the Americans the culture of this generous plant.[9]

The style of the notice tells us something about Legaux's promotional talents—"the first vintage ever held in America" was a fairly audacious claim to be making three hundred years after Columbus. It tells us something, too, about the reasons for his unpopularity with his neighbors, who were probably a bit sour at the thought of blessing Legaux's memory. The vintage yielded, so we learn from a later document, six barrels of wine plus a small quantity of "Tokay"; all were "preserved in perfection without the addition of another [sic] single drop of alcohol."[10]

Such publicity did little to relieve Legaux's money troubles. In 1794 he petitioned the U.S. Senate for support of his vineyard, without success.[11] An English traveller visiting Legaux that year was much disappointed by what he saw: the vineyard, he wrote, "does not succeed at all." When La Rochefoucauld-Liancourt called the next year, he found Legaux in desperate straits. Because Legaux could not meet the payments, his farm had been sold and he was reduced to living on fifteen rented acres, including the deteriorating house and the vineyard. There, wearing "stockings full of holes and a dirty night-cap," Legaux lived in penury, hiding from suspicious visitors, but still persisting in the care of his vines.[12] And by one means or another he clung to the Spring Mill estate. Whatever one might think of Legaux's behavior as a neighbor and of his unabashedness as a promoter, it is only fair to admit that his determination to succeed at winegrowing was deep and genuine.

Early in 1800 the Pennsylvania legislature passed an act to stimulate the lagging sale of Vine Company stock by making the terms of purchase easier. Thereupon an elegant prospectus—not signed, but doubtless written by Legaux—was put before the public. In this document the history of the vineyard since planting began at Spring Mill in 1787 is recapitulated.[13] Legaux is said to have begun with 300 plants from Burgundy, Champagne, and Bordeaux. Then follows an assertion that later, as we shall see, became the focus of a controversy not yet fully decided. After the first plants were obtained, the prospectus says, Legaux then "procured plants of the Constantia vine from the Cape of Good Hope." This was the vine for which, so Legaux told La Rochefoucauld in 1795, he had paid the remarkable sum of forty guineas,[14] and of which he did considerable advertising. It was not, however, the Constantia grape at all, or anything like it, being in fact the native hybrid best known as the Alexander. Legaux never gave up his insistence that the grape was what he said it was. Since he sold large quantities of it at premium prices under its attractive foreign name, the question has naturally arisen: Was he lying? Or was he honestly deceived? There is presumptive evidence both ways, but not of a kind to settle the matter.

Whatever the truth, the rest of the prospectus is straightforward. It declares that Legaux now had 18,000 vines set out in his vineyard and a nursery of several

27 | Entry for 15 April 1805 in Peter Legaux's journal, recording the receipt of vines from France for planting in the vineyards of the Pennsylvania Vine Company. The entry reads: "This day at 1/2 pass 10, o'clock at Night, I received a letter from Mr. McMahon with 3 Boxes of Grape- vines, sended by Mr. Lee Consul Americain from Bordeaux, all in very good order and good plantes of Chateaux Margeaux, Lafitte, and haut Brion. 4500 plantes for 230 # . . . and order to send in Town for more etc." (American Philosophical Society)

hundred thousand more, all ready to help produce the long-desired American wine. The scope of the company's proposed activity is set forth in detail, its main purposes being "the cultivation of the vine and the supply of wines, brandy, tartar and vinegar from the American soil, and the extension of vineyards and nurseries of plants of the Burgundy, Champagne, Bordeaux and Tokay wines, and to procure vine-dressers for America."[15] The last object was to be achieved by accepting apprentices at Legaux's vineyard for terms of three to five years, on conditions varying with the size of a shareholder's interest.

Legaux left no opportunity untried. He wrote to Jefferson in March 1801, just after Jefferson's first inauguration, to congratulate him on his election and offering to send him some thousands of vines from Legaux's nursery so that they might be tried in Virginia. When Jefferson politely declined, Legaux responded more boldly, sending him an account of his struggles to found the company and inviting the president to join the subscribers. His enemies were many, Legaux wrote in his charmingly Frenchified English, and especially "the medium classe of the people opposed more phase of this improvement than the richer."[16] Jefferson was either too cautious or too busy or both, for Legaux did not manage to add the dignity of the presidential name to his subscription list. He did, however, send vines to Jefferson the next year, and these were planted at Monticello by one of the Italian vine dressers brought over years before by Philip Mazzei.[17]

At last, in January 1802, the required minimum number of subscriptions to establish the Pennsylvania Vine Company was obtained, the company's incorporation was officially sealed, and Legaux was made superintendent of the company's vineyard at a good salary.[18] It had taken him nearly ten years to reach this official starting point, yet the names of his shareholders make a roster of the federal aristocracy—Citizen Genet, Stephen Girard, Alexander Hamilton, Aaron Burr, and Benjamin Rush, to name a few, were all investors in the Pennsylvania Vine Company.[19] Legaux was right when he told Jefferson that the "richer" rather than the "medium" class were his main support. It is comforting to think that these were, all of them, men of substance already, for they never made a penny from their investment in the Vine Company. The struggle to maintain the company's finances was

28 | William Lee (1772–1840), in uniform as American consul at Bordeaux. Lee had a hand in two notable, if unsuccessful, winegrowing enterprises in the early Republic. He sent vines from the great châteaux of Bordeaux to Legaux's Pennsylvania Vineyard Company in 1805; and in 1816 he was instrumental in forming the plans for the Alabama Vine and Olive Company. He also projected a book on winegrowing in the 1820s but did not publish it. (From Mary Lee Mann, ed., *A Yankee Jeffersonian* [1958])

always uphill, and the enthusiasm of the stockholders grew feebler as the struggle grew harder.

We can learn something about that struggle in detail because the journal that Legaux kept as a record of the Vine Company's work from 1803 onwards has survived in part.[20] It tells a story of such wasted labor and frustration that one wonders at the strength of Legaux's persistence—he seems never to have acknowledged to himself that the odds against him were hopeless. The record for the year 1803 will do as a representative instance. In the spring Legaux planted 14,000 vinifera vines at Spring Mill, or Montjoy, as his estate was called. The finances of the company were then relatively vigorous, after the recent completion of the incorporation proceedings, and Legaux was able to hire regular help for the company's vineyards, of which there appear to have been two, and for his own vineyard, which he maintained separately from the company enterprise. Some of the hands were of English stock—Joseph Nobbett and Abel Pond, for example; others were French, such as André Dupalais and Eustache Pailliase. From time to time the journal records the visits to Spring Mill of the managers and stockholders of the company, often accompanied by their wives and daughters, or by distinguished visitors come to see the interesting sight of a commercial American vineyard. But they saw no very cheerful sight in 1803. Heavy frosts in May and a severe hail storm in June blasted the new plantings, and by the end of the season only 582 vines out of 14,000 still grimly survived: "I am unable to make wine this year," Legaux sadly concluded,[21] and that failure made the end almost certain. The next year Legaux managed to make a few bottles of wine from his own vineyard, but the society's property was in bad shape "by want of supply and money."[22] A fresh start was made in 1805; William Lee, the American consul in Bordeaux, sent 4,500 cuttings from Château Margaux, Château Lafite, and Château Haut-Brion to guarantee the most aristocratic of all pedigrees to Legaux's republican vineyard.[23] These noble vines were supplemented by another 1,500 from Malaga. All shared a common fate. The heat and drought of the summer afflicted them, and though enough survived to be shown to the governor of Pennsylvania when he paid a visit the next year, Legaux was compelled to write in 1807 that all were neglected and overrun.[24]

The company had been authorized to conduct a lottery to raise funds in 1806, but the plan did not work out, and another lottery in 1811 also failed.[25] By this time the company seemed dead: such labor as was performed was performed by Legaux himself, who confided to his journal that in his lonely and unrewarding work "*Nobody* is my faithful Companion!!!"[26] Nevertheless, Legaux kept something going. He came to a definite—and correct—conclusion in 1809 when he observed that, of all his grapes, only the one that he called the Cape managed to grow: "all other sorte may be abandoned," he wrote then, and a year later he advised his journal that, in order to redeem the company's purposes, "the best will be to pull out all the plants, and planted again with the Cape of Good Hope."[27]

If Legaux's advice—dearly earned advice it was—had been acted on, the company might have succeeded in making wine, as Dufour was already doing from the Cape grape in Indiana, originally obtained from Legaux's own vineyard.[28] But protracted failures had destroyed Legaux's credit with the managers of the company. He had, indeed, made a first vintage from the company's vineyard with Cape grapes in September 1809,[29] but it was both too little and too late. The secretary of the company was a man who had notions of his own about how things should be done. He was Bernard McMahon, an Irishman who settled in Philadelphia as a nurseryman and seedsman and became the city's oracle on horticulture. His *American Gardener's Calendar* (1806) was the first thorough guide to the subject published in this country and remained a standard for half a century. McMahon, who took a special interest in the viticultural work of the company, now decided that a change was required. A new superintendent was appointed to oversee the company's vineyard in place of Legaux, but after a year Legaux had the bitter satisfaction of reporting that the man had bungled the job, the vines being pruned so badly that they would produce no grapes at all that season.[30] The dispirited stockholders were now ready to relinquish the entire thing back into Legaux's hands, while retaining title to the land and requiring that Legaux continue to keep up the vineyards. This Legaux was eager to do, but his eagerness had no reward. In the year after his restoration, the vines were devastated by a plague of caterpillars, and at the end of 1813 Legaux made this desolate entry in his journal: "No horses nobody no money and any assistance whatever to expect; what I shall do??"[31]

It is perhaps just as well that the journal for 1814–22 is missing; it could only repeat the tale of hapless vicissitude already clear enough. When the journal resumes in 1822 we hear no more of winegrowing. Legaux is old and ill, more interested in recording the details of the weather (a lifelong obsession with him) and in collecting information on the diseases that went round the neighborhood than in the state of his vines and the hope for a good American wine. His property at Spring Mill, though it had several times been put up for sale by the sheriff for debt, had at last been rescued by Legaux's son-in-law,[32] and there, in 1827, Legaux died, his dream of the Vineyard Company long since vanished. The forty years of vine growing at Spring Mill seemed to have led to nothing.

Other Pioneers in the Early Republic

Nevertheless, Legaux's name figures prominently in the efforts around the turn of the century that helped to determine what the actual course of successful American viticulture would be. The news of his vigorous, well-advertised, confident activity in its early years had the effect of stimulating others to a renewed attack on the great and still baffling puzzle of how to make an American wine. Legaux's nursery thus became the starting point from which a number of other vineyards grew and the source from which the historically important Constantia or Cape grape was distributed throughout the East. A contemporary eulogist of Legaux's states that the nursery at Spring Mill had furnished the vines for other vineyards not only in Pennsylvania but in New York, New Jersey, Maryland, Virginia, Ohio, and Kentucky.[33] Some of these can be identified: Johnson's in New Jersey has already been mentioned; Dufour's in Kentucky will be taken up shortly; and one, at least, in Pennsylvania has left a name. This was the vineyard of Colonel George Morgan, whose claim was to have planted the first cultivated vines west of the Alleghenies at his property Morganza in Washington County, Pennsylvania, on the western edge of the state. One authority dates this modest undertaking in 1796;[34] more likely, it did not begin until early 1802, for on 11 December 1801 Morgan wrote to Legaux requesting a shipment of 2,200 cuttings of "Champaign," "Burgundy," and "Bordeaux" vines.[35] Morgan called his work "an adventurous and expensive experiment," and he hoped by it to "render to my country more service than by a thousand prayers for its peace and prosperity, which I daily offer."[36] But he had the pioneer's inevitable result: only 84 of the vines sent by Legaux survived into 1803, and the vineyard was given up in 1806.[37]

The influence of Legaux's example extended even into Maine, where trials with grapes were made by the Englishman Benjamin Vaughan. Vaughan, a prominent sympathizer with the colonial cause in England before the Revolution, had helped with the peace negotiations between the Americans and the English; later he had had to flee England to revolutionary France, where he was imprisoned. After his release he had migrated to Hallowell, Maine. There, though he became a correspondent of, and adviser to, American presidents, he took no active part in politics but devoted himself to literature and to agriculture. Vaughan obtained grape vines from Legaux in 1807, and in that year wrote to his brother in Philadelphia asking for more cuttings, adding, "I can dispose of hundreds of cuttings for you, and make you a nice vineyard."[38] Vaughan persisted long and hopefully, for in 1819 he took the trouble to compile notes on wines and vines;[39] these are disappointing in their failure to comment on his experience, but something of what that had been is clearly implied by Vaughan's recommendation of native rather than imported vines.

Another positive result of Legaux's activity was to secure the interest of Dr. James Mease (1771–1846), a prominent Philadelphia physician and writer. When the Vine Company was promoted, Dr. Mease became one of the managers. A man of science, he had a technical as well as a commercial interest in the possibilities of grape growing and did what he could to advance the understanding of the subject. In 1802, when he was preparing a revision for American publication of an English work called the *Domestic Encyclopaedia,* he invited the Philadelphia botanist William Bartram to contribute an article on the native grapes of the United States. Bartram's article describes four species and three varieties of American origin. It was, of course, seriously incomplete, and did not clear up the confusions of nomenclature created by the great Linnaeus himself in naming the American vines, but it was the first published attempt to bring some order to the subject in this country.[40]

Mease himself extended Bartram's article by summarizing various authorities on viticulture and winemaking; he made a genuine attempt to consult local experience, citing Legaux, Antill, and Bartram as well as the more usual eighteenth-century French and English writers. Mease had the missionary zeal so common among the early propagandists: though he thought that the luxurious dwellers in the American seaports were probably too far gone in corruption to be able to leave their foreign wines, he hoped that the pioneers beyond the mountains would turn to making their own wine from native grapes. Mease recommended the Alexander (did he know that it was the same as the grape his associate Legaux called the Cape?), the Bland (another early native hybrid, from Virginia), and the southern bull grape (the muscadine).[41] By taking this position, Mease has been credited with "the first public utterance condemning the culture of the Old World grape and recommending the cultivation of native grapes."[42] This is not strictly true—we have seen that Estave in Virginia and the Society of Arts in London were both on public record in favor of the native grape before the Revolution, not to mention the many individuals from the earliest days who thought, either by logic or experience, along the same lines.[43] Mease's recommendations have, at any rate, the merit of being particular and had behind them more weight of authority than belonged to any earlier writer. His essay deserves Hedrick's compliment as "the first rational discussion of the culture of the grape in America."[44] Mease evidently hoped to expand his *Domestic Encyclopaedia* essay into a comprehensive treatise, for in 1811 he was at work on a "Natural History of the Vines of the United States," to be published with colored engravings.[45] There is no record of the publication of any such work, however.

The opening of the regions to the west of the original colonial settlements, which proceeded apace after the Revolution, certainly helped to stimulate fresh experiment, as in the instance of Colonel Morgan. Another, earlier, one had been made by Frenchmen along the Ohio, though Morgan evidently did not know it—his own experiment, he thought, was the first trans-Allegheny trial of grape growing. But before him, in about 1792, the unlucky Frenchmen who had been tempted by the blandishments of the Scioto Company—a land speculation that was for a time the rage of republican Paris—had taken up the cultivation of the native vines they found growing on the islands of the Ohio River near their settlement of Gallipolis. These vines, so they imagined, were the offspring of vines planted by the French at Fort Duquesne (built in 1754 on the site of Pittsburgh and burned in 1758); they thought that bears, who are fond of grapes, might have dropped the seeds and so have spread them along the banks of the Ohio.[46] Another fanciful explanation held that the French soldiers of Fort Duquesne, in order to deprive the British of the luxury of their vines, rooted them out when the fort fell to the enemy and threw them into the river; in this way they were washed down to the islands off Gallipolis.[47]

The writer who skeptically recorded this story did so as an instance of the unreliability of tradition among illiterate men; but there is something touching about this wish to see a French element in the utterly un-Gallic environment of Gallipolis. Visiting the damp, shabby, struggling settlement in 1795, the French historian Constantine Volney found that the round red grapes being cultivated for wine there produced a drink very little different from that yielded by the huge and undoubtedly native vines of the woods. The settlers, whatever their ideas about the origins of their vines, were under no delusions as to the quality of the wine they made, calling it, Volney tells us, "*méchant Surêne.*"[48] The wines of Suresnes, near Paris, were a byword for sourness; a *méchant* Suresnes would thus be a superlatively thin and sour wine. It was, incidentally, probably a straggler from the colony at Gallipolis who was reported in 1796 to be making wine from the sand grapes (*Vitis rupestris*) at Marietta, further down the Ohio.[49]

There were other Frenchmen who, despite such discouraging results as those at Gallipolis, continued to think well of the winegrowing prospects in this country. One of the earliest publications on viticulture in the new republic appeared at Georgetown about 1795 as *A Short and Practical Treatise on the Culture of the Wine-Grapes in the United States of America, Adapted to those States situated to the Southward of 41 degrees of North latitude.* This rare treatise, a single oversize leaf printed on both sides, was the work of a Frenchman named Amoureux, who was employed in an American merchant house but was hoping to take up viticulture in the developing settlements to the west—Kentucky, for example.[50] Amoureux's discussion, based wholly on European conditions, could not have led to practical results, but it is symptomatic of the interest that arose when the United States was new and hopes for all sorts of enterprise were high.

Another, slightly earlier, French contribution to the subject of American winegrowing had been made to a very different purpose by Brissot de Warville, whose visit to Legaux at Spring Mill has already been mentioned. Brissot, who had been in America on an antislavery mission, one of the earliest of such efforts, published an article in the *American Museum* in 1788 arguing against the development of a wine industry in the United States. Winegrowing only produced wretchedness, Brissot explained; for every man who was enriched by the trade, many more were reduced to poverty by its harsh necessities, which only the capitalist could cope with. Why not let the French bear the burden?[51] Since Brissot was manifestly French, this argument may have failed of its full force. It is, however, interesting to speculate about the reasons held to justify making such a statement in a country where after two full centuries of settlement no one had yet succeeded in making wine in any quantity.

Dufour and the Beginning of Commercial Production

With the appearance of Jean Jacques Dufour—or John James as he came to call himself in his American years—this history takes a new and positive turn. Dufour (1763–1827) was a Swiss, born in the canton of Vaud to a family long engaged in winegrowing. As a boy of fourteen, so he wrote years later in his history of his own work, he had been struck by reports of the scarcity of wine in the United States and had resolved some day to go there and do something about it.[52] The anecdote is revealing. Dufour was, it seems, one of those deliberate characters who can form a resolve and then stick to it, no matter what the obstacles and no matter how many years might intervene between the idea and the execution. It was just this power of perseverance in the service of a single idea that the cause of American winegrowing had to have. There had been any number of clamorous proclamations of assured certainties before; there had even been enthusiasts who persisted year after year, as Legaux had done. But no one yet had had quite the singleness of purpose and stubbornness of Dufour.

He began by studying viticulture in Switzerland in order to prepare for his call, and in 1796, at the age of thirty-three, he set out for the United States. It must have seemed an anxious gamble. Though not exactly impoverished, Dufour had very little money; as the eldest son, he was the hope of a large family; and he would not have impressed an observer as the ideal man for the hard labor of the pioneer, for, whether by accident or congenital deformation, Dufour's left arm ended at the elbow.[53] After his voyage in the steerage, Dufour, with characteristic thoroughness, at once set out on a survey of what had been done before him towards winegrowing in the new states and in the territories beyond. In the next two years he managed first to make personal inspection of all the vineyards around New York and Philadelphia; all, he found, were unworthy to be called vineyards, except for "about a dozen plants in the vineyard of Mr. Legaux."[54] Discouraged to find that things were even worse than he had imagined, Dufour then set off for the West to discover whether that region held any promise. Having heard someone in Phila-

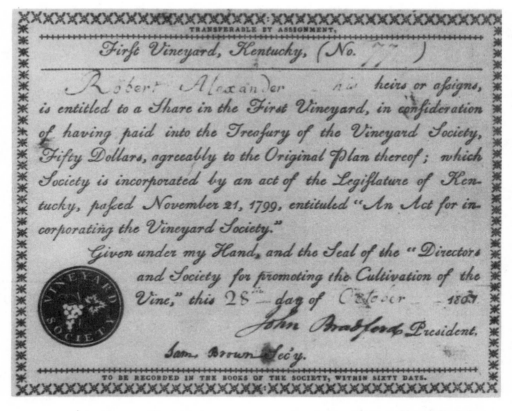

TRANSFERABLE BY ASSIGNMENT,

First Vineyard, Kentucky, (No. 77)

Robert Alexander his heirs or assigns, is entitled to a Share in the First Vineyard, in consideration of having paid into the Treasury of the Vineyard Society, Fifty Dollars, agreeably to the Original Plan thereof; which Society is incorporated by an act of the Legislature of Kentucky, passed November 21, 1799, entitled "An Act for incorporating the Vineyard Society." Given under my Hand, and the Seal of the "Directors and Society for promoting the Cultivation of the Vine," this 28 day of October 180

John Bradford President.

Sam. Brown Sec'y.

TO BE RECORDED IN THE BOOKS OF THE SOCIETY, WITHIN SIXTY DAYS.

29 | Certificate of a share in the "First Vineyard" of John James Dufour's Kentucky Vineyard Society. Though the act of incorporation is dated 21 November 1799, the society was organized earlier, and Dufour had already planted vineyards. By 1801 they were already beginning to fail, and the stock of the company was never fully subscribed. (From Edward Hyams, *Dionysus: A Social History of the Wine Vine* [1965])

delphia say that the Jesuits had productive vineyards at the old French settlement of Kaskaskia, on the river below St. Louis, Dufour dutifully made his way to that spot. There he found the remnants of the Jesuit asparagus bed, but the forest had swallowed up the vines: such, more or less, was the condition of almost all of the sites that Dufour had been told to see. Turning back east from St. Louis, he was led to Lexington, Kentucky, then the largest settlement in western America, the "Philadelphia of Kentucky" and the "Athens of the West," where enough professional men and merchants were already gathered together to support interest in winegrowing. Dufour was able in a very short time to organize the Kentucky Vineyard Society, a stock company modeled on Legaux's Pennsylvania Vine Company, which Dufour must have studied with interested attention.[55] The young Henry Clay, newly arrived in the booming town of Lexington, was the society's attorney and one of its subscribers.[56]

With the expectation of $10,000 in capital from the sale of two hundred shares at $50 each, Dufour, without waiting for the subscription to be completed, went into action. First he arranged for the purchase of 633 acres (and five slave families) on the banks of the Kentucky River at Big Bend, twenty-five miles west of Lexington. Then, early in the next year, 1799, Dufour travelled back to the Atlantic coast to collect vines for planting on the society's land; some he obtained from Baltimore and New York, but the bulk of his purchases were from Peter Legaux at Spring Mill—10,000 vines of thirty-five different varieties at a cost of $388. With this precious freight loaded on a wagon, Dufour crossed Pennsylvania to Pittsburgh and so back down the river to Kentucky. The cuttings were planted on five acres of the new property, which was then given the hopeful name of "First Vineyard."[57]

The vines grew well in the first two seasons; in the third they began, most of them, to fail. Dufour, like those hapless *vignerons* imported into Virginia nearly two centuries earlier, must have wondered what sort of curse the country was under, where the flourishing of the vines was the prelude to their death. Meanwhile, the experiment was much talked of in an expansive and confident way by its backers and by the patriotic press, so much so that, in 1802, the French naturalist François André Michaux, in America on a mission of scientific inquiry for Napoleon's government, felt compelled to pay a visit to Dufour to see whether his vines really did pose a latent threat to the French wine trade. Michaux was relieved to discover that First Vineyard, even at so early a stage, was not a success: "When I saw them, the bunches were few and stinted, the grapes small, and everything appeared as though the vintage of the year 1802 would not be more abundant than those of the preceding years."[58]

The symptoms described suggest that the vines were afflicted by black rot. No doubt mildew and perhaps both Pierce's Disease and phylloxera were at work as well. But from the general wreckage of his hopes, Dufour managed to salvage something. He had observed that two, at least, of the thirty-five varieties he had planted showed superior vigor and promised to be productive.[59] These were the vines that Legaux called "Cape," a blue grape for red wine, and "Madeira," for white. What the second and less important of these grapes was it is now impossible to say. So many grapes have been identified with the vines of the Wine Islands and especially with those of the privileged Madeira that one can only guess at what grape is actually meant in any given instance. Since it survived, it was no doubt a native hybrid, and such scant evidence as there is suggests that it was the grape known elsewhere as Bland's Madeira. The blue grape was, on Legaux's say-so, a grape that he had received from South Africa, where it was the source of those legendary wines known as Constantia (the actual source of Constantia is the Muscadelle du Bordelais). Whether Legaux maintained this statement in good faith or not is, as we have already seen, a question whose answer we can never know now. Whatever Legaux may have thought, the "Cape" is in fact the native labrusca hybrid grape once called Tasker's grape, originating in the region of William Penn's old vineyard on the Schuylkill and better known after its discoverer, James

30 | The Alexander grape, first of the American hybrids; it was propagated and sold by Peter Legaux as the "Cape" grape, and became the basis of John James Dufour's Indiana vineyards. It spread to all eastern vineyards, acquiring many synonyms (the name "Schuylkill" in this illustration is an instance). The Alexander is now a historic memory. (Painting by C. L. Fleischman, 1867; National Agricultural Library)

Alexander.[60] Legaux, to whom the Alexander owed its re-creation as a vinifera under the name of Cape grape, does not seem to have thought particularly highly of it at the time he sold quantities of it to Dufour. It was not even included in the vines listed in 1806 as under trial in the nurseries of the Pennsylvania Vine Company,[61] so that no importance seems then to have been attached to it. Within a few more years, however, as we have seen, Legaux recognized it as the only reliable variety of all the many varieties, foreign and native, that he had planted.

In defense of Legaux's good faith in calling a native labrusca a vinifera, it is important to note that the Alexander, unlike most pure natives, has a perfect (that is, self-pollinating) flower; every variety of unhybridized native vine bears either pistillate or staminate flowers that are, by themselves, sterile. Dufour himself was persuaded by this observation that the Cape was a genuine vinifera, and so he thought to the end, not knowing that the perfect-flowered characteristic is the effect of a dominant gene from vinifera that can enter into genetic combination; for all this was long before Mendel had provided any understanding of hybrid patterns. But Dufour's insistence that his grape was not a native probably owed much to sheer stubbornness. His half-brother, John Francis Dufour, stated publicly that the Cape grape was unquestionably a native variety;[62] if the elder Dufour denied this, he must have been holding out against strong evidence.

Once he had seen that only two vines gave him any hope, Dufour, with the decision of a practical man, determined to abandon the culture of all other varieties to concentrate exclusively on those two. First Vineyard was begun over again on this basis, and was made to yield at least a little wine. In 1803 Dufour's brother was despatched to Washington, D.C., leading a horse loaded with two five-gallon barrels of Kentucky wine consigned to President Jefferson.[63] We also hear of a toast, given by Henry Clay after the florid manner of the day and drunk in Kentucky wine at a banquet of the Vineyard Society. This was to "The Virtuous and Independent Sons of Switzerland, who have chosen our country as a retreat from the commotions of war" and who were assured that the wine of Kentucky would drive all painful memory of the Old World away.[64]

That moment may have been—probably was—the high point of the Vineyard Society's fortunes. Dufour had begun his work before all the subscriptions were paid in; the disappointing history of the vineyard provided a reason for not paying any more, and by 1804 the society was wound up, still in debt to Dufour for expenses.[65]

Even before the failure of First Vineyard was clear, Dufour had begun to set up another enterprise, one that became the first practical success in American wine-growing. Dufour seems from the first to have had the intention, once established, of bringing his family and others from his native place over to this country, where they could live secure from the disruptions and damage of the Napoleonic wars. In 1800, inspired by the first promising year in Kentucky, he sent word for his people to come. Seventeen of them, his brothers and sisters, their wives, husbands, children, and several neighbors, arrived in Kentucky in July 1801. There they found that Dufour had already begun to shape his plan for them. Congress had just created the Indiana Territory out of the old Northwest Territory, where settlers might obtain land at $2 an acre. Even at this rate, a purchase was beyond Dufour's means. But he was attracted to the shores of the Ohio, which looked like a region naturally appointed for the growing of grapes, and in 1801 he petitioned Congress for what he called "une petite exception" in his favor.[66] If Congress would grant him lands along the Ohio in Indiana Territory and allow him to defer payment for ten years, he, Dufour, would undertake, at a minimum, to settle his Swiss associates there, to plant ten acres of vines in two years, and to disseminate the knowledge of vine culture publicly. This was a minimum: but, as Dufour assured the gentlemen of the Congress, he foresaw a time when the Ohio would rival the Rhine and Rhone— when "l'Ohio disputera le Rhin ou le Rhône pour la quantité des vignes, et la qualité du vin."[67]

Congress was sufficiently swayed by the prospect to grant to Dufour the "petite exception" that he sought. In 1802, by a special act passed to "encourage the introduction, and to promote the culture of the vine within the territory of the United States, north-west of the river Ohio," Dufour was authorized to take up four sections of land along the north bank of the Ohio, just inside the present boundary of Indiana where it touches Ohio, and was allowed not ten but twelve years in which to pay.[68] Dufour himself did not leave Kentucky for the new grant; with two brothers and their families he stayed on at First Vineyard, evidently still determined to persist with it. The rest of the small Swiss colony went down the Kentucky River to the Ohio and their land grant, which they named New Switzerland (it is today in Switzerland County). There, in 1802, they began planting Second Vineyard with the Cape and Madeira varieties already selected by Dufour as the best hope of American growers.

In 1806 Dufour returned to Europe, ten years after his coming to this country, leaving the care of the Kentucky vineyards to his brothers.[69] The purpose of his trip was to settle the financial affairs of his family in Switzerland, especially with a view to paying off the debt on their Indiana lands. The dislocation of things in those days of protracted war could hardly be better shown than by the fact that Dufour did not return for another ten years! First, the English captured the ship on which he was a passenger and he was taken to England. Released, he made his way to Switzerland, but evidently the confusion of his and his family's affairs made it impossible to act efficiently—perhaps, too, Dufour was not reluctant to linger. The wife that he had married before leaving Europe for America had remained behind in Switzerland. Then the War of 1812 intervened. After such delay, he was compelled to petition Congress in 1813 for an extension of the time allowed for payment on his land grant,[70] and it was not until 1817, after his return to the United States, that the sum was paid.

In Dufour's absence the settlement at New Switzerland began to prosper. A first vintage was harvested in 1806 or 1807—the date is not certain—and for a number of years thereafter production rose pretty steadily through good years and bad: 800 gallons in 1808, 2,400 gallons in 1810, 3,200 in 1812. The greatest extent of vineyard—45 to 50 acres—and the largest volume of production—12,000 gallons—seem to have been reached about 1820.[71] By that time the Swiss of Vevay, as the town laid out in 1813 had been named, had acquired a good name up and down the Ohio. A Vevay schoolmaster was inspired by local pride to compose a Latin ode on the "Empire of Bacchus" to celebrate the accomplishments of the Swiss. It opens (in the English version provided by another Vevay classicist) in this lofty strain:

> Columbia rejoice! smiling Bacchus has heard
>   Your prayers of so fervent a tone
> And crown'd with the grape, has kindly appear'd
>   In your land to establish his throne.[72]

More sober commentators agreed that Vevay was one of the most interesting and encouraging of western settlements. The veteran traveller Timothy Flint wrote that he had seen nothing to compare with the autumn richness of Vevay's vineyards: "When the clusters are in maturity. . . . The horn of plenty seems to have been emptied in the production of this rich fruit."[73]

As a condition of their land grant, the Swiss at Vevay undertook to promote viticulture generally, and they honored the obligation, giving advice and instruction to those who sought it and distributing cuttings free. There is evidence that at least a few others in the region were able to imitate the success of Vevay. A Swiss named J. F. Buchetti, who was connected with Dufour's community, had, in 1814, a vineyard of some 10,000 vines, mainly the Alexander, at Glasgow, in Barren

County, south-central Kentucky. This was still extant as late as 1846, and had earlier produced wine that Dufour, no doubt prejudiced in its favor, had pronounced to be very good.[74] Besides Buchetti, James Hicks planted Cape and Madeira vines at Glasgow in 1814.[75] Another early Kentucky vineyard, that of Colonel James Taylor at Newport, across the river from Cincinnati, was described in 1810 by an English traveller as "the finest that I have yet seen in America." Taylor, a cousin of President James Madison's, made at least some wine for domestic purposes.[76]

As to the quality of the wine of Vevay, opinions vary according to the experience and loyalties of the critic. It was advertised in Cincinnati in 1813, where it sold for $2 a gallon, as "superior to the common Bordeaux claret";[77] a western traveller in 1817, buying at $1 a gallon at the winery door, found the wine "as good as I could wish to drink."[78] The candor of Timothy Flint (he was a preacher as well as a traveller and writer) compelled him to confess that the wine made from the Cape grape at Vevay "was not pleasant to me, though connoisseurs assured me, that it only wanted age to be a rich wine."[79] Flint's judgment is supported by the German visitor Karl Postel, who came to Vevay in the late, degenerate days of the vineyards and found their wine "an indifferent beverage, resembling any thing but claret, as it had been represented."[80] Whatever the quality of Vevay red—and the red wine from native grapes has always been less pleasing than the white—the producers sold all that they could make. Dufour wrote that people were at first unfamiliar with the flavor of native wine, but that by and by all came to like it, so that "consumption having pretty well kept pace with the product, old American wine has always been scarce."[81] What he might have said more to the purpose is that American wine of any age at all had always been scarce. But why they made red wine rather than white remains curious. The foxiness of such labrusca hybrids as the Alexander is intensified if the juice is fermented on the skins, and reduced if the skins are separated. White wine would be both better suited to the Swiss tradition and less strongly flavored.

While Dufour was absent in Europe, his brothers, in 1809, had finally abandoned First Vineyard, and gone to join the rest of the community on the Ohio.[82] When Dufour returned, then, he found the whole number of his family and friends around the new town of Vevay, where he himself built a house and spent the rest of his days. While he lived, he continued to work and the vineyards of the community continued to produce, though signs of decline were probably appearing among the vines before his death in 1827.

In the year before his death, Dufour published a book at Cincinnati briefly sketching his career as a pioneer of vine growing and embodying the fruit of his experience in this country. Called a *Vine-Dresser's Guide,* it may fairly claim to be the first truly American book on the subject. The works of Bonoeil, of Antill, of Bolling, and of St. Pierre are of course much earlier, but none of them has anything to say about an extensive experience of actual vine culture in this country. Adlum's book (see p. 145 below), though in some important ways genuinely American, and earlier than Dufour's by three years, is far more derivative. Dufour had earned his

THE
AMERICAN
VINE-DRESSER'S GUIDE,
BEING A TREATISE
ON THE
CULTIVATION OF THE VINE,
AND
THE PROCESS OF WINE MAKING;
ADAPTED TO THE SOIL AND CLIMATE
OF THE
UNITED STATES:

BY JOHN JAMES DUFOUR,

FORMERLY OF SWISSERLAND, AND NOW AN AMERICAN CITIZEN,
CULTIVATOR OF THE VINE FROM HIS CHILDHOOD, AND FOR THE
LAST TWENTY FIVE YEARS, OCCUPIED IN THAT LINE OF
BUSINESS, FIRST IN KENTUCKY, AND NOW ON THE
BORDERS OF OHIO, NEAR VEVAY, INDIANA.

Then said the trees to the vine, come thou, and reign over us:
And the vine said unto them, should I leave my wine, which cheer-
eth God and man, and go to be promoted over the trees?
Judges, c. ix. 12 & 13 vs.

Cincinnati:
PRINTED BY S. J. BROWNE,
AT THE EMPORIUM OFFICE.
....
1826.

31 | John James Dufour was the first American winegrower to succeed in producing wine in commercial quantities. This book, the fruit of his long experience of winegrowing in the remote American frontier states of Kentucky and Indiana, was published only a year before his death. (California State University, Fresno, Library)

authority; his readers, he wrote, might doubt some of his ideas, but that was because, as he wrote in his own special syntax, he had followed "the great book of
nature, from which most all I have to say has been taken, for want of other books,
and even, if I had them, among the many I have read on the culture of the vine, but
few could be quoted, for none had the least idea of what a new country is."[83]

"For none had the least idea of what a new country is"—the observation, logically so obvious, nevertheless took generations of experience before its truth was
fully realized.

Like all those who had earlier addressed the American public on this subject,
Dufour urges the great blessing of viticulture—but with a difference, for he is
more concerned with personal satisfaction than with transforming the economy
and enriching the nation. He wishes specially "to enable the people of this vast
continent, to procure for themselves and their children, the blessing intended by
the Almighty; that they should enjoy, and not by trade from foreign countries, but
by the produce of their own labor, out of the very ground they tread from a corner
of each one's farm, wine thus obtained."[84] Such eloquence on the virtues of doing it
oneself is very attractive, and suggests that the legion of home vineyardists and
winemakers in America today might well choose Dufour for their patron.

Dufour also hoped that the grapes available to American winemakers could be
improved. He was by no means satisfied with those that he had to work with. A
letter from him in 1819 notes that neither the Cape nor the Madeira ever ripened
properly at Vevay. They also suffered from exotic afflictions, including crickets;
these, Dufour says, had to be picked off the vines at night by lamplight.[85] The poor
Swiss must have felt themselves to be in a strange land indeed on those nights. In
his efforts to get a better grape, Dufour himself, he tells us, had made many experiments in grafting vinifera to native roots, but without any success in producing a
combination that could resist the endemic diseases.[86] He did not doubt that success
could be had, however, and he urged that others with better means should continue
trying. So, too, with hybridizing; that would have to be the work of others, but a
work absolutely necessary if better wine were ever to be made here.[87]

It was, perhaps, a good thing that Dufour died the year after his book was
published, for the wine industry at Vevay had not much longer to live. The immediate trouble was disease, especially the fungus diseases, of which black rot is the
chief in importance, and against which today a program of spraying must be maintained. At that time, no one knew what to do. A less immediate, but still important,
problem was the indifference of the second generation. To the pioneers—to Dufour
and his brothers, and their friends the Mererods and the Siebenthals—who had
come from Switzerland expressly to grow wine in a new country, that work was of
central importance. The second generation easily lost interest; there were many
other, and more secure, opportunities than winegrowing, with its heavy risks and
cruel disappointments, and who can blame them if they took them?[88]

There was also the important fact that the wine was not very good, so that,
when transport and commerce developed, the wine of Vevay lost the advantage

that it had when it was without competition. Nicholas Longworth wrote that when the Hoosiers and Buckeyes of the Ohio River country were at last able to get better wines, those of Vevay "became unsaleable and were chiefly used for making sangaree, for the manufacture of which they were preferred to any other."[89] Sangaree, incidentally, is one of those undisciplined concoctions that take many forms according to the inspiration of their compounder; we are familiar with it now in its Spanish form as sangria. In earlier times in America, however, the compound was any red wine, diluted with water or fruit juices, and invariably flavored with nutmeg. It is, clearly, no compliment to a wine to say that it was a favorite for sangaree. A frequently printed anecdote says that Dufour himself, on his deathbed, confessed that the wine of his Cape grapes was inferior to the wine from Longworth's Catawba grapes, a conclusion that he is supposed to have stubbornly resisted in his lifetime.[90] The anecdote, however, comes to us from a Cincinnati source and is therefore dubious. In any event, the wine industry of Vevay may be said to have died with its founder. The year after Dufour's death, the vineyards were described as "degenerated," and by 1835 they had effectively ceased to exist.[91]

Given all the confusions, misunderstandings, and wrong directions that had made the history of American winegrowing from the outset, it is appropriate that the basis of the first commercial wine production in the country should have been such a confused quantity as the Cape, or Alexander, grape, whose true name and nature nobody knew. The Alexander could not have made a good wine; not a great deal of that wine was ever produced at Vevay; and the winemaking enterprise there did not last beyond a generation. Nevertheless, it was with the Alexander grape, and at Vevay, that successful commercial viticulture and winemaking began in the United States. The time, place, and people deserve to be strongly marked and specially reverenced by everyone who takes a friendly interest in the subject.

The Spirit of Jefferson and Early American Winegrowing

The first decade of the nineteenth century was the period of Thomas Jefferson's administration; it is especially fitting that the early, tentative successes in American winegrowing should have occurred then, for Jefferson was, both in private and public, the great patron and promoter of American wine for Americans: in private, as both an experimental viticulturist and a notable connoisseur; in public, as the spokesman for the national importance of establishing wine as the drink of temperate yeomen and as the sponsor of enterprise in American agriculture generally. Agriculture was in his words "the employment of our first parents in Eden, the happiest we can follow, and the most important to our country."[92] As for wine, "no nation is drunken where wine is cheap," he had written in 1818.[93] America, he firmly believed, had the potential to yield wine both cheap and good: all that was wanted was "skilful labourers." No account of the history of wine in America is complete without at least a bare summary of "Jefferson and wine."[94]

We have already touched briefly on Jefferson's part in Philip Mazzei's Vineyard Society just before the outbreak of the Revolution. Soon after, Jefferson had been transformed from country gentleman and provincial lawyer into a world-famous statesman, but he had never lost contact with the soil of his own Monticello. Nor had he ever ceased to look for ways and means by which wine could be produced by American farmers. His extended residence in France as American minister from 1784 to 1789 greatly increased his knowledge of wine. An impressive number of pages in the edition of his *Papers* now appearing in slow and stately procession from Princeton is given over to his correspondence with French wine merchants and with friends for whom he acted as agent and counselor in their wine buying. He also had a collection of the finest French wines made for him by an expert, though whether they were shipped to Virginia does not appear. "Good wine is a daily necessity for me," he said,[95] and the documentary evidence of the trouble he took to secure the best and widest variety is ample proof of the assertion. He also made tours to the wine regions of France and Germany, where, with his habitual energy and curiosity, he questioned the experts and made copious notes, descriptions, and memoranda on the technicalities of viticulture and winemaking.

Jefferson was always ready to welcome a new enthusiasm, and his many remarks on wine show that he frequently changed his preferences: one year it was pale sherry that pleased him most and that he insisted on drinking exclusively; another year it was a light Montepulciano; another, a Bellet from the region of Nice; and yet another, white Hermitage. All of these loves were no doubt genuine, but as a connoisseur Jefferson was evidently as eager to be amused by a novelty as to be faithful to old loves. This propensity may help to explain some of the remarkable things that he had to say about American wines, remarks that will be noticed a little later.[96]

One of the first things that Jefferson did on his retirement from public life was to make a fresh attempt at vine growing: the thirty-five years of public activity that intervened between his part in Mazzei's experiments and his return to private life were only an interruption, not a change, in his purposes. By this time, however, Jefferson had had some experience of the wines that were beginning to be produced from improved varieties of the native grape. Dufour, it will be remembered, sent wine from his Kentucky vineyard to Jefferson. What he may have thought of that we do not know, but he has left a notable response to a sample of the wine produced by Major John Adlum in 1809 from the Alexander grape growing in Adlum's Maryland vineyard. This Jefferson praised in extravagant terms; he had served the Alexander wine to his friends together with a bottle of very good Chambertin of his own importing, and the company, so Jefferson told Adlum, "could not distinguish the one from the other."

Jefferson advised Adlum to "push the culture of that grape," and took his own advice by asking Adlum to send him cuttings to be planted at Monticello, calling himself a "brother-amateur in these things."[97] Adlum obliged, but the cuttings were long in travelling from Havre de Grace to Charlottesville; they arrived in bad condition, and all subsequently died.[98] This failure ended Jefferson's hopes for some years, during which he made no more efforts of his own. But when, late in 1815, Jefferson was approached by a young Frenchman named Jean David, newly arrived with a scheme for viticulture in northern Virginia, the old enthusiasm flared up again.[99] Jefferson at first cautiously replied to David that he was now too old to work in the cause of American wine and advised him to approach other sympathetic gentlemen: Major Adlum, for example, or James Monroe, then secretary of state, Jefferson's friend and neighbor, who had "a fine collection of vines which he had selected and brought with him from France with a view to the making wine."[100] Jefferson also urged David to concentrate on the native grapes.

David's proposal had evidently set the old ambition to work again, despite Jefferson's protest that he was now too old to take up the work again. By January 1816 Jefferson had decided that he would like to try again for himself. He wrote to Adlum to ask for cuttings as he had done in 1810, saying that he had an opportunity for fresh assistance and reaffirming his faith in the native vine: "I am so convinced that our first success will be from a native grape, that I would try no other."[101] He hedged his bet a little, though, for a few days later he wrote to Monroe to ask for cuttings from Monroe's French vines.[102] Unluckily, after stirring up this old passion in Jefferson, David seems to have backed out. A strange letter from him to Jefferson in February 1816, just when Jefferson had hoped to plant vines, says that, as a loyal Frenchman, he had been struck by a "*scrupule.*" If he were to succeed in making America abound in native wine, as he had no doubt that he would, would he not be doing an injury to the French wine trade? What could ever compensate him for such a painful thought? Well, perhaps a premium from the state for his intended services to American viticulture would be an adequate reward? And so on.[103] The relation between David and Jefferson ended here, and the author of the Declaration of Independence, the governor of Virginia, the American minister to France, the president of the United States, and the founder of the University of Virginia was once again frustrated in the matter of making grape vines clothe the slopes of Monticello.

Yet he never ceased to believe that the thing might be done by others. On the founding of the Agricultural Society of Albemarle County in 1817, Jefferson drew up a list of its objects that singled out "the whole family of grapes" for the society's "attention and enquiry."[104] He was also heartened by the success of certain gentleman growers in North Carolina with the Scuppernong grape, a variety of muscadine. He had some of the wine from this source in early 1817, the gift of his son-in-law, who praised it as of "delicious flavor, resembling Frontinac"[105] (that is, the sweet wine of Muscat de Frontignan grapes produced in the south of France; it was a favorite of Jefferson's). Jefferson, who had the patriot's tendency to exaggerate the virtues of the native produce, went even further in praise than his son-in-law had ventured: Scuppernong wine, he said, would be "distinguished on the best tables of Europe, for its fine aroma, and chrystalline transparence."[106] Those not partial to Scuppernong wine will not be much impressed by this evidence of

Jefferson's taste. Probably, like his judgment of the Alexander wine sent to him by Adlum, the intent of the remark was to be encouraging rather than impartially judicial. But there is no question that he enjoyed Scuppernong wine. Five years later he was still praising it, describing it as "of remarkable merit" and repeating the conviction that it would earn a place at the "first tables of Europe."[107] He also took pains to learn the names of the best producers so that he could have access to a good supply.[108] For the problem was to get it unadulterated by brandy, Jefferson complained; most was so saturated in brandy as to be, he wrote, "unworthy of being called wine."[109] In fact, according to a description published in 1825, the product called Scuppernong wine was really not a wine at all but rather fresh juice fortified and preserved by apple brandy, in the proportion of three gallons of juice to one of brandy.[110] Another writer, in 1832, dismissed North Carolina Scuppernong as "a compound of grape juice, cider, honey, and apple brandy."[111] Nearly a hundred years later an investigator for the state of North Carolina found that this, or something very like it, was still the practice.[112] We should, therefore, call the Scuppernong wine of the old South not a wine but a *mistelle* or cordial. It is hard to see how Jefferson could ever have had it in a form worthy to be called wine, but perhaps he had something the secret of which is now gone. His liking for this wine was by no means unshared; according to one good source, Scuppernong wine was always served as a liqueur with the dessert at the White House on state occasions during the presidencies of Madison, Monroe, John Quincy Adams, and Jackson— "a never-forgotten piece of presidential etiquette."[113]

At one point during his years in France Jefferson had come to the conclusion that viticulture, at least as he observed it in prerevolutionary France, was not a good thing for the United States: the grower either had too much wine or too little in most years, and got little for his produce no matter what. The result was "much wretchedness among this class of cultivators." Only a country forced to take up marginal land in order to employ surplus population was properly engaged in winegrowing, and for the United States "that period is not yet arrived."[114]

This was not, however, a fixed conviction. After his return to the United States, he was always quickly responsive to any new trial of American winemaking in whatever quarter. Though he planted vines of every description—natives and vinifera both—at Monticello over a period of half a century (the earliest record in his garden book is in 1771, the last in 1822), there is no evidence that Jefferson ever succeeded in producing wine from them, and probably after a certain time he ceased even to hope very strongly in the possibility for himself. But he cared much that others should succeed, and, by virtue of his zeal and his eminence, can be called the greatest patron of wine and winegrowing that this country has yet had.

6

The Early Republic, Continued

George Rapp and New Harmony

A kind of appendix to the chapter of winegrowing history at Vevay is that of the German religionists at New Harmony in western Indiana on the Wabash River, some twenty-five miles from its junction with the Ohio. The Harmonists, as they were called, combine two familiar elements in the history of early American winegrowing, being both an organized migration of non-English peoples traditionally skilled in viticulture (most of them came from Württemberg, in the Neckar valley), and a religious community. Led by the German prophet George Rapp, who preached that baptism and communion were of the devil, that going to school was an evil practice, and that Napoleon was the ambassador of God, the Harmonists, whose main social principles were communism and celibacy, left Germany for the United States in 1803.

George Rapp himself had been trained as a vine dresser in Germany, and the main economic purpose of his community was to grow wine. Following the example of Dufour, they tried to secure an act of Congress that would allow them to take up lands along the Ohio for this purpose on favorable terms. Difficulties arose, however, and they were at first compelled to settle in western Pennsylvania, where they were unhappy to find the land "too broken and too cold for to raise vine."[1] They turned instead to distilling Pennsylvania rye whiskey in substantial quantities, but did not quite give up the plan of carrying on the culture of the vine. In 1807 they laid out a hillside vineyard in neat stone-walled terraces, the standard practice of their native German vineyards but a novelty in the United States.[2]

There they planted at least ten different varieties of vine, probably all native Americans: the Cape and the Madeira as grown by the Swiss at Vevay were certainly among them.[3] In 1809 the Harmonists put up a new brick building with a cellar designed for wine storage, and by 1810 they were expecting about a hundred gallons of wine from their vineyard, now grown to ten acres.[4] The carefully kept records of the society show $1,806.05 received in 1811 for the sale of wine, a remarkable—indeed highly questionable—figure, since we are told that their total production two years later was still only twelve barrels.[5] What were the Rappites selling in 1811? In any case, they thought well enough of their 1813 vintage to send some bottles of it to the governor of Pennsylvania, who shared it with some friends and reported that one of them, "an expert," had found that it "resembled very closely the *Old Hock.*"[6]

The Pennsylvania settlement, sustained by the well-directed combination of agriculture and manufacture, quickly grew prosperous; but it was not what they wanted. In 1814 Rapp made a foray into the western lands, found an admirable site with a "hill . . . well-suited for a vineyard," and determined to lead the community there to resettle.[7] The whole establishment of Harmony—buildings and lands, lock, stock, and barrel—was put up for sale, the vineyards being thus described in the advertisements:

> Two vineyards, one of 10, the other of 5 acres, have given sufficient proof of the successes in the cultivation of vines; they are made after the European manner, at a vast expence of labor, with parapet walls and stone steps conducting to an eminence overlooking the town of Harmony and its surrounding improvements.[8]

In 1814 the move began to the thousands of acres that their disciplined labors had enabled them to buy along the banks of the Wabash. They brought cuttings with them from their Pennsylvania vineyards, some of which Rapp gave to the Swiss at Vevay, where he was well received on his way to his new domain.[9] Early in 1815 Rapp's community had planted their New Harmony vineyard; by 1819 they had gathered their second vintage, and by 1824, at the end of their stay on the Wabash, the Harmonists had about fifteen acres in vines producing a red wine of considerable local favor.[10] For the decade of their flourishing, roughly 1815–25, the two centers of wine production at New Harmony and at Vevay made Indiana the unchallenged leader in the first period of commercial wine production in the United States. The scale of production was minute, but, such as it was, Indiana was its fount. At New Harmony, as at Vevay, the successful grape was the Cape, or Alexander; they had also a native vine they called the "red juice grape."[11] The Harmonists naturally yearned after the wine that they had grown and drunk in Germany, and in the first hopefulness inspired by the hillsides of the Wabash, so obviously better suited to the grape than their old Allegheny knobs, they ordered nearly 8,000 cuttings of a whole range of German vines, including Riesling, Sylvaner, Gutedel, and Veltliner.[12] That was in 1816; more European vines were no doubt tried—another shipment was sent out in 1823, for example[13]—but of course all were doomed to die. The only thing German about the wine actually produced at New Harmony was Rapp's name for it, *Wabaschwein*.[14]

The Harmonists knew that it would not be easy to establish a successful viticulture, since, as hereditary vineyardists, they understood the importance of long tradition. When, in 1820, the commissioner of the General Land Office made an official request for a report on their progress in viniculture, they answered that they had yet to find "the proper mode of managing in the Climat and soil," something that "can only be discovered by a well experienced Person, by making many and often fruitless experiments for several years." It was all quite unlike Germany, "where the proper cultivation, soil, and climat has been found out to perfection for every kind of vine."[15] On the whole, their experience in Indiana was a disappointment, a disappointment reflected in these interesting observations, written about 1822, by an unidentified diarist who had just paid a visit to New Harmony:

> They have sent almost everywhere for grapes, for the purpose of ascertaining which are the best kinds. They have eight or ten different kinds of wine, of different colors and flavors. That from the fall grape, after a few frosts, promised to be good, as at the Peoria Lake, on the Illinois, where, it is said, the French have made 100 hogsheads of wine in a year.[16] But none has done so well as the Madeira, Lisbon, and Cape of Good Hope grapes. Here the best product is 3 to 400 gallons per acre, when in Germany it is 2 to 1500. They sell it by the barrel, (not bottled) at 1 dollar a gallon. Its flavor is not very good, nor has it much body, but is rather insipid. . . .
>
> The culture of it is attended with so much expense and difficulty, while it is so much subject to injury, that it results rather in a loss than a profit. . . .
>
> From all the experience they have had of it, they are only induced to continue it for the sake of giving employment to their people; and, although it does better than at Vevay and New Glasgow,[17] where it is declining, it will, they say, eventually fail, as it did in Harmony in Pennsylvania.[18]

Though they could not make German vines grow on Indiana hillsides, whatever else the Harmonists touched seemed to prosper—at least to the views of outsiders. The numerous travellers, American and foreign, who passed up and down the Ohio Valley in the decade of New Harmony all testify to the neat, busy, and flourishing air of the scene there: "They have a fine vineyard in the vale, and on the hills around, which are so beautiful as if formed by art to adorn the town," an Englishman wrote in 1823, "Not a spot but bears the most luxuriant vines, from which they make excellent wine."[19] How good the wine was in fact can hardly be known now, but one may doubt. One German traveller in 1819, though much impressed by the excellence of the New Harmony beer—"a genuine, real Bamberg beer"—was less pleased by the wine: "a good wine," he called it, "which, however, seems to be mixed with sugar and spirits."[20] The observation is one that could probably have been made of almost all early American vintages that aspired to any degree of palatability and stability: without the spirits the alcohol content would have been too low; and without the sugar the flavors would have been too marked and the acid too high. Jefferson, too, complained about the difficulty of getting wine free of such sweetening and fortification.

Another German traveller, the aristocratic and inquisitive Duke Karl Bernhard of Saxe-Weimar, called at New Harmony during the course of his extensive travels in 1826, just after the Harmonists had sold their community and moved back to Pennsylvania. They had left some wine of their produce behind them, which the duke described as having a "strange taste, which reminds one of the common Spanish wine." An old Frenchman whom the duke met at New Harmony told him that the Harmonists did not understand winemaking, and that their departure would allow better stuff to be produced. The remark probably says more about the relations between Germans and French than about actual winemaking practices. The duke carried his researches further, however, by visiting the newest and last of the Harmonist settlements; this was at Economy, Pennsylvania, where Rapp had taken his community to escape the unhealthy climate and the ill-will and harassment they faced on the remote frontier from the early, uncivilized Hoosiers. There, at Economy, the duke was served by Rapp himself with "excellent wine, which had been grown on the Wabash and brought from there; the worst, as I noticed, they had left in Harmony."[21] The morality of this conduct is a nice point, but however it might be settled, we know from it that the Harmonists took the trouble to select and specially care for their superior vintages.

Economy, a part of which is now preserved as a state park, lay on the Ohio just below Pittsburgh. As the first two Harmonist settlements had done, this third one quickly prospered; and as in the first two, this one also was furnished with a vineyard, and every home had vines thriftily trained along the walls on trellises of unique design. Within a year of the migration from Indiana, there were four acres of vineyards at Economy,[22] and they continued to be developed in succeeding years. A striking piece of information is that, after all the years of struggle at the two earlier sites, the Harmonists, on this their third and last site, were still persisting in trying to grow vinifera. A visitor in 1831, after noting the hillside vineyard at Economy, laid out in stone-walled terraces after the fashion of Württemberg, added that the vines had come from France and from Hungary.[23] If this were the case, and if they did not also plant some of the old, unsatisfactory natives, the Harmonists cannot have produced much wine at Economy.

Nevertheless, Economy itself did not merely continue to prosper after the death of Rapp in 1847; it was propelled into vast wealth through investments in oil and in railroads. In 1874 the historian of American communistic life, Charles Nordhoff, found the place in high good order, including "two great cellars full of fine wine casks, which would make a Californian envious, so well-built are they."[24] In 1889 the young Rudyard Kipling, on his way from India to England, looked in briefly on Economy and noted the contrast between its accumulating wealth and its declining vigor.[25] By that time, if the Harmonists still paid regard to winemaking, their pioneering work had long since been eclipsed by newer and more commercial efforts.

32 | A rare item testifying to the interest in winegrowing among the Germans of Pennsylvania in the 1820s. This reprinting at Reading, Pennsylvania, of a standard German treatise on winegrowing was published by Heinrich Sage, who tells us that he went to Germany expressly to acquire information on the subject. The title translated is *Improved practical winegrowing in Gardens and especially in vineyards, with instructions for pressing wine without a press . . . dedicated to American winegrowers by Heinrich B. Sage.* (California State University, Fresno, Library)

As for New Harmony on the Wabash, that had been sold in 1825 to the Welsh mill-owner and socialist Robert Owen, who intended to establish a revolutionary model community as an example to the world.[26] Too many theorists and too few organized working hands quickly put the experiment out of order, and the communitarian days of New Harmony ended two years after the shrewd and practical Rapp had peddled the place to the doctrinaire Owen. New Harmony today is notable among midwestern towns for its lively interest in its own past, but it has long since forgotten the "red juice grape" and its *Wabaschwein*.

Before the Harmonists had retraced their steps from Indiana, other significant ventures had been made in Pennsylvania in the new viticulture based on the Alexander grape. The pioneer in these was a Pennsylvania Dutchman named

Thomas Eichelberger, of York County, who, in an effort to put barren land to profitable use, engaged a German vine dresser and planted four acres of a slate ridge in 1818. By 1821 Eichelberger had a small vintage; by 1823 his four acres yielded thirty-one barrels and he had added six more acres. He planned to reach twenty. When the word got round that Eichelberger had been offered an annual rent of $200 an acre for the produce of his vines, there was a scramble to plant vineyards in the Dutch country. "There is land of a suitable soil enough in York county," one writer declared, "to raise wine for the consumption of all the United States."[27] The rural papers of the day are filled with calculations exhibiting the absolutely certain profits to be made from Pennsylvania grapes, and by 1830 there were, according to contemporary report, some thirty or forty vineyards around York and Lancaster.[28] Many amateurs throughout the middle states had also been inspired by the example of York County to attempt a small vineyard.

The grapes most commonly grown were called the York Madeira, the York Claret, and the York Lisbon—all, apparently, variations on the Alexander, though the York Madeira may be a different variety. Later, some of the new hybrid introductions that began to proliferate in the second quarter of the century were used, but these eventually succumbed to diseases and so put an end to the industry. Not before it had made a lasting contribution, however: as U. P. Hedrick writes in his magisterial survey of native American grape varieties, "a surprisingly large number have been traced back to this early center of the industry, so many that York and Lancaster Counties, Pennsylvania, must be counted among the starting places of American viticulture."[29]

Bonapartists in the Mississippi Territory

An unlikely agricultural colony, very different from the religious communities like Rapp's Harmonists, or refugees from religious persecution, like the South Carolina Huguenots, was formed in 1816 out of the refugee Bonapartists, mostly army officers, who had then congregated in considerable numbers in and around Philadelphia. On his second restoration, after the nightmare of the Hundred Days had been dispelled at Waterloo in 1815, Louis XVIII prudently determined to get rid of the more ardent partisans of the emperor, most of them officers of the Grande Armée or political functionaries under Napoleon. Decrees of exile were issued against some, and the fear of official vengeance determined others to leave. Most of them chose to go to the United States, and of these, many chose Philadelphia, not far from where Joseph Bonaparte was spending his exile at Bordentown, New Jersey. How the idea arose and by whom it was directed we do not know, but by late 1816 the French officers in Philadelphia, with various French merchants and politicians, had organized an association with the vague purpose of "forming a large settlement somewhere on the Ohio or Mississippi . . . to cultivate the vine."[30] They called themselves the French Agricultural and Manufacturing Society and included among their members Joseph Lakanal, one of the regicides of Louis XVI and the reformer of French education under the Revolution. He was sent out to explore the country for suitable sites, and ventured as far as southwestern Missouri on his quest.[31]

The plan soon grew more distinct. The Mississippi Territory was then being highly promoted and rapidly settled. It had, besides, the attraction of lying within the old French territory; Mobile was a French city, and New Orleans was not too remote. They would go, then, to what is now Alabama, where they had been assured that they would find a climate like that of France and a land adapted to the vine and the olive. An agent was sent to Washington to secure a grant of public lands, and in March 1817 Congress obliged by voting them four townships to be paid for at two dollars an acre on fourteen years' credit.[32] The financial arrangement was the same as that made with Dufour in 1802, and no doubt that precedent was consulted. But the scale of all this was much bigger than that of Dufour's project; this was not a family, but a whole community that was to undertake a new enterprise of large-scale winegrowing.

There were 350 members of the group, officially the "French Agricultural and Manufacturing Society," but more often referred to as the "Vine and Olive Association" or the "Tombigbee Association," after the river along whose banks they meant to settle.[33] Their grant extended over 92,000 acres. It was evidently the intention of Congress to make the experiment large-scale and coherent: no individual property titles would be granted until all the property had been paid for, and so, it was hoped, since the colonists thus could not sell their holdings, they would keep at their work. The whole vast tract was meant to remain exclusively French and was to be devoted mainly to vines and secondarily to olives, all tended by "persons understanding the culture of those plants." By the terms of the contract made between the association and the secretary of the Treasury, they were, within seven years of settlement, to plant an acre of vines for each section of land (that is, a total of about 140 acres at a minimum).[34]

Very shortly after receiving their grant, whose exact location was not yet determined, the first contingent of settlers, about 150 in number, sailed for Mobile, from there went up the Tombigbee to its junction with the Black Warrior River, staked their claim, and laid out the town of Demopolis.[35] The affair attracted much attention, and even the English were impressed: a London paper was moved to call the project "one of the most extraordinary speculations ever known even in America."[36] But the whole thing was grandiose, impetuous, and vague—grandiose because it was seriously maintained that the French would supply the nation's wants in wine;[37] impetuous because the would-be planters began settling even before they knew where they were to settle, with disastrous consequences, as will be seen; vague because no one knew anything about the actual work proposed or had any notion of ways and means. The idea that the veterans of the greatest army ever known, men who had been officers at Marengo, Austerlitz, Moscow, and Waterloo, would turn quietly to the American wilderness to cultivate the vine and the olive, emblems of peace, has a kind of Chateaubriandesque poetry about it, but little to recommend it to practice. There is a certain charm in the splendid incompetence displayed, but the charm is hardly sufficient to offset the fact that the emigrants paid a heavy cost in disease, death, and wasted struggle. They do not seem even to have heard, for example, of the work with native vines done by Dufour, and had no thought of attempting to grow anything but vinifera.

The first step in the debacle was the discovery, when the surveyors arrived, that Demopolis was laid out on land that did not belong to the French grant.[38] The settlers had to abandon their clearings and cabins and to found another settlement, which they called Aigleville after the ensign of the Grande Armée. Meantime, the distribution of lands within the grant was being drawn up on paper in Philadelphia after the first settlers had already made their choice on the spot, and of course the two divisions did not coincide. Once again the beleaguered French had to reshuffle their arrangements. Their lands, in the rich Black Belt of Alabama, were then a difficult mixture of canebrake, prairie, and forest, and were not even hospitable to the native grape, much less to the imported; as for the olives, the winters destroyed them at once. Fevers killed some of the settlers; discouragement sent even more to look for their fortunes elsewhere, a circumstance that at once made the original contract impossible of fulfillment. That had stipulated that no title would be given until all the contracting parties had met their terms, and if some of them simply abandoned the work, then the remnant were left with no means of satisfying the requirements. The provision was altered in 1822 when it was clear that the original plan was not going to work out.[39] Stories, apocryphal no doubt, but expressive, were told of the French officers at work felling trees in their dress uniforms and of their ladies milking or sowing in velvet gowns and satin slippers.[40] *Toujours gai* was the watchword; no matter how desperate the circumstances, in the evenings the French gathered for parties, dancing, and the exchange of ceremony. Such stories sound like Anglo-Saxon parodies of French manners, and probably are. But they testify to the fact that the French of Alabama struck their neighbors as very curious beings, almost of a different order.

It is sometimes suggested that these French soldiers were merely trifling—that they never seriously intended to labor at agriculture but were simply biding their time before Napoleon should return, or some other opportunity for adventure turn up.[41] That was certainly true of some. But others seem to have worked in good faith. Some vines were reported to be planted in 1818; by the end of 1821 there were 10,000 growing, though the French complained that most of the cuttings that they persistently imported from France arrived dead or dying.[42] A few vines lived long enough to yield a little wine, but it was found to be miserable stuff, coming as it did from diseased vines picked during the intensest heats of summer and vinified under uncontrollably adverse conditions.[43] Nevertheless, the usual optimism of ignorance was still alive; on meeting several of the Frenchmen, one traveller through Alabama in 1821 reported that "they appear confident of the success of the Vine."[44]

Since the settlers were under contract with the Treasury to perform their

33 | One of five panels of hand-painted French wallpaper showing idealized scenes from the Alabama Vine and Olive Colony. This one presents the building of Aigleville. The street signs—"Austerlitz," "Jena," "Wagram"—bear the names of Napoleon's victories. (Alabama Department of Archives and History)

promise, the Congress made inquiry into their progress from time to time. From the report for 1827 we learn that there were 271 acres in vines, but that these were not set out in the form of ordinary vineyards; instead, they stood at intervals of 10′ x 20′ on stakes set in the midst of cotton fields! By this time, the spokesman for the association had acquired at least one item of wisdom, for he informed the secretary of the Treasury that "the great question seems to be the proper mode of cultivation, and, instead of seven, perhaps seventy years may be required correctly to ascertain this fact."[45] The last official report, dated January 1828, states that the drought of the preceding summer had killed their vines, but that the French were "now generally engaged in replanting."[46] On this note of stubbornness in the face of defeat, the French Vine and Olive Association died out; some members returned to the eastern cities, some to Europe; others went to Mobile or points west.

The net result of the French ordeal in Alabama was to make it clear that, if any grapes were to grow there, they must be natives. In 1829 an American who had managed to obtain lands within the French grant reported that he had observed the repeated failures of the French over several years and attributed the result to their using vinifera. The only grape that ever succeeded was one—unnamed—that had been sent to them from New Orleans by the agent there of the Swiss at Vevay, and which the French *vigneron* who planted it called the Madeira.[47] Thus, circuitously and accidentally, was confirmed what they might have learned directly from Dufour's experience: with the natives there was a chance; without, none.

John Adlum, "Father of American Viticulture"

It is now time to take up a story of success, the episode that is traditionally identified as the true beginning of commercial winegrowing as it developed in the eastern United States. The man who is familiarly called the "Father of American Viticulture"—how well-deserved that title is will appear from this sketch of his work—was Major John Adlum (1759–1836), of The Vineyard, Georgetown, District of Columbia.[48] Adlum was born in York, Pennsylvania, and as a boy of seventeen marched off with a company of Pennsylvania volunteers to join the Revolution, but was captured by the British at New York and sent back home. Though he later held commissions in the provisional army raised in 1799, from which he derived his title of major, and in the emergency forces raised in the War of 1812, Adlum, after his brief experience of war, took up surveying as a profession. He chose a good time, for after the Revolution the western lands of Pennsylvania and New York filled up rapidly, allowing Adlum to make a modest fortune through the ready combination of surveying and land speculation. By 1798 he was able to retire, and he settled then on a farm near Havre de Grace, Maryland, at the mouth of the Susquehanna River, along whose course he had often travelled in his surveying work. He probably planted a vineyard at once at Havre de Grace, for he seems to have been interested in grapes even before his retirement; while carrying out his surveys he took notes on the native grapes growing wild in the woods and along the streams of Pennsylvania—red and white grapes growing on an island of the Allegheny, black grapes at Presque Isle, where the French were said to have made wine from them, and black grapes along the Susquehanna all came under his notice and suggested that, from such fruit, "excellent wines may be made in a great many parts of our Country."[49]

Nevertheless, his first plantings were of European vines, evidence of the strength of the grip that, at this late date in American experience, the foreign vine still had upon the minds of American growers. It did not take Adlum long, however, to decide that he had made a mistake. When insects and diseases overwhelmed his vinifera vines, he had them grubbed up and planted native vines instead.[50]

One of these was the Alexander, and from it Adlum succeeded in making a wine that had a significant success—he later admitted that his method with that batch was an accident that he could never afterwards duplicate.[51] Nevertheless, he made the most of what he had, which was, in the first place, an astute sense of publicity; he sent samples of his wine to the places and persons where they might have their most effective result. One went to President Jefferson, and with him the

34 | John Adlum (1759–1836), whose Georgetown vineyard produced the first commercial wine in the settled regions of the country. Adlum gave a tremendous boost to the development of winegrowing by his introduction of the Catawba grape and by his publications on grape growing and winemaking in the 1820s. (Portrait attributed to Charles Willson Peale, c. 1794; State Museum of Pennsylvania / Pennsylvania Historical and Museum Commission)

wine made a home shot. It was, the president wrote, a fine wine, comparable to a Chambertin, and he advised that Adlum look no farther for a suitable wine grape but press on with the cultivation of the Alexander. He should forget about foreign vines, "which it will take centuries to adapt to our soil and climate."[52] Adlum agreed, but observed with the doubtfulness of experience that Americans were not yet quite ready for wine from American grapes—as soon as they knew what they were drinking, they objected to it, though they might have been praising it a moment before.[53] The remark is one the truth of which most eastern winemakers even today will regretfully assent to. But Adlum was determined to persist, even though he knew that, as a prophet of American wine, his own country would likely be the last to honor him.

In 1816 Jefferson wrote again to Adlum, having been stirred by a fresh prospect of planting wine vines, and learned that great changes had occurred in his correspondent's circumstances. Adlum was now living in Georgetown, on property near Rock Creek, above the Potomac, where he had settled after leaving Havre de Grace in 1814.[54] At the time of Jefferson's letter, Adlum had not yet set out a Georgetown vineyard. It may have been Jefferson's inquiry that aroused Adlum again; it may have been that Adlum had the thought in mind himself; in any case, he was soon back at planting vines, this time on a different basis and with a wholly different success.

The Vineyard, as he called his farm, was a property of some 200 acres; the vineyards themselves were on the south slope of a hill running down to Rock Creek, now part of Rock Creek Park in Washington, D.C. A poetically inclined visitor in the early days found that they made a quiet, sequestered scene; rows of vines, ranged one above the other, rose from the base of a hill washed by a willow-fringed stream, beside which a black vine dresser gathered willow twigs for tying up the shoots of the vines that lined the hill above.[55] The picture is attractively idyllic, but perhaps a bit *en beau*. What Adlum had was in fact quite a modest establishment, with nothing of the grand château about it: from the vantage of another observer, the vineyard was seen as a "patch of wild and scraggy looking vines; the soil was artificially prepared, not with rich compost, but with pebbles and pounded oyster-shells."[56] The whole property was not large, and the vines occupied but a small part of the whole—some four acres by 1822.[57]

The first vintage at Georgetown of which we have report was made in 1822 and consisted of 400 gallons, in no way distinguishable from other vintages yielded by native vines before.[58] There was this difference, though: it was the produce of the nation's capital, and therefore noticeable and promotable in a way that, for example, the vintages of Dufour's Swiss on the remote banks of the Ohio were not. Here, for example, is how the editor of the *American Farmer,* a superior publication emanating from Baltimore, greeted Adlum's first offering:

FOURTH OF JULY PARTIES

Would manifest their patriotism by taking out a portion of *American* wine, manufactured by Major Adlum of the District of Columbia. It may be had in varieties of Messrs. Marple and Williams, and the Editor of the American Farmer will be thankful for the candid opinion of connoisseurs concerning its qualities.[59]

If any patriot-connoisseurs heeded the request, their responses do not appear in the *American Farmer,* but the publicity can have done Adlum no harm. Yet one wonders what Adlum could have been offering? July is too early by any stretch of the imagination for the vintage of 1822 to have been put on sale. And in any case, Adlum wrote to the *American Farmer* on 17 September 1822 that he had just then completed his winemaking.[60] The vintage of 1821, we know from Adlum's testimony, had all turned to vinegar.[61] Possibly wine from 1820 was what was advertised in 1822, but there is no record of any production in 1820.

As Adlum himself explained in the *American Farmer,* in 1822, he had only just begun his work then: he had some vines of "Constantia" and some vines of what he called "Tokay"—not anything like real Tokay, as we shall see, but something portentous nonetheless. He had cuttings for sale, Adlum added, and he hoped himself to have some ten acres in vines soon.[62]

In the next year, Adlum's work was translated to a different plane. His "Tokay" had fruited for the first time in 1822, and the wine that he had made from it in that season developed into something better than any native grape had yielded before. Adlum lost no time in advertising his success, and, as others began to admire, he did not let any consideration of modesty restrain his high claims for the quality of the "Tokay" grape. Jefferson, of course, was one of the first to receive a bottle of Adlum's Tokay; James Madison was another.[63] Jefferson's reply, though polite, must have been a disappointment to Adlum, who may have hoped for something as extravagant as the great man's earlier comparison of Alexander wine to Chambertin. This time, Jefferson restricted himself to the observation that the Tokay was "truly a fine wine of high flavor."[64] That was good enough for promotional purposes; Adlum sent Jefferson's letter (and a bottle of Tokay) to the editor of the *American Farmer,* where a notice appeared in the next month. Later, Adlum reproduced Jefferson's letter in facsimile as the frontispiece of his book on winegrowing.

The history of the "Tokay" grape, which thus first came to public notice in 1823, is fairly circumstantial, though a number of questions remain as to its origin and early distribution. In sending a bottle to Jefferson, Adlum stated that the vine came from a Mrs. Scholl in Clarksburgh, Maryland, that a German priest had said the vine was "the true Tokay" of Hungary, but that Mr. Scholl (now dead) had always called it the Catawba.[65]

Adlum took cuttings from Mrs. Scholl's vine in the spring of 1819; by 1825 he had determined that "Tokay" was a misnomer, and reverted to the late Mr. Scholl's name, Catawba,[66] which belongs to a river rising in western North Carolina and flowing into South Carolina. Traditionally the grape was found first not far from present-day Asheville, in a region of poor, thinly timbered soil. Whether Scholl had any information to justify the name he gave the grape is not known. After the success of the grape had led to its wide distribution, a good many different stories about its origin were published, but none authoritative enough to settle the matter.[67]

The same uncertainty attends the botanical classification of the Catawba. Early writers called it a labrusca; Hedrick agrees, but adds that it must have a strain of vinifera as well.[68] It has the self-fertile flowers of vinifera, a trait that combines with its improved fruit quality to confirm its vinifera inheritance. As to the character of the grape, that is well established. After more than a century and a half of cultivation, it still remains one of the important native eastern hybrids; for winemaking, it is one of the three or four most valuable of such grapes. The fruit of the Catawba is

35   The Catawba grape, introduced by John Adlum in the early 1820s, the first native hybrid to make a wine of attractive quality. Its origins are uncertain, but after more than a century and a half of cultivation, it still retains a place in eastern viticulture. (Painting by C. L. Fleischman, 1867; National Agricultural Library)

a most attractive lilac, a light purplish-red, yielding a white juice which is definitely foxy, after the nature of its labrusca parent, but which may be transformed into a still white wine that Philip Wagner describes as "dry to the point of austerity" and having "a very clean flavor and a curious, special, spicy aroma."[69] Its superiority to the other grapes available in its day quickly led to its trial all over the inhabited sections of the United States; growers then learned that it presented some severe problems, being susceptible to fungus diseases and, in northern regions, failing to ripen except in special locations. It found a home in Ohio, first along the Ohio

A MEMOIR

ON THE

CULTIVATION OF THE VINE

IN

AMERICA,

AND THE

BEST MODE OF MAKING WINE.

BY JOHN ADLUM.

Wine is as good as life to a man, if it be drunk moderately; what is life then to a man that is without wine? for it was made to make men glad. " Wine measurably drank, and in season, bringeth gladness of the heart, and cheerfulness of the mind."

ECCLESIASTICUS, c. 31, v. 27, 28.

WASHINGTON:

PRINTED BY DAVIS AND FORCE, (FRANKLIN'S HEAD,)

PENNSYLVANIA AVENUE.

::::::::::::

1823.

36 John Adlum's was the first book on winegrowing to be published in the United States as opposed to the British North American colonies. It was also the first book to assume that American winegrowing would have to be based on native American varieties. Both facts give the *Memoir* a special status in the early literature of American winegrowing. (Huntington Library)

River and later in the Lake Erie district, and in New York in the Finger Lakes country. It remains, in both states, a staple grape for winemaking, particularly in the production of sparkling wine.

From the evidence of his own descriptions of his winemaking methods, and from the remarks of some critics, it appears that Adlum himself did not make very good wine from his Catawba. Though he disapproved of the established American practice of adding brandy (most often fruit brandy of local production) to wine in order to strengthen and preserve it, he did not hesitate to add large quantities of sugar to the must, so much that the juice would not ferment to dryness. The horticultural and architectural writer Andrew Jackson Downing, a good judge, remembered Adlum's wine as "only tolerable";[70] Nicholas Longworth, who may be said to have succeeded to Adlum's work with Catawba, agreed that Adlum's wine was poor, not only for its artificial sweetness but because, he reported, Adlum was not above eking out his superior juice in lean years with the juice from the wild grapes growing in the woods that surrounded his vineyard.[71] This practice Longworth politely attributed to Adlum's "poverty" (whatever the size of Adlum's fortune when he retired in 1798, it does not seem to have been adequate to carry him easily to the end in 1836). After all these qualifications and reservations have been made, the main point remains: Adlum had found a grape from which good wine might be made; he had been quick to recognize the fact; and he had been able to publicize it effectively. At the time, and given the circumstances, he had done precisely what the long struggle to create an American winegrowing industry needed.

By some providence, the introduction of Adlum's Catawba wine coincided with the publication of Adlum's book on grape growing and winemaking: his *Memoir on the Cultivation of the Vine in America, and the Best Mode of Making Wine,* published in Washington early in 1823,[72] appeared almost together with the first distribution of Catawba. Perhaps he planned it that way. In any event, the two strokes, the new book and the new wine together, have made Adlum's mark on the record of American winegrowing permanent and visible to a degree hardly matched by any other individual's. His book is interesting, and original to the extent that it chronicles his own experience with vine growing and winemaking, going back to his residence at Havre de Grace at the end of the eighteenth century. As a treatise on viticulture, it is derivative; Adlum did not pretend otherwise, and freely acknowledged the fact that he was following the lines laid down by established European writers. He thus has little or nothing to say on such crucial subjects as the diseases that had to be faced by any American viticulturist. He spends more time on winemaking, but here, too, his achievement is not remarkable. His disposition to use too much sugar in his wine has already been noticed. Moreover, he recommended such practices as fermentation at high temperatures—up to 115° Fahrenheit!—which would horrify winemakers today.[73] But one may make many allowances for Adlum. He wrote with as much independence as could be expected in his circumstances, he clearly understood the importance of native vines, he firmly opposed the bad practice of drowning wines in brandy, and, in company with all of his notable predecessors, he acted with a conscious sense of patriotic selflessness: "a desire to be useful to my countrymen, has animated all my efforts," he declared in the preface to his *Memoir.* As he wrote to Nicholas Longworth not long after the triumphant introduction of the Catawba, "in introducing this grape to public notice, I have done my country a greater service than I should have done, had I paid the national debt."[74] And his confidence was infectious. James Madison, in sending two copies of Adlum's book to the Agricultural Society of Albemarle, wrote that now "nothing seems wanting to the addition of the grape to our valuable productions, but decisive efforts."[75]

For the next half-dozen years after he had brought Catawba wine to the public for the first time, Adlum was the recognized oracle on the subject of wines and vines in America. He wrote frequently to the agricultural press—a significantly larger and more influential part of the national press in those rural days than now—describing his practices and setting forth his prescriptions for others. He circularized the great men of the day to attract their attention to the cause of winegrowing, usually sending a bottle of his produce to help make the point; he lobbied the agricultural societies to get them to recognize viticulture and winemaking as activities worthy of official encouragement; he tried to get the federal government to establish a national vineyard in the District of Columbia in which the many varieties of native vines might be planted "to ascertain their growth, soil, and produce, and to exhibit to the Nation, a new source of wealth, which had been too long neglected."[76] Since the intensity of his enthusiasm far exceeded that of the institutions to which he appealed, he did not get very far immediately. But probably much of what we now have is owed to the example he set.

Certainly Adlum's activities had something to do with the noticeable growth of interest in winegrowing that spread over the United States in the 1820s. Adlum himself published exciting figures on the profits to be made from small vineyards, such as almost every American might reasonably plant. In 1824 he notified the public that the demand for cuttings from his vineyard was already growing beyond his ability to supply.[77] In 1825 he was able to boast that he had aroused national interest: "I have correspondents from Maine to East Florida, on the sea-board, and in the states of Ohio, Kentucky, and Tennessee, to the north and west, on the subject of planting vineyards and making wine."[78] It was in this year, probably, that the wealthy Ohio lawyer and landowner Nicholas Longworth visited Adlum and obtained from him cuttings of the Catawba vine:[79] the results of that encounter form part of another chapter. In 1827 Adlum had the dubious pleasure of inspiring a new contribution to the literature of American winegrowing. The work was a treatise in verse called *The Vigneron,* published in Washington, D.C., by one Isaac G. Hutton.[80] This strange performance, touching on temperance, soils, planting, cultivation, and other subjects, prints an essay by Adlum "On Propagating Grape Vines in a Vineyard" as an appendix, and also makes such familiar allusion to Adlum as to show that, if he did not beget the poem, he must at least have known that it was being perpetrated.[81]

All over the country waves were felt and echoes heard from the stir that Adlum had made. From South Carolina to New York, farmers, nurserymen, and journalists paid a new attention to the grape, not wholly because of Adlum, but in large part because of the fact that he had done well with a native grape at last and was equipped to publicize what he had done. In Maryland, for example, Adlum had been particularly aggressive in advertising his work, but met a disappointing reluctance on the part of the state agricultural society to do anything about viticulture.[82] Then, in 1828, a company of private gentlemen received a charter from the state to form the "Maryland Society for Promoting the Culture of the Vine," capitalized at $3,000, and furnished with many respectable names among its officers.[83] The intention of the society was to show the way towards scientific advance in vine growing and winemaking. Its plan, evidently inspired by Adlum's notion of a national vineyard, was to establish a small vineyard in which trials could be made of both European and native grapes, and, by its example, encourage the formation of other such societies. After a good deal of early publicity, however, not much seems to have been done. The society still had not managed to find land for a vineyard a year after its founding, and hence could do nothing towards hiring apprentices, selling cuttings, holding exhibitions, and diffusing information as it proposed to do. Perhaps the most interesting thing about the society is the fact that, even though it was called forth by Adlum's success with the Catawba, it still proposed to experiment with vinifera; it marked, as Hedrick has noted, the last organized effort to grow European grapes in eastern America—or rather, the last before the renewed trials of the late twentieth century.[84] Of course, the untried assumption that vinifera would grow here continued to be widespread among individuals. S. I. Fisher, for example, in his *Observations on the Character and Culture of the European Vine* (Philadelphia, 1834), argued that if we would only imitate the vine growing practices of the Swiss, we would succeed in acclimating the foreign vine. Fisher recommends, too, that Legaux's old Pennsylvania Vine Company should be revived for the purpose.

In 1826 Adlum published another treatise—a pamphlet, really—under the title of *Adlum on Making Wine*,[85] but his importance now was less as a winemaker than as a nurseryman promoting the wide distribution of native grapes in a country now at last prepared to believe in them. Adlum used a part of his *Memoir* as a catalog of his nursery, offering cuttings for sale: the list of the varieties he had available is an instructive record of the state of varietal development then. He includes a number of vinifera grapes, but the heart of the list lay in the native vines: "Tokay" (as he then called the Catawba), Schuylkill Muscadel (Alexander), Bland's Madeira, Clifton's Constantia (a variant of the Alexander), Muncy (later affirmed to be Catawba), Worthington, Red Juice, Carolina Purple Muscadine, and Orwigsburgh. The Red Juice grape is presumably that which the Harmonists are reported to have grown along with the Alexander; the Worthington is probably the variety better known as Clinton, a hybrid of riparia, labrusca, and some vinifera; it was later much used for red wine, but without giving much satisfaction—the fruit, Hedrick says, is "small and sour," the wine "too raucous."[86] Bland's Madeira is a labrusca-vinifera hybrid like the Alexander, and of almost as early discovery as the Alexander. Colonel Theodorick Bland, of Virginia, brought it to notice just before the Revolution, and there are reports of it under various names—Powel or Powell is the most common—in vineyards in New Jersey, Pennsylvania, and elsewhere in the early nineteenth century. Bland's Madeira was probably the "Madeira" that Dufour obtained from Legaux and grew in Kentucky and Indiana, but we cannot be sure.

In 1828 Adlum brought out a second edition of the *Memoir,* in which the list has been increased by the addition of four more grapes: an unnamed variety from North Carolina, two labruscas called Luffborough and Elkton, and Isabella. The last is a superior chance hybrid of vinifera and labrusca, introduced and promoted by the Long Island nurseryman and viticulturist William Prince as early as 1816. Originating, probably, in South Carolina, it was the chief alternative to Catawba for many years, for it ripens earlier than Catawba and is therefore preferred by growers in the middle Atlantic and New England states. Had Prince made wine in commercial quantities from the Isabella and publicized it, he might well have challenged Adlum for the position as the first to sponsor a good native grape. Adlum's list is a reasonably complete enumeration of what an American winegrower had to work with at the end of the first quarter of the nineteenth century. All of these varieties were accidents, the result of spontaneous seedlings; both the Isabella and the Catawba, the best two of the lot, have serious cultural defects and are susceptible to diseases that could not then be controlled; none was fit for the production of red wine, a severe limitation if one agrees that it is the first duty of a wine to be red. It was not, in short, much of a basis to work on, but it was all that was available up to the decade before the Civil War. Then there was a great and sudden increase in the number of varieties available, thanks to a belated but enthusiastic outburst of interest in grape breeding.

One of the last episodes in Adlum's career as a propagandist of winegrowing was his petition addressed to the U.S. Senate in April 1828 stating his claim to recognition for his work as a vineyardist and winemaker and requesting that the Senate take steps to make the newly published second edition of his *Memoir* "useful to the United States, *and of some advantage to your petitioner.*"[87] The Senate committee on agriculture, to which the petition was referred, proposed that the Treasury buy 3,000 copies of Adlum's book for distribution by members of the Senate, but the proposal struck the senators as unorthodox and was defeated.[88] It seems reasonable to suppose that Adlum needed the money; Longworth, as we have already seen, noted Adlum's "poverty," and there is further evidence of his neediness in 1831, when Adlum laid claim to a tiny pension for which he was eligible as a soldier in the Revolution.[89] From 1830 until his death in 1836 he does not figure in the public discussion of grapes and wine, though that went on in full flow. Adlum's name fell into obscurity after his death; his modest home in Georgetown stood until, derelict, it was demolished early in this century; the knowledge of his burial place was, for a long time, lost; and the record of his work was forgotten until brought back to light by the researches of the great botanical scholar and writer Liberty Hyde Bailey at the end of the nineteenth century.

As with most "Fathers" of institutions or of complex inventions, like the airplane or the automobile, Adlum can hardly be claimed to have been sole father to American viticulture. His establishment was at no time anything but a very small affair; he was not the first to introduce a usable hybrid native grape; he was certainly not the first to produce a tolerable wine; nor was his *Memoir* the first American treatise on the subject. It would be more sensible to say that he came at the right time in the right place, and that he is fully entitled to the credit of introducing the Catawba and of knowing how to promote it. After Adlum, the history of wine in eastern America is a different story.

The South in the Early Republic

A brief look at the South will close this chapter. The South was not merely the source of usable native hybrids—the Isabella and Catawba from the Carolinas; Bland's grape and the Norton from Virginia. It also had a part in the many winemaking trials made after the Revolution.

Despite the presence of such distinguished amateurs as Jefferson, Madison, and Monroe, Virginia was not one of the leaders in the development of viticulture and winemaking in the early days of the Republic. No doubt many private gentlemen kept up their interest in the subject: Adlum reported that the Virginians were more eager for cuttings from him than any others.[90] Josiah Lockhart, for instance, of Frederick County, bought 2,000 vines of Catawba from Adlum and was producing a few gallons of wine by 1827.[91] One notable event, of considerable importance for the future, was the introduction of the Norton grape by Dr. D. N. Norton of Richmond, Virginia. Sometime around 1820 Dr. Norton planted seed from a vine of the native grape called "Bland" that had fruited near a vinifera grape; one of the resultant seedlings he selected for its superior qualities, which would later be recognized by commercial plantings in Virginia, Missouri, and elsewhere.[92]

Something has already been said about the Scuppernong wine of North Carolina, which had reputation enough to attract Jefferson's interest. "Scuppernong" properly refers to a white variety of the species rotundifolia, the muscadine grape, a variety first brought to notice in North Carolina and much cultivated there from the early nineteenth century on. The popularity of the variety has led to the name Scuppernong being used for muscadines generally, but I restrict it to its original reference. The wine that Jefferson drank and liked was the produce of well-to-do planters around Edenton and Plymouth in the low country on Albemarle Sound; some of this, at least, came from cultivated vineyards. Whether grapes from wild vines were also used is unclear, but seems highly likely. Farther south, Scuppernong wine was almost a *vin de pays* for the poor; all along the Cape Fear River for a distance of seventy miles, we are told, farmers made wine from the wild grapes and used it "as freely as cider is used in New England."[93] Observers from time to time noted the ease with which such wine was produced, prompting them to wonder whether it might not be promoted from a hobby or cottage industry to become a staple product for the enrichment of the state.[94] Certainly North Carolina needed such a thing, for its agricultural economy in the first part of the century was well-nigh desperate, the consequence of feckless farming and exhausted soils. More land lay abandoned than was actually in production, and the population declined with emigration.[95] The State Board of Agriculture recognized the possibility of grape culture by distributing vines in the state from 1823 to 1830; but, though the newspapers wrote of what might be done, little in fact came of the effort to turn the worn-out lands of the state into vineyards.[96]

The possibilities of the high ground in the western part of North Carolina, so different from the low and swampy coastal plain favored by the muscadine, were also explored. Around 1827 the state legislature made a grant of 500 acres in the Brushy Mountains of Wilkes County, in the Blue Ridge country, to a Frenchman who undertook to grow grapes experimentally there.[97] What he did, or whether he did anything, are questions for which, as so often happens, no record has been found to answer.

It is in South Carolina, with its intermittent but persistent history of grape growing, going back to the early Huguenot emigration, that much of the interesting work is to be found. Towards the end of the century, the South Carolina Society for Promoting Agriculture (later the Agricultural Society of South Carolina) attempted to assist winegrowing along the familiar lines of importing cuttings from Europe and distributing them for trial,[98] with the usual result: the members were "inexperienced in the peculiar culture of the vine, their labourers were hirelings who did but little, and finally their funds failed them."[99] The one essential thing omitted from such a recital is that the climate and diseases killed the vines quite independently of all the other failures. After this disappointment, the society tried another tack by subsidizing a self-proclaimed expert to cultivate vines near Columbia. A contemporary historian says laconically that "their liberality was misapplied."[100] It is not clear whether this person was the same as "one Magget" who obtained a grant from the legislature around 1800 for the purpose of developing viticulture.[101] Perhaps so; and perhaps it was the same person who in November 1798 gave the address to the Agricultural Society published anonymously as "A Memorial on the Practicability of Growing Vineyards in the State of South Carolina." This was filled with extravagant claims and unreal calculations, demonstrating that, unlike cotton, rice, tobacco, and indigo, the grape presented "an inexhaustible source of riches and opulence."[102]

More productive than the publicly supported efforts were those of individual vineyard owners, of whom there had always been many in South Carolina. The focus of activity after the Revolution shifted from the coast at Charleston, or along the Savannah River, to higher ground around the newly established capital at Columbia and beyond. Benjamin Waring raised grapes and made wine as early as

1802 at Columbia; he was evidently working with a superior selection of native grapes, for he was able to produce wine without added sugar, though with one gallon of brandy to every twelve of juice—a considerable dose to us but a modest measure then.[103] Another, later, Columbia grower was James S. Guignard, who for many years grew Catawba and Norton grapes, as well as one that he called "Guignard."[104] Samuel Maverick, best known for his pioneering work in establishing the cotton culture of the South, was an enthusiastic viticulturist too. At his estate of Montpelier, at Pendleton in the far western corner of the state, Maverick made trials of various grapes, both native and foreign, and of different methods of training, as well as experimenting with soils, fertilizers, and horticultural methods. By 1823 Maverick had nearly fifty varieties growing and with the typical optimism of the time predicted that wine would soon be as valuable to the South as cotton then was.[105] When Caroline Olivia Laurens, wife of Henry Laurens, Jr., visited Maverick in July 1825, she found him full of proselytizing zeal. First he presented the party with "wine of his own manufacturing, equal to Frontinac," and then "he conducted us to his vineyard, which covers an acre or more of land. . . . The old man seemed very desirous that his neighbors should try the cultivation of the vine; he said that he thought this as good a country for grapes as the South of France, and he had no doubt that in a few years wine will be as lucrative a commodity as cotton."[106]

The most active and effective grower was Nicholas Herbemont of Columbia, who began growing grapes about 1811 and who did much to advertise the possibilities of winemaking in South Carolina for the next twenty years. I have not been able to learn much about him. He was evidently French-born, rather than a descendant of the South Carolina Huguenots.[107] He is sometimes referred to as "Doctor," but, on his own authority, he had no claim to the title.[108] In any case, he was an articulate and literate man, writing often for the agricultural press. Like Adlum, he was interested in the technicalities of winemaking and in the search for better native varieties. It is no surprise that, as a Frenchman, he did not immediately concentrate upon the native grapes; it is said that he returned to France in order to bring back vinifera vines to his adopted country.[109] But experience made it clear that success lay with the natives.

Herbemont's best wines came from a grape that he called Madeira, and that others called Herbemont's Madeira; it is now known simply as Herbemont. A member of the subspecies of aestivalis called Bourquiniana, the Herbemont grape probably contains vinifera blood as well. It is eminently a southern grape, sensitive to cold and requiring a long season; given the right conditions, Herbemont is that rare thing among natives, a grape with a good balance of sugar and acid. The white wine that Herbemont made from this grape he called "Palmyra wine" after his farm at Columbia.[110] It is much to be regretted that this excellent practice of naming the wine after the place of its production did not set a clear precedent and so spare us the clarets, madeiras, champagnes, burgundies, and ports whose borrowed names have confused and obstructed the development of a distinctive range of

American types and terms. Herbemont's other favored grape was the Lenoir, another variety of Bourquiniana, also restricted to the South, and giving a red wine better than the average expected from other native grapes—a very guarded praise. Herbemont was not the discoverer or the exclusive promoter of these grapes, both of which had an earlier history quite independent of him. But he did bring them to public notice in connection with his own successful manufacture of wine and he deserves to have his name perpetuated by the first of them.

Like all native winegrowers, he had to overcome much prejudice. The South Carolinian lawyer and politician William John Grayson reported that he and other legislators once sampled the wine of the "urbane and kind hearted" Herbemont. Grayson thought the wine "very pleasant. But not so my more experienced colleagues, adepts in Old Madeira and Sherry; they held the home article in very slender estimation. They thought it, as they said, a good wine to keep, and were content that it should be kept accordingly."[111]

Unlike Adlum, Herbemont did not produce a book on winegrowing, though a series of his articles on grape culture contributed to the *Southern Agriculturist* (1828) was reprinted as a pamphlet in 1833.[112] Perhaps for this reason in part, and perhaps too because he worked in the relative obscurity of the new, raw town of Columbia, he did not achieve the same effect as Adlum; in every other respect he seems entitled to the same recognition as his better-known contemporary. One might fairly think of them as sharing a divided labor, the one appealing to the mid-Atlantic states and to the North, the other to the South.

The uncertainties of a cotton-based agriculture on exhausted soils and in competition with new lands to the west made the search for alternative crops a familiar business in the seaboard states of the South. Viticulture was a frequently suggested possibility, and, as we have seen, the legislatures of both Carolinas supported experiments that would, it was hoped, bring it into being. Herbemont had his own special ideas about the public usefulness of a winegrowing industry. He was frightened by the future of a South with a slave population whose occupation—cotton—was disappearing from the older regions. What would happen if the slave population continued to grow while the work for which it was destined continued to diminish? What was wanted was a new industry—winegrowing—and a new kind of labor—"suitable labourers from Europe."[113]

In 1827 Herbemont presented his ideas to the South Carolina senate in the form of a memorial urging that the state subsidize the emigration of "a number of *vignerons* from France, Italy, Germany and Switzerland" who could be established in small communities throughout the state to turn the unprofitable pine barrens and sand hills into rich vineyards. The idea is one familiar from the beginning of southern colonization, but this time, at least, Herbemont recognized that European practices could not be simply transferred unchanged to the United States: "Experience has shown, that the mode of cultivation must be very different here from what it is in Europe." Nevertheless, Europeans could be quickly taught, and would then form a source of labor fit to carry out the agricultural transformation of the state.

The senate received the memorial with murmurs of praise for the "unwearied perserverance, untiring industry, and botanical research of the memorialist," but noted with regret that the state of the treasury would not allow the scheme to be acted on.[114]

A comparable scheme had been submitted to the South Carolina legislature a few years earlier by two promoters named Antonio Della Torre and James C. W. McDonnald. They proposed in 1825 to bring over Italian farmers—"a well conducted free white body of labourers"—to introduce the cultivation of that classic triad in the dream of American prosperity, wine, silk, and oil. Forty thousand dollars, they thought, would be enough to meet expenses through the necessary waiting time before profits started to roll in. Except that the language of their memorial is in a later idiom, one might be reading a prospectus of the sixteenth century—with the difference that the nineteenth-century visionaries were aware of earlier failures. These, however, were easily explained away, and appeal made to the unanswerable evidence of the native vine: "Your memorialists . . . feel assured also that the Great Author of nature would not have caused festoons of the wild grape to adorn many parts of this state, if He intended to declare—'this shall not be a wine country.'"[115] To this theological argument the legislature was politely respectful, but it did not see fit to support the faith with $40,000.

In Georgia, too, winemaking was thought of as a possible way out of agricultural depression. The committee on agriculture of the Georgia legislature reported in 1828 that the desirable commodities of which there was hope were—wine, silk, and oil! The persistence of the original vision, intact, after all the years since the colony's founding says much about the power of the wish over experience. But the committee had, it said, evidence that "very good wine was made in the state as early as 1740."[116] Is it possible that the evidence was that pathetic single bottle of Savannah wine presented to Oglethorpe by Stephens (see above, p. 51)?

Any genuine evidence in favor of the practicability of winegrowing in Georgia would have come from the examples of enthusiastic amateurs. The best known was General Thomas McCall, who, since 1816, had been tending a vineyard on piney land in Laurens County and making wine in small commercial quantities. His experience, which recapitulates the general American pattern, is interesting partly because it went back so far. McCall had known Andrew Estave, the Frenchman who directed the luckless public vineyard at Williamsburg in the early 1770s; McCall also read and made use of St. Pierre's *Art of Planting and Cultivating the Vine*.[117] He thus bridges the gap between the unbroken failures of prerevolutionary efforts and the tentative successes of the early nineteenth century. McCall, like everyone else, first planted vinifera grapes; when they failed, he fell back upon native vines, particularly one he called Warrenton, now identified as Herbemont. From a local fox grape he also made a wine with the delightful name of "Blue Favorite."[118] McCall had a technician's turn of mind: he kept careful notes on weather and on his winemaking procedures, and contributed an essential improvement to technique by making use, for the first time in the American record at any rate, of a hydrometer to measure sugar content and so make possible accurate adjustment of the must.[119] This was a great and necessary development if well-balanced, light, dry table wines were ever to displace the over-sugared, brandy-bolstered confections that appear to have been the standard of such wine as Americans had contrived to make. The reputation of McCall's wines was such that the governor, in his message to the legislature in 1827, proposed that the state subsidize their production as a basis for a larger industry.[120] When he began his efforts, McCall said, he had for many years been unable to make "a single convert to the faith . . . they call me a visionary, and other names, as a reward for my endeavours."[121] In time, he succeeded in interesting other amateurs to dabble in winemaking, and there was a period in the 1820s and early 1830s when Georgian connoisseurs were beginning to talk boastfully about the select vintages of their state. The impulse died with the individuals who imparted it, however; another generation would pass before anything resembling a continuing industry arose.

In 1830, at Philadelphia, the eccentric and unfortunate botanist and savant-of-all-trades, Constantine Rafinesque, born in Constantinople, but long resident in the United States, published the second volume of his *Medical Flora,* a comprehensive treatise on the plants of North America having pharmaceutical value. Rafinesque, an original but undisciplined observer, who died in obscure poverty in the next decade, and whose classifications are the despair of later students, included in his work a long treatise on *Vitis,* with special reference to American vines and American conditions. He had, he tells us, worked in the vineyards of Adlum at Georgetown in preparation for his opus,[122] and he evidently thought highly enough of the sixty-odd pages that he devoted to the subject in his comprehensive treatise to republish them separately in the same year under the title of an *American Manual of Grape Vines and the Method of Making Wine.* Though his classifications are fanciful, and his advice on winemaking of no particular originality, Rafinesque obviously cared much about the possibilities of winegrowing in this country, and took the trouble to survey the state of the industry not once but twice, first in 1825 and again in 1830.[123] It is this information that still gives his curious treatise some authority after a century and a half have lapsed.

Dufour, we remember, had surveyed American grape growing at the end of the eighteenth century, and had found scarcely a single vineyard worthy of the name from New York to St. Louis. The changes made in the next quarter of a century are indicated by Rafinesque's summary. In 1825, he learned, there were not more than sixty vineyards to be found in the entire country, ranging from one to twenty acres, and aggregating not more than six hundred acres altogether. That was just after Adlum's introduction of the Catawba, the plantings of the Dutchmen around York, and the experiments of McCall, Herbemont, and others in the South; their contributions had not yet had their chance to take effect. Five years later, in 1830, Rafinesque found that the pace of things had accelerated in unmistakable fashion. There were then, he reported, two hundred vineyards of from three to forty acres, making a total of five thousand acres—a miniscule amount measured

37 | Among his many interests, the unfortunate Constantine Rafinesque (1783–1840) paid special attention to grapes and wine. He worked in John Adlum's vineyard to gain experience, published an *American Manual of Grape Vines and the Method of Making Wine*, and made two surveys of American winegrowing activity. Rafinesque was an inveterate traveller and writer. His main work was in botany and ichthyology, but he taught modern languages, worked as a merchant, and wrote on banking, economics, and the Bible before his death as a neglected pauper. (From Rafinesque, "A Life of Travels," *Chronica Botanica* 8, no. 2 [1944])

against the undeveloped expanses of the United States, but still an impressive increase in a mere five years, testifying to a new confidence and a new sort of success in viticulture, so long attempted and so long frustrated in this country. Approximate and even doubtful as Rafinesque's figures are, they are at least symbolically valid as an expression of what was happening at last in the first part of the nineteenth century. As an act of piety towards the pioneers, Rafinesque set down the names of the vineyardists who had done the work: in New York, Gibbs, Prince, and Loubat; in Pennsylvania, Legaux, Eichelberger, Carr, Webb; in Maryland, Adlum; in Virginia, Lockhart, Weir, and Noel. The list goes on and does not bear quoting in full. But it marks the first time that such a thing could have been compiled, and for us it marks the point from which the growth of an industry can be measured. There have been many changes, diversions, obstructions, and failures since Rafinesque compiled his list, but there has not, since then, been any further doubt that the work of winegrowing in this country was a permanent fact rather than a prophecy—at least so far as nature's assent is concerned.

7

The Spread of
Commercial Winegrowing

Nicholas Longworth and
the Cincinnati Region

T he defrauded settlers at Gallipolis, the nameless Frenchman making wine at Marietta, Rapp's Germans at Economy, Dufour's Swiss at Vevay, and all the other earliest
winemaking settlers along the banks of the Ohio, from Pittsburgh almost to the
junction with the Mississippi, were vindicated at last by the success of Nicholas
Longworth at Cincinnati. As the main highway from east to west during the period
of early settlement, the Ohio had inevitably seen repeated trials of viticulture, suggested by the combination of southward-facing slopes and broad waters. Dufour,
as early as 1801, had assured Congress that the Ohio would rival the Rhine; it has
never done so, but it was the scene of the first considerable wine production in this
country, flourishing around Cincinnati from the early 1830s till after the Civil War,
and unashamedly flaunting the naive slogan "The Rhineland of America."[1] An account of what lay behind this too-ready formula is instructive as to the chances and
changes of commercial winegrowing in the era when useful native varieties had
been found but before effective controls against diseases had been discovered.

The first person to plant a vineyard on the site now occupied by Cincinnati, on
the great double curve of the Ohio, was a Frenchman named Francis Menissier, a
political refugee who had once sat in the French *parlement*. At the end of the eighteenth century he laid out a small vineyard of vinifera on a slope of the new town
(now the corner of Main and Third).[2] There he had success enough—or claimed
that he had—to petition Congress in 1806 for a grant of land for vine growing on

the strength of his experiments.[3] The petition was denied, but Menissier's example was not lost.

In 1804 a young man named Nicholas Longworth (1782–1863) arrived in Cincinnati from Newark, New Jersey, to make his fortune in this new and burgeoning town, soon to be a city.[4] Longworth had already discovered a consuming interest in horticulture, but he put that aside while he studied law and began a successful practice. He soon found himself doing even better in land than in the law, and in no very long time he was recognized as having the true Midas touch: property that he bought for a song became worth millions, and Longworth joined John Jacob Astor as one of the two largest taxpayers in the United States. Longworth was a little man, and eccentric in dress, speech, and manner. But he was also strong-willed and successful, so that he could afford to do as he wished. By 1828 he was able to quit a regular business life and devote himself to his horticultural interests. These were fairly wide—he helped to establish the scientific culture of the strawberry, for example—but his first and most enduring love was the grape.

His attention was caught by the work of the Swiss at Vevay, and as early as 1813 Longworth had begun to experiment with grape growing in a backyard way—this was even before the return of Dufour from his long European sojourn.[5] His first commercial beginnings, in 1823,[6] were with the grape grown at Vevay, that is, the Cape or Alexander, which Longworth set out on a four-acre vineyard in Delhi township under the care of a German named Amen or Ammen. Longworth had the idea—a good one—that by making a white rather than a red wine from the Alexander he might get an article superior to that which the Swiss were selling along the Ohio. What he got, according to his own recollection, was a tolerable imitation of madeira, a white wine that required amelioration with added sugar and fortification with brandy.[7]

That was not what he wanted. The next step—again, as in the case of so many other pioneers, we recapitulate in miniature the general history of vine growing in America—was to try European varieties. He planted these by the thousands, from all sources, over a period of thirty years, and did not publicly repudiate the possibility of using vinifera until 1849.[8] He saw, however, that the development of good native varieties was the most important job to be done. He never faltered in that conviction, and even after his success with the wines of the Catawba, he continued to offer a $500 reward for a variety that would surpass that grape for winemaking.[9] He received and made trial of native vines from all over the United States, but did not succeed in finding a new variety to eclipse the Catawba.

Longworth's primary object was the production of an attractive dry table wine from the native grape, both in the name of "temperance" (already a rallying-cry among the moralists of the United States) and because such wine is the necessary basis of any sound winemaking industry in any country. The American idea of wine was, in Longworth's judgment, thoroughly corrupt: the wine favored by a public without a native winegrowing tradition, and long accustomed to rum and

38 Nicholas Longworth (1782–1863), the man who made Cincinnati and the banks of the Ohio the "Rhineland of America," at the height of his reputation as the leading Ameri-can winemaker. The Catawba grapes on the table and the vineyards in the background are the emblems of Longworth's achievement. (Portrait by Robert S. Duncanson, 1858; Cincinnati Art Museum)

whiskey, generally contained 25 percent alcohol, and, Longworth added, "I have seen it contain forty percent."[10] After his unsatisfactory trials with the Alexander and with imported vinifera, Longworth got his chance when Major Adlum provided him with cuttings of the Catawba in 1825. Why Longworth should have been so slow to respond to this possibility I do not know: he must have known of the new grape as early as 1823, when Adlum began to publicize it. In any case, 1825 is the date of record.[11] Precisely when he got his first wines from the Catawba is not clear. But by 1828, the year in which he retired to devote himself to winegrowing, he was already well embarked on the plan with which he persisted through the rest of his life. Young Thomas Trollope, the brother of the novelist, who had accompanied his family to Cincinnati in 1828 on its hare-brained scheme for a frontier emporium selling exotic bijoux, made Longworth's acquaintance then and remembered him as "extremely willing to talk exclusively on schemes for the introduction of the vine into the Western States."[12] Young Trollope's mother, the redoubtable Frances, was quite unflattering about the wine of Cincinnati. A note to her *Domestic Manners of the Americans* (1832) provides what may be the first published judgment on Longworth's wines. It is not encouraging:

> During my residence in America, I repeatedly tasted native wine from vineyards carefully cultivated, and on the fabrication of which a considerable degree of imported science had been bestowed; but the very best of it was miserable stuff. It should seem that Nature herself requires some centuries of schooling before she becomes perfectly accomplished in ministering to the luxuries of man, and, perhaps as there is no lack of sunshine, the champagne and Bordeaux of the Union may appear simultaneously with a Shakspeare, a Raphael, and a Mozart.[13]

The basis of Longworth's plan for viticulture was to make use of—or exploit—the labor of the German immigrants flowing into the Cincinnati region and giving it that German flavor that it still retains. When Trollope knew him, Longworth was employing Germans to cultivate vineyards on his own estate at a wage of a shilling a day (Trollope's figure) and food—a peonage advantageous to Longworth and perhaps tolerable to the new immigrants.[14] The Germans were in fact doubly necessary: they not only grew and made the wine, they drank it as well. The dry white catawba that Longworth succeeded in making was unappreciated by Americans used to sweeter and more potent confections; Longworth used to tell about how even the choicest *Rheingaus* were mistaken by American tasters for cider or even vinegar. The Germans, however, were better instructed, and for many years, Longworth wrote, "all the wine made at my vineyards, has been sold at our German coffee-houses, and drank in our city."[15]

Like all American winegrowers before him and afterwards, Longworth was troubled by the tendency of Americans to prefer wines with European names to those that were honestly, but too adventurously, given names that meant nothing to an uninstructed consumer: "catawba" was dubious at best; "hock" meant familiarity and security. So, at some time in the 1830s, he wickedly put counterfeit labels on his bottles of catawba: *Ganz Vorzuglicher* (Entirely Superior); Berg Tusculum (Mount Tusculum, after the actual name of one of his vineyard sites); and *Versichert* (Guaranteed).[16] He did not actually put these labels on the market, but they helped to make his point—still a familiar one—that there were many who could not abide native wine under its own label but who acclaimed it under a foreign one.

Longworth continued, as he had begun, with his system of using German labor, though the terms became more liberal than those described by Trollope in 1828. Typically, Longworth sought to settle a German *Weinbauer* on a small

JOHN P FOOTE.   A.H.ERNST.   F.PENTLAND.   S.S.JACKSON.   J.SAYER.   DF J.A.WARDER.
E.J.HOOPER.

GABRIEL SLEATH. GEO.GRAHAM. R.BUCHANAN.   N.LONGWORTH.

39 | Members of the Cincinnati Horticultural Society, founded in 1843. At least three of these men—Dr. J. A. Warder, Robert Buchanan, and Nicholas Longworth—were leading winegrowers in Cincinnati. Note the grapes prominent among the fruits displayed on the table. (Cincinnati Historical Society)

patch—four acres at most—and to leave him to himself to plant and cultivate. When a crop came in, Longworth would buy the grapes or the must or the wine, and split the profits with his tenant.[17] As the business developed, more and more of the processing went on under Longworth's own control, but the growing continued to be the business of the Germans, who had, as he said, been "bred from their infancy to the cultivation of the vine."

Longworth's earliest public account of his work in winegrowing appears to be an essay he contributed to a local compendium of agricultural advice published in Cincinnati in 1830, in which he urged that silk culture, the perennial rival of viticulture in the American dream, ought to be postponed in favor of the grape, and gave his own experience as his reason for thinking so.[18] In succeeding years the increasing number, frequency, and prominence of his contributions to the press on winegrowing provide an approximate measure of his growing success and recognition. His writings remained irregular and scattered, usually taking the form of letters addressed to particular topics, but they helped to make him the best-known and most frequently consulted expert on the subject of wine in his generation.

Longworth's scale of operations remained small through the 1830s; in 1833, for example, when he took the County Fair prize for his "pure Catawba," the produce of the nine scattered vineyards on which he had tenants was only fifty barrels, or about 3,000 gallons.[19] The development of viticulture in the ensuing ten years is witnessed by the establishment of the Cincinnati Horticultural Society in 1843; it at once took an interest in winegrowing, and made its first report on the subject in the year of its founding.[20]

The explosive expansion of the industry occurred after 1842, when Longworth, quite by accident, produced a sparkling catawba (as it was always called: never "champagne").[21] Even if he did not know how to make one, Longworth decided that a sparkling wine would be his means of opening a market beyond the *Weinstuben* of Cincinnati. After trying and failing to duplicate his first accidental success, he sent for a Frenchman in 1845. Unluckily, the poor man drowned in the Ohio before he could apply the secrets of his knowledge. Longworth found a successor, who commenced his work in 1847. Though the winemaker was French, Longworth was quite firm about his intent to develop a native wine. "I shall not attempt to imitate any of the sparkling wines of Europe," he wrote in 1849; instead, he aimed to provide "a pure article having the peculiar flavor of our native grape."[22]

By 1848 Longworth had built a 40' x 50' cellar expressly for the production and storage of sparkling catawba; by 1850 he was turning out 60,000 bottles a year and had plans for national distribution of his wine. This he began in 1852, by which year he had two cellars devoted to his sparkling wine, and a production of around 75,000 bottles.[23] The wine was made by the traditional *méthode champenoise,* in which, after a dose of sugar was added to the wine following its first fermentation, a second fermentation was carried out in the bottles, and the resulting sediment cleared by the tedious process of hand riddling. Losses from bottles bursting under the intense pressure of fermentation were sometimes catastrophically high: when 42,000 of 50,000 bottles were thus lost in a season, Longworth naturally wondered whether it was worth continuing.[24] Something, however, was saved from these losses by distilling the spilled wine into catawba brandy, as a brochure put out by Longworth's firm innocently admits.[25]

A third cellar manager, one Fournier, from Rheims, arrived in 1851 and did better.[26] The troubles and losses of the first years were rewarded; if Americans had been put off by the tart, dry taste of still catawba, they knew without instruction how to be pleased by bubbles. Suddenly, Cincinnati's winegrowers, and Longworth in particular, had a national winner, a widely advertised and widely enjoyed proof that the United States could produce an acceptable wine.

Longworth thoroughly understood the value of advertising. His letters to the press were progress reports on the promising development of his enterprise. He sent his wine to editors and to the competitions of horticultural and state agricultural societies: as early as 1846 he was exhibiting samples of catawba at the annual fair of the American Institute in New York City.[27] In common with a number of other Cincinnati producers, he sent samples of his wine to the Great Exhibition of

1851 in London, the original ancestor of and the model for all subsequent international exhibitions and fairs. The produce of native American grapes was, of course, powerfully strange to British palates; as the official *Catalogue* of the Exhibition politely remarked, "With many persons the taste for [catawba] is very soon acquired, with others it requires considerable time."[28] The publicity was bound to be helpful back in the United States. One of the great sensations of the Exhibition, the demurely naked *Greek Slave* of the American sculptor Hiram Powers, was the source of immense national pride in the United States when it was known that the British admired the piece. Powers, as it happened, was a Cincinnati boy whose first patron had been Longworth, another well-publicized fact that helped put Longworth in an attractive light—was he not domesticating both Bacchus and the Muses?[29]

Longworth also sent samples of his wine to eminent men as a way of promoting it. Powers, in Italy, was a useful agent in presenting catawba to politely interested Italians. Perhaps it was during his years in Italy that the poet Robert Browning heard of catawba wine. He knew of it, at any rate, for it is referred to in his curious poem "Mr. Sludge, the Medium" (1864).[30] Longworth made a lucky hit with the poet Longfellow, who responded to a gift of sparkling catawba with some hasty verses (injudiciously included in his collected poems) that have often been reprinted since. A very few lines are enough to show such merit as the poem possesses:

> Very good in its way
> Is the Verzenay
> Or the Sillery soft and creamy;
>   But Catawba wine
>   Has a taste more divine,
> More dulcet, delicious, and dreamy.
>
> There grows no vine
> By the haunted Rhine
> By Danube or Guadalquivir,
>   Nor on island or cape
>   That bears such a grape
> As grows by the Beautiful River.[31]

In 1855 Longworth was able to boast that he had sent a few cases of his wine to London, where it had been successfully sold in the regular way of trade.[32] By this time, Longworth, his large house called Belmont, on Pike Street, adorned with the work of Powers, and his vineyards on a hill (now part of Eden Park) had long been established as premier attractions among the sights of Cincinnati, to be exhibited to all the many interested travellers who made their way to the Queen City of the Ohio before the Civil War.[33] Longworth was a national figure, celebrated for his wealth, his wine, and, most of all, for being a "character," shabbily dressed, laconic, unpredictable, and—according to the press at any rate—prodigal of charity. The English journalist Charles Mackay, travelling through the United States as the correspondent of the *Illustrated London News* in 1858, will do to represent many

40 | Longworth's vineyards recorded in 1858, perhaps more after the fashion of European models than as unadorned documentary truth. The steamboat and the train represent American progress, but the style of the *vendangeurs* and *vendangeuses* is distinctly Old World, as is the single-stake training of the vines, like that practiced on the Moselle and the Rhine. (From *Harper's Weekly*, 24 July 1858)

others. Cincinnati did not impress him as quite so enlightened a place as its inhabitants liked to think; as they had been to Mrs. Trollope thirty years earlier, pigs were too much in evidence for Mackay's taste, those pigs that, barreled as pickled pork and shipped up and down the river, gave Cincinnati the name of Porkopolis and made it wealthy. Longworth and his wine moved Mackay's unreserved admiration, however; dry catawba, he reported to the English, was better than any hock, and sparkling catawba better than anything coming from Rheims. When prose seemed inadequate to his rapture, Mackay (a facile song writer) broke forth into verse:

> Ohio's green hilltops
>   Grow bright in the sun
> And yield us more treasure
>   Than Rhine or Garonne;
> They give us Catawba,
>   The pure and the true,
> As radiant as sunlight,
>   As soft as the dew.[34]

Not everyone was so well pleased by Cincinnati's wines: the native character of the Catawba, its labrusca foxiness, was a shock to any uninitiated taste, and some visitors were candid enough to say so. When the Englishwoman Isabella

WINE LIST.

Each Waiter is provided with Wine Cards & Pencil.

Champagne.

Schreider,	$2 00
Heidseick,	2 00
Mumm's Cabinet,	2 50
Longworth, Bogen and Park's	
Sparkling Catawba,	2 00

Port.

Old Brazil Port,	2 00
Roriz,	2 50
Offley's Old Port, most choice,	2 00

Madeira.

Symington's,	1 50
Extra choice London particular	2 50
Pure Juice,	2 50
Jenny Lind;	2 50

Sherry.

Reigbedere's Brown Sherry,	2 50
Harmony Pale,	1 50
Ramano's Brown Vintage of	
1798, very dry & not strong,	3 00
Amontillado,	2 00

Hock.

Marcobrunner,	2 50
Rudesheimer,	3 00
Cabinet Rothenberg, 1842,	2 50
Buchanan's Catawba,	1 00
Sparkling Hock,	2 50
Park's Catawba,	1 50

Burgundy.

Glos de Vougeot,	2 00
Chambertin,	1 00
Romanee,	6 00
Sparkling Burgundy, St. Peray	2 00

Claret.

St. Julien, 1846,	75
Medoc Pouillac,	1 00
St. Estephe,	50
Chateaux Margeaux,	1 50
Chateau La Rose,	2 00
Chateau La Rose, 1844,	3 00
Mouton, 1844,	1 50
Palmer Margeaux,	2 00
Chateau Lafitte,	3 50

LIQUORS, ALE AND PORTER.

REGULATIONS.

Children occupying seats at the first table, will be charged full price.

An extra charge for meals sent to rooms.

Persons having extra meals, will please make known at the office.

Guests of the House leaving by the Morning Cars, will make it known at the office the evening previous. Those going by the afternoon Cars, will give early notice, so that their baggage may be aetende to.

An Omnibus in attendance to convey Passengers to each Train of Cars.

41   A menu from the Gibson House, Cincinnati, dated 15 November 1856. Sparkling Catawba from the local vineyards is listed on the same terms as some distinguished *grandes marques* from Champagne; so, too, among the "Hocks," one finds "Buchanan's Catawba" listed along with Marcobrunner and Rudesheimer. (California State University, Fresno, Library)

Trotter and her husband visited Cincinnati in 1858, almost at the same time as the well-disposed Mackay had been entertained there, they were regaled by their hosts with "most copious supplies of their beloved Catawba champagne, which we do not love, for it tastes, to our uninitiated palates, little better than cider. It was served in a large red punch-bowl of Bohemian glass in the form of Catawba cobbler, which I thought improved it."[35] To balance the record, one may quote a more enthusiastic description of catawba cobbler, provided by the Cincinnati wine-grower W. J. Flagg. The wine, he says, should be young, and sugar and ice added to it help to temper the heat of an Ohio valley summer: "A cobbler of new wine, grown in the valley of the Ohio, or Missouri, where the Catawba ripens almost to blackness, drunk when the dog-star rages, lingers in memory for life."[36]

Longworth was always the leading name in Cincinnati winemaking, and sparkling catawba was always the glamorous item. But they could not have long stood alone, and in fact a supporting industry developed quickly. Longworth's part of the whole diminished in proportion as others set up and began to develop their vineyards and wineries. In 1848 there were 300 acres planted, of which 100 were Longworth's; in 1852, there were 1,200, distributed among nearly 300 proprietors and tenants. In 1859, perhaps the peak year in the history of Cincinnati wine-growing, some 2,000 acres produced 568,000 gallons of wine, putting Ohio at the head of the nation's wine production.[37] Almost all of this was white, and almost all from the Catawba, which was now indisputably confirmed as the grape of the region. But it did not quite exclude all its rivals. In 1854, at the New York Exhibition of that year, it was Longworth's sparkling Isabella that took the highest award among American wines.[38]

Among the early growers who followed Longworth into viticulture were Robert Buchanan, John Mottier, William Resor, C. W. Elliott, A. H. Ernst, and a string of doctors: Stephen Mosher, Louis Rehfuss, and John Aston Warder, the last-named becoming later one of the country's most distinguished horticulturists. Not all of them were actual Cincinnatians; at least, not all of them confined their activity to Cincinnati proper. Dr. Mosher, for example, lived and grew his grapes on the Kentucky side of the river, as did others, including the actor Edwin Forrest.[39] Other vineyards in Ohio lay outside Hamilton County, in which Cincinnati stands; vineyards flourished in Brown and Clermont counties, and extended down the river well into Indiana at least in a minor way, and sometimes in more than a minor way. Clark County, Indiana, across the river from Louisville, had 200 acres of Catawba by 1850, and the calculations of the production along the Ohio included the grapes of Kentucky and Indiana as significant additions to those of the immediate Cincinnati region.[40]

Like Longworth, most of the Ohio River proprietors seem to have relied upon tenants, German by choice, to perform the labor in the vineyards (and then it was usually the woman rather than the man who did the work, as Longworth was fond of pointing out).[41] At this uncertain stage, only a man who had other resources could sustain the vicissitudes of such a pioneering enterprise. The actual wine-making was carried out on the tenanted properties in the early days, with predictably uneven results. As production rose, and the reputation of the wine began to be established, winemaking came increasingly under the control of commercial houses whose business it was to perform the vinification, storage, and distribution of the wine. By 1854 Longworth had two such houses; over his main cellars he had built a sort of barracks, four stories high, where poor laborers and their families might live. They showed their gratitude by frequently breaking into the wine vaults below and stealing their landlord's choicest wine, or so it was reported.[42]

VIEW OF WINE HOUSE OF Mᴿ CORNEAU & SON
LATONIA, NEAR CINCINNATIO

42 A winery on the Kentucky side of the Ohio River, in the region of Cincinnati. The vintage scene in this picture is described thus: "The grapes, when fully ripe, are gathered in baskets containing about a bushel, as well as in a sort of 'pannier' of wood, made very light and strong, and which is supported by straps or thongs of willow, on the back of the picker; . . . they are brought from the vineyard in this manner and thrown upon the picking tables, where they are carefully assorted." (*Western Horticultural Review* 1 [1850])

Other *négociants,* as the French would call them, were G. and P. Bogen, Zimmerman and Co. (associated with Longworth), Dr. Louis Rehfuss, and, in Latonia, Kentucky, the firm of Messrs. Corneau and Son at their Cornucopia Vineyard, some four miles south of Covington, across the river from Cincinnati. The figures for 1853, a good year, give some idea of the scale of production. The commercial houses bottled 245,000 bottles of sparkling wine in that year, and 205,000 of still wine, the value of the whole being estimated at $400,000 at prices ranging from $1.50 a bottle for the finest sparkling wine to 40 cents a gallon for the lowest-quality table wine.[43]

The accounts of winemaking methods in Cincinnati show that the general practice in the 1850s was excellent. Longworth himself was emphatic about the necessity of making "natural" wines and confident of his ability to do so. He set a good example. Grapes were picked at full maturity, and all green or unsound berries were removed from the bunches by hand. The grapes were then stemmed

GREEN TOWNSHIP
NATIVE WINES

FOR SALE BY
M. WERK & CO.,
11 MAIN ST.
Cincinnati.
And at the cellars in Green Township.

I beg leave to recommend the above wines, as an agreeable and fine variety of the Sparkling and Still Catawbas of Ohio. They are steadily growing in favor on this side of the mountains, and at home bear a high reputation as wines of the very first class. They are for sale in single cases of one dozen quarts each, Sparkling at $13. Cases of two dozen pints Sparkling at $14, and the Still Catawba at $7 per dozen quarts, hock bottles. In quantities of five cases and upwards, a discount of 50 c. per case.

FRED. S. COZZENS,
Sole Agent, 73 Warren street, N. Y.

43 Michael Werk, an Alsatian who prospered by making soap and candles in Cincinnati, joined the growing number of Cincinnati vineyardists in 1847. In less than a decade he was taking prizes for his wines. Later, when disease threatened to extinguish the Cincinnati vineyards, Werk developed large vineyards on the Lake Erie shore and then on Middle Bass Island in Lake Erie. (*Cozzens' Wine Press*, 20 August 1856; California State University, Fresno, Library)

and crushed, and the juice fermented without the addition of sugar whenever possible. The French technique of rubbing the bunches over wooden grids in order to remove the stems was introduced by 1850.[44] The hydrometer was a standard tool, so that the winemaker knew whether he had sufficient sugar to insure a sound fermentation; if not, then the addition of sugar before fermentation was allowed— "allowed" by local agreement as to its utility, that is; we are talking about an industry in its Innocent Age, wholly unregulated and subject only to its own sweet will. Modern producers and dealers may try to imagine what that condition is like. The juice was fermented at low temperatures, under water seal, and quickly racked from its lees, without undue oxidation, and then stored in clean casks in cool cellars.[45] Modern technology could not prescribe better methods, so far as they went. One irregularity Longworth did, it was whispered, allow himself. He was convinced that Americans were partial to the "muscadine" flavor of rotundifolia grapes. In order to get it he bought large quantities of Scuppernong juice in the Pamlico and Albemarle regions of North Carolina and added that to flavor his Ohio catawba.[46] In the spring the wine may have undergone a malo-lactic fermentation, and then was ready for bottling. There was then, as there is now, some disagreement as to the proper length of aging for white wine. Longworth favored a long time in the wood, keeping his superior wines for four or five years. Others thought that a year in cask was enough: "There are many who think the Catawba wine is better at this period than ever afterwards" is how the writer in the U.S. Patent Office *Report* for 1850 puts it.[47]

Cincinnati wine may be said to have come of age at the beginning of the 1850s. The commercial wine houses, insuring the stability and distribution of the region's produce, were founded then. In 1851 the growers met in Cincinnati and organized the grandly named American Wine Growers' Association of Cincinnati. Its objects were to publish information useful to growers through its journal, the *Western Horticultural Review,* and to promote the interest of the industry generally, especially by insuring that only pure, natural wine was sent to the market.[48] The association sponsored a "Longworth Cup," awarded annually to the producer of that year's best catawba,[49] and was the first such organization concerned with wines and vines in this country that is entitled to be called an industry organization.[50]

At the Great Exhibition in London, to which, as has already been mentioned, the growers of Cincinnati made a respectable contribution, the official *Catalogue* explained that Cincinnati was now the "chief seat of wine manufacture in the United States" and that though yet in its infancy, the trade was "attracting much attention, and growing in importance in America."[51] In vindication of the claim, five producers besides Longworth exhibited specimens of catawba wine: Buchanan, Corneau and Son, Thomas H. Yeatman, C. A. Schumann, and H. Duhme. Yeatman, who took a prize for his wine in London, made visits to the vineyards and wine estates of France, Germany, and Switzerland in 1851 and 1852 in order to study European methods.[52] Longworth sent both catawba and unspecified "other wines" to the Exhibition—a reminder that he never ceased experimenting with alternatives to the Catawba grape in hopes of finding a variety without its defects. In the year following the Exhibition, Longworth began the promotion of his wine on a countrywide basis,[53] and with that event the wine of the Rhineland of America may be said to have arrived.

Cincinnati wine had only a very fragile tenure, however, more fragile than was yet recognized, though of course sensible men understood that the obstacles to be

44 The label of T. H. Yeatman, from the year in which his wine took a prize at the Great Exhibition, London. (*Western Horticultural Review* 1 [1851])

surmounted were considerable. Robert Buchanan, for example, a successful Cincinnati merchant who began growing grapes in 1843, and who, with Longworth, was a founder of the Cincinnati Horticultural Society and a scientific student of viticulture and winemaking, took a modest view of what he and his fellows had accomplished. In his little *Treatise on Grape Culture in Vineyards, in the Vicinity of Cincinnati* (1850), the best practical handbook that had yet appeared on the subject in the United States, he wrote simply that "we have *much* to learn yet in the art of making wines."[54] But, as we have seen, the general principles of production at Cincinnati were in fact quite sound. The real—and soon fatal—weakness in the industry lay in the vine growing rather than in the winemaking. The Catawba did not always ripen well, and the average production was not very large; it seems to have run around one and a half tons per acre, though production as high as four tons was known, and ten was claimed.

Most ominous was the damage done by diseases, powdery mildew and black rot chief among them. In the first years of Catawba growing, these diseases were

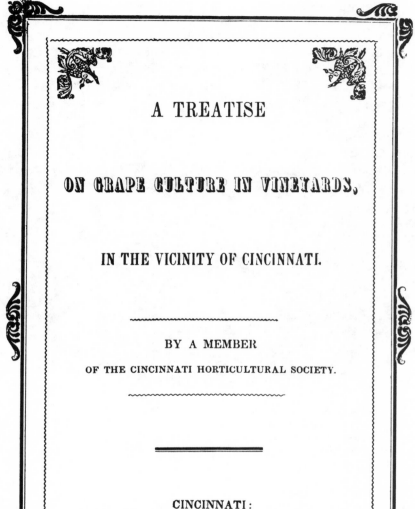

A TREATISE

ON GRAPE CULTURE IN VINEYARDS,

IN THE VICINITY OF CINCINNATI.

BY A MEMBER

OF THE CINCINNATI HORTICULTURAL SOCIETY.

CINCINNATI:

PRINTED BY WRIGHT, FERRIS, & CO.

SOLD BY J. F. DESILVER, MAIN STREET, AND D. M'AVOY,

SEEDSMAN, FIFTH STREET.

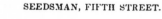

1850.

45 Robert Buchanan's little book, first published anonymously, is one of the earliest and best accounts of winegrowing around Cincinnati. Buchanan, a Cincinnati merchant, had had a vineyard since 1843. His book, which went through seven editions in the next ten years, was unlike any of its American predecessors in being based on the practices of an established industry. No writer in this country before Buchanan had had that advantage. (California State University, Fresno, Library)

only a minor problem in the Cincinnati region, so that the early confident assurances of the unchecked profits to be made by viticulture seemed perfectly justified. But the growth of planting and the passage of years saw mildew and black rot
increasingly more frequent, as they had a homogeneous and extensive population
of grapes to work upon. The record of each successive year's vintage, so far as this
can be reconstructed, shows alarming ups and downs according to the lightness or
the heaviness with which the infestations, especially black rot, struck the vineyards
in a given year.[55] Even before 1850 black rot and mildew were evident, and the
growers were unable to take any action against them. The fungous character of the
rot was not generally understood—some attributed the disease to worms, some to
cultivating methods, others to the atmosphere or to a wrongly chosen soil[56]—and
so when the Catawba, a variety peculiarly susceptible, was touched by the blight,
all that men could do was to resign themselves to their loss and speculate on the
causes and cures.

Among the other diseases that attacked Ohio grapes, powdery mildew was the
most important after black rot. This disease, native to the United States, first attracted serious attention not in its native place but after it had been exported to the
Old World. In the 1850s Madeira saw its vines, upon which nearly the whole
population depended, ravaged by powdery mildew (generally called *oidium* in Europe). The people of the island, driven to starvation, were forced to abandon their
homes and to emigrate in large numbers. The island's wine trade has never fully
recovered from the catastrophe—made more bitter still by the fact that it came
from the country where Madeira's wines were held in esteem beyond all others.
But Madeira was only the worst-afflicted among many: Portugal, Spain, France,
and Italy suffered too. In Italy, the appearance of the disease coincided with that of
the first railroads. Peasants, putting these things together, blocked new construc-
tion and tore up miles of rails already laid in order to fight the disease.[57]

The control of powdery mildew by sulfur dusting was now successfully tested
and developed in Europe, but it did little for the growers of Cincinnati. Native
vines, unlike vinifera, are sometimes injured by sulfur, so the cure in this case
might not have been much preferable to the disease. Against black rot, even the
most perfect application of sulfur would have had no effect. For that disease the
effective treatment is a compound of copper sulphate and lime called bordeaux
mixture, and that was not developed until 1885, much too late to be of use to the
growers of Cincinnati.

Throughout the 1850s rot and mildew were increasingly present in the vineyards of Cincinnati. In that decade, only three good years—1853, 1858, and 1859—
were granted to the growers by weather conditions inhibiting the rot.[58] By the end
of the decade it was clear that the very existence of the industry was now problematical, for who could endure such helplessness and such uncertainty? Some efforts
were made to introduce different and more resistant varieties—the Delaware, for
example, seemed at one time to promise a better basis for viticulture, but it did not
fulfill the promise. Ives' Seedling, a local introduction that had gained the premium

offered by Longworth's Wine House for the "best wine grape for the United States," also had some vogue, but was not good enough for wine or resistant enough to disease to provide a new basis for the trade.[59] The outbreak of the Civil War reinforced and accelerated the process begun by diseases. Though shortages brought high prices for wine, the vineyards were neglected, and new plantings ceased. A visitor to Cincinnati in 1867 reported that "the wine culture" was "somewhat out of favor at present among the farmers of Ohio."[60] By 1870 the vineyards, though still occupying a substantial acreage, were largely moribund. In that year, the brief flourishing of the Rhineland of America came to a symbolic close when Longworth's wine-bottling warehouse was taken over by an oil refinery.[61]

Longworth himself lived long enough to see the end coming, but refused to admit its certainty. As W. J. Flagg, his son-in-law and the manager of his wine business, wrote of Longworth at the end: "It was well enough he should pass away without knowing how nearly had failed the great work of his life. Among his last words before losing consciousness was an inquiry if [Flagg] had arrived: he wanted to tell him, he said, of a new vine he had found which would neither mildew nor rot. He never found it in this world."[62] The extinction of viticulture around Cincinnati was complete, and so powerful was the effect of the failure that even when, later, it became possible to control the diseases that had overwhelmed the vineyards, no one came forward to take the opportunity. Only in very recent years have tentative efforts been made to revive the industry there: more than a century has been needlessly lost in the interval.

Yet there *had*, after all, been a flourishing winemaking industry in Cincinnati: to show the possibility of such a thing was the historical importance of Longworth and his fellow growers. After many years of loss, Longworth had, before the end, even made money from winegrowing, and the possibility of doing so again waited only upon better cultivars and effective fungicides.

Meantime, the Cincinnati region had generated a sort of colonial extension of itself upon the shores and islands of Lake Erie, two hundred miles to the north. As early as 1830 a gentleman named H. O. Coit was growing vines and making wine in Cleveland, and he prophesied then that the shores of Lake Erie would someday be famous for their vineyards.[63] The success of viticulture along the Ohio River stimulated experiment with Catawba and other varieties along the lake shore in the 1830s. But it was not until late in the 1840s that anything like a commercial scale of viticulture was approached in this region. Northern Ohio had two centers of grape growing, from Cleveland eastward to the Pennsylvania border on one side of the state, and around Sandusky and the Lake Erie Islands on the other. It was in the second of these that winemaking particularly flourished. Here it was discovered that an ideal matching of variety and site had been stumbled upon: the limestone soil of lake shore and islands is classic grape-growing soil; the delayed springs and protracted autumns that the moderating effect of the lake brings to the islands just suited the Catawba; there, too, the diseases that destroyed the Catawba along the Ohio River did not pursue it with the same destructive effects. There has been an

OHIO WINE COMPANY;

MARTIN'S FERRY, BELMONT COUNTY, OHIO.

REV. AND DEAR SIR:

*Having given close observation and study to the preservation of the product of the grape in various portions of the United States for twenty years, I feel justified in the conclusion that this portion of the Ohio Valley, with its fertile and rolling hills, gives a more **perfect** basis for a pure and good article of Wine than to be had in **any** other locality.*

*Upon the result of my experiments, we have erected here **one** of the largest and best adapted cellars in the United States, for **the preservation** of wine made from grapes grown in this immediate **vicinity**.*

*In full sympathy with the reverend Clergy, required to take wine while fasting, particular attention has been given, not only **to** the pure condition of our production, but also to its preservative **qualities**, as our large supply constantly on hand enables us to send only the thoroughly prepared by age.*

Where personal attention or reliable care cannot be given, we respectfully suggest to order by case of one, two, or three dozen, particularly for Altar purposes, as the use of well preserved wine, WHILE FASTING, *will save many physical infirmities.*

Give one case of our Altar Wine a trial, and if this observation is not found correct, we will forfeit the hope of future orders.

Most Respectfully,

WM. LIPPHARDT.

---

3 year old White Wine (Catawba), per Gallon,		$1.25.
3 " " " " " " Case of 12 Bottles,		4.50.
3 " " Claret " (American), " Gallon,		1.20.
3 " " " " " " Case of 12 Bottles,		4.50.

46   Not all Ohio winegrowing was confined to Cincinnati or to the Lake Erie shores; this undated (c. 1850) trade circular offers altar wine from Martin's Ferry in far southeastern Ohio, just across the river from Wheeling, West Virginia. Noah Zane, the founder of Wheeling, is credited with having introduced grape culture to the region. (California State University, Fresno, Library)

uninterrupted history of Catawba growing on Kelley's Island and the Bass Islands since the first vineyards were set out, a record of continuity unmatched in the erratic history of American viticulture.[64]

So long as the Cincinnati region prospered, development along Lake Erie was not notably rapid. The boom commenced as the Cincinnati industry declined: large plantings began just before 1860, and the years 1860–70 were remembered as the era of "grape fever."[65] Seven thousand acres had been planted by 1867, and though growth inevitably slowed, there were 33,000 acres in Ohio by 1889, most of it in the Lake Erie counties. The growers, as at Cincinnati, were largely Germans; indeed, some of them were Cincinnati Germans looking for alternatives to the disease-ridden banks of the Ohio.[66]

The Missouri Germans

Cincinnati had sent out its influences in another direction too—down the Ohio to the Mississippi, up that river to St. Louis, and thence upstream along the Missouri to the German settlement of Hermann. Winegrowing of one kind or another was already a venerable activity in the central Mississippi basin. We remember the Jesuits of Kaskaskia, the reputation of whose vineyards Dufour had heard of in Philadelphia before the end of the eighteenth century. The early dominance of the French in the Mississippi Valley meant that many experiments by small communities and by individuals of that vinophile race—clerical as well as lay—were certainly made with both native and imported grapes. In the 1770s the French settlers at Vincennes on the Wabash made red wine of native grapes for their own consumption that gained a good report.[67] Dufour recorded that vines were growing well in the gardens of St. Genevieve, Missouri, below St. Louis.[68] Cahokia, another old French settlement, also made wine before the coming of the British. But these were strictly domestic efforts. The statement is repeatedly made that the French government in the eighteenth century forbade viticulture in its American territories for fear of injury to the home industry.[69] I have not found proof of this; if it is true, it expresses a fear for which, so far as the record shows, there was very little ground in fact. In Missouri, as in Ohio, a winegrowing industry waited upon the appearance of the Germans.

The flow of German emigration that reached Cincinnati in the 1820s moved through and beyond it to St. Louis and the Missouri Valley in the next decade. A large part of it had been attracted there by the idealized, romantic description of the region published in 1829 by Gottfried Duden, a wealthy German who was convinced of the evils of overpopulation in the Old World and sought a new beginning in the American West.[70] He bought a farm along the Missouri River in Warren County in the new state of Missouri and wrote of the rich pastoral beauties of the land in order to draw new settlers. They came in large numbers, hastened along by the repressive politics of the reaction to the revolutionary outbreaks on the Continent in 1830. When they arrived, they found a wilderness not exactly like the smiling land of overflowing plenty that Duden had led them to expect, but neither did they fare badly. St. Louis and the lands along the Missouri for many miles to the west soon took on a distinctly German character.[71]

It was this fact that caught the attention of the directors of the Philadelphia Settlement Society (*Deutsche Ansiedlungs-Gesellschaft zu Philadelphia*). This organization was formed in 1836 to carry out an ideal of German cultural nationalism by founding a colony in the remote West that should be German through and through in every particular.[72] The society sent an agent to the Missouri lands, and there, in the angle formed by the junction of the Gasconade and Missouri rivers, he bought some 11,000 acres for the society, which in turn sold the land to its stockholders. Settlement began in late 1837, and within two years Hermann, as the new town was called (after the German national hero Arminius who defeated the armies of Caesar Augustus), had a population of 450 souls: it was laid out with ambitious amplitude, its Market Street being deliberately made wider than Philadelphia's splendid Market Street by its visionary designers. They also included a "Weinstrasse" in the plan of the city's streets.[73] The difficulties of administering a frontier settlement from Philadelphia quickly led to a new arrangement, by which the Philadelphia Society's assets were transferred to the corporation of Hermann and the society dissolved. The aim of fostering a center of distinctively German culture was not abandoned. Hermann was substantially all German throughout the nineteenth century and was a center from which German settlement spread through east-central Missouri in Augusta, Washington, Morrison, and other towns.

The character of the immigrants was far higher than ordinary: most were men of education, and some were of high professional standing. Their distinction is crudely recognized in their local nickname of *Lateinische Bauern*—"Latin Peasants"—that is, farmers who could read the learned languages. Earlier, organized German settlements associated with winegrowing in this country were typically religious, on the model of the Pietists of Germantown in the time of William Penn, or of the Rappites in Indiana and Pennsylvania. The Hermannites, however, were thoroughly secular, inclining even, here and there, towards free thought. They cared more for literature, music, theater, and public festivals than for church. In Hermann, stores remained open on the Sabbath, and the early settlers did not trouble themselves to put up a church building, though they were quick to establish a theatrical society and to build a music hall.[74] It is perhaps no cause for wonder that a community so disposed should take to winegrowing and succeed at it as no one yet had succeeded.

The first settlers of Hermann had ventured west with the idea that they would become farmers on the wide prairies, but they found that the land their agent had bought was in broken, hilly, stony country, unfit for the agriculture they had in mind.[75] Viticulture was an experiment obviously worth trying, and though the long history of failure in this country was cause for skepticism, they had the current example of Longworth and his early successes as a hopeful sign to guide them.

47 The Poeschel Winery building, erected about 1850, near Hermann, Missouri, by the first winemaker in the region. Even in the beginning the Germans built solidly. (From Charles Van Ravenswaay, *The Arts and Architecture of Germans in Missouri* [1977])

Inevitably—almost as a ritual gesture it seems—some vinifera vines were tried before the end of the 1830s.[76] But the Hermannites were quick to accept the implication of Longworth's work and turned to the native varieties, using cuttings obtained from Cincinnati.[77] The first cultivated grape to produce at Hermann was an Isabella vine planted by Jacob Fugger that fruited in 1845. The first wine, from Isabella grapes, was made in 1846 by Michael Poeschel;[78] there were already 150,000 vines set out in Hermann then, and the economic promise was such that the town established a nursery for vines and offered land for vineyards on extravagantly easy terms.[79] The responses were immediate and strong: six hundred "wine lots" were snapped up, and by 1848 Hermann commenced its era of commercial winemaking with a modest but symbolically important production of 1,000 gallons of wine. The occasion was marked in good German style by a *Weinfest* that fall. The town cannon was fired in honor of Bacchus, and a steamboat-load of ladies and gentlemen from St. Louis came to join the festivities:[80] the rumor of wine spread instantly through that region, proof of the eagerness with which it was hoped for. One of the St. Louis gentlemen, a lawyer named Alexander Kayser, was inspired to offer three premiums of $100 for the best specimens of Missouri wine, the first of which was gained in 1850 by a catawba of vintage 1849 from the vineyards of Hermann.[81]

Though the Isabella was the first variety to be used, it satisfied no one. Other varieties were soon tried: the first Catawba crop was produced in 1848; the Norton began to be cultivated around 1850, the Concord in 1855.[82] When mildew and rot began to devastate the Catawba vineyards, as they quickly did, the Germans along the Missouri, unlike their compatriots along the Ohio, had acceptable alternatives to turn to. The Concord, thanks to its tough, productive nature, was not long in occupying the largest share of the acreage in vines, but Hermann would never have established a reputation for wine if it had had only the Concord. The variety for quality was the Norton, a seedling grown by Dr. D. N. Norton, of Richmond, Virginia, before 1830. It had been tried without much enthusiasm in various places, including the vineyards of Cincinnati, where Longworth pronounced that it was good for nothing as a wine grape.[83] The growers at Hermann, however, could venture to disregard the great Longworth's judgment, for their need was desperate. Thus when a Herr Wiedersprecher brought Norton cuttings from Cincinnati, they gave them a trial. To Jacob Rommel belongs the honor of producing the first wine from Norton at Hermann.[84] Thus the Norton caught on in Missouri at a time when the Catawba crop had already been repeatedly damaged by the diseases to which it is vulnerable and the growers were casting about for something to take its place.[85]

A black grape, the Norton yields a dark and astringent wine without foxiness, capable of developing into a sound and well-balanced table wine. Yet the early practice at Hermann was apparently to ferment on the skins for only one or two days and thus to produce wine more pink than red.[86] This was reportedly done to avoid excess astringency. By 1867 the Missourians had learned enough about handling the Norton to please at least one discriminating critic. The philanthropist and writer Charles Loring Brace, reporting on his disappointment with the wines of California that he had sampled on a tour of that state, concluded that "no red wine has ever been produced in America equal to that made by the Germans of Missouri from [the Norton]."[87]

The prominence of the Norton at Hermann links the region with Virginia and the South rather than with Ohio and the northern tradition of white winemaking in the eastern United States. For white wine, the winemakers of Hermann also used a southern grape, the Lenoir. The Catawba persisted, too, but subject to the same wild ups and downs in annual yield, the effect of disease, that plagued the variety at Cincinnati.[88]

By 1855 Hermann was surrounded by 500 acres of vineyards and was producing enough beyond local demand to be able to send wine up the Ohio River to the wine houses of Cincinnati, where Missouri catawba was added to the wine of Cincinnati.[89] By 1861 the volume was great enough to justify the establishment of a large-scale winery at Hermann, built by Michael Poeschel, Hermann's first wine-

Nortons Virginia.

48 | The Norton grape, originally found in Virginia, came into its own in the vineyards of Missouri in the years just before the Civil War. It is that rare thing, a native grape from which an acceptable red wine can be made. (Painting by C. L. Fleischman, 1867; National Agricultural Library)

maker, and his partner, John Scherer.[90] This firm, which grew to be the largest winery outside of California, operated until Prohibition, and has, since 1965, been put back into the production of native wines.

The Civil War slowed agricultural development at Hermann, as it did along the Ohio. Nevertheless, the winegrowing industry continued a modest expansion. The Hermann vineyardists exhibited thirty-five varieties of grapes at the Gasconade County Fair in 1862—the only fair held in Missouri that year.[91] The war did brush the town, for the wine in George Husmann's cellar was all drunk by General Sterling Price's Confederates when they raided the town in October 1864. At the end of the war, Hermann had about a thousand acres of vines, more than half of which were not yet in bearing. The preceding season had yielded 42,000 gallons of wine. And the demand for cuttings from the nurseries of Hermann exceeded their capacity: some two million went out that year. Winegrowing was now spread far beyond Hermann, touching almost every corner of the state, and moving into Illinois and Kansas, the states flanking Missouri on east and west. Augusta in nearby St. Charles County, another center of German settlement, was producing a significant quantity of wine in the 1860s[92] (after many years of dormancy, wine production has been resumed at Augusta). After the war, then, winemaking around Hermann was ready to enter on a steady prosperity that lasted down to Prohibition.

One may ask why Hermann, on river lands not much different from those around Cincinnati, should have succeeded in setting up an industry that long outlasted the one created by Longworth at about the same time? The most obvious, and perhaps most important, reason is that the Germans did not invest everything in the Catawba and so could survive its failure. They had tried other varieties with success that came before they could grow disheartened, as the Germans of Cincinnati had been disheartened. Another reason, less apparent, and much more difficult to demonstrate, lies in the character of the Missouri Germans. They were not tenant farmers but independent proprietors, prepared to take an experimental and scientific interest in viticulture. Perhaps it is significant that many of the pioneers were not Rhinelanders or South Germans like Rapp's Württembergers, but Hessians and Prussians, without experience of winegrowing in Europe. Hermann's first winemaker, Michael Poeschel, for example, was a north German who had no knowledge of grape culture; on the other hand, those who briefly and futilely tried vinifera at Hermann *were* Rhinelanders, another instance of Old World experience as a handicap in the new.[93]

As for the Missouri Germans' scientific disposition, that is shown in the work of developing new varieties and in the quantity of technical writing devoted to viticulture for which Missouri was remarkable in the nineteenth century. The philanthropic and literary farmer Friedrich Muench, of Washington, Warren County, a man trained to the Lutheran ministry in the University of Giessen and one of the original emigrants attracted by the blandishment of Gottfried Duden's description of the Missouri country, published the earliest treatise that I have found issuing from the Missouri German community.[94] His "Anleitung zum Weinbau in Nordamerika" ("Directions for Winegrowing in North America") appeared in the *Mississippi Handelszeitung* in 1859; a later version in book form appeared at St. Louis in 1864 as *Amerikanische Weinbauschule;* this went through three editions, and was translated in 1865 as *School for American Grape Culture: Brief but Thorough and Practical Guide to the Laying Out of Vineyards, the Treatment of Vines, and the Production of Wine in North America.* Muench, or "old Father Muench" as he grew to be called, had been growing grapes since 1846 and continued to do so until 1881, "when he was found dead among his beloved vines, one fine winter's morning of that year, with the pruning shears still in his hand, in his 84th year."[95] Something of Muench's high-minded style may be had from this passage in his *School for American Grape Culture:*

49 Friedrich Muench (1798?–1881), trained as a Lutheran minister in Germany, typified the enthusiastic style of the German winegrowers of Missouri. "With the growth of the grape," he wrote, "every nation elevates itself to a higher degree of civilization." The winery he founded in Augusta, Missouri, is in operation today. (State Historical Society of Missouri)

If it prove but moderately remunerative, the vine-dresser, free, lord of his own possessions, in daily intercourse with peaceful nature, is a happier and more contented man than thousands of those who, in our large cities, driven about by the thronging crowd, rarely attain true peace and serenity of mind. With the growth of the grape every nation elevates itself to a higher grade of civilization—brutality must vanish, and human nature progresses. (P. 11)

Before Muench's book appeared, another essay on viticulture was published at Hermann by a second and more important writer, George Husmann, whose *An*

50 George Husmann (1827–1902), a pioneer winegrower at Hermann, Missouri, was one of the most devoted proselytizers in the cause of the grape in the nineteenth century. A viticulturist, winemaker, nurseryman, writer, and professor of horticulture in Missouri, he ended his days as a winegrower in California's Napa Valley. (State Historical Society of Missouri)

Essay on the Culture of the Grape in the Great West came out in 1863.[96] Husmann, whose father had been a shareholder in the society that founded Hermann, was a north German like Poeschel and Muench, not a Rhinelander.[97] He thus inherited no tradition of Old World winemaking, but had to learn his craft under native frontier conditions. His next publication was *The Cultivation of the Native Grape, and Manufacture of American Wines,* published in New York in 1866. This book, written as the Civil War was ending, is filled with a kind of visionary excitement over the prospects of a new viticulture in a newly united country, which may in part help to account for its success. In successive editions and under various new titles, it became one of the standard works on the subject, remaining in print well into this century.

The special emphasis of Husmann was on the power of the winemaker to control his work precisely. He explains the use of both the saccharometer and the acidimeter, by which the winemaker can know exactly how much sugar and how much acid, the two key ingredients in the raw material of wine, he has to work with. Husmann is also frankly on the side of the winemakers who make no bones about adding sugar to a deficient juice and water to an over-acid juice. The object is to reach an ideal balance of sugar and acid; with the help of analytic instruments, Husmann argued, no winemaker need ever be at the mercy of a bad season. His instructions lean heavily on the work of the German chemist Dr. Ludwig Gall, whose "Practical Guide" had been translated in 1860 for publication in the U.S. Patent Office Report, the forerunner of the reports of the Department of Agriculture. There is no doubt that Husmann exaggerates the quality of the wine produced by his methods; he was writing more as a chemist than as a traditional winemaker, and he did not go uncriticized. But, as he very sensibly maintained, since the eastern grower more often than not was compelled to work with fruit low in sugar and high in acid, the choice was simply between making a "natural" wine unfit to drink and an "artificial" wine that was quite palatable—and profitable.[98]

In 1869 Husmann founded a monthly journal called *The Grape Culturist* at St. Louis, the first to be devoted to the subject in this country. Though it expired in 1871, that it could have been born at all and then have survived for three years is some measure of the status of winegrowing in the Mississippi Valley. It was also evidence of the literary and technical culture of the Germans. The publisher of the magazine was Conrad Witter, a St. Louis German who advertised that he kept a "large assortment of books treating of the culture of grapes and manufacture of wines."[99] It is hard to imagine any other region in the United States at this date in which such a stock of books might have been offered in the hope of sale.

The Missouri Germans were soon at work developing new grapes for western conditions; indeed, they were among the very first in America to carry on sustained trials in grape breeding. Jacob Rommel, who was taken by his parents to Hermann in the year of its founding, began work with native seedlings around 1860 and produced a number of varieties that had some recognition in their day.[100] He was looking for vines that had hardiness against the continental winters of the Midwest, resistance to the endemic fungus diseases, and productiveness enough to be profitable, and he sought these qualities in a series of seedlings derived from a riparia-labrusca ancestor. One at least of Rommel's seedlings, the Elvira, a white grape yielding a neutral white wine favored for blending, is still grown commercially in eastern vineyards, mostly in New York and Missouri. In Canada it had a great success, and it was still the most widely grown variety in the vineyards of Ontario as late as 1979.[101] It is, or was, occasionally met with as a varietal, but more often anonymously as part of a sparkling wine blend. Nicholas Grein, called Papa Grein by the younger generation of Hermannites, also introduced a number of riparia-labrusca seedlings, the best known of which is the Missouri Riesling, still cultivated to some extent in the state of its origin (and often confused with Elvira).[102] It has a strong resistance to black rot for an American variety.

By far the most distinguished scientific contribution to viticultural knowledge

5 I   Dr. George Engelmann (1809–84) was the leading physician in St. Louis, and, at the same time, a botanist of international distinction; Engelmann was the most expert of American ampelographers in the nineteenth century. His career illustrates the high achievement of the Missouri German community. (State Historical Society of Missouri)

made by the Missouri German community came from Dr. George Engelmann (1809–84), an M.D. from the University of Würzburg whose passion was botany.[103] He came to the United States in 1832 as agent for his uncles, who wanted to find investments in the Mississippi Valley. Settling in St. Louis, he became the most sought-after physician in the city, yet still found time to keep up his original work in botany, to carry out observations in biology, meteorology, and geology, and to found the St. Louis Academy of Science. Only a fraction of his work was devoted to grapes, but that is nevertheless an important fraction. He published a number of

52 | The 1875 edition of the catalogue of Bush & Son & Meissner; it later grew to include a "grape grower's manual," was translated into French and Italian, and was used as a textbook in American agricultural schools. (National Library of Agriculture)

brief articles on the classification of native varieties, beginning with "Notes on the Grape Vines of Missouri" in 1860 and ending with an essay on "The True Grape Vines of the United States" in 1875. This appeared as part of the encyclopaedic and learned catalogue of Bush and Son and Meissner, a leading Missouri nursery founded in 1865 by Isidor Bush (not a Missouri German but a Prague-born Austrian).[104] The catalogue passed through numerous editions and was used rather as a text book than as a commercial list; it was even translated into French and Italian. Engelmann's description and classification of the native vines was the scientific standard for his time: on his death it could be said that "nearly all that we know scientifically of our species and forms of *Vitis* is directly due to Dr. Engelmann's investigations."[105]

When Engelmann first came to the United States, he made his way to a settlement of Germans on the Illinois side of the Mississippi, about twenty miles east of St. Louis. Here he had some connections, and here he made his base of operations while he explored and botanized before settling down to his medical practice. This was the region of the old French settlements, where grape growing had long been familiar, so familiar that even the American settlers readily took it up. Gustave Koerner, another German immigrant, a friend of Engelmann's, and later a distinguished lawyer, and a friend and political supporter of Lincoln's, recalled what he, Engelmann, and their friends found as they travelled for the first time to Belleville in 1833. Stopping at a farm, they were pleased to find Isabella grapes growing on the trellised house; even better, the farmer offered them a drink of his wild grape wine. "It was really very good," Koerner remembered, though sweetened a bit by added sugar, "the American having no liking for wine unless it is sweet."[106] The Germans themselves, when a group of them settled around Belleville, began at once to grow vines, and long continued to do so. Years later Koerner remembered giving a visiting German poet, who had said disparaging things about American wines, some "old, well-seasoned Norton Virginia Seedling" from the vineyard of a neighbor:

> He drank it with great gusto, remarking that it was a very fine wine; he supposed, he said, it was Burgundy. When I laughingly told him it was St. Clair County wine, he would hardly believe me. . . . I must do him the justice, however, of saying that good Norton has really the body of Burgundy, and can never be taken for Bordeaux.[107]

One of the most prominent men among the Belleville Germans was Theodore Hilgard, who had been a lawyer, judge, and man of letters in Zweibrucken and who, after emigrating to Illinois, produced a wine there that he fondly called "Hilgardsberger."[108] More important for this history, Hilgard's son, Eugene, became professor of agriculture at the University of California, director of the Experiment Stations, and dean of the College of Agriculture, positions in which he made contributions of the first importance to the winegrowing of California.[109] He is thus another claim to the historical importance of the Latin Peasants settled in the region of which St. Louis is the center.

St. Louis itself—including St. Louis County—with its layers of French and German history, has been a scene of winemaking since very early times, as these things are measured in American history. The first St. Louis wine on record was made for church use by the Jesuits of St. Stanislaus Seminary at Florissant, north of the city, in 1823; they later developed commercial production as well, and continued the business down to 1960.[110] The earliest purely commercial winery in St. Louis was the firm called the Missouri Wine Company, founded in 1853. It constructed underground cellars for storage (they still survive in downtown St. Louis) and went into business not only in Missouri wines but in wines from Ohio.[111] The well-known Cincinnati vineyardist Robert Buchanan, for example, sold his vintages of 1855 and 1856 in bulk to the Missouri Wine Company.[112] So the traffic in wine between Missouri and Ohio was a two-way street; we have seen that Hermann sent some of its wine up the Ohio to Longworth in Cincinnati, while Buchanan was shipping downstream to St. Louis. The Missouri Wine Company was advertising its sparkling catawba in the St. Louis papers in 1857, and the probability is that this was Ohio wine. Another interesting, but indistinct, St. Louis enterprise was carried out by Isidor Bush's partner, Gustave Edward Meissner, who planted 600 acres of vines on Meissner's Island, below the city.[113] These may have been intended as a nursery planting; in any case, no wine production is recorded from Meissner's Island.

The main claim of St. Louis to a place in the history of wine in America rests with the American Wine Company, which took over the Missouri Wine Company in 1859 and, through many changes of fortune, persisted up to the early years of World War II. The president was a Chicago hotelkeeper and politician named Isaac Cook, who, despite the struggles of political faction in Illinois, still managed to take an interest in wine as both a connoisseur and a producer. In 1861 he left Chicago for St. Louis, and built up the American Wine Company to a leading place in the American trade.[114] The main stock in trade was called Cook's Imperial Champagne, a label still in use, though it has passed through various hands and been applied to wines of various origins in its more than a hundred years of currency. Under Cook, the American Wine Company bought vineyards in the Sandusky region of Ohio, and though the finishing of the wine was carried out in St. Louis (in the cellars originally built for the Missouri Wine Company), the history of the business belongs perhaps more to Ohio than to Missouri. The American Wine Company also dealt in such wines as Missouri catawba and Norton.

Missouri is the farthest western reach of winegrowing at this stage of American history (excluding for the moment California and the regions of Spanish-American cultivation in the Southwest). After recounting all the early trials and modest successes in Missouri we may glance briefly, by way of reminder, at the obstacles that the pioneers had to face, and that their successors still face. They cultivated a region at the heart of a continent, untempered by any great body of water. The winter cold there sweeps down from the arctic regions of Canada, or off the high mountains and high plains that form the western, windward, edge of the Missouri basin. Even the hardiest grapes may expect to be killed to the ground from time to time in the freezes that flow from these sources. Phylloxera is at home here. Not too far to the south and east is the home of Pierce's Disease. Mildews, both powdery and downy, are alternately favored by heat and by damp; black rot is always present. If the early growers had known all this, would they have ventured at all? In any case, they did not know, and they did venture. The reviving efforts to establish a significant viticulture in Missouri today have an honorable pioneer tradition behind them of successful struggle against very tough odds.

The Development of Winegrowing in New York State

New York presents four different viticultural regions, running from east to west across the state, whose development is roughly parallel to the westward movement of population. The first is around New York City, especially on Long Island; next is the Hudson Valley; then the Finger Lakes of the central part of the state; and last the so-called Chautauqua region, an extension into western New York of the shorelands along Lake Erie.

The gardeners of Long Island, having a large concentrated market just beyond their doorsteps in the city, were naturally interested in seeing if they could succeed in growing wine for it. Not surprisingly, one of the first was a Frenchman, a merchant named Alphonse Loubat, who came originally from the south of France. At a date unrecorded but probably in the 1820s, he set out a vineyard of some forty acres—a notably ambitious effort—at New Utrecht, as it was then known; it is now a part of the Brooklyn waterfront, where the idea of any growing crop is impossible to conceive. Loubat's vines were vinifera, as a Frenchman's would be. Black rot and powdery mildew descended upon him, and he set himself to struggle against them. In the process he is said to have invented the practice of bagging the clusters against their depredations. But at last he was compelled to admit that they were too much for human effort to overcome.[115]

Loubat left a permanent memorial in the shape of a curious little book with the same title as Dufour's, *The American Vine-Dresser's Guide,* and published just a year later than Dufour's, in 1827, in New York. The book, in French and English on facing pages, opens with a delightful dedication "To the Shade of Franklin"—"À L'Ombre de Franklin." The great man's ghost is invoked to "Protect my feeble essay" and to "protect my vine, and cause it so to thrive that I shall soon be able to pour forth upon thy tomb libations of perfumed Muscatel and generous Malmsey."[116] At the time that he published his *Guide,* Loubat seems to have had no suspicion at all that his vinifera were doomed, or that the failure of winegrowing in the United States was owing to anything but the inexplicable neglect of a splendid opportunity. The instruction conveyed in his *Guide* is without any reference to American conditions, and assumes that French practices can be taken over unaltered. He soon had reason to think otherwise, and in 1835 the enterprise that he strove to establish along the banks of the East River came to a rude end when the vineyard property was sold for building lots.[117]

Still, before the end, his work had attracted some attention. Longworth's early trials in Ohio of vinifera were made with vines that he got from Loubat.[118] Another Long Islander, Alden Spooner, the editor of the Brooklyn *Long Island City Star* and one of the leading citizens of that pastoral community, had watched Loubat's struggles with sympathetic interest, and around 1827 began, in imitation, to plant vinifera grapes in his Brooklyn vineyard, now a part of Prospect Park.[119] Unlike Loubat, however, Spooner soon concluded that the native vines were the only safe bet. He planted the Isabella grape instead, and with this he had success enough to

53 Alphonse Loubat, a New York merchant born in France, planted a large vineyard of vinifera vines in Brooklyn in the 1820s and published a book, in both French and English, called *The American Vine-Dresser's Guide* (1827). Interesting chiefly as a late memorial to the futile belief that vinifera would do well in the American East after two hundred years of unbroken failure, it was, for some inexplicable reason, reprinted in 1872, when its views had long been discredited. (From Loubat, *The American Vine-Dresser's Guide* [New York, 1872])

lead him to publish a book (he commanded a press and a bookstore, as well as a newspaper). Spooner's *The Cultivation of American Grape Vines and Making of Wine* (1846) is a scissors-and-paste job, of the sort that journalists know so well how to do, but it preserves some authentic anecdotes and is useful evidence of the interest in grape growing around New York City at that time.

The most important by far of the early Long Island grape growers was William Robert Prince, the son, grandson, and great-grandson of nurserymen.[120] The Princes operated the elegantly named Linnaean Botanic Garden at Flushing, Long Island, where, among other horticultural specialities, they kept a large collec-

54 A member of the fourth generation of a family of Long Island
nurserymen, William Robert
Prince (1795–1869) made a special study of
the grape and published the first comprehensive book on the subject in this country, *A
Treatise on the Vine* (1830). Prince introduced
one of the most successful of the early
hybrids, the Isabella grape. (From U. P. Hedrick,
Manual of American Grape Growing [1924])

tion of grapes, both native and foreign, for sale: their catalogue for 1830 lists 513
varieties.[121] The youngest Prince, as his father had before him, took a special interest in viticulture and became one of the recognized experts on the subject in the
first part of the century, writing frequently for the horticultural magazines and developing the section devoted to vines in his nursery catalogue into a substantial
essay on the subject. In 1830 he published a separate work called *A Treatise on the
Vine,* an ambitious and expansive discourse that undertakes, in the easy and incon-
sequent style of those prespecialized days, to provide a history of the vine from

Noah downwards, a description of two hundred and eighty varieties of grape, and instruction on the "establishment, culture, and management of vineyards." The work is dedicated to Henry Clay in recognition of his part in founding the Kentucky Vineyard Society many years before.

Compared to anything else on viticulture by American writers, the *Treatise* was a work of an entirely different and higher order—"the first good book on grapes," as Hedrick says.[122] Prince made a serious effort at straightening out the tangle of names used to identify native grapes, and, in his description of native varieties, organized a great deal of local historical information; his prominence as the proprietor of America's best-known nursery made it possible for him to obtain information that no one else could have. Prince promised to publish a second part of his *Treatise,* to include a "topographical account of all the known vineyards throughout the world, and including those of the United States";[123] for whatever reason, this never appeared, and we can only regret what would have been an unparalleled description of early nineteenth-century viticulture in the United States. He did, at least, print a list of his correspondents and sources, which includes some familiar names: Bolling, whose "Sketch" had been given to Prince; Thomas McCall of Georgia, "who has presented me with a detailed manuscript of his experiments and success in making wines"; and Herbemont, Eichelberger, and Spooner.[124]

Since Prince was able to grow vinifera vines successfully under nursery conditions, he was slow to give up faith in them. A large part of his book is devoted to foreign grapes, which he was confident would grow well in this country. He particularly recommended the Alicante. And no matter what the variety of vinifera, its failure, he thought, could in every case be explained by bad management.[125] An equally large part of Prince's *Treatise* is devoted to descriptions of some eighty native varieties, far and away the most comprehensive account of the subject that had yet appeared. His own experience showed him the need for improved American varieties, and he was himself one of the earliest of the country's hybridizers, though he does not seem to have introduced any grape of his own breeding. The variety with which Prince's name is associated is the Isabella, which his father obtained in 1816 from Colonel George Gibbs of Long Island, an amateur grower, and named after Gibbs's wife. The grape itself is of disputed origin, but it is generally supposed to be from South Carolina.[126] The Princes did not promote the Isabella at once, but, after Adlum's success in creating notoriety for the Catawba, they began to put forward the Isabella as a superior rival.[127] Unlike Adlum, William Robert Prince was under no illusion as to the value of his labrusca seedling compared to the standard vinifera; still, he wrote of the Isabella, "I have made wine from it of excellent quality, and which has met with the approbation of some of the most accurate judges in our country."[128]

Prince has little to say about mildew and black rot, the diseases that were the bane of native hybrids throughout the East; there is plenty of evidence that these afflictions plagued grape growers around New York when Prince was writing, but he gives them no particular emphasis in his discussion of grape culture. One no-

Isabella and Catawba Grape Vines.

OF PROPER age for forming Vineyards, cultivated from and containing all the good qualities which the most improved cultivation for over fifteen years has conferred on the Croton Point Vineyards, are offered to the public. Those who may purchase will receive such instructions for four years, as will enable them to cultivate the Grape with entire success, provided their locality is not too far north. All communications addressed to R. T. UNDERHILL, M. D., New-York, or Croton Point, Westchester County, N. Y., will receive attention. The additional experience of three past seasons, gives him full assurance that by improved cultivation, pruning, &c., a crop of good fruit can be obtained every year, in most of the Northern, all the Middle, Western and Southern States.

Also, Apple and Quince Trees for sale as above.

N. B.—To those who take sufficient to plant six acres, as he directs, he will. when they commence bearing, furnish the owner with one of his Vinedressers, whom he has instructed in his mode of cultivation, and he will do all the labor of the vineyard, and insure the most perfect success. The only charge, a reasonable compensation for the labor.

Nov. 8—w4tm2t   R. T. U.

55 An advertisement for vines from the Croton Point Vineyards of Dr. Robert Underhill (1802–71). Note the offer to send a vine dresser to take care of the vines "when they commence bearing." After a generation of successful grape growing along the Hudson, Underhill was himself just beginning to make wine for the New York City market. (*The Cultivator*, December 1855)

table thing he does do, however, is to call attention to the efficacy of spraying with a mixture of lime and sulfur against mildew. He was the first to do so in this country.[129]

Long Island may be imagined in the early part of the nineteenth century as a rural spot where grape growing for ornament and home use was widespread—local patriotism favored the Isabella, which "soon became the cherished ornament and pride of every garden and door-yard."[130] There, Colonel Gibbs, from whose garden the Isabella came, amused himself with a vineyard, as did Colonel Spooner; there, poor Loubat struggled and failed to compel vinifera to grow on a commercial scale; and there the learned Prince poured out, through his catalogues and monographs, information to the country at large from his base in the Linnaean Botanic Garden. Grapes *did* grow in Brooklyn (and there are wineries there today; that is a different story). One should also mention the famous nursery and botanic garden founded on twenty sterile, rocky acres at the junction of Jamaica and Flatbush Avenues in 1825 by the Belgian emigré André Parmentier. This quickly became a flourishing garden, complete with rustic observation tower. Parmentier collected and distributed an unprecedentedly comprehensive variety of imported and native plants, including grapes.[131] All of his grapes were, unluckily, imported, and so his work in that line was more enterprising than fruitful. Also unfulfilled was Parmentier's intention to publish an "Essay on the Cultivation of the Vine," left unfinished at his untimely death in 1830.[132] Long Island thus presented the spectacle of much hopeful activity, but did not get beyond the promise of interesting beginnings.

North from Manhattan, along the Hudson, a landowner named Robert Underhill, using vinifera vines from Parmentier, laid out a vineyard at Croton Point sometime before 1827—probably just a year or so earlier. By 1827 the failure of the vines was clear to him, and he replaced them with Catawba and Isabella.[133] These grew, and their fresh fruit found a ready and profitable market in New York City. Underhill died in 1829, but his two sons, Robert, a doctor who gave up his practice for vine growing, and William, continued the vineyard at Croton Point in separate holdings; by 1843 the Underhills had twenty-seven acres of vineyard; ultimately, they had seventy-five acres in vines.[134] The scale and the long life of their vineyards give them a claim to be the real founders of the winegrowing industry in New York. But they were not, at first, winegrowers, merely grape growers. Then Robert Underhill, while continuing to sell grapes, began to make wine for himself, and, at last, in 1859, he began to send Isabella and catawba wine to the New York market.[135] Croton Point wines, sold from the "Pure Wine and Grape Depot" in New York City, were advertised as "the pure product of the grape, neither drugged, liquored, nor watered, recommended by leading physicians in all cases where a stimulant of bracing character is required."[136] One notes the emphasis upon therapeutic value, forgivable perhaps in the case of wine produced by a physician, but almost always a sign of the puritanical suspicion of simple sensuous gratification. Dr. Underhill, it may be mentioned, was the first sponsor in the

THE VAULTS AT CROTON POINT
ON THE HUDSON

ESTATE OF

D.R. R. T. UNDERHILL

CONTAINING VINTAGES
FROM 1860 TO 1871

NO WINES NEWER
THAN THE ABOVE ARE
ON SALE THE MANU-
FACTURE OF WINE
HAVING CEASED WITH
THE DEATH OF D.R. UN-
DERHILL IN 1871 SINCE
WHICH THE GRAPES
HAVE BEEN MARKETED.

56 | Dr. Robert Underhill died in 1871, a little more than a decade after he began making wine at his Croton Point Vineyards. This advertisement offers the wines left after his death, all manufactured in the years 1860–71. (Huntington Library)

United States of the so-called grape cure, one of the many regimens designed to clean out the overfed systems of prosperous Victorians, and then fashionable in Europe. Since the cure consisted in eating five or six pounds of grapes daily, Underhill obviously had an interested motive in sponsoring it.[137]

The Underhills made another contribution to New York viticulture in the form of William's son Stephen, who, between 1860 and 1870, introduced a number of hybrid varieties of his creation and sold them through his nursery. The three generations of Underhills working at Croton Point are a first dynasty in American viticulture (their property is now a county park). [138]

A few miles north of Croton Point, a Frenchman named Thomas Gimbrede was experimenting with native vines at West Point, where he taught drawing to the cadets. Starting about 1820, Gimbrede had collected every variety that he found growing wild in the woods and transplanted them to his garden, "manuring, stimulating and pruning them with great care, in the hope of changing and ameliorating their character." After fifteen years of such experiment, Gimbrede was candid enough to admit that he had had no luck whatever: the natives remained obstinately unimproved by their pampering.[139] But perhaps this barren result may have helped put an end to the notion, so long and fondly entertained, that the "wild" grape could be "tamed" by so simple a process of cultivation in which, as one writer has said, the experimenter acts as a sociologist instead of a geneticist.[140] One hears little of the "taming" idea afterwards.

The first successful commercial winery in New York was founded by a Frenchman named Jean Jaques in 1839, at Washingtonville, on the west bank of the Hudson. Under the name of Blooming Grove, the winery business did well enough to be continued by his sons. In the 1870s the surviving son sold the winery to a firm of New York wine merchants who also dealt in the wines from the original Brotherhood Winery in Brocton, New York. The name of the Washingtonville winery was then changed to Brotherhood, for though the Brocton firm no longer existed, its name continued to have market value. Grapes are no longer grown on the Washingtonville property, and the firm has passed through many transformations, but it survived Prohibition by making sacramental wine and is still going. The winery may fairly claim to be the oldest such enterprise in continuous operation in this country and helps to bolster New York's claim to a central place in the commercial history of wine in America.[141]

One hundred and fifty miles west of the Hudson Valley lie the long, narrow, deep strips of water whose arrangement on the map like the outstretched fingers of a hand has given them their name of Finger Lakes. As Philip Wagner has written, "their beauty is famous and their geology fascinating."[142] But for Wagner and for us, their main interest is in their status as a winegrowing region. The lakes, with their adjacent highlands, keep the climate of the valleys much more equable than in the nearby regions, producing warmer winters and cooler summers and so favoring the grape.[143]

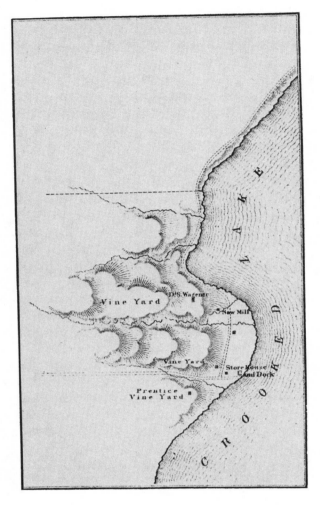

57   The first vineyards in the Finger   Keuka Lake (then called Crooked Lake) begin-
     Lakes region were planted on   ning in 1836. (From Goldsmith Denniston, *Grape*
     this spot along the west bank of   *Culture in Steuben County* [1865])

The Finger Lakes district is, and has long been, the main source of fine table wine, including sparkling wine, in the eastern United States. Its rise to this eminence was not particularly early or rapid, however; the history of the region's development largely belongs to the period after the Civil War, as is also the case in Ohio and Missouri. But, as in those states too, the beginnings at least were clearly made before the war. According to the received account, the first cultivated grapes in the Finger Lakes district were set out about 1830 (the date is disputed) by the Reverend William Bostwick, rector of the newly founded Episcopal Church in

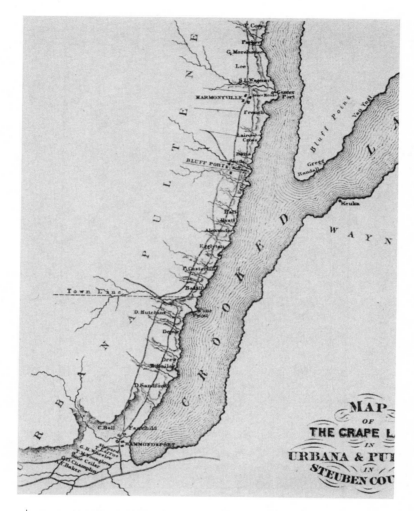

58 The viticultural region of Keuka Lake (Crooked Lake) as it developed after 1836. The Pleasant Valley subregion lies at the far lower left corner of the map, behind the town of Hammondsport. It was here that the large-scale winemaking enterprises of the valley developed. (From Goldsmith Denniston, *Grape Culture in Steuben County* [1865])

Hammondsport, at the south end of Keuka Lake (or Crooked Lake, as it was then called).[144] There is no record that Bostwick ever made wine from his grapes—he had only a few vines of Catawba and Isabella—but it is pleasant to have his example to show that the ancient tradition linking wine and the church included, in this country, not only the Catholic, the Huguenot, and the German Protestant, but the Anglican communion as well.

Bostwick's example was followed by his neighbors, perhaps with the greatest enthusiasm by J. W. Prentiss, who beginning in 1836 developed a three-acre vineyard on the shores of Keuka in the township of Pulteney with vines from Bostwick's garden.[145] Another significant event in the district was the arrival, after 1848, of experienced German vineyardists, refugees from the political revolutions of the Continent. One of these, Andrew Reisenger, after observing Prentiss's success with his small vineyard, set out two or three acres of his own in the same region of the western lake shore, at Harmony, in 1853.[146] The excellent results of Reisenger's professional practices—unknown until then in the neighborhood—showed what crops and profits might be made from viticulture. Local men of substance soon followed Reisenger's lead: planting began in 1855 on the land south of Hammondsport, a shallow valley once a part of the lake and now called Pleasant Valley.[147] The presence of the new German immigrants gave the region an advantage by providing a ready source of experienced labor. By 1859, Hedrick estimates, there were four or five hundred acres of grapes around Keuka Lake.[148] Planting had extended not only south to Pleasant Valley but north into Yates County and to the eastern shore of the lake around Wayne. It included all the established native varieties: Catawba, Isabella, Delaware, Diana, Iona for white wine; Concord, Norton, Ives, and Clinton for red. The market—at first mostly for fresh fruit—was so good that local enthusiasts proclaimed that "a bearing vineyard was as good as a gold mine."[149]

To take advantage of this considerable source, the first winery at Hammondsport, which has been from that time the center of the Finger Lakes industry, was founded in 1860 as the Hammondsport and Pleasant Valley Wine Company, incorporated for the purpose of producing wine, brandy, and champagne.[150] The head of this enterprise was Charles Champlin, one of the gentlemen growing grapes in Pleasant Valley, who was joined in the founding of the company by other Pleasant Valley growers. The handsome stone building that Champlin and his associates put up on the slope looking over Pleasant Valley still stands there. The first winemaker was a German named Weber,[151] but the winery aimed at a French style. The plan to produce a sparkling wine meant that a champagne maker would have to be imported: Longworth had already established that pattern in Cincinnati, and so had the Sainsevains in California. To make the French claim even plainer, the winery obtained the post office address of Rheims, and long continued to use it. The first champagne master was Joseph Masson, who was followed by a brother, Jules, and Jules by his son, Victor.[152] Both of the Masson brothers, originally from France, had come to this country to make sparkling wine in Cincinnati.[153] Thus did the production of sparkling wine in the East, after the decline of the vineyards along the Ohio, reappear and prosper under a succession of Frenchmen. But if the winemaking was French, one must remember that the vine growing owed much to the Germans.

The Pleasant Valley Wine Company shipped its first wine in 1862, and by 1864 its production had risen to around 30,000 gallons.[154] In 1867, at a banquet in Boston, its fame was made. That was a time when the literati of Boston were the tastemakers of the country, and they not merely approved of Champlin's sparkling

59 | The first winery erected in the Finger Lakes region, the Pleasant Valley winery building still stands and is still an operating winery. (*Harper's Weekly,* 11 May 1872)

wine, they gave it a name. From the point of view of Boston—the Hub, as they would have said—Pleasant Valley wine came from the remote reaches of the great West: it should be known, therefore, as "Great Western" sparkling wine, and so it has been since.[155] The name of the firm remains Pleasant Valley, but the name on its labels is always "Great Western."

Over the ridge to the west and north of Hammondsport the next valley is that of Canandaigua Lake, where grape growing on a commercial scale was begun in 1854 by a lawyer named Edward McKay, who planted Isabella vines on an acre of ground.[156] In a few years he had an excellent crop, and so his friends and neighbors began to plant vines too. The first winery was put up in 1861 at Naples, on Canandaigua Lake, by the town banker, Hiram Maxfield.[157] After the war a considerable migration of Germans and Swiss to the region took place, and the continued development of winegrowing in the Naples Valley was largely their work. Other sites along the Finger Lakes were being developed as vineyards in the 1850s and 1860s:

60 Jules Masson, who succeeded his brother Joseph as champagne master at the Pleasant Valley Wine Company in the 1860s. They founded the manufacture of sparkling wine in New York State. (*Harper's Weekly,* 11 May 1872)

Union Springs, on Cayuga Lake, was one center;[158] the hillsides of Seneca, largest of the Finger Lakes, began to be planted in 1862.[159] Winemaking, however, stayed close to Keuka and Canandaigua lakes, where it has mostly remained ever since.

Central New York, since the time of its first prosperity through the Erie Canal, has had an honorable place in the history of American horticulture. Generations of orchardists, vineyardists, nurserymen, and, latterly, plant scientists, have introduced and experimented with a great variety of fruits, and have especially attended to the grape. The great monument to this activity in the nineteenth century is the magisterial tome—it can hardly be called a mere book—entitled *The Grapes of New*

York, produced by the New York Agricultural Experiment Station at Geneva (also in the Finger Lakes region) in 1908. This work, of some 564 large quarto pages, lavishly illustrated with color plates, was published at the expense of the state under the supervision of the plant scientist U. P. Hedrick, and covers a far wider range than the title indicates. It is in fact an encyclopedia of the history of grape growing in the eastern United States to the time of its publication; it makes clear how large and important a part the work of growers, hybridizers, and scientists in upstate New York has had in that history. No doubt mere historical accident had something to do with all this: while others sought out chance seedlings, as Adlum did in Maryland, or undertook the expensive and frustrating labor of developing sound winemaking practices in unfamiliar conditions, as Longworth did in Cincinnati, the horticulturists of New York were not at all in the forefront of winemaking. When their moment came, however, they were ready, and since the early years of experiment along the Hudson, the state of New York has counted in eastern viticulture and winemaking as no other state has. This need not be a permanent condition of things, but the fact deserves to be recognized here.

The fourth and westernmost region of New York viticulture is along the shores of Lake Erie. The lake shore, which stretches over Ohio, Pennsylvania, and New York, provides the largest developed grape growing belt in the United States outside California. Planting began around Cleveland in the 1830s and around Sandusky in the next decade, though commercial development did not go very far before the 1860s. The pattern was pretty much the same in the New York section of the shoreline, which lies mostly in Chautauqua County, famous for the Chautauqua Institution as well as for its grapes—an ironic combination, given the prohibitionist character of the Chautauqua movement (the Woman's Christian Temperance Union was conceived at Chautauqua Lake in 1874).

The "grape belt" of western New York, as it has been called since the nineteenth century, occupies a narrow terrace between the waters of the lake and the high ground called the Allegheny Escarpment; the belt extends on one side to Erie, Pennsylvania, and on the other into Erie County, New York, south of Buffalo. The soil is thin, gravelly, and well drained, and though not sufficiently fertile for general farming it is well suited for grapes. More important than soil is climate: excellent air drainage retards fungus diseases, and helps to prevent frost. The combined effect of the lake and of the escarpment makes the growing season notably longer, the winters milder, the summers warmer than in the surrounding hills and valleys. The annual rainfall is less than that of the neighboring lands, to the advantage of the grape. Tradition says that the first grapevines planted in far western New York were cuttings from Massachusetts set out in 1818 on his farm in Brocton by Elijah Fay, a transplanted Yankee among the early settlers of the region. When these vines failed to do well, Fay obtained some plants of Catawba and Isabella from the Long Island nursery of William Prince and planted those in 1824.[160] From that beginning the Chautauqua region began its slow development into what became, later in the century, a virtual monoculture economy of the grape.

Elijah Fay began making wine for himself in 1830 and continued to do so until

61 Deacon Elijah Fay (1781–1860). A Massachusetts Yankee who migrated to the shores of Lake Erie in 1811, Fay is credited with planting the first grapes in the Grape Belt of New York State. He began winemaking in 1830, in part to supply sacramental wine to the First Baptist Church of Brocton, of which he was an early deacon. (From John B. Downs, *History of Chautauqua County* [1921])

his death in 1860. He was a deacon of the Baptist Church at Brocton, and so maintains the tradition of church and vine. His example does not seem to have inspired many imitators, but here and there small plantings were made, and Fay's family carried on the work. Joseph Fay, son of Elijah, planted the first commercial vineyard of the region in 1851;[161] Lincoln Fay, a nephew, was responsible for introducing the Concord grape in the late 1850s.[162] That was a decisive step, for in the Chautauqua grape belt the Concord quickly succeeded in driving out the Catawba and the Isabella, and has ever since remained the overwhelmingly dominant grape. This fact has served to distinguish the eastern, or New York, end of the Lake Erie shore from its western, or Ohio, end, where the Catawba held out against the Concord. In consequence, the Ohio end has always maintained its identity as a winegrowing region, while the New York end has for many years been the great national source of grape juice. That, however, was a late nineteenth-century turn of affairs.

The sudden expansion of the industry in Chautauqua County dates from the end of the 1850s, as it does also in the Finger Lakes and along the Ohio shore of Lake Erie. In 1859, when there were but a scant forty acres of vines in the county, the first winery, the Brocton Wine Cellars, was founded by three men, one of whom was a son and another the grandson of Elijah Fay, the original vineyardist of the region. The winery produced a modest 2,000 gallons in its first season, from which beginning it grew into a large and profitable business. In 1865 the winery had an inventory of 37,000 gallons, and the forty acres of vines around Brocton had jumped to four hundred: the rapid establishment of a "grape belt" was under way.[163] Western New York thus joined the pattern that was clearly developing in the northern states just before and during the Civil War, a pattern in which the long, intermittent, and frustrating preparations for a winemaking industry were at last completed and the basis laid for the production of wine in significant quantities from native grapes. Despite the years lost to the Civil War in the first half of the decade, the 1860s were the years of a "grape boom," years in which the acreage of vines in New York, Ohio, and Missouri increased at geometrical rates, when wineries were opened to take advantage of the new production, when new varieties were introduced almost daily to an eager public caught up in what the papers called the "grape mania." Some other elements that helped to generate the mania are taken up in the next chapter.

8

Eastern Viticulture Comes of Age

The Rise of Hybrid Grapes

W e have seen how it was that the beginning of American winegrowing depended not so much upon the skills of the winemaker as upon the contributions of the vine grower. The problem, in short, was not how to make wine but how to find a grape that would, first of all, survive, and second, yield a juice worth converting into wine. The answer came at first by accident, through the discovery of chance native seedlings that exhibited new and desirable characteristics. The Alexander was the first of these to be put on record; the Catawba the first to be good enough to maintain itself against the competition of later introductions. The discovery of such grapes was typically made by an amateur or professional horticulturist ranging the woods, or checking out the rumor of a promising vine growing in some domestic garden; again, the Alexander and the Catawba are examples of this pattern. Such plants then passed into the hands of commercial nurserymen, who performed the indispensable service of propagating them and making them widely and regularly available. Legaux and the Alexander, Adlum and the Catawba, and Prince and the Isabella illustrate this phase.

The thought that the accidental process of discovery might be systematized and controlled occurred to many people from time to time. Why wait upon the chances of nature when one could create and select one's own varieties? The simplest and most direct means for doing this lies in the fact that grapes are among those plants that do not breed true from seed. Every cultivated variety is already a storehouse of diverse genetic material, full of dominant and recessive traits ready to enter into new mixtures and relations in each successive generation. Furthermore, the receptivity of the grape to cross-fertilization means that any grape flowering in the neighborhood of another may easily be interbred. New mixes of good and bad traits may thus be readily generated by planting two or more varieties in proximity and allowing casual cross-fertilization at bloom time.

If the seeds of a Catawba, or of a Cabernet, or of any other grape, are planted, each seedling will show a greater or lesser difference from the parent. This is just what the vineyardist wishes to avoid; he wants the characters of his vines to be reliably perpetuated. Luckily for him, the vine is readily and consistently propagated vegetatively—that is, by cuttings taken from the wood of the vine—and the vineyardist therefore multiplies and maintains his stock by cuttings (or by other vegetative means, such as layering). He has nothing to do with seeds, which would only produce instability and confusion in his materials. But to the plant breeder, the genetic plasticity revealed in the vine's seedlings is just what he wants: it gives him his opportunity. The principles of Mendelian genetics were of course utterly unknown to plant breeders before the end of the nineteenth century. But the tendency to variation in grape seedlings has been known in a practical way for as long as the grape has been cultivated, and it was by taking advantage of the fact that the uncounted varieties of the European vine have been produced. It is surprising, therefore, that deliberate experiment with seedlings of native varieties was so long in coming. But so it was.[1]

As a further refinement of his methods, the plant breeder may control the mixture of qualities he seeks by artificially cross-fertilizing plants that he has selected beforehand for their desirable characters. This is the method of truly scientific hybridizing, requiring delicate manipulation of the vine's flower parts so that pollen from one plant is introduced to the ovary of another. The seed produced by this deliberate cross-fertilizing is then planted and the seedlings selected as they would be in the case of random crossings. Crosses may be made between varieties of the same species, in which case the more precise term *métis* rather than *hybrid* is used to describe the offspring. Or crosses may be made between different species, in which case the result is a true hybrid. In this very untechnical discussion I shall pay no attention to the distinction and speak indifferently of crosses and hybrids.

The understanding of the larger elements involved in the phenomenon of hybridization was, both in theory and in practice, quite well developed by the beginning of the nineteenth century. Hybridizing depends upon the principle of the sexuality of plants, a discovery established in the late seventeenth century and fully worked out in the eighteenth; by the middle years of the latter century, genuinely scientific experiment in plant hybridization was being carried on. But for some reason nobody bothered in those early days to work with grapes. Even in the nineteenth century, a time of unparalleled advance in the scientific understanding and improvement of agriculture generally, the work was rather slow to begin. The Europeans, perhaps, had no special reason to carry out grape hybridizing, since they were on the whole well suited with what they had.[2] But the Americans, with abundant reason to look for something better than the pure native vines, were not particularly forward in the business either.

The fact that certain received varieties were actually chance-produced hybrids was first recognized in print by the Philadelphia seedsman Bernard MacMahon: there were, he wrote in 1806, a number of varieties derived from crosses between different varieties of native grapes, or from crosses between native grapes and vinifera; such crosses included the Alexander[3] and the Bland. From these grapes, called "hybrids or mules," MacMahon thought it "probable that good wine may be produced."[4] Another reference to the possibilities of hybridizing grapes occurs in Dufour's *Vine-Dresser's Guide,* where Dufour expresses the hope that public-spirited people who, unlike him, have the leisure needed for such lengthy affairs, will try the "raising of new species of grapes, either by seeds or grafts." Even better, he thought, would be a public garden where hothouse experiments could be carried out in the actual cross-breeding of selected species.[5] A few years after Dufour, William Prince, in his *Treatise,* quotes the opinion of Professor Thomas Nuttall of Harvard that "hybrids betwixt the European vine (*Vitis vinifera*) and those of the United States, would better answer the variable climates of North America, than the unacclimated vine of Europe."[6] Nuttall's opinion is now the orthodox view, guiding all the work done to provide better varieties for the eastern United States.

Whether Nuttall inspired him to the experiment or whether it occurred to him independently, Prince did undertake to breed new grape varieties, being the first on record in America to do so. In his *Treatise on the Vine,* he states that he has 10,000 seedlings growing "from an admixture under every variety of circumstance."[7] Like Nuttall, Prince recommended that crosses be made between vinifera and the natives, and he believed that the native species ought to be the summer grape, aestivalis, rather than the labrusca, to avoid the foxy flavor of the latter.[8] It is curious that no further record of Prince's seedlings exists, though when one considers how many thousands of seedlings a modern plant breeder may have to raise before obtaining even one promising specimen it seems quite possible, even likely, that Prince's 10,000 yielded him nothing worth propagating. Another early experimenter with seedling selection was Samuel Pond of Massachusetts, who sometime before 1830 grew a seedling he thought worth introducing for general cultivation. Pond's Seedling, as it was known, has been called the first improved native American grape whose appearance was owing to deliberate experiment rather than chance discovery.[9]

In 1852 the list of approved grapes issued by the American Pomological Society, the standard guide for nineteenth-century horticulturists, named only two varieties, both of them native seedlings. These were the familiar Catawba and Isabella, both of which had been available since the first quarter of the century. There had, of course, been a good many introductions of other seedlings in the years up to 1852, but with very few exceptions they had proved to be disappointments, and they were invariably chance-found seedlings or the result of mixed plantings (as was, for example, the Diana, once a much-promoted grape, introduced in 1843).

What has been called the "novitiate stage"[10] of our grape breeding came to an end in 1852 when Dr. William W. Valk, a physician of Flushing, Long Island, exhibited before the American Pomological Society some grapes from a vine that he had produced by crossing the native Isabella, a labrusca, with the vinifera Black Hamburgh. The variety, called Ada, is now recognized as the first deliberately produced hybrid of the native and European grapes.[11]

Valk had begun his experiments in 1845, but even before that another grape breeder had begun to create hybrids of native and vinifera species. He was John Fisk Allen, of Salem, Massachusetts, the author of a book entitled *The Culture of the Grape* (1847). In 1843–44 he had fertilized an Isabella vine with pollen from Chasselas de Fontainebleau. From the produce of the resulting seed, he eventually selected a seedling that was introduced in 1854, two years later than Valk's Ada, as Allen's White Hybrid or simply Allen's Hybrid.[12] This was the first such grape actually to be distributed for cultivation, and so had the important function of establishing the fact against all doubters that the native-vinifera cross could be made practical. The vine was, according to Hedrick, grown for a generation everywhere that grapes were grown in this country and in Canada.[13] Under these testing circumstances, it soon began to show the weaknesses of all primary hybrids, as they are called: a tenderness to cold and a susceptibility to the diseases that had always devastated its European parent in the eastern United States. Its cultivation was therefore given up, and Allen's Hybrid has now joined the Alexander on the list of grapes of historic memory.

By a curious coincidence, a second, even more important, hybridizer was also at work in Salem, a small town in a region where there is no commercial viticulture. This was Edward Staniford Rogers, the son of a Salem merchant, a shy recluse who worked in an old, choked garden adjoining the family home (inevitably one thinks of Hawthorne's House of Seven Gables and its old New England inmates, also denizens of Salem).[14] Inspired by an article summarizing what was then known of the principles of plant hybridization, Rogers made his first and most successful crosses in 1851. For the pistillate (female) parent, he chose the wild Mammoth or Sage grape of New England, vigorously described by a contemporary as "a fox of the strongest odor, and of the most execrable and uneatable quality," but having the desirable characters of vigorous growth, earliness, hardiness, and large size of bunch.[15] Rogers fertilized flowers of this variety with pollen from both Black Hamburgh and White Chasselas vines, and from these crosses he ultimately obtained forty-five seedlings. By the end of the decade he was sending out cuttings of his hybrids, all of them identified by numbers only, to the later confusion of things. Some did acquire names as they entered cultivation: Rogers' No. 1, for example, was christened Goethe; No. 3 became Massasoit; No. 4, Wilder; and so on through ten more names, the best known of which is Agawam (originally Rogers' No. 15). None of these grapes has ever established itself as a leading variety (though one may note that Salem, Rogers' No. 22, was until recent years sold as a varietal wine by Widmer's Winery in New York State). Yet their quality

as a group was astonishingly high, considering the wretched character of the labrusca mother. This demonstration of what hybridizing could do towards quality
was not lost. The eminent horticulturist Marshall P. Wilder, president of the
American Pomological Society and the namesake of one of Rogers' grapes, proclaimed in a letter to Rogers: "You have achieved a conquest over nature, and your
efforts will constitute a new era in American grape culture."[16]

The stir created by Rogers' new grapes excited an unparalleled interest in
viticulture generally: "Never before or since," asserts one writer, "has grape growing in the United States received the attention given to it during the decade following the introduction of the Rogers Hybrids."[17] Everywhere in the country, amateurs and professionals took up the challenging sport of grape breeding—a sport
in which, at least, some six or seven years might elapse before any fruit could be
produced for judgment, and in which the effort of years might well produce
nothing at all of any distinct value. Among the notable names—the list might be
prolonged through scores and hundreds—a few may be specified. George W.
Campbell, a merchant of Delaware, Ohio, was led by his interest to become a professional nurseryman specializing in grapes, of which he produced thousands of
seedlings; James H. Ricketts, a bookbinder of Newburgh, New York, introduced
flashy new varieties with names like Bacchus, Don Juan, and Lady Washington.
George Haskell, a lawyer of Ipswich, Massachusetts, specialized in labrusca-
vinifera crosses like his compatriot Rogers.[18] In Missouri we have already noticed
Jacob Rommel, whose emphasis was not on hybrids of the natives with vinifera but
on crosses between the native species of labrusca and riparia, selected with an eye
to the requirements of the Middle West. In Kansas, as early as the 1860s, when the
territory had barely been converted into a state, John Burr, a transplanted Connecticut Yankee, began to produce a series of hybrids at his vineyard in Leavenworth, where his neighbor and friend, Joseph Stayman, also produced new varieties of grapes as part of his more extensive work in plant breeding (the Stayman
apple has survived better than any of Stayman's grape varieties).[19]

With such widespread activity and interest surging through the country, the
press inevitably began to talk of a "new era," as Wilder had said it would be. It
was, and it was not. It was, in virtue of the possibilities of scientific breeding that
had been vindicated by Allen and Rogers at midcentury. It was not, in virtue of the
fact that despite the flood of new varieties poured out in the latter half of the century, eastern viticulture remained based for the next one hundred years almost entirely upon exactly the native varieties already available by 1860.

The defects of such primary hybrids as those we have just been describing
were quickly recognized: too much vinifera meant susceptibility to all its weaknesses; too much native vine meant a dominance of all those undesirable fruit
qualities, the elimination of which was the very object of the hybridizing in the first
place. The next step was to undertake secondary hybrids—crosses of hybrids with
natives, or of hybrids with hybrids. The two pioneers of this phase were Jacob
Moore, of Brighton, New York, and Andrew Jackson Caywood, of Marlboro, New

York, both commercial nurserymen. Moore, described by Hedrick as a man of "a high degree of intelligence and an unusually keen sense of the latent possibilities in plants,"[20] spent half a century in the unwearied pursuit of a grape that would combine the best of old and new. Moore's most successful introduction, the Diamond (or more often Moore's Diamond) is a cross in which the vinifera strain is dilute, yet strong enough to have its effect upon the fruit quality; it is still used in the sparkling blends of the Finger Lakes, and occasionally in still, dry wines. Caywood's contribution to the permanent varietal stock of eastern viticulture is the grape called Dutchess; it is really a tertiary hybrid, or more, for its parentage of White Concord, Delaware, and Walter combines vinifera, labrusca, Bourquiniana, and aestivalis. Caywood's vineyard at Marlboro is still growing as part of Benmarl Vineyards;[21] and the Dutchess grape still commands the highest prices for native grapes in New York.

Dutchess, Diamond, Elvira, and other varieties that came out of the active ferment of plant breeding following Rogers' hybrids still survive in a modest way in eastern vineyards; they never achieved any moment of dominance. Yet it would be wrong to overlook their share in contributing to the development of American winemaking. The marked improvement in vine and fruit quality that they provided encouraged later experimenters to continue. Furthermore, scientific hybridizing required exact study of the native varieties to establish their characters for vigor, resistance to insects and diseases, hardiness, and fruit quality. Only when such things were determined could intelligent combination of characters be possible, and so the interest in hybridizing had as a necessary consequence the effect of stimulating the essential work of analyzing the material available.

The logic of plant breeding also required that the climate and soils of vineyard sites be studied in new detail and with exactitude, for specific characters implied specific circumstances in which they might best develop. One can see just such knowledge being accumulated in the literature of the latter half of the century; it is fair to say that the emergence of the controlled hybrid had something to do with that accumulation, for it was now, prospectively at least, worth determining such matters so that improved grapes could be grown in proper conditions. In the perspective of European winegrowing, all winegrowing in the rest of the world is still in its infancy. But in the brief chronicle of American winegrowing, the innocent age of viticulture ended with the appearance of the controlled hybrid.

Controlled hybridizing was by no means the only source of new varieties. The chance seedling found in the wild, or the botanical sport growing in a small town garden were still very much part of the picture, and, indeed, have provided the varieties that dominate it still. Of the uncounted number of such grapes, three may be singled out for remark, not just for themselves but because their histories are representative of so much in the story of American winegrowing.

The first of these three, the Delaware, is the fruit of a wild seedling, like the Alexander, the Catawba, and the Isabella. No one knows where it came from, or even who it was, for certain, who had the merit of first cultivating it. Yet it is as

good a native grape—pure-bred or hybrid—as has ever grown in eastern America.
It is derived from labrusca, but is so ameliorated by crossing that it is without any
foxiness. A well-made Delaware is among the very best white wines, and therefore
among the very best wines, that the East produces today from native vines.
Hedrick's claim that "there is no variety of *Vitis vinifera* more richly or more deli-
cately flavored or with a more agreeable aroma"[22] is extravagant, but at least indicates Delaware's standing at the head of the old native varieties.

Delaware came into public knowledge in 1849, when the editor of the local
newspaper in Delaware, Ohio (north of Columbus), saw some grapes of this variety brought in from a farm in the neighborhood. On inquiry, he learned that the
farmer had brought the vine from New Jersey more than twenty years earlier. Its
source in New Jersey appeared to be the garden of a Swiss named Provost, of
Frenchtown, Hunterdon County, on the banks of the Delaware River—though
that is only a coincidence of names: the grape is named for the town in Ohio, not
the river. By this time, Provost was dead, and where he got his vines remains a
mystery: some said they came from Italy; some said from a German newly arrived
in this country; some said from Virginia by way of Philadelphia.[23] Others disagreed
with all such stories of exotic origin and maintained that the vine was a seedling
from Provost's own garden. These stories and counter-stories, assertions and contradictions, flowed through the columns of the horticultural press pretty freely in
the generation after the Delaware was brought forward, and they have left the
question of the variety's origin just where it was before the controversy started.
The experts also disagree over the hybrid constitution of the Delaware. As Bailey
has said, "It is one of those fortuitous riddles which nature now and then produces,
the genesis of which, if known and well considered, might afford new light to the
intending breeder of plants."[24] The excellence and the inexplicability of the Delaware are a reminder to the grape breeder not to claim too much for his art. In any
case, the qualities of the Delaware as a wine grape were quickly recognized, so that
it was established in general cultivation before the end of the 1850s.

The proprietary claim to the second of our exemplary new varieties is quite
clear. The grape called Iona was introduced by Dr. C. W. Grant, a dentist originally of Newburgh, New York.[25] Newburgh was a notable spot in these years as
the home of the grape breeder A. J. Caywood and of the distinguished horticulturists
and journalists Andrew Jackson Downing and his brother Charles. Perhaps Grant
acquired some of his enthusiasm for viticulture from them. In 1849 Grant bought
Iona Island, an island of 119 acres in the Hudson River near Peekskill; after 1856
he made his home there and devoted himself to the cultivation of his vineyard and
to the sale of vines from it. Grant's main stock in trade was his Iona grape, which
he identified as a seedling of Diana (itself a seedling of Catawba), and introduced
in 1863. Coming into the market as it did towards the close of the Civil War, it
coincided with the height of the grape mania sweeping the eastern states, and
Grant was astute enough to see that the moment favored him. "Next to oil," as the
Gardener's Monthly remarked in 1865 (it was the era of the Pennsylvania oil boom

too), "nothing is so much spoken of in the cars, on the street, by the roadside, everywhere, as the grape, and grape native wine."[26] This was the time when, as one old nurseryman remembered, he had carried over a thousand dollars worth of grape cuttings on his back from his nursery to the shipping office in one trip.[27] Itinerant plant salesmen travelled the country peddling "guaranteed" varieties of vines to eager customers. There was a good deal of honest, but premature, promotion of newly introduced varieties that had not been proven and that, after a few years of trial, belied all the imaginary qualities claimed for them. Worse than that were the inevitable frauds generated by an inflated and heated demand for vines.

Grant well understood how to work in such an atmosphere. He advertised extensively and aggressively in the press, using all the machinery of testimonials, premiums, and self-assertion. A typical advertisement modestly declares that the Iona "equals the best European kinds in richness, purity and refinement . . . it is unequalled for fine, rich, enduring wine. . . . It is only with such grapes as this that we can equal the fine wines of Europe."[28] Grant secured the kind of frequent and respectful mention in magazines and books that comes from applying what we now call public relations, but for which there was not yet, in those days, any name other than "puffing." An extreme, yet characteristic, piece of promotion occurred in 1864 when Grant and his agents proclaimed a grand "Fruit-Growers' Convention" to be held for the encouragement of national horticulture at Grant's Iona Island.[29] By disingenuous means, Grant got a whole raft of New York public men to patronize the "Convention"—William Cullen Bryant, Horace Greeley, and Henry Ward Beecher among them. An ambitious program of papers and demonstrations was outlined, and a special steamer was laid on to bring the crowds upriver from the city to Iona Island. Grant, his island vineyards, and his Iona grape were all prominent in the print promoting this exciting affair.

The whole thing was a bold sham. No steamer appeared on the day appointed. Still, many people made their way to Peekskill by train, to find that no adequate preparations had been made to receive them and that most of the advertised talks and entertainments had not been arranged. What they did find was an unannounced auction of 10,000 cuttings of Dr. Grant's Iona grape at which they were encouraged to bid. No other activities would begin until the auction had been carried out. The notabilities—Bryant, Greeley et al.—had prudently been taken off to lunch and kept in good humor by Grant while the general public was taken for what it would give. When, towards the end of the day, a horticultural meeting was at last held in a huddled up sort of way, only some random and unconcerted speeches were given. Whether Grant was wholly responsible for the details of this dubious enterprise, and whether it did him more good than harm in the long run, we do not know. The episode tells us at any rate that somebody judged that the public interest in grapes at this time would stand a good deal of abusing, and that any publicity was good publicity.

The price of the Iona was kept high, and Grant's exclusive interest in its propagation and sale jealously guarded (the right of securing a patent in new plants was not obtained in this country until the next century). But Grant did not have a wholly smooth success with his new grape. There were skeptics who doubted out loud that it had anything like the virtues that Grant attributed to it; he had rivals in whose interest it was to denigrate it noisily; and the very intensity of the promotion it received inevitably provoked reaction. It is not surprising, therefore, that, as Hedrick says, "probably no American variety has been the subject of more caustic discussions than this one and it is only within the last few years that its merits could be impartially estimated."[30] And what are the merits? The truth is that the variety has great good qualities and equally great defects. The fruit is sweet, delicate, and juicy, yielding a wine that Wagner describes as "one of the best of those produced by the American hybrids—pale, very clean and dry, with a racy aroma that shows up particularly well under champagnization."[31] The vine itself, however, is condemned as "the poorest in the vineyard"[32]—troublesome to grow, lacking hardiness and vigor, vulnerable to all diseases, demanding special soils. It has for these reasons almost disappeared from commercial cultivation. As for Iona Island, that passed into the hands of the U.S. Navy and served as an ammunition depot until, in 1965, it became a state park. Parking lots and picnic grounds now occupy the land where Iona grapes once grew. So much for the second of our representative hybrids.

Hedrick estimates that in the fifty years following the introduction of Rogers' hybrids, some 2,000 new American hybrids were named and in some way made public.[33] The list of varietal names in *The Grapes of New York* runs from Abby Clingotten, Ada, Adelaide, Adelia, through Leon, Letovey, Lewis, Lexington, to Zane, Zelia, Zinnia, Zita, and Zoe. In such a spate of new varieties, relatively few might be expected to survive; one would suppose, however, that no one grape would emerge to dominate all others. Yet that, or something very like that, is what happened from the fateful moment when Ephraim Bull noticed a chance seedling growing just outside his garden in Concord, Massachusetts.[34] Bull was a goldbeater by trade, making and selling gold leaf for a living. His passion, however, was horticulture, and especially grape growing, with which he had experimented since childhood. He had left Boston for Concord partly in order to indulge his taste for gardening, and now lived in a house called Grapevine Cottage (where, later, his neighbor to the west was Nathaniel Hawthorne).

The sight of the seedling near his garden suggested to Bull that he might test the theory of the Belgian horticulturist Jean-Baptiste Van Mons that successive generations of seedlings would produce a greatly ameliorated plant. Accounts of the circumstances conflict, and some points remain obscure, but in one tradition (I follow Bailey) the seedling is explained as the result of wild grapes scattered by some grape-eating boys the summer before. This was in 1840. Three years later, Bull obtained fruit from the wild vine and planted whole berries from it in his garden. One of the resultant seedlings fruited in 1849 and seemed so superior that Bull destroyed the other seedlings in order to concentrate on the survivor, a blue-black grape he named Concord, which, he prophesied, would be the basis of a new in-

62   Ephraim Bull (1806–95), of Concord, Massachusetts, shown here with the original vine of the Concord grape that he propagated and named. By far the most popular and widely planted grape ever introduced in this country, the Concord still defines "grape" for most Americans. (From Kansas State Horticultural Society, *How to Grow and Use the Grape in Kansas* [1901])

dustry: "I venture to predict," Bull wrote, "that the man is now born who will see New England supplying herself with native wines, and even exporting them."[35]

Bull exhibited his new grape before the Massachusetts Horticultural Society in 1853, and in 1854 it was offered for sale by Hovey and Company, the leading Boston nursery. From that moment it spread throughout the country with astonishing rapidity. So astute was the promotion and so eager the demand that in March 1854 Concord was selling for $5 a plant![36] It reached western New York, the newest region of viticulture, in the year of its release, and it was established as a major variety in Missouri, the western edge of settlement, before the Civil War. No one can calculate the number of fences and back-yard arbors that Concord has adorned throughout America (even on the West Coast), where it has provided the archetypal idea of "grape" for generations of Americans. Its fruit and its foliage and its color are the model for most pictures of the grape in this country, so that the Concord image as well as the Concord flavor is standard for us. The reason for its success is concisely put by Bailey: "It was the first variety of sufficient hardiness,

63   The first offering of the Concord grape, which was to sweep the country and dominate eastern winegrowing for the next century. Note that no claim is made in this notice for the Concord as a wine grape. (*The Cultivator*, April 1854)

The Concord Grape.

Messrs. HOVEY & CO., 7 *Merchants' Row, Boston,*

HAVE the pleasure of announcing that thay will offer for sale on the 1st of April next, Mr. Bull's new Seedling Grape, the whole stock of which has been placed in their hands for disposal.

This remarkably fine new American variety is the greatest acquisition that has ever yet been made to our hardy grapes, and supplies the desideratum so long wanted, of a superior table grape, sufficiently hardy to withstand the coldest climate, and early enough to mature its fruit in any part of the Northern or New-England States. It is *four weeks* earlier than the Isabella, and nearly *two weeks* earlier than the Diana. It was fully ripe the last season (1853) about 3d *of September*, when Messrs. Hovey & Co. exhibited fine specimens from Mr. Bull's original vine, before the Massachusetts Horticultural Society.

It is a most vigorous growing vine, perfectly hardy, with bunches of large size, often weighing a pound, and with large roundish, oval berries, frequently measuring an inch in diameter; color very dark, covered with a thick blue bloom; flesh free from all pulp; flavor very rich and luscious, with a fine sprightly aroma. The foliage is large, broad and thick, and the berries have never been known to *mildew, rot*, and drop off, under any circumstances during the five years since it has first borne fruit. All good judges who have tasted it, pronounce it far superior to the Isabella in its ripest condition. A full description of it with an engraving, appears in the February number of the Magazine of Horticulture.

Opinions of the Fruit Committee of the Mass. Hort. Society.

1852. Sept. "Seedling Grape, from E. W Bull, large, handsome and excellent."

1853. Sept. "Fully equal to specimens last year, and proves to be a remarkably early, handsome, and very superior grape."

Fine strong one year old vines will be ready for delivery April 1st, at $5 each, and to the trade at $40 per dozen. All orders will be executed in the rotation in which they are received.

Messrs. Hovey & Co. will also offer for sale, at the same time, the BOSTON PEAR and HOVEY CHERRY. two new and superior varieties of fruit, particulars of which will be given hereafter. Feb. 23—w2tm1t productiveness and immunity from diseases to carry the culture of the vine into every garden of the land."[37] Its tough and fruitful nature, and its adaptability to a wide variety of conditions, have made Concord almost irresistible to commercial growers.

Yet one may regret that our American standard of the grape was set by such a variety as the Concord. It is a pure-bred labrusca, with all the foxiness of its kind; the skin is tough and astringent, the seeds large; the sugar content is not high, and the juice will not make even a barely tolerable wine without considerable artificial sweetening. In consequence the wine of Concord is typically sweet, and so has reinforced the American tendency to prefer a sweet to a dry wine. Nor has its wine any delicacy or complexity of flavor: the strong labrusca aroma and the taste of sugar pretty much exhaust its appeal. Like nearly all tastes, the taste for Concord wine can be acquired, but acquiring it entails a considerable lowering of the powers of discrimination. It would be impossible to estimate how much the taste for Concord and for the vinous confections made from it have retarded the development of a civilized tradition in which dry table wines for everyday use are taken as the standard. It is equally impossible to doubt that the Concord has had much to do with the fact that such a development has been greatly retarded. There is, perhaps, a form of Gresham's Law operating on wine as well as on currency, so that the bad drives out the good. But currencies can be reformed, and we can hope from the many signs in America today that a national taste in wine can be reformed too. The withering away of the taste for Concord is a necessary first step.[38]

In 1864 Horace Greeley, who liked to appear as, among other things, a patron of agriculture, offered a prize of $100 to be awarded to the man who should produce the best grape for general culture in America (the "best" being understood to mean the highest possible vinifera character in the fruit and the highest possible native character in the vine). Later that year, obviously impressed by the fanfare that accompanied Dr. Grant's introduction of the Iona, the committee awarded the prize to that grape. This hasty decision at once caused a flap—including charges of fraud—and the prize was withdrawn so that more experience might be gained before a decision was given. Two years later the prize was bestowed on Bull for the Concord, and this time the committee's decision stood firm. Concord—a pure native of the natives, without a suspicion of vinifera genes—was crowned, in Greeley's words, as "the grape for the millions."[39]

Ephraim Bull lived to be ninety before his death in 1895 at the house in Concord where he had developed his celebrated grape. He had grown thousands of seedlings since his discovery of the Concord, but that lightning was to strike only once in his plant-breeding career. He made little or nothing from the fabulous success of the Concord, other growers having quickly propagated and advertised the vine without restraint. His last days were impoverished and embittered. The legend on his tombstone in Sleepy Hollow Cemetery at Concord reads: "He sowed, others reaped." A modest memorial stone commemorating Bull and his grape was erected by the town of Concord and is now set into the fence running around the old garden where the original vine grew. It reads thus:

Ephraim Wales Bull planted seeds of a wild Labrusca grape found growing on this hillside which after three generations[40] through his work and wisdom became in this garden in September 1849 the Concord grape.

One has no wish to denigrate Bull, who was, by all accounts, a man of simple virtue and homely eccentricity. Still, as Philip Wagner has well said, the winemaker who approaches the shrine erected to the Concord grape does so with "mingled emotions."[41] That mingling is complicated even more by the knowledge that Bull himself was a teetotaller. Though he made wine, he did not drink it.[42]

The abundance of new varieties of American grapes and the rapidly spreading cultivation of the vine throughout the country began to form a curious new taste: people began *eating* grapes, as they might do with apples or peaches or cherries, instead of making them into wine. Of course, the fact that grapes were good to eat was no mystery: ancient laws prohibit the casual picking of grapes from vineyards, sufficient testimony that people would do so unless prevented. The French language recognizes both *raisins de table* and *raisins de cuve,* and of the former there are enough varieties to show that the taste is one going far back into botanic history. But table grapes, in the countries of vinifera, were strictly secondary; the destiny of the grape as a source of wine was so obvious that it was not thought of as a crop for any other purpose (one has to except the raisin grape, while noting that the raisin is, like wine, another form of preserved, not fresh, grape). In America the case was different. On the whole, the native varieties, even improved, were not up to wine-making standards, nor would they make raisins, the ratio of sugar to water being too low. But they had strong flavors (much more marked than those of the relatively bland vinifera), and enough sugar to make them palatable, if not enough for sound, stable wine. Gradually, the native grapes became a staple of the fresh fruit market instead of the winery.

Underhill's vineyards at Croton, for example, were first developed to supply fresh fruit to New York. But grapes for the table were still a new idea: one story says that when the first fresh grapes were sent to Buffalo for sale from the Chautauqua district, no one at first knew what they were meant for.[43] By the end of the century, for some parts of the community at any rate, the grape was almost divorced from its immemorial role as the mother of wine and was thought of rather as a fruit for eating or as a source of pasteurized, unfermented grape juice—a strange transformation! The force of the prohibition movement no doubt had much to do with this development. But the nature of the native grape in itself made it possible. The change is clearly described by Liberty Hyde Bailey (no prohibitionist). North America, he writes, "has given the world a new fruit in its grapes. This American grape is much unlike the European fruit. It is essentially a table fruit, whereas the other is a wine fruit." And, he adds, "it was not until the middle of the present century that the modern table use of the native grape began to be appreciated and understood."[44] In contemplating the phenomenon of the grape boom of midcentury and after, then, one must keep in mind this new American taste for grapes as table fruit as an element in it.

The Creation of Institutional Supports for Winegrowing

In the central decades of the nineteenth century, viticulture and winemaking became permanent institutions in the United States. Before that could happen, however, certain conditions had to be met; and when they were, still others had to be met so that the achievement could be sustained. Information, research, organization, publicity, legislation—all these complicated matters had to be provided for, and to do that a number of different agencies, some with overlapping functions, grew up. Not all can be dealt with here, but the more elementary forms of support may be briefly described.

The agricultural societies, local and state, were among them. Before the days of a vast scientific establishment such as we know, in which the results of research carried on at hundreds and thousands of laboratories, experiment stations, and universities are quickly collected, organized, and published, it was impossible for one man to profit readily from another's experience in this country. Viticulture was especially subject to the penalties of ignorance, as growers kept repeating over and over what were, in the circumstances, their futile trials of vinifera. Even into the nineteenth century the situation persisted: we have seen, for example, how the emigré French of 1817 went off to grow grapes in Alabama in entire ignorance of Dufour's work in Kentucky and Indiana—they learned too late, to their cost, what he might have quickly told them.

The earliest efforts to fill this large vacuum of experimental and practical knowledge in agriculture were made by societies whose interests were much wider than agriculture. We have already seen the work of the London Society for the Encouragement of the Arts in the colonial period; its domestic equivalent, the American Philosophical Society, earned a place in the records for its publication of Antill's pioneer treatise in 1771. But these were societies only incidentally interested in agriculture, and only intermittently in viticulture. The pattern of development since the middle of the eighteenth century has naturally been the formation of groups having more and more narrowly focused special interests—from learned groups like the American Philosophical Society the movement was to general agricultural societies and from them to horticultural societies; that interest was then narrowed to pomological societies and next to associations of grape growers, until at last we reach the departments and special branches of agricultural experiment stations and universities devoted exclusively to research in viticulture or winemaking. The whole process follows a fairly regular chronological sequence, as viticulture and winemaking become more secure and extensive and their requirements more distinct.

Organizations specifically concerned with agriculture appeared soon after the Revolution—the Agricultural Society of South Carolina and the Philadelphia Society for the Promotion of Agriculture, both formed in 1785, were the earliest. Both took an interest in viticulture, too. The example they set was widely imitated in the first half of the nineteenth century, and as state and local agricultural societies proliferated, they made it possible for the next phase to develop. This was the organization of horticultural societies—*horticulture* being understood as the art of cultivating those plants that grow in gardens, among which grapes are by tradition numbered. Such societies began with the New York Horticultural Society in 1818, but far and away the most prestigious and opulent through the nineteenth century was the Massachusetts Horticultural Society, founded in 1829, expensively housed in Horticultural Hall in Boston, and the proprietor for many years of a thirty-acre experimental garden. The society's library is a major collection, and its publications extend through many notable volumes. The exhibitions of the society around midcentury were important popular and scientific occasions; it was at one of them that the Concord grape was brought before the world. Its long-time president, Marshal Wilder, was enthusiastically interested in viticulture; it was he who presided over the dinner at which Great Western champagne received its name, and it was for him that Rogers named one of his pioneering hybrid grapes.

The next phase of specialization was to restrict horticulture to pomology—the science of fruit growing. The Ohio Pomological Society was founded in 1847, with grape growing as a major, though not exclusive, interest. The increasing importance of fruit culture in the rest of the United States led to the formation of the American Pomological Society, which quickly became the largest and most active organization of pomologists in the world.[45] This was the agency that, during the years of the grape mania, had a major share in publicizing, testing, and passing judgment on the hundreds of varieties that tried to crowd into the market. Its list of approved varieties was always kept to an austerely limited number, no doubt for the real security and comfort of the amateur.

The last refinement of specialization in the middle of the century came about with the formation of societies confined exclusively to grape and wine growers. The first, so far as I can find, was the Gasconade Grape Growing Society of Hermann, Missouri, chartered in 1849 to promote winegrowing in the county of which Hermann is the seat.[46] The next was the American Wine Growers' Association, founded at Cincinnati in 1851.[47] In the next few years the number of comparable organizations formed is rather remarkable, considering the still very small scale of viticulture in this country: the record is perhaps better evidence of the gregarious tendencies of nineteenth-century Americans in their lonely, underpopulated country than it is of the economic importance of the industry. In any case, there were associations organized in Pleasant Valley, New York; Aiken, South Carolina; Evansville, Indiana (this one German-speaking); on the Lake Erie shore; in Nauvoo, Illinois; St. Louis, Missouri; Richland, Missouri; and generally for the states of New York and Illinois.[48] None of these societies has left a trace today, except for a few mouldering files of their publications to be found in scattered libraries. But in their day they provided a structure where none had existed before; they made the efficient exchange of information possible and provided a basis for mutual support and enterprise.

Another service to winegrowing in this country was provided by the fairs and exhibitions. By midcentury state and county fairs were ritual events in rural America, and in urban America too, at a time when the city was still in touch with the country. Most such fairs accepted wine among their regular exhibits, and many of them made wine judging and the award of premiums part of their activity. The nineteenth century was not only the golden age of the agricultural fair but the era of the international exhibition. The model not just for the first but for *all* subsequent instances of this sort of exposition sprang full-blown from the brow of Prince Albert in 1851 and was triumphantly revealed to the world as the Great Exhibition. Wine from Cincinnati was among the exhibits sent over to represent American industry at this archetypal exhibition. Thereafter there was no important congress, exhibition, exposition, or world's fair without its contingent of American wines among the competitors. A few labels adorning commercial bottlings today still display the proud golden medals collected in those palmy days—Turin, Vienna, Paris, Rome, London, Lisbon, Rio de Janeiro—all acknowledged the humble efforts of the United States to produce wines worthy to be judged with those of the established wine countries.

It was not only at the local and state level that supporting organizations for winegrowing were at work. The national government, too, gave a strong helping hand to the early commercial wine industry, a fact likely to surprise many readers. Any American who has grown up in the twentieth century, after the great chasm made in our winegrowing history by Prohibition, is conditioned to think that the federal government has nothing to do with winegrowing. The subject is not referred to in federal publications; it is not provided for in the sums granted to the appropriate research agencies; it is not an issue in anyone's campaign. This state of affairs is, we may hope, an accident following from the bad old days of the Noble Experiment. The long history of the country's interest in winegrowing was suppressed then, and after Repeal the sensitiveness and timidity of politicians towards the question made it easy for a few aggressive, well-placed legislators to obstruct any effort to restore the industry to a place among the legitimate objects of the government's interest. It is enough to say here that the present situation is an anomaly, and that the federal government was not always derelict in its duty in this respect, as it has been now for more than a generation. Quite the contrary. All of the founding fathers were, without exception, not only steady friends of wine, but active propagandists for it. Washington, Jefferson, Madison, and Monroe were all interested in practical viticulture, and would have been winegrowers themselves if they could have found the way to success.

The best evidence of the official disposition in favor of wine is the fact that, in the early years of the republic, no tax was laid on it. Instead, the government did what it could to help those who undertook to provide the country with native wines. We have already seen how Dufour, in 1802, and the French emigrés, in 1817, were granted large tracts of land on favorable terms in the hope that they could turn the trick of making wine in considerable quantities. Both of these episodes, one may note, were essentially repetitions in the federal era of the experiments made in colonial Virginia and South Carolina to achieve a winegrowing industry through the assistance of the state.

When both Dufour and the French failed to make good on their promises, Congress quite naturally drew back from further trials of that kind.[49] But when, in the 1840s and the 1850s, it began to appear that viticulture was, after all, going to be successfully established in this country, the federal government again began to contribute to the work. This first took the form of articles on viticulture and wine-making published in the annual reports of the agricultural branch of the Patent Office, the forerunner of the U.S. Department of Agriculture.[50] The articles were of every kind, both historical and technical, and were gathered from both domestic and foreign sources. Translations of French treatises on winemaking, notes from middle western growers on the adaptation of native varieties to new conditions, and remarks on diseases, pruning methods, and the best modes of planting and propagation were all gathered and published for general distribution. One of Longworth's best and most informative articles on the wine industry of Ohio, for example, appears in the Patent Office *Report* for 1847. The office was also a clearing house for information about new varieties, and it collected and sent out cuttings to be tried by interested growers all over the country.

In 1857 the Patent Office determined to make a systematic effort to collect and study native vines to learn which were best for table and wine. One agent, H. C. Williams, was sent from Washington to explore Arkansas, the Indian Territory (Oklahoma we call it now), and northern Texas. In the next year, 1858, Williams travelled to New Mexico over the Santa Fe Trail, and thence into the valley of the Rio Grande down to El Paso, where he found that a small wine industry, going back to the seventeenth century and based on vinifera, was still in existence. Methods were exceedingly primitive: cowhides, for example, did duty for barrels in that woodless country. But to Williams' eye, the possibilities were spacious: the Rio Grande Valley in west Texas, he informed his superiors in Washington, is "the Eden of the Grape."[51]

At the same time that Williams was making his western explorations, another agent, John F. Weber, was sent on a similar mission to the middle Atlantic and New England states. He collected thirty-eight different varieties that seemed worth examination, and reported that people in the East were keenly interested in grape growing:

> I found, in general, a lively interest among all classes for this noble and lucrative branch of horticulture. The intention of the Patent Office to encourage the culture of the vine through the whole country, by collecting and disseminating knowledge relating to it, and the best methods of wine-making, was well appreciated, and especially so on account of the direct way which had been chosen.[52]

One of Weber's specimens had been provided from Concord, Massachusetts, not by Ephraim Bull but by another celebrated Concordian, Ralph Waldo Emerson, who had growing on his house a large labrusca of the variety called Sage, or Mam-

64   The United States Propagating Garden, Washington, D.C., established under the Patent Office in 1858 (the Department of Agriculture did not yet exist); the collection, propagation, and dissemination of grapes was an important part of the garden's work. The trellis that runs behind the ornamental gazebo in this engraving and connects the two greenhouses was exclusively for the training of native grapes; elsewhere in the garden there were 25,000 vines of some fifty varieties by 1859. (*Report of the Commissioner of Patents: Agriculture, 1858* [1859])

moth. All of the specimens were then sent to Boston for chemical analysis by the distinguished American scientist Charles T. Jackson (the co-discoverer of ether, and, incidentally, Emerson's brother-in-law); the results of Weber's collecting and of Jackson's analyses, published in the official *Report* of the Patent Office, gave a clearer and more accurate picture of the winemaking promise of the native vines than anything else yet available.

Besides gathering information in the field and from the published literature, the Patent Office did work of its own in Washington. An experimental garden was set up there in 1858, and work with grapes was a large part of the activity carried on.[53] Thus was realized, at last, and in a modest way, that "national vineyard" for which so many early growers, including Antill and Adlum, had prayed. The superintendent of the garden, William Saunders, made grapes a speciality, and published several papers on the subject. Within a year of its establishment, the garden had 25,000 seedlings of fifty different varieties of grapes growing; these included not only natives but vinifera as well, to be used in hybridizing experiments. By 1863 there were one hundred varieties in the garden; from this stock cuttings were sent out for trial in various parts of the country, and to it additions were regularly made from all available sources.

The scale and importance of American agriculture made it inevitable that a separate department of the government would need to be devoted to its interests. This came about in 1862, when the agricultural division of the Patent Office was separated from its parent and reestablished as the Department of Agriculture. The change made no difference to the policy of encouraging viticulture and winemaking; both subjects remained part of the regular concern of the department, and continued to do so until Prohibition. Since that time, as has been said, the department has, even after Repeal, yielded to prohibitionist pressure and studiously avoided any association with winemaking. It is agreeable to report the first signs of a turn back towards the department's original tradition; the 1977 *Yearbook* of the department, devoted to the subject of home gardening, contains not merely a brief article on viticulture by a department specialist, but another on home winemaking. It is significant of the lost ground yet to be made up that the winemaking article was written, not by a member of the department, but by the distinguished professional Philip Wagner. Nevertheless, the appearance of the book marks a turn, a welcome turn, in the right direction.

The literature of winegrowing kept pace with the growth of the industry. Articles and books devoted to the subject in the seventeenth and eighteenth centuries can be counted on one's fingers. By the middle of the nineteenth century the flow of print on vines and wine, if not precisely a flood, had at least become a substantial and steady stream.

The pioneer agricultural magazine was the *American Farmer,* published in Baltimore from 1819; it was followed by magazines with specialized regional appeal such as the *New England Farmer* (1822), the *Rural New Yorker* (1849), and the *Southern Cultivator* (1843); all of these took practical winegrowing as part of their province. Next came the more highly specialized publications: magazines devoted to horticulture, to pomology, and then to grapes and wine. *The Horticulturist,* founded in 1846 by the eminent writer and botanist Andrew Jackson Downing, was a type of the best of these.

The first periodical entirely devoted to winegrowing was the *Grape Culturist,* published in St. Louis from 1869 to 1871 and edited by George Husmann. The magazine was premature: there was not yet a sufficiently widespread commercial interest to sustain it. Yet there are many excellent things in it. In 1854, in New York, a different sort of journal began to appear, this one given over, not to the practical sciences of viticulture and enology, but to what may be called the lore of wine—anecdote, popular history, remarks on current trends, and the like. Wine, as a hobby and as a subject of connoisseurship, has always fostered this sort of interest. It was met in this country by the magazine called *Cozzens' Wine Press,* issued from 1854 to 1861 by Frederick S. Cozzens, by trade a grocer and wine merchant in New York and by avocation a humorous writer. Cozzens was a loyal champion of American wines, and there is much to be learned about early American wines from his pages, including such exotica in New York City as Kentucky and Virginia catawba, sweet wines from Orange County, New York, and the North Carolina scuppernong wines of J. H. Weller.

Down to the year 1850 there were published in the United States, by a liberal count, only ten books on the subject of vines and wines—the landmarks are Adlum's in 1823, Dufour's in 1826, and Prince's in 1830. But in the decades of the

1850s and 1860s some thirty-seven books, at least, on winegrowing were published in this country. The figure more than triples the output of the preceding fifty years, and the information in many of these books—not all, but many—was fuller and more accurate than it could have been earlier. They include Robert Buchanan's *A Treatise on Grape Culture in Vineyards, in the Vicinity of Cincinnati* (1850), a modest, but intelligent, brief work; the works of Husmann and Muench based on their experience in Missouri; Agoston Haraszthy's contribution from California, *Grape Culture, Wines, and Wine-Making* (1862); and, in the South, Achille de Caradeuc's *Grape Culture and Winemaking in the South* (1858). By the end of the Civil War, a man who wanted to collect a technical library on winegrowing in America could do so.

How good was the technology? That, too, is a question better deferred till later, when the revolutions brought about by Pasteur's studies and by the crises of disease in Europe can be discussed. By way of brief summary, however, it may be said here that at the end of the Civil War there was an impressive accumulation of knowledge about the habits and requirements of the native vine, and there was beginning to be, at least, some experience in knowing how to handle it for wine. The study of individual varieties had been carried pretty far, both in the vineyard and in the chemist's laboratory, and new methods of training had been devised to suit the vigorous habits of the native vines.[54] The techniques of hybridizing were well understood. Control of disease was still at a primitive stage, but that was about to change. The crucial importance of climate to winegrowing had been clearly grasped, and the Patent Office was publishing a detailed series of studies of climatological regions. If none of these things had passed beyond the beginnings, they were at least well begun.

The Grape Boom in the Old South

The main movements in eastern American winegrowing before the Civil War—main in the sense that they led to a continuing industry—were in New York State, northern Ohio, and Missouri. It would be quite wrong, however, to neglect the scattered but frequent efforts at winegrowing throughout the old South. We have seen how, in New York, Ohio, and Missouri, winegrowing not only continued but made considerable advances in size and prosperity throughout the war. In the South, however, it was severely cut back, and it is therefore of some historical interest to see just how widespread interest in it was before Fort Sumter stopped all that.

In Virginia, home of the oldest of all winegrowing traditions in this country, the record is meager. There was evidently a good deal of farm-scale winemaking from native grapes, but nothing more. Perhaps the state's best contribution was the Norton grape, which became so important in the vineyards of Missouri; there is some evidence that commercial plantings of Norton were made in Virginia too before the war, around Charlottesville.[55]

Scuppernong wine continued to flourish as the *vin de pays* of North Carolina. Its most energetic sponsor was a Yankee named Sidney Weller, a graduate of Union College in New York State, who took over a worn-out farm of some three hundred acres at Brinckleyville, Halifax County, in the late 1820s and began to carry out his progressive ideas on agriculture.[56] In addition to general farming, he went in for winegrowing, based largely on the Scuppernong but including the Norton and a labrusca called Halifax as well.[57] Weller was a good promoter, who filled the agricultural press with accounts of what he called his "American system" of viticulture: this was, in substance, simply to allow his Scuppernong vines unchecked growth on trellises instead of controlling them by any system of pruning: such freedom, presumably, could only be called "American."[58] From grapes grown in this liberated fashion on some twelve acres of vineyard (the largest in the South, Weller thought), he produced several thousands of gallons yearly of scuppernong "hock" and "champagne," which he was able to sell at prices from $1 to $6 a gallon to markets as distant as New York, New Orleans, and St. Louis.[59] He also made his vineyards a place of public resort, charging admission to picnickers and so adding measurably to the land's revenue. In the hands of his son John, Weller's winemaking business continued down to the Civil War.[60] It was afterwards the basis from which Paul Garrett's important winemaking business grew to national prominence.[61]

There were enough other producers of scuppernong wines in North Carolina besides Weller to make the state the nation's largest producer in 1840;[62] grapes were, according to one account, the main crop of the coastal "Bankers and islanders." The wine they made, however, was really only a fortified grape juice.[63] The hope of growing something better than Scuppernong persisted, but instead of sticking with such natives as the Herbemont, Lenoir, or Norton, all of which had been proven in the South, some experimenters, at least, went back to vinifera, with predictable results. Around 1849 Dr. Joseph Togno established a vineyard near Wilmington that he called the North Carolina Vine Dresser and Horticultural Model Practical School.[64] Togno's experience went far back—he claimed to have cultivated vinifera in Fauquier County, Virginia, in 1821 and 1822. His "School" advertised in 1849 that it stood ready to receive "pupils, over 14 years old, attended with or without slave, to learn all the manipulations of the Vineyard, the orchard, and horticulture in general." Togno had imported European vines for his vineyard, and after a year he reported that they were doing well and that he intended to graft them to native rootstocks. But then the enterprise failed. After their first delusive growth, the vinifera vines succumbed to the local diseases. That, however, might have been surmounted, since Togno had learned to appreciate the possibilities of the native vine, especially the Scuppernong, which he proclaimed the "American champagne grape par excellence; its aromatic bouquet making it superior to the Pinot, or Pineau of Champagne."[65] It was one thing to grow grapes; it was quite another to attract young southerners to the study of winemaking. As Togno sadly wrote in 1853, after four years he had had not a single application for admission to his school, and the local Tarheels called the place "Dr. Togno's Folly."[66] Not long

65 Henry William Ravenel (1814–87), member of the Vine-Growing and Horticultural Association of Aiken, South Carolina, founded in 1858. Ravenel, descended from one of the old Huguenot families of South Carolina, continued in the nineteenth century the trials of wine-growing that the Huguenots had begun in the seventeenth century. One of the most eminent of botanists in nineteenth-century America, he maintained a vineyard at his home, Hampton Hill. (From *The Private Journal of Henry William Ravenel, 1859–1887* [1947])

after poor Togno's debacle we hear of a Frenchman named Kron growing vines and making wine in the far western part of the state around 1860; he had native grapes, especially the Herbemont, but he had also imported vines from France.[67] They would not have survived even if war had not come.

In South Carolina the interesting development just before the war was the formation of the Aiken Horticultural and Vine-Growing Association in 1858, which addressed itself to the central problem of obtaining satisfactory varieties. It hoped to do so "by the raising of seedlings," and offered "handsome premiums towards that object."[68] The leaders of the association included Dr. J. C. W. McDonnald[69] and H. W. Ravenel of Aiken; D. Redmond of Augusta, Georgia, well known as the editor of the *Southern Cultivator* and as an enthusiastic propagator and grower of grapes; and Achille de Caradeuc of Woodward, who had been making wine since 1851[70] and who published his *Grape Culture and Winemaking in the South* in 1858.

Ravenel, who was president of the association in 1860, was a descendant of the South Carolina Huguenots and so a link in that chain of winegrowing tradition. He was a botanist of international distinction, and though his special interest was in fungi, he did not neglect the grape. He produced wine from his vineyard, took a prize for "the best foreign grapes" at the association's competition, read a paper on pruning vines to the association, and, after the war, published articles on viticulture.[71]

There were other vineyards then scattered about the state at Charleston, Kalmia, Columbia, Orangeburg, Bluffton, Kaolin, and Redcliffe. The war, obviously, was a severe check to their activity, yet within a year after the war the region around Aiken was reported to have from three to five hundred acres of vines, and wine was being made there in commercial quantity.[72]

The Aiken people, in common with many others in the latter years of the 1850s, were responding to the prospect that the news of *oidium* in Europe seemed to open. While production in Europe declined precipitously, how could production in the United States fail to enrich the grower? To southerners especially the proposition seemed foolproof, for they had slaves to do the work: as one enthusiast put it, "with all the facilities we possess at the South, with our soil, climate, and more particularly our slaves, nothing can prevent ours from becoming the greatest wine country that ever was."[73] Since the Civil War, to look no farther for reasons, did in fact prevent any such development, the prophecy now looks notably foolish. Yet the writer was talking sense. Grapes had certainly been grown in the South, and who knows what concerted and determined experimentation might not have done? Hope persisted against the heaviest discouragement. During the dark days of the war, the old South Carolinian politician William John Grayson, retired to the country and writing his recollections, noted that the making of wine had not ceased in South Carolina but was "gradually extending in various parts of the state. Some centuries hence our State may be as famous for wine as for cotton or rice." This was taking a very long view indeed.[74]

The Aiken people were also responding to the activity of a German, a Rhinelander named Charles Axt, who had come to Georgia in 1848, had been mightily struck by the vitality of the native vines, and had gone about the Piedmont region of the state since the early 1850s propagandizing for grape culture in broken English—the "itinerant Grape Missionary" he was called.[75] Since the cotton farmers of the region needed another cash crop, and since their lands were running more and more to gullies and washed-out red dirt under the destructive practices of cotton monoculture, Axt found men willing to listen. They especially liked the numbers that he used. He would, he said, undertake to plant and supervise a small vineyard of a quarter of an acre on a client's land; he would tend it for three years at $50 per annum; and at the end of that time he would deliver 350 gallons of wine. That was only a beginning, to show what might be done. After five years, he claimed, he could make an acre yield 2,500 gallons (or roughly the yield from an impossible sixteen tons of grapes). Probably no one ever held him to his claim.

By 1855 he was doing well, supervising vineyards in Georgia, South Carolina, and Alabama, and operating his own at Crawfordville, not far west of Augusta. This was not bad for a man who had come to Georgia with no capital and little English just seven years earlier. Catawba seems to have been the vine of choice for Axt, but the vineyards of Georgia contained the old southern varieties such as Herbemont and Lenoir too. In 1856 a Vine Growers' Association of Georgia was formed; by 1857 Axt had commercial quantities of catawba in local markets, and had won over all opinion in favor of his vision of the Piedmont as wine country. The Belgian horticulturist Louis E. Berckmans, who had migrated from New Jersey to Augusta to operate a nursery there, described the prospect thus:

> In places where no corn or rye will grow I have seen many a goodly acre covered with Catawba and Warren grapes, and yielding from four hundred to six hundred dollars, in soils abandoned as unfit for every other cultivation. South Carolina and Georgia will soon be awake to this new enterprise and acres upon acres of land not worth five dollars are going to be converted into vineyards to supply the union with wine, equal if not superior to any Hock or Madeira.[76]

The last few years before the war saw a grape mania in the South quite as intense as the one sweeping the North at the same time. Vineyards large and small sprang up in Mississippi, Alabama, and Louisiana, as well as in the older seaboard states and in the less cotton-dominated states of Kentucky and Tennessee. The southern agricultural papers were filled with a lively correspondence reporting developments, offering advice, disputing questions, and prophesying the future of southern wines and vines. The climactic moment may be located in August 1860, when, on the initiative of the Aiken Horticultural and Vine-Growing Association, a general convention of all interested vine growers in the United States was summoned to a grand meeting at Aiken.[77] The response from the North was chilly—it could hardly be expected, as one northern paper remarked, that people would wish to visit a southern town at the height of the summer.[78] Growers from the South were less troubled by the thought.

When it met at the Baptist Church in Aiken, the convention was largely made up of delegates from Georgia and South Carolina, who called themselves the Southern Vine Growers' Convention and were presided over by James Hammond, a former governor of South Carolina who was himself a winegrower. One of their objects was to establish exact botanical descriptions of grape varieties; another was to "determine upon some manner of naming the different wines"[79]—a subject bristling with problems that are still far from resolved. Varietal naming, which many think of as a recent introduction, was in fact already the standard American practice.[80] But it seemed most unsatisfactory in place of the traditional European principle of naming by place, for the plain reason that, as the prospectus of the convention put it: "the same grape will make totally different wines in different places"—a proposition as true today as it ever was then. As one convention speaker argued, with hundreds of catawba and Warren wines available, and no two of them alike, the names "catawba" and "Warren" could guarantee nothing at all. Place names, brands, or private names were what were wanted.[81]

Furthermore, varietal naming made no proper provision for blends of more than one sort of grape. How could you call it catawba if it was really Catawba, Lenoir, and Scuppernong? The proposals for labelling recommended by the convention were, first, the name of the state, followed by the town or other local name (river, hill, valley, or the like), and then the maker's name or brand. Nothing was allowed for the variety or varieties of grape.[82] The scheme is evidently not a perfect one, but it is interesting evidence of the way in which the difficulty—still being agitated as I write—of naming the wines of a new country was recognized.

The production of wine in Georgia in 1860 was 27,000 gallons, not in itself an impressive figure, but remarkable in comparison to the virtual absence of any production at all in 1850. In 1870, five years after the Civil War had ended, Georgia made 21,000 gallons.[83] Obviously the war did not put an end to winemaking on the scale that it had reached just before it began, but it is equally clear that the expansive and enthusiastic interest of those days had been killed. As for Charles Axt, who inspired the grape growers of Georgia, he was murdered in his bed with a hatchet in 1869; his slayer remains unknown.[84]

One interesting episode, at least, took place in Tennessee before the war. This was in Polk County, high in the hills of the extreme southeastern corner of the state. The enterprise was a sort of religious charity, yet without any distinct religious or economic ambitions, and it left so little record that even local tradition has hardly anything to say of it. Some time in the late 1840s the family of the emigrant Long Island horticulturist André Parmentier bought land in the Sylco Mountains of southeastern Tennessee, and, by 1850, had settled on it six Catholic families—about twenty people—of French, German, and Italian origin.[85] The Parmentiers, a married and an unmarried daughter, were devout Catholics, active in the lay affairs of the church, and they evidently conceived of their Tennessee settlement as a Catholic community. The place was called Vineland, or, in one account, Vinona. There, under the direction of a Monsieur Guerin, and in the midst of forests abounding in bears, panthers, and rattlesnakes, they planted vineyards of Isabella and Catawba grapes and made both white and red wines. There is also evidence that some wine, at least, was made from wild grapes. Because of the great steepness of the slopes—up to 45°—the vineyards were terraced. Polk County is credited with only 613 gallons of wine in the census of 1860, and even supposing that the Catholic communitarians of Vineland made more wine than was officially counted, they still had an industry on only the tiniest scale. What rule of life—religious or political—if any, that they lived by, we do not know. Indeed, everything about the place is unclear, except for the fact that for a decade at least, until the war dispersed it, an exotic little group of Catholics was tending native grapes and making wine for sale in the Scotch Presbyterian territory of the southern Appalachians.

Tennessee, in large part no doubt because of the unfitness of its eastern highlands for anything else, was beginning to be presented as a potential site for wine-growing. As early as 1854 the *Horticultural Review* noted that a Colonel James Campbell had a prosperous vineyard on the French Broad River near Knoxville

66   The symbolic—and prophetic—seal of the state of Connecticut: laden grape vines as the emblems of divine care in the New World. The motto may be translated as "who transplants, sustains." (From *The Public Records of the Colony of Connecticut, 1706–1716* [1870])

and concluded that Tennessee was a good place for grapes;[86] in 1856 a Frenchman named Camuse was reported to be producing good wine in the state.[87] David Christy, the geologist, abolitionist, and journalist, published a pamphlet at Cincinnati in 1858 entitled *The Culture of the Vine in the South West Alleghenies,* calling attention to western North Carolina and eastern Tennessee as places peculiarly suited to the vine. But there was little experience to prove the claim. Mark Twain's luckless father owned a large property in Tennessee (Fentress County, also in the eastern part of the state), a legacy he left to his children that tormented them with false hopes of speculative profits for years. The land, Mark Twain wrote, was in "a natural wine district . . . there are no vines elsewhere in America, cultivated or otherwise, that yield such grapes as grow wild here." Twain's father sent some samples to Longworth in Cincinnati, who graciously replied that "they would make as good wine as his Catawbas." But that promise was never acted on. When a buyer appeared with a scheme to settle foreigners on the land and turn it into wine country, Twain's erratic brother Orion, in a transient moment of teetotal conviction, refused to sell the land to a buyer who wished to put it to the wicked work of winegrowing. Such, at least, is the story Mark Twain tells.[88]

In 1859 and in 1860 two surveys of the wine industry appeared; one was written by the British consul in Washington, Edwin Morris Erskine, who, at the request of his government, undertook to gather statistics on the winegrowing industry in the United States. The other was contained in the national census of 1860. Together they give a picture—incomplete, indeed, but reliable within its limits—of the state of things after the first fifty years of more or less successful production in the United States, and with that picture this chapter can fitly close. In Erskine's account, which he put together in part through his own independent travel and inquiry, California was not yet a factor, though reports of its potential were beginning to be heard in the eastern states. Neither was New York State, where the commercial beginnings were still too new to have made themselves visible. But, Erskine reported, the promise was almost unlimited:

> About 3,000 acres are cultivated as vineyards in the state of Ohio; 500 in Kentucky; 1,000 in Indiana; 500 in Missouri; 500 in Illinois; 100 in Georgia; 300 in North Carolina; 200 in South Carolina, with every prospect of a rapid increase in all. It is calculated that at least 2,000,000 gallons of wine are now raised in the United States, the average value of which may be taken at a dollar and a half the gallon.[89]

A total of at least twenty-two of the thirty-two states then in the Union contained "vineyards of more or less promise and extent," leading Erskine to prophesy that "the culture of the vine in the United States will extend itself and improve very rapidly; and that, at no distant period, wine will be produced as cheaply and abundantly as in Europe."[90]

The figures of the 1860 census, gathered a year after Erskine's, are less expansive and no doubt nearer to the mark. The national production was put by the census-takers at just over 1,600,000 gallons. California was already yielding a significant quantity of wine—the figure given is 246,000 gallons, almost certainly too low. But the industry was still firmly centered upon Cincinnati, with its outlying provinces of Kentucky and Indiana. Kentucky made nearly 180,000 gallons, Indiana 102,000, and Ohio led all the rest with 568,000. Eleven other states, including—surprisingly—Connecticut, produced more than 20,000 gallons in 1860;[91] New York, for example, though it had gone unnoticed by Erskine, was up to 61,000 gallons. The United States, as it stood on the brink of the Civil War, was not yet making wine enough to supply a nation of wine drinkers—it does not do so even now—but it had increased its production eightfold in one decade. Mr. Erskine had the right notion of the way things were headed.

THE DEVELOPMENT OF CALIFORNIA

9

The Southwest
and California

Early Winegrowing in New Mexico

The earliest winemaking in the continental United States is credited to the Spaniards of Santa Elena, South Carolina, around 1568. The earliest successful viticulture and the oldest continuous tradition of winemaking, however, was established in the seventeenth century by the Spanish in those vast and barely populated regions of the Southwest that remained parts of the Spanish empire into the nineteenth century. Here the Jesuits and Franciscans planted grapes as they founded missions, and long before the days of Dufour, Adlum, and Longworth, the Spaniards and Indians of the widely scattered settlements from El Paso to the Pacific were drinking the wine of the country, though, to be sure, not a great deal of it. Even more important, this was wine from vinifera grapes, authentic wine as it had been known in Europe since the first apparition of Dionysus. In the dry, hot, stony soils of the Southwest the vine recognized something like its Mediterranean home and readily grew without suffering those afflictions of weather, disease, and insects that invariably devastated it in the East. All of this, however, went on invisibly so far as the United States was concerned. The great Spanish province of New Mexico, stretching from modern Texas to the Gulf of California, was wholly isolated from the developing country to the east; there was no line of communication whatever between them, and foreign trade was forbidden in the Spanish possessions.

The first wine grapes in New Mexico were planted at the mission of Socorro, on the Rio Grande, by Franciscan missionaries about 1626;[1] the mission, abandoned in 1680 on the great Indian uprising of that year, has now vanished without trace, but the valley of the Rio Grande has remained the site of a permanent viticulture. There is no record of the grape selected by the Franciscans in the earliest days; it may have been the same one they used later, the so-called Mission grape, grown wherever the missions might arise in order to provide wine for the celebration of the mass. This grape, so important in the history of wine in the Southwest, remains something of a mystery. It is, or is like, the grape called the *Criolla* in Mexico and in South America—"Creole," as we would say, meaning a New World scion of an Old World parent, adapted to the new conditions. The Criolla is not identified with any grape now known in Spain, though it must ultimately trace its origins to Spain; it is most likely a seedling of some Spanish variety brought over in the early days.[2] Whatever its origin, it is not well suited for making table wine, being too low in acid and without distinctive varietal character, so that its dry wines are flat and dull. It was a good choice—or a lucky accident—for the early days, though, because it likes hot country, is very productive, and yields quite good sweet wines, much easier to preserve in difficult conditions than low-alcohol dry wines. The Mission is and will remain a significant grape in California for the production of sweet wines. Though one rarely or never sees the Mission grape identified on wine labels today, there were 1,800 acres of Mission vines in California in 1986, linking the modern industry to its origins.

Colonial New Mexico (including much of present-day west Texas and all of Arizona) remained Spanish until Mexican independence in 1821; not until that time was there any communication or commerce between this remote northern outpost of Spain in the New World and the United States. After 1821 the opening of the Santa Fe Trail brought Americans into the valley of the Rio Grande—the Rio del Norte as it was then commonly called—and reports of its grapes and wines began to make their way back to the East. Small vineyards were scattered along the hundreds of miles of the river from Bernallilo southwards, but there was no trade in wine. The New Mexicans had no transport, few wooden vessels, and even fewer bottles, so that the wine they made was strictly for local consumption. The methods of New Mexican viticulture were described in 1844 by Josiah Gregg, the historian of the Santa Fe Trail. The grape vines grew unsupported, and by being pruned back heavily were made to grow as low bushes; this allowed the grower to dispense with any complicated apparatus of posts and wires and trellises, and it also made it possible to cover the vines with earth in winter to protect them against freezing. For, though New Mexico is hot in summer, it lies high and dry and is subject to some sharp winter weather. From these low shrubs the Mexicans obtained "heavy crops of improved and superiorily-flavored grapes," as Gregg rather confusedly put it—though clearly he found them good.[3]

After the annexation of the New Mexico territory in 1848, making it supply the nation with wine was at least conceivable. As the young U.S. attorney of the territory, William Davis, wrote in 1853: "No climate in the world is better adapted to the vine than the middle and southern portions of New Mexico, and if there was a convenient market to induce an extensive cultivation of the grape, wine would

67 | El Paso, Texas, whose "Pass wine" was known throughout the Southwest in the era of the Santa Fe Trail. This was the first region added to the United States in which wine from vinifera grapes was produced. (From William H. Emory, *Report of the United States and Mexican Boundary Survey* [1857])

soon become one of the staples of the country, which would be able to supply a large part of the demand in the United States."[4] The prospect was not necessarily illusory, but the history of New Mexico has not worked out that way. The production of wine in the state down to the most recent years cannot have been much greater than it was in colonial days. That is now changing, however, as New Mexico is currently the scene of large-scale investment—mostly of European money—in vineyards and wineries. It is far too early even to guess what the outcome of this sudden transformation of things will be, but it is particularly interesting as a renewal of winegrowing at one of its earliest sites in the United States.

Far to the south, at El Paso, where the Rio Grande comes out of the mountains to flow through a warm, low valley, winegrowing was extensive enough to support a trade and to acquire a reputation. The region—the American part of which is now in Texas—saw its first settlement in 1659, on the site of the present Mexican city of Juarez. Here orchards and vineyards flourished under irrigation; the vines, a Franciscan reported in 1744, "yield abundantly and produce fruit of good flavor and a rich wine in no way inferior to that of our Spain."[5] Early in the nineteenth century El Paso wine was the only revenue-producing crop in the whole province of Spanish New Mexico: "In no other country in America (so travelers declare) can wine be found with the taste and bouquet of the wine of New Mexico, especially that produced in the large vineyards of El Paso del Norte. Its abundance is shown by its price, which is one real per pint, two hundred miles from the place where it is produced."[6] The reputation of El Paso wines was perpetuated by the Santa Fe traders, though one may doubt that they were very discriminating judges. "Pass Wine," they called it, and gave it preference over the wines produced closer to Santa Fe. El Paso brandy—*aguardiente*—was also famous, and perhaps even more in demand among the men of a trader's wagon train.

Most enthusiastic of all about El Paso wine was a young Missourian named John T. Hughes, a private in Colonel Alexander Doniphan's military expedition to New Mexico in 1846 who afterwards wrote a history of the affair. In that book, Hughes prints a copy of a letter that he was moved to send to the War Department after he had had a chance to look around him in the "fruitful valley of El Paso," where Doniphan's troops had arrived in December 1846:

> The most important production of the valley is the Grape, from which are an-
> nually manufactured not less than two hundred thousand gallons of perhaps the richest
> and best wines in the world. This wine is worth two dollars per gallon, and constitutes
> the principal revenue of the city. Thus the wines of El Paso alone yield four hundred
> thousand dollars per annum. The El Paso wines are superior, in richness of flavor and
> pleasantness of taste, to anything of the kind I ever met with in the United States, and I
> doubt not that they are far superior to the best wines ever produced in the valley of the
> Rhine, or on the sunny hills of France.[7]

It was obvious to Hughes, and so he advised the War Department, that an energetic American population should displace the languid Mexicans; production of wine would then increase tenfold, and a link—road, railroad, or canal—between the valley and the United States would take the wine to a ready market. Hughes favored the plan of canalizing the Rio Grande from the Gulf to the falls at El Paso.[8] What answer the War Department made we do not know. No canal was dug, and the vineyards of El Paso seem to have declined through the rest of the nineteenth century under gringo auspices. When the Patent Office's viticultural explorer H. C. Williams arrived in the valley in 1858, he found that very few vineyards had been established on the American side of the river, and that the production of the whole region was declining.[9] There were then three qualities of wine produced by the El Paso vintners: a first-quality light red wine; a second-quality darker wine, the one properly called "Pass Wine"; and a third-quality wine left to the poor.[10] Here is how Williams described the methods of production he found in El Paso:

> An ox hide is formed into a pouch, which is attached to two pieces of timber and laid
> on two poles supported by forks planted in the ground-floor of the room in which the
> vintage takes place. The grapes are gathered in a very careless manner, and placed in
> the pouch until it is filled. They are then mashed by trampling with the feet. In this
> condition the mashed fruit, stems, and some leaves remain until fermentation takes
> place, which requires from fifteen to twenty days. An incision is made in the lower part
> of the pouch, through which the wine drips; it is transferred to barrels. The wine now

has a flat, sourish taste. Should it be desired to make sweet wine, grape syrup, made by evaporating fresh juice, is added until the wine has the desired sweetness. It is not afterwards fined, or racked off, but remains in the cask until used.[11]

It was just this pastoral simplicity that so annoyed the Americans who observed winemaking in El Paso. Colonel William Emory, who conducted the official survey of the Mexican-American border, saw the neglected potential with exasperation. He had, he wrote in his official *Report,* drunk wine in El Paso "which compared favorably with the richest Burgundy." But there was no control and so no consistency—the next wine might well be "scarcely fit to drink." The promise was great, for, he wrote, "in no part of the world does this luscious fruit flourish with greater luxuriance than in these regions, when properly cultivated." The reason that nothing adequate to develop the promise had been done was, in the colonel's judgment, quite simple:

> No one of sufficient intelligence and capital, to do justice to the magnificent fruit of the country, has yet undertaken its manufacture. As at present made, there is no system followed, no ingenuity in mechanical contrivance practised, and none of those facilities exist which are usual and necessary in the manufacture of wine on a large scale.[12]

Despite the optimistic views of writers like Hughes, Williams, and Emory, the Americans never took hold of the chance to develop the winegrowing of the Rio Grande Valley. There were reasons enough for this state of affairs: the isolated, underpopulated character of the region, the imperfect harmony between the Mexican-Indian cuisine and wine (compare the relative unimportance of wine in Mexico itself); and most of all, no doubt, the quick growth of California and its wine industry within a few years of the transfer of New Mexico to the United States. The situation is now undergoing a rapid and dramatic change, and the development of winegrowing in Texas and New Mexico will be one of the most interesting ventures in the history of American wine in this decade.

Winegrowing in the California Mission Period

Hundreds of miles to the west of the Rio Grande, along the Pacific coast, the widely scattered small mission communities and the great, isolated *ranchos* of Mexican California were beginning to be infiltrated by Yankee adventurers and traders at just about the same time as such people began to appear in New Mexico. Grapes and wine were among the first things to interest them there, as they had done in New Mexico, for there was in California, as in New Mexico, an already established tradition of winegrowing. Though of much younger date, it was, like that of New Mexico, developed in connection with the missions, was directed by the Franciscans, and was based on the Mission grape. Unlike that in New Mexico, it survived Americanizing and secularizing, flourished under alien hands, and grew rapidly into a major economic force. Since the years just after the Civil War, the story of American wine has been dominated by California, and by an industry inherited directly from the Franciscan founders.

The first mission in Alta California—the region that became the American state—was founded by Fray Junípero Serra at San Diego in 1769, where, accompanied by soldiers and priests, he took the first step in the spiritual conquest of the Indians and towards the secular control of the coast, so long neglected by European powers, against all rivals. It is convenient to date viticulture in the state from this event; it was, indeed, so dated when the state celebrated the bicentennial of the wine industry in 1969. But that was a mistake. True, General Mariano Vallejo late in the nineteenth century affirmed that his father, who was among the first contingents of soldiers sent to Alta California, told him that Padre Serra brought the first vines and planted them at San Diego; another source (Arpad, son of the famous Count Agoston Haraszthy) says that this was done in 1769 or 1770.[13] These are both impressive witnesses. Yet such documentary evidence as exists for the earliest mission years plainly contradicts their testimony. As Father Serra moved back and forth along the coast, founding mission after mission in the chain that ultimately stretched north of San Francisco Bay to Sonoma, he regularly complained of the difficulty of obtaining a supply of wine for the celebration of the mass; such wine as he did get was clearly imported from Mexico or Spain, not the produce of local missions.[14] In the early part of the nineteenth century, for example, Mission San Gabriel was recognized as the largest producer of wines in California, yet as late as 1783, fourteen years after the first mission had been founded and twelve years after the founding of San Gabriel, Serra wrote that San Gabriel had no wine at all, the barrel sent to it on muleback from the coast having slipped and broken so that all the wine was lost.[15]

The first clear reference to the planting of grapes at a California mission comes from San Juan Capistrano in 1779, ten years after the arrival of the Franciscans in California.[16] These vines might have produced a small crop as early as 1781, but the evidence points to 1782 as the likeliest date for California's first vintage. In an original and important essay Roy Brady has not only established this chronology for the first California wine but has also plausibly identified the means whereby the vines were first brought to the state; they came, he suggests, in May 1778 on board the supply ship *San Antonio* under the command of Don José Camacho.[17] If so, the state has a neglected benefactor long overdue for public recognition.

The beginning made at San Juan Capistrano (and perhaps at San Diego in the same season) grew, in time, to include the entire system of missions, with uneven but substantial success. Santa Cruz, at the north end of Monterey Bay, was not successful in growing grapes. Neither was Mission Dolores in San Francisco, being too cool and foggy; yet the California pioneer William Heath Davis reported that in 1833 he had frequently drunk the wine of Mission Dolores, as fine a California red as he ever had, "manufactured at the mission from grapes brought from the missions of Santa Clara and San Jose."[18] Mission San Gabriel, a few miles east of

68 | Mission San Gabriel, painted in 1832 at the height of its prosperity by the German Ferdinand Deppe—the only known painting of a California mission from so early a date. Its wine, for the celebration of the mass, for the occasional use of the fathers, and for the entertainment of visitors, was highly regarded in Spanish California. From the vines of San Gabriel developed the vineyards of Los Angeles, from which, in turn, the winegrowing industry of California grew. (Santa Barbara Mission Library-Archive)

Los Angeles, eventually developed into the largest and most prosperous of all the mission establishments; it stood first in the size of its winemaking operations, too, and for some judges at least, in the quality of the wine it produced. The original vineyard at San Gabriel was called the Viña Madre—"Mother Vineyard"—a name that has created some confusion by its implication that this was the original of all the mission vineyards. It was not that, but was, instead, the first of the several vineyard properties that the mission developed in the large surrounding valley it presided over.[19] Father José Zalvidea, a tough, capable Biscayan, is credited with developing viticulture at San Gabriel, over which he ruled from 1806 to 1827.[20] By 1829 the American merchant Alfred Robinson wrote that the San Gabriel grapes annually yielded from four to six hundred barrels of wine and two hundred of brandy, from which the mission received an income of more than twelve thousand dollars.[21] Robinson's figures are unquestionably exaggerated, but they tell us clearly that observers were impressed by what they saw being done under Father Zalvidea and his successors.

Reliable statistics for the mission period do not exist. San Gabriel is said to have had 170 acres in vines and to have produced 35,000 gallons a year[22]—a modest figure if the acreage is accurately given: but then a good deal of wine was turned into brandy. Father Duran, a Franciscan who enjoyed a good reputation for the wines and brandy that he produced at his mission of San Jose, thought that the best wines of the whole mission system were those of San Gabriel.[23] But it was not without competition. General Vallejo is reported by Haraszthy as saying that the wine of Sonoma, last and most northern of the missions, "was considered by the Padres the best wine raised in California."[24] But then Vallejo had taken over those Sonoma vineyards and had an interest in promoting their reputation (so, too, did Haraszthy for that matter). The Sonoma Mission vineyard was tiny, so that not many can have known its wines, whatever their reputation may have been. Another judgment on mission wines was delivered by an observant Frenchman, Captain Auguste Duhaut-Cilly, who in 1827 decided that it was at San Luis Rey, between Los Angeles and San Diego, that there were "the best olives and the best wine in all California." He acted on his judgment by taking some of the mission's wine back with him to France: "I have some of it still," he wrote in 1834. "After seven years, it has the taste of Paxaret, and the color of *porto depouillé*."[25] This makes it clear that the wine was of the sweet fortified kind, on the model of angelica. *Paxeret* or *Pajarete* is an intensely sweet Spanish wine of the Pedro Ximénes grape grown in the town of Paxarete. *Porto depouillé* means literally a well-fined port, perhaps suggesting one that through age has begun to lose color. It is not clear to me whether Duhaut-Cilly's description indicates a red wine grown pale with age, or a white one grown brown—the latter, I suspect, for that would agree with the report described below of the mission wine drunk by a curious gourmet in the twentieth century.

After San Gabriel, the next largest of the mission vineyards was at San Fernando, also in the region of Los Angeles. San Fernando had only about a fifth of the winemaking capacity of San Gabriel, yet it was considerably larger than those next in line, the missions at Ventura and San Jose.[26] Many of the figures on the missions are more than ordinarily untrustworthy, being taken from inventories made after the secularization of the missions, when the vineyards, along with the other temporal interests of the Franciscans, had long been neglected or even abandoned. It is enough to say that at one time or another almost all of the missions made wine both for the table and for religious purposes, and that at a few the production of wine and brandy was a business of modest significance.

At San Gabriel, about which more seems to be known than any other of the missions, there were four sorts of wine produced, described in a letter from Father Duran to Governor José Figueroa in 1833. Two were red—one dry, "very good for the table," the other sweet. Two were white, one unfortified and the other strengthened with a quantity of grape brandy.[27] In all probability, though the description is not as clear as one would like, the fortified white wine of San Gabriel is the original of the wine called angelica, once the most famous produce of the Los

Angeles county vineyards. Angelica, as it used to be made (and apparently is no longer), was not so much a wine as a fortified grape juice, such as the French call *mistelle* and the Spanish *mistela:* this is a drink that properly belongs to the class of cordials rather than of wine (compare the Scuppernong wines of North Carolina). To a must that has not yet begun to ferment, or has only partially fermented, brandy is added in such quantity as to arrest the action of the yeast. This was an effective way to handle the Mission grape, which under the hot skies of southern California gave a fruit almost raisined, rich in sugar but low in acid, so that its dry wines were flat and unpalatable. With the sweetness retained, and the preserving alcohol supplied by the addition of brandy, the juice, christened angelica after the City of the Angels, became a popular wine—some will say deservedly, others not.

The methods used in the missions were of the simplest, though such descriptions as exist do not always agree and are not always very clear. As in New Mexico, the ready availability of cowhides and the relative scarcity of wood determined the choice of materials. The standard method of crushing seems to have been by pouring grapes onto a cowhide, perhaps suspended over a receptacle, and then setting an Indian to treading the grapes with his feet. The juice expressed by this means was caught in leathern bags, in barrels, or in brickwork cisterns (some of these remain at San Gabriel), where it fermented; red wine, of course, fermented on the skins and stems of the crushed grapes; for white wine, the juice was drawn off to ferment separately. The skins might then go into a primitive still for brandy.[28] Most of the Franciscan fathers were natives of Spain and may be supposed to have had at least a general notion of how wine was made. We know that at one mission there was a copy of a winemaking guide, the second part of Alonso de Herrara's *Agricultura general,* in an edition published at Madrid in 1777.[29] The work was originally published in 1513, a fact that sufficiently indicates the conservative instincts of the Spanish, whether in the Old World or the New.

Whether the missions had wine in sufficient quantity to make it an item of commerce, how extensive that commerce was, with whom it was carried on, and how long it lasted, are all questions without distinct answers.[30] Until the overthrow of Spanish rule, all foreign commerce was forbidden, so at best the trade in mission wine was restricted to the brief span from the beginning of Mexican rule in 1821 to the secularization of the mission properties in 1833. The reports of travellers from the 1820s and afterwards make it sufficiently clear that mission wine then was at least available for the priestly table as well as for the altar—"plenty of good wine during supper" is the remark of one of Jedediah Smith's party at San Gabriel in 1826;[31] and we have seen how in the next year Duhaut-Cilly was able to take wine from San Luis Rey to France, and how, in 1829, Robinson could speculate on the large income brought to Mission San Gabriel by its wines. There is nothing coherent or distinct in all this, however. Father Payeras, president of the missions, made a contract in 1823 with an English firm trading to Lima to supply mission produce for a term of three years.[32] Among the goods listed as items of trade, wine and brandy are named; but no price is attached to them, and it is not likely that

69   Wall painting in the *sala* of the fathers' dwelling, c. 1825, Mission San Fernando, California, showing the Indian "neophytes" harvesting grapes—a unique combination of native American art and the Mediterranean tradition of winegrowing. The painting was destroyed in the earthquake of 1971. (Courtesy Dr. Norman Neuerberg)

much can have been shipped to Peru. At best one may cautiously suppose that during the 1820s a few of the missions could afford to manage an intermittent trade in wine, largely with and through the ships that coasted the shores of California.

Whatever trade the missions may have had in their hands came to an end beginning with the decrees of secularization passed by the Mexican government in 1833. By this act the Franciscans were stripped of their temporalities and restricted to the spiritual care of the missions, *presidios,* and *pueblos* of Alta California. The decree did not take effect at once or uniformly: the work of expropriation proceeded unevenly; some missions held out longer than others; and California was in any case far distant from the central authority in Mexico. Thus we find that years after the decree some missions were still cultivating their vineyards.[33] But the back of the enterprise had been broken. At San Gabriel, to take that place again as an image of the whole, the father superintendent ordered the large vineyards of the mission to be destroyed in the face of the decree of secularization. His order, so the tradition goes, was refused by the Indians, who, one supposes, were not about to destroy the source from which their *aguardiente* flowed.[34] Nevertheless, the good days were over. By 1844, so a modern historian of the Franciscans in California writes, "the mission had nothing left but some badly deteriorated vineyards cared for by about thirty neophytes" (Indians attached to the missions).[35] And at San Diego, a couple of years earlier, a French traveller had sadly observed vineyards stretching around the ruined mission that were "capable of furnishing the best wine in California" but that now lay uncared for and idle.[36]

Mission wine, which thus became practically extinct in the second quarter of the century, nevertheless had a curious survival in an unlooked-for part of the world. In the 1920s, in Paris, an English wine lover encountered an expatriate Pole who told him that, at the turn of the century, at Fukier's, the best restaurant in Warsaw, "the choicest and most expensive dessert wine" came from California. The Englishman, finding himself not long after in Warsaw, remembered what he had been told, went to the famous restaurant Fukier and asked for its California wine. He naturally supposed that it must be California wine such as other restaurants had, and was curious to know how it could be both the most expensive and the best available in a distinguished restaurant. The waiter told him that, fortunately, there were a few bottles still left, some of which were brought to the curious diner: "Imagine my surprise when I found that they were of wine from the Franciscan missions of California grown during the Spanish period, a century and a half or so ago. The wine was light brown in colour, rather syrupy, resembling a good sweet Malaga in taste, and in good condition."[37] The age is a bit exaggerated—in all likelihood the wine was from the 1820s and therefore just a hundred years old—but the recrudescence of such a wine in so unexpected a place is sufficiently surprising and pleasing. The description is pretty much what one would expect if the wine were an angelica type such as described earlier. And it is curious to note that this latter-day description agrees with one of the earliest accounts of mission wine: the German traveller Langsdorff, calling at Mission San Jose in 1806, noted that the wine of the place is "sweet, and resembles Malaga."[38] It is not likely now that anyone will ever have a chance again to taste the Franciscan wine of Old California.

The Beginning of Commercial Winegrowing in Southern California

Even before the expropriation of the mission lands, a small, very small, beginning of a secular viticulture, parallel to that of the missions, had been made. There is indirect evidence of vineyard planting in the *pueblo* of Los Angeles in the first decade of the nineteenth century or even earlier.[39] After Spanish rule, with its jealous exclusion of all foreigners, had been replaced by the loose, inefficient, and more hospitable Mexican rule, outlanders began to arrive in small numbers in California, some of them planting vines and making wine along with their Mexican neighbors. Los Angeles, in the brief interval between California's Spanish and American phases, became a quite cosmopolitan village, including miscellaneous Yankees and a sprinkling of Irishmen, Englishmen, Frenchmen, Italians, and Germans, not to mention Hawaiians, who were the most sought-after crewmen for ships in the Pacific trade.

In writing about early California—that is, California at any time before the Gold Rush—one must be careful to emphasize how tiny the extent of settlement throughout the state was. At the beginning of the century there were, through all the hundreds of miles of the state's length, only the missions, plus four *presidios* (army posts) at San Diego, Santa Barbara, Monterey, and San Francisco, and three *pueblos* (civilian communities)—Los Angeles, Santa Cruz, and San Jose. A few families would also have lived on the great *ranchos* belonging to the missions. The total number of inhabitants, exclusive of the Indians (fast dying out under the fatal impact of the West), could be counted in the hundreds.[40] After the end of Spanish rule, this number of course grew, but not by much. If we keep this circumstance in mind, it is clear that to talk about the development of a wine industry before the 1850s is a bit comic, the term *industry* having an absurd grandiloquence when measured against the actual scale of things. Nevertheless, there were interesting beginnings, some quite distinct phases of development, and a good many names that deserve to be perpetuated.

Since the situation is very different now, it is worth stressing the fact that commercial winegrowing in California after the mission era began around Los Angeles, and that southern California continued to dominate the scene for the next fifty years. The dusty *pueblo* of Los Angeles, founded in 1781 on the bank of the Los Angeles River, lived, like the missions, mainly on the trade in hides and tallow. The town stood at the foot of bluffs, but on three other sides the land was a flat plain, easy to irrigate, so that fruit trees, olives, and vines did well. To travellers coming up over the flatlands leading from the landing place at San Pedro on the south, or from the east through the mountain passes, Los Angeles was a green oasis, its low-roofed adobes embowered in willows, vines, and fruit trees. The vines were from the missions, and those who grew them had probably learned what they knew of viticulture from the missions too, so that California winegrowing is continuous with the mission tradition; there was no hiatus between the end of the one and the beginning of the other, for they had overlapped for a long time before the missions came to an end.

When the men of Gaspar Portola's expedition came, in 1769, to the site along the river where, later, Los Angeles was to be settled, they found growing there "a large vineyard of wild grapes and an infinity of rosebushes in full bloom,"[41] so the indications for grape growing were excellent from the start. We do not know who it was who planted the first vineyard in or around Los Angeles not belonging to a mission. He would certainly have had a Spanish name, though, and he must have planted before the end of the eighteenth century. A possible candidate is José Maria Verdugo, who planted a vineyard before 1799 on the Rancho San Rafael north of the *pueblo*.[42] Antonio Lugo, who planted a vineyard not long after 1809, is the earliest vineyardist in Los Angeles itself whose name we know.[43] By 1818 the town was reported to have 53,000 vines, and ten years later an official report noted that a succession of good vintages had given encouragement to winegrowing there.[44]

The name of the first American grower in Los Angeles, and therefore in California, is on record. He was Joseph Chapman, from Massachusetts, who came to California on a buccaneering expedition to Monterey in 1818, was captured and jailed by the Spanish, and, on his release, drifted to the southern part of the state. At San Gabriel he became a general handyman, functioning as carpenter, blacksmith, and apothecary at the mission.[45] In return, Chapman—called José Huero, "Blond Joe," by the Californios[46]—learned at the mission whatever he knew of grape growing and winemaking. By 1822 Chapman had moved to Los Angeles; in 1826 he bought a house there and set out 4,000 vines.[47] Here, for the next decade or so, Chapman grew grapes and, presumably, made wine, for there was no other economical use for his harvest. After the secularization of the missions, Chapman moved on to Santa Barbara, and then to property in Ventura County; he died at Santa Barbara in 1849. A vineyard in Los Angeles remained in the hands of Chapman's son Charles as late as 1860, however, so that this first American vineyard had a reasonable longevity.[48]

As California began to draw Americans both by sea and overland, others took up vine growing: Richard Laughlin, who had arrived overland as early as 1828 in Los Angeles, at some time unrecorded set out a vineyard; so did William Logan in 1831 and, later in the decade, William Chard and Lemuel Carpenter.[49] But in polyglot Los Angeles the Americans were merely one element among several in the general activity of vine growing. Besides, most Americans moved on to other parts of the province after only brief stays, and most tried their hands at all sorts of enterprises, among which viticulture had no very important place. At least one grower in Los Angeles was a Dutchman, going under the name of Juan Domingo (John Sunday). His real name was Johann Groningen; he was a sailor, whose ship had been wrecked in San Pedro Bay on Christmas Day, 1828, a Sunday. When he reached the shore in safety, he sensibly resolved to abandon the sea and to settle where he found himself. The locals gave him his name as a symbol of his experience. So the story goes; but since Christmas fell on a Thursday in 1828 it must need adjusting in some details.[50] Juan Domingo worked as a carpenter, planted a vineyard, married, raised a family, and spent the rest of his days in Los Angeles. Several growers were French: Louis Bouchet (or Bouchette or Bauchet—the spelling varies), a cooper by trade and a veteran of the Napoleonic wars, came to California in 1828 and must have been among the earliest of the newcomers to plant a vineyard. On his death in 1852 the inventory of his property included two vineyards and such winery equipment as a still, some casks, and earthen jars.[51] Victor Prudhomme and Jean Louis Vignes were other Frenchmen established among the vine growers of Los Angeles in the 1830s.[52] Most were of course Mexican: Manuel Requena, Tiburcio Tapia, Ricardo Vejar, and Tomas Yorba are among the names of notable early vineyardists in the Los Angeles region.[53]

Theirs was strictly a cottage—or backyard—industry. One estimate gives Los Angeles 100,000 vines so early as 1831, but this is almost certainly too high.[54] By an exceedingly moderate computation, such a quantity of vines would have yielded 30,000 gallons of wine a year, and it is hard to see how the local market of a few hundred men, women, and children could have blotted up all that liquid, even supposing that much of the vintage was converted into brandy, as it must have been. There is no reason to think that the wine and brandy produced in early Los Angeles was destined for any but a purely local trade, including the ships that put in at San Pedro at not very frequent intervals. The wine, coming as it did from the Mission grape, and handled under conditions of primitive simplicity, could not have been good. One judgment, expressed in 1827, was probably fair enough: the grapes of Los Angeles, Captain Duhaut-Cilly wrote, were quite good, but the wine and brandy made from them were "very inferior . . . and I think this inferiority is to be attributed to the making rather than to the growth."[55] Yet even had the making been better, the result would still have been limited by the inherent defects of the Mission grape.

Winemaking in Los Angeles was raised from a domestic craft to a commercial enterprise by a Frenchman with a name too good to be true, Jean Louis Vignes— because of his name, a French compatriot has written of him, "he seemed predestined to become the Noah of California."[56] Given his destiny, Vignes was not only well named but well born, for his native place was Cadillac, a winemaking community in the Premières Côtes de Bordeaux, where his father was a cooper. Jean Louis learned the cooper's trade, married, and lived quietly until 1826, when, at the age of forty-seven, and for reasons still quite obscure, he left home, wife, family, and trade to go to Hawaii. He could not get satisfactory work in the islands, however, and he had to live from hand to mouth for a time. At last, in 1831, he left for Monterey. The precise date of his arrival in Los Angeles is not known, but he was established in that town by 1833, perhaps drawn there by the reputation of its vineyards and the presence of a Frenchman or two.

He was somehow able to buy a hundred acres of land.[57] The property lay on the east side of the *pueblo,* along the river, and was marked by a great sycamore tree of venerable age called El Aliso, to give it the capital letters that all observers agreed that it deserved. Vignes himself came to be called Don Luis del Aliso in honor of his splendid tree. Here Vignes laid out a vineyard that ultimately occupied thirty-five acres and began the manufacture of wine and brandy.

It did not take him long to recognize the inadequacy of the Mission grape, for in 1833 Vignes imported European varieties from France, sent to him by way of Boston and then around the Horn.[58] Vignes thus lays claim to be the first to take the crucial step of obtaining better varieties. We do not know what varieties he imported, however, nor what success he may have had with them, nor whether they

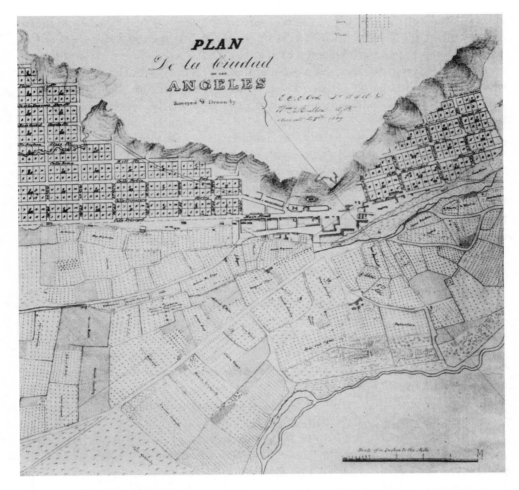

70 | Edward Ord's map of Los Angeles, 1849, from the copy in the Huntington Library. This is the earliest map of the town after the American annexation. The fields between the town and the river shown closely dotted are planted in vines. Just above and to the right of the island in the river are the vineyards of Jean Louis Vignes.

entered importantly into the wine he made. The high reputation that his wines established in competition with others from Los Angeles suggests that perhaps they did, but it is also clear that the Mission continued as the overwhelmingly dominant variety in Los Angeles vineyards. If Vignes did actually show a better way, no one yet troubled to follow him. For many years in California it was the custom to call all grapes other than the Mission "foreign." The Mission is an unquestioned vinifera, and so just as "foreign" as any other European grape: but the distinction made by the locals is an interesting reflection of their experience.

By making acceptable wine in considerable quantity, Vignes was able to take another step forward in 1840, when, through the agency of his nephew Pierre Sainsevain, newly arrived from France, he made the first recorded shipment of Los Angeles wines. Sainsevain loaded a ship at San Pedro with white wine and brandy and took it to Santa Barbara, Monterey, and San Francisco; at each of these places he was able to get good prices for his cargo.[59] This venture does not seem to have been regularly followed up, but it at least showed the way to an important later trade.

One of Vignes's most enthusiastic admirers was the pioneer California merchant William Heath Davis, whose classic *Seventy-Five Years in California* is the source of much detail about Vignes and his El Aliso vineyard. Davis regarded Vignes as "one of the most valuable men who ever came to California [he and Davis had arrived on the same ship in 1831], and the father of the wine industry here." Davis, who dealt in wines among other commodities, gave a present of "fine California wine" from Vignes's cellar to the American Commodore Thomas Ap Catesby Jones when the latter was at Monterey after his premature capture of the city.[60] Later (1843), when Jones was in Los Angeles, he and his officers called on Vignes at El Aliso: they inspected his cellars, sampled his wines, and accepted a gift of several barrels of "choice wine." Vignes asked them to save some of their gift wine to present to the president of the United States, "that he might know what excellent wine was produced in California."[61] On an earlier visit to Vignes in 1842, Davis, too, had been impressed by the cellars and the old vintages they contained. Vignes himself was full of prophetic enthusiasm about California as a wineland. It would, he said, rival "la belle France," and he had urged a number of his relatives and of "his more intelligent countrymen" to come to California and enter the business of winegrowing.[62]

How many Frenchmen Vignes may have enticed to California is not known (estimates vary widely as to the French population of those days), but when Captain Duflot de Mofras called at Los Angeles in 1842, Vignes, "on behalf of the French colony," presented the captain with a barrel of California wine to be offered to Louis Philippe. Unluckily, as we learn, the wine, having survived the hazards of shipment from California, was destroyed by fire in Hamburg before it could be presented to the king for his royal judgment.[63]

Vignes, who was born in 1779, continued to cultivate his vineyard and make wine until 1855, when he sold his property to his Sainsevain nephews for $42,000, one of the greatest commercial transactions that Los Angeles had ever seen.[64] Seven years later, Vignes died. The huge sycamore, El Aliso, that stood at the gate of his property, lasted some years longer, but was cut down before the end of the century; the remarkable grape arbor that ran from Vignes's house down to the river, perhaps ten feet wide and a quarter of a mile long, has long since been displaced by industrial building. It was, while it stood, one of the public places of Los Angeles, where receptions could be held and parties given under the grateful shade. Vignes himself is still remembered for his effective pioneering, a fact that would have pleased his friend Davis, who wrote in affectionate memory of Vignes that "it is to be hoped that historians will do justice to his character, his labors and foresight."[65]

Almost as prominent as Vignes in the same generation was a winegrower of very different origin and background. William Wolfskill was a frontiersman, born in Kentucky but growing up in Missouri at a time when the territory was still Indian country.[66] In 1822 he accompanied the first American trading expedition to Santa Fe, and for some years afterwards he lived and traded in New Mexico. At one point he travelled to El Paso to buy "Pass Wines" and "Pass Brandy" for trade, and so established the only link I know of between the winemaking history of Mexican New Mexico and Mexican California. In 1830 Wolfskill led an expedition for the purposes of fur trapping from New Mexico to California, along what later became known as the Old Spanish Trail, through Colorado, Utah, and Nevada, and into California across the Mojave to the Los Angeles basin, where the party arrived in 1831. Fur trapping was no longer particularly rewarding—around Los Angeles the prey was the sea otter—and after an unremunerative effort in the first ship known to have been built in Los Angeles, Wolfskill decided to try another line. He bought land already planted with vines by an anonymous Mexican and settled down in Los Angeles in 1833. Three years later he added more land, and then, in 1838, traded for a hundred-acre tract on the southeast outskirts of the town, where he developed a substantial vineyard and produced wine steadily until his death in 1866.[67]

By that time his vineyards and orchards covered 145 acres; the vineyards had been recognized as "best in the state" at the California State Fair in 1856 and again in 1859, and his wine production was up to 50,000 gallons.[68] Besides that, much of his produce went to market as fresh grapes, some he sold to other winemakers, and another part went into brandy. Wolfskill and Vignes were neighbors—everyone was in the Los Angeles of those days—and presumably friendly rivals for the lead in Los Angeles winemaking. Wolfskill had his partisans. Edwin Bryant, whose visit to California in 1846 resulted in one of the first in the long string of books boosting the Golden State, paid a call on Wolfskill at his rancho, by then one of the small town's showplaces. Wolfskill, Bryant wrote, "set out for our refreshment three or four specimens of his wines, some of which would compare favorably with the best French and Madeira wines."[69] And as Vignes had sent wine to President John Tyler, so Wolfskill sent wine, including the sweet red wine called "Port" for which Los Angeles was then gaining a reputation, to President James Buchanan in 1857.[70] There is no evidence that Wolfskill made any effort to introduce new and better varieties into California, as Vignes is said to have done.

When, as an episode in the Mexican War, American forces occupied California, the wines of Los Angeles found a new clientele. The Americans entered the town in January 1847, having among them the Lieutenant (later Colonel) Emory whose remarks on New Mexico viticulture we have already met with. "We drank today," Emory wrote on 14 January, "the wine of the country, manufactured by Don Luis Vignes, a Frenchman. It was truly delicious, resembling more the best description of Hock than any other wine."[71] Another American who took an interest in the local product was John Griffin, a surgeon with General Stephen Watts Kearny's army, who kept a diary. The entry for 12 January 1847 tells us that a large quantity of wine and brandy had been seized and secured in order to keep it out of the hands of the sailors of Commodore Robert Stockton's squadron; Griffin added that the wine was "of fine flavour, as good I think as I ever tasted."[72] Griffin gave practical meaning to his praise of Los Angeles wines by returning to the city in 1854 and spending the rest of his days there. He is remembered as often talking of a marvelous wine that he had had in his army days—surely it was the wine of Jean Louis Vignes? Perhaps from a barrel looted by the soldiers, and without any identity beyond that?[73]

Vignes and Wolfskill, by virtue of their early start and the large production to which they eventually attained, stand out among the first generation of commercial winegrowers in Los Angeles. A good many other men joined them in no very long time, however, and by the 1850s it is possible to speak without exaggeration of a real industry in and around the city. William Workman, an Englishman, and his associate John Rowland, planted vineyards at their La Puente Ranch in the 1840s.[74] Hugo Reid, a Scotsman, put in a vineyard in 1839 at his Rancho Santa Anita, northeast of the town, and made wine there until he sold the property in 1846;[75] Matthew Keller, an Irishman who had once studied for the priesthood, arriving in Los Angeles in 1851, soon developed vineyards third only to those belonging to Vignes and Wolfskill. Keller also deserves mention as one of the pioneers in importing new varieties to supplant the unsatisfactory Mission, and as the author of a report describing Los Angeles winegrowing in 1858, published in the U.S. Patent Office's annual report; this was the earliest authoritative description published for a national audience.[76]

Keller's enterprise outlasted those of Vignes and Wolfskill, and to the vineyard he established at the corner of Alameda and Aliso Streets in Los Angeles were later added hundreds of acres more at the Rising Sun Vineyard south of the city and at the Malaga Ranch, above Santa Monica. By 1875 Keller was described as a "wine making millionaire," and in that year one of the most splendid social occasions in Los Angeles was Keller's "First Annual Vintage Feast and Ball," at which the guests were offered "Claret, Eldorado, Madeira, Angelica, White Wine, Sherry, Port."[77] The financial crises of the 1870s brought Keller into trouble soon after. So did the much-complained-about practice of eastern dealers of adulterating and misrepresenting California wines. Keller went to New York in 1877 in order to act as his own agent, a move necessitated, as he sadly wrote, "to save my property and to get out of the wine business—and to do this I have risked my life in my old age in N.Y. in the depth of winter to try and accomplish it. . . . The wine business has been a millstone around my neck. . . . It has swallowed up all I made on land sales and any other way."[78]

The troubles that Keller faced were shared generally: financial depression and overproduction in California combined to hurt most winegrowers. But the quality of at least some of his wines may have helped to injure Keller's business. In answer to Keller's question about how a certain sherry had been made, for example, his winemaker and manager, Thomas Mahony, sent this astounding reply:

> All I know about it now is that it was made of white wine, Spirits, Grape Syrup, Hickory nut infusion, Quassia, Walnut infusion and Bitter aloes, the proportions I could not tell to save my life. At the time I made it I noted down on *cards* the contents of each vat, so that I could continue to make it if it turned out well, but when I received your letter saying it was no account I tore up the cards.[79]

How, one wonders, would the eastern dealers manage to adulterate this compound? It was, perhaps, something more than business rivalry that led another Los Angeles winemaker to say of Keller in 1877 that "he has done more damage to the California wine trade than any other man in it."[80] Yet Keller is said to have been in correspondence with the great Pasteur on the problems of winemaking, and to have received an inscribed copy of Pasteur's *Études sur le vin.*[81] Keller was at last freed of his difficulties by his death in 1881, when the wines and vines of the Los Angeles and Rising Sun Vineyards with which he had made his name passed to the Los Angeles Vintage Company.

Other names among many that might be mentioned testify to the continuing international character of early Los Angeles: there were the Frenchman Michael Clement, the Swiss Jean Bernard, the Englishman Henry Dalton, and the Swiss father and son Leonce and Victor Hoover (originally Huber), all active among the viticulturists and winemakers of the *pueblo*. In a town with a population still fewer than 2,000, the grape growing and winemaking activity of Los Angeles must have been visible and dominating to a degree that few, if any, American towns have since known. When Harris Newmark arrived in Los Angeles from his native Germany in 1853, he found more than one hundred vineyards in the area, seventy-five or eighty within the precincts of the town itself; and, best evidence of all of the degree to which wine had established itself, he found that the Angelenos generally patronized the local product, which was so cheap that it sold for fifteen cents a gallon and was usually served free with meals.[82] Leonce Hoover patronized the local product to a remarkable degree: a committee of the State Agricultural Society, visiting Los Angeles in 1858, reported that he drank nothing but wine the whole day through, excepting one cup of coffee on rising: "At his meals, when at work, around the social board, on retiring at night—at any and all times, he drinks his pure juice of the grape with perfect freedom, and, as he assures us, without the least intoxicating effect."[83]

One should mention, too, the vineyards that had been established beyond the environs of Los Angeles, at Cucamonga and at Rancho Jurupa (now Riverside), many miles to the east. The Cucamonga Rancho, about forty miles from Los Angeles, had been granted to Tiburcio Tapia in 1839; he planted vines there in the spot now known as Red Hill.[84] Since Tapia's death in 1845 the property has passed through many hands and many vicissitudes, but a winery still stands there. It is no longer a producing facility, but serves as a retail outlet for another local wine producer under the banner of "California's oldest winery." It may be. Cucamonga wines enjoyed a special reputation, apparently based on the high alcohol content generated in them by the hot sun in this interior valley. As one journalist wrote in 1861, "the wine made here is the most celebrated in the country, on account of its peculiar, rich flavor, being some twenty per cent above Los Angeles wine in saccharine matter."[85]

A few miles east and south of the Cucamonga vineyards is the Rancho Jurupa, where the city of Riverside now stands; the original grantee, Don Juan Bandini, built a home there in 1839, and probably began planting vines at the same time. He soon sold a part of his grant, and by the 1850s the new proprietor, Louis Robidoux, had 5,500 vines growing.[86] Both Cucamonga and Riverside continued to be wine regions after these beginnings, though urbanization has now, after nearly a hundred and fifty years, almost put an end to the vineyards that were planted in those early days. Other vineyards were scattered in various places at the eastern end of the Los Angeles basin—Dr. Benjamin Barton's ranch near San Bernardino, for example—but they did not compete in importance with the plantings around Riverside, and, especially, Cucamonga.

The main vineyard district of the city of Los Angeles itself was quite distinct and compact: it ran along both sides of the river, mostly on the west or city side, from Macy Street on the north to Washington Street on the south, and from Los Angeles Street to Boyle Heights going west to east. This section, in the heart of old Los Angeles, has long since been covered over by railway tracks, warehouses, the buildings of Little Tokyo, and freeways; even the banks of the Los Angeles River are now sheathed in concrete. But it is remarkable how the names that belong to its viticultural past persist. To the instructed eye the contemporary street map of Los Angeles reveals a generally unrecognized memorial to the early growers and winemakers who lived there long ago. Aliso Street remembers Don Luis Vignes's great sycamore; the street itself, which was once the main route across the river, is now a mere remnant of its old self, functioning as a sort of high-speed alley giving access to the San Bernardino Freeway. In the same region, Keller Street, after Don Matteo Keller, and Bauchet Street, after Don Luis Bauchet, commemorate two of the vineyardists who once made the region green. A little to the south, Kohler Street preserves the name of the enterprising German who first brought Los Angeles wines into large-scale commerce. Just across the river, to the east, Boyle Heights reminds us of the Irishman Andrew Boyle, whose house on the heights looked down to his vineyards and cellars on the bottom lands along the river below.

A visitor to this section of the city today must use all the power of his imagination to reconstruct the vineyards that once fringed the river, making the dusty town appear a green haven to the weary traveller. The Hoover vineyards, the Keller vineyard, the Domingo vineyard, the Vignes vineyard, all on Aliso; the Wolfskill and Wilson vineyards on Alameda; and those of Antonio Lugo, John Moran, Julius Weyse, and John Philbin on San Pedro, to name no more, now seem as remote as the hanging gardens of Babylon. Only the names on the street signs attest that here once grew the vines that made Los Angeles the fount and origin of wine in California.

Yet they did once grow there, and from them Los Angeles made its red and white wines, especially the whites for which it was most celebrated, including the sweet angelica. Brandy, too, was distilled, as it had been from the mission days. And fresh grapes formed a large and lucrative part of the traffic between Los Angeles and San Francisco, at least in the first few years after the rush of gold miners to the northern part of the state. Another continuity between commercial viticulture in Los Angeles and the mission days was the reliance upon Indian labor: as Matthew Keller wrote in 1858, "most of our vineyard labor is done by Indians, some of whom are the best pruners we have—an art they learned from the Mission Fathers."[87] Indians also did the hard labor of treading the grapes in those places where the simplicities of the mission style were still preserved. Harris Newmark, who arrived in Los Angeles in 1853, remembered how he was both fascinated and repelled by the sight of Indians in the vintage season, "stripped to the skin, and wearing only loin-cloths," trampling out the juice in large, elevated vats:

> These Indians were employed in the early fall, the season of the year when wine is made and when the thermometer as a rule, in Southern California, reaches its highest point; and this temperature coupled with incessant toil caused the perspiration to drip from their swarthy bodies into the wine product, the sight of which in no wise increased my appetite for California wine.[88]

The Indians' reward was to be paid on Saturday evening. Then, as Newmark writes, they drank through Saturday night and all of Sunday; three or four were murdered each weekend, the invariable consequence of the general debauch, but such of them as survived were ready for work again on Monday: thus, at any rate, runs the account of an early settler.[89]

The wine trade of Los Angeles moved into its next phase in the middle of the 1850s, when two commercial wine houses, like those developed in Cincinnati at about the same time, were set up to consolidate the production, storage, and distribution of the region's wines. Second in order of founding, but older by virtue of continuing an already operating winery, was the firm of Sainsevain Brothers, Jean Louis and Pierre, the nephews of Jean Louis Vignes. When they bought out their uncle in 1855, they immediately proceeded to expand the scale of operations at the old El Aliso vineyard. They bought wine from other growers, as well as making it from their own grapes and those purchased from local vineyards. In 1857 they opened a store in San Francisco; by 1858 they led the state with a production of 125,000 gallons of wine and brandy.[90]

The *fata morgana* of the Sainsevain brothers was the wish to make champagne. Pierre, the younger, returned to France in 1856 to study the manufacture, and brought a French champagne maker back with him. In the season of 1857–58 sparkling wine was produced at the San Francisco cellars of the Sainsevain brothers.[91] They called it Sparkling California Champagne, and it was greeted with much interest, shipments being made to New York and Philadelphia to give it the widest publicity. It was not, however, a success. The Mission grape was a poor basis for sparkling wine, which calls for a far more acid juice than the Mission can provide; besides, the Sainsevain methods were not good enough to prevent large losses from breaking bottles and from other causes. The brothers were soon in financial difficulties as a result of their investment in sparkling wine—they are reputed to have lost $50,000 in the venture.[92] Their partnership was dissolved some time early in the 1860s, and only Jean remained at the El Aliso property in 1865 when it was sold. Both Sainsevains, at different times and at different places, kept their hands in the California wine trade thereafter, but the firm was no longer a factor in Los Angeles.

More stable and successful was the enterprise of Kohler & Frohling, as it was also the earliest of the Los Angeles wine houses. It might in fact be said that the real commerce in California wines begins with the advent of Kohler & Frohling. Charles Kohler was a German violinist who emigrated to New York in 1850 and then went on to San Francisco in 1853, where he helped to found the Germania Concert Society and provided San Francisco with its introduction to classical music. Among the musicians in his orchestra was a flutist named John Frohling. Late in 1853, Kohler, Frohling, and a third musician, an operatic tenor named Beutler, inspired by some delicious Los Angeles grapes at a picnic lunch, resolved to go into the wine business. None of them knew anything about it; indeed, Kohler and Frohling had never even seen a vineyard. Beutler, however, was from Baden, and his enthusiasm for the vine apparently fired the others, who were certainly shrewd enough to see an opportunity and resolute enough to pursue it.[93]

They raised a capital of $12,000, and made their first step by purchasing a small vineyard of Mission vines in Los Angeles in May 1854; that autumn they crushed their first vintage with the help of some Rhinelanders they had been able to hire. Beutler, for personal reasons, soon dropped out of the partnership,[94] leaving its management to Kohler, the salesman, who remained in San Francisco to oversee the firm's marketing activity. Frohling was the production manager, operating out of Los Angeles, where the vineyards were. Whether this assignment of responsibilities was made for any special reason we do not know, but both men did their jobs well. They rented a cellar in the Montgomery Block of San Francisco to store the few hundred gallons of wine that they had made, and began to acquire a clientele among the French and Germans of the city. The example was not lost on the Americans, who also began to buy the wines of Kohler & Frohling; the business thereupon grew quickly. Not so quickly, though, that the partners could afford to give up their musical careers entirely. Until 1858 Kohler continued to depend upon his fiddle, and Frohling upon his flute, to make up by night the money that the firm may have lost by day. They were, evidently, musicians of ability, for they did not lack for work when they needed it.[95]

In that same year, 1858, Kohler & Frohling took the prize at the state fair for "best wine"; they had already garnered a "diploma" for their Los Angeles port in

71 | Charles Kohler, the German immigrant musician turned wine merchant who, with his partner, John Frohling, first put the sale of California wine on a national basis. The portrait is from about 1875. (Author's collection)

1856 from the United States Agricultural Society meeting in Philadelphia.[96] Their success was such that they almost at once dominated the Los Angeles wine trade, buying and crushing the produce of some 350 acres of vineyard each year. Their method was to send a crew from vineyard to vineyard, where some of the men would pick the grapes and others stem, crush, and press them. The whole wine-making process was thus entirely in the hands of the firm, even though they might be working on the property of other vintners—Wolfskill, or Keller, for example, with whom they had contracts. The Kohler & Frohling vintage crew, under the direct supervision of Frohling, is thus described in action at William Wolfskill's vineyard and winery in 1859:

He [Frohling] has in his employ four men who are cleaning off the stems; this they do by pushing the grapes through the sifter [a wire sieve] with their hands; two men turn the mill [of two grooved iron cylinders] by cranks; two feed the hopper; one weighs the grapes; three or four attend to the wine as it comes from the mill and the presses; five or six do the pressing and carry off the pommace to the fermenting vats; one, two or three attend to washing, cleansing and sulphuring of grapes; and three teams are constantly employed in hauling the grapes. Every night all the presses and appliances used about them are all washed thoroughly to prevent acidity. Everything that comes in contact with the grape juice from the time the grape is bruised till it reaches the cask is kept as pure as abundance of water and hard scrubbing can make it.[97]

The year 1859 yielded a small vintage in Los Angeles, but even then Kohler & Frohling made more than 100,000 gallons. The next year was a poor one too, yet Frohling had to rent space from the city under the Los Angeles court house in order to accommodate all the wine he then had on hand. He advertised the place by first holding a harvest home celebration there; afterwards, he set up a bar to which thirsty Angelenos could go to buy a glassful of the young wine drawn from the 20,000 gallons reposing in the cool cellar.[98]

From the account of Frohling's winemaking methods in 1859, it is evident that he had an enlightened notion of how to do it at a time when others in Los Angeles were still using Indian foot-power. Frohling died in 1862, but the standards he set were maintained and the reputation of the firm made secure. Among other improvements, the firm of Kohler & Frohling brought in new varieties to the Los Angeles Valley, especially the varieties used for the production of port and sherry, and so helped to reduce the region's dependence on the unsatisfactory Mission.[99] In the history, not just of Los Angeles, but of the whole state of California with respect to winegrowing, Kohler and Frohling occupy a place of particular distinction. They showed the way the trade should go, and they deservedly prospered.

Los Angeles was where the grapes grew and the wine was made; San Francisco was, at first, the place where the wine was sold and drunk—130,000 gallons were shipped from south to north in 1861, for example, where it was Kohler's business to sell it.[100] The next and crucial step, as production grew, was to secure recognition outside of the state—no easy task when the Pacific Coast was still largely unpopulated and the western center of wine production was separated from the eastern centers of population by a continent uncrossed by road or railroad. Kohler & Frohling nevertheless began to make shipments to the east, and it is for that reason, especially, that the firm is important in the history of California wine. How soon it entered into out-of-state trade is not clear; it could not have been long after the beginnings, for by 1860 Kohler & Frohling had shipped over $70,000 worth out of California and had exclusive agencies in New York City and Boston, opened in that year.[101] In 1861 the Sainsevain brothers also opened a New York City branch,[102] and from this point the wines of California grew, more and more, to be the dominant element in the native wines that flowed through the country.

California wine—Los Angeles wine, really—was soberly examined and reported on by the gentlemen of the Farmer's Club, a section of the American Institute in New York City, in 1862, the earliest tasting notes on the state's wines made outside California that I know of. The Sainsevains' white wines, under the Aliso label, received good marks. Their sparkling wine was highly praised too—"well fined, fermented in the bottle, is entirely clear and free from sediment, and is truly a good, sound, dry wine" at $13 a dozen; given the failure of the Sainsevain champagne to secure a market, the New Yorkers were evidently being more than kind in this judgment. The wines from Kohler & Frohling were not specifically identified in the published report, but perhaps they included the port, at $8 a dozen delivered in New York, and an angelica that did not please the taste of the New Yorkers—"it is too strong for a 'ladies' wine,' and a bottle full of it contains I don't know how many headaches," one judge concluded. But on the whole the examination was a success for the Californians: "I think the samples shown to-day," one taster declared, "prove that America is capable of producing its own wine, and that we are really independent of the wine countries of Europe."[103] This must have gratified Kohler, who, in 1857, had written to one of his Los Angeles correspondents complaining of competition and the difficulties of selling native wines, yet jauntily concluding that "on the long run we will beat Europe anyhow."[104]

When Mark Twain, newly famous as the author of the "Celebrated Jumping Frog of Calaveras County," left California for New York in 1866, he took California wines with him to help promote them in the East.[105] He may have done some good, for by 1867 the shipments of California wine to New York for sale there and elsewhere in the East had reached impressive figures: 80,000 gallons of angelica, 150,000 gallons of Los Angeles port, and half a million gallons of white wine from Los Angeles and Sonoma (then the region second to Los Angeles in production) were said to have been shipped that year. These figures are, without doubt, on the inflated side, but even making a large allowance for hopeful exaggeration, they show that, as the writer who reports them put it, "the viniculturist of California has good prospects before him."[106] Ten years later Kohler & Frohling could boast that no town or city of middle size or more was without its wines, which included the following range of types (I follow Kohler's own enumeration): hock, riesling, muscat, tokay, gutedel, claret, zinfandel, malvoisie, burgundy, sherry, port, angelica. The firm, by that time, had permanent establishments in Sonoma and in St. Louis, in addition to its San Francisco and Los Angeles properties, and was crushing up to two and a half thousand tons of California grapes a year.[107]

California wines did not make an instant or uncontested capture of the eastern market for native wines; the producers in Ohio and New York had an interest to protect, and did not scruple to accuse the Californians of adulterating their wines and using fraudulent labels. The Cincinnati people were especially truculent, proclaiming that so-called California wine for sale in the East was in reality native eastern wine. According to Kohler's recollection, the president of the American Wine Growers' Association in Cincinnati "made himself prominent in circulating and reiterating this charge," but was at last compelled to recant.[108] Shipping costs, too, were an obvious disadvantage for the Californians, and so was the lack of bottles on the remote Pacific frontier. The last difficulty was much reduced by the founding of the Pacific Glass Works in 1862; Kohler & Frohling had a one-sixth interest in this venture, and after it produced its first wine bottle in 1863 the firm had a secure source of supply.[109]

The later fortunes of Kohler & Frohling need not be recounted here. The firm survived, and even helped to direct, the shift of California's winemaking from south to north; as early as 1865 it had purchased a Sonoma County vineyard property. When Kohler, the immigrant violinist, died in 1887, he left to his sons an impressive estate: the largest wine merchant's firm in California and winegrowing properties in Los Angeles, Sonoma, Fresno, and Sacramento counties.[110] Kohler has been called "the Longworth of the west," and he may be allowed a clear claim to that modest title in virtue of his having been the first man to make a name for the wines of California outside the place of their origin, as Longworth had done for the wines of Cincinnati.

The Beginnings in Northern California

Winegrowing in northern California did not wait upon the Gold Rush, though of course that event transformed it. Like the southerners, the early settlers in the north had the winegrowing example of the missions before them—San Jose, Santa Clara, and Sonoma especially. The vineyards and wine production of these establishments were, however, much smaller than those of the missions to the south, and though their wines and brandy enjoyed a good reputation, they cannot have been in very great supply: the vineyard at Sonoma, for example, seems to have been less than an acre in extent, and of the two vineyards at Mission San Jose that survived secularization, the larger contained only 4,000 vines.[111]

The first layman to grow grapes in the north was, so far as the record goes, the original *commandante* of Alta California, and later the governor of the province, Pedro Fages, who planted a garden with vines at Monterey around 1783.[112] Despite this precocious beginning, however, winegrowing in the northern part of the state was very slow to spread and develop. There were vineyards here and there, of course, besides those of the missions. Kotzebue mentions the grapes of the *pueblo* of Santa Clara in 1824,[113] and later visitors to the place also remarked on the local vineyards. General Vallejo, who presided over the secularization of the mission at Sonoma in 1835, took over the mission's vineyard, located just off the plaza of the tiny village he had founded there. In view of the later importance of Sonoma to the California industry, much has been made of the importance of this beginning; it remained only a beginning, however, until after 1849. Sir George Simpson, the British administrator of the Hudson's Bay Company's territories and an intrepid explorer, visited Vallejo at Sonoma in 1841. The general had, Sir George wrote, a vineyard of only about three hundred square feet, inherited from the mission priests but replanted by Vallejo, yielding around 540 gallons of wine.[114]

Other growers in the north before 1849 were so few that almost all of them may be mentioned. George Yount, a mountain man who came to California with William Wolfskill and moved to the north, has the distinction of having planted the first grapes in the Napa Valley (where he had settled two years earlier, at what is now Yountville but was then the Caymus Rancho) in 1838. Yount's vines grew from cuttings taken from Vallejo's at the Sonoma Mission; Napa Valley wine, therefore, is originally derived from the Sonoma Valley, a fact that will give pleasure to the partisans of Sonoma in the rivalry between California's two best-known wine valleys.[115] Yount's beginning was followed by Dr. Edward Bale, an Englishman, who planted vines at his home north of St. Helena on a ranch he acquired in 1841 (he got it through Vallejo, whose niece he had married). Some time around 1846 Florentine Kellogg, a settler from Illinois, also planted grapes at St. Helena, as did Reason P. Tucker. To the north, in Tehama County, the county's pioneer settler, Peter Lassen, a Dane, set out a small vineyard in 1846 that was ultimately transformed into the huge Vina Vineyard of Leland Stanford later in the century.[116] To the east of Napa, in what is now Solano County, an outpost of southern California viticulture was established at the Rio de los Putos Rancho, the joint property of William Wolfskill and his brother John. John took up residence on the property in 1842 and set out a small vineyard of Mission grapes in the spring of 1843.[117]

In Contra Costa County, across Suisun Bay at the foot of Mount Diablo, Dr. John Marsh had a small vineyard in 1846, from which he made wine. Besides Mission vines he had Isabella and Catawba—a not uncommon circumstance in the early days. Easterners were familiar with their native grapes and were probably profoundly skeptical about vinifera's chances, even in a country where it was known to succeed. Marsh, a Yankee and a difficult man, was later murdered, so that his contribution to California's early winemaking history did not come to much.[118] A few more names make the list of early northern growers before the Gold Rush substantially complete: Nicholas Carriger, Jacob Leese, and Franklin Sears in Sonoma, Antonio Sunol and Juan Bernal in Santa Clara County.[119] Perhaps the most telling remark at this time is William Heath Davis's statement that, when in 1846 he gave an elaborate engagement party on board his merchant ship anchored in Monterey Bay, he served wine, but not local wine: "California wine was not in general use at that time as a beverage," he explains.[120] The southern part of the state was not yet exporting it with any regularity, and the north was not yet growing enough.

At the end of 1848 California is estimated to have had about 14,000 inhabitants, exclusive of Indians—probably the number was not really even that large. Four years later, after the crisis of gold at Sutter's Mill, the official state census recorded a population of 224,000.[121] The explosive rise in numbers is not exactly paralleled in viticulture, but it is certainly true that from 1849 onwards, winegrowing in California enters on a different order of magnitude from what it had known

COLOMA VINEYARD,

SUTTER'S OLD MILL.

Located on the South Fork of the American River, at Coloma, El Dorado County, California, (where the first discovery of gold was made, in 1848.)

The soil and climate of this locality is peculiarly adapted to the culture of many foreign varieties of grapes—such as Burgundy, Green Hungarian, Muscatella, and others.

The wines produced by these varieties—as well as from the Catawba and Isabella grapes—have been pronounced by connoisseurs (both in Europe and America) as equal in quality to any Foreign Wines.

At this Vineyard, the following Brands of Wines are manufactured:

GREEN HUNGARIAN (very choice); MUSCATELLA (Dry and Sweet;) RISELING; CATAWBA; ISABELLA; NATIVE (White and Red); TOKAY; HOCK; ANGELICA; SHERRY; PORT; BURGUNDY (Port and Dry.)

These Wines received the Gold Medal at the State Fair in 1875.

Blackberry Wines, Cordials and Brandies, Catawba Wine Bitters

Also Brandies which are now from one to four years old, and in great demand.

ROBERT CHALMERS, Proprietor,

COLOMA, CAL.

Orders Solicited and Promptly Attended to.

72   The vines of the Coloma Vineyard went back to 1852, planted by the German Martin Allhoff and the Scotsman Robert Chalmers. The winery was built by Allhoff, but on his death came into the hands of Chalmers. This advertisement, from T. Hart Hyatt's *Hand-Book of Grape Culture* (2d ed., 1876), is notable for the prominence still given to the old American hybrids in California—Catawba, Isabella, and, perhaps, "Native (white and red)." (California State University, Fresno, Library)

before. One of the first districts to show the results of extensive new vine planting was the Mother Lode country itself, especially in Amador, El Dorado, Sutter, and Tuolumne counties. Vines were planted as early as 1849 at Coloma in El Dorado County and at Bear River in Sutter County.[122] By 1856, the first year for which any figures are available, the four counties named above had some 70,000 vines; two years later the figure was 205,000, the largest number growing in El Dorado County, followed by Tuolumne, Sutter, and Amador.[123] These were all small plantings, and, though the Gold Rush country continued to be a significant section of California viticulture, it is not where the most important parts of the nineteenth century industry developed. That was in the counties to the north and south of San Francisco Bay, in the valleys and along the foothills of Sonoma, Napa, and Santa Clara counties especially, where winegrowing had been tentatively begun before the Gold Rush. Other northern counties had vineyards too: vines were planted at Stockton, in San Joaquin County, in 1850; the first vineyard in Stanislaus County was planted in 1852, and the first in Yolo County went in about the same time.[124]

Since the Gold Rush had attracted every sort of person from every part of the world, the early winegrowers were a diverse lot—Germans and Dutchmen, Frenchmen, Yankees, and Englishmen were all among the pioneers. Sutter himself, the Swiss adventurer and feudal-style landholder on whose land gold was first found, after losing most of his property in the rush that followed, turned to winegrowing on his Hock Farm, as he called it, on the Feather River south of Yuba City, where a vineyard had been set out in 1851.[125] Sutter, sad to say, was an alcoholic, whose interest in his wines was neither wholly commercial nor at all good for him. The man who actually made the discovery of gold, James Marshall, a native of New Jersey, also owned a vineyard in Coloma County where the discovery had been made.[126] In Tuolumne County, in 1853, a group of five Frenchmen planted a vineyard that, in five years, is said to have grown to 30,000 vines and to have yielded over sixty tons of grapes.[127] Many other names might be given to illustrate the international style of pioneer winegrowing in the north—names such as Gerke, Justi, Thee, Lefranc, Krug, Wubbena, Fabricius, and Votypka—but the point is sufficiently plain: just as it had been in the south around Los Angeles, winegrowing in the Gold Rush country and around San Francisco Bay was a cosmopolitan enterprise in which Maine fishermen and Illinois farmers were equally welcome with *viticulteurs* from Bordeaux and *Weinbauern* from the Rhine.

It was not until the middle of the 1850s that a genuinely booming development in winegrowing came about in the north. By that time the first and most violent years of the gold fever were over, and men were ready to think about more permanent bases for the state's economy. Winegrowing looked especially attractive, for the considerable trials that had already been made showed that the vine would grow almost anywhere in the state. At the same time, news of the great vine disease, the *oidium*, in Europe, led the papers to prophesy the imminent demise of winegrowing in the Old World and an unlimited opportunity for the New. Bacchus would be compelled to emigrate, and would become an American citizen with all those Frenchmen and Germans who had preceded him. After 1855, under the rally-ing cry of "California, the vineyard of the world,"[128] plantings increased by leaps and bounds. The statistics, even though they are probably quite unreliable in de-tail, tell a plain story. Santa Clara County, for example, is reported to have had 30,000 vines in 1855; in the next year the figure was 150,000; in 1857, it was 500,000.[129] Another significant first for these years occurred in 1857, when the first wine shipped from Napa County to San Francisco went to market—a modest quantity of "six casks and six bottles."[130] For the state as a whole the increase in plantings was quite dramatic: in 1856 there were, according to figures published in the *State Register*, 1,500,000 vines; in 1857, 2,265,000; and in 1858, 3,954,000. The total thus more than doubled by a good deal in the short space between 1856 and 1858. Nor was the growth confined to the north: Los Angeles made the greatest advance, doubling its plantings in the years in question.[131] By 1862 there were 8,000,000 vines in the state.[132]

The spirit of these first boom years is well expressed in the report made by the committee on grapes at the annual exhibition of the California Horticultural So-ciety in 1858:

> When it is remembered that the grape grows to the greatest perfection next to the very placers of gold—that some ten millions of acres of land in our state can be cultivated in this noble fruit—that the commercial value of the products of the grape trade in Eu-rope is worth two hundred and two millions of dollars, and employs some five millions of people in making wines, brandies, raisins, tartar, and in an infinitude of trades as coopers, coppersmiths, carpenters, glass makers, cork cutters, etc., and also employs a commercial marine of some two thousand ships, it will be seen what a glorious pros-pect of advancing power and greatness the cultivation of this ancient and valued fruit opens to our State. It is absolutely as valuable and as feasible a mine of wealth to us, as our mines of gold, silver, copper and quicksilver, besides being a more grateful and humanizing employment.[133]

The level of knowledge and experience at the beginning of the boom in the mid fifties was not yet very high. The *California Farmer*, a San Francisco weekly that made the promotion of winegrowing a special mission, was still, in 1855, drawing most of its advice and information about grape growing and winemaking from sources outside the state—typically from Ohio, or even from Massachusetts. It also recommended the eastern hybrids—Catawba especially—to the growers of California, a sure sign that not much local experience had yet accumulated.[134] Nevertheless, the means for assisting and developing the state's winegrowing were quickly forming in these years. In 1854 the California State Agricultural Society was chartered, and it at once began to help the wine industry. It sent visiting com-mittees throughout the state to report on vine growing and winemaking; it made competition between the growers for premiums an important part of the annual state fair, and it disseminated information through its *Transactions*. The best-known publication of this sort that it commissioned was the "Report on Grapes and Wine of California," written by the remarkable Colonel Haraszthy of Buena Vista, Sonoma County. Haraszthy's treatise, which was devoted mostly to practical notes on vine growing and winemaking, appeared originally in the society's *Transactions* for 1858, and was then reprinted in quantity for statewide distribution. It is in keeping with the international character of the state's winemaking tradition that Haraszthy was a Hungarian who had reached California by way of Wisconsin.

By 1859 the industry was large enough to become visible to the state legislature; an act of that year exempted new vine plantings from taxation until they were four years old, so that growers would not have to pay on their investment until they had a crop to enable them to meet the tax.[135] Apart from the useful work of the State Agricultural Society, this was the first official act in favor of the wine industry in California. It was soon followed by another in 1861, when the legislature established a "Commission upon the Ways and Means best adapted to promote the Improvement and Growth of the Grape-vine in California";[136] the work of this body will be described later in connection with its most active member, Colonel Haraszthy.

The work that Haraszthy is best remembered for was his importation of large quantities of European grape varieties to supplant the Mission grape, which dominated in the north as well as in the south. He has been given far too much credit for pioneering in the business, however, as a quick review of other men's contributions before Haraszthy will show. It did not take even uninstructed vine growers long to discover that something better than the Mission must be found if California wines were ever to improve. Jean Louis Vignes and Kohler & Frohling have already been mentioned as pioneers in introducing other varieties than the Mission to the southern vineyards. In the north, in the 1850s, there were a good many others who were active in trying to improve the stock of varieties available to the California vineyardist. Their efforts constitute a distinct chapter in California history and are worth emphasizing all the more since they have been so little recognized until quite recent years.

The growers and nurserymen of Santa Clara County were the leaders in this work, and among them the French were the most prominent: unlike most Americans, they knew for certain that one could do better than the Mission. The first grower known to have introduced superior varieties to the north was Pierre Pellier, who brought vines with him from the Bordeaux region about 1852 (the exact date is disputed), to be planted in his brother's nursery and vineyard near San Jose. In 1854 Pierre returned to France for more and better cuttings; it is said that, on the return voyage in 1856, the ship's supply of water was nearly exhausted by the long voyage and the cuttings were in danger of dying. Pellier bought up the ship's supply of potatoes, slit them, and saved his cuttings by inserting them into the moist potatoes. By this ingenious means, California received its first Grey Riesling, French Colombard, and Folle Blanche.[137]

Among other Santa Clara Frenchmen, Louis Prevost of San Jose had some sixty different varieties of grape planted in the 1850s.[138] Antoine Delmas, his neigh-

IFORNIA FARMER.

NURSERY BUSINESS.

SMITH'S GARDENS

SACRAMENTO.

Seed Warehouse,

No. 40 J street,

BETWEEN SECOND AND THIRD.

Now ready to be mailed to applicants, our General Catalogues of Fruit, Ornamental Trees, and Grape-vines. Also, our General Price-Catalogue of Garden-seeds, and a Wholesale Catalogue of Garden and Field-seeds for

WHOLESALE DEALERS.

For particulars and more minute information, please address as above, and we will promptly forward any or all of the above Catalogues, which will give our customers all the information they may require upon each of the subjects treated upon.

We offer

200,000 Choicest Foreign

GRAPE VINES,

The largest and best selected stock of

WINE AND TABLE GRAPES

IN THE STATE.

We are prepared to sell the above in large or small quantities, at greatly reduced prices from previous years, and lower than the same kinds are sold, as per Eastern Catalogues.

Write to Us Before Purchasing Elsewhere.

ALSO

150,000 California

GRAPE-VINES.

Our general Nursery-stocks of

FRUIT, Ornamental Trees,

Shrubs, Roses,

Are unusually large and fine.

GREEN-HOUSE PLANTS:

Our collections of Green-House Plants were never better. They are worthy of particular attention, and will be sold in lots at greatly reduced prices from former years.

NURSERY BUSINESS.

Fruit Trees!

ORNAMENTAL TREES AND SHRUBS,

Grapes, Green-House Plants,

ETC., ETC.,

—AT THE—

San Jose Nursery.

Always on hand the best varieties of APPLES, PEARS, CHERRIES, PLUMS, APRICOTS, PEACHES, GRAPES, CURRANTS, GOOSEBERRIES, STRAWBERRIES, Etc., Etc. Also, ORNAMENTAL TREES and FLOWERING SHRUBS. A great variety of EVERGREENS, cultivated in pots to insure their growth.

My collection of ROSES received the FIRST PREMIUM at the State Fair at San Jose. The best Varieties of MULBERRY TREES for Silk Culture.

—ALSO—

CALIFORNIA GRAPES,

OF ONE AND TWO YEARS OLD,

By the hundred or thousand,

FOR SALE AT VERY REDUCED PRICES.

The Trees and Shrubs carefully labeled and packed up in bundles or boxes, according to the distance they have to go. CATALOGUES SENT GRATIS ON APPLICATION. Direct to

L. PREVOST,
San Jose, California,

Or to my Agents,

MR. DELARIGNE,
59 Clay street, or
MR. L. PINCHARD,
Sonora, California.

143

French Garden

VINEYARD,

SAN JOSE.

THE UNDERSIGNED HAS THE honor of informing the public that his former partner,

MR. J. B. LÉGER,

I as just returned from France, bringing with him a comp, etc

APPARATUS FOR DISTILLING,

and one also

FOR MAKING WINE.

They wish to turn their attention to WINE-MAKING, and to make it a

SPECIAL BUSINESS.

They think that, by entering againin partnership, one being from BORDEAUX and the other from BOURGOGNE, they cannot fail to

PRODUCE GOOD LIQUIDS.

They will undertake, at reasonable terms, to

Make Wines and Cognacs,

Within their vicinity. for all persons who will hono them with their confidence.

A. DELMAS.

WE WOULD CALL THE AT-tention of GRAPE-GROWERS, to our

SPLENDID COLLECTION OF

Grape-Vines.

Already well noted for the

MOST BEAUTIFUL KINDS OF GRAPES,

BOTH FOR

TABLE AND WINE.

We have also lately added several varieties,

FROM BORDEAUX AND BOURGOGNE,

Which we will sell at REDUCED PRICES.

With us will also be found—

Fruit Trees,

One, two, and three years old, of all kinds. And the best Ornamental Trees, embracing—

ELMS, LOMBARDY POPLARS, AND SILVER-LEAF POPLARS.

Our whole assortment is in very fine order.

We beg our Friends and Customers to honor us with their confidence, and we will do all in our power esati-fy their wishes.

Catalogues sent to applicants.

A. DELMAS & J. B. LÉGER.

San Jose, Nov. 5th, 1860.   11

30,000 Locust Trees,

1000 LOMBARDY POPLAR,

FOR SALE BY

---

73 | Advertisements for grapevines in the *California Farmer,* 21 March 1861. On the left Smith's Gardens of Sacramento offers 200,000 cuttings of "foreign" vines (that is, any vinifera other than the Mission grape); on the right, Antoine Delmas of the French Garden, San Jose, offers assistance with winemaking and distilling as well as grapes for table and winemaking. The "California grapes" offered by Louis Provost were presumably the Mission variety. Such were the resources available to California vineyardists well before Agoston Haraszthy left California for Europe.

---

bor and fellow Frenchman, had the most extensive of all early varietal collections in California.[139] Delmas had imported 10,000 cuttings from France in 1854, when he received a special premium from the State Agricultural Society for the "best and largest varieties of foreign grapes."[140] When Delmas took the first prize for wine at the state fair of 1859, his superior grape varieties were probably a reason for his success. By 1858 Delmas's collection had swelled to 350,000 vines of 105 different varieties.[141] Still another Santa Clara County Frenchman, Charles Lefranc, set out a vineyard of foreign varieties in 1857.[142]

The French were not the only ones to follow this line towards improving California wine. Jacob Knauth, the son of a Johannisberg winemaker, imported the Orleans grape from the Rhine for planting near Sutter's Fort in 1853; this furnished the basis for his well-known Orleans Hill Vineyard in Yolo County, beginning in 1860.[143] Another German, Frank Stock, in 1858 introduced to San Jose such great varieties from his native country as the Riesling, Sylvaner, and Traminer.[144] And various Americans contributed too: Bernard Fox, of the Stockton Ranch Nursery, was advertising nineteen varieties of vinifera as early as 1854; three years later Fox moved his business north of San Jose, where by 1858 he had eighty-six different varieties in his stock.[145] L. A. Gould and William Thomburg of Santa Clara and the Englishman James Lowe of San Jose all had vineyards of different varieties by 1858—Gould had seventy, Thomburg, sixteen.[146] In San Joaquin County, adjoining Santa Clara on the northeast, the nurserymen William and George West imported forty varieties of grape from Boston in 1853; from this stock, it is said, the earliest vineyards of the county were propagated. The Wests themselves developed the El Pinal Vineyard, one of the famous names in the winemaking of the nineteenth century.[147] In Napa County, varieties other than the Mission were being grown at the vineyard of the Thompson brothers south of Napa City by 1856; two years later they had some forty-five different varieties available in their nursery.[148] Sam Brannan, who began developing his Calistoga vineyards in 1859, collected thousands of cuttings from France, Spain, Germany, and Italy.[149] And in Sonoma, with which the introduction of superior varieties to California is particularly associated on account of Haraszthy's work, the first new varieties seem to have been brought in by the brothers Shaw, transplanted Vermonters who brought their "foreign grapes" from Los Angeles in 1856.[150] As a final instance, one may name A. P. Smith of Sacramento, who offered more than a hundred varieties of vinifera for sale in 1859 after several years of experimental trials. Smith had also made wine from some twenty of the varieties he offered for sale; one of them was the Black St. Peters, which there is reason to think may have been a variant name for the Zinfandel.[151]

It is evident from this rapid summary that the need for better varieties was well recognized and that the work of introducing them was well begun a good many years before Haraszthy made his famous collecting tour of the wine regions of Europe in 1861. To call attention to this fact is not to deny Haraszthy's contribution but to put it into a more sensible historical perspective. Like most critical events, the introduction of new and better varieties into California did not happen all at once, nor was it the work of a single hand. Haraszthy was one among many contributors, and far from the first. One should not forget, either, that the U.S. government was actively identifying and disseminating improved varieties of native grapes for the eastern states. The example would not have been wholly lost on the Californians. Eastern vines, as has been noted, were included among those tried by California vineyardists in the 1850s. Longworth's success with Catawba naturally led the Californians to imitate what he had done, but though Catawba wines were made in California, and others from such native hybrids as the Diana and the Isabella, it was pretty generally concluded that the future did not lie that way. The natives persisted for some time in a small way, however. Nurserymen continued to offer the old favorites like Catawba and Herbemont, and when the State Vinicultural Society commissioned the handsome illustrated *Grapes and Grape Vines of California* in 1877, one of the ten varieties represented was the Catawba. As late as 1886 A. Langenburger of Anaheim was offering "*genuine* LeNoir wine" for sale.[152] According to Leon Adams, the last Catawba vineyard in California, in Santa Clara County, endured until 1969.[153]

At the end of the 1850s, the northern region of California, where ten years earlier no commercial winegrowing had existed at all, was a serious competitor to the southern part of the state. The census of 1860, whose figures for wine production are certainly far below the actual gallonage, reports that California made 246,518 gallons of wine in that year. Of this, Los Angeles produced 162,980 gallons; San Bernardino and Santa Barbara Counties, the other contributors from the south, added some 19,000 gallons more. The rest—some 64,000 gallons—came from the new northern regions of the Mother Lode counties and the lands around San Francisco Bay.[154] It was evident that, at this rate, Los Angeles and the south would soon be overtaken, as in fact happened within the next ten years. The advantage of the north lay not only in its relation to the much larger population of metropolitan San Francisco but also in its topography and climate. About soils it is difficult to generalize—the vine takes to all sorts, and a demonstrable correlation between soil type and wine quality is not uniformly possible (at least it has not been in this country: the French think differently). But one can say that the terrain of the north was much more varied than that of the south, cut up as it is into a myriad hills and valleys ranging from the regions of coastal fog to the high, snowy Sierra. In the south, the coastal range is higher and more sterile, the valleys are larger and flatter, and the influence of the contiguous desert more troublesomely felt.

Climate is demonstrably the most important of external factors for the vine, and within the notion of climate, sunshine and rain are the key elements. Though the southern region has by no means a single, uniform climatic character, it is, to put it as simply as possible, both hotter and drier. The cooling effect of the ocean is lost when one has penetrated only a few miles into the interior valleys; the rivers flow only during the winter rainy season, and irrigation is the necessary condition of growing crops, with unimportant exceptions. In these circumstances of dryness and heat, the grape will respond quite vigorously, but not in the way best adapted to the making of fine, well-balanced table wines, the standard by which any winemaking country is to be measured. Instead, as the grapes swell with rich, sugar-laden juice under the generative power of the sun, the acid content sinks proportionately. The result, even when one has the best varieties available, is a wine flat and flabby, or, as tasters say, out of balance. Without very sophisticated means of measurement and control, then, means quite unavailable in the nineteenth century, the grower in a region like the south of California will not be able to make a superior table wine; more often than not he cannot make even a good one. Owing to the high sugar content and low acid of his grapes, he can make admirable, even outstanding, sweet wines, and it was on that style of wine that Los Angeles grew more and more to concentrate. But if it is not to be a mere supplier of aperitifs and dessert wines, an industry must depend on good, sound dry table wine, and for this requisite the north had an irresistible advantage over the south. In favored northern districts, the sunshine is long enough and strong enough to bring grapes to full ripeness, yet not so strong as to raise the sugar out of balance with the indispensable acid content. Winter rains are sufficient to allow the vines to grow without summer irrigation; the circumstance is important, because irrigation, for complex chemical reasons, has the result of causing the vine and its fruit to flourish vegetatively at the expense of winemaking quality.

The men in the north must have begun to realize their advantage in no very long time, but the judicious among them knew that so young an enterprise had most of its work still in front of it—that is, indeed, still true, for the refinements of winegrowing can only arise out of long-continued experience of a kind still not attained in the United States; the two millennia and more of European experience remind us that we need not be particularly anxious on this score. On the other hand, it is remarkable how quickly the winegrowing possibilities of the state had been explored, at least by way of beginning: the south, the San Francisco Bay region, and the foothills of the Sierra were all tested in a significant way by the middle of the century. Among today's important winegrowing regions, only the great Central Valley and the Salinas Valley were untried by that point—although of course these are very large omissions.

On the whole, while admitting the precocity of California's development, the historian should probably emphasize how young and untaught the wine industry was. In 1860 the Committee on Wines of the State Agricultural Society confessed that "most of our people have never seen a vineyard. Whoever will enlighten [them] on the most approved modes of culture, and, above all, the scientific and practical treatment of the grape juice in the making of wine will be a great public benefactor."[155] At the state fair of the year before, for example, the judges analyzed one specimen of table wine and found it to have 15 percent alcohol and 0.28 percent acid—a grotesque imbalance. They concluded, with gentle understatement, that the state's winemakers had not yet "reached that standard of perfection which our climate and soil must one day enable them to attain."[156]

After a tour of vineyards and wineries north and south, a not very friendly Yankee visitor in 1867, Charles Loring Brace, affirmed less charitably that "in fact, on a broad scale, the wine-making of California has been a failure." The wines lacked character and were too alcoholic, he said—faults both of the varieties from which they came and of the methods by which they were made. There was no good, light, cheap table wine, and at the same time the industry had too self-congratulatory an opinion of itself; everybody conspired to compliment the wine-growers, whereas, Brace thought, "there is nothing that California needs so much in developing her resources as a little truth-speaking"—especially in making judgment on her wines.[157]

Brace was perhaps too harsh. Another voice, that of a Californian devoted to promoting the resources of the state, and himself a winegrower, puts the case more mildly and dispassionately. John S. Hittell, the author of *The Resources of California* (1863), after making the standard observation that "California is a favorite land of the grape," goes on to say that growers do not yet know what the right soils are or the right grapes for them in the large and varied territories of the state. Nor have the winemakers learned their trade:

> It is certainly no easy matter to make fine wine out of the Mission grape, and most of our wine-makers have little experience in the business. Again, they send their wine to market too soon after it is made. They often use old barrels and bottles, which may give a taste to the wine. They have also been too careless in pressing grapes before they were fully ripe, and without picking out the green and rotten fruit.[158]

It is no disgrace to the early growers that such things could be said of them; but it would be many years before they could say that the charges did not apply.

10

The Haraszthy Legend

T he United States, though rather an old country now as standards of national identity go, still feels itself to be young and therefore takes an anxious interest in its founders and fathers. The California wine industry has had, according to the stories repeated over and over in the press at every level since the late nineteenth century, a "father" named Agoston Haraszthy.[1] In 1946 the title was officially sanctioned by the state of California at ceremonies dedicating a memorial in Sonoma to Haraszthy as the "Father of California Viticulture": one may still contemplate the bronze assertion on the north side of the old plaza in Sonoma. The same formula identifies a vine planted in Haraszthy's memory in 1961 by Governor Edmund Brown in Capitol Park, Sacramento.

How good is Haraszthy's claim? Is it only the result of effective publicity? Does it mean something solid? Or is it just a mistake? On a simple documentary level the answer is clear. As the preceding chapter has shown at some length, viticulture and winemaking in California were thoroughly established long before Haraszthy made his way to the state in 1849. By that time there was a history of nearly three-quarters of a century of practical winegrowing, and a strong effort towards improving the selection of grape varieties was already well under way. But if one tries to answer the question in a more critical way, the case grows a little complicated. "Father," after all, is not a very useful metaphor: a literal father must have an exclusive claim, but a man who pioneers in a decisive way may share credit with a good many predecessors. The best thing to do, then, seems to be to tell Haraszthy's story as well as it can be reconstructed (many important questions have never been answered), and to let that stand as an argument for or against the alleged paternity connected with his name.

74 Agoston Haraszthy (1812–69), the Hungarian who developed the Buena Vista Vineyard in the late 1850s. He has since been given credit as a pioneer of California winegrowing out of all proportion to his actual contributions. (Wine Institute)

Both the beginning of Haraszthy's life in the old Austro-Hungarian empire and its ending in the forests of Nicaragua are quite indistinct so far as the record goes. What were his activities before he came to the United States? And was he, at the end, devoured by an alligator? No one seems to know. But between those two points, the busy, confident, multifarious, and striking activities of Haraszthy left a strong impression that remains clear enough today.[2] The son of a landed proprietor, Agoston Haraszthy was born in 1812 at Futak, on the east bank of the Danube at the end of its long run from north to south across the great Hungarian plain. The place was then in southern Hungary but is now a part of Yugoslavia. Young Haraszthy is said to have studied law, to have been a member of Emperor

Ferdinand's bodyguard, and to have served as private secretary to Archduke Joseph, palatine of Hungary. At some point—indistinct like all of the details of the early years—Haraszthy retired to his estates and pursued the life of an enlightened agriculturist; winegrowing and silk culture were among his interests. In this period, Haraszthy served in the Hungarian Diet; he also married a Polish lady, by whom he had six children: four sons named after the heroes of Hungarian history—Geza, Attila, Arpad, and Bela—and two daughters.

In 1840, together with a cousin, a boy of eighteen, Haraszthy left Hungary for the United States; the reason, according to Haraszthy's statements afterwards, was political. The failure of Louis Kossuth's liberal movement, with which he was in some way associated (indistinct again), is supposed to have forced him to flee.[3] Haraszthy has, in consequence, traditionally been represented as a hero of the liberal cause in Europe. But the claim is not clearly made out, to say the least. For one thing, Kossuth had just been *released* from jail when Haraszthy first left Hungary. For another, Haraszthy's cousin and travelling companion on that first visit to the United States later affirmed that he and Haraszthy had left Hungary "for no reason, except to wander."[4] Whatever the truth of that matter, Haraszthy was able to return to Hungary in 1842 to sell his estate there and to bring his whole family, father and mother included, back to the United States. If he was a political exile, he was evidently under no very severe persecution.[5]

Haraszthy had, on his first visit to America, bought land on the prairie bordering the Wisconsin River where the town of Sauk City now stands. From 1842, when he settled there with his family, until 1848, when he left for California, Haraszthy was the prince of this Wisconsin property. With a partner he set about developing a town—at one point it was called Haraszthy—and he took a hand in all sorts of pioneer enterprises: a brickyard, a sawmill, a general store, a hotel. He sold lots; he operated a ferry across the Wisconsin River and a steamboat on it; he held a contract for supplying corn to the soldiers at Fort Winnebago, and raised large numbers of pigs and sheep; he planted the state's first hop yard (prophetic of Wisconsin beer). He also published *Travels in America,* a two-volume account of his American impressions, in Hungary in 1844, partly in order to stimulate immigration to his Wisconsin lands (the publication is further evidence that Haraszthy was not a political exile). Despite the pressure of these affairs, Haraszthy seems to have spent much of his time as an enthusiastic outdoorsman, riding and hunting with a flamboyance that amazed the simple Wisconsin settlers: one anecdote tells of his killing a wolf with his bare hands.[6] He was tall, dark, fiercely mustached, and given to wearing aristocratic boots and a green silk shirt with a red sash. It is no wonder that the natives always called him "Count," though he was not a member of the Austro-Hungarian nobility.

From the point of view of his later work in California, Haraszthy's most interesting project in Wisconsin was his attempt to grow wine there, high up above the forty-third parallel, in the middle of a continent. He set out vines in 1847 and in 1848, and built a forty-foot cellar to receive the fruit of his vines. But winter frosts killed the vines and there is no evidence that Haraszthy succeeded in producing a Wisconsin wine before he left the state.[7]

At the end of 1848 Haraszthy turned his back on all this—probably he was dissatisfied with the financial results of all his speculations—and prepared to travel overland to California with his family. They left St. Joseph via the Santa Fe Trail in the spring of 1849, ahead of the main wave of forty-niners and apparently without any intention of literal gold-seeking. The news of gold in California had reached the East at about the time that Haraszthy left the village he had founded in Wisconsin, but instead of heading for the Mother Lode, Haraszthy made his way to the unprepossessing hamlet of San Diego, hundreds of miles to the south. There he was at once energetically busy in his old omnicompetent way. He and his sons briefly experimented with a plan to take over the derelict mission gardens at San Luis Rey, but soon returned to San Diego, where Haraszthy and others had established a market garden in Mission Valley; there, in March 1850, Haraszthy began to plant the first of his Californian vineyards, with cuttings taken from the Mission San Luis Rey's surviving vines. Haraszthy is also said to have ordered roots and cuttings of vinifera vines from Europe and planted them in 1851, the first of the many importations that he was to bring into the state. The evidence for this, however, is not reliable.[8] Haraszthy diversified his time in San Diego by Indian fighting, land speculation, and politics: he was elected the county's first sheriff in 1851, and city marshal in the same year, when he also built the town's new jail on a speculative contract (the jail proved incapable of holding prisoners). Haraszthy's brief episode in San Diego came to an end late in 1851, when he was elected state assemblyman for San Diego County and went off to his legislative duties far to the north in Sacramento. He never returned to live in San Diego, and his vineyard there was abandoned.

Haraszthy must have had his mind on growing things as well as on making laws when he left the south of the state for the north; within two months after the legislature had convened in Sacramento he had bought an extensive property near Mission Dolores, south of the city of San Francisco as it then was. At this place, which he called "Los Flores," he began to develop a nursery, including grapevines. But this was no better a place to grow grapes then than it had been in mission days, when the Franciscans found that they could not succeed with grapes there. Haraszthy sold part of the property in 1853 and began buying land farther south on the peninsula in the hills near San Mateo (the land now lies under the waters of the Crystal Springs Lakes reservoir); by 1854 he had planted thirty acres of grapes there.[9]

He had also begun to operate as an assayer and refiner of gold in San Francisco in partnership with two fellow Hungarians. In 1855 he was made official smelter and refiner at the branch mint in San Francisco, and, despite his public appointment, joined in a private gold and silver refinery as well. Haraszthy came to serious grief in this activity, for in 1857 a grand jury brought in a charge against him for the "embezzlement" of $150,000, the value of the gold for which he was unable to account after a tally of the mint's gold had been made. Haraszthy was forced to mortgage or sell the larger part of his properties and to hand over his assets to the government in pledge, while a complicated inquiry and trial took place. What was finally determined was that, under the strain of extraordinary operation night and day, the furnaces of the mint had allowed gold to escape up the chimneys in quantities beyond the officially permitted measure of waste. Haraszthy—who by this time had made enemies as well as friends—was cleared, but not until 1861.[10] In the meantime, he had begun the work for which he is now remembered in California.

Haraszthy had already learned that the cool wet fogs of the peninsula made his Crystal Springs property unsuitable for successful grape growing, and so he began to cast about for another place—his fourth in California and fifth in the United States, if we count the Wisconsin venture—where grapes might do well. He found it across the bay to the north, ouside the town of Sonoma, where Vallejo, who had already been growing grapes for a generation, had since the Gold Rush built a new house, laid out a larger vineyard, and begun taking prizes for his wines at the newly founded state fair. On a property nearby were some sixteen acres of vines called the Sonoma Vineyard, said to have been planted by an Indian as early as 1832.[11] The wine from it was good enough to convince Haraszthy that he could do even better there. Accordingly, in 1856, in the very midst of his troubles with the Mint, Haraszthy bought about 560 acres of Sonoma property, lying northeast of the town, including the Sonoma Vineyard, and extending up the slopes of the Mayacamas Mountains. Work began at once in transferring vines from the San Mateo vineyards to the new property in Sonoma; Haraszthy himself moved there in May 1857 and made it his home until he left California some ten years later.

The astonishing confidence and energy of the man is abundantly illustrated in his operations now. He was now always known as the Colonel, for "Count" would not have sat well on the freely elected member of a representative assembly, such as Haraszthy had been in California: the claim to "Colonel" presumably was based on Haraszthy's service in the imperial bodyguard—or perhaps it was based on nothing but personal style. In any case, the Count-Colonel christened his new estate Buena Vista, and at once proceeded to transform it. Within a year he had 14,000 imported vines growing and another 12,000 in his nursery, the whole consisting of some 165 varieties.[12] He also planted extensively for other landowners, among them such names later famous in California winemaking as Krug, Gundlach, and Bundschu: by the end of 1857 Haraszthy and others had more than tripled the total grape acreage of Sonoma County.[13]

In preparation for the abundant harvests that were soon to come, he set his Chinese coolies to digging tunnels back into the hillside to serve as wine cellars: one was 13 feet wide and 100 feet long; the other, 20 feet wide, was driven back 240 feet into the hill.[14] To crown his vineyards he built a large white villa in Pompeian style, boasting a pillared porch and a parapet surmounted by statues of classical figures (so at any rate the pictures show it). From this vantage he could look south and west over the vines and grain fields of the valley all the way to San Pablo

75 The villa in "Pompeian" style built by Agoston Haraszthy on his Buena Vista ranch property, Sonoma County. This was the final touch to Haraszthy's flamboyant development of Buena Vista. No trace of the house remains today. (From Haraszthy, *Grape Culture, Wines, and Wine-Making* [1862]; Huntington Library)

Bay. When Haraszthy was entertained at Schloss Johannisberg in 1861, he politely admired the splendid view that Prince Metternich, the owner, enjoyed of the Rhine, but he thought to himself that his own Buena Vista did quite as well: "The Prince may boast of the view from his palace, as I can from my ranch in Sonoma; or, rather, I may boast of having scenery equal to that of the Prince Metternich. It is true that I have no River Rhine, but in its place there lies the St. Pablo Bay."[15]

The rapidity with which Haraszthy established himself once he had settled in Sonoma may be documented by various details: he set out 300 acres of vineyard between 1858 and 1862, and in 1859 he was able to claim first prize for the best exhibit of wines at the state fair, "with reference to the number of varieties, vintages, and quality"; among the items of his exhibit were a tokay and a wine obscurely called "Menise" or "Monise" (the name is spelled both ways in the record).[16] Two of Haraszthy's sons, Geza and Attila, soon had vineyards of their own in Sonoma, and Arpad had been sent to France in order to study, among other things, the manufacture of champagne at Epernay. Haraszthy continued to import grape varieties from Europe to augment his collection: the 165 varieties in it early in 1858 had grown to 280 later in that year. By the beginning of the 1860s he claimed to have the largest vineyard in the state, or, sometimes, "the largest vineyard in the world."[17] For a man who had just been compelled to resign his official appointment, to mortgage his properties, and to face a criminal trial, all of this was evidence, not merely of a remarkable insouciance, but of a powerful determination to do just what he chose to do. He must have outraged his enemies, and he must have had great pleasure in so doing.

The remarkable improvements that Haraszthy had made at Buena Vista attracted attention at once; in the first year of his settlement there, the gentlemen of the California State Agricultural Society asked him to write a treatise on the science and mystery of winegrowing in the state. The difficulty of such a task was nothing to Haraszthy, who, by February 1858 had dashed off a "Report on Grapes and Wine of California"; it may be regarded as the first native Californian treatise on the subject, and though, like all first words, it could hardly have the authority of a last word, California was lucky to have anything so intelligent. The "Report" was published in the *Transactions* of the society for 1858, and was, as well, separately reprinted for extensive distribution throughout the state.[18] There is nothing particularly notable or original in this essay, unless perhaps we except Haraszthy's instructions for making a tokay wine; these called for raisined grapes pressed by their own weight, the classic method of Hungarian tokay *Eszencia*.[19] Perhaps that was the method that produced Haraszthy's prize-winning tokay of 1859; if so, it was not likely to be imitated widely in California.

On the matter of the choice of varieties, Haraszthy agreed with what many others were already saying: the quality of California wine, he wrote, would never be what it might be so long as the Mission grape was the standard. He also thought that California should study the art of blending:

> To illustrate this more to every man's mind, I will compare the wine-making with the cooking of a vegetable soup. You can make from turnips a vegetable soup, but it will be a poor one; but add to it also potatoes, carrots, onions, cabbage, etc., and you will have a fine soup, delicately flavored. So it will be with your wine; one kind of grapes has but one eminent quality in taste or aroma, but put a judicious assortment of various flavored grapes in your crushing-machine, and the different aromas will be blended together and will make a far superior wine to that manufactured from a single sort, however good that one kind may be.[20]

Haraszthy's prosperity crested in 1861. In that year production at Buena Vista was large enough to allow him to open a branch office in San Francisco.[21] Even better, the long court case against him growing out of his work at the Mint was decided in his favor in March, and the property that he had had to place in trust was then returned to him:[22] one must remember that all of Haraszthy's enthusiastic labor at Buena Vista up to this point had been carried out under the cloud of his protracted trial. In April, very shortly after his release from the Mint charges, Haraszthy was appointed by Governor John Downey one of the state commissioners to report "upon the Ways and Means best adapted to promote the Improvement and Growth of the Grapevine in California." The commission, created by joint resolution of the assembly upon the urging of the California State Agricultural Society, had three members: one was to report on California; one was assigned to South America; and one—Haraszthy—to Europe.[23] A month later he was on his way, at the beginning of a trip whose consequences, though not easy to specify or to assess, have long been regarded as having profoundly affected wine-making in this country, so profoundly indeed that in the popular version the whole history of winemaking is divided into two parts, before and after Haraszthy's European tour. Let us see what that was.

Armed with his commission from governor and assembly, and accompanied by his wife and by their daughter Ida, Haraszthy set out at his own expense, for the commissioners were not to be paid for their work. On reaching the East Coast, he first stopped at Washington to get a circular letter of introduction to the American consular corps from Secretary William Henry Seward. He then went to New York, arranged there with the publishers Harper & Brothers to produce a book on his mission, and, on 13 July, sailed for Europe. The purpose of his trip, according to the terms of his commission, was simply to make observations upon European practices in viticulture and winemaking and to report on these to the state. But in his own mind Haraszthy seems to have had the collection of grape varieties as his first and most important business. At any rate, he talked in that way before his departure, and he spent a good deal of energy that way during his tour.

It was not a very extensive tour, compared to the possibilities that might easily be imagined. Making his first headquarters at Paris, he visited Dijon and several great Burgundian sites—Gevrey, Chambertin, Clos Vougeot. Then he moved on into Germany to visit such wine towns and noble estates as Hochheim, Steinberg, Kloster Eberbach, and Schloss Johannisberg. In Germany he made his first purchase of vines, a hundred varieties from a nursery in Wiesloch. Haraszthy now went into Italy, to Turin and to Asti, where he bought a second collection of vines, including the Nebbiolo, the preeminent grape of the region. He had originally thought of taking in Rome and Naples, but he now abandoned the idea, since, as he explained, he had friends through whom he could order cuttings there. At the same time he abandoned any thought of travelling farther east—not even to his native Hungary. "It is true that my original intention was to visit Greece and Egypt," he wrote in the published account of his travels; but, he added as a sufficient reason, he learned that the plague had broken out in Syria, so that "I, of course, decided not to go."[24]

Instead, he turned back to the west, travelling to Bordeaux via Marseilles and Cette—a town then infamous for its trade in adulterating wines and the source, Haraszthy asserts, of most of the wines that Americans drank as Château Margaux, Château Lafite, and Chambertin. For some reason, the Bordeaux region did not especially interest Haraszthy. He paid brief visits to Château Margaux and to Château Rauzan (then still undivided) but did not, according to his report, pursue his inquiries any further. On the nineteenth of September he set out for Spain, where the conditions of travel were much the most difficult of his entire tour. Railroads were being built, but the system was not linked up yet, and travellers had to fill in the gaps by taking passage in huge *diligences* pulled over the breakneck mountain roads by teams of mules. After four days of such travel Haraszthy reached

Madrid, and then pushed on to Malaga. The wines of Spain he did not care for, since he found that they were all invariably fortified. He bought vines at Malaga, however, and again at Alicante, where he had gone from Malaga by steamer. That marked the end of Haraszthy's inspection of European viticulture, for from Alicante he returned to Paris, and shortly thereafter set out on a stormy crossing of the Atlantic to New York. By the fifth of December he was back in California, having completed his travels from San Francisco to the Mediterranean and back in just six months.

Haraszthy's first business was to make his report to the state legislature, which he did, briefly, under date of January 1862. In this he reaffirmed his belief that California had more natural advantages as a wine region than any European district; he also urged the creation of a state agricultural experiment station, state support of plant exploration, and the appointment of a state agency to handle the commerce of wine in California in order to eliminate frauds.[25] The book that Haraszthy had contracted for on his way to Europe followed soon after as *Grape Culture, Wines and Wine-Making, with Notes upon Agriculture and Horticulture,* published by Harpers in New York. This was a very hasty production, and, for that reason, very disappointing: though it touches on a number of matters incidentally, it quite fails to give a clear picture of Haraszthy at work on his mission. He does not tell us what questions he had to ask, or how he went about getting them answered, nor has he much to say about the wines he encountered, or the problems faced by European wine-growers—just the things, one would suppose, that would occupy him most. He gives instead a sort of journal narrative of his travels, noting down as many miscellaneous items about architecture, topography, general agriculture, and the like as about the vines and wines of those European parts that he succeeded in visiting. Many another traveller might have done as much—and have done it better.

The narrative occupies a good deal less than half of the volume; the rest is bulked out by a melange of pamphlets and treatises picked up in Europe—for example, Professor Johann Karl Leuchs's *Wines and Their Varieties;* Dr. Ludwig Gall's *Improvements in Wine-Making;* and even *The Sorgho and the Impee,* an American pamphlet on those newly introduced crops. Haraszthy also included his treatise on wines and vines in California written in 1858 for the state agricultural society, now slightly modified in the light of his subsequent observations on pruning practices and the spacing of plantings. He adds the interesting information that his Buena Vista vineyard now extended over 400 acres and was, he thought, "the largest in the United States."[26] And that is all that there is to the book. It may rightfully claim to be the first book by a California winemaker to be given national circulation, but it has only very incidental remarks to make about California, and then mostly about Haraszthy's affairs, and pitifully little about European practices. The writers—and they are many—who refer to it as a monument in the literature of American winemaking have not, perhaps, looked at it very critically, or have not been able to put it in an adequate historical context.

Haraszthy's Buena Vista vineyards, already the largest in the country, were

GRAPE CULTURE,

WINES, AND WINE-MAKING.

AGRICULTURE AND HORTICULTURE.

BY

A. HARASZTHY,

COMMISSIONER TO REPORT ON THE IMPROVEMENT AND CULTURE OF THE VINE IN
CALIFORNIA.

With Numerous Illustrations.

NEW YORK:

HARPER & BROTHERS, PUBLISHERS,

FRANKLIN SQUARE.

1862.

76 | Title page of Agoston Harasz-thy's record of his European tour in the interest of the California winegrowers. Though largely about European vineyards, its last chapter is devoted to California. The first discussion in book form of California as a winegrowing region, it inaugurated a still-vigorous tradition of unrestrained boasting: "No European locality can equal within two hundred per cent. [California's] productiveness." (Huntington Library) soon to be even larger, for the vines that he had amassed in Europe were on their way to California—100,000 of them. Haraszthy first reported that his collection included 1,400 varieties[27]—an unreal number—but even after inspection and comparison had reduced this figure, he still had some 300 varieties in his newly imported collection. On the arrival of the vines in late January 1862, Haraszthy reported to the governor that he had prepared the vines for propagation, and that there would be "300,000 rooted vines ready for distribution next fall."[28]

Though Haraszthy wrote as though he expected the state to take responsibility for the distribution of his vines and pay his expenses, he had not been authorized to buy vines or to incur any expenses of any description whatever to be charged to the state. The terms of his commission instructed him only to observe European practices, not to buy large quantities of nursery stock for a state already abounding in vines of every description. Haraszthy knew, of course, that this was the case, just as he knew that the commissioners were not to be paid: the resolution of the assembly authorizing the commission contained this explicit proviso: "Such commissioners who may accept the office shall not ask, or receive, any pay or other compensation for the performance of the duties of their offices." Nevertheless, Haraszthy did ask for compensation—he estimated his expenses at $12,000—and a bill to indemnify him was introduced in the state senate. The senate committee appointed to report on it recommended against it in April 1862, and the bill was stifled.[29]

This has for many years been described as an act of gross injustice and ingratitude to Haraszthy, who has been made to appear a martyr to political faction or to some even worse villainy. The tradition that Haraszthy was cheated is by now so well established in California that it has almost mythological status. Yet the facts, so far as they can be known now, tell a very different story. Haraszthy knew from the outset that he was not going to be paid, just as he knew that he had no official charge to buy vines for importation. Why then did he buy them? Evidently for the simple purpose of making money. Before he left for Europe he was advertising a scheme for buying vines and other plants in Europe for subscribers: $25 would buy twenty-five varieties of vine, $50, fifty varieties, and so on up to $500, in return for which the subscriber would receive "two cuttings of every variety of grape now in cultivation in the civilized world."[30] The coolness of that last offer tells us a great deal about the man. When Haraszthy returned from his European visit and announced that he was having a large quantity of vines sent after him, the *Los Angeles Star* wrote simply that Haraszthy "will make a handsome profit from their sale."[31] Probably he did. There is nothing wrong with that. But it was an astonishing piece of effrontery to pretend that he was owed compensation for his expenses, and to pretend to be aggrieved when it was denied.

What vines does California owe to Haraszthy's importations? Since it has long been taken as uncontested truth that Haraszthy greatly improved the standards of California through the introduction of superior varieties, it would be interesting to know what some, at least, of those varieties were. There is no clear, positive evidence on the matter. Even at the time, there was much confusion as to what varieties Haraszthy had obtained: many of them had been collected not directly by Haraszthy but by the agency of friends and by members of the consular service; the chances of mislabelling in the process of shipping, transshipping, and planting were considerable; and there was no guarantee of authenticity at the source. Haraszthy himself, as we have seen, thought at first that he had some 1,400 varieties, suggesting that many vines of the same variety had been given different names.

After the vines had arrived and been put into his keeping in Sonoma, and after his bold attack on the public purse to pay for them had failed, Haraszthy prepared a catalogue of the varieties that he had for sale. This included both his recent importations and those that he had earlier imported into California, or had, perhaps, obtained from other California nurserymen. It makes a sufficiently exotic and interesting list, a total of 492 varieties.[32] Hungarian kinds figure notably: Bakator (both white and red), Boros, Csaszar szolo, Dinka, Furmint, Jajos, and Kadarka are among the many names. None of these is now commercially grown in California, if any of them ever was. Other striking exotics are a red Corinthe from the Crimea, the Kishmish from Smyrna, the Marocain Noir from Morocco, the Tautovina of Carinthia, and Torok Malozsla from Turkey. There are many, many more unfamiliar varietal names on the list, most of them probably familiar varieties masquerading under unfamiliar local names, but some of them at any rate varieties that did not "take" in California—the German Affenthaler, for example, and the French Calytor.

Of the varieties now either most prominent or most highly regarded in California, many are represented on the list: Cabernet Sauvignon, Carignane, Pinot Noir, Sauvignon Blanc, Semillon, Riesling, Sylvaner, Gewürztraminer, and perhaps the Chenin Blanc, if that is what is meant by the item identified as "Pineau blanc." Among the varieties one misses are the Chardonnay, the Grenache, and the Syrah. It is, perhaps, safe to say that many of the varieties named in Haraszthy's catalogue were first imported into California by Haraszthy, but that among them were very few, if any, of the varieties that have any importance now. Since the importation of superior varieties of vinifera into California goes back to the early 1830s, Haraszthy had long been anticipated with respect to the most highly regarded varieties.

By far the most sensational omission in Haraszthy's catalogue of his imported vines is the variety called Zinfandel. Haraszthy's association with this grape, almost the trademark variety of California winemaking, is just as hallowed a part of his legend as his claim to be the "father" of California winemaking. The received account of the connection goes like this. After Haraszthy had left San Diego and had bought his Las Flores property south of San Francisco, he received a shipment of vines from Europe, including the Zinfandel, a variety from his native Hungary. He planted his Zinfandel, the first ever known in California, in the spring of 1852. When he moved from Las Flores to Crystal Springs, and then from Crystal Springs to Sonoma, the Zinfandel went with him, and there, in Sonoma in 1862, ten years after its importation into the state, Haraszthy produced California's first zinfandel wine.[33]

Such is the story, but against it there is overwhelming evidence, both positive and negative. On the negative side, why is there no mention of the variety in Haraszthy's catalogue of 1862? Two years later, in an article that Haraszthy wrote for a national audience in *Harper's,* an article of unashamed advertising for his Buena Vista property and its wines, there is still no mention of Zinfandel, though every other possible boast and claim that he can make is duly made.[34] On the positive side there is indisputable evidence that the Zinfandel was known in California before Haraszthy came to the state. Even more to the point, the Zinfandel was a familiar variety on the East Coast when California was still a Mexican province. The Zinfandel (called "Zinfindal") was exhibited at the Massachusetts Horticultural Society in 1834 and regularly thereafter; it became a favorite among the fashionable amateur gardeners who could afford to grow grapes under glass in eastern American cities. It is described by Andrew Downing in his *Fruits and Fruit Trees of America* in 1845, and is frequently mentioned in the agricultural press of the 1840s and 1850s. It may even have been known to William Prince earlier than this, for in his catalogue of varieties published in 1830 Prince includes a variety he calls the "Black Zinfardel of Hungary" among those propagated and for sale at his Linnaean Garden. Whether Prince's Zinfardel is merely a typographical error for Zinfandel or a wholly different variety no one can say now, but the contemporary descriptions of the East Coast's "Zinfindal" show that it is the grape called Zinfandel in California.[35]

The earliest published record of the variety in California is in 1858, when the Sacramento nurseryman A. P. Smith exhibited "Zeinfindall" at the state fair.[36] There is no proof for the supposition, but it seems simplest and likeliest to think that Smith got his "Zeinfindall" from eastern American sources of supply, perhaps as early as 1855. Many years later the San Jose grape grower and nurseryman Antoine Delmas claimed that he had imported the Zinfandel from France to California in 1852, but under the name of Black St. Peters.[37] If so, he would have to be awarded the claim of introducing the variety to the state; we do not have evidence to settle the question. But we do know that the grape was beginning to attract favorable notice before the end of the 1850s: examples were exhibited again at the state fair in 1859, and more than one grower was making wine from it by 1860. During the sixties it attracted more and more attention as the most promising among the many varieties that were competing to replace the Mission, and by the end of the 1870s it was established as the first choice for California's vineyards.

The presence of Zinfandel in eastern America in the 1830s and its importation into California before the end of the 1850s are beyond doubt; the European origin of the variety, however, has not yet been determined, though there is, of course, no doubt that it is wholly vinifera; the most promising claim that has yet been put forward is that it is identical with a grape known in Italy as the Primitivo di Gioia.[38] The mystery we have to do with here, though, is not that of the Zinfandel's European identity, but that of its association with Haraszthy: how did it happen that Agoston Haraszthy was identified as the man who introduced the Zinfandel to California?

The first statement to this effect that I know of was made in 1879 by the San Gabriel winegrower L. J. Rose, who wrote in the *Transactions* of the California State Agricultural Society of that year that the Zinfandel was "introduced by the late Colonel Haraszthy from Hungary."[39] Rose gives no authority for the statement, but the probability is that he heard it from Haraszthy's son Arpad, who was certainly the most zealous proponent of the claim. Arpad's friend and colleague on the Board of State Viticultural Commissioners, Charles Wetmore, was probably echoing the same source when he wrote in 1880 of "the princely gift to this State made by Col. Agoston Haraszthy in 1860 [i.e., 1862], who brought us hundreds of varieties of valuable grapes from Europe, including our now famous Zinfandel."[40] Later, Wetmore recognized that he had been misinformed; in 1884 he wrote that the Zinfandel "was in this State long before Colonel Haraszthy visited Europe as a State Viticultural Commissioner."[41] There were others who publicly denied the invented Haraszthy claim, but they did not succeed in persuading the public. For one reason or another, the notion that Haraszthy brought the Zinfandel to California has persisted, and now it seems to be so firmly fixed that no amount of historical bulldozing can dislodge it. Still, it is not true.

Even opportunists like Haraszthy, who care nothing for the obstacles and difficulties that other men see all too clearly, may at last find themselves overextended. By 1863 that was the case with him. He was immediately out of pocket for his European tour and the large purchases of vines he had made. The development of Buena Vista into the largest of American vineyards was expensive; the cost of establishing a vineyard then was estimated at $50 an acre, not counting the cost of the land, and though this seems a laughable sum to us, it was substantial enough then. Labor costs were notably high in California, so that Haraszthy was an eager advocate of cheap Chinese labor; he was hurt in the pocketbook when, in 1862, the legislature imposed a tax of $2.50 a month per head on Chinese labor.[42] There may have been other reasons, too, for his financial difficulties; in any event, Haraszthy was willing to listen when he was approached by San Francisco bankers interested in the future of wine who had a scheme to propose to him.

Haraszthy, an irrepressible "developer," had at one time thought of promoting small, independent wine farms by selling parcels of his Sonoma lands and supervising their development as vineyards.[43] Now, however, in 1863, he sold his lands, vineyards, and winery to an organization called the Buena Vista Vinicultural Society. The society, incorporated in April, announced in its prospectus that it had a variety of purposes: to develop land, to quarry stone, and in any other way to exploit its property; but its main aim was to become the biggest winemaker in California, and soon.[44] Haraszthy himself, who held 2,600 of the society's 6,000 shares, was a trustee and the superintendent of the firm; he was joined by such winegrowing Sonoma neighbors as Isidor Landsberger, Emil Dresel, and Major

Jacob Snyder. The crucial backing, though, was provided by the reckless banker and speculator William J. Ralston, lord of the Comstock Lode and builder of San Francisco's Palace Hotel. The prospects of the society looked unbeatable: good vineyard land in a proven area, planted to superior varieties (in part at least—there is evidence that Haraszthy was not so quick to give up the Mission as has been supposed);[45] a winemaking establishment superior to everything else in the state, complete with steam-powered grape crusher and press; and the experience, confidence, and energy of Haraszthy himself presiding over all. The society's declaration that it would, within ten years from 1863, produce more than two million gallons of wine and one million of brandy did not, at the time, seem extravagant.[46]

Scores of Chinese were fed and housed on the Buena Vista property and set to work in the fields and the winery, adding to the vineyard acreage and expanding the winery and its cellars. Wine began to be produced in large quantities, and the profits at the end of the first year surpassed even the optimistic expectations of the promoters. After that first year, however, things did not go well at all. Arpad Haraszthy, back from his studies in the cellars of Epernay, was entrusted with the production of champagne, with dubious results and substantial losses to the company.[47] Business did not grow at the rate so confidently predicted, and there were other sorts of difficulties too—new taxes, for one. The wines were not all they should be either. The Massachusetts editor Samuel Bowles visited Buena Vista in 1865 and was not impressed. It did not, he said, seem a "well managed" enterprise; "nor," he added, "do we find the wines very inviting. . . . I have drank, indeed, much better California wine in Springfield than out here."[48] In short, the Buena Vista venture was not paying dividends, and Haraszthy, the central figure, quickly came under fire. Stockholders accused him of extravagance and irresponsibility, and it is to be feared that he did not always keep to the windward side of the law: there was a scandal in 1864 about an attempt to defraud the revenue by a scheme for distilling "brandy" from molasses brought in from the Sandwich Islands.[49] At last, Haraszthy had to give way. In 1866 he resigned his position and left forever the property that he had developed so spectacularly in a brief decade.

Haraszthy took refuge at the vineyard and winery near Sonoma owned by his son Attila, but accident and bad luck dogged him there too. The upshot was that in 1868 he left California. The scene of the fourth and final phase of his life—after Hungary, Wisconsin, and California—was Nicaragua, where, somehow, he had managed to obtain a sugar plantation near Corinto, on the Pacific coast, and a permit from the government to produce rum for export.[50] A year later he met his death in circumstances that are not likely ever to be made clear. The sole authority is a letter from his younger daughter Otelia reporting that he disappeared on 6 July, and that his path had been traced to where a large tree grew with branches stretching across a stream:

About the middle of the stream, a large limb seemed to be broken [Otelia wrote], and at the same place, a few days before, an alligator had dragged a cow into the stream from the bank. We must conclude that father tried to cross the river by the tree, and that losing his balance, he fell, grasping the broken limb, and then the alligator must have drawn him forever down.[51]

Perhaps this was a fitting end for a man who allegedly killed wolves with his bare hands; certainly it maintains the note of the unusual that Haraszthy so strikingly set.

Now that the outline of Haraszthy's activity in California has been sketched, what can we say of his role in the development of the state's winegrowing? He may claim to be the author of California's first treatise on grapes and wine. He was not the first to advertise California wine to the wider markets of the East Coast, but perhaps he did it better than anyone else had so far through his *Grape Culture, Wines, and Wine-Making* of 1862, and in the articles that he sent to the press throughout the 1860s. His work in bringing the Buena Vista winery to a high level of production was a notable exhibition of entrepreneurial skill. But the three main claims in the Haraszthy legend are all false: he was not the "father" of California winegrowing; he was not the man who first brought superior varieties of grapes to California; and he was not the man who introduced the Zinfandel. Incidentally, he was not a martyr to public ingratitude whose financial sacrifices for the good of the state went uncompensated. He certainly was an energetic and flamboyant promoter, combining the idealist and the self-regarding opportunist in proportions that we can now only guess at. He will remain an interesting and highly dubious figure, of the kind that always attracts historians; but we should no longer take seriously the legend that has grown up about him.

11

The Fate of
Southern California

The Rise and Fall of Anaheim

A bout the time that Haraszthy migrated to Sonoma another enterprise began in the south of the state that, in its unlikely origins, its rapid prosperity, and its even more rapid demise, presents a number of points of interest. This was the invention and development of the Anaheim colony, now celebrated as the site of Disneyland but originally a well-planned, well-executed agricultural experiment devoted to the production of grapes and wine.[1]

Its remotest origins were in the operations of the firm of Kohler & Frohling. As soon as the two German musicians began to sell their wine successfully, they saw that they needed a larger supply of grapes than Los Angeles yet afforded; they also saw that the empty spaces of Los Angeles County might be quickly and cheaply developed into vineyards. The catch was to find people willing to do the work; the answer was the German population of San Francisco, a population that Kohler and Frohling, of course, already knew and understood. There was a considerable colony there by 1857, all of them drawn by the Gold Rush. Many of them were now both disenchanted with golden prospects and dissatisfied with crude and violent San Francisco as a place in which to raise families and pursue the life of *Gemütlichkeit*.

The work of forming an agricultural colony out of these San Francisco Germans was assigned to another German, George Hansen (an Austrian, actually), who had served as deputy surveyor to the county of Los Angeles for six years, knew the region well, and had been in consultation with Kohler and Frohling

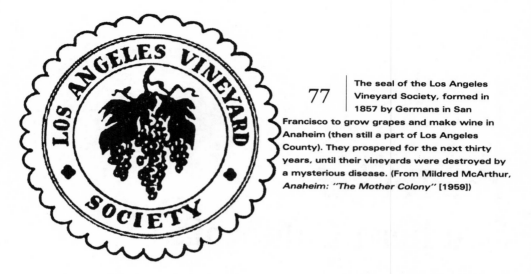

77   The seal of the Los Angeles Vineyard Society, formed in 1857 by Germans in San Francisco to grow grapes and make wine in Anaheim (then still a part of Los Angeles County). They prospered for the next thirty years, until their vineyards were destroyed by a mysterious disease. (From Mildred McArthur, *Anaheim: "The Mother Colony"* [1959])

about the practicability of their plan from the beginning. In February 1857 Hansen held a meeting with the San Francisco Germans at which the plan was unfolded and the Los Angeles Vineyard Society was formed.[2] The scheme was simple. The society would issue fifty shares at $1,400 each (originally the figure was lower, but this was the sum eventually arrived at); with the capital thus raised, the society would buy land, divide it into twenty-acre parcels, of which eight were to be in vineyard, and assign one to each shareholder. But—and this was the distinctive idea of the whole scheme—before anyone moved onto his property, everything was to be put in readiness. By this arrangement, the participants would avoid the rigors of the first pioneering years and—more important—they could remain at their jobs in San Francisco while they earned the money to pay for their shares. This was capitalism on the installment plan. A down payment would secure a share; with the capital thus generated the work could begin; and the shareholder could stay gainfully employed right where he was until he had paid up his share and the new land was ready for him.[3]

The scheme worked quite well. Hansen was made the general manager for the Vineyard Society and set to work scouting for a property to buy in the southland. His first intention, to buy land along the Los Angeles River, did not work out. Under pressure of the impatience of the society's members, he fell back on the knowledge he had acquired as a county surveyor: in 1855 he had surveyed the Rancho San Juan Cajon de Santa Ana, owned by Juan Ontiveros, lying along the Santa Ana River some twenty miles south of Los Angeles. The grapes of the Santa Ana region had a reputation as the "sweetest and best grapes in the state";[4] whether they deserved that or not (and there cannot have been many vines in the Santa Ana Valley then), the important fact was that Ontiveros was willing to sell to the society. In September 1857 Hansen completed the purchase from Ontiveros of a 1,165 acre tract, with water rights providing for an irrigation canal from the river, some six

78 | George Hansen, the Austrian surveyor who purchased the Anaheim property, built the irrigation works, laid out the site, and planted the vines in readiness for the arrival of the colonists. (Anaheim Public Library)

miles away. Hansen's first order of business then was to lay out the irrigation system—the gravity flow from northeast to southwest determined the disposition of the Anaheim streets as they exist today—and to arrange the site for occupation.[5] Within two years, working with a motley crew of Indians and Mexican irregular labor, he had done it: the irrigation channels had been dug, the vines—400,000 Mission cuttings[6] mostly from the vineyards of William Wolfskill in Los Angeles—had been planted, and the whole property surrounded by a fence of 40,000 six-foot willow, alder, and sycamore poles, later to grow into a living hedge as a protection against wild animals and range animals alike. The whole expense of two years' labor of preparation was $60,000.[7] Inevitably, Hansen had to encounter grumblings from his impatient stockholders, but he seems to have done a remarkably capable job of laying the foundations of a successful agricultural community from scratch on land that was nothing but rough, dry, lonely range in every direction. The little house that Hansen built in 1857 as a place to live and from which to direct the operations of his Indians still stands in Anaheim, now a museum called the Mother Colony House.

In September 1859 the first shareholders arrived to claim their twenty-acre homesteads in the colony that now had a name: Annaheim. The name—soon altered from the German *Anna* to the Spanish *Ana*—signifies "home on the Santa Ana River"; it had narrowly beaten out the rival name of "Annagau" by vote of the shareholders in 1858.[8] It is a curious circumstance in the history of a successful winemaking colony that most of the Anaheim colonists—there was but one exception—had not only no experience of winemaking but no farming experience at all. They were small tradesmen, craftsmen, and mechanics. They had only their Germanness in common, and so they present a very different case from the earlier German agricultural colonies—Germantown, Pennsylvania; New Harmony, Indiana; and Hermann, Missouri, are instances—so important in the history of wine in this country. The Anaheimers were of diverse origin: they came from Saxony, Hanover, Schleswig-Holstein, Baden, and elsewhere; they were not co-religionists; and, after the colony's land had been bought, laid out, irrigated, planted, and distributed, they ceased to have any further cooperative arrangement.[9] Each shareholder was an individual proprietor, competing with his neighbors just as much as if he still lived in San Francisco, Los Angeles, or Frankfurt. But there was, nevertheless, an intense spirit of community in Anaheim, given the common nationality, the common enterprise of winegrowing, and the common isolation of life on a raw, remote site.

The reality of life in early Anaheim must have been hard, without much margin or amenity. The site was unattractive, a sandy alluvial fan watered by a thin stream flowing through a shallow ditch; it lay, too, in the path of the dessicating Santa Ana wind of winter, booming down off the high desert through the mountain passes to the ocean and leaving a wake of blown sand and jangled nerves behind it. And it would be years before the work of man could do much to ameliorate the scene. A writer in 1863, one of the shareholders, noted that nearly 600 acres—half of the entire tract—still lay vacant, and yet "the welfare of the vineyards requires that this land should be cultivated, for it is now covered with weeds and brush and is the home of innumerable hares, squirrels, and gophers, which eat the vines, young trees, and grapes."[10]

Even from the very earliest years, however, the accounts of the place tend almost invariably to stress the tranquil, harmonious, pastoral simplicity and fruitfulness of the colonists' life. No doubt the idea of a frontier settlement that combined a real community of language and habits of feeling with the poetic labor of winegrowing made this inevitable. And certainly Anaheim was different from the western model of town life. In any case, to conclude from the language of the many

79   James Bullard, M.D., bottling
wine behind his office on Los Angeles Street, Anaheim, c. 1885.
Wine was a familiar object throughout Anaheim. (Anaheim Public Library)

newspaper articles generated by curiosity about the Anaheim experiment, all was
peaceful and prosperous in the colony: "Their soil is good, their climate, also, their
wine is fine, and their tables well supplied" as an envious reporter for the *Alta
California* put it in 1865.[11] Whatever the fantasies about Anaheim, though, the plain
fact is that the wine business did succeed, for reasons having perhaps less to do
with the quality of the wine or the efficiency of the organization than with the demand for wine on the coast. The wine was made by the various proprietors separately, with the result that Anaheim wine was not a uniform but a highly unpredictable product, at least at first.[12] Later, consolidation and cooperation did come about,
but a high level of individualism seems to have persisted to the end.

The wine was not long in acquiring a reputation. The eastern traveller Charles
Brace, who did not flatter California wine in general, found Anaheim wine "unusually pleasant and light. . . . It cannot be stronger than ordinary Rhine wine."
He also observed that it was the only wine that could be found throughout the
state in 1867: "I found it even in the Sierras, where it was sold at $1.00 a bottle."[13]
Much of the crop, too, went to Kohler & Frohling in the early years, as had been
the original intention, and their standards certainly helped to establish the reputation of the wine of Anaheim.

There were forty-seven wineries—that is, individual winemaking proprie-

80 | The Dreyfus Winery, Center and East streets, Anaheim, c. 1880. This establishment was later replaced by a larger winery that never func- | tioned, owing to the death of the vineyards from the Anaheim disease. (Anaheim Public Library)

tors—in the first decade; two decades later there were fifty, though some of them were by no means small. From a token 2,000 gallons in 1860, the year of the first vintage, production had reached 300,000 gallons in 1864.[14] Twenty years later, at the moment when the Anaheim wine industry was just about to come to its sudden and unforeseen end, production had reached its highest point. Some 1,250,000 gallons of wine were produced by the town in that year, along with 100,000 gallons of Anaheim brandy.[15] In the roster of winery names, German still predominated—Kroeger, Koenig, Langenberger, Zeyn, Lorenz, Reiser, Dreyfus, Korn, Werder—though there were also by that time a Browning Brothers and a Golden Belt Wine Company. Anaheim had also attracted two most unlikely characters, the famous Helena Modjeska, the Polish actress, and a young Polish gentleman later to be quite as famous as the Modjeska, Henryk Sienkiewicz, the author of *Quo Vadis*. They had come to join a Utopian colony in Anaheim that had only a very brief life, and neither stayed long. Modjeska later bought a summer home in the Santa Ana mountains not far from Anaheim, and Sienkiewicz makes a few references to Anaheim in some of his American sketches, but neither was much taken by the place.[16]

The king of Anaheim winemakers was unquestionably Benjamin Dreyfus, a Bavarian Jew.[17] He was not a member of the San Francisco group that formed the

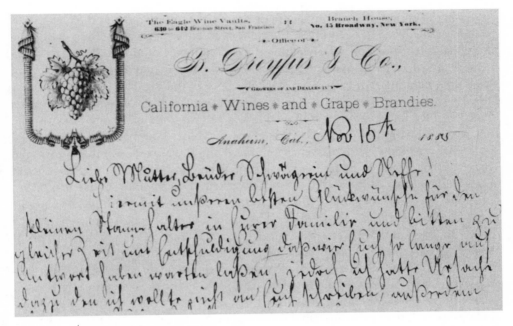

81 The letterhead of B. Dreyfus & Co., in the year that the vines were being devastated. Note that the letter is in German. (Anaheim Public Library)

Los Angeles Vineyard Society, but he was a resident of the Anaheim site even before the first shareholders arrived. Dreyfus had opened a store there in 1858 in anticipation of the new community, had welcomed the first settlers to the place, and soon showed that he had gifts as a salesman that were just what was needed by the growers. In 1863 Dreyfus went to San Francisco to manage the depot of the Anaheim Wine Growers' Association (there, incidentally, he made Kosher wine in 1864—perhaps a first for California).[18] Shortly thereafter he opened the firm of B. Dreyfus and Company in New York and San Francisco, through which he sold Anaheim wines. Among his clients was his own winery in Anaheim, supposed at that time to be the largest in the state and using the produce of some 235 acres by 1876.[19] Dreyfus eventually owned properties in Cucamonga, San Gabriel, and the Napa Valley as well as in Anaheim. By the end of the sixties, through Dreyfus and other agents, the city of New York had a wide variety of Anaheim wines available to it: Anaheim hock, claret, port, angelica, sherry, muscatel, sparkling angelica, and brandy are all listed in a promotional pamphlet of the time.[20] The array is striking evidence that the California practice of producing a whole "line" of wine types from one site and from a limited number of grape varieties is no new thing.[21] Dreyfus is said to have made genuine riesling and zinfandel, but the Mission was always the staple grape of Anaheim so long as grapes grew there.[22]

As in the design of a well-made tragic drama, the high point and the collapse of Anaheim winegrowing occurred at the same moment. That was in 1883, when the fifty wineries of Anaheim were yielding their more than a million gallons and when the acreage of vines in the Santa Ana Valley was estimated at 10,000, including substantial plantings for raisins and for table use. In the growing season that year the vineyard workers noticed a new disease among the Mission vines. The leaves looked scalded, in a pattern that moved in waves from the outer edge inwards; the fruit withered without ripening, or, sometimes, it colored prematurely, then turned soft before withering. When a year had passed and the next season had begun, the vines were observed to be late in starting their new growth; when the shoots did appear, they grew slowly and irregularly; then the scalding of the leaves re-appeared, the shoots began to die back, and the fruit withered. Without the support of healthy leaves, the root system, too, declined, and in no long time the vine was dead.[23] No one knew what the disease might be, and so no one knew what to do. It seemed to have no relation to soils, or to methods of cultivation, and it was not evidently the work of insects. Not all varieties were equally afflicted, but the disease particularly devastated the Mission, far and away the most extensively planted variety in the vineyards of Anaheim. By 1885, according to one doubtless exaggerated report, half the vines of Anaheim were gone; in the next year, "there was not a vine to be seen."[24] In fact, some vineyards persisted long after this, but the assertion, made by a longtime resident, expresses the sense of sudden, unsparing destruction that the disease created in the Anaheimers as they looked over their blighted vineyards. The official government report estimated the loss to the disease at Anaheim and elsewhere in the Los Angeles region at $10,000,000.[25]

The disease was not confined to Anaheim; much of the San Gabriel Valley and the Los Angeles basin east through Pomona to Riverside and San Bernardino was seriously affected too; the flourishing trade of the San Gabriel region never fully recovered. Anaheim, and the neighboring vineyards of the Santa Ana Valley at Orange and Santa Ana, planted after the success of the Anaheim experiment, were the hardest hit in the midst of the general affliction. The Anaheimers appealed to the state university for expert opinion, and the Board of State Viticultural Commissioners hired a botanist to study the problem. But the disease baffled all inquiry, and meantime its effects were rapid and sure.

In response to repeated appeals, the U.S. Department of Agriculture belatedly sent an investigator to the Santa Ana Valley in 1887; he was puzzled by all that he saw, but reported hopefully that the trouble would "probably disappear as quietly and mysteriously as it came."[26] In 1891 the department sent another investigator, Newton Pierce, whose careful investigation showed that the disease was none of those currently known and that no remedies existed for it. Pierce's reward for his careful and thorough studies was to have the disease named after him. By the time his report was completed, in 1891, the region of Anaheim was reduced to fourteen acres of vines and its identity as a center of winegrowing utterly annihilated.[27] The fate of the bold new winery building that Benjamin Dreyfus, the Anaheim wine

82   A vineyard of Mission grapes in Los Angeles County killed by the Anaheim disease. The vines, planted more than twenty-five years earlier, were dead by 1890, when the picture was made. Mission vines were peculiarly susceptible to the disease, but all were vulnerable. (From Newton B. Pierce, *The California Vine Disease* [1892])

king, had erected in 1884 is symbolic. This was an imposing stone building, far larger than anything else of the kind in the area, but when it was completed and ready to receive a vintage, there was no vintage to receive. The building thereafter passed through various humiliating roles as a warehouse, as a factory for chicken-feeding equipment, even as a winter quarters for a circus. When the freeway went through in the 1960s, part of the building was lopped off by the right of way; it was at last put out of its long agony by demolition in 1973.[28]

Anaheim recovered from the disease by turning to the new crops that were just at that time rapidly developing in southern California, especially oranges and walnuts. The Germans of Anaheim had long since set up breweries, and these, of course, were unaffected by the grape disease. So the settlement, which became otherwise indistinguishable from its neighboring communities in making its living from tree crops, still managed to enjoy some notoriety for its beer, its beer gardens, and its beer drinkers. These gave a welcome scandal to their Orange County neighbors, who would otherwise have had little diversion in their rural lives.

What was the Anaheim disease? The plant pathologists have not yet arrived at satisfying answers, but they have continued to study the question because the disease still exists and still threatens California vineyards. In quite recent years, it has been established that the carrier of the disease is a leafhopper, and that the pathogen, as Pierce suspected, but could not prove, is a bacterium. It is also known that the incidence of the disease varies with the populations of its leafhopper carrier, so that wet years favor it, and sites having abundant weedy and bushy growth surrounding them are vulnerable—both circumstances mean more leafhoppers and so more danger of infection. So far, the only known effective treatment is to pull the infected vines and to start with others, hoping to keep them free of infection.[29] The University of California at Davis is carrying on work to develop a vine specifically resistant to Pierce's Disease by modern means of genetic manipulation, but success has yet to be achieved.[30]

One other thing is known: that the home of the disease in this country (to which it seems so far confined) is in the states bordering on the Gulf of Mexico. The native grapes of that region are the only ones to show any power of resistance to it, and the presence of the disease there doubtless helps to explain why the repeated trials of grape growing in that region met with such poor success. There are abundant other reasons for that result, of course, but the potent destructiveness of Pierce's Disease was certainly a factor in the deaths of any vines brought in from the outside.[31]

The San Gabriel Valley

Even before the Anaheim colony had been planted in the late 1850s, another section of the Los Angeles region was beginning to develop as a major winegrowing area: the San Gabriel Valley, immediately to the east of Los Angeles, stretching for forty or fifty miles. The San Gabriel Mission had originally presided over the territory, and it was the old mission vineyards that gave the idea to later proprietors that winegrowing belonged to their land. This third division of the southern California vineyard, though earlier in its beginnings than Anaheim, reached its heyday a bit later; dominated by ambitious, large-scale proprietors, its spacious ranchos, sprawled over the slopes of the San Gabriel mountains, made it the most splendid of winegrowing regions.

The lines of descent from the mission fathers may be traced through Hugo Reid, a Scotsman who drifted to California, married an Indian woman, and, through his wife, became possessed of the 8,500 acres of the Santa Anita Rancho, once the property of the San Gabriel Mission. Grapes still grew there, and Reid gave some attention to them; by 1841 he had a walled vineyard of 22,000 vines at Santa Anita and boasted, "I consider myself a first-rate wine maker."[32] Reid also owned a small property of some 128 acres, called La Huerta de Cuati, just to the west of his Santa Anita Rancho, and this formed the next step in the growth of San Gabriel Valley vineyards. While Reid lay on his deathbed in 1852, the Huerta de Cuati was bought by Benjamin D. Wilson, who renamed the property "Lake Vineyard," after the shallow lake that lay there, where the Franciscans had built a dam to run a mill and to supply water to the Mission San Gabriel.[33] Here Wilson began one of the most successful of southern California winegrowing enterprises.

Wilson was a model instance of the sort of versatility and mobility that went

83 Benjamin Wilson (1811–78), of the Lake Vineyard, Pasadena, with his second wife, probably around 1860. After a commercial and political career in Los Angeles beginning in 1841, Wilson settled in the San Gabriel Valley and helped to make it the leading wine region of the state in direct succession to the work of Mission San Gabriel. (Huntington Library)

with being a California pioneer.[34] A Tennessean by birth, he had been a New Mexico trader before pushing on to California in 1841. There he had married a Mexican wife and had begun to acquire land—at various times he held the Rancho Jurupa, now the city of Riverside; the Rancho San Pedro, now the site of Wilmington and San Pedro; the Rancho San Jose, where Westwood and UCLA now stand; and, finally, the properties now occupied by modern Pasadena, South Pasadena, San Marino, Alhambra, and San Gabriel! He prospered by running cattle, by keeping a store and lending money, and by acquiring ever more land. Wilson may be tracked all over the Los Angeles region: he was one of the party whose exploits in lassoing bears gave its name to Big Bear Lake; he had a rather unheroic part in the Mexican War, and was briefly a prisoner at Chino; he was, after the war, the first *Anglo* mayor of Los Angeles, where he had a vineyard on Alameda Street; he built a trail up the high peak behind his San Pascual ranch in order to bring out the timber there, and so that landmark is now called Mount Wilson. One may add that he was twice a member of the state senate, that he went to Washington to lobby for a railroad in southern California, and that he helped to promote the building of Los Angeles harbor. But for us his interest is as a winegrower.

Wilson, despite his long years in Los Angeles, remained a thorough southerner in style, always wearing the white linen collar, ruffled shirt front, and flowing black tie of the plantation gentleman.[35] Despite the expansiveness of his sartorial style and of his hospitality at Lake Vineyard, from his correspondence Wilson appears to have been an undemonstrative, reserved, perhaps slightly melancholy, man. But he nourished a strong passion for his Lake Vineyard. By the time that he bought it, he was wealthy enough to move back east and to live there in style, as some of his friends urged him to do. His new property decided him to stay: he built an adobe house there, and moved in permanently in 1856; the Lake Vineyard, he said, was "the prettiest and healthiest place in California."[36] He planted fruit of all kinds, especially large groves of oranges; he brought in water, planted ornamental trees, laid out avenues, and so adorned the property that it quickly became the unrivalled showplace of the region: no visit to Los Angeles was complete without a visit to Wilson and his Lake Vineyard.[37]

Vines were already on the property when Wilson took over: his granddaughter remembered the original Mission vines there as having trunks six feet high before they succumbed to the Anaheim disease in the eighties and nineties; they may have been planted as early as 1815, for the Lake Vineyard in 1876 was thought to contain vines as much as sixty years old.[38] Wilson went beyond the inheritance of Mission vines, however, and made continuing experiments with new and superior varieties in the hope of discovering what the region would yield best.[39] He also experimented with different wine types; he has the credit, for example, of having made the first sparkling wine in California, though this was a severely limited success.[40] In 1856, the year after the sparkling wine had been created, Dr. H. R. Myles, Wilson's partner in the Lake Vineyard wine business (he had a nearby vineyard of his own), wrote to Wilson that the "old man" who was their champagne master "has been pottering at the sparkling wine ever since you left. . . . The truth is he never will make anything of it. . . . I believe him to be a *humbug*."[41] The old man thereafter disappears from the record, and the making of sparkling wine was pretty soon recognized to be one of the things that southern California was not destined to do well.

Wilson also had some local hazards to deal with: the vintage of 1856, over 12,000 gallons, had not yet fallen clear by January 1857. The reason, Myles suggested, was at least in part that they had had "about fifty earth-quakes in the last two weeks, three of which rocked the house very much" and had stirred up all the sediment in the wine;[42] one recalls that the San Gabriel River, which drains the valley, had originally been named the Rio de Temblores by the Spaniards—the River of Earthquakes.

The unsatisfactory old man's replacement was a Swiss named Adolf Eberhart, who came in 1857;[43] after that, things went better. Wilson continued to acquire land and to plant grapes, so that in a few years he was in a position to seek markets wherever he could find them. His vineyards exceeded 100 acres in 1861, and he was then still adding to them. By 1862 Wilson had a San Francisco agent, who, in addition to supplying the trade in that city, was able to add the exotic touch of a shipment of twenty-five cases to Japan only eight years after that country had been "opened" to foreign trade.[44] More significant was the trade opened with the East Coast; the Sainsevains and Kohler & Frohling had made the first contact between California and the East about 1860. Wilson was not far behind. In 1863 his San Francisco agent shipped fifteen pipes of white wine, sixteen of port, and twenty-one of angelica to Boston; the speculation evidently paid, for Wilson continued to send wine to that city. But the trade was not without its difficulties. As Mr. Hobbs, the agent, complained to Wilson in July 1863, the Bostonians were so accustomed to adulterated wine they no longer believed in the possibility of anything else; in consequence they mostly drank whiskey.[45] Yet if Boston found it hard to accept unadulterated wine, other places found the problem reversed. In St. Louis, in 1866, the local horticultural society, after sampling five different Lake Vineyard wines, pronounced them all "doctored" and unfit to recommend.[46] It is hard to know what the truth was: were the wines pure and thus unaccustomed, as was said in Boston? or adulterated, and thus unpleasant, as was said in St. Louis?

Still, during these years of the Civil War the reputation of Wilson's wines gradually grew both in and out of California; in 1863 two gentlemen from Chicago proposed to set up in the wine business in that city with wine supplied by Wilson because, as they said, "your wines are far superior to those of old Nich. Longworth of Cincinnati";[47] and from his San Francisco agents Wilson heard that his only competition there was from the other Los Angeles producers, Kohler & Frohling and the Sainsevains, because, they reported, "the Anaheim and Sonoma wines are not as good as the wine from Los Angeles."[48] By 1865 the San Francisco trade was large enough to make the old commission agency arrangement no longer satisfactory, and Wilson accordingly set up his own firm in that city.

Like his near neighbors in Los Angeles and in Anaheim, Wilson produced a variety of wines from a variety of grapes: early records show, in addition to the standard Missions, such varieties as Carignane, Zinfandel, Grenache, Mataro, Trousseau, Burger, and Folle Blanche.[49] It was already recognized that the dry light table wines from the Zinfandel and the white wine varieties grown in Los Angeles County were not so good as those produced in more northern regions, and from an early time there was a considerable trade in buying such wines in bulk from northern sources for resale. Sweet, fortified wines—port, angelica, and sherry especially—quickly became and remained the characteristic product of the Lake Vineyard; brandy, too, became increasingly important. But table wines, more white than red, did continue to be produced, even if in less quantity than the dessert wines.

The vicissitudes of commerce began to wear on Wilson as his business grew larger: wines were spoiled in the shipping; agents often adulterated what was sent to them pure; the American public went on preferring whiskey; competitors under-sold one with inferior products; competent help was hard to find and harder to keep; and, in short, Wilson began to think that making and selling wine from the "prettiest place in California" was more trouble than it was worth. Just when he began to weary of the trade, Wilson acquired an energetic son-in-law, who quickly took over the business and was later to lead it through a major transformation. This was a young man named James De Barth Shorb, a native of Maryland, who had come to California in 1863 at the age of eighteen looking for oil in Ventura County. He had soon turned to other things, and had taken his first step towards the considerable prosperity he later enjoyed for a time by marrying Benjamin Wilson's daughter Sue in 1867. The history of the Lake Vineyard under Shorb, though it takes us into another era, is so clear an illustration of the opportunities and disasters of California winegrowing in the later nineteenth century that it will be instructive to tell it here.[50]

Shorb had many of the qualities of the southerner; he talked and wrote fluently and flamboyantly, was quick to take offense, exuded confidence, and loved to pro-mote large but untried enterprises. He was as well a splendid host, a prominent Catholic layman (he now lies buried in the small, select cemetery of the San Gabriel Mission), and the father of eleven children. The undefined and expansive character of California exactly suited him: as he was able to boast in 1888 to the reporter sent round by the historian H. H. Bancroft to record Shorb's impressions for posterity, he had come to California with $700 in his pocket and was now worth from one and a half to two million dollars.[51] Once established as heir pre-sumptive to the Wilson property (Wilson's only son John was a ne'er-do-well who committed suicide in Los Angeles in 1870), Shorb wasted no time in setting to work. With a San Francisco partner, he leased all of the Lake Vineyard and its cellars under the name of B. D. Wilson and Co., his father-in-law lending only his name to the firm. That was in 1867, when, for purposes of the lease, an inventory was made; in this we learn that in addition to a copper still, large iron screw press, grape crusher, and such impedimenta as funnels, wine baskets, measures, dippers, syphons, hoses, bungs, bottles, and boxes, Wilson had thirty tanks of 1,500 to 2,000 gallons' capacity each at the Lake Vineyard.[52] From this it appears that Wilson op-erated with a storage capacity of, say, about 50,000 gallons. Within fifteen years, Shorb was building a winery of 1,250,000 gallons' capacity.

At first, Shorb took over personal direction of the firm's San Francisco agency, where, he informed his father-in-law, in one year he would "sell more wine than the whole of them put together."[53] But the expansion of the enterprise soon brought Shorb back to the Lake Vineyard, where new vineyards were being planted and large additions made to the cellars. Another novelty for which Shorb was respon-sible was the introduction of Chinese laborers in 1869: they had not before been used in southern California. As Shorb wrote in 1870, the experiment was a great success: he thought the Chinese "a more intelligent class of labor" than "the old Mission Indians or Sonorans from Mexico," and found that they could be safely trusted to work alone after only a few days' instruction.[54]

84 | A label from the Wilson vineyard in the era of Wilson's son-in-law J. De Barth Shorb, some time | after 1867, when Wilson's Lake Vineyard wines were sold under the name of B. D. Wilson & Co. (Huntington Library)

The example of Wilson and of Shorb had its effect on their neighbors, more and more of whom planted vineyards and sold their grapes to Shorb or to the wineries of Los Angeles. The San Gabriel Valley was becoming the most extensive vineyard of the state. General George Stoneman, former governor of California, was perhaps the most eminent among the new vineyardists of the region stretching from Pasadena to the east, but he was only one of many who laid out vineyards in the 1870s there: Colonel Edward Kewen, General Volney Howard, Michael White, Alfred Chapman, and John Woodworth may be named among others.[55]

By 1875 Shorb was boasting that "we are the largest wine manufacturers on the Pacific Coast": average production of the Lake Vineyard was 150,000 gallons of wine annually, and 116,000 gallons of brandy.[56] Despite Shorb's expansive optimism, there were inevitable difficulties in selling California wine, the greatest of which was to obtain responsible and intelligent agents who would follow honest practices in the struggle to educate a recalcitrant American public to the virtues of wine from California. As Shorb reported from New York City in 1869 about the firm's agents there:

> They have a double fight before them: first to introduce a new article which all importers are fighting against, and secondly to remove the bad effects and strong prejudice against all California wines, created by the horrible stuff offered here as California wines on this market. Out of one hundred and ten dealers in Cal wines on this market alone, there are but four or five who ever buy a gallon—they manufacture it here in their cellars.[57]

The invoice book of B. D. Wilson and Co. for the five years 1873–78 shows that Shorb was trying to develop markets here and abroad, but with somewhat irregular and dissatisfying results. There are sizeable shipments to the firm's agents in New York, Chicago, and San Francisco, though the New York agency seems to be frequently changed: Wilson, Morrow, and Chamberlin give way to B. Dreyfus, then to J. F. Carr, and then to J. H. Smith's Sons. One may guess at some of the troubles implied by this sequence from Shorb's exasperated outburst to a correspondent who offered to do business with him: "My strong predilection," Shorb wrote, "even in business is to deal with gentlemen, and God knows our wine business has been handled almost exclusively by another class."[58] Lake Vineyard wines were also regularly shipped to Cleveland, and, less regularly and in smaller quantities, to Baltimore (the Baltimore agent did not pay his bills), Wilmington, Detroit, and a scattering of smaller places. More interesting are the records of efforts to open a foreign market. Early in his career, Shorb had seemed confident of establishing a large trade in South America and Mexico.[59] Nothing seems to have been achieved in that direction, however. In 1876 Shorb shipped eight barrels of wine and brandy to a William Houston of England; probably these were samples of the winery's whole range. In the same year fifteen barrels went to A. C. Jeffrey of Liverpool. There is no record of repeat orders. Before the shortages and fears created by the onslaught of phylloxera in Europe, England was not ready for California wine.

Yet another market that Shorb sought to develop was that for altar wine; he had an advantage here, being Catholic, and so particularly eligible for recommendation by the church. "We are getting up a circular," he wrote to his New York agent in 1875, "intending to attract the attention of the Catholic trade to our wines for 'Altar purposes,' and will have certificates from the Bishop [of Los Angeles] accompany the same. This trade will consume all our white wines at high prices if it can be secured. Your firm will have a 'lift' in the circular." The "communion wine," he wrote again, "is the dry Lake Vineyard or Mound Vineyard white wine— and be careful to offer none other."[60]

In Shorb's opinion, the wines of the Lake Vineyard were the best in the state, and so the best in the country: "We make the best wines of California," he wrote in 1872, "and we only ask of the trade that they *compare* our wines with others to satisfy themselves."[61] The profits of the business were low, however, and from time to time Shorb would determine to sell out and occupy himself with other things—real estate, for choice. In 1875 he unsuccessfully sought a buyer, on almost any terms, for the firm's entire inventory—some 80,000 gallons of wine and 7,000 gallons of brandy, besides about 30,000 gallons on hand in New York—explaining that "my time is too much occupied to give that attention required to successfully prosecute the business."[62]

It is certainly true that Shorb had plenty of other things he might do. In 1873 he and Wilson had formed a new partnership, under the old name of B. D. Wilson and Co., to carry out livestock and grain-growing operations as well as those of the Lake Vineyard and Winery.[63] And that was only a beginning for Shorb. The Wilson property also included extensive orange and lemon groves, whose produce was shipped widely under Shorb's management. Shorb was also preparing for his later extensive dealings in real estate development by establishing land and water companies and building irrigation systems in the San Gabriel Valley and elsewhere. He was interested in mining in the Mojave; in a furniture factory at Wilmington; in water and land development in the Arizona territory; in railways; in electric power; and in exploiting patents for everything from arc lamps to milling machinery and cable car systems. Nor did he neglect Democratic politics at the local and state levels.

In 1877, on property from his father-in-law, Shorb gave expression to his civic and commercial importance by building the big house, rich with carpenter's ornaments, called "San Marino" after the estate of the same name that had belonged to his grandfather in the Catoctin mountains of Maryland. As Wilson's Lake Vineyard had been before it, San Marino became the showplace of the Los Angeles region, a center of lavish hospitality, the place that every visitor had to see and where every transient dignitary might expect to be entertained. After Shorb's death, the house was bought by Henry Huntington, who razed it and built on the site his own mansion, now the Huntington Art Gallery. Few visitors to that lovely place know that it stands where once the leader of southern California viticulture lived, and that all around them once spread the vineyards of the San Gabriel Valley.

Benjamin Wilson died early in 1878, and though he had long before ceased to have any active part in the wine firm bearing his name, his death seems to have been a signal for it to go dormant for a time. The winery and vineyards remained, of course, but the wine company withdrew from the public marketplace. Instead, Shorb sold his production in bulk to the San Francisco firm of Lachman & Jacobi for a couple of years, and then to Benjamin Dreyfus.[64] But the quiet life of a bulk wine producer was not enough to satisfy the ambitious Shorb, and he soon began to develop plans for a new enterprise on a scale not yet attempted in California.

The second phase of Shorb's winegrowing career, which saw the Lake Vineyard transformed into something very different, opened in 1882 with the formation of the San Gabriel Wine Company, capitalized at $500,000, and financed, in large part, by English investors;[65] prominent and moneyed Californians were in on it

85   J. De Barth Shorb on the steps of San Marino with a part of his large family. The picture is probably from the 1880s, when Shorb had established his San Gabriel Winery and hoped to flood the markets of Europe with the wine of southern California. The site where the house stood is now occupied by the Henry E. Huntington Art Gallery. (Huntington Library)

86 | A view of the San Gabriel Wine Company, "the largest in the world," begun in 1882 at Alhambra, California, between Los Angeles and San Gabriel. With the backing of English investors, the winery, designed for a capacity of over a million gallons, was intended to put California wines into the world market as European production collapsed through the ravages of the phylloxera. (From Norman W. Griswold, *Beauties of California* [1884])

too, notably the Los Angeles banker Isaias Hellman and a group of San Franciscans including Senator F. G. Newlands and Senator William Gwin. Their intentions were, to put it mildly, grand beyond precedent. It had long been thought "by persons interested in the manufacture of American wine," a prospectus statement ran, that California could compete in the world wine market, given enough capital and intelligence: "This Anglo-American enterprise is the first of its kind which seems to us to have been undertaken on a scale of sufficient magnitude and under all other conditions to solve, exhaustively, the problem of California wine-making."[66]

What can have attracted this kind of interest in the provincial winegrowing industry of a country that did not yet drink wine? The answer lies in the scourge of phylloxera, which was then at the very highest pitch of its destruction of the vineyards of Europe.[67] It did not, at that time, seem an alarmist notion, but rather the sober judgment of informed observers, that Europe would soon be unable to supply its own demand for wine. If wine was going to be produced, it would have to come from unspoiled new sources—California prominent among them. Against this almost surefire prospect of immediate profits, Shorb promoted his San Gabriel Winery. He had another attraction to offer as well: land. Southern California was ripe for development; the railroad from the East would soon run through the San

Gabriel Valley; the nation at large was beginning to grow aware of the Southland's golden climate; the future was immense. The old ranch property accumulated by Ben Wilson would soon be valuable real estate. And so the San Gabriel Wine Company was launched on Shorb's land at the same time that the town of Alhambra, in which it stood, was being invented and promoted by Shorb. Stockholders had shares in land as well as in the company, and dividends could be provided by land sales if, by any unlikely chance, the wine trade should prove insufficient to provide them.

The San Gabriel Wine Company itself owned 1,500 acres; 200 of these were planted to vines in 1883, a further 400 in 1884—or that, at least, was what one prospectus stated. A further 400 were planned for 1885.[68] As for the winery itself, that was planned on an unprecedented scale. The buildings, costing $125,000, were to provide a winery meant to be, quite simply, "the largest in the world." The fermenting capacity was a million gallons, the storage, a million and a quarter.[69] Some of the stockholders expressed doubts about beginning on so grand a scale, but Shorb was confident and swept aside such timid hesitations. The winery, brick-built and steam-powered, duly arose in the new town of Alhambra according to the original plan.

The San Gabriel Wine Company did not need to wait for the growth of its own vineyards before it began to make wine: grapes were available from the many vineyards already established all the way from Los Angeles to the foothills above San Bernardino, many miles to the east. The company was able, thus, to crush some 2,000 tons of grapes in the vintage of 1882 and a larger quantity the next year; the plan was to hold back sales until 1885, when the wine would be ready for market.[70] Shipments began as early as 1884, however, by which time the company had chosen agents for its wine in New York. Problems began at once. It was all very well to grow grapes and make wine in the rural simplicity of Los Angeles County, but once the wine left the hands of the producer no one could tell what might happen. After a visit late in 1884 to their New York agents, Evan Coleman, one of the San Francisco investors, wrote to Shorb that "the more I see of the wine business the less I like it; it seems impossible to do an honest, straightforward business and compete with others, all of whom are lying, adulterating, etc., etc." The agents, in turn, were dissatisfied with what was sent to them: "They have many complaints about the Co.'s wines," Coleman reported, "and doubt that Watkins, the wine-maker, is competent."[71]

Such complaints persisted long after changes had been made and experience accumulated. The port wine produced at San Gabriel, a staple of the winery's trade, gave persistent trouble: it was "nothing but trash," wrote one Philadelphia merchant. "I would not give it away much less sell it to my customers."[72] The stuff spoiled during the long rail journey through the southwestern deserts and across the midwestern plains. Appeals to the University of California for analyses and remedies did not much help, but the addition of cherry juice seemed to turn the trick, and so shipments of cherry juice (so-called; in fact not juice but highly alcoholic cordial) were discreetly made to the San Gabriel Wine Company in wine puncheons ("by this means we can avoid advertising the fact that we use it," the plant manager wrote to Shorb).[73] Capable help was hard to find; and even the design of the splendid new buildings created difficulties: an expert from the university concluded that the winery was too dry, so that evaporation losses were excessive and the wines did not develop well, while the storage building was too hot. Shorb had had in mind the example of the great above-ground *bodegas* of the sherry region in Spain in designing it, but, as the expert dryly noted, if you wanted to get the results that the Spaniards got, you had to build like them.[74] No wonder that, in the face of all these troubles, the temptation to cheat was powerful. "If we have to go into the 'doctoring' business in order to meet the market," the secretary of the company wrote Shorb, "can we not find some book that will give us the necessary formulae and suggestions so as to avoid the delay and expense of experiments?"[75]

Shorb was full of resource and suggestion in the face of all difficulties. A key possibility, one that had been part of the original idea in founding the new winery, was the development of foreign markets. This proved harder in practice than in theory, but not for lack of trying. It was evident, for one thing, that they could not send anything less than their best to new markets if they hoped to succeed, and so it was necessary to wait until they had properly made and properly aged stocks. A start was made by sending angelica to Canada; France was considered that year, but the idea was not acted on.[76] France, in fact, was never a market for California wines, despite the possibilities that the phylloxera had seemed to open. The French preferred to buy American rootstocks on which to reestablish their own vineyards. England was more accessible; by 1891 the company's London agent was writing that "California wines are becoming quite the rage here and I hope in a few years time to make a very large business indeed in them."[77] By that time, however, the company's prolonged financial illness made "a few years" too long to wait.

The cost of transport from the West Coast to Europe was a major obstacle, and a splendidly simple way of getting around it seemed to be discovered in 1886. This was by the method of concentrating the must, or unfermented juice of the grape, for shipment to foreign parts, where, upon the addition of water, it could be fermented into wine. Since concentrating the must got rid of the water, the product was economical to ship; and since it had not been fermented at the time of its importation, it avoided the duties upon alcohol. Here, it seemed, was the solution to the problem of finding an export market for the product of California's grapes.

The technology of the process had been developed by a German named Dr. F. Springmuhl, and its promotion was in the hands of a San Francisco German, Paul Oeker. Shorb was soon interested in their propositions, and by early 1887 the American Concentrated Must Company of Clairville, California, J. De Barth Shorb, president, was incorporated and awaiting the next vintage. England was to be the main target—the English already had (and still have) a trade in "British wines," which is to say, wines fermented in England from musts brought in from the Mediterranean or other regions of the grape-growing world. They were thus familiar with the product and could also provide a source of experienced labor. All that was necessary was to persuade the market of the superiority of the raw material from California. An agent was despatched to London to watch over the business at that end (from the charming address of 10, Camomile Street); at the California end, Shorb was busy signing up growers to supply his vacuum condensers. This was a period of deep commercial depression in the California wine trade, so that Shorb had no trouble in finding interested growers: they included Charles Krug, of Napa, Leland Stanford and his Vina Winery in Tehama County, the Italian Swiss Colony of Asti, and Kohler & Frohling.[78]

Dr. Springmuhl went to London to supervise the crucial operation of fermenting the condensed must into wine, and then the troubles of the new company began to mount even before operations properly began. The process seems to have worked all right, but Springmuhl was contentious and litigious, and his principals back in California did not trust him. The quarrel was at last smoothed over: Springmuhl remained to supervise the technical operation, while a new manager was set up and the name of the firm changed to the California Produce Company in 1888.[79] Still, the business did not prosper under these new arrangements. Five years after the company had been formed, one of the chief investors wrote that "the Must business . . . is the d-dest most disagreeable thing any of us ever encountered," and that the only thing to be done was to get rid of it to anybody on any terms.[80] So ended this early phase of California's struggle to find a footing in the international export market.

Things were not much better with the parent enterprise, the San Gabriel Wine Company. From the outset it had never had quite enough money to operate easily, for the capital stock was never fully subscribed, and in order to meet its needs it had to depend more and more upon the sale of its lands. The boom year of 1887, when land was eagerly sought by speculators, was fairly easy for the company. But the boom died as quickly as it had come, and year followed year not only without dividends but with a growing indebtedness weighing on the company. As early as 1884, one major investor had come to the conclusion that "a great mistake was made in the beginning in building on such a grand scale. We should have built a winery and cellars of not over one half the capacity of that constructed and had $40,000 more by that means on hand, instead of in buildings which we cannot use to their full capacity for ten years to come."[81] Sales of the company's wines in 1886 amounted to $94,000; in 1888 they had risen to $114,000. Early in that year, after the company had shipped twenty cars of wine to the East in March, the manager reported that "everything is going along nicely."[82] At that moment, when at last the prospects began to look good, the Anaheim disease hit the San Gabriel region, and though its effects do not seem to have been catastrophic, as they were around Anaheim, they added just enough weight to the San Gabriel Wine Company's burden to put a stop to its progress.

"But for that fatal disease the outlook for the future would be good," Evan Coleman, one of the investors closest to the operation of the company, wrote in

September 1888.[83] But if Coleman seemed to despair, Shorb, as always, was quick to take action in response to the new problem. Quite improbably, he was able to find in Los Angeles an Englishman with the resonant name of Ethelbert Dowlen, a graduate of the South Kensington School in London (now the Imperial College of Science), where he had studied botany with the great Thomas Huxley. Dowlen volunteered to devote himself to an examination of the disease in the hope of finding its causes and cure, and Shorb at once engaged him.[84] As a member of the Board of State Viticultural Commissioners, Shorb was able to make the appointment official and to provide Dowlen with laboratory equipment and an experimental greenhouse on the San Gabriel property. By the first week of October 1888, Dowlen had issued number one of the weekly reports that he would produce over the next two years. Though he labored with admirable thoroughness, both in the field and in the laboratory, Dowlen was entirely unable to explain the disease or to provide anything like a remedy. Growers could do little except to replant, and then to wait, and though the intensity of the disease in the San Gabriel Valley faded rather quickly, confidence in the future of viticulture was greatly injured. As they had around Anaheim, oranges became the crop of the future.

Shorb and the San Gabriel Wine Company were in dire straits by 1890: he was on the verge of losing his entire investment and had only his wife's estate (itself heavily mortgaged) between him and destitution.[85] The possibility of selling the company now became the main hope of its stockholders, but the chances of doing so diminished as the company's troubles grew. To make matters worse, a group of British investors had bought out the Sunny Slope Winery of Shorb's neighbor L. J. Rose in 1887 and had failed to make the profits they hoped for: the result was that investments in California wine properties went begging in the English money market.[86] Since the San Gabriel Wine Company could not make a profit and could not be sold, it ought to have gone out of business. But Shorb would not submit to that logic yet. A form letter from the company addressed to "Our Patrons and the Trade" on 1 March 1892—just ten years after it had been founded amid such euphoric expectation—announced that there was no possibility of earning "an adequate return on the capital invested" in the wine business. Therefore, it went on, "we . . . beg to inform you that we have determined to discontinue the manufacture and sale of wines and confine our operations henceforth exclusively to the manufacture of brandy."[87] So, Shorb seemed to say, if we can't make it in the wine trade, at least we will stay in business and make brandy. In the next year, we hear of Shorb busily planting citrus orchards on the company's land—an activity that angered the powerful Isaias Hellman, whose bank held the mortgage on Shorb's own estate and who was one of the company's stockholders. "It is all nonsense," Hellman expostulated; "I insist that the San Gabriel Wine Co., must go out of business as other similar corporations have done down South; pay our debts and divide the land and property amongst the shareholders."[88] But Shorb went out of business only on his death, which occurred just a few years later, in 1896, at the rather early age of fifty-four; it is easy to imagine that the scrambling required by his many enterprises, not least among them the San Gabriel Wine Company, had worn him out.

When the company pulled out of the wine business in order to concentrate upon brandy, its stocks of wine were offered for sale at a heavy discount and were bought up by the New York agency that had represented it from the beginning— evidence, at least, that what the company made was saleable, though at the price of 35 cents a gallon it need not have had much quality to attract a buyer.[89] The kinds and quantities of wines put up for sale at this time make an interesting list: there were nearly 150,000 gallons of wine on hand, 90,000 gallons of which were port and 25,000 gallons sherry; the rest was red and white table wine. Of brandy there were nearly 50,000 gallons, from stocks going back to 1882, the year of the company's founding. The company still owned 1,170 acres of land, and had assets of just over $700,000.[90]

The aftermath of Shorb's brief, busy career is rather sad. The San Gabriel Wine Company struggled on until around the end of the century and then at last expired. Its buildings were taken over for other purposes but have now been demolished. With the proverbial heartlessness of bankers, Isaias Hellman foreclosed the mortgage on Shorb's widow, and the splendors of San Marino, as we have seen, passed into the hands of Henry Huntington. The family migrated to the San Francisco Bay area, where their paths led them far away from the wine business that had so deeply engaged their father and grandfather before them. In the city of Alhambra, which Shorb had both christened and developed, a number of street names commemorate Shorb and his numerous children—Shorb Street itself, and Ramona, Ynez, Marguerita, Campbell, Benito, Edith, and Ethel. Otherwise, his work seems to have left no trace. One looks in vain for anything like a vineyard along the slopes that run for miles up from the San Bernardino freeway to the foothills of the San Gabriel range, and most people living there today are surprised to learn even that grapes once grew in the area; the idea of the valley's once having contained "the world's largest winery" is even more strange.

Shorb's story, as I have said, seems in essentials to be exemplary of the history of winegrowing in southern California: at one end it links up with the era of the missions, through B. D. Wilson and his Mexican wife, whose daughter Shorb had married; at the other, it reaches out to the modern era of large-scale and international commerce; and then it disappears. But good work in one form or another always persists, and it is perhaps not wrong to think that the bold and ambitious example that Shorb set his fellow winemakers helped to change their ideas of what their industry's future might become.

This chapter may conclude on a minor but pleasant note. Somehow, a few bottles of the San Gabriel Wine Company's wines managed to survive to so late a date as 1955, when one California connoisseur, on sampling a San Gabriel cabernet, 1891, found it "a wine to be savoured with pleasure and respect," faded, indeed, but still retaining its character. (One must hint a doubt here as to whether the wine was in fact from San Gabriel: Shorb regularly bought table wine in bulk from the north to put out under his own label—perhaps it came from Isaac De Turk in Santa Rosa?) As for the 1893 port, that may have been of the San Gabriel Winery's own production (though in 1893 it had already withdrawn from the wine market), and it is gratifying to learn that it was pronounced, upon tasting, "a benediction."[91] *Requiescat in pace.*

12

California to the End of the Century

Changing Patterns and
the Development of New Regions

T he simplest way to show what happened in California between, say, 1869, when Haraszthy left the state, and 1900, after a full generation of development had taken place, is by some statistics, graphically presented. A few details of graph 1 may be noted. The plateau from 1874 through 1877 conceals the fact that plantings increased mightily through those years—by an estimated 13,000 acres—so that the consequent overproduction destroyed prices. In 1876 grapes did not pay the cost of their picking, and many acres were uprooted or turned over to foraging animals. Through such drastic means, the industry had come back to a reasonably stable situation by 1880. The relatively small decline from 1886 to 1887 conceals another disastrous break in prices that year, which plunged the industry into a prolonged depression.

Accompanying the rising curve of production was another change, the rapid shift of dominance from south to north. Graph 2 comparing the San Francisco Bay counties to Los Angeles County will make this plain. The redistribution would be even more obvious if one took into account the continuing production of the Sierra foothill counties and the new production coming from the Central Valley counties. The reversal is clear enough, however; in the thirty years from 1860 to 1890, Los Angeles's share of the state's total sank from near two-thirds to less than a tenth; in the same span the Bay Area counties saw their share rise from little more than a tenth to near two-thirds, an almost symmetrical exchange.

The decline of the Southern Vineyard (as Los Angeles was called and as its newspaper styled itself) was relatively sharp and quick. But that does not mean that winegrowing there disappeared, or was even much diminished to a casual eye. The news of phylloxera in Europe stimulated ambitious new planting, as we have seen in the case of Shorb and the San Gabriel Winery. Shorb's neighbor at the Santa Anita ranch, the Comstock millionaire E. J. "Lucky" Baldwin, built expansively in the late 1870s and early 1880s. He had 1,200 acres in vines in 1889, and promoted his Santa Anita Vineyard wines and brandies far and wide.[1] Another neighbor, L. J. Rose of the Sunny Slope Winery, tried, like Shorb, to exploit the opening created by phylloxera in European vineyards. Rose had been growing grapes and making wine for a decade when, in 1879, he determined on a great expansion. In that year he built what was called the largest and most modern winery in the state, with a capacity of 500,000 gallons to accommodate the yield of his 1,000 acres of vineyard. But the moment of the San Gabriel Valley's prosperity had passed for Rose as for Shorb. In 1887 Rose managed to sell the Sunny Slope Winery to a syndicate of English investors, who never recovered their money and whose experience considerably tarnished whatever appeal Los Angeles County winegrowing had as an investment.[2]

The onset of the Anaheim disease, which put an end to viticulture in Orange County, also helped to discourage the farmers of the San Gabriel Valley about the future of grapes and to turn them more and more to the all-conquering orange. Winegrowing in the south of the state therefore tended to shift eastwards to the region of Cucamonga, where viticulture was long established and the soil, a deep deposit of almost pure sand, was hardly suitable for anything else. When phylloxera appeared in California, this sandy soil protected the vines from the pest and so invited further plantings. Thus, the district, which had produced 48,000 gallons of wine in 1870, was producing 279,000 gallons in 1890.[3] It was here that Secondo Guasti, beginning in 1900, developed the "world's largest vineyard" (it ran to some 5,000 acres at its peak) and created a strong market for Cucamonga wine among the Italian communities of the East Coast.[4] The vineyards of the region persisted through Prohibition, depression, and war in the twentieth century, but fell victim at last to tract homes, freeways, airports, and industrial parks. Only rapidly diminishing vestiges survive in the 1980s.

Santa Barbara, Ventura, and San Diego counties all produced wine, but never very much—the total was 45,000 gallons in 1890, for example, and this was the work of scattered small producers. Nothing resembling an economically important industry ever arose in those counties, though there were some interesting enterprises. One of these was the Caire ranch on Santa Cruz Island, off Santa Barbara. The Frenchman Justinian Caire, a successful merchant in San Francisco, acquired the island around 1880; there, in addition to running sheep and cattle over the island's hills and valleys, he planted extensive vineyards and built a substantial winery of brick baked on the island. The island community was a varied mix of French, Indian, Mexican, Anglo, and Italian ranch hands and field workers. Winemaking was in the hands of French experts and the vineyards were tended by Ital-

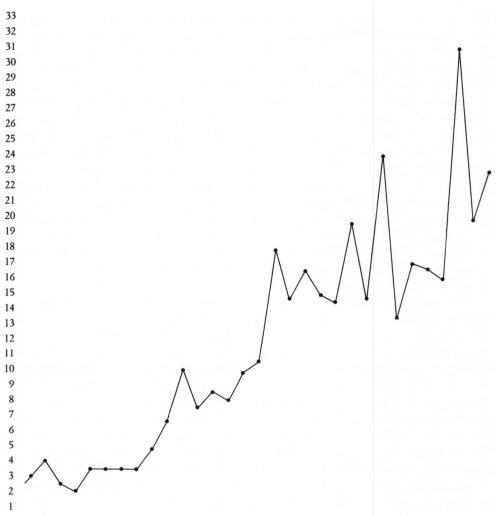

I | **Wine Production in California in**
Millions of Gallons, 1870—1900
Source: Report of the California
State Board of Agriculture, 1911 (Sacramento, 1912)

ian workers, some of whom "spent their lives on the island and spoke no English."
Among the hazards to viticulture on Santa Cruz were the wild pigs with which
the island abounds. The vineyards included such varieties as Cabernet Sauvignon,
Pinot Noir, Petite Sirah, and Zinfandel, and the wines acquired a good reputation,
only to disappear, with so many others, under Prohibition.[5]

In San Diego County in 1883, through their El Cajón Land Company, a group
of northern California wine men, including Charles Wetmore, Arpad Haraszthy,
and George West, promoted the prospects of "viticulture and horticulture" on the

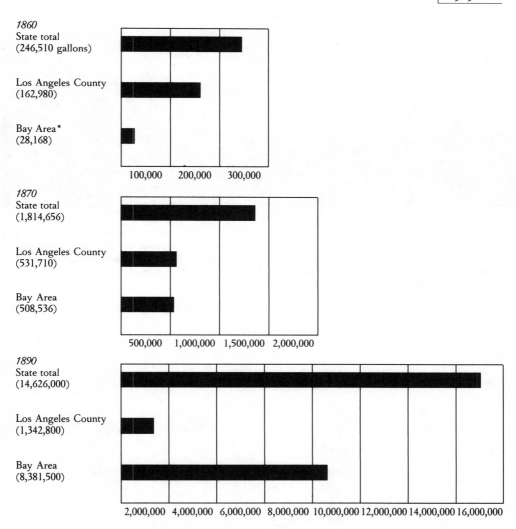

1860
State total
(246,510 gallons)

Los Angeles County
(162,980)

Bay Area*
(28,168)

100,000   200,000   300,000

1870
State total
(1,814,656)

Los Angeles County
(531,710)

Bay Area
(508,536)

500,000   1,000,000   1,500,000   2,000,000

1890
State total
(14,626,000)

Los Angeles County
(1,342,800)

Bay Area
(8,381,500)

2,000,000 4,000,000 6,000,000 8,000,000 10,000,000 12,000,000 14,000,000 16,000,000

*Alameda, Contra Costa, Napa, Santa Clara, Solano, Sonoma, and Yolo counties

2 | **California Wine Production,
North and South, 1860–90**
Source: *Report of the California
State Board of Agriculture, 1911* (Sacramento, 1912)

27,000 acres of land they held for speculation.[6] Despite the high qualities claimed for Zinfandel wine grown in the county, winemaking was at best a sideline on San Diego ranches. There was, however, a considerable flurry of planting in San Diego following the collapse of the Anaheim region; the Italian investigator Guido Rossati reported that there were 6,000 acres in production in San Diego County in 1889, and 7,500 acres of vines not yet bearing.[7]

87 | The Sunny Slope vineyard and winery of L. J. Rose in the San Gabriel Valley. With its thousand acres of vines and half-million-gallon winery, this was one of the giants of the valley. It shared in the general decline of the southern California vineyards, however, and after its sale to an English syndicate in 1887 did not prosper. (Huntington Library)

88 | A label of Justinian Caire's Santa Cruz Island Company, the only wine producer on California's Channel Islands. (Author's collection)

A new development in the southern region was the growing of grapes for raisins rather than wine. Commercially successful trials with raisin grapes were made in Yolo County in 1867, but the great bulk of the trade soon shifted southwards. In 1873 raisin vineyards were set out in Riverside, in the El Cajon Valley of San Diego County, and along the Santa Ana River in Orange County, and these places soon became centers of raisin production.[8] The future lay with the region around Fresno, however, where planting also began in 1873 and where success was so rapid and complete that in barely more than a decade raisins were Fresno County's major crop. The raisin growers belong to the history of California winemaking because the grapes they grow have traditionally formed a part of the supply for the state's winemaking—rightly or wrongly. The mainstay of California raisin growing is the Thompson Seedless grape, introduced in 1872, which makes raisins of quality but at best a wine of entirely neutral flavor. Nevertheless, substantial tonnages of this grape in California have long been made into wine for blending or distilled into brandy for fortifying.

By 1870 the credibility of the idea that California was destined to be a great winegrowing country had been well established; it was also becoming clear that the southern part of the state had not succeeded in the essential matter of producing an attractive table wine: the combination of semidesert heat and the Mission grape stood in the way. A straw in the wind showing the new direction appeared in 1865, when the astute Charles Kohler of Los Angeles and Anaheim bought vineyards in Sonoma County. By 1870 he had "discovered" the Zinfandel, and from that time he planted his northern vineyards to it.[9] What Kohler was doing, and what Haraszthy and others had done before him, showed their opportunity to the smallholders and ranchers of the north. They had a reasonable selection of varieties, especially the Zinfandel, to replace the Mission grape, and these would yield acceptable dry wines from their more temperate valleys and hillsides. Anyone who possessed land not suited for irrigation or too rough for standard farming could put it into vines, as the newspapers, promotional agencies, and agricultural experts of the state were all urging everyone to do. The spirit of this time is expressed by Arpad Haraszthy, who had inherited his father's flair for publicity as well as his optimism, writing on "Wine-Making in California" in the Overland Monthly in 1872. The early winegrowers, he wrote, had not understood the importance of good varieties and proper soils, but that had now changed: "Every season brings us better wines, the product of some newly discovered locality, planted with choicer varieties of the grape, and entirely different from anything previously produced." Ultimately, he prophesied, California would produce a wine fit to take its place among the handful of the world's very finest.[10] All sorts of individuals and organizations were drawn into the work, and one can see several distinctive and clearly marked patterns taking shape in the 1870s.

First and most important was the individual farmer working on his own account and in his own style. More often than not the vine grower was also his own winemaker. Scores of the farm winery buildings put up at this time still stud the towns and hillsides of the counties surrounding San Francisco Bay; typically they were simple, solid buildings, often of stone (or brick) or mixed stone and wood, providing a gravity-flow operation from upper to lower floor and a cool place of storage behind the stone walls of the lower stage.[11] A hand crusher and a hand press would suffice for the modest tonnage to be vinified, and the wines produced would perhaps go into vats and casks of native redwood—California's contribution to the medieval craft of the cooper, though not adopted as early as might be supposed.[12]

Many of the pioneering names of the 1850s continued to flourish: Jacob Gundlach in Sonoma, Charles Krug in Napa, and Charles Lefranc and Pierre Pellier in Santa Clara County, to name some of those whose wineries continue in operation to this day. To these pioneers, many new names were now added. Some of those still operating in California go back to this time, but very few indeed: Inglenook and Beringer in Napa County and Simi in Sonoma are notable; Cresta Blanca, Wente, and Concannon, all (originally) in the Livermore Valley, belong to the early 1880s, as do Geyser Peak and Italian Swiss Colony in Sonoma County and Chateau Montelena in Napa. The overwhelmingly greater number of the new establishments of this era were destined to briefer lives, and even the hardier of these could not survive Prohibition: Aguillon, Bolle, Cady, Chauvet, Cloverdale, Colson, Cralle, Delafield, Doma, Dry Creek, Eagle, Fischer, Glassell, Gobruegge, Green Oaks, Gunn, Holst, Laurel Hill, Lehn, Live Oak, Meyer, Michaelson, Naud, Nouveau Médoc, Palmdale—such a list of vanished names might be extended into the hundreds.

There are no reliable statistics on the number of winemaking establishments in California in the nineteenth century. What is certain is that there was a rapid and unstable growth. The instability is well illustrated by the figures (perhaps approximately reliable) for the number of registered wineries in 1870 and 1880: in the first year there were 139 wineries; in the second, after the crash of 1876, only 45.[13] These figures must be for the more visible wineries only: the number of people actually making wine at any time was far greater. In the survey made by the Board of State Viticultural Commissioners in 1890, for example, 711 growers reported that they made wine, and even that figure is well below what must have been the case.[14] But whatever the actual number may have been, the point is that it kept going up and down.

The counties ringing San Francisco Bay, though they were clearly coming to dominate the industry, were not the only scenes of new development; the attraction to winegrowing was felt throughout the state wherever the chances seemed good. The expatriate Englishman (afterwards a prolific and exceedingly bad novelist) Horace Annesley Vachell put in a vineyard on the Coast Range in San Luis Obispo County in 1882, and viticulture on the Estrella Creek (or River) in that county went back a number of years earlier,[15] as it did in the town of San Luis Obispo itself, where, not long after 1859, Pierre Dallidet planted a vineyard and opened a winery.[16] In a few other counties that are now, in our time, coming to be important in California winegrowing, only the barest of starts was made in the nineteenth century. In Mendocino County, for example, there were only two wine-makers listed in the state board's 1891 directory; the same source lists but two for Lake County, and for Monterey none at all, though there were some ten names listed as grape growers. The possibilities of the central coast of California, roughly between Monterey and Los Angeles, though not exactly unknown, lay unrecognized and undeveloped until very recent years. The fact is good evidence that the winegrowing map of California is far from its final form.

In an unsystematic way much was being learned about the possibilities of the vast number of soils, sites, and microclimates in California, but one can hardly say that the diverse regions of the state had been fully prospected. Nor have they been even today. It would not be anything like as soon as Arpad Haraszthy and others thought before the possibilities of the state's territories were sufficiently known to allow the right varieties of grape to be matched to the right soil and climate. That is a work that still has many years before it in California, to say nothing of the rest of the United States. But certainly much had been done in a rough-and-ready way by the end of the 1880s.

A new region, hitherto unattractive to settlement, begins to be heard from in the 1870s. The interior of the state, south of San Francisco and between Coast Range and Sierra, now the gigantic cotton, almond, tree fruit, and grape factory called the Central Valley, was then still pretty much what the Spaniards had called it, *tierra incognita*. Its main products for many years would be raisins and other fruit unfit to drink: the huge modern wine production of Kern, Tulare, Kings, Stanislaus, and Fresno counties lay in the future. But significant work had begun. And it was evident, from the beginning, that the growers of the Central Valley were going to make a *lot* of wine. Even if the bulk of the grapes they grew went to raisins, the scale of winemaking operations was much bigger here on an average than elsewhere.

Token plantings of grapes had been made in scattered parts of the Central Valley in the 1850s and 1860s, but the region was almost wholly given over to cattle grazing until the opening of the railroad through it at the beginning of the 1870s. Then speculators began to try what the possibilities of this virtually untouched territory might be. The center of development was the new town of Fresno, laid out in the middle of the valley and named by the Central California Railroad in 1872. An experiment in irrigated farming in that year produced sensational results on the Easterby ranch ouside Fresno, and the agricultural exploitation of the region was off and running.[17] The valley was hot and arid, but the touch of water seemed to release a magic fertility.

The honor of introducing the grape belongs, by all testimony, to Francis Eisen, a Swedish-born San Francisco businessman who had just bought property in Fresno County, and who put in vines to see what they might do. That was in 1873. These grapes, as a writer put it in 1884, turned out to be "the key which has unlocked nature's richest stores."[18] Eisen went on to develop his property on a scale that was to be a model for agricultural development generally in the Central Valley: by the end of the seventies he had 160 acres in vines; in 1883 he had 200 acres; by 1888 he had 400, and his winery had been built up to a capacity of 300,000 gallons.[19] Eisen's original vine plantings had included raisin varieties as well as wine varieties, and it was the raisin that was to dominate Fresno County viticulture in the early days, as it does still. But winegrowing was established at the same time, and grew only less rapidly than the raisin trade. It is interesting to note that Eisen, in the untried Central Valley, experimented with a wide range of varieties, including a number of the American hybrids such as Lenoir, Cynthiana, and Norton.[20] The great object of the early Fresno growers was to find a way to prove that they could grow something other than sweet wines in the blazing heat of their valley, and the native American varieties were tried for the sake of their higher acids in blends with such vinifera as Zinfandel. It is also notable that the Mission was not part of the varietal mix in Fresno; its defects were now too well known to be doubted, and there was, by this time, no need to depend on it.[21]

Agriculture in the Central Valley was never an affair for the small proprietor. Only irrigated farming was possible, and the costs of preparation for that were too great for most individuals: the main irrigation works had first to be provided; then the ground had to be levelled, ditches dug, dikes and levees built, hedges planted, roads made—all before any planting went on. In these circumstances two kinds of proprietorship grew up. Either the land was developed by wealthy individual capitalists or corporations, or it was developed by the "colony" system, something on the model of the Anaheim scheme twenty years earlier. A group would form for the purpose of pooling its resources, buying land, and then dividing the property, to be paid for on long terms. The first of these was the Central California Colony in 1875. That was followed by a string of others—the Washington Colony, the Scandinavian Colony, the Fresno Colony, and, ominously, the Temperance Colony. Several of these associations had winegrowing as an object: the original Central California Colony, for instance. The Scandinavian Colony, founded in 1879, developed a considerable winery; it had a capacity of 100,000 gallons in the nineties, when it was taken over by the California Wine Association.[22]

The large-scale example set by the pioneer firm of Eisen was followed by a number of other Fresno vineyards and wineries. Among the most notable of these were the Eggers Vineyard, the St. George Vineyard, the Barton Vineyard, and the Fresno Vineyard Company. They may be dealt with briefly. The Barton Vineyard, founded in 1879, was the showplace of the region, splendid on a level of display that put it high among California attractions. Robert Barton, a former mining engineer, spared no expense to make his new property elegant and handsome in every detail: his fences, his hedges, his pleasure grounds, his winery, his barns, his mansion, his vineyards—all moved the admiration of the journalists who wrote about it: "a princely domain," one called it; "a paradise," said another.[23] Barton had five hundred acres of bearing vineyard by 1884, from which he made both dry and sweet wines from standard varieties such as Zinfandel and Burger; he also had a

89 | The bareness of the scene and the large scale of the operations that characterized Central Valley winegrowing are both clearly evident here. (From Jerome D. Laval, *As "Pop" Saw It* [1975])

90 | The Barton Estate Vineyard at Fresno, the unchallenged showplace of the Central Valley in the pioneer days; founded in 1879, it was sold only eight years later to a syndicate of English investors for $1 million. To contemporaries, the Barton Estate was "a princely domain" by contrast to the bare flats of the valley around it. (From Frona Eunice Wait, *Wines and Vines of California* [1889])

mixture of other, more exotic varieties for trial, especially for sweet wines. In 1887, at the high point of English interest in California vineyard property, Barton sold his estate to a syndicate of English investors for a million dollars—a sensational transaction for Fresno, where winemaking was barely more than a decade old. Unlike the Sunny Slope Winery of L. J. Rose, which was sold to English investors at about the same time, the Barton Vineyard continued to grow; by 1896, as the Barton Estate Company Ltd., it had a capacity of half a million gallons, supplied by over 700 acres of vineyard. Its manager, installed by the English owners, was a Colonel Trevelyan, a survivor of the Charge of the Light Brigade.[24]

The other early wineries of Fresno had little notable about them apart from their tendency to grow to great size. The St. George Vineyard was the work of an immigrant Silesian named George Malter, who, like Robert Barton, had been a mining engineer before becoming a grape grower and winemaker, beginning in 1879. His vineyards covered 2,000 acres by the end of the century, and his winery was one of the largest in the state before Prohibition put an end to it.[25] The Eggers Vineyard and Winery, of 225,000-gallon capacity, was the property of a San Francisco land company that began vineyard development in 1882;[26] the Fresno Vineyard Company was also the work of a San Francisco corporation, in which the wine merchants Lachman & Jacobi had an original interest.[27] It was begun in 1880 and was soon developed to a capacity of 500,000 gallons. The Eggers Vineyard and the Fresno Vineyard Company were both essentially bulk wine producers, whose wines were shipped in volume to San Francisco and elsewhere to disappear into blends. All of these big Fresno district wineries were largely devoted to sweet wine production by the end of the century, though all had begun with a determination to make dry table wines. They failed to convince the skeptics that good dry wines could come from the heat of the Central Valley and were forced to turn to the production of vast quantities of anonymous sweet wine. This development was probably inevitable at the time: the production of good dry wines would not be possible until a much more scientific control, both of grape growing and of winemaking, had been worked out. Meantime, the growth of the Fresno vineyards went on. In 1908 there were 100,000 acres of grapes: 60 percent of this acreage was in raisin varieties, 38 percent in wine varieties, and 2 percent in table varieties. Acreage would go on increasing even after Prohibition.[28]

Perhaps the most highly regarded of the new regions exploited for vines around this time was the Livermore Valley in Alameda County, a pleasant region of oak-studded coastal hills a few miles inland from San Francisco Bay. Here an English sailor named Robert Livermore had made his way in 1844 and had set up as a rancher. He planted vines and made wine, but only, as most ranchers did, for his own needs.[29] The floor of the valley is a deep gravel bed, suited to the vine and not fit for much else; the valley, shut off from the Bay by the Berkeley hills, is hot, and yet, surprisingly, it has from the outset made good dry white wine, for many, many years a thing that the rest of California had trouble in producing. From a token 40 acres in the 1870s the valley's vineyards leaped to over 4,000 acres by

1884, a development largely owing to the promotional genius of Charles Wetmore, who invested in Livermore in 1882 and thereupon persuasively declaimed its virtues to a responsive state.[30] Livermore also profited from the fact that good varieties of the grape—notably the Semillon—were planted there in the first days of development. The region never had to pass through a phase of dependence on the Mission. It was, moreover, a region largely developed by wealthy men, as the glamorous names of their properties suggest: Chateau Bellevue, Olivina, Mont Rouge, Ravenswood, La Bocage. The small farmers did not lead here but followed.

Large-Scale Investment in California Winegrowing

Livermore was hardly alone in the combination of wealth and winemaking. While hundreds of farmers and small businessmen were planting vines and making wine in commercial quantities, there were at the same time a good many individuals and organizations of great wealth busied in the same work. They define the second pattern of the development of this generation in California. The vine has always been one of the ornaments of wealth and power. Greek and Roman aristocrats owned vineyards and competed with their wines as they might compete in racing fine horses or in collecting rare manuscripts. In the Middle Ages princes of the church as well as secular princes owned vineyards and patronized the arts of viticulture and enology. The same attraction operated in California. The early San Francisco banker William Ralston, who had a hand in California enterprises ranging from silk mills to mines, all financed by lavish and irregular loans from the Bank of California, was a major promoter of the Buena Vista Vinicultural Society, Haraszthy's ambitious organization in the 1860s. The collapse of the bold schemes of the Buena Vista Society and the bizarre death of Haraszthy were matched by Ralston's fall to ruin and his death in San Francisco Bay. As early as 1859 one of the state's first millionaires, the hard-drinking renegade Mormon Sam Brannan, sank a large part of his fortune in a property in the northern Napa Valley where, having named the place Calistoga, he set out to create both a health resort at the local hot springs (California plus Saratoga Springs yielded "Calistoga") and large-scale vineyards. He failed in the speculation, though the vine-growing part was successful enough. Brannan commissioned an agent to send thousands of cuttings of the best varieties to him from Europe, and in a couple of years had some 200 acres in vines. Brandy rather than wine seems to have been Brannan's main production for the market, and he was trying to get Ben Wilson of the Lake Vineyard to take over the Calistoga wine interest by 1863.[31] Though Brannan was the first Californian of great wealth to take up winegrowing, he did not take it very far.

The most ambitious and sustained application of California's early wealth to winegrowing came from Leland Stanford, one of the Big Four with Collis P. Huntington, Charles Crocker, and Mark Hopkins; wartime governor of California, U.S. senator, and founder of the university named for his son, Stanford was one of the great powers in the state throughout the latter half of the nineteenth century. Stanford's interest in California wine went back at least as far as 1869, when he bought property at Warm Springs, along the southern shores of San Francisco Bay in Alameda County, from a Frenchman who had some seventy-five acres of grapes planted there. Stanford installed his brother Josiah on the property, and there the brothers began making wine in 1871. By 1876 production at Warm Springs Ranch was up to 50,000 gallons.[32]

In 1880 Stanford travelled with his family to France and there paid visits to some of the great chateaux of Bordeaux: Yquem, Lafite, and Larose among others. Whether this experience was the direct inspiration for what followed next is not known, but it seems likely, for on his return Stanford determined to become a great wine producer. The flourishing enterprise of L. J. Rose at Sunny Slope, with its big new winery, may also have stimulated Stanford's competitiveness. In 1881 Stanford began buying large quantities of land along the Sacramento River in Tehama and Butte counties, between Red Bluff and Chico, with the announced aim of growing wines there that would rival the best of France. The property was part of the old Lassen grant and already had a winegrowing history. Peter Lassen himself had planted Mission vines as early as 1846; in 1852 he had sold what remained of his grant to a German named Henry Gerke, who extended and improved the vineyards and successfully operated his winery through most of the next three decades.[33]

When Stanford took over, things changed dramatically: in one year a thousand acres of new plantings were added to Gerke's modest seventy-five; vast arrangements of dams, canals, and ditches for irrigating the ranch were constructed, fifty miles of ditch for the vineyards alone; a number of French winegrowers were brought over and housed in barracks on the ranch; a winery, storage cellar, brandy distillery, warehouses, and all other needful facilities were built, no expense spared. The new-fangled incandescent lights were installed in the fermenting house so that work could be carried on night and day during the critical time of the vintage. All the while Stanford continued to add to the acreage of his ranch, now called the Vina Ranch after the nearby town that Henry Gerke had laid out. Lassen's original grant from Mexican days extended over 22,000 acres, but Lassen had not been able to hold it long, and by the time Gerke appeared Lassen's ranch had dwindled to about 6,000 acres. Gerke, too, had sold off parts of the property, so that Stanford's first purchase was but a fragment of the original Mexican grant. Stanford simply kept on buying once he had started, however, and by 1885, when he appears to have thought that he had enough for his purposes, the Vina Ranch spread over 55,000 acres of foothill pasture and valley farmland—some 20,000 acres of the latter.[34]

The moral of this enterprise, larger and more costly than anything else ever ventured in California agriculture to this point, was not long in appearing: size and wealth are not enough to make up for lack of experience. The circumstances were all wrong for what Stanford wanted to do, and though the Vina property was lovely to the eye and richly productive in all sorts of crops, it did not and never

91 Workers at Leland Stanford's Vina Ranch on the verandah of their boarding house. There are thirty-seven men and one dog in this picture, taken in 1888, and they were probably only a fraction of those employed on the ranch and in the winery. The picture was taken by George C. Husmann, son of Professor George Husmann. (Huntington Library)

could have made fine table wines. It was, in the first place, too hot in the summer for the grapes from which the noble wines come. The ranch lies in what is called, in the classification of California winegrowing lands, region five, the hottest of the five classifications, more like Algeria than Alameda. Its soil, too, was richer than that which good wine grapes need—they always prefer the poorer to the richer; and, finally, there was not enough experience yet in California with the bewilderingly wide range of Old World grape varieties and their possibilities. As has already been said, the matching of the right varieties with the right soil and climate is a work still going on and bound to continue for many years. It cannot be hurried, since not until the trial has been made can one know whether the right match has been found and one can hardly expect that what has required centuries in Europe will occur overnight here.

The force of these considerations was made clear within a year or two of the first vintage at Vina, which took place in 1887 with a harvest of several thousand tons (three earlier harvests had been sold to other winemakers). By this time there were 3,575 acres of vines planted, and a wine cellar with a capacity of two million gallons of storage had been built to receive the yield from this sea of vines. To supervise the work, Stanford had hired one of the master winemakers of the state,

Captain H. W. McIntyre, who had been winemaker to Gustave Niebaum at Inglenook in the Napa Valley and president of the state association of grape growers and winemakers.[35]

Evidently, all that could be done had been done, and yet the wine was a disappointment. No clear report about the character of the table wine produced is on record, but the circumstantial evidence is eloquent. The original selection of varieties, for one thing, was mistaken. Stanford planted Burger, Charbono, Malvoisie, and Zinfandel in his first expansion of the Vina vineyards; the cuttings, incidentally, came from the San Gabriel Valley vineyards of L. J. Rose, and this itself was a bad sign.[36] Burger wine was a Rose specialty, and he had particularly promoted it as greatly superior to the Mission. That was true, no doubt, but still faint praise. Burger, for white wine, does not make a distinguished table wine no matter where it is grown; the Malvoisie is an excellent source of sweet wines; only the Charbono and Zinfandel, red wine grapes, can be expected to yield good sound wines for the table, but that is when they are grown in the cooler hills and valleys of the state. Later, Stanford introduced a selection of other varieties, including the Riesling (though Gerke seems to have had this grape before Stanford's day), Cabernet Sauvignon, Malbec, Sauvignon Blanc, and Semillon.[37] But the lesser varieties continued to dominate, and in any case the finer varieties could never have produced wine comparable to what they yield in a suitable climate. As though to underline the uncertainties of Stanford's experiment, native American grapes were also included in the mix of varieties that were tried at various times: the Catawba, Herbemont, and Lenoir, varieties that have since entirely disappeared from California viticulture.

By 1890, only the fourth vintage at Vina, the entire huge production of 1,700,000 gallons of wine from 10,000 tons of grapes was distilled into brandy.[38] No more telling comment could be made on the collapse of Stanford's hope to rival the best that Bordeaux could produce. This is not to say that the vineyards and winery were a failure; only that the much-publicized aim of producing outstanding table wine was not met, and could not have been met. What *could* be done was to produce quite good sweet wines—baked sherry, angelica, port—and large quantities of brandy that acquired a high reputation. One experienced New York dealer of the time recalled Vina brandy as "more like cognac than anything made in this country,"[39] and there are other testimonies more or less agreeing with this. The Vina angelica was judged the best of that sort exhibited at the great Columbian Exposition in Chicago in 1893.[40] But these compliments, and a scattering of others like them, are a sad anticlimax after the high and boastful intentions with which the Vina experiment started.

Stanford's winegrowing was not confined to Vina or to Warm Springs. He had grown grapes on his Palo Alto ranch in San Mateo County ever since he purchased it in 1876; in 1888 he built a winery there, perhaps in recognition of the fact that something better was needed than Vina was able to provide. Wine was produced and sold there under the Palo Alto label, on the Stanford campus, down to 1915, but the scale of the enterprise was not comparable to that at Vina, and Stanford does not appear to have put a special effort into its success.[41]

For all the fact that it was widely and regularly written up in the California press, as a sort of standing feature subject, the Vina Ranch seems to have had curiously little impact on the life of the state. Its practices in grape growing and winemaking did not point the way to the future but gave only a sort of object lesson of what was to be avoided. The labor on the ranch was mostly provided by Chinese and Japanese workers, isolated from the general life around them.[42] And the production of the ranch was almost entirely sold to New York markets, so that a bottle of Vina brandy or of Vina wine was rarely seen by a California buyer.[43] The whole thing seemed to exist outside the view of the ordinary citizen of the state.

Stanford died in 1893. The Vina Ranch had already passed into the endowment of Stanford University, and once Stanford himself was no longer around to indulge his hobby interest in the property, his widow and the university trustees followed a very different style in its management. Captain McIntyre took his departure; Mrs. Stanford fired 150 employees and cut the salaries of everyone who remained. Vineyard acreage was reduced and land planted to other crops like alfalfa and wheat.[44] All the while, the university grew more and more embarrassed by its position as a major producer of wine and brandy in the face of growing prohibitionist disapproval of such an unholy connection between Demon Rum and godly education. Worst of all, David Starr Jordan, the university's first president, was a vocal prohibitionist himself. Stanford University's somewhat shamefaced part as proprietor of a great vineyard persisted, however, until 1915, when a final harvest of 6,000 tons from the vines of Vina was sold off to Lodi winemakers and the vines themselves uprooted. A few more years and the ranch itself had been dispersed by sale. After passing through different hands, the central part of the old ranch, including the vast cellar, with its two-foot-thick walls of brick, was sold to the Trappist monks in 1955; now they cultivate their gardens in silence there, at Our Lady of New Clairvaux.[45]

To judge from a number of the published accounts of Stanford's "failure" at Vina, their writers take a barely concealed satisfaction in the thought of a very rich man's inability to buy what he wanted. The Vina Ranch was in fact a double disappointment for Stanford, for he had meant it not only to produce fine wines but to be an inheritance for his beloved son, Leland, Jr., whose early death in 1884, at the very moment when the great vineyard plantings were going on at Vina, must have taken the heart out of the enterprise for the father.

But if the story invites some threadbare moralizing, it did not discourage other men of wealth from venturing on the chances of winemaking. Nothing so grandiose has since been attempted by an individual in California, but the record of late nineteenth-century winemaking in the state is studded with the names of the rich, the fashionable, and the powerful. Two of Stanford's fellow millionaires and fellow senators owned extensive vineyards and made wine: the Irishman James G. Fair—now remembered for his Fairmont Hotel in San Francisco—at his Fair

Ranch in Sonoma County, and George Hearst, father of William Randolph, at the Madrone Vineyard in Glen Ellen, Sonoma County.[46] In Napa, the Finnish sea captain Gustave Niebaum, made rich from the traffic in Arctic furs, bought the Watson vineyard, called Inglenook, near Rutherford, in 1879 and proceeded to make of it not merely a model winery but a successful model. Niebaum could afford to take his time, being a wealthy man, and wisely did so, with distinguished results. Not until after he had had a chance to study the subject in Europe did he make his decisions. He chose superior varieties, constructed a state-of-the-art winery, and put the work in the hands of experts. The results were excellent, and were quickly recognized as such.[47] In the Livermore Valley Julius Paul Smith, with a fortune derived from the California borax trade, made a speciality of fine winegrowing at his Olivina Vineyard; like Stanford, Smith had visited Europe to study its vineyards and wines; unlike Stanford, he chose a site that rewarded his expectations. Olivina Vineyard wines had a great success in New York, where Smith opened a large cellar.[48]

Smith had two prosperous neighbors who also took up winegrowing: at his estate of Ravenswood, south of Livermore, the San Francisco Democratic boss Christopher Buckley—the "Blind White Devil," as Kipling tells us he was called[49]—amused his intervals of rest from the implacable wars of city politics by making wine from his 100 acres of grapes.[50] At the Gallegos Winery, in nearby Irvington, Juan Gallegos, a wealthy coffee planter from Costa Rica, built a winegrowing enterprise on a large scale, and had the technical assistance of the distinguished Professor Eugene Hilgard of the university. The Gallegos vineyards, of 600 acres, incorporated the old vineyard of Mission San Jose from the days of the Franciscans. When the Gallegos Winery was destroyed by the great earthquake of 1906, it had become a million-gallon property.[51]

Far away in the south of the state, General George Stoneman, Civil War hero and governor of California, set out a large vineyard and built a winery in the early 1870s at his magnificent estate of Los Robles, near Pasadena (or the Indiana Colony, as it then was); another governor, John Downey, joined with the banker Isaias Hellman in developing their winemaking property in Cucamonga.[52] Downey, it will be remembered, was the governor who had appointed Haraszthy a state viticultural commissioner in 1861. Just south of Los Angeles, Remi Nadeau, once mayor of Los Angeles, developed a mammoth vineyard of over 2,000 acres beginning in the early 1880s; poor Nadeau committed suicide in 1887, and the vineyard property seems to have gone into residential subdivisions in the land boom that swept over southern California in that year. Not, however, before a winery, an "immense affair" according to contemporary description, was built to receive the expected flow of grapes from the Mission, Zinfandel, Trousseau, and Malvoisie vines on the property.[53] Nadeau's was not only the largest but the last moneyed plunge into winegrowing in Los Angeles County.

Winegrowing on a big scale was undertaken not only by wealthy individuals but by stock companies, after the earlier model of the Buena Vista Vinicultural Society. The most notable of such attempts in the eighties was that of the Natoma Vineyard, near Folsom in Sacramento County, the property of the Natoma Land and Water Company, itself one of the enterprises of Charles Webb Howard, one of California's baronial landowners. The company first experimented with different varieties, and then began planting vineyards on its land in 1883; by the end of the decade, it had 1,600 acres of wine grapes and had built a winery of 300,000 gallons' capacity. The operation was self-contained and tightly organized: a foreman's house and barns were provided for each 400 acres of vines, and at the winery itself, at the center of the property, there were houses for the superintendent, an accountant, and their families.[54] The expert George Husmann, writing in 1887, declared that the Natoma Vineyard was the most exciting development in California, "a most striking illustration of the rapid advance of the viticultural interests in the state,"[55] and an influence for the general improvement of the industry through its experiments with different varieties suited to California. The original mover and shaker of the project, Horatio Livermore, left in 1885, however, and his plans were not carried through as originally drawn up. The California wine trade had entered into its long depression, and by 1896 the company had leased its vineyards to other operators.[56]

Italian Swiss Colony and the Italian Contribution

Another sort of big-scale enterprise begun in California in the eighties recalled earlier experiments like that at Anaheim, but with considerable difference. Andrea Sbarboro was a native of Genoa who had arrived in this country in 1850, aged twelve, and earned prosperity by organizing building and loan societies in California. As a way to help his fellow-countrymen in the state, he had the idea of creating a large grape-growing business on the principle of the savings and loan society. The original investments would be made by capitalists who could afford them, but the workers would, through payroll deductions, acquire shares in the company and could, if they liked, convert their property into land. Sbarboro's intention was to provide steady, dignified work for the many Italians who had arrived in San Francisco in large numbers and sunk to the bottom of the labor pool. No doubt, as a prudent man of business, Sbarboro hoped to make money, but as a student of the many cooperative experiments of the nineteenth century, and as a devoted reader of John Ruskin and Robert Owen, Sbarboro also hoped to create a work of genuine social philanthropy. Thus the Italian Swiss Colony was born (there were originally a few Swiss from Ticino in the affair, but it very soon became exclusively Italian).[57]

The first steps went well. In 1881 a company was formed, and 1,500 acres of hill and valley were bought far north in Sonoma County, near Cloverdale. Here, in a village called Asti after the Piedmont town famous for its wines, the workers were settled and planting began in 1882. Workers were easy to recruit, for the company gave good terms: $30 to $40 a month, plus room, board, and as much wine as a man could decently drink. Preference was given, according to the bylaws, to Italians or Swiss who had become U.S. citizens or who had declared their intention of becoming citizens: this was to be a permanent community.[58] Two developments, however, soon altered the original purposes. The first was that the Italian workers wanted no part of Sbarboro's investment scheme. The proposal to deduct $5 each month from their wages looked to them like financial trickery. Suspicious to a man, they all refused to participate. Thus, as a company publication put it some years later, "they rejected the future that their more sagacious fellow-countrymen had planned."[59] The Italian Swiss Colony had, therefore, to be carried on like any other joint stock company, though it continued to be marked by a strong paternalistic tendency. A second change in the original purposes came about through the collapse of the market in 1886. The idea of an Italian Swiss Colony specializing in grape growing had been formed when wine grapes were bringing $30 a ton; by 1887, when the first substantial tonnage appeared, the price was $8, not enough to meet the costs of production. The directors determined that the colony would enter the wine business itself and authorized the construction of a 300,000-gallon winery. By these steps the cooperative vineyard of Sbarboro's original vision became an integrated winemaking company.[60]

By very careful management, and by the severe discipline of paying no dividends for its first sixteen years, the Italian Swiss Colony gradually made its way. It was lucky in its officers: Sbarboro continued to take a close personal interest in the work; Charles Kohler, the dean of California wine merchants, was a shareholder and a member of the company's auditing committee; Dr. Paolo de Vecchi, the vice president, was a highly successful San Francisco surgeon; the president and general manager was Pietro Rossi, a graduate in pharmacy of the University of Turin. Despite the phylloxera then spreading through California, they managed to develop extensive vineyards, as well as coping with the wild fluctuations of an unstable wine market. When the company at last had its wine ready, the California dealers' best price was a derisory seven cents a gallon. Rossi responded by organizing the company's own agencies in order to reach the eastern markets.[61] They were able to ship in quantity to New York, New Orleans, and Chicago—the three cities where the still very restricted American wine market was concentrated. Before long, Italian Swiss Colony wines were being sent to foreign markets as well, through agents in South America, China, Japan, England, Germany, Switzerland, Belgium, Denmark, Norway, and Sweden. The New York branch held stocks of a million gallons. The company did a good trade in altar wines. And it industriously collected prizes and awards at expositions around the world, to be displayed on its labels.[62]

By the turn of the century, the Asti premises were the largest source of table wine in California, and the huge wine cistern—500,000 gallons' capacity—that Sbarboro had had built to hold the bumper vintage of 1897 in order to keep it off the market had become one of the tourist wonders of California.[63] By 1910 the vineyards of the Italian Swiss Colony extended over 5,000 acres, including properties at Madera, Kingsburg, Selma, and Lemoore in the Central Valley in addition to the original Sonoma plantings. Company literature boasted that there were more superior varieties of grape grown at Asti than anywhere else in the United States, and certainly the winery poured out a profusion of kinds: Italian Swiss varietals included zinfandel, carignane, mataro, barbera, cabernet, pinot, riesling, pinot blanc, and sauvignon blanc. The company developed a sparkling moscato, and distilled large quantities of both brandy and grappa. Its banner wine, familiar in all American markets, was its "Tipo," sold in imitation chianti *fiaschi* in both red and white varieties.[64]

The shareholders who endured the long years of profitless operation were finally well rewarded. The company's winery capacity in 1910 had reached 14,250,000 gallons, and the stock, originally worth around $150,000, was now valued at $3,000,000 and would continue to grow.[65] Sbarboro and Rossi both built handsome "villas" at Asti, which they used as summer retreats, from which they could survey their work—the winery, the village houses, cooper's shop, post office, school, railroad station, and church—the latter built in the shape of a barrel among the vineyards. Sbarboro could, with pardonable pride, look on the evidence of a success rather different from, but probably far greater than, anything he had imagined back in 1881. Unluckily, he had also the misfortune of living long enough to see the catastrophe of the Eighteenth Amendment, which wiped out all the results of his philanthropic labor. Sbarboro was one of the first among the leaders of California winemaking to perceive the threat of prohibition, and he became a leading publicist in the national campaign for wine and temperance. He had the bitter fulfillment of seeing all that he had worked for fail.

It is not necessary by this point to repeat that the growth of winemaking in this country was the work of a wide variety of different immigrant communities; but the success of the Italian Swiss Colony reminds us that the Italians were a relatively new element. There had been Philip Mazzei in eighteenth-century Virginia, but he seems to have had no successors, or at least none who left a record. That changed very quickly now. Italian immigration to the United States had formed only one half of one percent of the total immigration in the decade of the Civil War. By 1881–90 it had increased more than tenfold, and in the next decade it tripled again. Much of this tide came to California. The Italians were all the more welcome after the Oriental Exclusion Act of 1882 shut off the flow of Chinese labor to the vineyards and wineries of the state.

Though it can be given only incidental mention, the Chinese contribution to California wine deserves more than that; it is, however, largely undocumented, and so much of it is lost to history. What can be said is that in the thirty years between their first immigration in 1852, when they were sent to the gold mines or to the railroad embankments, and the Exclusion Act of 1882, they were widely used in the California wine industry, from vineyard to warehouse. Scattered remarks in print attest this, and a few old prints and photos show Chinese at work in vineyard and press house, but no connected account of the Chinese in California winegrowing

92 | A Chinese worker tends the receiving bin for grapes at the Fair Oaks Winery in Pasadena. Chinese workers appear to have been as much a part of the winemaking scene in the south as in the north of the state. (Huntington Library)

has yet been put together.[66] As early as 1862 Colonel Haraszthy was employing Chinese labor at Buena Vista and defending his practice against an already strong public hostility.[67] In the south, as we have seen already, J. De Barth Shorb had discovered the virtues of Chinese labor in his vineyards by 1869; his neighbor and rival L. J. Rose had followed Shorb's lead in using Chinese labor by 1871,[68] and thereafter one may reasonably suppose that they were a standard part of southern California winemaking as they already were in the north. Perhaps the best-known picture of winemaking in nineteenth-century California, the drawing made by Paul Frenzeny in 1878, has as one of the most prominent parts of its design the figures of Chinese coolies bringing in baskets of grapes from the field and treading them out over redwood vats.[69]

To return to the Italians, the earliest of them in California winemaking were very early indeed: the Splivalo Vineyard and Winery in San Jose went back to 1853, though Splivalo did not acquire it until the late fifties. Earliest of all, perhaps, was Andrea Arata, who planted his Amador County vineyard in 1853. These were isolated instances, however.[70] And when there was a considerable Italian immigration to California, few of the newly arrived Italians were in a position to set themselves up independently—a fact to which Sbarboro's cooperative scheme of the Italian Swiss Colony had been a response. The fate of most who went on the land, then, was to labor in the fields. There were exceptions: Vincent Picchetti was in business in Cupertino by 1877, Placido Bordi at the same place in 1881;[71] but it was not until the late eighties that Italian names began appearing with any regularity among the proprietors. In the south, Giovanni Demateis founded his winery at San Gabriel in 1888; Giovanni Piuma his in Los Angeles in 1889; Secondo Guasti opened his Los Angeles winery in 1894.[72] In the Central Valley two wineries founded in the 1880s followed the expansive tendencies of that region by growing to a great scale: the Bisceglia brothers at Fresno, who opened in 1888, eventually built their enterprise to a capacity of eight million gallons; Andrew Mattei at Malaga, near Fresno, processed the yield of some 1,200 acres of vineyard.[73] In the north, Bartholomew Lagomarsino was established in Sonoma County; G. Migliavacca was one of the earliest of all, for he set up as a winemaker in Napa in 1866.[74]

Though they were beginning to make an important contribution to California winegrowing before the nineteenth century was over, the Italians were far from dominating the scene, as they have sometimes seemed to do since Repeal. Certainly one would get that impression from the fiction and drama written about the families who make wine in California: the writers almost all choose Italians as their image of the California winegrower.[75] The French family Rameau in Alice Tisdale Hobart's *The Cup and the Sword* is a rare exception. Perhaps it is true that the Italians were more loyal to the vine than any other group during the trying times of Prohibition, so that the names that first came forth on the morning of Repeal were those of the faithful Italians: Rossi, Petri, Martini, Gallo, Cribari, Vai. But the prominence of Italian names on the winemaking scene of California is an effect of our particular perspective. To an observer of the California industry at the moment when Prohibition shut it down, its character would have been thoroughly mixed, perhaps a little more evidently European than most American institutions, with its many Beringers, Schrams, Lefrancs, Gallegoses, Niebaums, and Sbarboros, but not clearly dominated by any one of these nationalities and not excluding an abundance of people with names like Tubbs, Baldwin, Dalton, and Keyes. If I were to make a guess on the question (and it would be something more than a guess), I would say that there were more growers and winemakers of German descent, both in California and in the rest of the country, than of any other origin before Prohibition.

Communal Organizations and Winegrowing

The traditional link between religious communities and winegrowing went back to the beginnings of California, when the missions introduced the art and mystery of wine. It is interesting to note that one, at least, of the old mission vine-

93   Leader of the Brotherhood of the New Life, Thomas Lake Harris (1823–1906) founded wine-growing communities in both New York and California. Their produce was, he held, not mere wine but the divine breath of God. At Fountain Grove, outside Santa Rosa, the Brotherhood developed a major winery that prospered even after Harris, the founder, had been driven from California. (Columbia University Library)

yards was brought back about this time, in the eighties, when California wine-growing had entered on a new order of importance. Under the patronage of the archbishop, Father Kaiser at Mission San Jose began making wine for the church from the vines still growing at the Mission.[76] But, as wine had never been an important part of the economic life of the missions originally, neither was it to be so now. For some latter-day religious communities, however, it *was* to be important—most notably for a strange melange of diverse people brought together on the basis of an equally strange compound of mystical principles and calling themselves the Brotherhood of the New Life. The founder, Thomas Lake Harris, was English-born, but brought up in the "burnt-over" region of upstate New York, the most fertile source of new religious growth in the whole United States. Harris gradually pieced together all sorts of elements—Swedenborgian, Universalist, Spiritualist—into a new rule of life and attracted to himself a small community to carry out the practices of his invention: the members included Englishmen, Yankees, Southerners, even a few Japanese. Among the Englishmen was Laurence Oliphant, a writer and traveller of some fame, who had once sat in the British Parliament. With his wife, he brought a good deal of money into Harris's community.[77]

The New Life began in Dutchess County, New York, in 1861, first at a village called Wassaic, and then in the town of Amenia, where, it is said, winemaking was the business of the community. Since the Brotherhood were there only four years, their winemaking cannot have progressed very far. In 1867 Harris moved the community to Brocton, on the shores of Lake Erie, in Chautauqua County, New York, where he had purchased some 1,200 acres. This was the era of the grape craze in the East, and of expansionist activity in the winegrowing industry of the Lake Erie region. Harris decided to join the action, or, as he put it, to devote the community to "the manufacture and sale of pure, native wine, made especially for medicinal purposes."[78] For this was not to be just ordinary wine. The community's produce would share in the special virtues of its religious practice: the wine of the New Life was infused with the divine aura and opened the drinker to the creative breath of God Himself. More prosaically, Harris meant to make wine from the Salem grape, one of the hybrids produced by E. S. Rogers, in which Harris had put his faith and his money, for he had paid for the rights to grow it.[79] One wonders whether he chose this grape for the sake of its winemaking qualities or for its religious name? His "New Found Salem Wine," as it was called, did not prove entirely satisfactory, however (though whether on divine or merely sensuous grounds is not clear), and the Brotherhood at Brocton soon tried other varieties as well as the Salem. Harris himself kept a vineyard at his house, called Vine Cliff, where he could experiment with different varieties. Meantime, in 1869, he sold all of his stock of Salem vines to a Lockport nurseryman.

In his work at Brocton, Harris had the advantage of good help. A Dr. J. S. Hyde, from Missouri, was his wine expert, assisted for a time by a Dr. Martin, from Georgia. Another member, Rensselaer Moore, who came from the grape-growing Iona Island in the Hudson, understood the propagating and growing of vines. Between them, these men made a success of the community's venture. By 1870, only three years after their move to Brocton, the small community—it numbered between 75 and 100 members—had a vintage of 15,000 gallons and had built a solid masonry underground storage vault a hundred feet long.[80] The winemaking enterprise was called the Lake Erie and Missouri River Wine Company, though why it had that name is not clear.[81] Perhaps Hyde's Missouri origins were thus indicated, or perhaps they used Missouri wines in their own production?

No sooner were things running smoothly at Brocton than Harris decided to move to California, probably for the same reason that urges people today to leave the wintry shores of Lake Erie for the Pacific Coast, though Harris gave religious reasons as well. In any case, in 1875 he bought 400 acres of land just north of Santa

Rosa (where Luther Burbank arrived in the same year), named the property Fountain Grove, and set about to develop it. The community at Brocton continued to operate, selling its wine to a New York firm using the "Brotherhood" label until the gradual shift to California was complete.[82] Not all the New Yorkers went to California, but the Brocton establishment was wound up in 1881.

At first the California colony supported itself by dairying, but vines were soon planted and by 1883, when Harris hoped for a vintage of fifteen to twenty thousand gallons, the entire estate had been concentrated on winegrowing.[83] From this point on Fountain Grove prospered. By continued purchase Harris ultimately enlarged the property to about 2,000 acres, of which 400 were in vines, and nearly as many more in orchards. The winery, brick-built, three stories high, steam heated, and scientifically equipped, had a capacity of 600,000 gallons, and production grew rapidly to use that capacity: 70,000 gallons were made in 1886; 200,000 in 1888.[84] The winemaking remained under the charge of Dr. Hyde, who had accompanied Harris west from New York. The vineyards grew good varieties—including, it is said, Pinot Noir, Cabernet, and Zinfandel—and red table wine was the staple product. This was sold mainly in the East, through a New York agency that included a wine house, restaurant, and bar at 56 Vesey Street. The winery even published its own illustrated journal, the *Fountain Grove Wine Press*. So far as I know this is the first example of a house journal or newsletter in the American wine industry.[85]

Harris, who held the title to all this property, lived in something like splendor compared to the provincial standards of Sonoma County in those days. His house, of many rooms, was finished in fine woods, ornamented with stained glass, and surrounded by gardens and fountains. It also contained what a contemporary described as "perhaps the most extensive library in northern California," where Harris could play at science and poetry.[86] The other members of the community lived in two buildings, men in the "Commandery" and women in the "Familistery."

Though Fountain Grove prospered, no one so striking and controversial as Harris could expect to lead a tranquil life, especially not when he propounded sexual theories that could only scandalize a California farm community in the 1880s. Harris taught that God is bisexual, and that everyone, man and woman, has a celestial counterpart with whom to seek eternal marriage. Unluckily, the counterpart is elusive: it may move from one body to another, and in any case it is hard to know for sure where it dwells, and when. Yet the main business of life is to find one's counterpart. Hunting the counterpart, then, looked to outsiders like simple promiscuity, never mind about the celestial sanctions. It did not help the reputation of Fountain Grove that the partners in civil marriage were supposed to be celibate, since civil marriage did not, except by the rarest accident, bring together genuine counterparts. And Harris, a copious writer who set up a printing press at Fountain Grove before a wine press, put forth stuff about how the world is filled with tiny fairies who live in the bosoms of women and sing heavenly harmonies inaudible to worldly ears. It is no wonder that rumors grew until scandal broke. It is perhaps more remarkable that Harris stayed on at Fountain Grove so long as he did. At last in 1892, urged by newspaper furor, he left for England, never to return to Fountain Grove.[87]

In 1900, six years before his death, Harris sold out to a small group of the faithful, including Kanaye Nagasawa, a Japanese variously styled baron or prince, who had been one of the earliest converts to the New Life and one of Harris's closest assistants.[88] Nagasawa kept the winery and vineyards until his death in 1934, after which they passed into other hands and at last expired in 1951. The Fountain Grove label was purchased by a neighboring winery and may still be seen on bottles of California wine, but it is not what it was.[89] The estate itself has been eaten away by the city of Santa Rosa, and so this phase of the New Life, at any rate, has returned to the spirit.

While Fountain Grove's wine business was developing, another Sonoma County community, some distance to the north, almost within sight of the Italian Swiss Colony at Asti, had been founded on the basis of communistic winegrowing. This was the Icaria Speranza commune, and its example completes the sequence of communal groups that chose winegrowing as a way to realize the dream of self-fulfillment in a new land. The Huguenots, the German Pietists, and the Rappites were seeking religious freedom; the French in Alabama and the Germans in Missouri were seeking to transplant a European culture intact; the colonists of Anaheim and Asti were looking for simple economic sufficiency. The Icarians of Cloverdale were looking, in a way, to combine all of these things.

They were a secular group, but professed the religion of True Christianity; they were communists but not political, preferring to change the world by the force of good example; they taught universal brotherhood, but required the ability to read and speak fluent French for membership.[90] Their roots in this country went back to 1848, when a group of Frenchmen, inspired by the utopian communism of Etienne Cabet revealed in his *Voyage en Icarie*, arrived in Texas to create a model community. They soon migrated to Illinois, then to Iowa, suffering dissension, schism, and material hardship along the way.[91] The California venture was a last gasp in the struggle that had begun over thirty years earlier for the original Icarians. Armand Dehay, an idealistic barber associated with the Iowa community, led the way to California, where in 1881 he purchased 885 acres along the Russian River three miles south of Cloverdale and at once began laying out a vineyard of Zinfandel grapes. The Icarians, good Frenchmen all, had planted a Concord vineyard during their sojourn in Iowa, and the main hope of the California colony was to make viticulture the basis of independence.

The times were propitious—the Italian Swiss Colony venture began the same year, inspired by the same expansive market for grapes—and the Icarians, consisting of a few families only, began work with good hope. In one year's time they had 45 acres in vines, and were planning a distillery as well as a winery. In 1884 they were joined by a further migration from the Iowa colony, raising their numbers to about fifty-five people. They held their property in common, but they lived their lives in fairly usual fashion. In the main house they met to dine and to enjoy their social occasions, but the different families lived in separate dwellings rather than in some regulated communal arrangement.[92]

Their luck soon ran out. They had counted on the sale of their Iowa property to meet their California debts but ran into legal trouble and got nothing; they lacked both labor and money to carry out the developments that their scheme required; and finally, as had happened to the Italian Swiss colonists too, when they at last had a grape harvest to sell, they had nobody to buy it. The writing on the wall was clear by 1886; in 1887 the society could not meet its debts and was dissolved, the property passing to the ownership of some of the individual colonists, several of whom remained to tend the vineyards and make wine as small proprietors rather than as the communitarians they had hoped to be.[93] Armand Dehay, the prime mover of the group, was one of those who remained; with his brother he grew grapes and made wine at the Icaria Winery. Thus the three different community experiments made within a few years and a few miles of one another in Sonoma County—the Fountain Grove Brotherhood, the Italian Swiss colonists, and the Icarians—all failed to reach their spiritual or political goals. They all succeeded at viticulture, however.

Winegrowing in Sonoma County: A Model of the Whole

Winemaking had been tried by almost every imaginable sort of person or agency in nineteenth-century California—rich men, poor men, large companies and small companies, Godless cooperatives and religious communities. But the standard remained the relatively small independent grower, more likely to be tending a vineyard of ten or twenty acres than of a hundred or more. These were the people who had been attracted into the industry in the sixties and seventies, and not many of them would have moved beyond their modest beginnings into anything very large or impressive. As George Husmann wrote in 1887:

> We have thousands, perhaps the large majority of our wine growers . . . who are comparatively poor men, many of whom have to plant their vineyards, nay, even clear the land for them with their own hands, make their first wine in a wooden shanty with a rough lever press, and work their way up by slow degrees to that competence which they hope to gain by the sweat of their brow.[94]

To get an idea of the character of California winegrowing in the eighties one may look in some detail at the scene in a particular region. Sonoma County, a larger and more diverse winegrowing region than any other of the north coastal counties, provides a rich source, a sample of which will provide the flavor of the whole.

The king of Sonoma County in those days was Isaac De Turk, of Santa Rosa, who came to California from Indiana in 1858, began planting vines in 1862, and a quarter of a century later presided over the biggest business in Santa Rosa: his winery had a capacity of a million gallons, and took up an entire block along the railroad tracks on the west side of town, where, the historian reports, it was "no uncommon thing to see a train load of cars leave his warehouse loaded with wine for Chicago, St. Louis or New York."[95] "Claret" was De Turk's great speciality, made from the Zinfandel for which Sonoma was already famous. Other wineries in the state bought their claret from De Turk to sell under their own labels.[96] His standing in the industry was recognized by his appointment to the original State Board of Viticultural Commissioners in 1880.

At the other extreme from De Turk's large, factory-scale enterprise were great numbers of individual farmers, still unspecialized, who grew grapes among other crops and who perhaps made wine themselves or sold their crops to nearby wineries. Such farmers were scattered all over Sonoma County and represent hundreds of others like them to be found up and down California. These are typical descriptions: Joseph Wilson, near Santa Rosa, had "forty-five acres . . . devoted to the cultivation of wine grapes of the Zinfandel and Grey Riesling varieties. . . . Twelve acres are planted with apples, pears, cherries, and plums. . . . The rest of his land is devoted to hay and grain." John Laughlin, of Mark West Creek, had "twenty acres of orchard, twelve acres of wine and table grapes, and seventy acres of alfalfa." Edward Surrhyne, in the Vine Hill district west of Santa Rosa, tended a little of everything. His orchard grew peaches, pears, apples, prunes, "and other fruit." He had fifty acres of grapes, including Zinfandel and something called Ferdeges for wine, which he made on his own property.[97]

A few of these farmers, incidentally, were women: Mrs. Eliza Hood, widow of the Scotsman William Hood, ran the Los Guilicos Ranch, including its winery and 100 acres of vines; Mrs. Ellen Stuart presided over the Glen Ellen Ranch at the little town named for her, Glen Ellen, where her neighbor Mrs. Kate Warfield operated the Ten Oaks Ranch. Both of these ranches included grape growing and wine-making in their activity.[98]

In between De Turk's huge enterprise and the domestic operations of the Sonoma farmers, there were a number of substantial wineries going back to the days of Haraszthy's Buena Vista in the 1860s. Buena Vista was now much decayed, but others were prospering. Jacob Gundlach, for example, made highly regarded wines on his Rhinefarm, neighboring Buena Vista, and sold them through wine vaults in San Francisco and New York. At Glen Ellen the pioneer Los Angeles wine man, Charles Kohler, had made a showplace of his Tokay Vineyard and winery, producing all kinds of wine on a large scale for sale through his own agencies.[99]

Most striking of all in the survey of Sonoma's winegrowing industry as it stood in 1889 is the mix of nationalities, which contains most of the elements already identified in California's history. There were Italians other than those at the Italian Swiss Colony: the Simi brothers, whose winery still operates today, had set up at Healdsburg in 1881; not far away, and beginning in the same year, the brothers Peter and Julius Gobbi ran their Sotoyome Winery; at Windsor, to the south, B. Arata had settled in 1884 and set out a vineyard of 18 acres (he was, like the

Simi brothers, from Genoa, and like so many Genoese he had been a sailor; now he tended Zinfandels in the valley of the Russian River).[100] There were, rather unusually, several Englishmen in the business. Thomas Winter, a sailor originally from Nottingham, raised vines on his ranch on Dry Creek. Near Sonoma, Thomas Glaister, a north countryman from Cumberland, after episodes in Chicago, New York, and Australia, had built up an estate including 150 acres of vines and a winery of 100,000 gallons' capacity specializing in white wine. Another native of Nottinghamshire, John Champion, raised grapes near Cloverdale and also managed the Gunn Winery near Windsor, a small new property owned by an absentee proprietor. Earliest of the Englishmen was John Gibson, a Kentishman, who settled in the Sonoma Valley in 1856, planted a vineyard, built a winery, and operated a hotel halfway between the towns of Sonoma and Santa Rosa.[101]

There was a higher than usual proportion of French to be found too. The little community at Icaria has already been described, and it may be that it was attracted to the county in part by the example of the French growers and winemakers already established there. The first to come was Camille Aguillon, the son of a winemaker from the Basse Alpes. Aguillon had been drawn to California by the Gold Rush, but worked mostly as a gardener before making his way to the town of Sonoma. He planted no vineyard, but instead specialized in making wine in a building on the town plaza; it eventually became the town's largest—"Aguillon's famous winery," Frona Wait calls it.[102] Next was the Alsatian George Bloch, who made the transition from a restaurant in San Francisco to a vineyard at Dry Creek in Sonoma in 1870. With another Frenchman, Alexander Colson, Bloch founded the small Dry Creek Winery in 1872. Bloch continued to operate it after Colson left the partnership in 1884, when with his brother John he founded a winery, also on Dry Creek, called Colson Brothers. The brothers were from the Department of Haute Saône, the sons of a *vigneron* and winemaker. Jean Chauvet, a native of Champagne, had been settled near Glen Ellen since 1856 but did not begin winemaking until 1875; by 1888 he was producing 175,000 gallons, making him one of the major individual producers in the county. In the same year that the Colson brothers built their winery, another pair of French brothers, Auguste and N. C. Drayeur, natives of Lorraine, opened their "Two Brothers Wine Store Vaults" in Healdsburg. Like Aguillon, they grew no grapes but selected from the local vineyards. Finally, there was Jean Baptiste Trapet, a native of the Côte d'Or brought up in viticulture; he had a five-year adventure in California in the 1850s but returned to France, lived as a vine grower, and served on the town council of Beaune. The phylloxera drove him back to California in 1877, where he settled as a neighbor of the other Frenchmen in the Dry Creek region, growing his own vines and making his own wine.[103]

Despite the presence of the French, English, and Italians, Sonoma County was in the first generation after Haraszthy preeminently a region of Germans. Gundlach has already been mentioned. To his one might add a long list of good German names, many of them borne by men who had come from the winegrowing regions

94 The Geyserville Winery of Julius Stamer and B. W. Feldmeyer, proudly flying the American flag in token of its owners' identity as American citizens. Stamer, the winemaker, came from Hamburg; Feldmeyer, from Oldenburg, was a carpenter. The two men met in St. Helena in the early 1880s and founded their Sonoma County winery in 1884. Producing dry red and white wines only, with a capacity of 75,000 gallons, the winery typifies the industry in Sonoma at the end of the nineteenth century. (From *Illustrated History of Sonoma County* [1889])

of the old country. Conrad Haehl, for example, of the Mount Vineyard and Winery near Cloverdale, though not German-born, was the son of a Bavarian winegrower. George Friedrich Fischer, who operated a small vineyard and winery south of the town of Sonoma, came from Baden, where he had been the winemaker on the family farm. Charles Knust, owner of the Sulphur Creek Vineyard and Winery near Cloverdale, though born in Hamburg, learned the wine business along the Rhine before emigrating to America. Conrad Wagele, who cultivated twenty acres of grapes and made his own wine in the Dry Creek region, came, like George Fischer, from Baden. But it was not necessary to have that sort of background, and more often than not the Sonoma Germans did not. They included Frank Bohlin, a Hanoverian who managed the Stegeman Winery at Cloverdale; Henry Weyl, a cooper from Bingen (close enough to winemaking), who owned a vineyard in the county; Charles Lehn, of Frankfurt-am-Main, who grew grapes and made wine near Windsor; Ernst Rufus, one of the very early settlers in Sonoma (he was imprisoned with Vallejo during the bumbling Bear Flag Revolt) came from Württemberg and ended his days as a vineyardist; Charles Schnittger, another of the Dry Creek vineyardists, came from Hanover, as did L. Michaelson in the Alexander Valley; the proprietors of the Geyserville Winery were Julius Stamer, of Hamburg, and B. W. Feldmeyer, of Oldenburg—they too grew their grapes on Dry Creek; finally, one may add another Dry Creek German, though this one was in fact a Swiss—Charles Dunz, a native of the canton of Berne, the proprietor of the Laurel Hill Vineyard and Winery.[104]

According to the directory of winegrowers and winemakers compiled by the Board of State Viticultural Commissioners in 1891, there were some 736 vineyard proprietors in Sonoma County in that year. By far the greater part of them were growers only, but 118 growers made wine as well, in quantities varying from a few thousand to hundreds of thousands of gallons each year, the average running perhaps to around 15,000 gallons.[105] Individual, small-scale, unspecialized in the midst of a general agricultural economy: that was the character of the winegrowing trade in Sonoma County in the eighties, and by and large that was its character in the state as a whole.

13

California: Growing Pains and Growing Up

Organizations and State Support: The Board of State Viticultural Commissioners

T he earliest organizations of winegrowers in California were essentially *ad hoc,* the *hoc* almost invariably being some question of taxes or tariffs. The first such group was formed at the end of 1862 as the "California Wine-Growers' Association"; its objects included general "encouragement" to the industry and "discouragement" of the adulterating of California wines, but its real business was to protest a new federal tax on domestic wine and to ask for tariff protection against imported wine. After its first flurry of activity, the association quickly languished, and it was dead within a year.[1] It was galvanized back to life in 1866 by the renewed threat of a tax on domestic wine. The association sent a lobbyist to Washington and, whether for that reason or not, the tax bill did not pass.[2] A satellite group in Los Angeles was also created in 1866; this had life enough in it to survive through at least the next three years, for it met in 1869 to protest against new regulations for the collection of taxes.[3]

In 1872 another and more sustained effort to establish a statewide society began with the creation of the cumbersomely named California Vine Growers' and Wine and Brandy Manufacturers' Association. B. D. Wilson, of the Lake Vineyard in the San Gabriel Valley, was president, the headquarters were in Sacramento, and the state gave the society official recognition by a grant of $1,000.[4] The society—its name soon shortened to a tolerable length as the California State Vinicultural Society—was more than a protest group: it held an annual fair, set up a committee on the cultivation of the vine, and called its officers to regular meetings.[5] But its

341

activity was most notable when it came to the old questions of taxes and tariffs. A sharp flurry broke out in 1878 when the French proposed a trade treaty with the United States and the Californians took alarm: preferential treatment for French wines would spell doom for them, they argued through the society, and meetings of protest were held up and down the state.[6]

There were also local bodies of growers and winemakers organized in counties that had established a viticultural industry. A "Grape-Growers' Association" was formed by the farmers of Napa, Solano, and Sonoma counties as early as 1870. The Santa Clara growers also organized early.[7] But these were groups whose work was strictly local and largely devoted to the technical problems of production.

The pressure of demand for an official body to direct and assist the California wine industry as a whole grew intense towards the end of 1879. The crop had been short that year, sending prices up. At the same time, when the prospects of wine-growing in Europe looked hopelessly bleak owing to the ravages of phylloxera, the future of California as winegrower to the world looked more glamorous than had ever been imagined before. The feeling of the period is conveyed in this prophecy by the respected grower and winemaker H. W. Crabb, proprietor of the To Kalon Vineyard in Rutherford, Napa County:

> Whoever lives a half a century hence, will find the grapes of California in every city of the Union; her raisins supplying the whole Western hemisphere; her wines in every mart of the globe, and then, with her golden shores, her sunny clime, her vine-clad hills and plains, will California, indeed, be the Vineland of the world.[8]

The economic possibilities of wine took on a new attractiveness in the light of this vision, and politicians began to listen to the promoters. There had been a Committee on the Culture of the Grapevine in the state assembly since 1861; it now began to take information from winegrowers and dealers such as Arpad Haraszthy, son of Agoston and to some extent his father's heir as the leading publicist for California wines; from scientists like Hilgard; from established producers like Krug and De Turk; and from bodies such as the California State Agricultural Society. The upshot was the passage of a bill on 15 April 1880 creating a Board of State Viticultural Commissioners.[9]

The board, which had the very general charge to "promote the viticultural industries of the state," consisted of nine commissioners, one for each of the seven districts into which the state was divided[10] and two for the state at large; the president was selected from among the commissioners, and all served without pay. The prestige of the board was established at once by the original commissioners appointed, for they were all men of high standing in the industry. Arpad Haraszthy was the first president, and his fellow commissioners included Charles Krug, Isaac De Turk, George West, L. J. Rose, and J. De Barth Shorb. The executive officers, who were paid, included a secretary, and, after modification of the original act in 1881, a chief executive officer.

95 — California's rising confidence as a winegrowing region is illustrated by this ebullient frontispiece to E. H. Rixford's *The Wine Press and the Cellar* (San Francisco, 1883). The figure of Liberty pops a cork while the California bear holds his glass to be filled on a barrel whose head displays the state seal. Cases of mission, "pineau," riesling, and zinfandel wine fill the foreground. Rixford, a San Francisco lawyer, had just purchased vineyard property in San Mateo County. His book was evidently the fruit of his study in preparation for becoming a winegrower. The wines that he afterwards produced at his La Questa Vineyard, particularly the cabernet, acquired a high reputation. (California State University, Fresno, Library)

The first urgent business of the board was to meet the problem of phylloxera. The insect had been discovered as early as 1873 in California, in a vineyard near the town of Sonoma.[11] For some reason the winged form of the insect did not regularly develop in California, and so its spread was relatively slow. By 1880, however, growers had to face the fact that they were in serious trouble from phylloxera: some 600 acres of vines had already been destroyed in Sonoma County,[12] and infestations had been found in every other winegrowing region of the state except Los Angeles. For years growers in the afflicted regions had pretended that the

Prepared especially for killing

Squirrels, Gophers, Rats, Ants, Moths,

WEEVILS, PHYLLOXERA, SCALE, LICE, Etc.

Sold by Druggists and dealers in general merchandise.   May also be obtained direct from the manufacturer,

JOHN H. WHEELER.

Manufacturer, also, of Su'phocarbonates, Disinfectants for Vine Cuttings, Diseased Vines, Trees and Plants in general.   Vineyards treated for Phylloxera; Injectors for Bisulphide Sulphur for Vineyards, and all kinds of Fertilizers furnished.

Office, 111 Leidesdorff St., San Francisco.

96 — An advertisement for carbon bisulphide as, among other things, a specific against phylloxera. John H. Wheeler was the first secretary of the Board of State Viticultural Commissioners, and the address given in this advertisement is that of the board. Since the board was then engaged in a search for a remedy for phylloxera, Wheeler's use of his official position for commercial purposes seems highly irregular. But no one seems to have complained. (*Pacific Rural Press*, December 1881)

threat was not serious, or that it was under control, or that it did not exist, or that it would go away by itself. But the time had come when such pretense could no longer be kept up. Now the board acted vigorously. It surveyed the infested areas; it made and published translations of the standard French treatises on reconstituting vineyards after phylloxera attack; it tested the innumerable "remedies" that had been hopefully proposed since the outbreak of the disease in France in 1863.[13] In a very few years, after some dallying with the attractions of carbon bisulphide as a cheap and ready remedy, the board was able to make clear and positive recommendations to California growers. Resistant rootstocks of native American varieties were the only sound solution, just as they were in Europe. In fairness, it should be noted that the University of California experts had earlier come to the same conclusion, so that the board was in effect endorsing a finding made by the university.[14] This was one of several issues in which duplicated work by board and university created jealousies.

Many, perhaps most, vineyardists in California were slow or negligent in acting on the advice given by board and university alike. Fewer than 2,000 acres, it was estimated, had been replanted to resistant rootstock by 1888, while phylloxera continued to spread.[15] In Napa County, for example, even after clear evidence had been provided both of the destructiveness of the affliction and of the certainty of the remedy, one writer estimates that 10,000 acres were destroyed by phylloxera between 1889 and 1892. By 1900 there were only 2,000 bearing acres in Napa, and though the recovery was rapid thereafter, the statistics are interesting evidence of how slow growers were to respond even when they must have known what awaited them if they did nothing.[16]

It was not, however, merely human stubbornness or parsimony that slowed the fight against phylloxera. Though the solution was known in general, much remained to be learned about *what* resistant native stocks should be used, and how they should be matched to varieties and soils. Wetmore and others, without much evidence, recommended the native *V. californica,* but results over a period of years showed this to be a mistake.[17] Later, growers thought Lenoir could be indiscriminately used, and then Rupestris St. George. Finally, California appealed to the U.S. Department of Agriculture, which undertook a program of systematic testing up and down the state, beginning in 1904. The scientist in charge of this work was George C. Husmann, the son of the Missouri pioneer grower George Husmann. How large and difficult the problem to be met was, and how slowly the recovery proceeded, appears from the younger Husmann's report in 1915: at least 250,000 acres of vines had been lost in the preceding decades; worse, only a few had been replanted in the past ten years, and of those, many were still not planted on resistant rootstock.[18]

Though the phylloxera question was the most difficult of the technical questions faced by the Board of State Viticultural Commissioners, their work touched on a number of other things too. It included an extensive program of publication, mostly in translations from the French on such topics as pruning, training, and grafting, and on cellar practices and techniques of vinification; original American contributions on such matters were still rare, though Charles Wetmore did publish a short ampelography (as the scientific description of vines is called) of California for the board.[19] The board opened an experimental cellar in San Francisco in 1886, where tests with different varieties and methods could be made, including experiments with brandy making; and in 1887 it made arrangements for an experimental vineyard in Napa County.[20] The question of varietal selection was given particular attention, as were the related matters of varietal identification and nomenclature—all questions of first importance in California. The board also studied such subjects as the soils and climates of California regions, and advised on the choice of sites.[21]

The board's work towards identifying superior varieties for California and encouraging their planting throws an interesting light on the state of things in the

Make Your Vineyards Permanent.

Resistant Vines the Only Safety.

I OFFER FOR SALE THE FOLLOWING varieties of vines and cuttings, all grown in the State, fresh and healty:

Riparia. Elvira, Taylor, Clinton, M'ssouri Riesling and Uhland, Lenoir. Herbemont, Cynthiana, Norton's Virginia.

Also, rooted vines of the following Vinifera varieties:

Zinfandel. Queen Victoria, Chasselas Rose, Black Burgundy and others.

Price list and circulars sent on application. Address,

GEORGE HUSMANN,

TALCOS VINEYARD, Napa, Cal.

---

97 George Husmann had been brought from Missouri to California to help save the state's vineyards from the ravages of phylloxera, but his words of wisdom contained in this advertisement went unheeded by California vineyardists: "Resistant Vines the Only Safety." Husmann had supplied the French with large quantities of resistant rootstocks from Missouri in their fight against the phylloxera and knew what he was talking about. But by the turn of the century the vineyards of northern California, which might have been made secure, were largely devastated. (*Pacific Rural Press*, 29 December 1883)

early 1880s. We have already seen how French and German growers in the 1850s brought in the major varieties of vinifera; but very few of these, it appears, took hold commercially at the time. Zinfandel caught on in the Bay Area counties, but did not displace the Mission; and the superior white wine varieties seem not to have succeeded at all. The evidence of the trade press and of the exhibitions and wine judgings in the early 1880s is that the Mission remained the dominant variety; Zinfandel was the uncontested leader among grapes regarded as producing fine red wines, and for the whites the Gutedel (Chasselas) was the variety of choice; there was also some of a variety called Riesling, but whether authentic Riesling or not is doubtful, for many varieties have masqueraded under that name.[22]

Comments by two of the leading growers and winemakers, one from Sonoma and one from Napa, make the situation clear. Julius Dresel, writing in 1880 for George Husmann's book on *American Grape Growing and Wine-Making,* stated that the Riesling, Gutedel, and Burger were the leading varieties for white wine; for red, there was only the Zinfandel. H. W. Crabb, the owner of the celebrated To Kalon Vineyard in Napa County and a man who had experimented for years with a vast range of vinifera varieties, affirmed in the same work that the prime white varieties were Riesling, White Pineau (Chenin Blanc?), and Chasselas (Gutedel); as for red wines, he added Black Burgundy (perhaps Pinot Noir) and Charbono to Zinfandel.[23] The varieties that Dresel named were undoubtedly far more familiar than those named by Crabb, but the lists given by both men are notable for the varieties that they fail to name—Cabernet, Syrah, Chardonnay, Semillon, Sauvignon Blanc, and so on.

A few skilled growers—Pierre Pellier and Charles Lefranc in Santa Clara County were notable instances—succeeded in keeping some noble varieties in cultivation. But when Charles Wetmore, as chief executive viticultural officer of the board, reported in 1884 on the state's vineyards, he did not have a very advanced condition of affairs to describe. Not "a single bearing vineyard," he wrote, was "planted systematically with the varieties necessary to reproduce the types of Bordeaux clarets, Burgundies, Sauternes, Hermitage, Portuguese port, Spanish sherry, Madeira, or Cognac."[24] Cabernet, for example, was "only experimentally known here at present"; Pinot Noir was not yet cultivated "in any quantity sufficient to give token of its merits in this State"; Chardonnay was "not practically known to us." Wetmore himself had recently imported Semillon vines but had none for distribution; as for the true sherry varieties, he observed, they "are practically unknown to us, although during the last year some stocks have been imported for trial."[25] And so it went.

Wetmore attributed the failure of earlier importations of the noble varieties to the old Spanish tradition of short pruning—good for heavy-bearing varieties but not for the shy-bearing fine varieties. The early growers, finding that their methods did not succeed with the noble varieties, abandoned them and went back to their proven varieties. But now, in the eighties, the prospects were rapidly changing, and Wetmore wrote with confidence in the future. For one thing, there was a considerable list of experiment with superior varieties: Malbec, Frontignan, Verdelho, Cabernet Sauvignon, Petite Syrah, and Semillon are among those that Wetmore names.[26] And for another, the plantings made since the founding of the board had vastly extended the stock of superior varieties actually available: Wetmore estimated that in four years the state's acreage had tripled, and that most of the increase was accounted for by varieties better than those already growing in California vineyards.[27]

Wetmore's optimism was not wholly mistaken. A decade later, on the occasion of the great Columbian Exposition in Chicago in 1893, the display of California wines showed that many of the varieties practically unknown in 1880 were now

98 | Charles A. Wetmore (1847–1927), journalist, speculator, and winemaker, the founder of Cresta Blanca Winery, was the most energetic and effective member of the Board of State Viticultural Commissioners in the first and most useful decade of its life. (Bancroft Library, University of California)

assimilated into the repertory of the state's production. The varietals exhibited there included Riesling, Semillon, Cabernet, Barbera, Malbec, and Carignane—though still no Chardonnay. The same exhibit also included such astonishing names as a "Chambertin" from J. Gundlach, a "Hermitage" from H. W. Crabb, and a "Chateau Yquem" from Wetmore himself; one may hope that these were made in part at least from Pinot Noir, Petite Syrah, and Semillon. All of those varieties were established in the state by that time.[28]

Carrying out experiments, collecting scientific information, and spreading it to the members of the industry may be thought of as the board's internal affairs. The external affairs lay largely in political and promotional work. The board kept an eye on legislation at both the state and national level, especially on anything that bore on the touchy question of taxation, and took a hand where it could in trying to affect the process of lawmaking. But more and more, as the years passed, the work of the board tended to concentrate on promoting California wine. After the collapse of the market in the late eighties, this was clearly its main job. From the beginning, the board was responsible for an annual state viticultural convention, which was officially intended to be a means for organizing and instructing winegrowers throughout the state, but which had perhaps the even more important function of advertising the winemaking industry widely and regularly. The board also took responsibility for seeing that California wine was represented at international fairs and exhibits—for example, at Antwerp and Louisville in 1885, at London in 1887, Paris in 1889, and Bordeaux in 1895.[29]

The Chicago Columbian Exposition of 1893 has already been mentioned. This was far and away the most splendid American fair held during the active years of the board, and the Californians had high hopes for promoting their wines through the Exposition. They were disappointed. The arrangements for the display of wines were confused; the concession for selling wine went to a man who bought French wine cheaply and prohibited the sale of the California article, and the wine judging satisfied no one. The French withdrew their wine exhibit in anger over the qualification of the jurors, and the matter was settled only by the absurd expedient of giving awards to *all* of the exhibitors, as in the caucus race in *Alice in Wonderland*.[30]

Next year there was a major fair on the Californians' home ground, the Midwinter Exposition in San Francisco, and here things went better. At the Midwinter Exposition the California winemakers erected a "Palace" adorned with plaster statues of Bacchus and Mercury, with an abundance of roccoco twiddles and scallops in plaster, and with tags and verses from a variety of sources and languages: "Hail, California, glory to thee! / Nature's great wonder, noble and free" was one; Martin Luther's "Wer nicht liebt Wein, Weib und Gesang, / Der bleibt ein Narr sein Leben lang" another. Here there were displays of some fifty-two winemakers and merchants, and visitors could sample the wines on display in a *Weinstube* adjoining the Palace. The rules for the wine judging were written by Arpad Haraszthy, and on these terms prizes went to some of the best of California's producers. If the fair did not extend the fame of the exhibitors as the grand show at Chicago might have done, it at least helped to smooth some ruffled feelings.[31]

Two other promotional schemes sponsored by the board may be mentioned. In 1888 it opened a permanent exhibition of California wine in connection with a cafe in downtown San Francisco. The cafe menu offered such exotica as "concombres à la Charles Krug," "pieds de mouton à la Olivina," and "anchois à l'huile de Kohler and Frohling," as well as a choice of any of the wines displayed in the permanent exhibition; they could be drunk with the meal (and what, one wonders, went with the anchovies?) or taken home in any quantity.[32] At the other end of the country, the board hired the celebrated American actress, journalist, and lecturer Kate

Field, the friend of Robert Browning and Anthony Trollope, to give a lecture on California wine in the cities of the East Coast. This she did in the season of 1889, with mixed results. She ran afoul of the temperance movement, already strongly established in this country, and though the board expressed satisfaction with her effort, the arrangement was not continued.[33]

From its founding in 1880 the board's dominating member was Charles Wetmore, one of the first graduates of the University of California, a San Francisco journalist, and a restless, tactless, enterprising man of considerable talent and great confidence.[34] Arpad Haraszthy was president of the board for the first eight years of its existence, but the energy behind most of its activities came from Wetmore. He was one of the original commissioners, representing the county of Napa; when the office of chief executive officer was created in 1881, Wetmore stepped into the position and held it for the next six years. It was he who directed the surveys, collected the statistics, translated European technical treatises, arranged for publication of the board's reports and instructions, set the research policies of the board, and supervised its experiments. He travelled up and down the state to address meetings and inspect vineyards; he lobbied in Washington, publicized and promoted in New York, represented California wine at expositions. And all the time he poured out an inexhaustible flood of articles on every subject connected with grapes and wine in California, both technical and popular. In the eighties he was virtually synonymous with California wine to the public.

He did not do all this without stepping on toes, for he was quick to take the initiative against what he saw as obstructions and enemies. He resigned as chief executive officer in 1887, but remained a commissioner; a year later he became president of the board; in the next year, 1889, he became chief executive officer again, adding the title to that of the presidency. Though his presidency ended in 1890, he remained chief executive until 1891, when his connection with the board ceased.[35] It is probably more than a coincidence that the energetic days of the board ended with Wetmore's departure. But the Wetmore connection was not yet broken, for Charles's brother Clarence, who had also served the board in various ways, succeeded as chief executive.[36] Charles Wetmore is now best remembered as the founder of the original Cresta Blanca Winery in the Livermore Valley in 1882; he should also be remembered for his vital part in the operation of the Viticultural Commission in the first ten years, the effective decade of the board's work.

The Board's Rival: The University of California

Wetmore's most prominent enemy in his years at the board was the university itself. The act that created the board also created a department of viticulture in the University of California's College of Agriculture, to be supported out of the same budget that paid for the board's work. Such an arrangement was obviously headed for trouble, and it was not long in coming. The board naturally wished to have a part in every kind of activity affecting its work; the university, with equal reason, wanted to have full and unobstructed support for its work. In Professor (later Dean) Eugene W. Hilgard, the College of Agriculture had a skilled and bold defender, a worthy antagonist for Wetmore at the board. The two men at first treated each other with guarded respect, then differed, then fell into open controversy. They traded insults and squabbled over almost every point of advice to the industry, and on every occasion of public display. The rivalry came to a head in 1885 over the allocation of a grant of $10,000. This matter was eventually compromised, but the conflict between the two men went on unchanged.[37]

One way or another, Wetmore managed to keep the bulk of the viticultural work and the larger share of the annual appropriation in the hands of the board. The university, handicapped though it was in its rivalry with the board, nevertheless carried out work of great importance at this time. Its contribution to the fight against phylloxera has already been mentioned. Another, and one of its most important and sustained labors was begun almost at once, in fulfillment of plans made by Hilgard. When the university received its money from the state, it immediately constructed a model wine cellar on the campus next to South Hall and began to carry out experimental fermentations with grapes grown around the state. The wines produced thus in small (seven-gallon) experimental batches were carefully analyzed and the results published in a long series of reports covering the years 1881–93. Hilgard's aim was to make what he described as a "systematic investigation of grape-varieties with respect to their composition and general winemaking qualities in the different regions of the state."[38] The jealousy of the board was not Hilgard's only obstacle in this: he had to convince skeptics that wine made in small test batches could produce representative results—many believed that only wines produced in commercial quantity could do that. Other, more stubborn, doubters held that chemical analysis of any kind was a mere impertinence and that the professor was wasting his time and distracting the industry with his analyses. Hilgard persisted, however, and in the decade of his experiments produced an impressive body of objective information on this vital subject.

Grapes were collected from as many regions of the state as possible. Vineyards at Fresno, Mission San Jose, Cupertino, Paso Robles, and in Amador County were among the most prominent sources: Napa and Sonoma contributed much less.[39] The varieties examined made what was probably a comprehensive inventory of those then growing in the state, and included all of the varieties both red and white now recognized as having commercial value in California—from Aleatico and Cabernet to Tinta Cão and Valdepeñas. When the grapes were received at Berkeley, they were crushed and fermented in the university's experimental cellar under the supervision of F. T. Bioletti, assisted by A. R. Hayne. Bioletti, who ran things under Hilgard's direction, later became the director of the university's wine program and lived to train the first generation of post-Repeal wine scientists in California.[40] Before fermentation the musts were analyzed by Hayne, and after the fermentation the resultant wines were analyzed for sugar, acid, solids, alcohol, and

99 Eugene Hilgard (1833–1916), dean of the College of Agriculture of the University of California, a leading soil scientist and the head of viticultural and enological research in California, was the son of an Illinois *Lateinische Bauer* who grew a wine called "Hilgardsberger" on his midwestern farm. As champion of the University of California's work in viticulture and enology, Hilgard was in frequent conflict with Charles Wetmore, representing the rival Board of State Viticultural Commissioners. (Bancroft Library, University of California)

tannin. The reports sometimes went on to add details on the aging of the sample wines and on the results of tastings. On the solid basis of information thus provided, Hilgard and his associates could then make positive recommendations on what to plant and where to plant it. This work, going back to the very earliest days of the university's interest in viticulture, has continued to the present day pretty much along the lines that Hilgard laid down at the beginning.

Of comparable importance to its varietal studies was the university's work on the process of alcoholic fermentation, a subject that biochemists were just then beginning to grasp. Fermentation, of course, had been known and used in a practical way for millennia, but it was known as a mysterious and magical power, more spiritual than material, and all sorts of ritual and superstitious proceedings for directing and controlling it had grown up. During the course of the nineteenth century the problem of discovering the actual mechanisms of fermentation engaged the attention of researchers in many parts of the world; by the end of the century the general understanding of the means whereby the strange transformation of sugar into alcohol and carbon dioxide is achieved had been carried far beyond the limits of the old knowledge. It was, unromantically enough, the demands of the great brewers of beer in Europe that most stimulated research into the subject, but winemakers profited immediately from the results.

The chemical changes produced by fermentation had been well described by Lavoisier in France at the end of the eighteenth century. And the presence of yeasts in fermenting liquids had been known from the late seventeenth century. The unanswered question was, How are yeasts connected with the chemical changes that come about in fermentation? Not until the work of Pasteur in the 1850s and 1860s was this question answered, and then only in a general way. Pasteur was able to show that the chemical changes took place inside the cells of living microorganisms—the yeasts—and that the process was therefore a physiological one rather than, as some had maintained, a mechanical one. Exactly *how* the yeasts produced the change was far from being explained (it is still a subject of research, though the steps have been worked out in detail); but by the 1890s, when the university began active work in fermentation science, the idea that fermentation depended on the enzymes in the yeast cell was more or less established.[41] Pasteur had also suggested that different yeasts produced different results—some desirable, some highly undesirable—and that it was therefore of the first importance for the winemaker to get the right sort of yeast for his purposes. The yeast of winemaking is, generically, *Saccharomyces ellipsoideus,* but, just as there are many varieties of the wine grape, *Vitis vinifera,* so there are many varieties of the wine yeast, *ellipsoideus.* Fruit brought in from the field is covered with the spores of a multitude of yeasts, and in a fermentation left to itself there is no way to know which strain will prevail. If it is not a sound wine yeast that dominates, the fermentation may not "go through," as the winemakers say, or it may go through to bad results—to vinegar, for example, or to a fluid in which all sorts of undesirable bacteria and molds may develop. Work on isolating and propagating "pure" strains of yeast was first successfully carried out by the Danish scientist E. C. Hansen in the 1880s, with results that allowed a degree of control over the process of fermentation never before possible. By 1891 the French researcher Georges Jacquemin had established a commercial source of pure wine yeasts, and within a few years their use had become a widespread commercial practice in Europe.[42]

The university was quick to take advantage of the achievements of European research by applying them in California. The first experiments with strains of pure yeast began in Berkeley in 1893, with striking results: "In every one of the experiments at Berkeley," Bioletti wrote, "the wines fermented with the addition of yeast were cleaner and fresher-tasting than those allowed to ferment with whatever yeasts happened to exist on the grapes."[43] Samples of pure yeast cultures were sent out to commercial producers in Napa, Sonoma, St. Helena, Asti, San Jose, and Santa Rosa, with equally positive results.

Once the crucial importance of controlling fermentation had been clearly understood, university research was extended into other variables in the process. The role of temperature was investigated, especially the damaging effects of the high temperatures typically encountered in California. Other investigations were made on such topics as the decrease of color in fermentation, the control of temperature through refrigeration, the special problems of high sugar musts (also typical in California), the extraction of color, and the use of pasteurization. The latter process was first made known in 1865 and was quickly adapted in Europe and abroad, but often rather uncritically.[44]

The practical conclusions of all this work were passed on to the industry, and, if the industry was in many cases slow to adopt them (as it was), one could say at least that the California winemaker at the end of the century had, in theory, a mastery of his art that would have astonished the preceding generation. The work of Pasteur and others on the understanding of fermentation had, in one generation, literally transformed the powers of the winemaker to control what he was doing. As the distinguished enologist Maynard Amerine has written, the contributions of biochemistry to wine "have changed winemakng more in the last 100 years than in the previous 2,000," delivering us from a state of things in which "white wines were usually oxidized in flavor and brown in color" and most wines were "high in volatile acidity and often low in alcohol. When some misguided people wish for the good old days of natural wines, this is what they are wishing for."[45]

In retrospect, the work of the university, carried out against the hostility of the board and the skepticism of the state's farmers, had a permanent importance that far outweighed the better-advertised activities of its rival. At the time, however, it may well have been the case that the board's promotional work was more immediately necessary. That both agencies were of the greatest utility in advancing the state of the industry in California is unquestioned; it is a pity only that a better design for their cooperative working could not have been devised.

Though the board was able to keep its university enemies at bay, it had others to face as well. Some winegrowers resented its methods as high-handed and unresponsive; others thought simply that its work was not worth doing, or that, if it was, it was being badly done. The prolonged depression of trade in the wine industry, beginning in 1886, made the board seem clearly ineffective, and the research work of the university appeared all the more valuable by contrast. At the same time, a reformist campaign against all "useless and expensive" state boards and agencies was under way. The Board of State Viticultural Commissioners could hardly hope to escape indefinitely. Although a bill to abolish the board introduced in 1893 was killed, a comparable bill was passed in 1895.[46] Thus the board came to an end, and was forced to yield up its assets and properties—including a valuable library of technical literature—to its rival, the university's Department of Viticulture in the College of Agriculture.[47]

Marketing Problems in the Late Nineteenth Century: The California Wine Association

The problems of viticulture and winemaking such as the university and the state board devoted themselves to were mostly manageable problems. Given time, they could be, and were, successfully worked out. Another, and more difficult, problem was how to sell the wine once it was made, a problem that became acute in the season of 1886. The decade had opened with the prospect of California's taking over the first position in supplying the world's wine, with the result that planting and production leaped up: the ten million gallons that California had produced in 1880 had soared to eighteen million in 1886. Yet, after all, European winemaking had not died. The heroic labor of the French scientists and officials had first checked, then reversed the decline of the vineyards, so that the vast export markets that Californians imagined were only briefly opened to them. Some expansion of markets had taken place in South America and the Pacific, and a beginning had been made in England.[48] The export of condensed juice as an expedient to evade the taxes on wine was also tried; we have already noted Shorb's experiments. These things were at best only palliatives, however, and could not avert a long depression of prices and sales.

Part of the problem, at least, lay in the failure of the California industry to impose itself upon the eastern trade. California wine lacked prestige as compared to anything imported, and the New York merchants wanted it only to supply the cheap market. Charles Wetmore charged that the New Yorkers in fact knew nothing about the possibilities of California wines, and that, since they never visited the state, they missed their opportunities to buy good wines before they disappeared into undistinguished blends for the standard market. On the other hand, Wetmore conceded, the Californians handled their own wines badly: uncontrolled secondary fermentations, storage under conditions of damaging heat, aging too long in wood, and other bad practices meant that the wines they shipped east would be heavy and dull at best and, at worst, simply spoiled.[49]

The failure to develop a market for wines of quality from California was particularly damaging to the industry, for it destroyed all incentive to take the trouble and run the risks required to grow the best varieties and to make the highest standard of wine. "The man who gets ten tons of grapes to the acre gets 10 cents for wine; the man who, on a steep hillside, gets two tons and a half, gets 12 cents; and the 12-cent wine is mixed with the 10-cent," said Charles Wetmore in 1894.[50] He went on to describe the languishing of the industry: growers were allowing diseases to run unchecked through their vineyards; some were grafting over their superior varieties to high-yielding, low-quality kinds; and some 30,000 acres of grapes had been withdrawn from the state's total in the past six years.[51]

By 1892, for example, Zinfandel grapes sold for $10 a ton—not enough to pay the costs of picking. Wine at wholesale fetched 10 cents a gallon.[52] In such circumstances, the wish to eliminate competition in favor of some sort of cooperation, legal or otherwise, grew irresistible. At the lowest point of the industry's fortunes, in 1894, the decisive step was taken when seven of the state's largest and most powerful merchants, all based in San Francisco, joined together to form the California Wine Association (CWA). Together they represented much of the wine-growing history of California, and so large a part of the state's wine traffic that they at once dominated the market and continued to do so until Prohibition.[53]

The distinction between winegrower and wine merchant was not sharply drawn at this time in California. Most of the members of the CWA were vineyard owners, and all of them operated wineries that produced at least a part of what they sold. The association was thus in a position to operate a fully integrated enterprise, beginning with the grape and ending at the retail shelf, and this on a scale without precedent. Among the association's many and various properties from the beginning were such items as the Greystone Cellars at St. Helena, biggest in the state, the Glen Ellen Vineyards in Sonoma County, the Orleans Hill Vineyards in Yolo County, and the Cucamonga Vineyards in San Bernardino County. Other properties were absorbed into the system in ensuing years. By 1902 the CWA controlled the output of over fifty wineries, producing some thirty million of the state's forty-four million gallons of wine in that year. By 1910 a company brochure could boast that the association "cultivates more vineyard acreage, crushes more grapes annually, operates more wineries, makes more wine, has a greater wine storage capacity than any other wine concern in the world."[54] The company's wineries were scattered throughout every winegrowing region of the state: they included, to name but a few, the Uncle Sam Winery in Napa, the Tokay Winery in Glen Ellen, the Pacific Winery in San Jose, and the Calwa and Wahtoke wineries in Fresno County.

Their produce was sent to central cellars in San Francisco where the wines were stored, blended to a uniform standard, bottled, and then shipped for sale under the Calwa brand, with its trademark of a young Bacchus, accompanied by the California bear, standing at the prow of a ship whose sail bore the seal of California. Thus the idea of a standard, unvarying product bearing a brand identity was introduced into the California wine trade. The care of the cellars and the crucial work of blending was under the exclusive charge of Henry Lachman, famous as one of the two best tasters in the state (the other was Charles Carpy, also an official of the CWA).[55]

Retirement, death, business vicissitude, and the consequent sale of stock greatly altered the original ownership of the CWA, and after about a decade of operation, when it had proven its profitability, control passed into the hands of certain California bankers, notably those of Isaias W. Hellman.[56] Since Hellman, through his

The imposing scale of the operations of the California Wine
Association appears in its headquarters building in San Francisco. The building
was destroyed in the earthquake and fire
of 1906. (From a California Wine Association
brochure, c. 1910; Huntington Library)

Farmers' and Merchants' Bank of Los Angeles, had been instrumental in financing such pioneer wineries as B. D. Wilson's and the Cucamonga Vineyards, his investment in the CWA made a link between the old phase of the industry, centered in Los Angeles, and the new, centered in San Francisco.

Well provided with capital, and strongly entrenched in the wine markets of the country, the CWA was able to withstand the catastrophe of the San Francisco earthquake, when the ten million gallons of wine in its cellars were lost to shock and fire.[57] A year later, the resilient company was building its final monument, a huge red-brick bastion on the shores of San Pablo Bay near Richmond. With its satellite buildings, it covered forty-seven acres and combined a winery, distillery, and warehouses. An electric railway threaded the premises, linking the docks where ocean steamers loaded, with the transcontinental railroad tracks on the landward side of the plant. The storage capacity of Winehaven, as this little commercial city-state was named, was originally ten million gallons, later raised to twelve million; besides the wine produced on the spot, Winehaven also handled the flow of wine that came in from all of the many outlying properties of the CWA.[58] From the turn of the century to the coming of national Prohibition, the CWA was the most prosperous establishment in the most prosperous period that the California wine industry had yet known. As a monopoly, or rather, near-monopoly, it belonged to

IOI   Winehaven, the central facility of the California Wine Association on the shore of San Francisco Bay at Richmond, photographed in 1910. Winehaven was the phoenix which rose from the ashes of the fire in 1906 that consumed the association's San Francisco headquarters. From its ten million gallons of storage, wine was shipped by direct ship and train connection all over the country. (Huntington Library)

the rapacious business style of the late nineteenth century, and, no doubt, if the full record could be known it would show a long tale of sharp practices and dubious moves. Whether the combination represented by the CWA was a necessary or even a particularly effective way to restore the California wine trade to health no one can say now. But its flourishing did coincide with a span of years in which prices remained fairly stable while production gradually gained.

The leading antagonist of the CWA was a rival organization dominated by winegrowers, as the CWA was dominated by wine merchants. In 1894, foreseeing that growers would be entirely at the mercy of the CWA unless some alternative home for their grapes could be found, a combine of growers and wineries formed the California Wine Makers' Corporation (CWMC).[59] The manager was the former secretary of the Board of State Viticultural Commissioners, John H. Wheeler, and the main promoters were Andrea Sbarboro and Pietro Rossi, the leaders of the Italian Swiss Colony. Their plan was to contract for a large part of the California crop, have it made into wine by wineries outside the CWA network, and stored until such time as a favorable sale could be made. (It was to assist in carrying out this plan that the famous giant cistern was built on the Italian Swiss Colony grounds at Asti.) In this way the CWMC could reasonably hope to negotiate with the CWA instead of helplessly accepting whatever terms the merchants cared to dictate. The CWA chose not to fight at first; it bought the corporation's wines at the corporation's prices in the first year of their dealings, 1895. Thereafter they began to draw apart, and by 1897 were engaged in full-scale war in the major markets of the country. The CWMC undertook to sell its own wines direct instead of through the CWA; the CWA responded by ruthlessly cutting prices. By 1899, when a short crop drove prices up for the whole industry, the CWMC was glad to take the opportunity to retreat. It was quietly dissolved in that year, and the field left open to the victorious CWA.[60]

Whatever else the CWA may have accomplished, it permanently transformed the idea of how California wine was to be sold. The trade in the early days had come to be dominated by the San Francisco merchants, whose practice was to buy the entire annual output of producers at a fixed price and then to blend it according to their own notions of what was suitable. On this system there was obviously no incentive for winegrowers to aim at making wines of special quality, since all went at a single price and all was blended so as to smooth out whatever peaks and valleys occurred in the produce of a given vintage. Later, as some individual growers grew large enough to handle their own production—including aging, blending, and shipping—they could set their own standards. Even then, however, most wine in California left the winery in bulk—in barrel, puncheon, or cask. And most such wine went from producer to large wholesalers in distant parts of the country, who might or might not know how to handle the wine properly, supposing, as must rarely have been the case, that they even had the facilities to do so. The wholesalers would label the wine as their own taste and experience dictated, or they could sell to a retailer who might then label the wine according to *his* own notions. The succession of intermediaries meant that the wine ran all sorts of risks in the handling, especially the risk of spoiling.

Even more prevalent, according to the dark imaginings of the California producers, was the risk of the wine's being adulterated. The claim that unscrupulous easterners adulterated California wine before selling it is a constant theme of the California winemakers, and an explanation for all the ills of the trade. No doubt much wine was injured in handling, but it does not follow that deliberate adulteration was a very frequent practice. George Husmann, writing from California in 1888, doubted that adulteration took place to the extent that his fellow winemakers claimed. Bad handling and bad methods were the real cause of trouble for California wine; so, too, was the "prevailing custom of selling whole cellars of wine, good, bad, and indifferent, to the merchant, and compelling him, so to say, to take a lot of trash, if he also wanted the really good wines a cellar contained."[61] This is interesting evidence that the merchant was not always the villain and the grower the innocent victim.

Growers also ran the risk of having their wines given French, German, or Italian labels. Robert Louis Stevenson tells in *The Silverado Squatters* of a San Francisco merchant showing him a cupboard filled with a profusion of "gorgeously tinted labels, blue, red, or yellow, stamped with crown or coronet, and hailing from such a profusion of *clos* and *châteaux,* that a single department could scarce have furnished forth the names"—and all to be used on innocent bottles of California wine.[62] There might be *some* French wine in the bottles so labelled. Henry Lachman, the pioneer San Francisco wine merchant and director of the CWA, recalled that for many years it was standard practice in San Francisco to blend California wine with French wine that had arrived as ballast in ships calling to load California grain for Europe.[63] Given the anarchic methods for distributing and identifying wine that prevailed through the nineteenth century, even the largest California producers had little chance to control the condition of their wines or to establish any kind of market identity and customer loyalty.

The system was not all bad, by any means. Since the small producer did not have to worry about marketing his wine, he did not have to develop a "line" and could therefore concentrate on producing what he did best. If he had a stable arrangement with a wine merchant, a sound and enduring reputation might be built up. But in general, the received pattern in California did not encourage the ordinary winegrower, or do much to make a reputation for the integrity of California wines.

The sheer size of the CWA's operations made it possible to change the prevailing system. The company could afford to store vast quantities of wine, to keep it on hand to insure uniform blending, and to advertise and distribute its own brand throughout the country. Calwa brand wines were bottled at the winery and sold only in glass;[64] if there was anything to object to in a bottle, at least the company stood behind it. Another forward-looking practice of the CWA was to avoid using European names for its wines. They might be described as "table claret" or "burgundy type" or "good old sherry type," but they were called by their own names— Winehaven, La Loma, Hill Crest, Vine Cliff. Not very imaginative, perhaps, but at least distinctive, and impossible to confuse with the wines of some other country. A few CWA wines were what we should now call varietals, and were identified as such: Vine Cliff, for example, was riesling; Hill Crest, a "finest old cabernet claret," selling, in 1910, for $8 a case.[65]

One of the unnoted casualties of the great San Francisco earthquake and fire was the plan of the CWA to mature specially selected California wines in its cellars to demonstrate to the trade what such care could do for the state's wines. These special selections were among those millions of gallons of wine destroyed in the fire, and the loss, according to a rival eastern winemaker, was "one of the greatest calamities that ever visited the California wine business."[66] Such wines, if they had survived to be distributed, would have made the reputation of the state, according to one who had been privileged to taste, a decade later, a few of the bottles that had escaped the general destruction.[67]

The CWA carried on an export program under the "Big Tree" brand of Cali-

Fine Matured Bottling Wines

"CALWA" BRAND

	Per Case of		
	12 Large Bottles	24 Half Bottles	48 Quarter Bottles
RED			
WINEHAVEN—A Matured Table Claret......	$4.00	$5.00	$6.00
LA LOMA—Fine Burgundy type	6.00	7.00	8.00
HILLCREST—Finest Old Cabernet Claret.....	8.00	9.00	10.00
WHITE			
GREYSTONE—Good Light Hock type	4.00	5.00	6.00
ROCKDALE—Chablis type	4.00	5.00	6.00
CERRITO—Fine Dry Sauterne type	6.00	7.00	8.00
GLENRIDGE—Fine Haut-Sauterne type.......	8.00	9.00	10.00
VINE CLIFF—Finest Riesling........................	8.00	9.00	10.00
DESSERT WINES			
WAHTOKE—Good Old Sherry type	8.00	9.00	10.00
MADRONA—Fine Old Port type	8.00	9.00	10.00
DULZURA—Finest Old Tokay type	8.00	9.00	10.00
CALHETA—Malaga type	8.00	9.00	
SAN MARTINHO—Madeira type	8.00	9.00	
ANGELICA—Finest Old................................	8.00	9.00	
BRANDY			
Finest Old Calwa Brandy..............................	15.00	16.00	
Fine Muscat Brandy	12.00	13.00	
SPARKLING WINES			Magnums 6 to the case
RUBY CLIFF—Sparkling Red Burgundy type	11.00	12.00	11.00
GOLD CLIFF (Sec)—Sparkling Moselle type	11.00	12.00	11.00
GOLD CLIFF (Brut)—Dry Champagne style	11.00	12.00	11.00

Assorted Cases of any of the above at proportionate cost.

The fine dry "Calwa" Wines are exclusively supplied in bottle, but the fine Dessert Wines and Brandy are also supplied in bulk on the following terms:

	Per Gallon
"Calwa" Port, Sherry, Tokay, in Casks........................	$2.50
"Calwa" Muscat Brandy, in Casks..............................	4.00
"Calwa" Finest Cognac type Brandy, in Casks	5.00

The Charge for Casks Holding

5 Gallons, $1.00	10 Gallons, $1.35	15 Gallons, $1.85
20 Gallons, 2.25	25 Gallons, 2.25	50 Gallons, 2.90

CALWA WINE VINEGAR—Red or White .... $2.50 per Case

The list of Calwa wines around 1910; these wines, blended to standard and bottled at the winery, were available for national distribution. Customers could, however, order wine from the California Wine Association in five-gallon casks or larger containers, freight prepaid to "the nearest main line railway depot." (From a California Wine Association brochure; Huntington Library) fornia red and white wines, familiar items of commerce in England by the end of the century. "Big Tree" wines, sold in flat-sided flagons of brown glass with the image of a huge sequoia stump blown in relief on one side, were advertised in the catalogue of London's elegant Harrod's store in 1895 thus: "Zinfandel, good table wine . . . very soft and round and free from acidity, most wholesome and blood-making," at 18 shillings a dozen. One notes the typical English recommendation— "most wholesome and bloodmaking"—on grounds of health rather than of pleasure. The number of old "Big Tree" bottles still available for sale in antique shops and at jumble sales in England attests to the success of the approach.

With the establishment of the California Wine Association, the wine industry in California had acquired the shape that, with little essential change, would continue down to the advent of Prohibition. The dominance of the CWA was such that its old competitors were absorbed into the system—notably the Italian Swiss Colony, which had been instrumental in forming the rival California Wine Makers' Association in 1894. By 1901 it was ready to slip quietly into the fold of the CWA. It retained, to all external appearances, its old identity, but its policies were now those of the CWA.[68]

Though it controlled the market by the power of its size, the CWA did not prevent others from joining the trade; there were, for example, 187 winemaking establishments in California in 1900 (the figure does not take account of the many farm producers), a considerable increase over the 128 in 1890, and most of these new establishments would have been created after the formation of the CWA. The figure of 181 reported in the 1910 census shows only a marginal decline from the point reached in 1900. Almost all of the new establishments would have been small enterprises, exploiting local markets and thus almost invisible on the national scale of the CWA's operations. The extent to which winemaking was still a domestic occupation is suggested by the national census of 1910, which reported that wine and grape juice were manufactured on 2,163 farms in California in 1909. One quite large firm did arise in this period, however, the Italian Vineyard Company of Secondo Guasti, on the sandy slopes of the Cucamonga district east of Los Angeles. Beginning in 1900, Guasti was able to develop a vineyard that ultimately grew to some 5,000 acres and was, inevitably in California, proclaimed "The World's Largest"; the winery he built to receive the tide of grapes from his sea of vines had a capacity of five million gallons.[69]

The decades from the nineties down to Prohibition were not notable for innovation in the wine industry. Its position as a distinctive and favored element in the general economic system of California was well established after several generations of promotion, experiment, legislation, and hard work. Technical work went on quietly at the university, as it had done since 1880, but the pioneering on such basic matters as varietal selection, the identification of the different viticultural regions in the state, and the discovery of winemaking techniques adapted to California conditions had already been well begun. Such work is never finally done, but no remarkable changes were made in the general scheme of things in these years.

The notable change was only in the slow growth of wine production. In 1895, one year after the formation of the CWA, the state of California produced a little less than 18 million gallons of wine. There were great fluctuations in the annual production thereafter—the 31 million gallons of 1898, for example, were followed by a mere 19 million the next year—but overall the graph of production kept moving steadily up. There were 23 million gallons in 1900, 31 million in 1905, and 45 million in 1910. Production thus doubled in a decade, and in a state whose population in 1910 was only a little more than two and a quarter million, winemaking was evidently a matter of great importance. In the early days much, perhaps most, California wine was sweet; and so it would be again, after the repeal of Prohibition and down to 1967, when dry table wine at last edged ahead of the sweet wines. But in these prosperous decades before Prohibition, the wine of California was dry table wine, both red and white. The proportion was two to one in favor of table wine in 1900, and though the share of the sweet wines crept up in following years, it did not overtake table wine; it was 13 million against 18 million in 1905; 18 million against 27 million in 1910.[70]

The Growth of Related Trades and a Literature of Wine

To supply an industry on this scale, the trades related to winemaking gradually developed in California. Coopers, of course, had been in California almost from the beginning, for in a world without tin cans, paper boxes, plastic buckets, and cheap disposable bottles, the art of the cooper will be urgently required. The coopering skills available in California from an early period are suggested by the diploma awarded in 1857 at the Mechanics' Institute Industrial Exhibition to Eck & Chicolot of San Francisco for a brandy cask, "all of oak, in the French style, with willow-bound hoops, and of superior workmanship and good finish."[71] By the 1870s there was a specialized branch of the state's cooperage industry devoted to the needs of the wine trade: the Santa Rosa Planing Mill could produce tanks up to 5,000 gallons' capacity, and in San Francisco there was a rivalry between the firms of Fulda Brothers and David Woerner, both of which undertook to supply a complete range of locally manufactured wooden containers.[72] It is interesting to note that West Coast woods were not regarded as suitable for wine storage and aging. It was one of Haraszthy's claims that he had been the first to show that California redwood could be satisfactorily used to make the vats and barrels for California's wines.[73] If so, the demonstration was slow to take effect. The Committee on Wood Work and Cooperage of the Mechanics' Institute Exhibition reported in 1868 that the cost of casks was one of the heaviest expenses for winegrowers, and that "the discovery on the Pacific Coast of wood suitable for wine cooperage would be very valuable."[74] And twenty years later the complaint was still the same. The committee noted in 1888, apropos of David Woerner's exhibit of cooperage, that Woerner's factory, the largest on the coast, consumed an "incredible" quantity of lumber, most

DAVID WOERNER,

COOPER,

No. 104 and 112 Spear St., San Francisco.

Wine Casks, Tanks, Tubs, Pipes, Beer Barrels, etc., Manufactured at Short Notice
and LOW RATES.

a LUMBER for CASKS, etc., TANKS, etc. Steamed
nd Dried if required.

eow–bp.

Woerner's firm was the largest
producer of cooperage on the
West Coast, all of the work
being done by hand, without machines. (*Pacific
Rural Press*, 20 February 1875)

of which would continue to be imported "until some adequate substitute for eastern oak is found."[75] There is no doubt that redwood *was* being used for wine cooperage; the Korbel brothers of the Russian River Valley in Sonoma County were advertising vats made from their redwood in 1885. But such vats were for fermenting, not for aging wine. It must have been later that what was done out of necessity came to seem a virtue and that California winemakers boasted of their redwood storage vats. The precipitous decline in the use of redwood storage in California in recent years confirms the earlier reluctance to use it.

The more complicated and specialized machines peculiar to the making of wine—crushers, stemmers, presses, and pumps, especially—required a little longer for local industry to provide. It is still true today, as a matter of fact, that the wine industry of the United States depends to an important extent on machines and supplies from Europe. Still, Californians made a beginning towards self-sufficiency in these things at least by the sixties; a press designed and made in California was being offered as early as 1863 by a Sacramento firm.[76] In the Mechanics' Institute Exhibition of 1869 were exhibited an "improved grape crusher and stem separator" and a hydraulic wine press.[77] There was, thereafter, a fairly steady number of entries at the annual exhibition of machines for winemaking, machines that grew more and more sophisticated and complex. The combined stemmer-crusher exhibited by Schoenstein & Klein in 1874, for example, improved on the old batch-process models by making a continuous feed possible: "With one of these machines nine tons of grapes have been crushed and the stems automatically discharged in a thoroughly separated condition without the necessity of stopping or varying the operation of the machine."[78] The early stemming devices in question were no doubt on the model of the perforated tray, the standard design until 1878, when the first design based on the revolving cylinder was introduced.[79] The exhibition of 1888 showed that the combining of multiple functions in compound machines had continued: two exhibitors in that year showed combined crushers, stemmers, and presses. The crusher operated with adjustable rubber rollers, and though the press was still the old basket style, it had the strength of the double-action lever principle.[80] At some indeterminate later date the continuous screw press was introduced; such presses were certainly in use in California before Prohibition, but they were not general.

The machines basic to the process of winemaking—crushers and presses— were naturally the staple items of manufacture, but in 1877 J. M. Curtis exhibited a "wine heater," that is, a pasteurizing mechanism suitable for wine.[81] It would be interesting to know how widely used the process was in nineteenth-century California. Special designs for vineyard tools were also experimented with: plows specially made for use in the vineyard were exhibited in the seventies and eighties, including the "Napa Plow Company's Vineyard Plow" in 1874, and a "side-hill vineyard plow" in 1884.[82] The first must pumps (as distinguished from ordinary force pumps) did not appear until 1896, and they made a significant difference to winery practice and winery design. Up to that time, a California winery was likely

The GOLDEN STATE LATEST IMPROVED WINE & CIDER PRESS.

This is a Compound Screw and Lever Press, is very powerful, strong and durable, and does not easily get out of order. It is easily worked by one man, who stands in one place and moves the lever up and down, the same as a pump-handle. This manner of operation is much easier than the old way where the operator is compelled to walk back and forth.

Send for Circu'ars.   F. W. KROGH & CO., 51 Beale St., S. F.

104 An advertisement directed at the California wine trade in 1892: hydraulic presses were available by that time, but the traditional screw press went on being "improved." Small producers—and most were small producers—would not have needed anything more. (*Pacific Rural Press*, 8 October 1892)

to be sited against the side of a hill, so that grapes could be delivered directly to the top floor of the building to be crushed; thence the must could flow down to the fermenting and storage tanks by force of gravity. Often the means used to convey the must down from crusher to fermenting vat was an open wooden chute, so that the must was exposed to oxidation and contamination. A must pump allowed the use of pipes, to the greater protection of the must. At the same time, since gravity was no longer required as the moving force, wineries could move away from the hillsides to the flatlands, where they could be expanded or altered much more easily.[83]

It would be fair to say that by the end of the 1880s the California wine industry came close to being self-sufficient. Some materials had to be imported still: corks, most obviously,[84] but, as we have seen, wood from eastern oak too. The only

105 An arrangement for pasteurizing wine, from Pasteur's *Etudes sur le vin*. Pasteurizing machinery was available to California winemakers by the 1870s, but it is doubtful whether many made use of it. (California State University, Fresno, Library)

chemical in much use for winegrowing and winemaking was sulfur—as a pesticidal dust in the vineyard, and as a disinfectant gas in the winery—and that had to be imported too, though there was some native supply.[85] Nurseries to supply the vines, coopers to make the necessary barrels and vats, foundries and iron works to make the machines, glass blowers to make the bottles, and printers to print the labels were all in good supply, and the scale of operation was large enough to allow at least some specialization. The Union Machine Company and the Atlas Iron Works in San Francisco, J. L. Heald of Crockett, Contra Costa County, and W. Worth in Petaluma all stood ready to provide the mechanical needs of winemakers.[86] Heald was the leading specialist, who would undertake to advise on the design and equipment of an entire winery and to furnish the machines: presses, crushers, stemmers, elevators, pumps. The list of his customers in the early eighties is a roster of the industry: Krug, Beringer, Niebaum, Gundlach, De Turk, and so on.[87] Thus, a man who wanted to enter winemaking in California in, say, 1890, stood in a radically different position from a beginner just a generation before not only in technical knowledge but in equipment and supply. There was plenty of pioneering still to be done, but the pioneer was now surrounded by help.

The wine industry in California was recognized fairly quickly as a subject for journalism, and it was not long before it began to attract specialized publications to report its activities. Early newspapers, like the *Star* in Los Angeles, and the *Alta California* in San Francisco, took an interest in the state's winegrowing as early as the 1850s: buried in their old files is much local detail about pioneer viticulture and winemaking that has not yet been exhumed. The general agricultural magazines of the state, such as the *California Farmer* (San Francisco, 1854–84) also made wine-growing a regular subject of coverage from an early period. The first periodical known to proclaim wine as a central item of its interest was a monthly called the *California Wine and Wool Register,* which began publication in Sacramento in January 1863 and expired at some indeterminate date not long thereafter. Close on its heels, and bearing almost the same name, was the *California Wine, Wool and Stock Journal,* published in San Francisco from 1863 to 1864. A *Wine Dealer's Gazette* began publication in San Francisco in 1871. Interest in the southern part of the industry was served, after 1877, by the Los Angeles journal called the *Rural Californian.* In 1879 the *San Francisco Merchant* began publication, without any special reference to the wine industry among its commercial subjects; in the early eighties, the boom in California vineyards brought about a change in emphasis, however, and beginning in 1884 the *Merchant* proclaimed itself "the only viticultural paper in the state." In 1889 the journal was renamed the *Merchant and Viticulturist,* and by this time it had come to dominate the field. In 1890 it was renamed again, now as the *Pacific Wine and Spirit Review,* and so continued down to its demise in 1919, a victim of Prohibition. It is remarkable that only the unimportant *Wine Dealer's Gazette* among these early periodicals was exclusively devoted to wine. Even in the state producing the overwhelmingly larger part of the country's wine there was not a large enough readership to sustain a journal entirely given over to the industry.

Final evidence for the settled establishment of winegrowing in California was its use as a literary subject. Wine in California, so far as I know, has not yet found its poet, the writer who will by the force of his passion and skill impose his vision on the popular mind. There have been many to try their hands in recent years, especially since about 1970. But the victor has not yet been crowned. The earliest venture that I know of was made by George H. Jessop with a story called *Judge Lynch: A Tale of the California Vineyards,* published in Chicago and London in 1889. It is a poor affair, melodramatic and conventional; and though Jessop was a Californian, he shows no authentic understanding of the scene. The setting is somewhere in southern California, on the western slope of the Coast Range; a few purple patches of description about vines and wine cellars are sewn on to the fiction from time to time, though otherwise the story might just as well have transpired in the High Sierra—or in Patagonia, for that matter. But the book is at least interesting as evidence that California, as early as 1889, and as far away as London, was popularly thought of as a land of vineyards.

Climax and Collapse

The symbolic high point of California winegrowing before Prohibition overwhelmed it came, as in all well-made dramas, only shortly before the fall. In 1915, when the shadow of Prohibition was already moving rapidly over the country, California seized on the opportunity provided by the newly opened Panama Canal to promote its climate, its industries, and its future through the great Panama-Pacific International Exposition in San Francisco; it was also a dramatic way for San Francisco to show the world how it had risen, phoenix-like, from the ashes of 1906. California's wine men, now pretty well seasoned in the business of international exhibitions, were ready to make the most of their chance to show their best on their own ground. This sort of thing, though impressive, was not new. What was uniquely outstanding was the gathering of the International Congress of Viticulture at the Panama-Pacific Exposition, a gesture of recognition and honor to the California wine industry.

The congress had been authorized two years earlier by the Permanent International Viticultural Commission in the last days of uneasy European peace. When the time came, of course, Europe had been almost a whole year at war, a war of a destructiveness never imagined before. The consequence was that the Californians, once again, saw their hopes for effective international publicity disappear: Europeans had other things to occupy themselves with in July 1915. As the afflicted Prosper Gervais, secretary of the Permanent Viticultural Commission, wrote to the Americans, "My son, my only son, is dead on the plains of Flanders. I cannot come."[88] The dark note of war and death that such poignant excuses created was intensified by the less brutal, but still oppressive, influence of the prohibition movement, an obsessive topic throughout the congress. And, adding to the other causes that damped the enthusiasm and spirit of the occasion, the federal government had just laid a new tax on brandy, jumping the rate from 3 cents a gallon to 55 cents: the producers of fortified wines in California loudly proclaimed their imminent ruin, and so added another shade of gloom to an atmosphere already dark enough.

Still, the affair was notable for its scope and for the evidence it gave of the achievements made not just by the California winegrowers but by those of the country generally. If the European representatives, who were the most active members of the Permanent Viticultural Commission, could not come, at least the rest of the United States could. The presiding officer was from Virginia; delegates came from thirteen states, and officials from experiment stations in a half dozen states as well as from the U.S. Department of Agriculture read papers to the congress. They showed quite impressively the state of knowledge to which the subjects of viticulture and enology had been carried in this country: there were papers on the technical topics of pruning, breeding, fertilizing, and other matters, as well as reports on grape diseases and grape pests, on the contributions of engineering to winemaking, and on advances in fermentation science. To all this were added a series of reports on the history and status of grape growing in the East, in California, and in developing regions such as Washington, Idaho, Oregon, and Utah. The programs were in the charge of the distinguished viticulturist and administrator U. P. Hedrick of the New York Agricultural Experiment Station and clearly reflected his interest in the subject of winegrowing throughout the country. His own

contribution to the congress described the work of the New York station in growing vinifera varieties in the East, two generations before the possibility of doing so
again became a topic of current interest.

Though the delegates were sadly restricted in their numbers and in the variety
of countries they represented, they were given the full honors of the state's hospitality. After they were shown the rival attraction of the San Diego Exposition, they
were banqueted in Los Angeles, and then transported to the Stern Winery in Riverside and the Italian Vineyard Company's establishment at Guasti—there, in the
company's "immense plant," they were given lunch in "the huge storage cellars."
En route from Los Angeles to San Francisco, they stopped in Fresno, "where they
were shown not only the important sweet wine plants, but also the raisin grape
vineyards and the big packing houses": there would have been nothing like these
things where they came from. Following the sessions of the congress proper, the
delegates were taken on a further excursion to the great plant of the CWA at Winehaven, on San Francisco Bay, and then had to return to the Exposition grounds for
an official "wine day." The next day they went to Asti to view the much advertised
tourist attractions of the Italian Swiss Colony, with its marvelous underground
storage tank and its large-scale activities of every sort. There they lunched under
the vine arbors of Andrea Sbarboro and submitted to be recorded on moving picture film.

The Congress of Viticulture was a well-earned compliment to the winemaking
achievement of California in the relatively few years of its history. But if the
achievement had been rapid, its destruction was rapider still. When, only a few
years later, the official history of the Panama-Pacific Exposition came to be published, in five large and pretentious volumes, it gave the briefest description of the
wine industry's exhibit and then dismissed the subject: "This is history—closed by
the Eighteenth Amendment."[89]

THE INDUSTRY
ACROSS THE NATION

14

The Eastern United States: From the Civil War to Prohibition

W inemaking in the United States east of the Rocky Mountains—or rather east of the Sierra—gradually consolidated and extended the work that had been begun before the Civil War. There were no striking new departures, and the scale of grape growing and of wine production never was large enough to be very visible to Americans, the great majority of whom lived in the eastern states. The ordinary American was still anything but a wine drinker, so such growth as the market made probably had as much to do with a growing national population, and, especially, a large immigration, as with a change of taste. The statistics of per capita consumption show an erratic, but on the whole discouraging, pattern. Another obstacle to rapid growth was an old one—the endemic diseases of mildew and, above all, black rot. Despite a growing understanding of these diseases, they put every grower's crop at risk season after season. The major new factor for eastern winemaking was the competition from California, a significant force by the 1870s; thereafter California grew at a rate unmatched by all the other winemaking territories of the country put together. Still, California was a very remote place throughout the nineteenth century, despite the railroad; the United States was still a largely rural country, and many of the services and supplies now provided by large-capital, nationally organized enterprises were then a matter for local activity. In

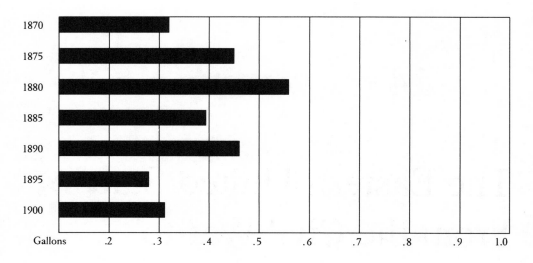

3	**Per Capita Consumption of Wine in the United States, 1870–1900**

Sources: U.S. Department of Agriculture, *Yearbook, 1898* (Washington, D.C., 1899); *Encyclopaedia Britannica*, 13th ed., 26: 581

these circumstances, winegrowing was a very good bet over a large part of the country, and it developed accordingly.

Eastern Wine and Eastern Grape Juice

New York, after its somewhat slow start, began to overhaul and soon passed all the other states outside California. In 1870, for example, New York stood sixth in wine production among the states, behind not only California and Ohio but Illinois and Pennsylvania too. By 1880 New York had closed to third, after California and Ohio; by 1890 New York stood second, and that was where it stayed until Prohibition put an end to the race.[1]

The regions of the state that stood out as winegrowing centers before the war remained in that position afterwards: the Hudson shores, the Finger Lakes, and the Lake Erie grape belt. Of the Hudson region there is little to add once it had been established: it maintained a fairly steady acreage of grapes but did not expand. Its nearness to the produce market of New York City made the Hudson region particularly attractive for growing table grapes, and its river climate made it attractive to fruit growing generally. Thus, instead of specializing in wine, the Hudson growers made grape growing a part of a general fruit-growing economy. The most encouraging development in the state was the spread of winegrowing in the Finger Lakes. Keuka Lake had been the original focus; there, by the end of the Civil War,

106 The vineyards of Pleasant Val-
ley, above Hammondsport, New
York, at the south end of Keuka
Lake, 1872. The view is of the region shown on
the map reproduced as figure 58 (*Harper's
Weekly,* 11 May 1872)

there were some 3,000 acres of vines divided among two hundred proprietors and
served by three wineries.[2] By 1890, the year in which New York took over the
second spot in the country, the Finger Lakes region had nearly 24,000 acres of
vines, mostly still centered on Keuka Lake but with other large acreages around
Seneca Lake to the east and Canandaigua Lake to the north and west. The vast
bulk of the yield from New York's vineyards did not go the wineries but to the
cities, in boxes and baskets, as grapes for the table.[3] The Keuka region, however,
specialized in winemaking, as did the developing Naples Valley at the south end of
Canandaigua Lake. After its beginning in 1861 with the Maxfield Winery, the wine
trade in the Naples Valley picked up speed in the 1870s and expanded very rapidly
in the 1880s. The leaders were largely Germans, as the pioneer Hiram Maxfield
was: he was followed by such names as Miller, Dinzler, Kaltenbach, and Widmer
(though the latter was, to be exact, Swiss).[4]

Finger Lakes wine was mostly white and came from the same varieties that
had been established at the beginning, mainly Catawba and Delaware, with significant plantings of Elvira, Isabella, Moore's Early, and other varieties.[5] Sparkling wine
continued to be a staple product, so that Finger Lakes "champagne" was almost
synonymous with American sparkling wine down to Prohibition. At the turn of the
century, for example, New York produced more than twice as much sparkling wine
as all other domestic sources—California, Ohio, and Missouri—combined.[6] Some
of that New York sparkling wine, however, was based on neutral California white
wine imported in bulk to modify the flavors and the acidity of the wine from native
varieties—a practice long established and still followed. The pioneer firms of the

Finger Lakes continued to be the major producers: Pleasant Valley ("Great West-ern," 1860) and the Urbana Wine Company ("Gold Seal," 1865). On Seneca Lake the first considerable commercial establishment was the Seneca Lake Wine Com-pany, which put up its stone-built winery in 1870.[7] The Germania Wine Cellars were founded in that year in Hammondsport, and the next quarter of a century saw such further additions to the Finger Lakes list as the Hammondsport Wine Com-pany, the Columbia Wine Cellars, the Lake Keuka Wine Company, the Empire State Wine Company, and the White Top Winery.[8] Something of an anomaly, but an important presence nonetheless, was the Paul Garrett Winery at Penn Yan, where, after 1912, the Garrett enterprises had their headquarters. Garrett's story properly belongs to that of North Carolina and will be told later in this chapter. Driven by a steadily encroaching zone of prohibitionist drought, Garrett left North Carolina for Virginia, then Virginia for New York, where he weathered Prohibition and reemerged as the genius behind the formation of Fruit Industries Incorporated, a combine of California and eastern interests that was the largest winemaking enterprise in the country. For a time, then, in virtue of Garrett's Penn Yan head-quarters, the Finger Lakes region was the capital of the American wine trade. But that was an accident of the dislocations produced by Prohibition.

To the west, along the shores of Lake Erie in the New York and Pennsylvania grape belt, the production of wine from traditional varieties such as the Catawba continued, but only in a small way. As the century went on, the region was devoted more and more to the supply of grapes for the table; thus, by the end of the cen-tury, it was overwhelmingly dominated by the Concord grape. The first carload of grapes for the table market was shipped from the region in 1877, from Brocton to Philadelphia;[9] within a generation hundreds of carloads left the grape belt each fall for eastern and middle western cities. The success of this trade created a "grape fever" in the 1880s: "Lawyers, teachers, doctors, and even ministers of the gospel turned vineyardists," a local historian recalled at the turn of the century.[10] The con-centration on table grapes rather than wine grapes was reinforced by the very strong local sentiment in favor of prohibition; Chautauqua County, the heart of the grape region, was also the home of the Chautauqua Institution, where the Woman's Christian Temperance Union was conceived,[11] and where the uplifting programs of "culture" purveyed at the institution were sustained on cold water and high thought alone. The shores of Lake Erie, ideally suited to viticulture, continued to be devoted to the grape, but increasingly less to wine. Not that winemaking was extinguished. The Brocton Wine Cellars, going back to the earliest days of wine production in the grape belt, continued to operate, and by 1900 had grown to a capacity of 250,000 gallons. Other wineries in the grape belt—the Lake Erie Cel-lars at Westfield, the Chautauqua Wine Company at Ripley, and the Portland Wine Cellars at Portland, to name a few—raised the region's total production to one and a half million gallons annually by the turn of the century.[12] A group of Italian winemakers concentrated in Fredonia also contributed to this total.[13]

Generally speaking, the development of table varieties received more attention in New York than did the work on wine varieties. The excited interest in breeding new native grapes generated by the grape boom of the 1860s had greatly subsided but not entirely disappeared, and a steady stream of new introductions appeared in the latter half of the century. One of the most effectively ballyhooed of these was the Niagara, a green grape, which for a time was the light-colored counterpart in eastern vineyards of the dark-colored Concord. Niagara may be, and is still, used for wine, but its chief market was for the table, as were such other new introductions, now largely fallen out of use, as Champion, Croton, Empire State, Jefferson, and many others in a long list of local and patriotic names.[14]

One extremely promising experiment in New York never got a chance to develop: this was the work with vinifera vines carried out by the state's agricultural experiment station at Geneva, in the Finger Lakes. A grape-breeding program was started at the station in 1890, based on the station's own varietal collection: this was largely made up of native varieties but included experimental plantings of vinifera. By 1911 the station undertook a deliberate program of growing vinifera, with the idea of developing hybrids; some 101 varieties were planted, and four years later the results were encouraging enough to allow U. P. Hedrick, the director, to report that it was certainly possible to make the vines grow under New York conditions.[15] Two years later, in 1917, one of Hedrick's fellow workers wrote in a station bulletin that they now had satisfactory means for protecting vinifera from all four of the major pests in New York: mildew, black rot, phylloxera, and winter injury.[16] On that confident note the work so well begun flickered out in the darkness of Prohibition. The episode is well worth reporting, now that extensive experiment with vinifera is again being made in New York and elsewhere in the East. In the publicity surrounding the current trials, the earlier contribution of Hedrick and his associates ought not to be forgotten.

In Ohio, the shift from the south, where Ohio winegrowing was first established, to the north of the state along the Lake Erie shore was quite complete within just a few years after the Civil War. Ohio enjoyed an unspectacular, but fairly steady, growth in winemaking throughout the latter half of the nineteenth century, but the Cincinnati *vignoble* was gone. Of the two regions where winegrowing was focused along the Erie shore, the one centered on Cleveland was first, by a little, to be developed. A Lake Shore Grape and Wine Growers' Association held a convention at Cleveland in 1866, and next year the members displayed their wines at the Paris Exhibition.[17] Like their neighbors to the east in Chautauqua County, New York, the growers in the Cleveland area felt prohibitionist pressure from a very early date. In 1869, when there were already three hundred members of the association, its fourth meeting, held at Temperance (!) Hall in Cleveland voted to change the name of the group to the Ohio Grape Growers Association, dropping any reference to wine; the meeting also voted to exclude wine from future exhibitions. There were loud protests at these moves, but not enough to prevent them. The dissidents seceded and formed their own group under the old name in 1869, while the temperance branch soon disappeared into the Ohio State Horticultural Society.[18] Thus winemaking continued around Cleveland. Most of the vineyards were planted to Catawba in the early days, but as happened throughout the eastern part of the Lake Erie grape belt, the Concord and other table varieties came more and more to dominate. Winemaking in northeastern Ohio never attained any very considerable proportions, but it managed to persist for a long time: among the wineries of greater Cleveland were the Dover Bay Grape and Wine Company, the Lake View Wine Farm, and the Louis Harris Winery.[19]

The other focus of Ohio winegrowing was at Sandusky and the islands that lie scattered north of Sandusky Bay, in western Lake Erie. Vineyards here began to be planted in a substantial way about the end of the 1840s, and developed rapidly in the 1850s, largely through the work of German immigrants, and, as has been noted earlier, by growers who migrated from the doomed Cincinnati vineyards to the promising region of Lake Erie. One of them, the Alsatian Michael Werk and his sons, had 400 acres of vines near Vermillion by the 1870s.[20] Another northern Ohio producer, H. T. Dewey, of Sandusky, was one of the first to open a New York agency for eastern wines. When Dewey sent a shipment of his wines to New York in 1865, he found that no merchant was interested in them, or in eastern American wines generally. He thereupon opened his own store and continued to sell his American wines there even after he shifted his winemaking from Ohio to New Jersey.[21] Before the century was out, the Sandusky region was the undisputed center of Ohio wine production, from such wineries as those of the Diamond Wine Company, Duroy & Haines, the Sweet Valley Wine Company, and M. Hommell, among other names now vanished.[22] Sandusky was also the scene of important cooperage works, specializing in supplying the wineries; and at Sandusky the firm of Klotz & Kremer made the machines—crushers, presses, pumps—that equipped wineries throughout the eastern states.[23] The most attractive sites in the Sandusky region were the Lake Erie islands, which were almost entirely given over to vineyards and thus presented a concentration of vines and wines unmatched anywhere else in the country. Some of the island methods were Old World traditions, like the practice of growing willows and rye to provide shoots and straw with which to tie up the vines, a tradition that persisted on South Bass Island long after cheap string was readily available.[24]

From about 1880 onwards, the vineyards of Ohio at the western end of Lake Erie furnished the main part of the state's statistics; here, too, the Catawba reigned as the premier grape for winemaking. In 1880 Ohio had twenty-one winemaking establishments; in 1890 when the state produced almost two million gallons of wine, there were fifty-eight; in that year the vineyards throughout the state reached their greatest-ever size, before or since, of 33,000 acres. From that high point a slow, but fairly steady, decline set in: there were fifty-two wineries in 1900, but just before Prohibition the number had dwindled to thirty-nine.[25]

This diminution was owing to some other causes apart from the threat of prohibition. The growth of the city of Cleveland, for one thing, forced some vineyards in that part of the state out of production; increased competition from the vine-

107 — Michel Hommel's winery, founded in 1878 in Sandusky, Ohio, by then the center of the Ohio wine trade. Hommel, a Frenchman from the great champagne town of Epernay, had a distinguished background in American wine: he had worked for Longworth in Cincinnati and for Cook in St. Louis. Like them, he specialized in sparkling wine and made a solid success with his White Star brand. (Author's collection)

yards of states on either side of Ohio—Pennsylvania, New York, and Michigan—accounted for other losses; so, too, did the diseases that Lake Erie growers for a long time had fondly hoped would not trouble them.[26] For a number of years, it is true, they escaped the rot and mildew that destroyed the vineyards along the Ohio River, but that time of immunity was only a postponement, not a permanent state of affairs. A heavy infestation of black rot showed up on the Lake Erie islands as early as 1862,[27] and though the disease was never as destructive as it was in the southern part of the state, it was a serious problem thereafter. The statistics of production show some violent swings from year to year, according to whether the rot or mildew did or did not appear in force in any given season. One estimate put the number of vines lost to disease throughout Ohio in the decade 1870–80 at 10,000 acres, a net decrease of 3,000.[28]

The extent to which the German influence permeated winemaking along Lake Erie in Ohio is at once apparent from a mere recital of winery names: Steuk (1855), Engels & Krudwig (1863), Miller (1865), Carl Lenk (1867), Peter Lonz (1884),

108 | The Golden Eagle Winery on Middle Bass Island, Lake Erie, Ohio, at one time supposed to have been the biggest in the United States. One of its proprietors, Michael Werk, had begun winegrowing in Cincinnati in the era of Longworth and had migrated successfully to the Lake Erie region to continue the work there after the industry around Cincinnati fell victim to disease. The building, much altered, still stands. (Author's collection)

Gustav Heineman (1886). The giant among these firms was the Golden Eagle Winery, founded in 1861 on Middle Bass Island by Michael Werk and Andrew Wehrle; with a capacity of 500,000 gallons it was, for a time at least, regarded as the biggest winery in the United States.[29]

Kelley's Island, the largest of the Lake Erie islands on the American side, and the first of them to be planted to vines, was the site of a considerable winemaking activity. The largest establishment was the Kelley's Island Wine Company, housed in a ponderous stone building looking like a feudal castle, and capable of storing 350,000 gallons of wine. Its operations were interestingly described by the French botanist J.-E. Planchon, on a visit of inspection in the vintage season of 1873. Grapes were brought in by wagons from all over the island, weighed, paid for on the spot, and sent by a steam-driven conveyor to the top floor of the winery, where they were crushed, destemmed, and the juice separated from the skins. The juice then went to the fermentation vats on the second floor, while the skins descended

KELLEY'S ISLAND

SWEET   CATAWBA.

109   The first of the Lake Erie islands on the American side to be planted, Kelley's Island flourished as a place of winemaking in the 1860s and 1870s. The Kelley's Island Wine Company crushed 9,000 tons of grapes in 1879, the produce of around 2,000 acres of vineyard. (From Bella C. Landauer, *Some Alcoholic Americana* [1932])

to the ground floor, where six great steam-powered presses, each one capable of handling three tons of material in six hours, awaited them. Below ground were two levels of vaulted cellars for the storage of wine in both casks and bottles, including champagne storage. The wines were made and bottled as varietals, including Concord, Ives Seedling, Delaware, Isabella, and Iona. There were nine other substantial wineries on Kelley's Island at the time, ranging from 50,000 to 350,000 gallons of storage capacity. Planchon was particularly struck by the cellar of the German Thomas Rush, with its rows of well-made and scrupulously maintained casks and vats; they reminded him, Planchon wrote somewhat extravagantly, of "the work of that race of powerful drinkers, who, in times past, symbolized the cult of Bacchus along the banks of the Rhine in the great Heidelberg tun." [30]

Planchon's observations, in Ohio and elsewhere, on the practices of American winemaking, are worth summarizing. In the first place, he tells us, the practice of chaptalizing—that is, of adding sugar to a must deficient in natural sugar—was standard in seasons when the grapes did not ripen sufficiently. This, he thought, was a perfectly innocent proceeding, especially if the sugar came from cane rather than potatoes: the latter sort gave the wine a strange flavor. More dubious was the equally widespread practice of making wine twice out of the same grapes: first the free-run juice was converted into white wine, and then the *marc,* the residue of skins and seeds, was fermented into a red wine by the addition of water and sugar. In this manner, Planchon noted, the Concord would give first a "white wine with a not very pronounced flavor, then an inferior red wine, agreeable enough and stable enough to keep." The practice of turning the residue of skins from the press into a thin, sharp wine called *piquette* was traditional in France, but the American product, according to Planchon, was better than that; the grapes had "superabundant quantities of acids, tannin and aroma" in their skins, and needed only sugar added to make a genuine wine.[31]

Planchon assured his French readers that despite the American winemakers' regular use of artificial methods, the average quality of American wine was higher than that of France—"superior not only to the frightful brews with which, under the name of wine, the public poisons itself in our cabarets, but superior to our *petits vins de consommation courante.*"[32] He reassuringly pointed out at the same time that the production costs of wine in eastern America were too high to raise a serious threat to the French, even though he was writing in the very depths of the phylloxera devastation in France. Far more likely, he thought, was the possibility that wines made from American vines grown in France would be exported to the United States.[33] It would be interesting to know whether such a thing ever did in fact happen, following the extensive planting of American vines as direct producers in France in the last quarter of the nineteenth century. Very possibly it did, though I have no evidence on the subject.

Michigan, like Ohio, Pennsylvania, and New York, a state where fruit growing was traditional thanks to the climatic influences of the Great Lakes, was a natural region for the extension of the viticulture already established along the Lake Erie shore. A vineyard was planted along the lake at Point de Peau, near Monroe, in 1863 by Joseph Sterling, and a few years later this region was proclaiming itself a new Rhineland.[34] As a matter of fact, the river in the region had been named the Raisin River by French *voyageurs* on account of the wild grapes growing there,[35] and the literal name "raisin" was doubtless closer to actuality than the poetic "Rhine," even though here, as so frequently elsewhere, the growers were largely German. By 1890 there were a half dozen wineries in and around Monroe, producing wine from the standard eastern native varieties.[36] The really considerable development in Michigan was in the "fruit belt" in the southwestern corner of the state, where the waters of Lake Michigan tempered the climate to suit the production of apples, cherries, and grapes. A sizeable beginning was made there shortly after the Civil War. By 1880 there were already more than 2,000 acres of vineyard.[37] Some of the traditional eastern wine varieties—Catawba, Delaware, and Dutchess—were grown and some wine produced, but Michigan was dominated by the Concord. In 1900, there were only five small wineries in the state, with a production of only 33,000 gallons, scattered in the region of Monroe (on the Lake Erie side) and Muskegon (on the Lake Michigan side).[38] The growth of Michigan as a wine-producing state did not really begin until after Prohibition.

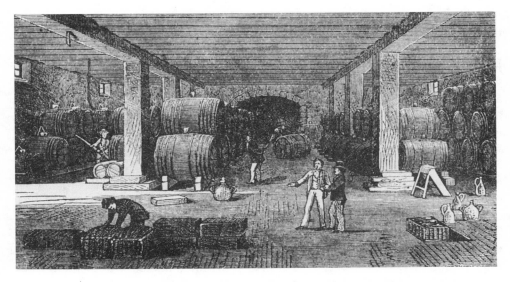

I IO   Vaults of the Egg Harbor Vineyards, Egg Harbor City, New Jersey, in the sandy flatlands of the southeastern part of the state, a center of red wine production in the eastern United States that was largely in the hands of German producers. (From *Industries of New Jersey* [1883])

Pennsylvania, to finish this brief review of winegrowing in the Great Lakes states, has its short stretch of Lake Erie shore in the far northwest of the state, in Erie County, linking the grape belts of New York and Ohio. Indeed, from Cleveland on the west to Buffalo on the east and north, the region is essentially one from the point of view of the grape, and the Pennsylvania section has shared the same development as the rest. Commercial winemaking began in Erie County as early as 1863, but after flourishing briefly was displaced by the spread of the Concord and the dominance of the table grape and juice markets. From a high of 97,000 gallons of wine in 1870, Pennsylvania—which largely meant Erie County—slipped to only 51,000 gallons in 1900.[39] Commercial winemaking on a modest scale also persisted in the German-settled parts of the state, where some success had been gained with the Alexander grape in the 1820s in York County. In the latter part of the century there were small wineries in and around Reading, all operated by Pennsylvania Dutchmen.[40]

In New Jersey the beginning made in the eighteenth century by Edward Antill and William Alexander had not been followed up in any effective way, though there are many sites in the state well suited to viticulture that might have encouraged continued experiment. The abundance and quality of New Jersey apples had suggested another sort of possibility to the farmers and orchardists. Jersey cider had been famous since early colonial times, and it was an easy step to make it sparkle and to offer the result to the public as "champagne." Newark was the center of this trade, well established by the 1840s. The Scottish traveller Alexander Mackay was told then that most "imported champagne" in America came in fact from Newark. Even under its assumed name, Mackay found it "excellent as a summer drink. Many is the American connoisseur of champagne who has his taste cultivated on Newark cider."[41] The fountain of cider that flowed through New Jersey also supplied the stills that made applejack, or Jersey Lightning. Essex County, where Newark is, alone produced 300,000 gallons of applejack in 1810, and though a growing temperance movement much reduced production thereafter, there were still 388 distilleries in New Jersey in 1834, some of them no doubt kept in operation by the state's bountiful apple crop.[42]

Proper winegrowing began at the time of the grape boom of the 1850s and 1860s, in the region of Egg Harbor City in the sands of south Jersey. Here an agricultural society was organized in 1859 and carried out tests of some forty different grape varieties to determine which were best suited to the local conditions.[43] The dozen varieties selected included the staple Concord and Catawba, but also the briefly popular but now forgotten Martha, and, most interestingly, several native varieties for the production of red wine: Norton, Ives, Eumelan, and Clevener.[44] At Egg Harbor City, as in so many other places, the first impetus was from the Germans; the *Gardener's Monthly* reported in 1865 that the town, which had hardly existed eight years earlier, was now full of Germans making wine, "as good as any in the world" according to the boast of one of them.[45] Julius Hincke, Jacob Schuster & Son, August Heil, Charles Saalman, and J. Furrer were among these early producers:[46] they were soon joined by H. T. Dewey & Sons, whose vineyards were originally on the Lake Erie shore of Ohio, and by L. N. Renault, who bought land in Egg Harbor City in 1864.[47] In the early days Hincke was the enterprising grower of the region. He exhibited his wines to good effect at the great Philadelphia Centennial Exhibition in 1876 and at the Paris Exposition of 1878, winning medals at both for wines that he called "Iohlink" and "Franklin"—the latter is the name of a native variety, but what was "Iohlink"?[48] The firm of Dewey was long known for its red wine from the Norton grape, and Renault for its New Jersey champagne—this one from grapes rather than apples. Production was considerable, but never large enough to make much of a difference to the market: by 1879 there were nearly 800 acres of vineyard around Egg Harbor City; in 1900, a year of peak production, New Jersey made about 220,000 gallons of wine from eleven wineries. Native red wines, never very common in the east, gave New Jersey its special place in American winegrowing.

Only a few miles away from Egg Harbor City, at Vineland, New Jersey, something was going on that would make a profound difference to the character of grape growing in the east. This was the invention of grape juice. Vineland was a real estate speculation promoted, successfully, by a Philadelphia lawyer named Charles Landis, beginning in 1861, on 32,000 acres of cutover and swampy land in southern New Jersey. "Intending to make it a vine country," Landis said of one of the towns he laid out on his acres, "I called it Vineland."[49] He did not, however, explain why it should also have a charter forbidding the sale of alcoholic beverages, but so it did. The combination of viticulture and prohibition, which strikes

III | Workers (and a proprietor?) at the Renault Winery in Egg Harbor City, New Jersey, enjoying the sparkling wine for which the firm was noted. The picture was taken in 1906. (Huntington Library)

us as so strange, is pretty clear evidence of the strength of prohibitionist sentiment and of the establishment of a table grape market as an alternative to winemaking so early as 1861: we have already noticed a comparable development in Chautauqua County, New York, just after the Civil War. Landis's temperance principles did not, however, prevent a large Italian community settled at Vineland in the 1870s from making wine in commercial quantities; a German named Peter Lenk also operated a winery in Vineland until black rot destroyed the supply of grapes at the end of the eighties.[50]

To Vineland there came in 1868 a dentist named Thomas Welch, a restless type of which the American nineteenth century seems to have had so many. English-born, but reared in upstate New York, he had been a Wesleyan preacher, then a

112 Four generations of the Welch family. Dr. Thomas Welch, the inventor of grape juice, is seated; his son, Dr. Charles E. Welch, the successful promoter of the invention, stands on the left. The picture dates from some time before 1903, when the elder Welch died. (From William Chazanof, *Welch's Grape Juice* [1977])

doctor, and then a dentist, practicing in New York State and in Minnesota before fetching up in Vineland. He liked to experiment and to diversify: he had invented a stomach-soothing syrup, had made a trade in compounding and selling dental alloys, and had devised a "Sistem of Simplified Spelling."[51]

In Vineland, where he was communion steward to the Vineland Methodist Church, he began to take thought about the problem of wine in the sacrament. To Dr. Welch, and to many other ardent prohibitionists, the centrality of wine in the service of the Christian church was a rock of offense and a stone of stumbling. To the riddle of how Our Lord could possibly have recommended the Demon Rum—anything alcoholic was so identified in the circles to which Dr. Welch belonged—as the symbol of His own sacrificial presence there seemed to be only one

113   Eliphalet Nott (1773—1866), Presbyterian minister, prohibitionist, and for sixty-two years president of Union College, Schenectady, New York. He revived the notion that there were two kinds of wine mentioned in the Bible, one fermented, the other not, and so helped to contribute to the invention of grape juice. (From Andrew Van Vranken Raymond, *Union University* [1907])

answer: the wine of these latter days was a sad corruption of the wine Our Savior knew, which must have been an innocuous temperance beverage suitable to divine purity. By what distortions and evasions of historical and philological evidence such people were able to sustain their conviction we need not trouble to discuss here.[52] The case is a clear instance, if one is needed, of the power of the wish over the fact.

But Dr. Welch, in Vineland, in 1869, had an unprecedented opportunity to re-alize that wish—in fact, to make a non-alcoholic "wine." For two things had come together for him: first, he had the vineyards of Vineland all around him, and second and most important, he had learned of the experiments of Pasteur in the control of fermentation. The process we call pasteurization had been made known only a few years before, but its obvious importance had spread it abroad quickly—it was dis-cussed in the *Transactions* of the California State Agricultural Society in 1867, for example. Now, thinking about how he, an incorruptible prohibitionist, could sup-ply wine for the communion services of his church, Dr. Welch was inspired to try the effect of heating an unfermented grape juice. I know of no positive evidence on the question, but the juice he used was presumably that of the Concord grape. By the simple expedient of bringing a liquid to a temperature of 140° Fahrenheit, as Pasteur had shown, one could kill whatever yeasts it contained and so preserve it against fermentation. Thus was the first preserved grape juice of which we have record created. It was certainly a new thing under the sun. The three great staples of classical Western civilization—bread, cheese, and wine—are all the products of a natural process of fermentation that both transforms and preserves the substances upon which it works. Now, in the name of the "natural," but in fact through the ap-plication of modern technological understanding, an American dentist had shown how to hold the blood of the grape in artificial arrest. It was the final insult to injured nature to call it, as its inventor did, "Dr. Welch's Unfermented Wine," and to sell it in burgundy-style bottles—a parody in name, appearance, and substance.[53]

Welch made some efforts to sell his product, but gave up after a few years, having met with little encouragement. In 1875, however, his son, Charles E. Welch, also in practice as a dentist, determined to resume the manufacture and sale of his father's invention. He evidently saw its commercial possibilities, but for many years after the younger Welch took it over, the business remained shaky. At last, in 1893, Charles Welch quit his dental practice and devoted himself wholly to the business of "grape juice," as he had now decided to call it (in England, though, it was sold as "Unfermented Port wine").[54] Shortly thereafter, the vineyards in New Jersey were smitten by black rot and the supply of grapes became a critical problem. Charles Welch at once moved his operations to upstate New York, first to Watkins Glen on Seneca Lake, and then, after only a year, to Westfield, in the grape belt of Chautauqua County. That was in 1897. In that year, Welch's Grape Juice Company pressed about 300 tons of Chautauqua County Concords and sold 50,000 gallons of the pasteurized juice; a decade later, sales had reached a million gallons annually.[55]

The success of grape juice in the American market clearly owed much to preexisting prohibitionist sentiment, as its invention had; but Charles Welch understood the importance of advertising, and he effectively combined moral uplift with commercial astuteness. He founded two magazines to promote his product, one called *The Acorn* in 1875, and five years later another called *The Progress:*[56] in these Welch could put his advertisements of grape juice together with editorial matter promoting the temperance cause and the virtues of Welch's grape juice, the whole flavored with fundamentalist Christianity and the offer of premiums. "If your druggist hasn't the kind that was used in Galilee containing not one particle of alcohol, write us for prices," as one ad put it.[57] And, since temperance and religion might not be attraction enough, grape juice was described as good for everything that might ail one: "Dr. Welch's Grape Juice is especially recommended in Typhoid Fever, Pneumonia, Pluritis [*sic*], Peritonitis, Rheumatis, for Lying-in Patients and for all forms of chronic diseases except Diabetes Melitus."[58] Since Charles Welch certainly did especially recommend his grape juice to all and sundry, there was that much truth in this claim, and, perhaps, not too much harm. One may note that for many years grape juice was a drugstore, rather than food store, item, which no doubt affected the character of its advertising.[59]

Welch did not confine his promotional efforts to print. He took advantage of the Columbian Exposition of 1893 to set up a stand and distribute samples of grape juice to the crowds gathered in Chicago, as he did later at the St. Louis World's Fair and at other expositions. He also set up a permanent stand on the boardwalk at Atlantic City to catch the holidaymakers in their thousands. In his program of national advertising, he made grape juice all things to all people: for the medical trade it was presented as a tonic; for the religious, as a scriptural necessity; for the secular, as a pleasant drink. Later, in the vacuum created by Prohibition, the company was even bold enough to proclaim Welch's grape juice "the national drink."[60]

The demands of the Welch Company for Concord grapes ensured that the Lake Erie grape belt would remain entirely dominated by that variety, and not only the Lake Erie grape belt. It was not long before new regions were devoted to the growing of Concords and the supply of Welch's grape juice. Welch had bought out a large competitor at North East, Pennsylvania, only a few miles away from Westfield, in 1911. As expansion continued, the company built a new plant at St. Catharine's, Ontario, in 1914, amidst the vineyards of the Niagara Peninsula; in 1918 the company acquired a plant at Lawton, Michigan, in the grape-growing southwest corner of the state.[61] Prohibition being a boon to the grape juice industry rather than the bane it was for the winegrower, Welch's added another factory in 1922, this one at Springdale, Arkansas, in the Ozarks, where 15,000 acres of company vineyards were planted, or so a company statement proclaimed in 1925.[62] Official figures are much more modest, though substantial.[63] By the end of this process of expansion grape growing outside of California was virtually synonymous with growing Concords for the provision of juice, jams, and jellies. That situation is now, at last, beginning to change, but only beginning. For most of its modern history, and apart from merely natural conditions, eastern viticulture has been shaped by three historic events in combination: the introduction of the Concord grape in 1854; Dr. Welch's invention of grape juice in 1869; and the institution of national Prohibition in 1920. Together they have powerfully retarded the growth of a healthy wine industry.

Missouri, Kansas, and the Midwest

In Missouri, the center of winemaking in the Midwest, there was an expansive mood immediately following the Civil War. We have already noted the excited enthusiasm of George Husmann about the future of winemaking in Missouri, and he evidently managed to communicate that enthusiasm to others in the state. The Cliff Cave Wine Company was organized in 1866 to develop 240 acres of vineyard site on the Mississippi River, thirteen miles south of St. Louis. It had cellars in a natural cave—like the one where Tom Sawyer spied on Injun Joe not far away in Mark Twain's Hannibal—and a storage capacity of 100,000 gallons by 1870. The director was Dr. C. W. Spalding, M.D., of St. Louis, the co-editor, with Husmann, of the short-lived *Grape Culturist*.[64] Another postwar enterprise near St. Louis was the vineyard operated by an Irishman named J. J. Kelley at Webster Groves; there he produced wine from such native varieties as the Delaware and Norton that the French scientist Planchon, visiting in 1873, found excellent.[65]

In the same year that the Cliff Cave Company was set up, another, larger enterprise was founded on the Missouri River, not many miles to the east of Hermann, at Bluffton. This was the Bluffton Wine Company, which secured over 1,500 acres in Montgomery and Callaway counties, laid out the town of Bluffton, and then leased the land to tenants who were to grow the grapes for the winery.[66] This sort of scheme was called a "colony," and in one form or another it occurred frequently in the history of American settlement in the latter half of the nineteenth century. Two of the leading names in Missouri viticulture were among the incorporators of the Bluffton Company, Husmann of Hermann, and Isidor Bush of St. Louis. Samuel Miller, of Pennsylvania, a well-known horticulturist who had introduced the Martha and other varieties of native hybrid grapes, was in charge of the viticultural work. Husmann himself took the presidency of the firm and migrated from Hermann to Bluffton in 1869 when the cellars of the firm were complete and ready to begin production. The party inaugurating the cellars in February 1869 attracted a large group of St. Louis notables, mostly drawn from the German community, and the hopeful officers of the firm announced that they had received an order for forty cases of their Missouri Cynthiana and other wines from President U.S. Grant himself.[67]

In 1867, shortly after the founding of the Cliff Cave and Bluffton wineries, Dr. Spalding and Husmann founded the Mississippi Valley Grape Growers' Association to organize growers on both sides of the river, north and south of St.

The ruins of high hopes in Missouri: the Boonville Wine Company's building, shown in a nineteenth-century view, a victim of the bad times for midwestern winemakers after the Civil War. (From Charles Van Ravenswaay, *The Arts and Architecture of Germans in Missouri* [1977])

Louis.[68] All this must have seemed good evidence of the secure beginnings and bright future of winegrowing in Missouri. But the young hopes of the growers were soon knocked on the head; the crash of prices in 1871 forced the Bluffton Wine Company into bankruptcy;[69] at the same time diseases, especially the black rot, began to ravage the vineyards beyond all precedent, and the horizon for wine-growers seemed dark indeed. When, in 1880, the irrepressible Husmann published his *American Grape Growing and Wine Making,* he was forced to admit that the preceding decade had almost entirely falsified the hopes with which it had begun, not just in Missouri but in other states: "Prices in consequence of over production of inferior grapes and wines, came down to their lowest ebb, diseases and other disasters have occurred, and for a time it seemed almost as if grape growing had become a failure."[70] All was not lost, however. There was reason to be hopeful as growers learned their business better, and as the control of winemaking methods became more secure.

One new development of crucial assistance was not far away. This was the discovery, by one of those happy accidents that help to make revolutions, of the fungicide called bordeaux mixture, a compound of copper sulphate and lime. The mixture was applied by a harassed French grower to his vines bordering a roadside to make them look unappetizing and so to discourage casual thefts. Its fungicidal properties were somehow noticed, and it was then tested and brought to the attention of the public by the French scientist Alexis Millardet of Bordeaux in 1885.[71] It was soon thereafter introduced into the United States through the Department of Agriculture. Trials were made in afflicted vineyards in South Carolina, Virginia, New Jersey, and Missouri, with spectacularly good results.[72] This work was, incidentally, one of the first significant contributions of the newly established state agricultural experiment stations. Called "the first broad spectrum fungicide,"[73] bordeaux mixture for the first time gave the embattled eastern grape grower an effective weapon against black rot and downy mildew.

Throughout the ups and downs in the rest of the state, the industry at Hermann had been continuous and expanding. The biggest of the town's wineries, the firm of Poeschel & Scherer, put up its main building in 1869, added a cellar in 1874, and was producing on the order of 200,000 gallons in the 1880s. In the next decade it was taken over by new owners as the Stone Hill Wine Company and the production capacity expanded to over a million gallons. When the battleship *Missouri* was launched in 1901, it was wine from Stone Hill that christened her.[74] Other successful growers at Hermann, though not on the same scale as Stone Hill, were Henry Henze, August Langendoerfer, Frederick Loehnig, H. Schus, and Julius Hundhausen.[75] Winegrowing also continued in and around Augusta, near where Friedrich Muench had pioneered years before. Some vineyards and winemaking also developed in the southwestern corner of the state, in the Ozarks, and around Kansas City on the Missouri River: a hundred acres of wine grapes were reported in that region as early as 1870.[76]

By far the most significant and interesting work in Missouri in the nineteenth century—a work of vital importance to winegrowing around the world—came about through the phylloxera crisis that began its career of devastation in France in 1867, about the time that winegrowing in Missouri was being energetically expanded. It happened that Charles V. Riley (1843–95), the first state entomologist for Missouri, was a leading expert on the phylloxera; he was able, in 1870–71, to establish the identity of the American insect with the unknown creature at large in the vineyards of France, a first step of essential importance in combating the pest.[77] As a resident of Missouri (though English-born), Riley knew something about native American vines; he was one of the first to suggest the idea of grafting vinifera to native American rootstocks, and his authority gave special weight to the suggestion. His work on phylloxera had made him well known in France; he had also visited that country, and he had assisted the experts sent over to this country by the French government to learn about phylloxera.[78] Riley was thus in a position of special importance for the French in their search for a means of fighting against phylloxera. After hundreds of futile and often pathetic "cures" for the phylloxera infestation had been vainly tried in France, and when it gradually became clear that grafting vinifera vines onto resistant American roots was the only reliable and practical way to save the French wine industry, Riley was again appealed to, this time for his advice on the selection of appropriate American varieties for the purpose. He in turn referred the French experts who were carrying out the necessary trials to the veteran growers and nurserymen of Missouri.[79]

115   The Stone Hill Vineyards and Winery, Hermann, Missouri, in 1888. Descended from the earliest winery at Hermann, it grew to be the largest. (From *History of Franklin, Jefferson, Washington, Crawford and Gasconade Counties* [1888])

In this way it came about that Missouri took the lead in furnishing the rootstocks that saved the vineyards of France. Three nurserymen in particular, all of them winemakers themselves, were in the forefront of this work. They were George Husmann, who, after the failure of the Bluffton Wine Company, had established himself as a nurseryman in Sedalia, Missouri; Isidor Bush, the learned Austrian whose Bushberg nursery and Bush Wine Company were in St. Louis; and Hermann Jaeger, a trained viticulturist from Switzerland who had come to Missouri in 1867 and planted a vineyard at New Switzerland, in the southwest Ozark region of Newton County. The combination of Riley, Husmann, Bush, and Jaeger probably could not have been matched outside of Missouri in the 1870s, both for relevant scientific knowledge and for practical experience in viticulture. It was highly fitting, then, that Missouri supplied the vines that, after extended trial in France, yielded the sorts that enabled the French to reconstitute their afflicted vineyards. Writing in 1880, Husmann reported that "millions upon millions of American cuttings and vines have already been shipped to France."[80] George Ordish has calculated that the potential market for American rootstocks sufficient to replant the vast vineyards of France was on the order of eleven billion plants[81]—a figure that might well make the Missouri nurserymen imagine wealth beyond the dreams of avarice. But of course the French soon began propagating from their own nurseries of imported American vines. The significant contribution of Missouri was to provide the original vines from which a stock could be propagated and disseminated in France by the French themselves. The years from 1873 to 1876 were the period of greatest activity in this movement of cuttings from Missouri to France.[82]

Missouri was also ideally situated to provide a variety of native vines, a point of great importance since it was quickly discovered that American vines were by no means uniform in their power to resist phylloxera. Labrusca varieties, for example, were almost as tender and vulnerable to the louse as was vinifera itself. It was also found that the American species differed widely in their ability to serve as rootstock for vinifera: some took well to grafting, some less well. Another variable was the Americans' tolerance of French soils. Many French vineyards are on chalky soils—those of Champagne, to take a famous example—and some American varieties have an intense, even fatal, dislike of chalk. It was thus necessary to proceed slowly and to try as wide a range of experiment as the material available allowed. Here Missouri could be most useful, for it is a state where southwestern, midwestern, and southeastern climates meet. Labrusca, aestivalis, riparia, rupestris, cordifolia, and other species all grow in Missouri, so that if one sort failed another could be provided. As it happened, the first varieties sent for experiment to France were labrusca and labrusca-riparia hybrids; they did not do well. Then varieties of aestivalis were shipped. In the end, it was found that riparia and rupestris varieties did best, and they provided the basis on which rebuilding could proceed. Jaeger, Husmann, and Bush shipped great quantities of them.[83]

One may mention here that the French did not confine their use of American vines to the roots alone. They also planted the vines for their fruit, and though officially disapproved, there are still many vineyards of old-fashioned American hybrids, known as *producteurs directs,* to be found in France: Noah, Clinton, Othello, and Lenoir among others. At the same time, experiments were made in hybridizing the American and French vines, just as American hybridizers had been doing on this side of the Atlantic since the middle of the century. The French have produced many valuable varieties through hybridizing, a work still actively carried on, and though the use of such hybrids is now officially discouraged in Europe, they are widely and increasingly planted in the eastern United States. The so-called French hybrids are an unlooked for, but welcome, consequence of the phylloxera disaster.

Hermann Jaeger deserves a word more. He was an indefatigable worker in developing and testing better varieties of grapes for American conditions. With this object he explored the Ozark region and originated hybrids and seedlings from his finds, many of them from the Post Oak grape (*V. lincecumii*).[84] Jaeger was also partial to rupestris varieties. When the French scientist Pierre Viala, searching for American vines adapted to chalky French soils, called on Jaeger in Missouri he was offered rupestris wine made by his host; it had, Viala said, "a very good color and a taste good enough."[85] It is interesting to know that one of Jaeger's hybrids found its way from Missouri to the Ardèche region of France, where it became the ancestor of the famous series of hybrids developed by Georges Couderc and Louis Seibel, now widely planted in this country as well as in Europe.[86]

George Husmann also deserves another and final word. In many ways his career was symbolic of the fortunes of winegrowing in the United States itself, for it touched many points of development and mirrored many representative changes. A brief outline will make the truth of this proposition clear. We have already looked at his origins in the winegrowing community of Hermann, at his embodiment of the scientific German style of experiment, and at his eager proselytizing for winegrowing through his publications. Then came his failure, in common with that of many others, in the incautious days after the war. Undaunted, he turned to the propagation of vines in a nursery business, and had a large part in supplying the French with native vines to combat the phylloxera. The rest of his story begins in 1878, when he was appointed the first professor of horticulture at the University of Missouri in Columbia. There he at once laid out a vineyard on university ground and had over 130 varieties growing by 1880.[87] In 1881, as though to symbolize the transference of power from the East to the West, Husmann accepted a position as manager of the Talcoa Vineyards in the Napa Valley, California, belonging to the James W. Simonton estate. The vineyards were being destroyed by phylloxera, and Husmann was a recognized expert who might save them. He had sent native root-stocks to California as well as to France in the years when he was a nurseryman.[88]

Husmann's migration to California in 1881 came at just the moment when phylloxera was at last recognized as a menace to the state, and at the same moment that saw the formation of the Board of State Viticultural Commissioners and the founding of the university's viticultural program. Husmann set to work with his invariable energy and enthusiasm, and soon had three hundred acres planted in native American vines for experiment to determine their resistance and their suitability for grafting to vinifera.[89] He also continued his interest in the whole subject of winegrowing, making inquiries into the various developments in California and taking part in the professional meetings of the state's winegrowers. The result was that within the decade of his arrival in California he had written a book, called *Grape Culture and Wine-Making in California: A Practical Manual for the Grape-Grower and Wine-Maker* (1888).

This was the third phase of Husmann's oracular performances before the American public: in the first, going back to his early days as a grower and wine-maker at Hermann, Missouri, he proclaimed the future of Missouri and the "great west" as the home of a marvelous winegrowing economy; in the second, as a somewhat sobered but still convinced prophet, he sold American vines to the French and wrote a book to encourage eastern American growers generally after a decade of sore disappointment and distress. In his final phase, he joined the growing company of visionaries who had found the future revealed to them in California. In all of this, there was nothing meretricious, nothing affected. Husmann was, clearly, a true believer, wherever he found himself, and a shrewd judge too of what was going on and what might be made of it. That California claimed him at last is no discredit to the rest of the country. I note it here only as completing his role as symbolic instance of the progress of American winegrowing in the century, a progress in which California was surely the culminating stage. Long before his death in

1902, Husmann had left the Talcoa Vineyard for his own property of Oak Glen, in the Chiles Valley of Napa County. The winery that he built there has now disappeared, but the professor's work and his example are still vivid.

As we saw in an earlier chapter, winegrowing in other midwestern states responded very quickly to the early successes in Ohio, Indiana, and Missouri. There were vineyards and wineries in Illinois and Wisconsin before the Civil War, and in Iowa, Nebraska, and Kansas not long after it. In Iowa, for instance, the State Horticultural Society reported in 1868 on the results of grape growing and winemaking in sixteen different counties with all the established varieties of native hybrids. The testimony was all optimistic, and one witness declared that "one man can tend three acres of grapes as easily as twenty acres of corn."[90] The fact that corn has long since triumphed over its rivals in Iowa does not necessarily mean that the grape could not still have a significant place there. In the same year as the Iowa report, 1868, Illinois produced 225,000 gallons of wine, more than Missouri and only barely less than New York.[91] The very heart of the Midwest was evidently a place where people thought well of the chances of grape growing and winemaking.

In a large and general view, the two most favored regions for winegrowing in the Midwest were along the two great river valleys of the Mississippi and the Missouri: along the first of these from southern Wisconsin to a point well below St. Louis; and along the second from Omaha to St. Louis. On the Mississippi there was significant viticulture at Dubuque, Nauvoo, Keokuk, and St. Louis; on the Missouri, at Council Bluffs, St. Joseph, Leavenworth, Kansas City, and, of course, at the old German settlements from Boonville to St. Louis. Grapes were not confined to the riverine slopes, however; they were raised on the prairies of the Illinois interior, on the Ozark hills of southwestern Missouri, on the rich black lands of central Iowa, on the arid bluffs of western Kansas, and any other sort of middle western site that might challenge the ambitions of a horticultural pioneer.

It should certainly be known that these middle western states were winemaking states, since the fact is largely forgotten today. Winemaking at Nauvoo, Illinois, is a notable exception in having persisted down to the present day. More typical is the history illustrated on the other side of the river from Nauvoo by the White Elk Vineyards of Keokuk, Iowa. Established in 1869 by Hiram Barney of New York, the one hundred acres of White Elk vines produced, by 1880, up to 30,000 gallons of Concord, Ives, Norton, and Clinton wines a year.[92] But they could not survive the unequal struggle against the growing power of prohibition on one side and the unremitting attack of endemic diseases on the other. There were a number of beginnings comparable to the White Elk Vineyards scattered over the wide distances of the flat Midwest, but to try to give a connected account of them would present a distorted idea of their importance in the general agricultural scene in the latter half of the nineteenth century. Winegrowing was always an exotic activity in most of this territory, at the mercy of unfriendly nature and regarded with suspicious hostility by large parts of the population. Still, though winegrowing was scattered and small-scale in these states, its history recapitulates the most familiar themes of pioneer American experience in this effort. In the first place, it was largely the work of continental immigrants, who were almost certain to be German, Swiss, or French. In the second place, it was sometimes an aspect of communitarian life, either religious or utopian. And it had to face the inevitable obstacles: powerful endemic diseases, and intolerant prohibitionist hostility. These themes may be briefly illustrated.

The Germans of Belleville, Illinois, have already been mentioned, and the Germans, it seems, almost always gave the lead elsewhere in the state, as they had at Belleville. John Bauer, the son of a German winegrower in Rhenish Bavaria, and John Tanner, a Swiss, introduced winegrowing to Nauvoo, Illinois, in the early 1850s, and one of the earliest wineries there belonged to a man from Liechtenstein named Rheinberger.[93] Louis Koch, a Saxon, operated a winery for many years before and after the Civil War, at Golconda, on the Ohio River.[94] As viticulture spread up and down Illinois along the length of its Mississippi River border, and into the prairies to the east, one continues to encounter German names: Theodore Engelmann operated his Looking-Glass Vineyard at Mascoutah; Dr. H. Schroeder his Marble Front Wine House in Peoria; Friedrich Hecker at Belleville, Fred Schneiter at St. Elmo, and Theophile Huber at Illinois City are other instances.[95] Hecker was a man of considerable eminence, a lawyer and politician from Baden who had been forced into exile for his revolutionary activities. He settled among the learned German farmers in the region of Belleville, fought with distinction in the Civil War, and afterwards cultivated his farm with success. He made viticulture a special interest and corresponded on American grape varieties with experts in Germany at the time of the phylloxera crisis.[96] Theophile Huber, whose vineyard went back to 1867, was an active experimenter in breeding new varieties of native grapes; so were Ludwig Hencke of Collinsville, and J. Balziger of Highland, G. A. Ensenburger of Bloomington, and Otto Wasserzieher of Nauvoo.[97] The German propensity to experiment was not restricted to such eminent names as Engelmann, Husmann, and Rommel, but was diffused widely and shared by many obscure, but useful, workers.

Perhaps no state has been thought of as more thoroughly and permanently "Dry" than Kansas: it was the first state to adopt constitutional prohibition; its politicians were usually notable among the public spokesmen for the Dry cause; it was the home of the absurd Carrie A. Nation, the ax-wielding destroyer of saloons. As the president of the State Temperance Union vaunted in 1890, "Kansas is the mausoleum of the saloon, the sepulchre of its vices, the tomb of its iniquities."[98] Besides, its rolling prairies seem utterly unfitted to grape growing: Bacchus loves the hillsides, and there are none in Kansas. In the popular imagery of the United States, Kansas is a place to grow wheat, and that, in fact, is what most of the state's acreage is devoted to. Yet there was a time when the future of winegrowing looked quite promising in Kansas, and perhaps such a time will come again.

Wild vines flourish in Kansas just as they do in every other part of the Midwest. Captain Etienne Venyard de Bourgmont, on an expedition to what is now the northeastern corner of the state in 1724, was supplied with grapes there by the local Indians; what is more, he and his men made wine from the wild summer grapes that they found growing in abundance along the Missouri River bluffs.[99] Eighty years later, when Lewis and Clark passed the site where Bourgmont had found his grapes, they saw the same abundance: "On the shores were great quantities of summer and fall grapes."[100] It would be another half century before much settlement had been made in Kansas, but when it came, the grapes were still there to meet the pioneer. One settler heading west from Kansas City just after the Civil War recalls the air of June on the Kansas prairie as "fragrant with wild grape blossoms."[101] Another early settler, describing how they used to go "graping" along the Kaw River bottoms, remembered that "one could drive the wagon under the vines as they hung from low tree tops and pick the fruit directly into the buckets and tubs provided."[102] I myself remember in the 1930s swinging across a Kansas creek on a great festoon of wild grape vine hanging from the trees along the bank.

Such an obvious invitation to try grape growing was responded to quickly. We have already noted the work of John Burr and Dr. Stayman around Leavenworth in the 1860s. Another pioneer in grape growing, a bold one, was a nurseryman named A. M. Burns, who set up a nursery on the arid plains of Riley County in 1857 and specialized in vines. In his catalogue for 1866 he wrote as one who had proved beyond doubt the harmony between Kansas and the grape: "I now think I can with safety predict a glorious future for the grape in Kansas. It is only a matter of time, and some who, when I commenced to test the vine, sneered at the idea, may yet live to see the day when our bluffs will be teeming with millions of dollars of wealth, while they ought to hang their heads with shame at their own ignorance."[103] To anyone who has had the patience to read to this point in my narrative, Burns's words will have a distinct pathos: they echo so closely what other intrepid pioneers had to say about their work and their vision in the two centuries before Burns wrote that one can hardly avoid the ironic connection between his boast and their failure. Yet we cannot say that Burns was wrong: only that the trial has not yet been sufficiently made. Burns offered a list of more than 150 varieties for sale, all of them native American vines, including such aboriginal hybrids as the Alexander and the Bland as well as the latest popular hybrids such as the Concord, the Iona, and Rogers' hybrids. He was also producing his own new varieties for trial in central Kansas.[104]

Burns was not just a voice crying alone in the wilderness, for there were many to share his faith. Who was the first to make wine in Kansas does not appear, but the Brenner family must have been among the earliest to do so, and they return us to the theme of the European element in the Midwest. The two brothers Brenner, Adam and Jacob, were born in the celebrated wine town of Deidesheim, Rheinpfalz, and migrated to Kansas in the 1860s. There they settled in Doniphan County, in the far northeastern corner of the state where the Missouri River forms the boundary and where the early explorers had noted the abundance of native grapes. Jacob Brenner planted his Central Vineyards in 1864 and developed sacramental wines as a specialty; Adam Brenner planted his Doniphan Vineyards in 1865; George Brenner, Jacob's son, planted his Bellevue Vineyards in 1869. The family's vineyards lay adjacent, and included such varieties as Elvira from Missouri, Goethe from Massachusetts, and Norton from Virginia. By 1883 they had, together, over a hundred acres of vines and a winery capacity of over 60,000 gallons.[105] There was at least a touch of French influence in Kansas as well. In Douglas County, just west of Kansas City, Isador Labarriere was growing grapes and making wine in the 1870s, and in the same county August Jacot built a wine cellar and planted a vineyard in the 1880s; there is still a hamlet called Vinland in the area, no doubt evoking thoughts of Vikings rather than of wine in the minds of its Kansas neighbors, who have long been out of the habit of familiarity with wine.[106] In Miami County, not far from Vinland, R. W. Massey had been growing grapes since just after the Civil War around Paola, on the Marais des Cygnes River, where, only a few years earlier, the fanatical John Brown had been preaching against the wickedness of slavery and slaying such proslavery men as he could find. Massey hoped to form a "grape colony" in the area, but there is no evidence that he did so.[107]

When the Kansas State Horticultural Society was formed, it at once made grape culture a part of its work—the grape forms a prominent part of the society's official seal. At the 1871 meeting it approved such varieties as Ives, Norton, and Clinton for "general culture for wine," and Creveling, Catawba, and Delaware for "amateur culture for wine." At the same meeting in 1871 "the manufacture of grapes into wine was ably discussed, *pro* and *con*."[108] In 1871 and 1872 the society heard lectures on the grape from Dr. Stayman of Leavenworth, and from the distinguished Dr. Warder, one of the pioneers of winemaking in Cincinnati.[109] The State Board of Agriculture, an official branch of the state, was also concerned with winemaking; M. Labarriere exhibited his wines to the board in 1873, and the *Transactions* of the board regularly report the statistics of viticulture in the state. These make rather startling reading for anyone who finds it hard to connect the ideas of Kansas and the grape. In 1872, for example, vineyards were reported in fifty counties, and the production of wine in that year was put at about 35,000 gallons.[110] A year later, though the production of wine had fallen off, there were more than five and a half thousand acres of vines reported in the state, from all but seventeen of its seventy-three counties.[111] The effect of these extensive plantings was evident by 1880, the year the state went Dry: the census of that year reported a production of 226,000 gallons of wine from Kansas. Even after Prohibition, the state took notice of viticulture by establishing an experimental vineyard at the Agricultural Experiment Station in Manhattan (where Burns's nursery was) in 1888. This began with 64 varieties of native grape and had grown to include 157 varieties by 1894; the vineyard was used for experiments in spraying and winter protection, as well as for determining what were the best varieties to recommend to Kansas growers.[112]

Working against all this interest, whether official, commercial, or amateur, was the powerful prohibitionist sentiment that seems somehow to be just as native to Kansas as its wild grapes are. At the meeting of the State Horticultural Society in 1871, in the very midst of the discussion on winemaking, one member suddenly offered a resolution condemning "the use and manufacture of wines,"[113] and, though the resolution was rejected, the threat that it expressed grew rather than diminished. The passage of constitutional prohibition in 1880 put an end to official encouragement of winegrowing, of course, though it does not seem to have shut down such wineries as already existed. The state of things in Kansas by the end of the century is exhibited by a curious volume published by the State Horticultural Society in 1901 called *The Grape in Kansas*. On the title page stands this remarkable declaration about "the grape":

> The oldest cultivated fruit. The finest of all table fruits. A fruit too good to be made a chief source of the degradation of the race as an alluring (yet intoxicating) principle. To the glory of Kansas, 99½ per cent. of this luscious fruit which grows freely all over the state is used without fermentation.[114]

In its treatment of the grape, the book gives recipes for canned grapes, grape jam, grape jelly, grape marmalade, grape pie, pickled grapes, spiced grapes, and grape syrup, but not a hint about wine. The entire discussion of fermentation is confined to this succinct assertion: "Ferment is decay, decomposition, rot. Alcohol is only produced by decay, decomposition, rot."[115] And that remained the official view of things in Kansas for the next fifty years. It is no wonder that grape growing gradually withered away in a state that its hopeful pioneers had declared—not altogether fancifully—to be "the home of the vine." There are now beginning to be heard in Kansas prophecies of new beginnings in winemaking. If they should be fulfilled, one may hope that the new winemakers of the state will hold the pioneers of the grape in Kansas in pious memory. They have long been lost in the oblivion thrust upon them by the state's history of prohibition.

About a hundred miles north of the early Kansas vineyards, in the same Missouri River country, at least one winegrower was active in Nebraska. Peter Pitz, who had been a winemaker on the Rhine before settling near Plattsmouth, Nebraska, had about twelve acres of vines and a cellar sunk thirty feet deep in the ground against summer heat and winter blasts. Pitz made three kinds of wine from his grapes—white, red, and yellow (!)—and he claimed to do so entirely without the assistance of added sugar or water. A report on his operations in 1896 noted that Pitz's success had stimulated "a number of German capitalists" to investigate the chances of winegrowing in Nebraska.[116] No extensive development followed, but a small industry has persisted in the region, especially on the opposite bank of the Missouri, in Iowa, around Council Bluffs. One may note, too, that back in the days of the grape boom of the sixties, when hybridizing was all the rage, Nebraska made its contribution: two varieties, at least, were introduced by R. O. Thompson, of Nursery Hill, Nebraska, and though neither had any success, they are good evi-

HOW TO GROW AND USE.

THE GRAPE

IN KANSAS.

The oldest cultivated fruit.   The finest of all table fruits.

A fruit too good to be made a chief source of the degradation of the race as
an alluring (yet intoxicating) principle.

To the glory of Kansas, 99½ per cent. of this luscious fruit which grows freely
all over the state is used without fermentation.

COMPILED AND REVISED FOR THE

KANSAS STATE HORTICULTURAL SOCIETY,

By WILLIAM H. BARNES, Secretary,

State Capitol, Topeka, Kan.

ISSUED BY THE STATE,

1901.

116 The extraordinary boast of this
title page—that it is the "glory"
of Kansas to consume its grapes
fresh rather than fermented—speaks volumes
about the attitudes of a constitutionally dry
state and about the cultural atmosphere in
which midwestern grape growers had to work.
(California State University, Fresno, Library)

dence of the hopefulness of those days. In the same spirit Thompson tested hundreds of varieties of native vines, looking for the elusive one that would yield good wine in the state's unfriendly climate.[117] Nebraska was later a source of resistant riparia rootstocks for California, shipped out by the carload when that state began to reconstitute its vineyards against the phylloxera in the 1880s.[118]

The communal pattern, which we have seen on both the East and the West Coasts, appeared in the Midwest too, though only in a flickering way. The Icarians of Cloverdale, California, were the remnant of a community of idealistic Frenchmen, inspired by utopian notions, who had settled in Nauvoo, Illinois, in 1849, not long after the Mormons who had founded and built the town had abandoned it for their migration to Utah. The Icarians did not pioneer grape growing at Nauvoo, but when others began it they joined in; not, however, without taking a backward step. They planted European vines, and so had to watch them fail first before finding their way with native vines.[119] Emil Baxter, an Englishman who had joined the Icarians, founded a winery at Nauvoo in 1857 that is still in operation.[120] Meanwhile, a series of bitter schisms among the Icarians, culminating in the exile and death of their leader, Etienne Cabet, had left the Nauvoo community weak and disorganized. In the hope of making a new start, some Icarians migrated to the southwestern corner of Iowa in 1860, not far from that stretch of the Missouri River where the borders of Iowa, Nebraska, Kansas, and Missouri approach one another between Omaha and Kansas City. Here they established a small vineyard of Concord vines expressly for winemaking and succeeded in maintaining it for many years.[121] Even after another schism had sent the last expedition of Icarians out to California, the Icarians who remained in Iowa kept their vineyard going. The example had some effect, for as early as 1870 nearby Des Moines County had 250 acres in vines and was producing 30,000 gallons of wine from standard American varieties.[122] It was reported in 1898 that the example of the Icarians had made grape growing a success in southwestern Iowa.[123]

Another communal experiment, also utopian rather than religious, is worth noting just because it repeats so many of the motifs that we have heard from the beginning of American colonization. Ernest Valeton de Boissiere, a wealthy and philanthropic Frenchman inspired by the communitarian theories of his countryman Charles Fourier, in 1868 bought 3,500 prairie acres in Franklin County, Kansas, a region then in rapid development immediately following the Civil War. There de Boissiere intended to make cheese, silk, and wine through the cooperative labors of a community living in a Fourierist phalanstery. Cheese making is a new note, but the combination of wine and silk takes us back to the dreams of Hakluyt and the first days of the Virginia colony. There were 1,000 vines planted by 1871, and ten years later a visitor noted the "acres of grapes then worked into wine." The community also succeeded in producing silk, a display of which was an object of interest at the Centennial Exhibition of 1876. But then Silkville, as the community was called, was abandoned in 1892, after twenty years of struggle.[124] The long double avenue of mulberry trees planted to supply the silkworms and the large, austere communal building of native sandstone long remained to remind the farmers on that windswept prairie of an exotic episode in the history of their county.

As for winemaking in religious communities, that, too, was represented in the Midwest, at least in a token way, in the Amana Colonies in southeastern Iowa, still flourishing 130 years after their founding by the German Community of True Inspiration in 1854. On 25,000 acres of splendid Iowa soil, the Inspirationists quietly developed a prosperous economy based on farming, cabinetmaking, meat smoking, and winemaking, carried out in seven small villages scattered over an area of some twenty square miles. Like the houses of the Rappites in Economy, Pennsylvania, those in the Amanas, often brick-built, had their walls covered in trellises for the growing of grapes. Winemaking was largely for local consumption; in the communal scheme of distribution, the average ration was about a gallon a month for adult men, half as much for women. As though to underline the connection between wine and the spirit, the colonists used the basement of their meeting house (they did not use the term "church") as their wine cellar.[125]

The obstacles that middle western winegrowing had to face were both natural—acts of God, as the insurance companies say—and cultural—acts of man. The obstacles that nature laid in the way were those already long familiar in the shape of weather, pests, and diseases. The special agent of the census bureau assigned to report on viticulture in the United States in 1890 declared gloomily that in Missouri and Kansas in the past ten years there had been "but little progress." The vineyards in Missouri, he affirmed, "have been devastated or ruined," and in Kansas the industry was stagnant (he does not refer to the circumstance that the state was constitutionally Dry).[126] This was too alarming a view, but it at least testified to widespread uneasiness and discouragement. The introduction of the fungicide called bordeaux mixture at about this time gave reason for new confidence, yet production did continue to decline, in the next decade, in Illinois, Kansas, and Missouri. Even more daunting than the struggle with diseases was the intensifying struggle with prohibitionists, enemies to winegrowing who were in fact to prove far more devastating than even the lethal black rot. The rising trend to oppose, obstruct, and forbid the sale of alcoholic drink in any and all forms had to be a severe inhibitor of the wish to plant vineyards and to make wine, not just in Kansas but in any state where organized "temperance" opposition was growing—and that was just about everywhere. The movement was not, perhaps, stronger in the Midwest than in other parts of the country, but the relative feebleness of the winegrowing industry there meant that it had little means of standing up to it.

15

The Southwest; the South; Other States

Arkansas, Texas, and Oklahoma

S outh of Missouri, in Arkansas, the first winegrowing began as almost a repetition of the Missouri development: as Missouri had begun with Germans along the Missouri River, so Arkansas began with Germans (and Swiss) along the Arkansas River. The place chosen, around 1880, was at the high point of the territory along the river's course between Fort Smith, on the western border, and Little Rock, in the center of the state. This high point, logically named Altus, was planted in native varieties such as Catawba, Ives, and Cynthiana (a variety often claimed as native to Arkansas, and just as often asserted to be identical with Norton).[1] The beginning thus made has continued to the present day, and the firms of Wiederkehr and Post may now claim more than a hundred years of operation. The Cynthiana, by the way, is a variety of which we perhaps ought to hear more. According to Hedrick, it is not only a variety distinct from the Norton (so he settles that argument), it is "the best American grape for red wine."[2] This judgment was confirmed in the nineteenth century by the French in their experiments with native American grapes suited to the direct production of wine in Europe. Only a handful of producers now offer a varietal Cynthiana, three in Arkansas and three in Missouri.[3]

A distinctive note in Arkansas winegrowing is provided by the Italians of Tontitown, who varied the otherwise overwhelmingly German character of the industry throughout the Midwest and Southwest. Tontitown, in the far northwestern corner of Arkansas on the Ozark plateau, began as a refuge from a disastrous experiment. About 1895 the New York financier Austin Corbin conceived the idea that his vast cotton-growing properties in the swampy flatlands along the Mississippi in south-eastern Arkansas could be better worked by Italian immigrants than by the freed slaves who had been the only labor employed before. Accordingly he arranged to have Italians shipped out directly from Italy to the cottonfields of Arkansas.[4] Corbin's plantation was an island in the river, and, ominously, had been a penal colony, though now it was renamed Sunnyside.[5] There the Italians, despite their ignorance of cotton-chopping, met and surpassed all expectations as field laborers. They also met malaria, with fatal consequences: in one year at Sunnyside 130 died out of about a thousand.[6] By 1898 there was almost a panic feeling of desperation; they knew that they had to get out, but did not know how or where. At this juncture the priest of the Sunnyside church, Pietro Bandini, took charge. He entered into negotiations with the Frisco Railroad, whose lines ran through Arkansas and whose officers were eager to encourage agricultural development along their route. One of the properties proposed by the railroad was almost symmetrically opposite from the Sunnyside plantation: it lay in the northwest corner of Arkansas, at the other end of the state from Sunnyside, and it stood high in the Ozarks instead of at water level. The land was poor, but at least it would be free from malaria.

In 1898, under Bandini's leadership, some forty families of Sunnyside Italians made the exodus to the new lands; the men went to work at once in the zinc and coal mines of the region in order to pay the mortgage on the land, and in the intervals of their breadwinning began to plant vineyards. They were, most of them, from the Romagna and the Marches, and so at least by association of birth they were familiar with an immemorial winegrowing tradition. They named their settlement for Enrico de Tonti, the Italian who served as La Salle's lieutenant in the exploration of the Mississippi region, including Arkansas.[7] By degrees, through very hard work, and against much sullen and ugly local opposition,[8] the Italians made their way as farmers and winemakers. The town was not a communal experiment: each householder had his property to himself. But the experience of common origins, common suffering, and common achievement gave the Italians a powerful sense of community. Father Bandini, who had remained with his flock, was rewarded by seeing the growth of a small, but flourishing, town, which to a remarkable degree retained its original Italian character. By 1909 there were seventy families, all Italian, living in Tontitown. They were making wine from their vineyards of Cynthiana and Concord (a trial of vinifera varieties had quickly failed and was not persisted in); and they were soon to form a cooperative association for the marketing of their grapes.[9] In common with almost all the other grape-growing regions of the Midwest and East, the Tontitown vineyards were more and more given over to the production of table grapes, and then of grape juice. Prohibition, which put an end to winegrowing, nevertheless swelled the vineyards—now exclusively Concord—to record size, enabling the growers to survive and prosper but putting an end to the interest of the region from the point of view of this history.[10]

I I 7 | Father Pietro Bandini (1853–1917), the priest under whose leadership Italian immigrants established Tontitown, Arkansas, and made it a center of winegrowing. (From Giovanni Schiavo, *Four Centuries of Italian-American History* [1952])

The ill-fated Sunnyside plantation was the source of two other small wine-growing colonies of Italians, both of these in Missouri. In Father Bandini's original negotiations with the Frisco Railroad, an offer had been made of land at Knobview, Missouri, along the route of the railroad as it ran southwest out of St. Louis. Bandini and that part of his flock who went with him to Tontitown rejected the offer, but a group of some thirty families closed with it and made the migration to Missouri in 1898.[11] Who the effective leader of the Knobview Italians was is not known—it would be interesting to identify who it was that took the initiative and made the crucial arrangements.[12] In any case, after hard days of struggle, the Knobview group, like that at Tontitown, began to prosper. At first many of them did track work for the Frisco in order to support their families while the slow work of agricultural development went on. Their town, which they later renamed Rosati, after the first bishop of St. Louis, did not flourish, most of its functions being absorbed by the neighboring town of St. James, so that Rosati lost its post office, its schools, and its stores. But the grape growing did well, so well that it managed to survive Prohibition and to serve as the basis for a newly revived winemaking industry around St. James in our day.

The third Sunnyside colony was the tiny town of Verdella, Missouri, consisting originally of only twelve families. They, too, devoted themselves to winegrowing, but beyond that their story remains obscure.[13]

In Texas, largest and among the most varied of the contiguous forty-eight states, the history of grape growing and winemaking was very much like what it had been in the earliest days of colonization: full of unmistakable promise but hard to bring to success. Over much of the state, especially in the eastern half, wild grapes of many varieties abounded—indeed, one expert affirms that Texas has "the most diverse population of wild grapes in the world."[14] The explorer sent out by the U.S. government in 1857 to report on the grapes of the Southwest found that in parts of Texas the Mustang grape "is multiplied to an extent almost incredible."[15] The grapes and wines of El Paso, at the far southwestern tip of the state, went back to the first days of Spanish colonization, but, as we have seen, that start was not carried further after the annexation of Texas. Even before that annexation, German immigrants in eastern Texas made repeated trials of vinifera varieties, with the predictable result. Texas, like Missouri, was the scene of very early and considerable German settlement, otherwise rather unusual in the Southwest. Much of this settlement was organized by a group of wealthy men in Germany for speculative purposes, beginning in the early 1840s.[16] The colonists they sent out scattered over an area of southeastern Texas that now centers on San Antonio, and there they founded their towns, giving them such names as Fredericksburg, Weimar, and New Braunfels. At the same time, but under different sponsorship, a settlement combining Alsatians, Germans, and Frenchmen was made at Castroville, a little west of San Antonio.[17] The speculative hopes of the promoters of these places were not realized, but the Germans continued to come anyway. By 1860, it is said, there were some 20,000 of them in Texas.[18] Germans and Frenchmen alike hoped to make winegrowing one of their important businesses and almost at once set out vines brought from Europe. When these failed, they turned to the unimproved native grapes and made wine from them, sometimes in commercial quantities.[19]

The Mustang grape (*V. candicans*) was the main variety used, and from all reports, it made a tolerable red wine, requiring added sugar but without the foxiness of labrusca.[20] Since it was so abundant a grape, it was natural to hope that it might also be a good wine grape. One Dr. Stewart, writing from Texas in 1847, reported that a "French wine maker and vineyardist" from Kentucky had come into Texas and pronounced the Mustang to be "the port wine grape, and of superior quality and yield." On this testimony, Dr. Stewart was moved to exclaim, "What resources our country possesses in this respect, if this be the fact, for the mustang grows every where in our fair land."[21] It is hard not to smile now, since the hope was so wide of the mark, but where little is known much may be hoped, and experts are not immune to the desire to please. It is probably also the fact that there *are* great opportunities for winegrowing in Texas that are only now beginning to be grasped.

The Mustang was the dominant native grape of Texas winemaking but not the only one used. Judge J. Doan, in the Texas panhandle, made well-regarded wine from a species of wild grape in Texas and Oklahoma Territory named after him *Vitis Doaniana*.[22] But such local and limited successes with the indigenous vines were disappointing when the early hopes had been to discover the Eden of the grape in Texas. Individuals continued to experiment through the rest of the century, trying all the native hybrids developed in the older eastern and southern states and gradually determining that the traditional southern varieties of aestivalis,

I I 8   Thomas Volney Munson (1843–1913), of Denison, Texas, nurseryman, grape hybridizer, ampelographer. For nearly four decades Munson produced a steady stream of native hybrid grapes and showed by his work the possibilities latent in the grapes of the American Southwest. (From T. V. Munson, *Foundations of American Grape Culture* [1909])

like the Lenoir and the Herbemont, seemed best suited to large parts of the state.[23] Nor did people entirely resist the seductive attraction of trying to grow vinifera: after all, such grapes were already long proven around El Paso. By the end of the century we hear of large plantings—200 acres—of vinifera around Laredo, on irrigated lands bordering the Rio Grande, of a group of Italians attempting to grow vinifera around Gunnison, Texas, and of a group of forty-seven French winemakers brought over by the Texas and Pacific Railroad to grow grapes in the alkali desert around Pecos.[24]

The more discreet growers contented themselves with the safer native varieties from the South, however: the oldest commercial winery now operating in the state, at Val Verde on the Rio Grande, goes back to 1883, and is still making its wines from vineyards of Lenoir and Herbemont grapes.[25] The success of these and other related varieties led one of the persistent German growers of the state to declare that they "make of nearly the entire state of Texas a natural wine-producing region of enormous capacity."[26] By now we know that no claim to "natural" status is worth very much, but the proposition is an interesting one once again now that very powerful interests in Texas, including the university in its character as a great landholder, are investigating anew the chances of winegrowing in Texas.[27] That those chances were never realized in the nineteenth century is clearly affirmed by the French viticulturist Pierre Viala, who found abundant native grapes on his visit of exploration to Texas in 1887, but who noted that "Texas is one of the least viticultural regions of the United States."[28]

Apart from its wide open spaces, its abundant native grapes, and its large promise, Texas's greatest claim to attention in this history is the work of a single man, Thomas Volney Munson, of Denison, on the far northern edge of the state. Munson (1843–1913), a native of Illinois, was educated at the University of Kentucky and worked in Kentucky as a nurseryman for some years.[29] He was thus familiar with the many native vines of the Midwest and upper South, and began to take a keen professional interest in their possibilities. In 1873 he migrated to Lincoln, Nebraska, to continue his business as a nurseryman. He experimented with grapes in the frigid blasts and searing droughts of that country of extremes for a few years, but was then glad to accept the invitation of a brother to transfer his business to the north Texas town of Denison, on the Red River. This he did in 1876, and for the next thirty-seven years, until his death, he operated the firm of T. V. Munson & Son and indulged his passion for collecting, describing, and hybridizing native American grapes.

Like his good friend Hermann Jaeger, not far away in southwestern Missouri, Munson was an indefatigable field worker; for many years during grape season he rode on horseback through the woods and fields of Texas, Arkansas, and Oklahoma in quest of new varieties. Travelling by train, he carried his search into all but six of the United States and into Mexico, hunting, as he tells us, from train car windows, jumping off to collect specimens at every stop, scheduled or unscheduled.[30] Munson was active in assisting the French in their great struggle to understand and to exploit the characters of native American vines for their own ravaged vineyards. For his contribution he was made a chevalier of the Legion of Honor in 1888. Munson also did notable work in the description and classification of native varieties and in publicizing the results of his work. He made an ambitious, comprehensive display of the native and foreign grape for the Columbian Exposition at Chicago, and he wrote several treatises on grape classification and grape varieties.[31] All this would have been work enough for a man who had his living to make as a practical nurseryman. But Munson's great passion was not for selling stock or for making classifications. It was for breeding native grapes. This is the work for which he is remembered today, work that he began soon after he removed to Texas and continued until his death. In that time he introduced about three hundred new varieties, derived from crosses making use of a large number of native vines.

Munson's objects were several: for one thing, he tried to create a series of grapes ranging from early to late so that the whole of a growing season would be filled with successively ripe grapes. Like every American breeder, he dreamed of creating grapes that would defy the endemic national diseases—the rots and mildews that had oppressed American viticulture from the beginning. And he also aimed at creating a series of wine grapes suited to all the varying conditions of the country.[32] He accomplished none of these things, but the example of his energy and resourcefulness in the work was widely impressive. No hybridizer before him had provided so large and steady a stream of new varieties. There were so many, in fact, that Munson had difficulty in providing names for them; many are named for his family or friends, and others have singularly graceless names, suggesting exhaustion of the poetic power. Who would be tempted to drink the wine of "Headlight," "Lukfata," "XLNTA," "Armalaga," or "Delicatessen"? These and others are all recorded in Munson's *Foundations of American Grape Culture*, a retrospect of his work that he published in 1909.

One of Munson's distinctive additions to the repertoire of American grape hybridizing was his extensive use of native southwestern varieties, especially those of the species *V. lincecumii* (Post Oak grape), *V. champini,* and *V. candicans* (Mustang). It is fitting therefore that he should be especially honored in the South, as he has been in recent years. The eclipse of experimental grape growing during Prohibition meant that many Munson varieties almost disappeared from knowledge and were in some danger of disappearing for good. In the past decade, however, a small and enthusiastic group has devoted itself to rescuing Munson's work from oblivion. Led by W. E. Dancy, an Arkansas businessman and amateur grower, they have succeeded in discovering living instances of most of the Munson hybrids. They have also established a Munson Memorial Vineyard, where the Munson hybrids are grown and propagated, in his home town of Denison. Another tribute to him has been paid in South Carolina, where a "Munson Park" vineyard of thirty-three Munson varieties has been planted at the Truluck Vineyard of Lake City. It is even possible, still, to buy wine from Munson grapes: the Mount Pleasant Winery of Augusta, Missouri, offers red, white, and rosé wines made from the Munson variety Muench (named for the venerable Missouri German winemaker Friedrich Muench); and the St. James Winery of St. James, Missouri, makes (or did make) a dry wine from the variety called Neva Munson, after one of Munson's daughters. So Munson's name is still alive in the land, as are his grapes.

Oklahoma, or the Indian Territory, where Judge Doan found his supply of *Vitis Doaniana* for winemaking, was not without some production of its own. In 1890, only a year after the territory was opened to white settlement, Edward Fairchild, a transplanted winegrower from the Finger Lakes of New York, acquired land near Oklahoma City for a vineyard and orchard. In 1893 he constructed a substantial cellar of native sandstone, and there, for the next fourteen years, he made wine for the local trade from Concord and Delaware grapes.[33] When Oklahoma Territory became the state of Oklahoma in 1907, it entered the Union as a Dry state. That put an immediate end to Fairchild's winemaking, and to any other such enterprises that had grown up in the brief history of Oklahoma settlement. It is a startling fact that, according to the census of 1910, Oklahoma had over 4,000 acres of vineyard, putting it eighth among all the states. Yet perhaps we ought not to be surprised. No less an authority than T. V. Munson pronounced Oklahoma to be a splendid grape-growing region.[34] In recent years the Fairchild Winery has been carefully restored and entered in the National Registry of Historic Places.[35] The restoration makes it possible to get an unusually distinct and accurate idea of the details of the actual operation.

The South

In the Southeast, as in the Southwest, the general picture in the period after the Civil War was one of widely scattered local enterprises in grapes and wine. The South had much to contend with: the economic and political disruptions of the war and Reconstruction, obviously; but besides that, the destructive effects of cotton culture, the bad old system of tenant farming, the backwardness of methods, and the poverty of things generally made any new venture precarious. And quite apart from economics and politics, the South was a place where nature itself had many kinds of bad news for grapes: humidity, heat, black rot, downy mildew, powdery mildew, anthracnose, Pierce's Disease, phylloxera, nematodes—after running the gauntlet of that list of afflictions, few vines that people wanted to grow for wine were likely to be left alive. Nevertheless, people did persist, and the conclusion one finally draws from the record is that the hope of making a success of winegrowing is indestructible, no matter what the obstacles and the defeats. What follow are examples of this general proposition.

In Florida, for instance, a state largely developed after the Civil War by an influx both of dispossessed southerners and of northerners looking for sun and land, there was a small sort of grape boom in the last thirty years of the century. The northerners, clustered around Orlando in the middle of the state, tended to plant the labrusca varieties; the southerners, in the north and panhandle of the state, were loyal to their native muscadines. By the 1890s, the high point of grape planting, there were about five hundred acres in the region of Orlando. Florida made 20,000 gallons of wine in 1890; by 1900 the figure was 31,000 gallons.[36] Much of what was made doubtless went unreported, however, for the muscadine growers in the north of the state were rarely more than household winemakers, a circumstance that probably has been true in the South almost from the beginning. By the end of the century, despite modestly rising production figures, it was clear that the northerners' idea that labrusca varieties would prosper in the humid warmth of Florida was a mistake. Inevitably, Catawba and Concord succumbed to fungus diseases, while the invulnerable muscadines continued to spread vigorously over the rambling trellises that supported them. Florida winemaking went on as it had begun; that is, as a domestic affair usually based on the possession of only a very few muscadine vines. Commercial production was carried on at the Ponce de Leon Wine Company of St. Augustine, which had a winery at Moultrie.[37]

One grower of distinction did emerge from Florida's brief affair with the grape. This was Emile Dubois, of Tallahassee, who was respected enough to be among the wine judges at the Chicago Exposition of 1893 and whose produce from his San Luis Vineyard of Cynthiana and Norton varieties was good enough to win a medal at the Paris Exposition of 1900. But Dubois was, ultimately, compelled by endemic diseases to give up his Florida vineyards, in common with less notable growers.[38]

Alabama, to take another sample of the South, might very well have developed a small, steady trade in wine but for the obstruction of prohibition. Two small colonies on Mobile Bay, named Daphne and Lambert, were founded in the 1890s for Italian immigrants by an Italian-American newspaper editor from Chicago named Alessandro Mastro-Valerio. Both colonies grew grapes and made wine as part of their general plan to make a living from truck gardening and fruit growing. The wine made in these small communities had some success in the markets of Mobile, but local prohibition put an end to viticulture in the pine lands along Mobile Bay.[39]

An entity called the Alabama Fruit Growing and Winery Association was incorporated in 1894 to exploit 20,000 acres in Cleburn County, in the northeastern part of the state along the Georgia border. This was a speculation headed by investors from the Chautauqua grape belt in New York State, including Garrett Ryckman of the Brocton Wine Cellars. The New Yorkers hoped to promote immigration to the district and to develop fruit growing through a cooperative scheme. They named the town on their property Fruithurst, and by 1896 the planting of native grapes—Ives, Delaware, Concord, Niagara, and other familiar varieties better suited to the North than to the South—was under way. Fruithurst attracted a good many settlers, among them a group of Scandinavians. At least one winery was built and wine produced, but marketing difficulties, the shadow of prohibition in the South, and, above all, the native vine diseases had made the enterprise uneconomic by the turn of the century.[40] In 1898 another outfit, called the Alabama Vineyard and Winery Company, promoted a property called Vinemont in the north central part of the state.[41] The hamlets of Vinemont and Fruithurst remain on the Alabama map, but these undertakings, so far as I can learn, have left no other trace and are interesting chiefly as evidence of the persistent glamor of the idea of winegrowing, even where history was not encouraging and local sentiment positively hostile.

In South Carolina, where the tradition of experiment with winemaking goes back to the beginnings in the seventeenth century and where, as we have seen, a great variety of men had tried a great variety of different approaches to the challenge, things were not much different than in the rest of the South. The vineyards at Aiken, established with such buoyant hope shortly before the Civil War, were still there afterwards, but the heart and means to develop them seem to have disappeared.[42] In the seventies there was a brief burst of activity in grape growing in a new region, the Piedmont area around Greenville in the far northwestern corner of the state. Here, it had been discovered, was a favored spot, a "thermal belt," where the climate just suited the grape and where, for a time, the quickly established vineyards yielded immense crops. Then, in the late eighties, black rot appeared and grape growing faded away.[43] A good instance of the optimism that prevailed for a time around Greenville is a M. Carpin, who came from France, where he had been a viticulturist, to the neighborhood of Greenville in 1876, determined, he said, to "make a wine farm on the French plan." He bought a hundred acres of hilly woodland, cleared it, and set out a mixture of native vines—Norton, Clinton, Concord, Ives, Martha, and Pocklington among others. By the end of a decade he had a vineyard of 80 acres and plans for 150 more; his wine production was 40,000 gallons annually, all of it disposed of through a Boston firm and most of it consisting of a dry red blended wine called "Bordeaux." Carpin himself, it was reported, was "much better pleased with the results of his labor than he ever was in France," and would "listen to no suggestions of failure."[44] Whether Carpin in the event did fail I do not know. Bordeaux mixture may well have arrived in time to save him (South Carolina was one of the first places where it was tried in this country),[45] but its effect was not powerful enough to preserve the Greenville area as a permanent center of winegrowing.

There were more positive developments in the South, too, though they were never quite uncomplicated or straightforward. In Virginia, for example, it might have seemed for a time that the spirit of Jefferson *redivivus* was at work. For there, in Jefferson's old territory in Albemarle County, grape planting and winemaking had been started afresh immediately following the Civil War. Just after the war, the Virginia farmers, with slavery gone, were forced to find a new basis for their work, and were desperately looking for different crops from those that they had used to grow. Grapes for wine were one of the first suggestions to be made: an advertisement in the *American Agriculturist* for July 1865, for example, invites investment from interested parties in a scheme for winegrowing in Virginia and North Carolina. This was within three months of Lee's surrender at Appomattox Court House. One of the places where vineyards actually were planted was at Charlottesville, and, as so often was the case, the pioneer was a German. William Hotopp, a native of Germany then residing in Hudson, New York, came south immediately after the war, in 1866, and bought land near Charlottesville on which he planted vines. Other Germans followed him, and by 1870 Hotopp ventured to build a winery.[46]

In 1873 a much larger enterprise, the Monticello Wine Company, was founded by a group of farmers led by another German, Oscar Reierson. The company built a four-story winery of 200,000 gallons' capacity to handle its native wines, and in only a few years was able to obtain awards at international expositions—such awards were apparently required of any American winery seeking respectability.

THE

VIRGINIA

WINE

AND

CIDER MILL

Is superior to any MILL now made, and more sold annually in this market than of all other kinds combined. It does not grate, but thoroughly crushes every fruit cell, insuring all cider the apples will yield.

Send for Catalogue.

jy–1y

CHAS. T. PALMER,
1526 *Main Street, Richmond, Va.*

119 | Advertised in *The Southern Planter* of 1875, this "wine and cider mill" shows that winemaking was still alive in Virginia, though such crusher-presses no doubt saw many more apples than grapes.

The Monticello Wine Company picked up its obligatory prizes at Vienna in 1876 and at Paris in 1878.[47] Charlottesville wine was largely sold in the New York market, and trade was brisk enough so that by 1888 there were 3,000 acres of vines planted in Albemarle County and a Grape Growers' Association had been formed.[48] The local boosters proclaimed Charlottesville the "Capital of the Wine Belt of Virginia," a modest enough boast, and no doubt true.[49]

An advertisement for the Monticello Wine Company in 1888 lists its products as delaware, catawba, Norton, cynthiana, clinton, Ives seedling, Virginia claret, "Extra Claret," and brandy.[50] Other establishments in the new Virginia wine industry presumably grew more or less the same varieties and made comparable wines. Among those others were Frash & Company in Orange County, Heineken & Peters in Prince William County, and Fritz Baier in Nelson County. In 1890 Virginia recorded a wine production of 461,000 gallons, fifth among all the states. And then the crash. The numbers for 1900 were a pitiful 38,000 gallons.[51] In 1910 Virginia reported nearly 50,000 gallons of wine produced, far behind such states as Iowa, North Carolina, Arkansas, and Indiana.[52] What had happened? Diseases, as always, were part of the answer; trade depression another part; and competition from California yet another. Finally, and probably most destructive of all, came the growing encroachments of local prohibition, culminating in a statewide measure in 1914. The combination was too much, so that the sources of Virginia wine dried up, not to be renewed until very recent years.

North Carolina, like its neighbor state to the south, had long been the scene of varied experiments aiming to prove that the state could have a profitable wine industry. Some of this experimenting continued to be carried out on a purely fanciful basis, with costly results. A Swiss named Eugene Morel, a pupil of the great French viticultural scientist Jules Guyot,[53] settled near Ridgeway, North Carolina, in 1870, convinced, as he later ruefully recalled, that the vinifera varieties of central and southern France would certainly do well there. He persuaded a group of French settlers to join him, and together they planted 100,000 cuttings of Aramon, Mourvèdre, Grenache, Carignane, Cinsaut, Mourastel, and Clairette vines. Five years later the failure was obvious. A penitent Morel moved on to California, where he employed his skills as a winemaker first in the Napa Valley and then, before his early death from tuberculosis in 1884, in Fresno for the pioneer vineyardist Robert Barton.[54]

When the French viticultural expert J.-E. Planchon visited North Carolina in 1873 he found considerable interest in winegrowing, stimulated by Morel's plantings at Ridgeway (Planchon was rightly skeptical about them). The successful vineyards, he observed, were given over to Scuppernong, and some of these were quite substantial plantings. Everywhere, however, he noted that the winemaking methods and machinery of the state were "entirely primitive."[55]

North Carolina's great success after the Civil War had direct links to a successful antebellum enterprise. The vineyards of Sidney Weller at Brinckleyville, where Weller had carried on a prosperous winemaking business for three decades before the war, were bought in 1867 by two brothers named Garrett.[56] They continued the winegrowing that Weller had begun, selling both still and sparkling wines, mainly from Scuppernong, the rotundifolia variety whose wine Thomas Jefferson had favored early in the century. In 1877 the firm was joined by Paul Garrett (1863–1940), the son of one of the Garrett brothers, and its transformation began. Paul Garrett was evidently born to be a salesman, and since wine was given him to sell, sell it he did. His ability to sell was so far in excess of the winery's ability to produce that he eventually left it to operate on his own as Garrett & Company, founded in 1900.[57] At first he contracted to sell New York State wines as well as those of North Carolina, but he soon determined to concentrate his efforts on the wine from the Scuppernong grape of his native state. He was inspired to call his most popular Scuppernong wine Virginia Dare, after the first child born to English settlers in this country, on the island where the Scuppernong vine itself was supposed to have originated.[58] So popular did Virginia Dare become, in fact, that its sales outstripped the supply of Scuppernong grapes. Garrett had constantly to exhort the farmers of North Carolina to plant more to feed his presses, and when his efforts fell short of his needs he had to resort to changing the formula: Virginia Dare may have begun as a pure Scuppernong wine, but as its popularity grew so did the volume of bulk California wine that Garrett was forced to add to it. In the end, it had only enough Scuppernong juice in it to "tincture the flavor."[59] Only less popular than Virginia Dare were other Scuppernong wines called Minnehaha and Pocahontas. Garrett also made wines from other native varieties, a claret from Norton and Ives grapes, for instance; but these were by the way.[60]

Ironically, Garrett's growing success was matched by the growing power of prohibitionist sentiment in North Carolina. As district after district voted to go Dry, Garrett escaped the net by moving his operation over the line to Norfolk, Virginia, in 1903. There, in an imposing five-story winery, the fresh juice of North Carolina grapes was turned into Virginia Dare wine. But the dessication of the South continued its inexorable spread, and Garrett was forced in 1912 to move again, this time to Penn Yan, in the Finger Lakes of New York.[61] By then he had expanded and broadened his operations in many ways, with large interests in wineries and vineyards in all the major winegrowing states: California, New York, Missouri, and Ohio, as well as in the muscadine-producing states of the Southeast. Thus, as the sources of the Scuppernong grapes with which he had made a national reputation progressively shrank, and as he had to move his operations farther and farther from their point of origin, his business persisted in growing. The eve of Prohibition found Garrett presiding over a complex of winegrowing establishments with a storage capacity of 10,000,000 gallons. But the North Carolina part of this empire was by that time only a minor territory.[62]

Garrett was not the only producer of native wines in North Carolina, only the most successful. In the 1870s wineries specializing in Scuppernong wines were founded at Whiteville, in the southeastern corner of the state, and at nearby Wilmington. The Bear Winery, also at Wilmington, flourished in the late nineteenth century, and by 1912 had reached a capacity of 200,000 gallons a year, mostly muscadine.[63] Fayetteville was another active center of winegrowing, dominated by the Tokay Vineyard of Colonel Wharton Green, whose hundred acres of vines yielded twenty to thirty-five thousand gallons of wine each year. The colonel made wine not only from the Scuppernong but from a varied mix of native grapes: some of the wines were labelled simply Dry Red, Dry White, Sweet Red, and Sweet White; others carried varietal names, such as Norton's Seedling and Delaware.[64] Around Raleigh there were some substantial vineyards, as there were also in the far western corner of the state at Tryon.[65] In 1893 the State Horticultural Society officially reported that the winemaking of North Carolina had "grown greatly in the past few years;"[66] it seems likely that if the growers had not been beset by Prohibition

120 | Starting from a small North Carolina winery that went back to Sidney Weller in the 1830s, Paul Garrett (1863–1940) eventually became the most successful of eastern winegrowers before Prohibition. His Virginia Dare wine, based on the native Scuppernong grape of the South, became the most popular of American wines. (From Clarence Gohdes, *Scuppernong: North Carolina's Grape and Its Wines* [1982])

There is more of this brand of wine used in the
United States than of all other brands
of bottled wines combined

See Page 33 for Prices.

I 2 I   A bottle of Paul Garrett's Virginia Dare wine, from a company brochure published around 1913. The quantity of Scuppernong juice in the blend grew steadily less as the sales of the wine outstripped the ability of southern growers to supply the grapes. Virginia Dare, for whom the wine was named, was the first English child born in the colonies. (California State University, Fresno, Library)

they would have continued to develop what they had so well begun. It is notable, however, that the most solid successes of North Carolina were all with Scuppernong wines. Without prejudice to those who admire these, it is possible to hint a doubt as to their acceptability nationwide and over the long run. Against that skeptical remark, though, one must set the fact that Paul Garrett's Scuppernong-based

122 | The Garrett Winery at Norfolk, Virginia, where, to escape prohibition in North Carolina, Paul Garrett moved his headquarters in 1903. According to company claims, the new building had "the largest clock on earth" and a wine capacity of four million gallons. But by 1912 prohibition in Virginia had forced Garrett to move once more, to New York State. (Huntington Library)

Virginia Dare, in versions both red and white, was the most popular American wine both before Prohibition and immediately after.

Other States

Here, at the end of this narrative of America's long struggle to discover the ways and means of winegrowing, what can be said about those states that have so far received no mention? In a few cases, almost nothing. So far as I know, the states of North and South Dakota, Colorado, Wyoming, and Montana do not figure even in a token way in the story I have to tell.[67] But given the meager historical materials on this subject, that is hardly a decisive statement. Much may have been done without having made its impress upon the record. All the rest of the contiguous forty-eight states have some experience to contribute to the general record, and most have, by this point in the book, been mentioned in one connection or another. New Hampshire and Vermont have not been so mentioned, but might well have been. They figure repeatedly in the discussions of grape growing and winemaking carried on in the agricultural and horticultural press of the nineteenth century. Both the Vergennes and the Green Mountain grapes, varieties of some commercial importance, originated in Vermont.[68] In the South, Mississippi had its share of viticultural experiment, though I have said nothing of it.[69] And, after its creation during the Civil War, so, too, did West Virginia, especially along the Ohio River, where grape growing was carried on when the state was still a part of Virginia.[70]

Another omission is Minnesota, but of course Minnesota contains wild grapes, and of course the first settlers tried their luck with cultivated varieties. They had success enough to encourage commercial grape growing at least in a modest way, for in the 1880s considerable quantities of local Delaware grapes were being sold in the markets of Minneapolis.[71] There was also some work done towards hybridizing grapes to withstand the Minnesota winters: the variety called Beta, for example, from a riparia-labrusca cross made by Louis Snelter of Carver, Minnesota, and another called Beauty of Minnesota, a labrusca-Bourquiniana cross made by J. C. Kramer of La Crescent; and there were others.[72] There is precedent, then, for the work towards developing a native hybrid fit for Minnesota conditions now being carried on by the University of Minnesota and by the Minnesota Grape Growers' Association.[73]

In the West, Utah, despite the prohibition of alcohol among the modern Mormons, grew grapes and made wine in the region called "Dixie" around St. George in the southwestern part of the state. Moreover, this work was carried out under the directions of Brigham Young himself, who wanted the wine both for use in the communion of the Mormon church and as an article of commerce.[74] A Bavarian-born Mormon, John Naegle, built a winery in 1866 at Toquerville in the Dixie region; this operated only briefly, but winemaking continued on a smaller scale thereafter.[75] Arizona, which has had no previous mention, was a place of grape growing long before it became a state. J. De Barth Shorb, of the San Gabriel Winery, had property interests around Phoenix in the 1880s and sent cuttings to be planted there. They did well enough so that in 1890 the Arizona Fruit Growers' Association seriously thought of promoting dessert wine production, and some 25,000 gallons of wine were made in the state that year.[76]

In Oregon and Washington, the history of winegrowing is practically a reversal of what happened in most other states. Usually, men tried to grow grapes in regions where they would not succeed; in Oregon, especially, but in Washington as well, *Vitis vinifera* will grow more or less unaided, but there were few who made the effort to grow it. Thus, though the possibility was always there, and though it was pretty clearly recognized in theory, no significant commercial winemaking developed in the Pacific Northwest until the second half of the twentieth century. The story of the region before that time is an irregular chronicle of isolated experiment.

Both Washington and Oregon are sharply divided, north to south, into coastal and inland regions by the Cascade Mountains. The narrower coastal part is wet, temperate, and fruitful; the high and wide inland regions, in the rain shadow of the mountains, are dry, hot, and barren, except where water for irrigation can be had. The coastal region was, of course, the earliest settled part of the Northwest, and the history of horticulture there goes back to the Hudson's Bay Company's establishment at Fort Vancouver on the Columbia River—actually in what is now Washington but belonging to the region of metropolitan Portland. Grapes were raised there from seed brought from England in 1824, and some of those vines were still living early in the twentieth century.[77] Since they came from England, they were presumably vinifera, and since they lived so long, they evidently took kindly to their situation. When the American settlement of Oregon Territory began in the 1840s, the Americans, familiar with the native grapes of the East, and no doubt taught to believe that vinifera would not grow in this country, did not follow the lead set by the English. Instead, they sent for cuttings of native vines: the first planter of record, the pioneer nurseryman Seth Lewelling, of Milwaukie, Oregon, came from Iowa, and the first vine that he planted, in 1847, was an Isabella.[78] From native vines the Oregon people made wine at least good enough to compete in California. William Meek, of Willamette, Oregon, took a special premium in 1859 at the California State Fair for his Isabella white wine; Oregon wines were also exhibited there by Lewelling and by A. Stanborn.[79]

The chances of vinifera were not entirely overlooked. At least as early as the 1860s, A. R. Shipley of Oswego, an enthusiastic amateur horticulturist, imported some vinifera as well as native vines into the Willamette Valley.[80] Both vinifera and native grapes were shown at the Oregon State Fair in 1869, and the fair offered premiums in the seventies for "foreign" as well as "American" grapes.[81] But in the next decade the "foreign" grapes disappear from the competition, while the number and variety of natives grows steadily: in the 1900 fair list, prizes were awarded for a whole spectrum of the familiar American varieties, now evidently well settled on the Pacific coast: Agawam, Concord, Delaware, Niagara, Worden, Diamond, Catawba, and others. These were, of course, mainly grown for the table; so far as I have been able to determine no commercial winemaking was carried on in the Willamette Valley, the main region of settlement and of fruit growing, in the nineteenth century.

South of the Willamette Valley, in the Roseburg and Grants Pass areas, things were a little different but not much. The region is essentially an extension of the coastal valleys of California: *Vitis californica* is native there, and so is *Sequoia sempervirens,* the redwood. Here the Van Pessl brothers planted vinifera in the 1880s, and at least one winery, that of Adam Doerner, opened in the 1890s and operated until 1965.[82] Thus a beginning in winegrowing was made, and though it had not grown beyond those beginnings when Prohibition cut off all development, it is fitting that the revival of Oregon winegrowing should have begun in these southern valleys in the 1960s.[83]

The potential economic importance of grape growing was recognized in 1890, when a vineyard was established at the Oregon Agricultural Experiment Station;[84] but the already flourishing wine industry in California, the remoteness of Oregon from the important markets, and the continued mistrust of vinifera all made winegrowing look too risky for almost anyone to venture. There were, of course, bold individual exceptions: one Oregonian took a silver medal for his riesling at the St. Louis Exposition in 1904.[85] In 1910 Oregon had some 381,000 bearing vines planted, enough to rank it eighteenth among the states; and in 1915, in a report presented to the International Viticultural Congress at San Francisco, both southern Oregon and the Columbia basin were identified as "splendid" locations for growing vinifera.[86] About that time the chronicle ends, not to be resumed for many years.

The beginnings in Washington were just as tentative as those in Oregon, and were not made so early. Still, they were early. Some vinifera were being grown at Walla Walla in 1869, and about the same time German settlers planted vinifera at Tampico.[87] The first vineyards leading to commercial production were in the wet western, not the dry eastern, part of Washington, and they were not of vinifera but of native American varieties; these were on Stretch Island, at the south end of Puget Sound, planted in 1872 by one Lambert Evans.[88] When the beginnings worked out well, other vineyards were planted on the Stretch Island site. The favored grape in the Puget Sound region was an eastern hybrid called Island Belle locally but known elsewhere as the Campbell Early, a black grape of labrusca parentage, introduced in 1892.

In eastern Washington fruit growing, including grape growing, could not develop in advance of irrigation works. When large-scale development of water resources began in the Yakima Valley in 1905, grapes soon became an important crop; but the grapes were largely Concord and they were destined to become grape juice rather than wine. By 1910 Washington had a respectable total of nearly 700,000 grapevines officially recorded—say about a thousand acres. Grapes grew at other places dotted around the great Columbia basin, even as far east as Idaho, along the Clear Water and Snake rivers, and some of them were vinifera intended for wine.[89]

The pioneer grower at Lewiston, Idaho, was Louis Delsol, a Frenchman, who planted vines there in 1872 and opened a winery not long after. Robert Schleicher, an Alsatian, began his Lewiston vineyard in 1880, and made wines that attracted attention in Portland, Seattle, and beyond.[90] But for Idaho, Washington, and Oregon alike, the dominance of California and the threat of prohibition made the risks of winegrowing too great. Washington was to develop as a source of grapes for the table and grapes for juice; it was thus relatively unaffected by Prohibition, but its promise as a winegrowing land was effectively unrecognized for the better part of a century.

At least forty-three of the contiguous forty-eight states had made some sort of beginning in grape growing and winemaking before the end of the nineteenth cen-

I 23 | The pioneer of grape growing in western Washington, Lambert Evans, a former Confederate soldier, planted vines on Stretch Island in Puget Sound. He sent his grapes to market in Olympia; winemaking came later. (From J. Elizabeth Purser and Lawrence J. Allen, *The Winemakers of the Pacific Northwest* [1977])

tury, and in at least a dozen of those states winegrowing had become an established enterprise. Now, in our day, there has been a return to the beginnings that were cut off by Prohibition. Societies of grape growers and winemakers are springing up in states that have long been wrongly supposed to have had no history of winegrowing: Tennessee, Kentucky, Mississippi, and Minnesota, for example. At the same time, both viticulture and enology, after long neglect by the state universities and agricultural experiment stations (except for those of California and New York), are being energetically taken up by those institutions in such states as Mississippi, Florida, Texas, Missouri, Kansas, Virginia, and Washington. State legislatures in New York, Pennsylvania, Indiana, Maryland, and a number of other states have in very recent years passed legislation enabling the operation of so-called farm wineries, so that the small grower-producer can sell his wine directly and without the burden of heavy licensing fees. These changes are both a response to the country's newly broadened interest in wine and a cause of it. Everything considered, the current scene in this country is more active, more exciting, and more promising than at any time since the middle of the nineteenth century, when successful winemaking had at last been established and when the economic possibilities of newly settled regions were being explored for the first time. The point I especially want to make is that the current ferment of interest in wine in America is not so much a new thing as it is a return to and a continuation of an earlier state of things. Prohibition and its lingering effects have obscured that fact from us. It is now time to consider what Prohibition was, where it came from, and what it did.

16

The End of the Beginning: National Prohibition

T he Eighteenth Amendment to the Constitution of the United States, forbidding all trade in alcoholic beverages, was ratified in January 1919; a year later national Prohibition went into effect. It remained in effect until the amendment was repealed in December 1933. For the fourteen years of Prohibition the wine industry, like the beer trade and the distilled spirits trade, was legally ended.[1] As it turned out, the measure intended to kill Demon Rum[2] in this country managed to give it hardly more than a flesh wound. Liquor of all kinds continued to be made by one means or another, and people, perhaps in larger numbers than ever before, continued to drink liquor of all kinds. Yet the interruption to the normal growth and functioning of winegrowing in this country had disruptive and destructive effects that are still being felt and will continue to be felt for as long as one can foresee.

It is often said, or suggested, that Prohibition was the result of a sudden aberration in the American public, something that came out of the dislocations of World War I. On this view, it was an unlucky accident rather than an expression of any important tendencies in our national life. That view is quite wrong. A little history will help us to understand what happened.

The ideal of temperance is perennial and permanent, as old as morality itself. It is an ethical ideal, to be achieved, if at all, by the inner will of the individual, acting freely. It is inclusive rather than exclusive, judicious rather than violent, permissive rather than dogmatic, complex rather than simple. It is also very difficult to achieve. Prohibition is everything that temperance is not: exclusive, violent, dog-

425

matic, and simple. It is achieved, if at all, not by the free consent of the individual, but by the communal imposition of external control. It, too, is very difficult to achieve. The story of this chapter is, in part, of how the American temperance movement turned into the prohibition movement, or, in other words, how the campaign to reform the individual drinker became a campaign to control the producers and sellers of drink.

Before the nineteenth century there were, of course, many advocates of temperance in drink, but they appeared intermittently, were unorganized, had no program, and can hardly be described as constituting a movement. Their typical plea was not for abstinence from drink but for decent moderation, not only in drink but in all sensual indulgence. In secular thought, Aristotle was the great authority for the ethical doctrine of "nothing too much." For the essentially Protestant culture of the United States, there were many authorities from the churches to provide the same counsel. It is a mistake to think that Christian temperance had anything austerely and rigidly prohibitory about it. Even the stern and unbending Calvin held that the pleasures of food and drink were given to us by God for our enjoyment, an evidence of divine benevolence not to be despised but welcomed. The Puritans, whose example was so powerful in the formation of early American cultural life, would have stared at the idea of prohibiting alcoholic drink. The greatest poet of the Puritan tradition, John Milton, praised wine; its greatest popular writer, John Bunyan, held that the Bible approved alcoholic drink. More practically, as we have already seen, the Puritans of Massachusetts Bay planted vineyards for wine almost as soon as they had set foot on dry land: no doubt they had the scriptural precedent of Noah in mind, without necessarily meaning to imitate him in detail. John Wesley, the founder of the Methodist communion in the eighteenth century, was in fact a prohibitionist so far as distilled spirits were concerned; the vastly increased production and consumption of gin and other spirits in Wesley's day had given a new character and scope to drunkenness. But Wesley had no idea of preaching, much less enforcing, total abstinence.[3] The first Methodist bishop in the United States, Francis Asbury, followed Wesley in preaching against hard liquor, but, like Wesley, never thought of suggesting prohibitory laws.[4]

Apart from the spiritual idea of moderation, there were arguments for temperance based on purely physiological grounds. The most influential of these was set forth by the distinguished Philadelphia physician, scientist, and patriot Benjamin Rush in a widely influential essay called "An Inquiry into the Effects of Spirituous Liquors on the Human Body," published in 1784. "Spirituous Liquors"—especially rum and whiskey—were cheap and abundant in late eighteenth-century America: rum came from New England, where the molasses to make it from came as part of the traffic in slave trading. Whiskey came from the corn fields of the western states, whiskey being a concentrated, portable, and saleable form of a corn crop otherwise difficult and expensive to transport to distant markets. In a society where whiskey and rum were everywhere available, and everywhere cheap, there was plenty of evidence of their destructive effect. The poor Indians, especially, had been devastated by firewater, and there were prohibitory laws passed to protect the Indians long before they were enacted for the whites.[5]

But one did not need to look to the Indians to find disease and social suffering produced by addiction to hard liquor. A generation of travellers and commentators on the American scene had noted the native style of excess in drink before Dr. Rush produced his essay, in which he took up and developed an already familiar theme. With zealous exaggeration, Rush attributed almost every physical malady and social problem to the abuse of strong drink: falsehood, fraud, theft, uncleanliness, and murder, as well as yellow fever, jaundice, dropsy, diabetes, gout, epilepsy, gangrene, and madness all flowed from strong waters.

The most vivid part of Rush's pamphlet was his scheme of a "moral thermometer," measuring the different degrees of moral and physical sickness caused by increasingly strong drink. Thus "toddy" would produce, on the moral side, "peevishness," and, on the physical, "tremors"; "grog," a stronger drink, led morally to "fighting" and physically to "bloatedness." The poor sinner who had progressed through grog, flip, and morning drams to the ultimate tipple of "pepper in rum" would find fraud, anarchy, and murder in his path, with the gallows at the end. But all of this extravagant denunciation was aimed against spirits. So far from prohibiting the temperate use of wine, Dr. Rush actually prescribed it for health and longevity. He was, we may remember, one of the investors in Legaux's Pennsylvania Vine Company, which was to be a source of wholesome wine to the new republic. "It must be a bad heart, indeed," Dr. Rush wrote in his "Inquiry into the Effects of Spirituous Liquors," "that is not rendered more cheerful and more generous by a few glasses of wine."

The principal ideas of the temperance movement are the two just described: first, the spiritual idea of the general virtue of moderation; and second, the secular idea of the physiological healthfulness of moderation in drink. Most of the early American temperance movements are clearly based on one or the other, or most often on both of these ideas, with varying degrees of religious sanction and clerical support behind them. The churches were associated from a very early period with temperance in America; but one must not think that the movement originated with the churches or that it in any way depended on them for its essential principles— not, at any rate, at first. In time, it is true, fundamentalist Protestantism and teetotalism became almost indistinguishable, but it is only an accident of our culture that the morality of bone-dry prohibition and of fundamentalist Christianity should have been so mixed up as they were, especially in the South and Midwest.[6] Biblical teaching is patently unclear and divided on the subject of alcoholic drink, and there have always been at least some churchmen candid enough to admit that there is nothing biblical about prohibition nor any demonstrable connection between abstinence and piety.

Who was "first" among organized American temperance groups is disputed, and is probably not a very important question anyway, since the early organized groups were not the causes of the temperance movement but were themselves the response to a feeling spread through the community at large. One of the very earliest of such groups was founded in 1808, at Moreau in upstate New York, under the inspiration of a local doctor. They called themselves the Union Temperate Society and had only a local purpose in mind; that is, by subscribing to a set of rules and by holding regular meetings, to help their members to do without strong drink. True to their name, the Temperate Society aimed at temperance rather than at strict abstinence. Hard liquor was prohibited, but wine and beer were not. A system of modest fines was the only safeguard against the dangers of backsliding.[7] Though the Moreau society did not remain active very long, it struck a responsive chord and was widely imitated in other communities of the Northeast. The purely secular and purely voluntary character of this early model are worth noting.

A rather different sort of model was created not far away and at about the same time. This was the Massachusetts Society for the Suppression of Intemperance, organized in 1813 by clergymen in Boston. It differed from the Union Temperate Society in two evident ways: its scope was statewide rather than local, and its direction was not in the hands of members who sought mutual support against their own weakness but of professional moralists who were bent on public reform.[8] The name of the society echoes those of the many reforming societies founded by the Evangelicals in England in this same period of intense reforming sentiment: the Anti-Slavery Society is the best known, but it was accompanied by a swarm of others, all christened after the same ungainly fashion: the Society for the Suppression of Vice, the Society for the Suppression of Mendicancy, the Society for the Suppression of Sabbath Travel, the Society for the Suppression of Blasphemy, and so on and on. The Massachusetts society also resembled its transatlantic models in another important particular. Like them, it was not content to work on individuals by moral suasion; it was out to change the laws. The main object of attack was hard liquor rather than wine and beer, so it was not devoted to total abstinence. But its concern with legislative means put it much closer to the later tendencies of the prohibition movement than were the easy-going and individualistic methods of the Union Temperate Society.

The Massachusetts society had its first legislative triumph in 1838 (by that time the original society had been several times reorganized and rechristened as it grew in strength and numbers); in that year the state of Massachusetts passed a law requiring the purchaser of spirits to buy not less than fifteen gallons at a time and to take his purchase off the premises.[9] Though this obstructive law was quickly removed from the books, it deserves notice as an early piece of prohibition law in this country. It was, despite its own brief life, a portent of the future. At the risk of being tedious, one may repeat that beer and wine were still not included among the objects of this kind of attack.

Whether by persuasive or by coercive means, the temperance people had much to do in the first third of the nineteenth century. All testimony agrees that this was a period of appalling public drunkenness in the United States. In the phrase of the

Reverend Lyman Beecher, one of the first and most prominent clergymen to advocate prohibition, Americans were "a generation of drunkards."[10] Beecher was no doubt exaggerating, but such statistics as we have give some color to his assertion. In 1810, for example, there were more than 14,000 distilleries reported in the United States; their production was estimated to be in excess of 33,000,000 gallons, a figure yielding a per capita consumption of spirits of 4.7 gallons.[11] In 1823, per capita consumption was put at 7.5 gallons.[12] By way of comparison, per capita consumption of distilled spirits in the United States in 1985 was 2.54 gallons.[13]

In early nineteenth-century America drinking was a part, and a large part, of almost every social occasion, sacred or profane: dances, barn raisings, weddings, militia meetings, elections, funerals, husking bees, college commencements, log rollings, ordinations, or "any other reason why," as the old song puts it, were occasions for breaking out the jugs. In the North some of those jugs would be filled with cider; in the South, with peach brandy; but North or South, rum and whiskey were sure to be in plenty. Beer was not a common general drink in the early republic—it had to wait on the large German immigrations after 1848.[14] And wine was even less common than beer. But distilled spirits were available everywhere. They were largely untaxed; the Jeffersonians had repealed Hamilton's modest whiskey tax in 1802, and except for a wartime tax from 1813 to 1817, whiskey and other spirits were tax-free commodities until the Civil War. In 1860 the average retail price of whiskey was 30 cents a gallon.[15] The combination of cheapness and availability would seem to be a sufficient explanation for the notorious American habit of heavy spirit drinking, though students of the subject have suggested any number of other reasons as well: the anxieties of pioneer life, for example, or the self-conscious spirit of democracy, which compelled a noisy, boozy, gregariousness even on those who would gladly have done without it. Whatever the reasons, the fact was clear to all: that Americans drank heavily and they drank hard stuff.

The style of much early temperance activity was to offer a kind of counter-attraction to the pleasures of social drinking. Meetings at which lectures were given and at which a kind of revivalist fervor could be enjoyed in the hearing of confessions and the receiving of pledges were the staple entertainment. Such groups as the Washington Temperance Society, founded in Baltimore in 1840, added the attractions of brass bands, parades, uniforms, and mass meetings to the business of redeeming the drunkard.[16] Another way that temperance societies could distract their members from the temptations of drink was to imitate the secret and fraternal societies, complete with oaths, rituals, regalia, degrees, honors, and mutual benefits. The Sons of Temperance, the Templars of Honor and Temperance, the Independent Order of Rechabites, the Independent Order of Good Templars, and others, all took this route.[17] For all of the temperance societies, whether open or secret, exclusive or comprehensive, the main means of enforcement was simply the Pledge. This had various forms, a familiar instance of which ran thus: "I hereby pledge myself, God being my helper, to abstain from the use of intoxicating liquors

PLEDGE of the

𝔚oman's 𝔠hristian 𝔗emperance 𝔘nion

✒ **PLEDGE** ✒

I hereby solemnly promise, GOD HELPING ME, to abstain from all distilled, fermented and malt liquors, including wine, beer and cider; and to employ all proper means to discourage the use of, and traffic in the same.

Name

Date

After signing this Pledge, retain it, but send name to Mrs. Geo. F. Pashley, 629 McDonough St., Brooklyn, N. Y., State Supt. work among Soldiers and Sailors.

124 | A late form of the temperance Pledge, probably from 1917 or 1918, by which time most of the loopholes had been closed and the commitment required was complete, though still quite voluntary. (From *The Temperance Songbook* [1971])

(including wine and cider), except in cases of necessity."[18] The only sanction for the pledge was the individual's uncoerced consent, however much that might be supported by solemn public profession in company with crowds of other penitents.

With no punishment beyond the guilt of the sinner, one may readily imagine that backsliding went on wholesale. Huck Finn's Pap illustrates the deplorable pattern: after tearfully taking the pledge at the new judge's house, Pap feels himself powerful thirsty in the night, gets hold of a jug of forty-rod, has a high old time, falls off the porch, and breaks his arm. When they find him in the morning he is nearly frozen to death. As for the new judge, "he felt kind of sore. He said he reckoned a body could reform the old man with a shot-gun, maybe, but he didn't know no other way."[19]

The judge's conclusion neatly summarizes what actually happened: if free will did not work, perhaps force would. Huck Finn's Pap was a low-down sort of human being, but there were enough who were not so very different from him to make the sterner reformers despair of any movement that depended on voluntary participation and that permitted any sort of indulgence—as in that saving clause of the pledge, "except in cases of necessity." The ultras in the temperance movement wanted legal compulsion, and they wanted total abstinence. Both of these ideas came into prominence in the 1830s, after a generation of temperance agitation seemed to have made no important difference to the drinking habits of the nation. It is interesting to note that in both England and the United States this development took place at about the same time. *Teetotalism* is in fact a word of English coinage,[20] expressing a sort of logic of despair. Since experience had shown that people who drank no spirits might still get drunk on beer and wine, and that people who drank no beer or wine might still get drunk on spirits, the only conclusion was total abstinence from alcohol, not moderation or temperance. And the prohibition should be binding on all, not just upon the weaker brethren.

A national temperance organization had been created in 1833 through the cooperation of dozens of county and state groups (the American Temperance Union, it was called), but it soon split apart on the rocks created by the extremist doctrines of legal prohibition and teetotalism.[21] As the conservative and moderate elements departed over these issues, control of the national organization passed to the ultras. Hereafter the story of prohibition in this country is the story of the successive legislative victories gained by the ultras—let us call them the Drys—working through a variety of organizations.

The first wave of laws passed in response to this pressure came in the 1840s: Portland, Maine, voted itself Dry in 1843, the first American city to do so; in 1844, the remote Oregon Territory passed a law forbidding the sale of spirits—striking evidence, on that distant frontier, of the general spread of prohibitionist sentiment. The most important and most publicized early legislation was the passage of a law prohibiting all intoxicating liquors in Maine in 1851.[22] The "Maine Law," as it was called, became the model for convinced prohibitionists throughout the country and the leading exhibit of American intolerance to liberals throughout the world—John Stuart Mill, for example, gravely condemned it in his classic essay *On Liberty*.[23] The Maine Law was quickly followed by similar laws all over the Union—Rhode Island, Massachusetts, Vermont, Connecticut, Delaware, Pennsylvania, New York, New Hampshire, Indiana, Michigan, Minnesota, and Nebraska Territory all followed suit in the next four years.[24] So did many smaller localities. Evanston, Illinois, for example, declared itself Dry from the very moment of its founding in 1855.[25]

These victories were, for the time at any rate, more apparent than real. It was comparatively easy to pass legislation that put an end to public drinking. It was quite another thing to enforce the legislation. The fact that liquor had been prohibited in state after state did not mean that people stopped making it, selling it, and drinking it. Whatever the law might say, where there were few means for enforcing it and even less will to do so, people went on doing what they wanted. Between 1850 and 1860, while the legislative triumphs of the prohibitionists were coming thick and fast, the per capita consumption of beer, wine, and whiskey in the country actually increased sharply.[26] So sensationally obvious a contradiction between law and practice greatly injured the cause. It might also have taught the Drys that legislation was not enough; yet that lesson did not seem to sink in. Not the least curious thing about the whole story of prohibition is the fact that the Drys always appeared to take it for granted that once the laws had been passed the laws would be obeyed. Thus, when national Prohibition was at last achieved, they were quite content to accept only the most rudimentary provisions for enforcing it, with, for them, catastrophic results.

The Dry cause was sharply, but only temporarily, set back by the Civil War, which gave the nation something else to think about. The war also led to a development that was afterwards to form a serious obstacle to the Drys. In order to raise money for the expenses of the war, Congress passed an Internal Revenue Act in 1862 that required a licensing fee from every retail liquor dealer and put a tax on every barrel of beer and gallon of spirits and wine produced in the country (the tax on wine was 5 cents a gallon).[27] Though it was intended simply to raise money, the act had the effect of "authorizing" the making and selling of liquor in the United States, since the government in effect recognized these as legitimate taxable activities.[28] It also provided a major argument in defense of the liquor interest, since the liquor trade was now important to the government's revenues. After the war, the taxes were reduced, but like so many emergency measures they remained in force when the emergency had long passed.

The war was, after all, only an interruption for the Drys; their activities were quickly reorganized and reenergized as soon as it had ended. Some sense of the quietly growing power of Dryness may be given by its effects in a region where the wine trade had once been important. In southern California, the cradle of California winegrowing, temperance communities grew up side by side with the vineyards. The town of Compton, founded in 1865 by the Methodist church, was teetotal from the beginning. So, too, was the bigger and richer settlement of Long Beach, where the deeds to town sites contained a provision by which the property would revert to the seller if the buyer engaged in the liquor traffic. And the city of Pasadena, which included several vineyards from the earliest days of viticulture in the San Gabriel Valley and which lay in sight of the great vineyards and wineries operated by Shorb, Rose, and Baldwin, declared itself a Dry town and kept itself so simply by force of community sentiment. When a merchant challenged the system by stocking liquor for sale, the city passed a prohibition ordinance and successfully defended its constitutionality before the state supreme court. By 1890 nearly fifty towns in southern California had local option in one form or another, in a place where, but a generation before, the prospect of winegrowing was being hailed as the brightest hope for the region's future.[29] California was far from Dry, but more than a small beginning had been made to that end. And as more and more migration from the Midwest poured into the state towards the end of the century, the Drys grew steadily stronger. There was plenty of opposition to the Dry campaign; but the opposition successes were tactical only. The direction of long-range strategy was in the hands of the Drys.[30]

Elsewhere, just as in California, the aim of that strategy was to get a firm legal basis for prohibition; the main work was therefore all concentrated on acquiring political power. At first the Drys worked to obtain laws obstructing or prohibiting the liquor traffic in whatever way seemed possible or appropriate. But experience showed that this piece-work, uncoordinated policy was unsatisfactory: statutory laws provided too many loopholes, too little uniformity, and too much vulnerability to the shifting fortunes of party politics. What the Democrats had passed the

Republicans could repeal; and while one administration might prosecute the saloon keepers without mercy, the next might allow the policeman to turn a blind eye to even the gaudiest saloons.

Furthermore, "Dry" was almost always a relative rather than an absolute term; large exceptions might be permitted, and special cases allowed, that made it possible for people to continue drinking in some fashion. When Virginia, for example, enacted statewide prohibition, it was at first proposed to allow the winemakers and brewers in the state to continue to operate on condition that they sold their product outside the state; and since Virginia is a large grower of apples, it was also proposed to allow 6 percent cider to be made and sold in the state. These proposals did not pass into law, but when Virginia did finally pass its prohibition law, it allowed every householder to buy, out of state, one quart of spirits, three gallons of beer, or one gallon of wine per month.[31] Niggardly measure, no doubt, but not exactly bone Dry. In fact, the distillers of Maryland prospered greatly from prohibition in Virginia, a contradiction that was bound to disturb any thoroughgoing Dry.

The Dry strategy was changed in the light of such results: the goal now became to base prohibition, not on state and local laws, but on a constitutional amendment, first in the states and then in the nation. The Drys did not abandon the work of getting state and local laws passed in their interest—indeed, they remained busy at that without interruption: but the new goal had been perceived and the policy of pursuing it became more and more distinct. Kansas was the first state to adopt prohibition by constitutional amendment (1880), but in the years immediately after, that hopeful example was followed by only four more states (Maine, Rhode Island, North Dakota, and South Dakota).[32]

The bold idea of amending the U.S. Constitution was first revealed in 1876, when the newly formed National Prohibition Party made it a plank in its platform. The party was pitifully weak at the polls, but it provided the idea that its stronger associates would ultimately succeed in carrying out. Chief among these were the Woman's Christian Temperance Union (WCTU), founded in 1874 and heroically directed by Frances Willard, and the Anti-Saloon League, founded in 1895 and the outstanding leader in the work of propaganda and politics for the Dry cause. The last, successful phase of the Dry campaign, culminating in national Prohibition, may be said to have been carried out by the Anti-Saloon League.

The league did not make national prohibition an explicit object all at once, but pursued whatever policy seemed likely to work in the circumstances. This kind of politic flexibility was the hallmark of league activity and its greatest strength. As Bishop James Cannon, the "Dry Messiah," once said, the league was "intensely practical" in seeking to "attain its ideal."[33] If it was expedient to deny any wish to achieve national prohibition, then it simply did so. But whatever the league people might say at any particular moment, they in fact aimed at national prohibition. And the league would support any candidate who could stay sober long enough to vote Dry.[34]

By the beginning of the twentieth century, the long and patient labor of the

Drys was at last making all obstacles yield. The most important practical element in this success was the Anti-Saloon League's policy of supporting any candidate, regardless of party, who was friendly to prohibition or could be scared into voting for it. By this means the Drys found themselves, in no very long time, in control of state legislatures throughout the South, the Midwest, and the West. And then began a dessication of states in rapid fashion. Georgia went Dry in 1907, Mississippi and North Carolina in 1908, Tennessee in 1909, West Virginia in 1912, Virginia in 1914. The process accelerated, so that by the time that the national prohibition amendment was passed in 1919, thirty-three of the forty-eight states were already Dry.[35] In 1913 a decisive victory had been won when Congress allowed Dry states to enforce their own laws on interstate commerce in liquor, a remarkable and troublesome exception to the commerce clause of the Constitution.[36] With this evidence of their new national power, the Drys determined that the time had come to strike for their ultimate goal, a prohibition amendment to the U.S. Constitution.

The last push turned out to be surprisingly easy. Dry influence on the elections of 1914 returned a friendly Congress, and by the end of 1914 a resolution proposing the Eighteenth Amendment had been introduced into the House and passed by a majority, though failing of the necessary two-thirds.[37] The Dry forces prudently waited for the next election, in 1916, and were rewarded. In the newly returned Congress a resolution to submit a prohibition amendment to the states passed the Senate in August 1917 and the House in December. Barely more than a year later the amendment had been ratified by the required two-thirds of the states: constitutional prohibition had been achieved.

The campaign that had at last succeeded in pushing it through had occupied only a very few years, but was the culmination of efforts stretching back over the better part of a century. And the victory, when it came, was apparently a popular victory, supported by large majorities in all but two states (for the record, Connecticut and Rhode Island refused to the end to ratify the amendment; yet Rhode Island had once had constitutional prohibition itself. Such were the ups and downs in the struggle between Wets and Drys). As Herbert Asbury has written, after surveying the complicated history of the prohibition movement, "it seems clear that the American people wanted prohibition and were bound to try it; for more than a hundred years they had been indoctrinated with the idea that the destruction of the liquor traffic was the will of God and would provide the answers to most, if not all, of mankind's problems."[38] "American people" is too sweeping a term, as the defiantly law-breaking behavior of millions during Prohibition made clear. But it is inconceivable that it could have been achieved without a wide and solid basis of support for the agitators.

And what were the terms of this experiment, "noble in motive and far reaching in purpose," to use the solemn phrase of President Hoover, so often sarcastically invoked afterwards? The article amending the Constitution was directed exclusively against the "traffic" (a favorite word of the Drys) in liquor, declaring that "the manufacture, sale, or transportation of intoxicating liquors within, the importation thereof into, or the exportation thereof from the United States and all territory subject to the jurisdiction thereof for beverage purposes is hereby prohibited." Turning this principle into enforceable law was the task of the National Prohibition Act, usually called the Volstead Act after its chief designer, that went into effect a year after the ratification of the Eighteenth Amendment. That act defined the "intoxicating liquors" of the amendment to mean any drink having more than one-half of one percent alcohol by volume, which meant that beer and wine were not excepted.[39]

Thus the hope that the winemakers had fondly clung to as Prohibition drew closer and closer, that wine would be recognized as an exception, was lost. There was, of course, a strong tradition, even in the United States, that wine was the drink of temperance rather than intoxication. Thomas Jefferson's is perhaps the best-known statement of the view: "No nation is drunken where wine is cheap," he had written in 1818. And there were many, both before and after Jefferson, to agree with him. Dr. Rush, in the very act of urging abstinence from spirits, recommended wine for pleasure and health alike. John Bartram dreamed of establishing viticulture in America for the sake of leading men away from strong drink. The federal government lowered the tariffs on imported wines in 1819 in order to encourage temperance,[40] and, as we have seen, granted lands to the Swiss in Indiana and to the French in Alabama in hopes of creating a plentiful source of native wines. And most of the early temperance societies had had no quarrel with wine, only with distilled spirits. Clearly, though, it was unwise of the wine men to think that this view of the question had much of a chance after the idea of total abstinence had come to dominate the prohibition movement, as it had from the 1830s onwards. The absolutist thinking of the confirmed teetotaller simply had no room for accommodating a "temperance" drink like wine, yet the wine men seemed to have gone on without recognizing that absolutist character. They hoped against hope that the reformers would see a clear distinction between the products of distillation and the milder products of unaided fermentation.

Their sense that they were different, not to be confused with the real enemies of temperance, appears to have confused and paralyzed their abilities to meet and respond to the threat of prohibition. If they separated themselves from the manufacturers of distilled spirits, the winemakers would seem to give their support to the prohibitionists; but if they threw in their lot with the distillers, they would then be identified with Demon Rum and be indiscriminately attacked with it. Finally, if they went their own way, they would have both distillers and prohibitionists as their enemies. Given these alternatives it is not surprising that the wine industry as a whole had no idea of how to fight the steady attack of the Dry forces. The one side knew what it wanted and how to get it; the other could merely protest its innocence and hope, in vain, for the best.[41]

National prohibition was enacted, but it had still to be enforced, and it was here that its unreality was made clear. The police arrangements of the Volstead Act were superficial. The Internal Revenue Service (not, as many thought should have been the case, the Justice Department) was put in charge of enforcement, through a commissioner who presided over a national system of regional directors and inspectors. They were armed with various powers of searching and seizing defined by the act, and the courts were empowered to impose appropriate fines and sentences on persons convicted of violating the act.[42] Yet the machinery of enforcement was absurdly slender and flimsy in relation to the job to be done, a fact that makes clear the innocent expectations of the Dry workers.[43] They imagined that once the law was made, compliance would follow. But that was not what happened. Prohibition instead created a nation of law breakers. All the provisions of the act were defied systematically and persistently by large sections of the population. And if the numbers of prohibition agents had been multiplied a hundred times, they would still have been powerless to stop what happened. The liquor "traffic," so far from being ended, was simply driven into the hands of bootleggers and gangsters; drinking, so far from being stopped, seemed actually to increase. And while the main objects of prohibition were being completely defeated, there was growing up in the country a general contempt of law. Seldom in the history of moral legislation can there have been a completer contradiction between expectation and result. It almost seems that the sharper and shrewder the Drys grew in political experience, the more simple-minded they grew in moral perception.

The intention of the law was simply to shut down all traffic in liquor—production, transportation, sales—and essentially it succeeded so far as the regular trade in wine was concerned. Spirits were far more attractive to the bootlegger than wine could ever be. And such wine as the bootlegger did deal in was likely to be homemade. All that most wineries in the country could do was quietly go out of business. And so they did. Production of wine in the United States in 1919 was over 55 million gallons; in 1920 it sank to 20 million; in 1922 it was just over 6 million, and by 1925 it reached a low of 3,638,000 gallons.[44] That some wine continued to be made was owing to special provisions in the Volstead Act. Sacramental wine could be legally made, under license, and so those wineries that managed to secure a license could maintain a precarious hold on existence. Wine could also be prescribed as medicine. Wine could be made for sale to the manufacturers of vinegar, and to the manufacturers of wine "tonics" of more or less medicinal character. Wine could also be used as a flavoring, in cooked foods and in tobacco, for instance. Since much sacramental wine was fortified and so required brandy, some wine could be made for the purpose of distillation into brandy to supply this need. There were thus several legal provisions allowing the continued production of wine, and since this very limited production could be legally carried on, it could be—and no doubt was—illegally extended. I have no figures that even suggest to what extent the legal permissions were abused. All writers on the subject take it for granted that abuses were widespread, but there do not seem to have been enough prosecutions to allow a guess at what was going on.[45]

Besides producing wine for the authorized purposes, some wineries tried to keep going by making juice (in the East especially, where Concord grapes were available) and other grape "products": jams and jellies mostly. And there were experiments with "non-vinous" commodities like concentrated juice and winebricks; the bricks were whole grapes pressed into solid form and wrapped for sale. Both concentrate and winebricks were sold with yeast tablets, and a caution against allowing illegal fermentation to take place.[46] Towards the end of the Prohibition era, a combination of wineries called Fruit Industries, organized by the resourceful Paul Garrett, undertook to deliver grape concentrate to the buyer's home and there to supervise its conversion into wine and to bottle it for storage and consumption. This complete domestic service was assisted by a large grant to the grape growers from the federal farm relief program, and it advertised itself in this remarkable way:

> Now is the time to order your supply of VINE-GLO. It can be made in your home in sixty days—a fine, true-to-type guaranteed beverage ready for the Holiday Season. VINE-GLO. . . . comes to you in nine varieties, Port, Virginia Dare, Muscatel, Angelica, Tokay, Sauterne, Riesling, Claret and Burgundy. It is entirely legal in your home—but it must not be transported. . . . You take absolutely no chance when you order your home supply of VINE-GLO which Section 29 of the National Prohibition Act permits you.[47]

The company's confidence in the legality of its operation was bolstered by the fact that it had succeeded in hiring as its attorney Mabel Walker Willebrandt, who for eight years had been assistant attorney general in charge of prosecuting violations of the Volstead Act. It is even stated that Willebrandt had helped to work out the terms of the Vine-Glo scheme before she left her public office to return to private practice.[48] In any case her quick change of sides inevitably provoked a lot of smart remarks, among the best of them this one by Al Smith, who had suffered much as the recognized leader of the Wets in American politics and who had no reason to feel kindly towards Willebrandt:

> I congratulate the Fruit Industries in securing the services of so competent a person as Mabel. She did two things for them, two wonderful things. She convinced the Department of Justice that this 12 per cent wine was not intoxicating. That was some stunt when you figure that old Andy Volstead fixed it at half of one per cent, and she jumped it up 11½ per cent and still robbed it of every intoxicating character. But she did something else for them that was equally important. She got the Farm Board to lend them $20,000,000.
>
> So when all is said and done, Mabel collected a beautiful fee for making the Volstead Act look like thirty cents.[49]

But, after all, Willebrandt failed to turn this astonishing trick. The Justice Department threatened to bring suit against Fruit Industries, and Vine-Glo was taken off the market at the end of 1931.[50]

The most striking paradox of Prohibition, in California at any rate, was that it led to a large increase in the planting of vineyards. The provision of the Volstead Act allowing the legal production of "fruit juices" in the home led to an immediate demand for fresh grapes all over the country. The result was remarkable: the price of grapes shot up from $10 to $100 a ton and even higher as the produce agents competed for each carload of grapes. An episode in Alice Tisdale Hobart's novel of the wine country, *The Cup and the Sword,* describes the California scene in the early days of Prohibition:

> Passing the station he saw a steady line of men coming out of the freight office, bills of lading in their hands. They did not get ten feet before they were accosted. Sometimes there were half a dozen men trying to talk to the same grapegrowers at once. Buyers from the East, was John's quick conclusion. . . .
> "What's up, Dietrick?" John called out.
> "Just sold my grapes for seventy the ton."
> John whistled.
> Dietrick grinned. "Sold 'em first for fifty. Bought 'em back when they went to sixty. Now I've got seventy."[51]

California had about 300,000 acres of vineyard in 1919; by 1926, after six years of Prohibition, that acreage had almost doubled, and shipments of grapes had grown by 125 percent.[52] Then, unluckily for the growers, the market was oversupplied. The boom went bust, and the years of Prohibition ended as they had begun, with the spectacle of discouraged growers pulling out their vines.

Worse than that, over the long run, was the fact that the grapes that shipped well and looked good in the market were not the best wine varieties. Alicante Bouschet, a splendid-looking grape, with large clusters of dark thick-skinned berries loaded with color, was the popular grape for amateur winemakers. But though it pleases the eye, the Alicante Bouschet at best makes only a mediocre wine.[53] Flame Tokay and Emperor, which are not wine grapes at all but table grapes, were also much favored. There was no encouragement to plant the superior, more delicate, yet less attractive-looking, varieties; indeed, there was every reason not to, when the market demanded the coarse, heavy-bearing sorts. The result was that the vast new plantings that went in during the Prohibition years were of the poorer sorts. The damage that this deterioration in the varietal quality of California's vineyards did to the reputation of California wines persisted long after Prohibition was a thing of the past. Table grapes, raisin grapes, and inferior, but productive, varieties of wine grapes were the overwhelming basis for California winemaking for years after Prohibition. Even as late as 1961, a whole generation after Repeal, there were only about 800 acres of Cabernet Sauvignon to supply the entire American wine industry! The same sorry figures held for the other distinguished varieties: 600 acres of Pinot Noir, 450 of Riesling, 300 of Chardonnay—absolutely appalling numbers at a time when California already had 424,000 acres of vines.[54] And no adage is truer in winemaking than the one that says the wine can be no better than its source. The degradation of the California source was a direct and lasting effect of Prohibition.[55]

Still, the "fruit juice" provision of the Volstead Act certainly helped to reduce the economic disaster of Prohibition for California grape growers. It also made an obvious, yet legal, mockery of Prohibition, since home winemaking did not need to be concealed. In San Francisco at vintage time, according to a *New York Times* reporter, this was the scene:

> A walk through the Italian quarter reveals wine presses drying in the sun in front of many homes. The air is heavy with the pungent odor of fermenting vats in garages and basements. Smiling policemen frequently help the owners of these wine presses to shoo away children who use them for improvised rocking horses.[56]

No doubt there were not many places quite so vinous as the Italian quarter of San Francisco, but what one saw there was only the extreme form of a situation to be found in every considerable town and city of the country.[57]

People are perfectly able to live with all sorts of contradictions and inconsistencies, but those created by Prohibition were impossible. Repeal, when it came in 1933, was met not so much with loud rejoicings as with a great public sigh of relief. Obviously the wine men had more reason than most to be joyful. But they had much to make them rueful too. The degenerate state of the vineyards has already been noticed. And of course the closing of the great majority of the wineries meant that the material basis of the industry had to be built all over again: buildings were out of repair or converted to other uses; machinery had been dispersed, or, if still in place, was out of order or obsolete; the vats and casks had been broken up or had dried out and fallen apart. More serious yet was the absence of experienced workers and managers: the continuity of tradition had been broken, and though there might be survivors who could pass on what they knew, there had been no young generation to receive it. That was the view on the production side. The market was equally derelict. The whole system of packaging, distributing, advertising, and selling wine had to be made anew.

Long before Prohibition the movement of wine through the United States had been complicated by the crazy-quilt patterns of local laws. Now, after Repeal, things were made even worse, perhaps more by accident than by design. The Drys, though they had been routed, were by no means dead; when the Twenty-first Amendment, the Repeal amendment, was drawn up, it recognized the persistence of Dryness in its section 2, which reads: "The transportation or importation into any State, Territory, or possession of the United States for delivery or use therein of intoxicating liquors, in violation of the laws thereof, is hereby prohibited."

Section 2 was clearly meant to allow *state* prohibition, even at the very moment that *national* prohibition was being swept away. A further question of interpretation was raised at once: did section 2 mean that "intoxicating liquors"—spirits, wine, and beer—were to be denied the protection of the commerce clause of the Constitution? They had been so denied even before Prohibition, when state and local option laws were upheld, beginning with a Supreme Court decision in 1847.[58] Now, after Repeal, that special status was affirmed by the language of the Twenty-first Amendment and supported by a number of decisions written by Justice Louis Brandeis of the Supreme Court. In effect, the states—not just Dry states but *all* of the states—were given absolute authority to do as they pleased in regulating the liquor traffic within their borders.

The result has been a chaos of varying and conflicting practices and regulations. Taxes vary wildly—from the 1 cent a gallon for table wine in California to the $1.75 a gallon exacted in Florida. Regulations vary wildly—some states have complete state monopoly of all liquor sales; some states have only a partial monopoly; some turn over everything to private licensees. In some states, you may buy table wine in a private store but dessert wine only in a state store, or wine by the bottle but not by the glass, or wine in drug stores but not in a grocery store, and so on through literally dozens and scores of other irrational permissions and prohibitions. In those states that allow for local prohibition, some put it on a county basis, some on a city basis, some on both. In other states, local option is not allowed at all.

Pricing is equally erratic, having little to do with costs; instead it is in large part the outcome of state and local taxes, licensing fees, and state-required minimum markups. A bottle of California wine in Washington, D.C., bought 3,000 miles from its source, may well cost less than the same bottle bought in Arizona or Nevada, states neighboring California. The catalogue of conflicting and arbitrary regulations is immense, so that any firm engaged in interstate commerce in wines requires the services of a professional staff to see that the rules are identified and complied with. The daily labor and confusion created by this tangle of balkanized regulations tells us at least two things: one, that we are still suffering from the legacy of Prohibition; and two, that we are still far from regarding wine as a simple commodity just as much entitled to unrestricted sale and consumption as, say, bread and cheese. If the federal government had simply undertaken to regulate alcoholic beverages on a national basis, this balkanizing would have been avoided; its failure to do so may be seen as another unwanted effect of Prohibition: after the failure of that experiment, the federal government seems to have wanted nothing so much as to wash its hands of further responsibility. Since then, it has confined itself to tax gathering and to monitoring such matters as the form and content of wine labels.

The Drys made themselves felt in another significant way just after Repeal. Among the projects of Franklin Roosevelt's first administration was one designed to help American winemaking get back on its feet. Rexford Tugwell, an assistant secretary of agriculture, planned to have the department again take up its historic role of assisting grape growing and winemaking through research and educational programs. Under his direction a model experimental winery was built and equipped at the department's Beltsville, Maryland, experimental station; another was put up at the department's research station in Meridian, Mississippi. Tugwell, who came to Washington from his position as professor of economics at Columbia, had a special interest in agricultural history and knew how important a role the federal government had played in the earlier history of American winegrowing. What he had not reckoned on was the entrenched strength of the Drys in strategic places. A power on the House Appropriations Committee was the veteran Missouri prohibitionist Clarence Cannon; when he learned of Tugwell's plans, Cannon threatened to block the whole departmental appropriation: the wicked work on "fermentation" must be stopped, or the whole work of the department would be brought to a halt. Faced with this desperate choice, the department gave way; the model wineries, still virgin, were converted to other uses and their machinery sold.[59] So shaken was the department that for the next generation it did nothing that could in any way be construed as having to do with winemaking. It hardly dared mention the word "wine" in its publications or to hint that grapes might in fact yield anything more exciting than "juice" or "jelly." As in the case of the government's abandoning the commerce in liquor to the chaos of state regulations, here was another evidence of the timid anxieties created by the experience of Prohibition. Repeal had been achieved, but not that frame of mind in which wine could be regarded as a valuable and decent commodity, to be produced, sold, consumed, and studied without apology.

That was the worst consequence of Prohibition—the way in which it had warped American attitudes towards drinking. The very extravagance implicit in the idea of enforced total abstinence seemed to have provoked an answering extravagance: if one was not austerely Dry, one had to be flamboyantly Wet.[60] The notion of decent moderation was overwhelmed in the conflict between these absurd opposites. Even now, more than half a century after the repeal of Prohibition, anyone who knows anything about the patterns of American drinking can observe the continuing effects of this conflict: for many Americans, it is hard to be natural and straightforward on the question, whether one drinks or does not drink. There remains something problematical and troubling in the subject, whatever side one takes.

The immediate question for the winemakers looking over the desolate scene left behind by the Dry years was to educate the American public in the renewed use of wine. If they were older Americans, they had forgotten what the civilized use of wine was; if they were younger, they had never known. How this was done lies outside of the scope of this history, which must shortly conclude. From what has already been said it will be clear that a hard and bitter labor faced the American winegrowers: their vineyards were debased, their wineries decayed, their markets confused by arbitrary and unpredictable barriers, and their public ill-instructed and corrupted by the habits of a hard-drinking bootleg style. Add to this the facts that Repeal did not take place until the country was plunged in deep economic depression, followed by the disruptions of a world war. Perhaps no activity ever knows anything like "normality," but it is hard not to feel that the American wine industry, passing through the uninterrupted sequence of Prohibition, depression, and war, has had particularly hard measure.

Yet it has, despite all these things, both survived and prospered. That it has managed to do so is a tribute to the persistence of many individuals—vineyardists, winemakers, scientists, publicists, dealers—who worked with a dedication more often associated with a cause rather than with mere commerce. Some of that growth was also owing to the roots already sent down during the life of American winegrowing before Prohibition. To make clear what that life was, and to suggest something of the connection between past and present, has been the aim of this history.

Appendix 1

Fox Grapes and Foxiness

There are two main questions connected with these terms: why *fox?* and what quality in the grape, exactly, is meant by *foxiness?* One must note first that more than one species of native American grape has been called "fox grape": at various times the name has been given to labrusca, rotundifolia, riparia, and cordifolia varieties. There is, furthermore, a difference in regional practice; in the North, labrusca is usually meant by "fox grape"; but in the South it usually means the muscadine or rotundifolia grape. If all of these possibilities have to be juggled, the task of explanation, bad enough to start with, grows hopeless. Fortunately, there seems to be something like agreement now that "fox grape" without further modification means some variety of the species labrusca. I shall take that as a starting place.

A second point to be noted is that "fox grape" occurs very early in American history. John Bonoeil, describing the grapes of Virginia in 1622, writes that "another sort of Grapes there is, that runne upon the ground, almost as big as a Damson, very sweet, and maketh deepe red Wine, which they call a Fox-Grape."[1] A report dated 1638 says: "I have not seene as yett any white grape excepting the foxgrape which hath some stayne of white"; John Parkinson writes in 1640 of "The Foxe Grape" that "hath more rugged barke"; and another writer in 1687 speaks of "The Fox-grape . . . in itself an extraordinary grape."[2] William Penn in 1683 writes of "fox grape" as an established name in American speech.[3] The usage thus established at least by the seventeenth century has continued to remain standard: Americans can still talk about fox grapes. *Why* they did so, and do so, remains a question.

After the historical evidence has been collected and compared, it appears that there are a number of rival theories, no one of them clearly preferable. The best thing to do in the circumstances is to present the details and let the reader judge.

One theory may, I think, be dismissed as purely fanciful: this is the notion that "fox grape" alludes to Aesop's fable of the fox and the grapes; on this account, the grape is named after the grapes that the fox in the fable could not reach and therefore called sour.[4] It is true that many native American grapes are sour, but they are all easily accessible, and there is simply no point in resorting to Aesop in order to account for the name of "fox." No early writer even suggests this explanation, and I conclude that it is a late, desperate effort at a solution.

For convenience of comparison I have put together under different headings the explanations that seem to me to be based on comparable principles.

1. Theories that *fox* means something other than fox

    a. Fox grape = *wild* grape: Waverley Root, *Food: An Authoritative and Visual History and Dictionary of the Foods of the World* (New York, 1980), asserts that *fox* in the seventeenth century was generally understood to mean "wild" but gives no evidence. The *Oxford English Dictionary* contains no support for this assertion, and though it seems on the face of it quite plausible, it has not been documented.

    b. "Fox grape" employs *fox* in the sense of "to intoxicate." This meaning is proposed by so eminent an authority as Liberty Hyde Bailey, but again without any evidence.[5] It is true that one of the well-established meanings of *fox* as a verb is to intoxicate, befuddle, or confuse (the last two senses obviously the result of being treated "foxily"); but there is no evidence that the American colonists meant such a thing at all in reference to the labrusca or other native grapes. They are almost all low in sugar and hence low in alcohol following fermentation. How, then, could such grapes have been regarded as filled with the power to "fox" in the sense suggested? Seventeenth-century Englishmen were not so weak-headed as that.

    c. *Fox* is a distortion of the French *faux*—that is, it signifies "false" grape. Robert Bolling, an eighteenth-century vineyardist in Virginia, calls the native grape the "faux" grape, and thus suggests this etymology for "fox" grape.[6] So far as I know Bolling is alone in doing so, and, given his fanciful notions, and his liking for French, one may doubt that he had anything but his own notions for evidence. It would have been just like Bolling to have converted the whole question to a matter of misunderstood French. Who were the French who gave the name?

2. Theories of appearance

    a. The grape is called "fox grape" because its leaf resembles the print of a fox's paw. Bailey reports this explanation, but without reference to his sources.[7] I have not found it before Bailey, and so I cannot criticize the grounds of its origin.

b. T. V. Munson affirmed that the name comes from the fox-colored wool or pubescence of the underleaf of the labrusca.[8] The unpersuasiveness of this explanation he later implicitly acknowledged by abandoning it in favor of a function theory (see 3b below). The suggestion was repeated by Eunice Fried as late as 1973;[9] thus the most arbitrary notion may be perpetuated long after its natural term of life is over.

3. Theories of animal attraction

a. Fox grapes are so called because foxes delight to eat them.[10] This seems to be one of those pieces of popular animal lore that no one has troubled to track to its source but that many have delighted to repeat. No doubt there is a biblical influence in the idea, from the "little foxes that spoil the vines" in the Song of Songs. I have found no early reference to the phenomenon of American foxes eating American grapes. The evidence seems to be that foxes take no particular interest in wild grapes.

b. Fox grapes are so called because their odor attracts small animals, including skunks, possums, and foxes. This theory was proposed by Munson in *Foundations of American Grape Culture* (1909) after he gave up his appearance theory (2b above). As a piece of animal lore, it seems as unsupported as that of 3a above; and even if there were evidence for it, why single out the fox, when skunks and possums are much more abundant?

4. Theories that *fox* refers to odor

These are the most common, and on the whole, most persuasive; but so far as I can show they are not conclusively supported by the evidence. Some representative statements follow:

a. "The Foxe Grape . . . smelleth and tasteth like unto a Foxe": John Parkinson, *Theatricum Botanicum: The Theater of Plants* (London, 1640).

b. The "fox" grape of Virginia is of "a rank Taste when ripe, resembling the Smell of a Fox, from whence they are called Fox-Grapes": Robert Beverley, *The History and Present State of Virginia* (1705).

c. "A strong scent, a little approaching to that of a Fox, whence the name of Fox-grape": Humphry Marshall, *Arbustrum Americanum: The American Grove, or an Alphabetical Catalogue of Forest Trees and Shrubs, Natives of the United States, Arranged According to the Linnæan System* (Philadelphia, 1785).

d. "There is another property of this grape which alone is sufficient to prove it to be the *Vit. vulpina*, that is, the strong rancid smell of its ripe fruit, very like the effluvia arising from the body of the fox, which gave rise to the specific name of this vine, and not, as many have imagined, from its being the favourite food of the animal; for the fox (at least the American species) seldom eats grapes or other fruit if he can get animal food": William Bartram, in James Mease, ed., *Domestic Encyclopaedia* (1803–4).

There is no need to multiply examples of this view of the question. One may note that the official statement of the U.S. Tariff Commission in 1939 declared succinctly that American fox grapes were so called for "the foxlike odor of their skins."[11] Where, one wonders, did they find their authority? The observation about the source of the odor being in the skins is correct. A very recent writer, Clarence Gohdes, adds the complicating detail that *foxy* was sometimes altered to *catty:* but this in reference to the southern muscadine, and then out of regional prejudice rather than in a sober effort to describe.[12] Another complication is added by William Penn, who wrote in 1683 that the fox grape is so-called by "Ignorance . . . because of the Relish it hath with unskilful Palates."[13] What does "unskillfulness" have to do with it?

A final theory may be mentioned. Liberty Hyde Bailey, in *Sketch of the Evolution of Our Native Fruits* (1898), holds that the term *foxiness* refers to the odor of the labrusca, as do many other writers, but that the meaning is a late development and was "suggested by the name of the grape" (*labrusca* means "wild vine"). In Bailey's view, *fox* originally referred to the intoxicating qualities of the wine made from such grapes; that meaning then passed out of currency, allowing the new one to arise. Bailey and Root (1a above) thus appear to agree on the general sense of "wild" as the meaning of *fox*.

Whatever the original intention of the name, the preponderant current usage holds that an aroma or taste peculiar to the labrusca grape is what *foxiness* refers to. Furthermore, that aroma is preponderantly defined as "musky," that is, "having a musky taste or smell, like a fox-grape" (Funk and Wagnalls, *Standard Dictionary of the English Language,* 1895); "the musk-like flavor of the wild *Vitis Labrusca*" (Bailey, *Evolution of Our Native Fruits*); "the strong, musky, odor and flavor is peculiar to this species" (Munson, *Foundations of American Grape Culture,* 1909); "the musky wine the native grapes yielded" (Peter Quimme, *Signet Book of American Wine* [New York, 1975]). Like most of our descriptive terms for tastes and smells, *musk* and *musky* do not take us very far towards a perception of what *foxiness* means. Musk is "an odoriferous reddish-brown substance secreted in a gland or sac by the male musk-deer" (*Shorter Oxford English Dictionary*). It is an element in many perfumes, it suggests wildness, and it provokes mixed responses, like anything strong: some people like it, some do not. I do not know what the informing substance is in the odor of musk or whether it has been discovered by chemical analysis. The flavor of the Concord grape, a pure labrusca, *has* been analyzed, and then synthesized so that the flavor can be used in soft drinks and other products. One of the main ingredients in that flavor is an ester called methyl anthranilate. But, to complicate things, the ester is not an important constituent of other labrusca grapes (e.g., Niagara).

Many American writers, in an effort to avoid the unflattering *foxy,* speak of the "grapey" character of labrusca grapes. As a description, this is logically hopeless, since it defines the thing to be defined by the thing to be defined. But, presumably, most Americans will know what is meant, since even if they are Californians and unused to eastern American wines, they will probably know the flavor of Concord grape juice or the taste of Concord grape candy.

It is interesting to look at other attempts to find flavor equivalents to express the aroma and taste of labrusca; some are rather attractive, some quite the reverse. The French scientist Planchon, an expert on American vines, regularly translates *foxy* as *gout de cassis*[14]—the taste of black currants; to me, this is a most attractive identification. At other times he compares the taste to that of raspberries; at others, to the fox, or perhaps even worse, to a fishy or gamey sea bird—*sauvagine.* Here is a passage combining all of these ideas: "Le gout de cassis ou de framboise (*foxy taste,* gout de renard ou de sauvagine, comme disent les Américains), que rend ces deux raisins peu agréables."[15] The comparison to black currants was also used by the New Zealand plant scientist S. F. Anderson in 1917. Anderson had much experience with American grapes, which are widely planted in New Zealand: he speaks of them as "inferior for winemaking, owing to a peculiar black currant, or, as it is generally termed, 'foxy' flavour that pervades the whole family."[16]

Unattractive descriptions of the foxy taste abound: I shall confine myself to two of them. The Englishman Michael Allen, long expatriated as a winegrower in France, writes: "The grapes of the American vine, when grown in Europe, have a totally unacceptable flavour which the French call *gout de fox* or even *gout de pipi de chat.* Once tasted never forgotten."[17] The Russian-born American winemaker, Alexander Brailow, recalled this even more surprising description: "People have tried to compare the smell and taste to things that they know. In Russia, for instance, they say that the grape Isabella, which is grown extensively in Crimea for red wine, smells like bedbugs. It all depends on the association and personal taste."[18]

Fox and *foxy* applied to grapes have passed into the French language since the phylloxera days. Larousse records the adjective *foxé,* and the Larousse *Dictionnaire des vins* the intransitive verb *renarder*—defined as what wines from American grapes do in the way of smell and taste. Frank Schoonmaker, in his *Encyclopedia of Wine* (1964), adds that the French speak of the *queue de renard* to describe the foxy taste. So, if we still do not know for sure why the labrusca is called the fox grape, or why its wines are called foxy, at least two languages agree to use those terms.

The Language of Wine in English

One cannot talk or write long about wine in English without discovering that the language is weak in words for the activities of vine growing and winemaking. The solution is either to Frenchify one's language, since French is rich in just those words that English lacks, or to invent English equivalents, or, most often, to strike some sort of compromise.

It was not always thus. In the days when England had vineyards and made large quantities of wine, there was a considerable stock of wine terms both in Old English and in Middle English: *wintre* (vine), *winberi* (grape), *wingetred* (press), *winegeard-naem* (harvest), *win-cole* (vat), *winwyrcend* (vine dresser), *drosna* (lees), *awilled win* (new wine), *win-aern* (wine cellar). In the days of King Alfred it was possible to speak of the *winegeard-naem* of the *winberis* from the *wintre*, the result of which went through the *wingetred* and was stored, as *awilled win*, in the *win-aern*.[1] Now we say that the harvest (*vintage*) of *grapes* from the *vine* goes through the *press* and, as *new wine*, goes into the *cellar*. All of the Anglo-Saxon terms have been driven out by French.

The triumph of the French was double. Not only did the Norman conquest impose the French language on the Anglo-Saxon, but French winegrowing put an end to that of the English. The process of borrowing into English had been going on since a much earlier time than these events, however. It is notable that there was no Anglo-Saxon term for wine itself: Anglo-Saxon *wine* is the Latin *vinum*. Other terms borrowed at a very early time include *barrel, bottle, cellar, grape, press,* and *vine,* all of which were known in Middle English. Some words that were borrowed early from the French have not survived into modern English, evidently because the things they named no longer existed in England: *vigneron* (winegrower) and *vynour* (vine dresser) are instances.

What was true of the language in England was even truer of the language in the North American colonies. The English colonists came without a winegrowing tradition, and were, for centuries, unable to build one in the New World. The vocabulary of wine would continue to wither away without anything to feed it. But we have now developed, or are developing, a tradition of our own, so that we can at least expect the possibility of a lively growth of novelty in our stock of wine words. The state of the vocabulary as it stands at this moment may be briefly outlined:

1. Words taken from the French, either replacing older English terms or having no English equivalent

    There are two levels in this category: the first level consists of those terms that have been accepted so long that they are no longer perceived as foreign; the second consists of words that are still felt to be French and therefore regarded as somewhat affected. Sometimes this is so because we lack the *thing* as well as the word.

    a. Accepted terms include: *barrel, bottle, butt, cellar, claret* (and a whole range of equivalent wine names used as typical), *ferment, funnel, gallon, gauge, graft, grape, press, puncheon, raisin, ullage, vine, vintage,* and *vintner.* Such words can change in interesting ways. *Vintner,* for example, is an instance of a specialized meaning becoming generalized. Originally a vintner was a wine dealer, a seller of wine; now the word and its derivations are used to mean not only a seller but one who has to do with the entire process of winegrowing, as in the phrase now common on American wine labels, "vinted and bottled by." *Vintage* is an instance of the opposite process of narrowed meaning: originally *vintage* meant harvest, but it is now generally understood to mean "good harvest," as in "vintage year" or "vintage wine."

    b. French terms still felt to be alien but in fact used by writers in English include: *appellation, brut, cave, cépage, chai, chambrer, chaptalization, climat, clos, cru, cuvage, cuvée, éleveur, marc, négociant, ordinaire, remuage, sec, sommelier, terroir, vigneron, vignoble.* One of these terms, *vigneron,* was anglicized as *vinearoon* in the days of Shakespeare, but it did not survive long. A word like *négociant* is an instance of a name for something unfamiliar but not quite unknown in the United States: the *négociant* is a merchant who selects young wines, then stores, ages, and blends them, before bottling and labelling them to sell wholesale. He thus performs many functions under one comprehensive name. *Terroir* is another unfamiliar concept; it refers, literally, to the contribution of the soil to the character of the wine, but in application it sometimes takes on almost mystical attributes. The French take *terroir* seriously; the Americans so far remain skeptical.

A few French terms may be regarded as on the borderline between naturalization and foreignness: *Château* used in American winery names is perhaps one of them; so, too, is the technical term *must* (French *mout*) for the yet-unfermented juice that comes from the crusher.

2.   Words of modern English origin now accepted as standard

This is a category containing, so far as I know, only two words: *winery* and *winegrowing*. *Winery*, formed on the analogy of *tannery* or *creamery*, is an American invention whose first recorded instances go back to the early 1880s. Before that time, Americans were likely to call their few wine-making establishments "wine houses," or "wine cellars." *Winery* obviously filled a gap, and has become absolutely standard.

Winegrower is a more tendentious word, perhaps not yet fully established. I have used it as one of my conventions in this book, but not without some hesitation. Its use is encouraged by the California Wine Institute, which recognizes in it the valuable implication that wine is not a manufactured but an agricultural product. Its currency goes back to the days not long after Repeal, when California winegrowers sought a marketing order under the Agricultural Marketing Act. Such an order gave legal authority to the wine trade association to collect mandatory assessments from all California wineries in order to pay the costs of research and promotion. But the enterprise had to be demonstrably agricultural. The wine people were at first refused as not qualified under the act, but later won recognition, partly through the "evidence" for the character of their work provided by the name *winegrower*. Jefferson Peyser, for many years the legal officer of the Wine Institute, claims the credit for having suggested the term when the marketing order was being sought.[2] The term was used as early as 1851 in Cincinnati, and doubtless elsewhere as early, or earlier than, that; the *Oxford English Dictionary* records an English instance from 1859. Thus Peyser cannot claim the invention of the word; but he may have been responsible for bringing it into wide and recognized use in this country.

3.   Words of modern English origin not yet accepted

I exclude from this category the technical terms of modern viticulture and winemaking—terms, mostly compounds, such as *T-bud grafting, mechanical harvester, dejuicer, field crushing,* and *ion exchange. Shermat* (from "sherry material") and *mog* (for "material other than grape") are genuine new words. Besides those, I know of only a very few instances of deliberate coinages, all of them efforts to solve the same problem: What do you call a person who takes a general interest in wine? *Oenophile* is one suggestion, from the Greek *oinos*, "wine." The variant *enophiliac* also exists.[3] Leon Adams has suggested *oenenthusiast*, with the same beginning but concluding not with the Greek *philos* ("loving") but with the Greek *enthousia* ("being possessed by a god"). I have also seen *vinophile*, mixing Latin and Greek. Whether as oenophiles, enophiliacs, oenenthusiasts, or vinophiles, we should be seeing an efflorescence of new names and terms for wine and its lore.

Notes

1. The Beginnings, 1000–1700

1. D. B. Quinn, *North America from Earliest Discovery to First Settlements* (New York, 1977), p. 32.

2. Samuel Eliot Morison, *The European Discovery of America: The Northern Voyages, A.D. 500–1600* (New York, 1971), ch. 3.

3. M. L. Fernald, "Notes on the Plants of Wineland the Good," *Rhodora* 12 (1910): 23–25, 32–38.

4. Quinn, *North America*, p. 32.

5. J. R. McGrew, "A Review of the Origin of Interspecific Hybrid Grape Varieties," American Wine Society Manual no. 10 (Royal Oak, Mich., 1981), p. 2; George Ordish, *The Great Wine Blight* (London, 1972), p. 8.

6. A. J. Winkler et al., *General Viticulture*, rev. ed. (Berkeley, 1974), p. 657; Philip Wagner, "Wine from American Grapes," *American Mercury* 28 (1933): 360.

7. Philip Wagner, *Grapes into Wine* (New York, 1976), p. 34. On American varieties in general, see Liberty Hyde Bailey, "The Species of Grapes Peculiar to North America," *Gentes Herbarum* 3 (1934): 149–244.

8. U. P. Hedrick, *The Grapes of New York* (Albany, N.Y., 1908), p. 28.

9. Samuel Eliot Morison, ed., *Journals . . . of Columbus* (New York, 1963), p. 242.

10. William Bradford, 16 November 1620, in Alexander Young, *Chronicles of the Pilgrim Fathers* (Boston, 1841), p. 130. *Labrusca* is the Latin word for the wild vine of Europe, but it was given by Linnaeus, confusingly enough, to this American species.

11. M. A. Amerine and W. V. Cruess, *The Technology of Wine Making* (Westport, Conn., 1960), p. 59.

12. Amerine and Cruess, *Technology of Wine Making*, p. 59.

13. *Wines and Vines* 69 (July 1978): 62.

14. McGrew, "Origin of Interspecific Hybrid Grape Varieties"; T. V. Munson, *Foundations of American Grape Culture* (Denison, Tex. [1909]); Winkler et al., *General Viticulture*. Other native species that have contributed to the development of useful hybrids include *V. berlandieri, V. candicans, V. champini, V. cinerea, V. lincecumii, V. longii,* and *V. monticola*.

15. Richard Hakluyt, *The Principal Navigations, Voyages, Traffiques, and Discoveries of the English Nation* (1589; reprint, Glasgow, 1903–5), 8: 430.

16. Morison, *European Discovery of America*, p. 298.

17. Hakluyt, *Principal Navigations*, 8: 430.

18. Ibid., p. 221.

19. Howard S. Russell, *Indian New England before the Mayflower* (Hanover, N.H., 1980), p. 85.

20. Hakluyt, *Principal Navigations*, 10: 51, 56.

21. Francisco Watlington-Linares, "The First American Wine," *Eastern Grape Grower and Winery News* 9 (October–November 1983): 50–52, based in part on the work of Dr. Stanley South for the Institute of Archaeology and Anthropology, University of South Carolina, 1980, 1981.

22. Ibid.

23. Hakluyt, *Principal Navigations*, 8: 298–99.

24. E.g., Hakluyt, *Divers Voyages Touching the Discovery of America* (London, 1850), p. 134; Hakluyt, *Principal Navigations*, 8: 355.

25. Quoted as motto to P. Morton Shand, *A Book of French Wines* (London, 1928), and roughly translatable as: "A good Frenchman, when I drink my glass filled with ardent wine I thank God that they haven't got any in England."

26. Léonie Villard, *La France et les États-Unis* (Lyon, 1952), p. 52.

27. Michael Drayton, "Ode to the Virginian Voyage" (1606), in *Poems,* ed. John Buxton (Cambridge, Mass., 1953), 1: 123-25.

28. George Percy, "Discourse" (1608?), in Philip L. Barbour, ed., *The Jamestown Voyages under the First Charter, 1606-1609* (Cambridge, 1969), 1: 138.

29. Francis Magnel's "Relation" (c. 1607-8), in Barbour, *Jamestown Voyages,* 1: 153.

30. Robert Johnson, "Nova Britannia," in Peter Force, ed., *Tracts Relating Principally to the Origin, Settlement, and Progress of the Colonies in North America,* 4 vols. (Washington, D.C., 1836-46), 1: no. 6, p. 16.

31. Robert Johnson, "The New Life of Virginia" (1612), in Force, ed., *Tracts,* 1: no. 7, p. 9.

32. Johnson, "Nova Britannia," p. 16.

33. Captain John Smith, *A Map of Virginia* (1612), in Barbour, *Jamestown Voyages,* 2: 346.

34. William Strachey, *The Historie of Travell into Virginia Britania (1612),* ed. L. B. Wright and Virginia Freund (London, 1953), pp. 121-22.

35. Alexander Brown, *The Genesis of the United States* (Boston, 1890), 1: 385.

36. "A True Declaration of the Estate of the Colony in Virginia" (1610), in Force, ed., *Tracts,* 3: no. 1, pp. 20, 23.

37. Lord De La Warr to Virginia Company (7 July 1610), in Brown, *Genesis of the United States,* 1: 409-10.

38. De La Warr's "Relation" (1611), in Brown, *Genesis of the United States,* 1: 482.

39. Ralph Hamor, *A True Discourse of the Present State of Virginia* (1615) (Richmond, Va., 1957), p. 22.

40. William Strachey, "For the Colony in Virginea Britannia, Lawes Divine, Morall and Martiall, Etc.," in Force, ed., *Tracts,* 3: no. 2, pp. 16-17.

41. Brown, *Genesis of the United States,* 1: 248, 353.

42. S. M. Kingsbury, ed., *The Records of the Virginia Company of London* (Washington, D.C., 1906-35) 3: 166.

43. Kingsbury, *Records* 3: 116.

44. Villard, *La France et les États-Unis,* p. 56; United Kingdom, Public Record Office, *Calendar of State Papers, Colonial, 1574-1660,* 8 April 1623; *William and Mary Quarterly,* 1st ser., 9 (1900-1901): 86; 13 (1904): 289; *Virginia Magazine of History and Biography* 2 (1894-95): 79, 310-11; 6 (1898-99): 241-42.

45. Warren M. Billings, ed., *The Old Dominion in the Seventeenth Century* (Chapel Hill, N.C., 1975), p. 34.

46. Clifford M. Lewis and Albert J. Loomie, eds., *The Spanish Jesuit Mission in Virginia, 1570-1572* (Chapel Hill, N.C., 1953), pp. 138-39, 141.

47. John Pury to Sir Edwin Sandys, 14 and 16 January 1620 (Kingsbury, ed., *Records,* 3: 254, 256).

48. Samuel Purchas, *Purchas His Pilgrimes* (Glasgow, 1905-7), 19: 153. This phenomenon is easily possible if the cutting includes a fruitful bud or buds from the parent vine. But the grower should remove the clusters that grow from any such buds until the vine is mature enough to sustain them. That the Virginia French apparently did not suggests that they had little experience in viticulture.

49. Ibid.

50. "A Declaration of the State of the Colony and Affairs in Virginia," in Force, ed., *Tracts,* 3: no. 5, p. 15.

51. Kingsbury, ed., *Records,* 2: 349.

52. Ibid., 2: 102 (5 September 1622); 3: 663 (9 July 1622).

53. John Bonoeil, *His Maiesties Gracious Letter to the Earle of South-Hampton . . . commanding the present setting up of Silke works, and planting of Vines in Virginia* (London, 1622).

54. Kingsbury, ed., *Records,* 3: 663.

55. Bonoeil, *His Maiesties Gracious Letter,* pp. 49-50.

56. Captain Butler, "Dismasking of Virginia" (1622), in Kingsbury, ed., *Records,* 2: 375, 384 (23, 30 April 1623).

57. Edmund S. Morgan, "The First American Boom," *William and Mary Quarterly*, 3d ser., 28 (1971): 169–98.

58. Kingsbury, *Records*, 3: 647 (10 June 1622).

59. Ibid., 3: 365–67 (July 1620).

60. Ibid., 4: 272 (31 August 1623).

61. Ibid., 4: 453 (30 January 1624).

62. Ibid., 2: 349 (12 April 1623).

63. Alexander Brown, *The First Republic in America* (Boston, 1898), p. 562.

64. "An Answer to a Declaration of the Present State of Virginia" (1623), in Kingsbury, ed., *Records*, 4: 142 (May 1623).

65. George Sandys to John Ferrar, March 1623 (Kingsbury, ed., *Records*, 4: 124).

66. *Virginia Magazine of History and Biography* 65 (1957): 21.

67. *Virginia Magazine of History and Biography* 20 (1912): 156.

68. Edward Williams, "Virginia . . . Richly and Truly Valued" (1650), in Force, ed., *Tracts*, 3: no. 11, pp. 16–18, writes as though all one had to do was to plant the vines; more than thirty years later the Reverend John Clayton writes in the same way (*Virginia Magazine of History and Biography* 76: [1968]: 427), and so do many others throughout the latter part of the seventeenth century.

69. William Waller Hening, ed., *The Statutes at Large: Being a Collection of All the Laws of Virginia* (Richmond, Va., 1819–23), 1: 115.

70. Ibid., 1: 135–36.

71. Ibid., 1: 161.

72. Williams, "Virginia . . . Richly and Truly Valued," in Force, ed., *Tracts*, 3: no. 11, p. 17.

73. United Kingdom, Public Record Office, *Calendar of State Papers, Colonial, 1574–1660*, p. 98.

74. William Bullock, *Virginia Impartially Examined* (London, 1649), p. 8.

75. "A Perfect Description of Virginia" (London, 1649), in Force, ed., *Tracts*, 3: no. 8, p. 14.

76. *Virginia Magazine of History and Biography* 76 (1968): 427.

77. Robert Beverley, *The History and Present State of Virginia*, ed. Louis B. Wright (Chapel Hill, N.C., 1947), p. 135.

78. Thomas Glover, "An Account of Virginia," in *Philosophical Transactions of the Royal Society*, vol. 11 (1676; reprint, Oxford, 1904), pp. 15–16.

79. This idea originated with Giovanni da Verrazzano, who also thought that he had found Arcadia on the east coast of North America (Boies Penrose, *Travel and Discovery in the Renaissance, 1420–1620* [Cambridge, Mass., 1952], p. 147).

80. Williams, "Virginia . . . Richly and Truly Valued," in Force, ed., *Tracts*, 3: no. 11, pp. 16–18, 28.

81. Hening, ed., *Statutes at Large*, 1: 470.

82. Lyman Carrier, *Agriculture in Virginia, 1607–1699* (Williamsburg, Va., 1957), p. 24.

83. John Clayton to Boyle, June 1687, *Virginia Magazine of History and Biography* 77 (1959): 427.

84. Villard, *La France et les États-Unis*, p. 59.

85. Conway Zirkle, "John Clayton and Our Colonial Botany," *Virginia Magazine of History and Biography* 67 (1959): 286.

86. Winkler et al., *General Viticulture*, rev. ed., p. 445.

87. J. R. McGrew, "Black Rot," *American Wine Society Journal* 9 (1977): 4.

88. It remains a question, however, why the European vine should succumb to, and certain American vines successfully resist, the phylloxera. Structurally, the vines in question are not all that different. The pathology is still under investigation. See Ordish, *Great Wine Blight*, pp. 106, 108, 184.

89. Liberty Hyde Bailey, *Sketch of the Evolution of Our Native Fruits* (New York, 1898), p. 13.

90. E.g., S. F. Field, *The American Drink Book* (New York, 1953), p. 242.

91. Alexander Young, *Chronicles of the Pilgrim Fathers*, p. 165.

92. Edward Winslow, "Good News from New England," in Young, *Chronicles*, pp. 231, 234.

93. Justin Winsor, ed., *Narrative and Critical History of America* (Boston, 1884–89), 3: 61n.

94. Alexander Young, *Chronicles of the First Planters of the Colony of Massachusetts Bay, from 1623 to 1636* (Boston, 1846), pp. 42, 43.

95. "New-England's Plantation" (1630), in Force, ed., *Tracts*, 1: no. 12, p. 7; Bailey, *Evolution of Our Native Fruits*, p. 12.

96. Samuel Eliot Morison, *Builders of the Bay Colony* (Boston, 1930), pp. 246, 247.

97. A. Holmes, "Memoir of the French Protestants," Collections of the Massachusetts Historical Society, 3d ser., vol. 2 (1830): 29–30; J. L. Bishop, *History of American Manufactures* (Philadelphia, 1866), 1: 272; Charles W. Baird, *History of the Huguenot Emigration to America* (New York, 1885), 2: 297–302.

98. Holmes, "Memoir," p. 80.

99. Carl R. Woodward, *Plantation in Yankeeland* (Wickford, R.I., 1971), pp. 50–52.

100. Lydia Sigourney, "On Visiting a Vine among the Ruins of the French Fort at Oxford, Massachusetts," Collections of the Massachusetts Historical Society, 3d ser., vol. 2 (1830): 82.

101. United Kingdom, Public Record Office, *Calendar of State Papers, Colonial, 1661–68*, p. 150.

102. William Hubbard, *General History of New England,* Collections of the Massachusetts Historical Society, 2d ser., vols. 5–6 (1815): 23.

103. Bishop, *History of American Manufactures,* 1: 270.

104. U. P. Hedrick, *History of Horticulture in America to 1860* (New York, 1950), p. 59.

105. Jasper Danckaerts, *Journal, 1679–1680,* ed. Bartlett Burleigh James and J. Franklin Jameson (New York, 1913), p. 59.

106. Israel Acrelius, *History of New Sweden,* Memoirs of the Historical Society of Pennsylvania, vol. 11 (1874): 37.

107. Bishop, *History of American Manufactures,* 1: 273.

108. Albert C. Myers, ed., *Narratives of Early Pennsylvania, West New Jersey, and Delaware* (New York, 1912), p. 228.

109. G. D. Scull, "Biographical Notice of Doctor Daniel Coxe, of London," *Pennsylvania Magazine of History and Biography* 7 (1883): 328.

110. Alice B. Lockwood, *Gardens of Colony and State* (New York, 1931–34), 1: 333.

111. Myers, *Narratives of Early Pennsylvania,* p. 398.

112. M. D. Learned, *The Life of Francis Daniel Pastorius* (New York, 1908), p. 160; *Germantown Crier* 34 (1982): 32–33.

113. William Hepworth Dixon, *William Penn,* new ed. (London, 1872), p. 304.

114. J. R. McGrew, "Brief History of Winemaking in Maryland," *American Wine Society Journal* 9 (1977): 60. The evidence for this vineyard is unclear, and though it seems probable that a vineyard was planned for the site, it is doubtful that it was in fact planted. The comments on its wine, then, if not wholly fanciful, are surely exaggerated.

115. Hedrick, *History of Horticulture in America,* p. 104.

116. *Calvert Papers, Number One,* Maryland Historical Society Publications, no. 28 (Baltimore, 1889), pp. 275, 296.

117. North Carolina, *The Colonial Records of North Carolina,* ed. William L. Saunders (Raleigh, N.C., 1886–90), 1: 51.

118. United Kingdom, Public Record Office, *Calendar of State Papers, Colonial, 1661–1668,* p. 159.

119. Lewis Cecil Gray, *History of Agriculture in the Southern United States to 1860* (Washington, D.C., 1933), 1: 44.

120. Thomas Woodward to the proprietors, 2 June 1665, in United Kingdom, Public Record Office, *Calendar of State Papers, Colonial, 1661–1668,* p. 304.

121. United Kingdom, Public Record Office, *Calendar of State Papers, Colonial, 1675–76,* and *Supplement,* p. 145.

122. United Kingdom, Public Record Office, *Calendar of State Papers, Colonial, 1669–74,* p. 34.

123. South Carolina Historical Society, *The Shaftesbury Papers and Other Records Relating to Carolina,* Collections of the South Carolina Historical Society, vol. 5 (Charleston, 1897): 175–76.

124. Ibid., 382.

125. St. Julien Childs, *Malaria and Colonization in the Carolina Low Country* (Baltimore, 1940), p. 157.

126. South Carolina Historical Society, *Shaftesbury Papers,* 5: 445.

127. Alexander Salley, ed., *Records in the British Public Record Office Relating to South Carolina, 1663–1690* (Atlanta, 1928–29), 1: 59.

128. Childs, *Malaria and Colonization,* p. 212.

129. St. Julien Childs, "The Petit-Guérard Colony," *South Carolina Historical and Genealogical Magazine* 43 (1942): 1–17; Arthur H. Hirsch, *The Huguenots of Colonial South Carolina* (Durham, N.C., 1928).

130. Thomas Ashe, "Carolina, or a Description of the Present State of that Country" (1682), in Alexander Salley, ed., *Narratives of Early Carolina, 1650–1708* (New York, 1911), p. 144.

131. Salley, ed., *Narratives of Early Carolina*, pp. 174–75.

132. Letter of Thomas Newe, 17 May 1682 (Salley, ed., *Narratives of Early Carolina*, p. 182).

133. Hirsch, *Huguenots*, p. 205.

134. South Carolina, *The Statutes at Large of South Carolina*, Thomas Cooper, ed. (Columbia, S.C., 1836–40), 2: 78.

135. Hirsch, *Huguenots*, p. 205.

136. Beverley, *History and Present State of Virginia*, p. 134.

137. Salley, ed., *Narratives of Early Carolina*, p. 310.

138. Ibid., p. 117.

139. Robert Bolling, "Pieces concerning Vineyards" (MS, Huntington Library), p. 118.

140. Sir Robert Montgomery, "Discourse concerning the Designed Establishment of a New Colony," in Force, ed., *Tracts*, 1: no. 7.

141. John Oldmixon, *The British Empire in America* (1741; reprint, New York, 1969), 1: 517.

142. John Lawson, *A New Voyage to Carolina* (1709), ed. H. T. Lefler (Chapel Hill, N.C., 1967), p. 118.

143. Frank Schoonmaker and Tom Marvel, *American Wines* (New York, 1941), pp. 162–67.

2. The Georgia Experiment

1. Georgia, *Colonial Records of Georgia*, ed. Allen D. Candler (Atlanta, 1904–16), 1: 11.

2. Benjamin Martyn, "Reasons for Establishing the Colony of Georgia" (London, 1733), in Charles C. Jones, *The Dead Towns of Georgia* (Savannah, 1878), p. 45.

3. Kenneth Coleman, *Colonial Georgia* (New York, 1976), p. 112.

4. "A New Voyage to Georgia, by a Young Gentleman," 2d ed. (1737), Collections of the Georgia Historical Society, vol. 2 (1842): 40–41.

5. Patrick Tailfer et al., *A True and Historical Narrative of the Colony of Georgia* (1741), ed. Clarence L. Ver Steeg (Athens, Ga., 1960), p. 60.

6. *Colonial Records of Georgia*, 1: 96.

7. James W. Holland, "The Beginning of Public Agricultural Experimentation in America: The Trustees' Garden in Georgia," *Agricultural History* 12 (1938): 278.

8. *Colonial Records of Georgia*, 3: 59.

9. *Colonial Records of Georgia*, 3: 126, 153, 156, 178.

10. John Perceval, 1st earl of Egmont, *Diary*, in *Manuscripts of the Earl of Egmont* (London, 1920–23), 2: 370 (16 March 1737).

11. *Colonial Records of Georgia*, 22, part 2: 113 (12 March 1739).

12. *Colonial Records of Georgia*, 22, part 2: 144 (19 May 1739).

13. Holland, "The Trustees' Garden in Georgia," 278–83.

14. Mills Lane, ed., *General Oglethorpe's Georgia* (Savannah, 1975), 1: 132.

15. Ibid., 1: 213.

16. Ibid., 1: 315.

17. Ibid., 1: 315–16.

18. *Colonial Records of Georgia*, 5: 63.

19. William Stephens, *Journal*, ed. E. Merton Coulter (Athens, Ga., 1958–59), 2: 197 (16 February 1745).

20. *Colonial Records of Georgia*, 7: 101 (4 February 1755).

21. Edith D. Johnston, "Dr. William Houston, Botanist," *Georgia Historical Quarterly* 25 (1941): 339.

22. U. P. Hedrick, *History of Horticulture in America to 1860* (New York, 1950), p. 136.

23. Francis Moore, *A Voyage to Georgia* (London, 1744), in Trevor R. Reese, *Our First Visit in America* (Savannah, 1974), p. 120.

24. John Wesley, *Journal*, ed. Nehemiah Curnock (London, 1909), 1: 402 (2 December 1737).

25. Tailfer et al., *True and Historical Narrative of the Colony of Georgia*, ed. Ver Steeg, p. 15.

26. *Colonial Records of Georgia,* 22, part 1: 251, 254 (19 September 1738); 23: 489 (12 February 1743).

27. *Colonial Records of Georgia,* 5: 91 (10 January 1739).

28. *Colonial Records of Georgia,* 5: 243 (2 November 1739).

29. *Colonial Records of Georgia,* 5: 347 (9 May 1740).

30. James Carteret to Lord Egmont, 22 April 1741, in *Colonial Records of Georgia,* 5: 500.

31. Stephens, *Journal,* 2: 71 (14 February 1744).

32. Mr. Christie to Lord Egmont, 6 March 1741, in *Colonial Records of Georgia,* 5: 461–62.

33. For Stephens, see E. Merton Coulter's introduction to Stephens' *Journal.*

34. *Journal of William Stephens, 1737–1740,* vol. 4 of *Colonial Records of Georgia,* p. 44 (6 December 1737).

35. Ibid., pp. 43–44.

36. He arrived on 10 July 1733: see E. Merton Coulter and Albert B. Saye, *A List of the Early Settlers of Georgia* (Athens, Ga., 1949), p. 71.

37. *Colonial Records of Georgia,* 23: 156.

38. John Brownfield to trustees, 19 June 1737, in *Colonial Records of Georgia,* 21: 483–84.

39. De Lyon to council, 12 April 1738, in *Colonial Records of Georgia,* 2: 228.

40. *Colonial Records of Georgia,* 2: 241; 22, part 2: 113 (12 March 1739).

41. *Colonial Records of Georgia,* 22, part 1: 327.

42. Tailfer et al., *True and Historical Narrative of the Colony of Georgia,* ed. Ver Steeg, pp. 61–62.

43. United Kingdom, Public Record Office, *Calendar of State Papers, Colonial, 1738,* p. 229.

44. *Colonial Records of Georgia,* 23: 157 (1 December 1741).

45. Tailfer et al., *True and Historical Narrative of the Colony of Georgia,* ed. Ver Steeg, p. 62.

46. *Colonial Records of Georgia,* 4, supplement: 135 (30 April 1741).

47. Coulter and Saye, *List of Early Settlers,* p. 91.

48. Richard Lawley to Lord Egmont, 6 February 1741, in *Colonial Records of Georgia,* 5: 451.

49. *Colonial Records of Georgia,* 6: 3 (12 October 1741).

50. See Malcolm H. Stern, "New Light on the Jewish Settlement in Savannah," *American Jewish Historical Quarterly* 52 (1962–63): 195.

51. Lane, *Oglethorpe's Georgia,* pp. 126, 302.

52. *Colonial Records of Georgia,* 3: 198.

53. Ibid., 4: 330–31 (4 May 1739).

54. Ibid., 4: 515 (18 February 1740).

55. William Stephens, "A State of the Province of Georgia," Collections of the Georgia Historical Society, vol. 2 (1842): 76.

56. Egmont, *Diary,* 3: 112–13 (5 February 1740).

57. Petition of 29 December 1740, in Lane, *Oglethorpe's Georgia,* 2: 522.

58. *Colonial Records of Georgia,* 4: 653 (1 September 1740).

59. Stephens, "State of the Province of Georgia," p. 71.

60. *Colonial Records of Georgia,* 5: 500 (22 April 1741).

61. Ibid., 22, part 2: 490 (15 January 1741).

62. Ibid., 4, supplement: 155 (29 May 1741).

63. Ibid., 4, supplement: 165 (12 June 1741).

64. Ibid., 4, supplement: 193 (16 July 1741). James Balleu, or Bailleu, or Baillou, arrived in Georgia in 1734, and was a storekeeper in 1741. He was also identified as a "vine dresser and hatter" (Coulter and Saye, *List of Early Settlers,* p. 3).

65. Ibid., 23: 157 (1 December 1741).

66. Ibid., 23: 138 (29 October 1741).

67. Edward Martyn, "An Impartial Inquiry into the State and Utility of the Province of Georgia" (1741), Collections of the Georgia Historical Society, vol. 1 (1840): 164.

68. *Colonial Records of Georgia,* 4: 537 (21 March 1740). "Bewlie" is the French *Beau Lieu* transformed by English mouths.

69. Stephens, *Journal,* 1: 42, 197–98 (13 February 1742, 26 April 1743).

70. Ibid., 1: 67 (20 April 1742); 2: 506 (17 August 1743).

71. Ibid., 1: 195–96, 221–22 (20 April, 30 June 1743); 2: 5–6 (17 August 1743).

72. Ibid., 1: 194 (26 April 1743).

73. Ibid., 2: 185–86 (8 January 1745).

74. Ibid., 2: 197 (16 February 1745).
75. *Colonial Records of Georgia,* 24: 227 (29 February 1744).
76. Stephens, *Journal,* 2: 124 (14 July 1744).
77. Ibid., 2: 125.
78. *Colonial Records of Georgia,* 24: 371 (19 March 1745).
79. Stephens, *Journal,* 2: 211 (29 March 1745).
80. Ibid., 2: 223−24 (5 July 1745).
81. Johann Martin Bolzius, "Bolzius Answers a Questionnaire," *William and Mary Quarterly,* 3d ser., 24 (1957): 242−43.
82. Royal Society of Arts, London, MS Guard Books, 12: 92.
83. John William De Brahm, *History of the Province of Georgia* (Wormsloe, Ga., 1849), p. 22.
84. William Bartram, *Travels,* ed. Francis Harper (New Haven, 1958), p. 291.

3. Virginia and the South in the Eighteenth Century

1. United Kingdom, Public Record Office, *Calendar of State Papers, Colonial, 1734−35,* pp. 290−91 (9 November 1734).
2. Johann David Schoepf, *Travels in the Confederation, 1783−1784* (Philadelphia, 1911), 2: 184−85.
3. *Journal of the Commons House of Assembly, 1742−1744,* ed. J. H. Easterby, in *Colonial Records of South Carolina* (Columbia, S.C., 1954), p. 553.
4. *Journal of the Commons House of Assembly, 1748,* ed. J. H. Easterby, in *Colonial Records of South Carolina* (Columbia, S.C., 1961), pp. 70, 105, 383 (26 February, 3 March, and 28 June 1748).
5. Royal Society of Arts, Journal Book, 24: 153−55.
6. Royal Society of Arts, Guard Books, 5: 20 July 1760; Royal Society of Arts, Minutes of Committee on Colonies and Trade, 1: 30 June 1756.
7. Robert Hilldrup, "A Campaign to Promote the Prosperity of Colonial Virginia," *Virginia Magazine of History and Biography* 67 (1959): 423.
8. Henry Laurens, *The Papers of Henry Laurens,* ed. Philip M. Hamer (Columbia, S.C., 1968−81), 4: 336 (7 July 1764).
9. David Ramsay, *History of South-Carolina* (Charleston, 1809), 1: 228.
10. Laurens, *Papers,* ed. Philip M. Hamer, 7: 362 (9 June 1772).
11. "Journal of Josiah Quincy, 1773," *Proceedings of the Massachusetts Historical Society* 49 (1915−16): 453 (22 March 1773).
12. *Travels,* pp. 213, 56.
13. Lewis Cecil Gray, *History of Agriculture in the Southern United States to 1860* (Washington, D.C., 1933), 1: 114.
14. E. P. Panagopoulos, "The Background of the Greek Settlers in the New Smyrna Colony," *Florida Historical Quarterly* 35 (1956): 95−97.
15. On Turnbull and New Smyrna, see Carita Doggett, *Dr. Andrew Turnbull and the New Smyrna Colony* [Jacksonville? 1919]; and E. P. Panagopoulos, *New Smyrna: An Eighteenth-Century Greek Odyssey* (Gainesville, Fla., 1966).
16. Schoepf, *Travels in the Confederation,* 2: 235−36.
17. John Lawson, *A New Voyage to Carolina,* ed. H. T. Lefler (Chapel Hill, N.C., 1967), p. 108.
18. Ibid., pp. 117−18.
19. North Carolina, *The Colonial Records of North Carolina,* ed. William L. Saunders (Raleigh, N.C., 1886−90) 4: 6, 16 (12 December 1734, 12 September 1735).
20. Ibid., 4: 919 (1749).
21. Ibid., 5: 316 (4 January 1755).
22. Clarence Gohdes, *Scuppernong: North Carolina's Grape and Its Wines* (Durham, N.C., 1982), p. 26n; Adelaide L. Fries, ed., *Records of the Moravians in North Carolina* (Raleigh, N.C., 1922−69), 1: 180; 3: 1085, 1189.
23. U. P. Hedrick, *The Grapes of New York* (Albany, N.Y., 1908), p. 38.
24. Robert Beverley, *The History and Present State of Virginia,* ed. Louis B. Wright (Chapel Hill, N.C., 1947), pp. 133, 135.
25. Ibid., pp. 315−16.

26. United Kingdom, Public Record Office, *Calendar of State Papers, Colonial, 1708–9,* p. 565.

27. John Fontaine, *The Journal of John Fontaine,* ed. Edward Porter Alexander (Williamsburg, Va., 1972), p. 86 (15 November 1715).

28. Hugh Jones, *The Present State of Virginia* (1724), ed. Richard L. Morton (Chapel Hill, N.C., 1956), p. 140.

29. Fontaine, *Journal,* p. 106.

30. Jones, *Present State of Virginia,* p. 91.

31. Robert Beverley, *History of Virginia* (1722; reprint, Richmond, Va., 1855), p. 260.

32. Jones, *Present State of Virginia,* p. 140.

33. Robert Bolling, *Virginia Gazette,* 24 February 1773.

34. Jones, *Present State of Virginia,* p. 140.

35. William Byrd, *Correspondence of the Three William Byrds of Westover, Virginia, 1664–1776,* ed. Marion Tinling (Charlottesville, 1977), 1: 380, 410 (c. 15 July 1728, 25 June 1729); Pierre Marambaud, *William Byrd of Westover, 1674–1744* (Charlottesville, 1971), p. 159.

36. *Correspondence of the Three William Byrds,* ed. Tinling, 1: 426, 427 (c. 1730?); 409 (25 June 1729); Westover MSS, Virginia Historical Society.

37. *Correspondence of the Three William Byrds,* ed. Tinling, 2: 493 (18 July 1736).

38. Ibid., 2: 513 (31 May 1737).

39. Ibid., 2: 518 (27 June 1737).

40. Pamela C. Copeland and Richard K. Macmaster, *The Five George Masons* (Charlottesville, 1975), p. 102.

41. *William and Mary Quarterly,* 1st ser., 16 (1907–8): 23.

42. William Waller Hening, ed., *The Statutes at Large* (Richmond, Va., 1809–23), 7: 567 (30 October 1760).

43. Ibid., 7: 568–70.

44. Hilldrup, "Campaign to Promote the Prosperity of Colonial Virginia," p. 410.

45. Ibid., p. 421.

46. Ibid., p. 415.

47. Robert Dossie, *Memoirs of Agriculture* (London, 1768–82), 1: 242. Dossie says that one of Carter's wines was "the product of vines brought from Europe."

48. Hilldrup, "Campaign to Promote the Prosperity of Colonial Virginia," p. 423.

49. Landon Carter, *The Diary of Colonel Landon Carter of Sabine Hall, 1752–1778,* ed. Jack P. Green (Charlottesville, 1965), 2: 1134 (4 October 1777).

50. Virginia, *Journals of the House of Burgesses of Virginia,* ed. John Pendleton Kennedy, 12 (Richmond, Va., 1906): 17 (25 May 1769).

51. Robert Bolling, "Incitation to Vineplanting" (MS, Huntington Library), pp. 112–14.

52. Hening, *Statutes at Large,* 8: 364–66.

53. A mile east of town on the old Yorktown Road, near Fort Magruder. The site is now identified by a state historical marker.

54. Virginia, *Journals of the House of Burgesses,* 12: 240 (13 March 1772).

55. Ibid., 12: 265: 23 March 1772; Virginia, *Legislative Journals of the Council of Colonial Virginia,* ed. H. R. McIlwaine (Richmond, Va., 1918–19), 1461 (25 March 1772).

56. Purdie and Dixon's *Virginia Gazette,* 20 June 1771–23 March 1776.

57. Rind's *Virginia Gazette,* 27 May 1773.

58. "On the night of May 4, 1774, a frost, caused by a northwest wind, ruined the corn and the wheat just above the ground, froze the small oak and other young trees, and caused all other trees to shed their leaves, which did not bud again until the following year. It was horrible to see the woods entirely stripped of leaves in summer, as if it had been midwinter. The bunches of grapes were already quite large, but they froze with the new crop. The old part of the vine, from which the branches had sprung, suffered too. But the vines put out new shoots, which produced about half the amount of grapes of the preceding years, and ripened at the usual season in the woods and gardens" (Philip Mazzei, *Memoirs, 1730–1816,* trans. Howard R. Marraro [New York, 1942], p. 207).

59. Virginia, *Journals of the House of Burgesses of Virginia,* 13 (1905): 111 (19 May 1774).

60. Dixon and Hunter's *Virginia Gazette,* 24 June 1775.

61. Hening, *Statutes at Large,* 9: 239 (October 1776).

62. Purdie's *Virginia Gazette,* 28 February 1777.

63. *William and Mary Quarterly,* 1st ser., 16 (1907–8): 32, 163. The sale was made in 1785.

64. Robert Bolling, "A Sketch of Vine Culture, for Pennsylvania, Maryland, Virginia and the Carolinas" (MS, c. 1774, Huntington Library), p. 36.

65. A complete copy of Bolling's MS, with what are probably his own corrections, is in the Huntington Library. A copy made for William Prince by Bolling's son, parts of which were published in the *American Farmer* in 1829 and 1830, is in the Prince Papers, National Agricultural Library.

66. Bolling, "Sketch," pp. 36, 41.

67. J. R. McGrew, "An Historical View of Early-Day Winemaking," *Wines and Vines* 57 (1976): 26.

68. Bolling, "Sketch," pp. 39–40, 110.

69. Virginia, *Legislative Journals of the Council of Colonial Virginia,* 3: 1482–83 (11–12 March 1773).

70. *Virginia Gazette,* 11 March 1773.

71. Purdie and Dixon's *Virginia Gazette,* 29 July 1773.

72. Ibid.

73. Purdie and Dixon's *Virginia Gazette,* 2 September 1773.

74. Robert Bolling, "Vintage of Parnassus," in "Pieces concerning Vineyards and Their Establishment in Virginia" (MS, Huntington Library), pp. 113, 122.

75. Bolling, "Sketch," p. 109.

76. Bolling, MS, Huntington Library.

77. *American Farmer,* 20 February 1829, p. 387.

78. Estave drifted to Georgia after the Revolution, where he intended to cultivate vines and where he was remembered as saying that "he would cultivate the native vines of any country, preferably to exotics" (Thomas McCall, *American Farmer,* 11 February 1825, p. 369).

79. On Mazzei, see Richard Cecil Garlick, *Philip Mazzei, Friend of Jefferson* (Baltimore, 1933); Philip Mazzei, *My Life and Wanderings,* trans. S. Eugene Scalia, ed. Margherita Marchione (Morristown, N.J., 1980); Giovanni E. Schiavo, *Philip Mazzei* (New York, 1951).

80. Garlick, *Mazzei,* pp. 27–29.

81. Garlick, *Mazzei,* pp. 32–39; Rind's *Virginia Gazette,* 2 December 1773.

82. Mazzei, *My Life and Wanderings,* p. 204.

83. Garlick, *Mazzei,* pp. 41–42.

84. Mazzei, *My Life and Wanderings,* p. 208.

85. Garlick, *Mazzei,* pp. 43–47.

86. Ibid., p. 52.

87. *The Papers of Thomas Jefferson,* ed. Julian P. Boyd (Princeton, 1950–), 1: 158.

88. Purdie and Dixon's *Virginia Gazette,* 28 July 1774.

89. Philip Mazzei, *Researches on the United States,* trans. Constance D. Sherman (Charlottesville, 1976), pp. 243–44.

90. Jefferson to Gallatin, 25 January 1793, in Garlick, *Mazzei,* p. 53.

91. Mazzei, *Researches,* pp. 243–44.

92. R. de Treville Lawrence, Sr., ed., *Jefferson and Wine* (The Plains, Va., 1976), p. 15.

93. Mazzei, *Researches,* p. 245.

94. Mazzei, *My Life,* p. 212.

95. Ibid., p. 212.

96. Schiavo, *Mazzei,* p. 177; Mazzei, *Researches,* p. 245.

97. *My Life,* p. 212.

98. Lawrence, ed., *Jefferson and Wine,* p. 14.

99. Jefferson to Gallatin, 25 January 1793, in Garlick, *Mazzei,* p. 53.

100. Edwin Morris Betts, ed., *Thomas Jefferson's Garden Book, 1766–1824* (Philadelphia, 1944), pp. 52–54 (6 April 1774).

101. *The Diaries of George Washington,* ed. Donald Jackson and Dorothy Twohig (Charlottesville, 1976–79), 2: 52 (11 April 1768).

102. *The Writings of George Washington,* ed. John C. Fitzpatrick (Washington, D.C., 1938), 27: 55 (Washington to François Barbé-Marbois, 9 July 1783).

103. Washington, *Diaries,* 3: 73, 80.

104. Dixon's *Virginia Gazette,* 10 June 1775; *Virginia Gazette,* 10 June 1775.

105. Bolling to Pleasants, 26 February 1775 (MS, Huntington Library).

106. *Southern Planter* 36 (1875): 655.

107. The Monticello Grape Growers Cooperative was organized in 1934 (Frank Schoonmaker and Tom Marvel, *American Wines* [New York, 1941], p. 184).

4. Other Colonies and Communities before the Revolution

1. *American Farmer,* 9 August 1822, p. 157; 22 December 1826, p. 318.

2. Governor Sharpe to Lord Baltimore, 15 June 1767 (Maryland Historical Society, *Archives of Maryland,* ed. William Hand Browne et al. [Baltimore, 1895]), 14: 402.

3. *Maryland Historical Magazine* 32 (1937): 213n.

4. J. R. McGrew, "Winemaking in Maryland," *American Wine Society Journal* 9 (1977): 61. The Carroll family once again maintains a vineyard in Maryland (*Wines and Vines* 55 [August 1974]: 24). One of the native vines planted in the eighteenth century in the Carroll vineyard is still alive (J. R. McGrew, "Some Grape and Wine Episodes in Maryland" [MS, 1986]).

5. U. P. Hedrick, *History of Horticulture in America to 1860* (New York, 1950), p. 113.

6. J. R. McGrew, "The Alexander Grape," *American Wine Society Journal* 8 (1976): 20.

7. Ibid.

8. Andrew Burnaby, *Travels through the Middle Settlements in North America* (London, 1798), p. 55.

9. Maryland Historical Society, *Archives of Maryland,* 14: 20.

10. Having been a delegate to the Albany Congress in 1754 along with Benjamin Franklin, Tasker may have learned of the interesting new grape found near Philadelphia from Franklin, who was attentive to such matters (information from Dr. J. R. McGrew).

11. Gottlieb Mittelberger, *Journey to Pennsylvania,* ed. and trans. Oscar Handlin and John Clive (Cambridge, Mass., 1960), pp. 55, 77.

12. Franklin to the Abbé André Morellet, in Morellet, *Mémoires* (Paris, 1823), 1: 303.

13. Reprinted in *The Papers of Benjamin Franklin,* ed. Leonard W. Labaree et al. (New Haven, 1960–), 2: 365–67.

14. See Ibid., 12 (1968): 4–7. For Hill's directions, see above, p. 70.

15. Ibid., 11 (1967): 183 (Benjamin Gale to Peter Collinson, 10 May 1754).

16. John Adams, *Diary and Autobiography of John Adams,* ed. Lyman Butterfield (Cambridge, Mass., 1961), 2: 125–26 (26 May 1760).

17. *Franklin Papers,* ed. Labaree et al., 9 (1966): 400 (10 December 1761).

18. Ibid., 20 (1976): 6 (4 January 1773).

19. Ibid., 14 (1970): 309 (18 November 1767).

20. Ibid., 15 (1972): 54 (20 February 1768).

21. J. McArthur Harris, Jr., "A Wissahickon Anthology," *Germantown Crier* 34 (1982): 81, 82.

22. Jared Eliot, *Essays upon Field Husbandry in New England,* ed. Harry Carman and Rexford Tugwell (New York, 1934), p. 200.

23. Johann David Schoepf, *Travels in the Confederation, 1783–1784* (Philadelphia, 1911), 2: 188.

24. American Philosophical Society, *Early Proceedings* (Philadelphia, 1884), pp. 15–17.

25. The vineyard site is now part of the grounds of the Waldron Academy, Merion, Pa.

26. F. J. Dallett, "John Leacock," *Pennsylvania Magazine of History and Biography* 78 (1954): 460–62.

27. John Leacock, Commonplace Book (MS, American Philosophical Society).

28. Dallett, "John Leacock," p. 464.

29. R. P. McCormick, "The Royal Society, the Grape, and New Jersey," *Proceedings of the New Jersey Historical Society* 81 (1963): 75–84.

30. *Franklin Papers,* ed. Labaree et al., 9 (1966): 321–22.

31. Royal Society of Arts, Minutes of Committee on Colonies and Trade, 17 February 1761.

32. McCormick, "The Royal Society, the Grape, and New Jersey," p. 80.

33. Edward Antill to Dr. Peter Templeman, 28 August 1765 (Royal Society of Arts, Guard Books, 9: 19).

34. McCormick, "The Royal Society, the Grape, and New Jersey," p. 79. Antill's remark is admirable rhetoric but poor geography; nature has denied to most parts of the world the means to grow wine grapes.

35. *Franklin Papers,* ed. Labaree et al., 2 (1960): 381 (14 May 1743).

36. Edward Antill, "An Essay on the Cultivation of the Vine, and the Making and Preserving of Wine, Suited to the Different Climates of North-America," *Transactions of the American Philosophical Society* 1 (2d ed., Philadelphia, 1789): 183.

37. Edward Antill to Dr. Sonmans, 31 January 1768: MS, Historical Society of Pennsylvania.

38. Royal Society of Arts, Guard Books, 10: 19 (28 August 1765).

39. Antill, "Essay on the Cultivation of the Vine," p. 192.

40. McCormick, "The Royal Society, the Grape, and New Jersey," p. 79.

41. Antill to Dr. Templeman, in Royal Society of Arts, Guard Books, 12: 38 (9 May 1766).

42. *New York Gazette and the Weekly Mercury,* 1 February 1768.

43. Evidence of Thomas Burgie, Stirling's gardener, in Royal Society of Arts, Guard Books, 11: 82 (6 October 1766).

44. McCormick, "The Royal Society, the Grape, and New Jersey," p. 77.

45. Royal Society of Arts, Guard Books, 11: 82 (6 October 1766).

46. McCormick, "The Royal Society, the Grape, and New Jersey," p. 80.

47. Schoepf, *Travels in the Confederation,* 2: 184.

48. Stephen William Johnson, *Rural Economy* (New Brunswick, N.J., 1806), p. 166.

49. *Proceedings of the New Jersey Historical Society,* n.s., 5 (1920): 126.

50. Robert Dossie, *Memoirs of Agriculture* (London, 1768–82), 1: 243.

51. Royal Society of Arts, Minutes of Committee on Colonies and Trade, 2 February 1768.

52. Richard Hakluyt, *The Principal Navigations, Voyages, Traffiques, and Discoveries of the English Nation* (1589; reprint, Glasgow, 1903–5), 8: 355.

53. Peter Force, ed., *Tracts Relating Principally to the Origin, Settlement, and Progress of the Colonies in North America* (Washington, D.C., 1836–46), 1: no. 6, p. 16.

54. Alexander Brown, *The Genesis of the United States* (Boston, 1890), 1: 410.

55. *Virginia Magazine of History and Biography* 76 (1968): 427; Albert C. Myers, ed., *Narratives of Early Pennsylvania, West New Jersey, and Delaware* (New York, 1912), pp. 227–28; Alexander Salley, ed., *Narratives of Early Carolina, 1650–1708* (New York, 1911), p. 310; for Beverley, see p. 64.

56. Hedrick, *History of Horticulture,* p. 145.

57. See above, p. 36.

58. Jean Pierre Purry, "Proposals" (Charleston, 1731), in B. R. Carroll, *Historical Collections of South Carolina* (New York, 1836), 2: 122, 131.

59. Collections of the South Carolina Historical Society, vol. 2 (1858): 83: "Ils se proposent . . . de s'appliquer principalement à la culture de vignes et des vers-a-soye."

60. Arthur H. Hirsch, *The Huguenots of Colonial South Carolina* (Durham, N.C., 1928), pp. 39–40; Nora Marshall Davis, "The French Settlement at New Bordeaux," *Transactions of the Huguenot Society of South Carolina,* no. 56 (1951): 28–57.

61. William Stork, ed., *A Description of East-Florida with a Journal Kept by John Bartram,* 3d ed. (London, 1769), p. 29.

62. For the date, see Davis, "French Settlement at New Bordeaux," p. 43.

63. Louis de Mesnil de St. Pierre, "Plan for the Culture of the Vine etc. at New Bourdeaux" (London, 1771); a MS copy is in the Library of Congress.

64. Davis, "French Settlement at New Bordeaux," p. 45.

65. Hirsch, *Huguenots,* p. 207; St. Pierre, "Plan for the Culture of the Vine."

66. Louis de Mesnil de St. Pierre, *The Art of Planting and Cultivating the Vine* (London, 1772), pp. xxviii–xxix.

67. It appears in an anonymous pamphlet entitled "A Memorial on the Practicability of Growing Vineyards in the State of South Carolina" (Charleston, 1798), p. 5. Lord Hillsborough himself told Henry Laurens that he regretted that public money was not available for St. Pierre's project, and it may have been Hillsborough who obtained a grant of 5,000 acres of land in South Carolina for St. Pierre through the Privy Council (*The Papers of Henry Laurens,* ed. Philip M. Hamer et al. [Columbia, S.C., 1968–81], 8: 139, 140n).

68. Royal Society of Arts, MS Transactions, 7 January 1772.

69. St. Pierre, "Plan for the Culture of the Vine."

70. *Papers of Henry Laurens*, 8: 139 (to John Lewis Gervais, 28 December 1771).

71. A MS copy of St. Pierre's "The Great Utility of Establishing the Culture of Vines . . ." (London, 1771) is in the Library of Congress.

72. Ibid., ff. 15, 19.

73. Louis de Mesnil de St. Pierre, "A Proposal for the Further Encouragement of the Production of Silk, and Growing of Vines, at the Colony of New Bourdeaux . . . ," in *Acts of Parliament,* 1772; *The Art of Planting and Cultivating the Vine,* p. xxvii.

74. United Kingdom, Board of Trade, *Journals of the Commissioners for Trade and Plantations, January 1768–December 1775* (18 March 1772).

75. St. Pierre, *Art of Planting and Cultivating the Vine,* pp. xiv–xx.

76. Ibid., p. 6.

77. Anon., "Memorial on the Practicability of Growing Vineyards in South Carolina," p. 5. Perhaps St. Pierre's reference to "A VERY GREAT AND EXALTED PERSONAGE" whose patronage was offered but whose name he could not disclose was the basis of this assertion (*Art of Planting,* p. xxix).

78. *Papers of Henry Laurens,* 8: 400n., and 566n. (report by Lewis Gervais, 6 June 1772).

79. Purdie and Dixon's *Virginia Gazette,* 22 July 1773, p. 2a.

80. Royal Society of Arts, Guard Book A: 159, 161, 163 (20 January, 19 November, 22 October 1770).

81. *Papers of Henry Laurens,* 9: 187.

82. John William De Brahm, *Report of the General Survey in the Southern District of North America,* ed. Louis De Vorsey, Jr. (Columbia, S.C., 1971), p. 70.

83. Ibid., p. 71. The story about the wine of the Jesuits in Mexico is more legend than fact. The Jesuit missions of Baja California did produce a trickle of wine, but not enough to supply their own needs, much less those of any others.

84. William Bartram, *Travels,* ed. Francis Harper (New Haven, 1958), p. 237.

85. MS note on Library of Congress copy of St. Pierre, "The Great Utility of Establishing the Culture of Vines," f. 21.

86. "A Memorial on the Practicability of Growing Vineyards in the State of South Carolina," p. 5.

87. [Fairfax Harrison], *Landmarks of Old Prince William* (Richmond, Va., 1924), 1: 188.

88. Durand de Dauphiné, *A Huguenot Exile in Virginia,* ed. Gilbert Chinard (New York, 1934), p. 126.

89. Robert Beverley, *The History and Present State of Virginia,* ed. Louis B. Wright (Chapel Hill, N.C., 1947), p. 134.

90. Louis Michel, "The Journey of Francis Louis Michel," *Virginia Magazine of History and Biography* 24 (1916): 123.

91. John Lawson, *A New Voyage to Carolina,* ed. H. T. Lefler (Chapel Hill, N.C., 1967), p. 119.

92. Cecil Johnson, *British West Florida, 1763–1783* (New Haven, 1943), pp. 151–52.

93. William Penn to Lord Halifax, 9 December 1683, in J. L. Bishop, *A History of American Manufactures from 1608 to 1860,* 1: 273; "A Letter from Doctor More . . ." (1687), in Myers, ed., *Narratives of Early Pennsylvania,* p. 287.

94. Myers, ed., *Narratives of Early Pennsylvania,* p. 227n.

95. Francis Pastorius, in Myers, ed., *Narratives of Early Pennsylvania,* p. 398. The passage from John reads: "I am the true vine, and my Father is the husbandman. . . . I am the vine, ye are the branches: He that abideth in me, and I in him, the same bringeth forth much fruit."

96. Myers, ed., *Narratives of Early Pennsylvania,* p. 291.

97. Ibid., p. 228n.

98. Ibid., p. 227.

99. Ibid., pp. 241–42.

100. United Kingdom, House of Lords, *The Manuscripts of the House of Lords, 1695–1697,* n.s., 2 (London, 1903): 471.

101. Albert Bernhardt Faust, *The German Element in the United States* (Boston, 1909), 1: 285.

102. Myers, ed., *Narratives of Early Pennsylvania,* p. 398.

103. Ibid., p. 383.

104. United Kingdom, Public Record Office, *Calendar of State Papers, Colonial, 1708–1709,* pp. 456–57 (30 August 1709).

105. Ibid., pp. 565–66.

106. Ibid., *1710–1711,* various entries.

107. Vincent H. Todd, ed., *Christoph von Graffenreid's Account of the Founding of New Bern* (Raleigh, N.C., 1920), pp. 43–49.

5. From the Revolution to the Beginnings of a Native Industry

1. *Pennsylvania Magazine of History and Biography* 47 (1923): 201–2.

2. Jacques Pierre Brissot de Warville, *New Travels in the United States of America,* ed. Durand Echeverria (Cambridge, Mass., 1964), pp. 204–7.

3. For Legaux generally, see S. Gordon Smyth, "Peter Legaux," *Historical Sketches* (Historical Society of Montgomery County, Pa.) 2 (1900): 92–125.

4. François, duc de la Rochefoucauld-Liancourt, *Travels through the United States of North America* (London, 1799), 1: 11–12.

5. Smyth, "Legaux," p. 105.

6. "A Memorial on the Practicability of Growing Vineyards in the State of South Carolina" (Charleston, 1798), p. 6.

7. Pennsylvania, *Statutes at Large of Pennsylvania from 1682 to 1809,* ed. J. T. Mitchell and Henry Flanders (Harrisburg, 1896–1908), 14: 356–60; 16: 438, 516.

8. Smyth, "Legaux," pp. 113–15 (26 January 1791).

9. Ibid., p. 116.

10. Ibid., p. 118.

11. *Annals of Congress,* 3d Cong., 1st sess., 19 May 1794, col. 101.

12. *Henry Wansey and His American Journal, 1794,* ed. David John Jeremy (Philadelphia, 1970), pp. 39–40; Rochefoucauld-Liancourt, *Travels,* 1: 11.

13. Smyth, "Legaux," pp. 117–19.

14. Rochefoucauld-Liancourt, *Travels,* 1: 11.

15. Smyth, "Legaux," p. 119.

16. Legaux to Jefferson, 4 and 25 March 1801; Jefferson to Legaux, 24 March 1801 (MSS, Jefferson Papers, Library of Congress).

17. Edwin Morris Betts, ed., *Thomas Jefferson's Garden Book, 1766–1824* (Philadelphia, 1944), pp. 277–78 (11 May 1802).

18. Smyth, "Legaux," p. 122.

19. Ibid., p. 121.

20. The extant journal is in the keeping of the American Philosophical Society, of which, one recalls, Legaux was a member. The journal for the years 1814–22, during which period the company collapsed and expired, is missing, perhaps deliberately suppressed.

21. Peter Legaux, Journal, 1: 38, 66 (see preceding note).

22. Ibid., 1: 135 (19 August 1804).

23. Ibid., 1: 171–72 (April 1805). Lee evidently formed a permanent interest in winegrowing but never fulfilled his promise to write a book on wines and vines. A prospectus for such a book, which was to include a general history, information on varieties, accounts of European vineyards, and advice on viticulture and enology, was noticed in the *New England Farmer* in 1823; four years later *Niles' Register* reported that Lee, now one of the auditors at Washington, was just on the point of going to press with his treatise on vine culture. I have found no further record of the book. It would have had an eager reception: James Madison, for example, wrote Lee on 16 December 1823 asking to be put down for two copies of the projected volume (MS, Historical Society of Pennsylvania). In 1816, after his return from France to the United States, Lee had been active in organizing the French Alabama settlement for wine and olive growing (see below, pp. 135–39, and Winston Smith, *Days of Exile: The Story of the Vine and Olive Colony in Alabama* [Tuscaloosa, Ala., 1967], p. 27).

24. Legaux, Journal, 2: 33, 84 (12 June 1806, June 1807).

25. *Pennsylvania Magazine of History and Biography* 48 (1924): 79.

26. Legaux, Journal, 2: 96 (October 1807).

27. Ibid., 3: 2, 31 (August 1809, 4 May 1810).

28. See below, p. 119.

29. Legaux, Journal, 3: 6 (26–29 September 1809).

30. Ibid., 3: 10 (1811).

31. Ibid., 3: 19, 35 (1813).

32. Smyth, "Legaux," p. 123.

33. S. W. Johnson, *Rural Economy* (New Brunswick, N.J., 1806), pp. 156-57.

34. U. P. Hedrick, *History of Horticulture in America to 1860* (New York, 1950), p. 84.

35. Copy, George Morgan Papers, Library of Congress.

36. Morgan to ?, 11 June 1802: copy, Morgan Papers.

37. Max Savelle, *George Morgan, Colony Builder* (New York, 1932), p. 233.

38. 28 February 1807 (MS, American Philosophical Society).

39. MS, American Philosophical Society.

40. William Bartram, in James Mease, ed., *Domestic Encyclopaedia* (Philadelphia, 1803-4), 5: 289-92. The *Catalogue* of Bartram's Gardens published in 1807 lists these species available according to Bartram's classification: occidentalis, labrusca, vulpina, taurina, and serotina, adding that "the varieties are infinite."

41. Mease, ed., *Domestic Encyclopaedia* 5: 292-96.

42. U. P. Hedrick, *The Grapes of New York* (Albany, N.Y., 1908), p. 43.

43. E.g., Joseph Cooper, who farmed on the banks of the Delaware across from Philadelphia. He had been making wine from native grapes and encouraging their cultivation since the time of the Revolution. He was a friend of Mease's and of Adlum's, and a grape of his introducing is described by Prince, so that it is clear that his work in favor of native vines was well known in quarters where attention was paid to such matters. See also p. 93 above for other evidence of interest in the native grape. For Cooper, see John Adlum, *A Memoir on the Cultivation of the Vine in America, and the Best Mode of Making Wine* (Washington, D.C., 1823), pp. 107-9, and Hedrick, *History of Horticulture*, p. 432.

44. Hedrick, *Grapes of New York*, p. 43.

45. Clarence Gohdes, *Scuppernong: North Carolina's Grape and Its Wines* (Durham, N.C., 1982), p. 12, quoting a letter from Mease published 7 March 1811.

46. Constantine F. Volney, *View of the Climate and Soil of the United States of America* (London, 1804), pp. 363-64.

47. John James Dufour, *The American Vine-Dresser's Guide* (Cincinnati, 1826), pp. 20-21.

48. Volney, *View of the Climate and Soil*, p. 364.

49. Dufour, *Vine-Dresser's Guide*, p. 20.

50. A copy of the broadsheet is in the Innes Papers, Library of Congress. Some years later the poet John Keats, writing to his brother George, who had emigrated to Louisville, Kentucky, wondered whether Kentucky could not grow a wine like his favorite claret: "Would it not be a good spec. to send you some vine-roots? Could it be done? I'll enquire. If you could make some wine like claret, to drink on summer evenings in an arbour!" (February 1819).

51. J. P. Brissot de Warville, "Thoughts on the Cultivation of Vines—and on the Wine Trade between France and America," *American Museum*, December 1788, pp. 568-71.

52. Dufour, *Vine-Dresser's Guide*, pp. 7-8. On Dufour generally, see Perret Dufour, *The Swiss Settlement of Switzerland County, Indiana* (Indianapolis, 1925).

53. Dufour, *Vine-Dresser's Guide*, p. 8. Dufour says that his left arm was "maimed"; Perret Dufour, *Swiss Settlement*, p. 8, says that it was the right.

54. Dufour, *Vine-Dresser's Guide*, p. 18.

55. Dufour, *Vine-Dresser's Guide*, pp. 18-19; 8.

56. Bernard Mayo, *Henry Clay* (Boston, 1937), p. 117.

57. Dufour, *Vine-Dresser's Guide*, p. 9; Perret Dufour, *Swiss Settlement*, pp. 9-10.

58. François André Michaux, *Travels to the Westward of the Allegany Mountains* (London, 1805), pp. 163-68.

59. Dufour, *Vine-Dresser's Guide*, pp. 9-10.

60. Partly because of uncertainty about what it really was, the Alexander has generated a more than usual number of synonyms, some of them clearly reflecting its mixed character, in which the perfect flowers of vinifera are mingled with the unmistakable flavor of a native grape. Among the names it has gone under at different times and places are Cape, Black Cape, Schuylkill Muscadel, Constantia, Springmill Constantia, Clifton's Constantia, Tasker's Grape, Vevay, York Lisbon, and York Madeira.

61. Liberty Hyde Bailey, *Sketch of the Evolution of Our Native Fruits* (New York, 1898), p. 42.

62. *American Farmer* 7 (22 July 1825): 140.

63. Perret Dufour, *Swiss Settlement*, p. 19.

64. Mayo, *Henry Clay*, p. 117.

65. Perret Dufour, *Swiss Settlement*, pp. 307–9; 315–17. The eminent botanist and writer Liberty Hyde Bailey visited the site of First Vineyard and published a description of it in his *Sketch of the Evolution of Our Native Fruits* (1898). At the end of the century, the property had become a sheep pasture, the old log house had disappeared, and only a pear tree and the vestiges of a stone wall marking the boundary of the vineyard remained to memorialize Dufour's struggles there to grow vines and make wine.

66. Dufour to Thomas Jefferson, 1 February 1801 (Jefferson Papers, Library of Congress).

67. Dufour to Thomas Jefferson, 15 January 1802 (Jefferson Papers).

68. *Statutes at Large of the United States of America, 1789–1873*, 6 (1846): 47–48 (1 May 1802).

69. Perret Dufour, *Swiss Settlement*, p. 18.

70. *Statutes at Large of the United States of America, 1789–1873*, 6 (1846): 126 (2 August 1813).

71. Perret Dufour, *Swiss Settlement*, pp. 33–34.

72. Ibid., p. 70.

73. Timothy Flint, *Condensed Geography* (1828), quoted in Harlow Lindley, ed., *Indiana as Seen by Early Travellers* (Indianapolis, 1916), p. 449.

74. Dufour, *Vine-Dresser's Guide*, pp. 24, 113; Karl J. R. Arndt, *A Documentary History of the Indiana Decade of the Harmony Society, 1814–1824* (Indianapolis, 1975–78), 1: 11–12.

75. *American Farmer* 2 (16 March 1821): 405.

76. John Melish, *Travels through the United States* (Philadelphia, 1812), 2: 131; John F. Von Daacke, "'Sparkling Catawba': Grape Growing and Wine Making in Cincinnati, 1800–1870" (M.A. thesis, University of Cincinnati, 1964), p. 7.

77. *Niles' Weekly Register* 4 (24 July 1813): 344.

78. William Cobbett, in Lindley, ed., *Indiana as Seen by Early Travellers*, p. 508: 17 June 1817.

79. Timothy Flint, *Recollections of the Last Ten Years* (Boston, 1826), pp. 59–60.

80. Lindley, ed., *Indiana as Seen by Early Travellers*, p. 522.

81. Dufour, *Vine-Dresser's Guide*, p. 33.

82. Perret Dufour, *Swiss Settlement*, p. 25.

83. Dufour, *Vine-Dresser's Guide*, p. 11.

84. Ibid., p. 7.

85. *American Farmer* 2 (26 November 1819): 281.

86. Dufour, *Vine-Dresser's Guide*, pp. 74–75.

87. Ibid., pp. 39, 41.

88. Perret Dufour, *Swiss Settlement*, p. 363n.

89. *Report of the Commissioner of Patents, 1847* (Washington, D.C., 1848), p. 462.

90. *Cozzens' Wine Press*, 20 February 1858, p. 172, citing the Cincinnati grower and winemaker Robert Buchanan.

91. Karl Postel in Lindley, ed., *Indiana as Seen by Early Travellers*, p. 522; Hedrick, *Grapes of New York*, p. 19.

92. Betts, ed., *Jefferson's Garden Book*, p. 572.

93. To M. de Neuville, 13 December 1818 (*Writings of Thomas Jefferson*, ed. Andrew A. Lipscomb and Albert Ellery Bergh [Washington, D.C., 1903], 15: 178).

94. The title of an instructive exhibition mounted in 1975 at the Wine Museum of San Francisco. See also R. de Treville Lawrence, Sr., ed., *Jefferson and Wine* (The Plains, Va., 1976).

95. Wine Museum of San Francisco, *Thomas Jefferson and Wine in Early America* (San Francisco, 1976), p. 11.

96. See *Vinifera Wine Growers Journal*, Fall 1984, p. 142a.

97. Jefferson to John Adlum, 7 October 1809 (Jefferson Papers).

98. Jefferson to John Adlum, 13 January 1816 (Betts, ed., *Jefferson's Garden Book*, p. 554).

99. Jean David to Jefferson, 26 November 1815 (Jefferson Papers).

100. Jefferson to David, 13 and 16 January 1816 (Jefferson Papers).

101. Jefferson to Adlum, 13 January 1816 (Jefferson Papers).

102. Jefferson to James Monroe, 16 January 1816 (Jefferson Papers).

103. Jean David to Jefferson, 1 February 1816 (Jefferson Papers).

104. Quoted by Rodney True, "Early Days of the Albemarle Agricultural Society," in *Annual Report of the American Historical Association, 1918* (Washington, D.C., 1921), 1: 245.

105. Betts, ed., *Jefferson's Garden Book,* p. 637.

106. Ibid., p. 572.

107. Jefferson to John Adlum, 13 June 1822 (Jefferson Papers).

108. They were identified to him as Ebinezer Pettigrew, of Edenton, and George E. Spruill, of Plymouth, who "owns the famous vine covering an acre of ground" (Francis Eppes to Jefferson, 21 April 1823, in *The Family Letters of Thomas Jefferson,* ed. E. M. Betts and J. A. Bear, Jr. [Columbia, Mo., 1966], p. 447).

109. Jefferson to John Adlum, 13 June 1822 (Jefferson Papers).

110. *American Farmer* 7 (29 April 1825): 45.

111. Nicholas Longworth, in *American Farmer* 15 (21 December 1832): 326.

112. F. C. Reimer in a report of 1909 cited in Lawrence, ed., *Jefferson and Wine,* p. 83.

113. *Cozzens' Wine Press* 4 (20 May 1858): 198.

114. Betts, ed., *Jefferson's Garden Book,* pp. 126-27 (to William Drayton, 30 July 1787).

6. The Early Republic, Continued

1. George Rapp, Petition to Congress, 1805, in Karl J. R. Arndt, *George Rapp's Harmony Society, 1785-1847* (Philadelphia, 1965), p. 86.

2. Arndt, *George Rapp's Harmony Society,* p. 114.

3. Karl J. R. Arndt, *Harmony on the Connoquenessing* (Worcester, Mass., 1980), p. 874.

4. Ibid., p. 422.

5. Arndt, *George Rapp's Harmony Society,* p. 125; id., *Harmony on the Connoquenessing,* p. 874.

6. Arndt, *Harmony on the Connoquenessing,* pp. 715-16.

7. Arndt, *George Rapp's Harmony Society,* p. 134.

8. Ibid., p. 137.

9. Karl J. R. Arndt, *A Documentary History of the Indiana Decade of the Harmony Society, 1814-1824* (Indianapolis, 1975-78), 1: 77 (29 November- 14 December? 1814).

10. Arndt, *Documentary History,* 1: 107, 745, 799; id., *George Rapp's Harmony Society,* p. 295.

11. Dufour, *Vine-Dresser's Guide,* pp. 20, 305.

12. Arndt, *Documentary History,* 1: 235-37 (20 July 1816).

13. Ibid., 2: 480n.

14. Arndt, *George Rapp's Harmony Society,* p. 322.

15. Arndt, *Documentary History,* 2: 18 (8 February 1820).

16. The story of the abundant wine produced from wild grapes by the French in eighteenth-century Illinois is a hardy perennial, but the evidence for it is shaky; the earliest published version I know of is in a newspaper item from the late eighteenth century promoting emigration to the Illinois country—a suspicious circumstance. Other stories about wine in early Illinois—such as that one that tells how the French government forbade vine planting for fear of competition with the home industry—are equally dubious. For the assertion about French wine production in Illinois, see, e.g., Liberty Hyde Bailey, *Sketch of the Evolution of Our Native Fruits* (New York, 1898), p. 3, and the Franklin Papers, American Philosophical Society, 58: ff. 11-12 (MS, c. 1772); the latter document affirms that the French remaining in Illinois territory had made French vines "flourish there and produce wine." For the newspaper reference, see Howard Mumford Jones, *America and French Culture, 1750-1848* (Chapel Hill, N.C., 1927), p. 303n.

17. In Barren County, Kentucky: the reference is to the vineyards of a Swiss, Buchetti, and of an American, James G. Hicks.

18. MS, c. 1822, courtesy Karl J. R. Arndt, German-American Archives, Clark University, Worcester, Mass.

19. Arndt, *George Rapp's Harmony Society,* p. 277.

20. Ferdinand Ernst, "Visit to Harmonie," 18 July 1819 (Arndt, *Documentary History,* 1: 745).

21. Lindley, *Indiana as Seen by Early Travellers,* p. 425; Arndt, *George Rapp's Harmony Society,* p. 341.

22. Karl J. R. Arndt, *Harmony on the Wabash in Transition* (Worcester, Mass., 1982), pp. 685–86.

23. Sandor Farkas, 4 October 1831, quoted in Karl J. R. Arndt, *Economy on the Ohio, 1826–34* (Worcester, Mass., 1984), p. 624.

24. Charles Nordhoff, *The Communistic Societies of the United States* (New York, 1875), p. 89.

25. Rudyard Kipling, *From Sea to Sea* (London, 1900), 2: 180.

26. Arndt, *George Rapp's Harmony Society*, pp. 296–98.

27. *American Farmer* 5 (31 October 1823): 251.

28. William Robert Prince, *Treatise on the Vine* (New York, 1830), p. 227. A list drawn up for Prince in 1829 provides these names of growers: in Lancaster County, Bauchman, Meitz, Gist, Miller, and Becker; in York County, Eichelberger, Bernetz, Lessus, Upp, Spengler, Hinkel, Small, Groll, Shelby, Ness, Sulsbach, Forembach, and Wildie. There were doubtless others as well (Prince Papers, National Agricultural Library).

29. U. P. Hedrick, *The Grapes of New York* (Albany, N.Y., 1908), p. 44.

30. *Niles' Register* 11 (23 November 1816): 208.

31. John Charles Dawson, *Lakanal the Regicide* (University, Ala., 1948), p. 104.

32. *Annals of Congress,* 14th Cong., 2d sess., p. 1313 (3 March 1817).

33. On the different names of the organization, see J. S. Reeves, *The Napoleonic Exiles in America,* Johns Hopkins University Studies in History and Political Science, 23d ser. (Baltimore, 1905), p. 558; Kent Gardien, "The Splendid Fools: Philadelphia Origins of Alabama's Vine and Olive Colony," *Pennsylvania Magazine of History and Biography* 104 (1980): 503.

34. *American State Papers, Public Lands* (Washington, D.C., 1832–61), 3: 387, 435.

35. Reeves, *Napoleonic Exiles,* pp. 560–61.

36. Reported in *Niles' Register* 13 (31 January 1818): 377.

37. *American State Papers, Public Lands,* 3: 435.

38. The summary in this paragraph is drawn from Hamner Cobbs, "Geography of the Vine and Olive Company," *Alabama Review* 14 (April 1961): 83–97; Anne Bozeman Lyon, "The Buonapartists in Alabama," *Gulf States Historical Magazine* 1 (1902–3): 325–36; Albert James Pickett, *History of Alabama,* 3d ed. (Charleston, S.C., 1851); Reeves, *Napoleonic Exiles;* Winston Smith, *Days of Exile: The Story of the Vine and Olive Company in Alabama* (Tuscaloosa, Ala., 1967); and Gaius Whitfield, Jr., "The French Grant in Alabama," *Transactions of the Alabama Historical Society, 1899–1903* 4 (1904): 321–55.

39. *American State Papers, Public Lands,* 3: 537.

40. Lyon, "Buonapartists in Alabama," p. 330.

41. Cobbs, "Geography of the Vine and Olive Company," pp. 89–90; *American State Papers, Public Lands,* 3: 396.

42. *American State Papers, Public Lands,* 3: 396, 537.

43. Pickett, *History of Alabama,* 3d ed., 1: 398.

44. Samuel Maverick to Thomas Jefferson, 4 March 1822 (Edwin Morris Betts, ed., *Thomas Jefferson's Garden Book, 1766–1824* (Philadelphia, 1944), p. 602.

45. *American State Papers, Public Lands,* 5: 15.

46. Ibid., p. 467.

47. Robert W. Withers, *American Farmer* 11 (5 June 1829): 91.

48. On Adlum generally, see Bessie Wilmarth Gahn, "Major John Adlum of Rock Creek," *Records of the Columbia Historical Society* 39 (1938): 127–39; Donald H. Kent and Mearle H. Deardorff, "John Adlum on the Allegheny: Memoirs for the Year 1794," *Pennsylvania Magazine for History and Biography* 84 (1960): 265–324, 435–80; John A. Saul, "Tree Culture, or a Sketch of Nurseries in the District of Columbia," *Records of the Columbia Historical Society* 10 (1907): 38–47.

49. John Adlum to Thomas Jefferson, 15 February 1810 (Jefferson Papers, Library of Congress).

50. John Adlum, *A Memoir on the Cultivation of the Vine in America, and the Best Mode of Making Wine,* 2d ed. (Washington, D.C., 1828), p. 11.

51. Adlum, *Memoir,* 1st ed. (Washington, D.C., 1823), p. 24n.

52. Jefferson to Adlum, 7 October 1809 (Jefferson Papers).

53. Adlum to Jefferson, 15 February 1810 (Jefferson Papers).

54. Jefferson to Adlum, 13 January 1816 (Betts, ed., *Jefferson's Garden Book,* p. 554); Adlum to Jefferson, 27 February 1816 (Jefferson Papers).

55. *New England Farmer* 2 (1824): 277.

56. *Cozzens' Wine Press* 1 (20 June 1854): 2.

57. Adlum to Jefferson, 5 June 1822 (Jefferson Papers).

58. Adlum to J. S. Skinner, 17 September 1822 (*American Farmer* 4 [1 November 1822]: 256).

59. *American Farmer* 4 (5 July 1822): 112.

60. *American Farmer* 4 (1 November 1822): 256.

61. Adlum to Jefferson, 5 June 1822 (Jefferson Papers).

62. *American Farmer* 4 (1 November 1822): 256.

63. Adlum to Jefferson, 24 March 1823 (Jefferson Papers).

64. Jefferson to Adlum, 11 April 1823 (*American Farmer* 5 [16 May 1823]: 63).

65. Adlum to Jefferson, 14 March 1823 (Jefferson Papers).

66. Adlum uses "Catawba" in *American Farmer* 7 (4 March 1825): 397.

67. The most circumstantial account, by Dr. Stephen Mosher, was published in the *Western Horticultural Review,* 1850; this is summarized by both Hedrick, *Grapes of New York,* p. 206, and by Liberty Hyde Bailey, *Sketch of the Evolution of Our Native Fruits* (New York, 1898), pp. 54–56.

68. Hedrick, *Grapes of New York,* p. 207.

69. *A Wine-Grower's Guide* (New York, 1965), p. 206.

70. *The Horticulturist* 5 (August 1850): 58.

71. *Report of the Commissioner of Patents, 1847* (Washington, D.C., 1848), p. 467.

72. It was republished in facsimile in 1971. The first edition is now a collector's item, bringing a price of many hundreds of dollars.

73. Adlum, *Memoir on the Cultivation of the Vine,* 2d ed., p. 37.

74. *Report of the Commissioner of Patents, 1847,* p. 462.

75. Madison to Mr. Randolph, 13 April 1823 (Pennsylvania Historical Society).

76. John Adlum, *A Memoir on the Cultivation of the Vine,* 1st ed., p. 4.

77. *American Farmer* 6 (7 May 1824): 53.

78. *American Farmer* 7 (2 September 1825): 188.

79. Gahn, "Major John Adlum," p. 136.

80. Isaac G. Hutton, *The Vigneron; an Essay on the Culture of the Grape and the Making of Wine* (Washington, D.C., 1827); copy in the Library of Congress.

81. Verse as a medium for popularizing technical subjects goes back to Vergil and was familiar in the eighteenth century, but it is unusual to find it being used as late as 1827: see, e.g., the poem *Cyder* by John Philips (1708) and Dr. Erasmus Darwin's *The Loves of the Plants* (1789).

82. Adlum to Jefferson, 5 June 1822, 24 March 1823 (Jefferson Papers).

83. *American Farmer* 10 (4 July 1828): 128; *Niles' Register* 36 (18 April 1829): 119.

84. U. P. Hedrick, *History of Horticulture in America to 1860* (New York, 1950), p. 224. Hedrick's is a general proposition subject to much modification in particulars. The attempt to grow vinifera in the East was never abandoned by private growers, and both state and federal agencies kept up experiments at different times during the century.

85. John Adlum, *Adlum on Making Wine* (Georgetown, 1826) was reprinted from the *National Journal.*

86. Hedrick, *Grapes of New York,* p. 214.

87. *Senate Documents,* 20th Cong., 1st sess., Senate Document 185 (Washington, D.C., 1828).

88. Ibid.; *Niles' Register* 34 (1828): 161, 192, 209.

89. Gahn, "Major John Adlum," p. 131.

90. Adlum to Jefferson, 24 March 1823 (Jefferson Papers).

91. *American Farmer* 9 (22 February 1828): 388.

92. Information from Dr. J. R. McGrew.

93. *American Farmer* 1 (1 October 1819): 214.

94. E.g., *American Farmer* 7 (29 April 1825): 45; *Niles' Register* 35 (25 October 1828): 130.

95. C. O. Cathey, "Sidney Weller: Ante-Bellum Promoter of Agricultural Reform," *North Carolina Historical Review* 31 (January 1954): 5.

96. C. O. Cathey, *Agricultural Developments in North Carolina, 1783–1860* (Chapel Hill, N.C., 1956), p. 155.

97. *American Farmer* 9 (6 April 1827): 22.

98. David Ramsay, *The History of South-Carolina* (Charleston, S.C., 1809), 2: 224.

99. *American Farmer* 7 (6 January 1826): 329.

100. Ramsay, *History of South-Carolina,* 2: 224.

101. Bailey, *Evolution of Our Native Fruits,* pp. 13-14.

102. Anon., "A Memorial on the Practicability of Growing Vineyards in South Carolina," p. 16. The speaker identifies himself as a "stranger" (p. 11) and a "foreigner" (p. 12).

103. John Drayton, *A View of South Carolina* (Charleston, S.C., 1802), p. 212; James Mease, ed., *Domestic Encyclopaedia* (Philadelphia, 1803-4), 5: 325.

104. James Guignard to William Prince, 30 December 1844 (Prince Papers, National Agricultural Library); *Report of the Commissioner of Patents, 1847,* p. 468.

105. Constantine Rafinesque, MS notes on vineyards, American Philosophical Society; Samuel Maverick to Thomas Jefferson, 11 August 1821, in Betts, ed., *Jefferson's Garden Book,* pp. 597-98.

106. "Journal of a Visit to Greenville from Charleston in the Summer of 1825," *South Carolina Historical Magazine* 72 (1971): 222.

107. *The Grape Culturist* 1 (1869): 173.

108. *American Farmer* 12 (2 April 1830): 21.

109. *American Farmer* 9 (4 January 1828): 333.

110. *American Farmer* 11 (9 October 1829): 237.

111. "Autobiography of William John Grayson," *South Carolina Historical Magazine* 69 (1949): 95.

112. "A Treatise on the Culture of the Vine" (Baltimore, 1833). I have not seen a copy.

113. Nicholas Herbemont, *American Farmer* 8 (8 September 1826): 196.

114. *American Farmer* 9 (4 January 1828): 332-33.

115. *American Farmer* 7 (6 January 1826): 329.

116. *Niles' Register* 33 (12 January 1828): 321.

117. *American Farmer* 6 (11 February 1825): 369-70; 8 (19, 26 May, 2 June 1826): 69-70, 77-78, 82-83.

118. James C. Bonner, "The Georgia Wine Industry on the Eve of the Civil War," *Georgia Historical Quarterly* 41 (1957): 21.

119. Adlum, "Adlum on Making Wine," p. 13; *American Farmer* 6 (11 February 1825): 369.

120. Stephen Franks Miller, *The Bench and Bar of Georgia* (Philadelphia, 1858), 1: 399.

121. *American Farmer* 6 (11 February 1825): 369.

122. Rafinesque worked in Adlum's Georgetown vineyard in 1825: "It was there that I began to study better our vines" (Rafinesque, "A Life of Travels," *Chronica Botanica* 8, no. 2 [1944]: 326). Rafinesque gave the name *Adlumia* to the Allegheny smoke vine.

123. Constantine Rafinesque, *Medical Flora, or Manual of the Medical Botany of the United States of America* (Philadelphia, 1830), 2: 159-60.

7. The Spread of Commercial Winegrowing

1. See, e.g., Robert Buchanan, *The Culture of the Grape, and Wine-Making,* 5th ed. (Cincinnati, 1854), p. 61.

2. Ophia D. Smith, "Early Gardens and Orchards," *Bulletin of the Historical and Philosophical Society of Ohio* 7 (April 1949): 72.

3. *American State Papers, Public Lands,* 1: 256-57 (3 February 1806).

4. On Longworth generally, see Clara Longworth de Chambrun, *The Making of Nicholas Longworth* (New York, 1933); and Louis Leonard Tucker, "'Old Nick' Longworth: The Paradoxical Maecenas of Cincinnati," *Cincinnati Historical Society Bulletin* 25 (1967): 246-59.

5. Nicholas Longworth, "The Grape and Manufacture of Wine," in *The Western Agriculturist and Practical Farmer's Guide* (Cincinnati, 1830), p. vii.

6. Date derived from Robert Buchanan's statement in 1850 that Longworth's oldest vineyard dated from twenty-seven years earlier (Buchanan, *A Treatise on Grape Culture in Vineyards, in the Vicinity of Cincinnati* [Cincinnati, 1850], p. 18).

7. *Report of the Commissioner of Patents, 1847* (Washington, D.C., 1848), p. 462.

8. Buchanan, *Culture of the Grape,* 5th ed., p. 106.

9. Ibid., p. 23. As early as 1832 Longworth had written: "I regret that more attention has not been bestowed in collecting native grapes from our forests and prairies. To them, and new varieties raised from their seed, we must resort, if we wish success" (Longworth to H. A. S. Dearborn, 10 October 1832, *American Farmer* 14 [21 December 1832]: 326).

10. Longworth, "The Grape and Manufacture of Wine," p. 305.

11. Liberty Hyde Bailey, *Sketch of the Evolution of Our Native Fruits* (New York, 1898), p. 61.

12. Thomas Trollope, *What I Remember* (New York, 1888), p. 122.

13. Frances Trollope, *Domestic Manners of the Americans,* 5th ed. (New York, 1927), p. 6n.

14. Trollope, *What I Remember,* p. 122.

15. Buchanan, *Treatise on Grape Culture,* p. 58.

16. John F. Von Daacke, "'Sparkling Catawba': Grape Growing and Wine Making in Cincinnati, 1800–1870" (M.A. thesis, University of Cincinnati, 1964), p. 39.

17. Ibid., pp. 18, 22, 41.

18. Longworth, "The Grape and Manufacture of Wine," p. 205.

19. Von Daacke, "'Sparkling Catawba,'" p. 22.

20. Committee on Wines, Cincinnati Horticultural Society, "Report on Wines" (1845), in *Report of the Commissioner of Patents, 1845* (Senate Documents, 29th Cong., 1st sess., no. 307, pp. 950–52).

21. *Horticulturist* 2 (1847–48): 318.

22. *American Agriculturist* 9 (1850): 119.

23. *Horticulturist* 2 (1847–48): 383; Buchanan, *Culture of the Grape,* 5th ed., p. 58.

24. *The Cultivator,* 3d ser., 6 (September 1858): 276.

25. "Longworth's Wine House" (Cincinnati, n.d. [c. 1864]). Copy in the Library of Congress.

26. *The Cultivator,* 3d ser., 6: 275. Fournier may have brought other Frenchmen from Champagne with him: a visitor to Longworth's wine cellar in 1855, after remarking that the practice there was identical with that followed in Epernay, added: "Indeed, all the men employed in the cellar are from that neighborhood" (Charles Weld, *A Vacation Tour in the United States and Canada* [London, 1855], p. 209). After ten years in Cincinnati, Fournier returned to France "with a snug fortune acquired in America" (William J. Flagg, *Three Seasons in European Vineyards* [New York, 1869], p. 148).

27. *American Agriculturist* 5 (1846): 351.

28. *Official Descriptive and Illustrated Catalogue of the Great Exhibition* (London, 1851), 3: 1433.

29. Louis Leonard Tucker, "Hiram Powers and Cincinnati," *Bulletin of the Cincinnati Historical Society* 25 (January 1967): 37–38.

30. Sludge says of Champagne, "I took it for Catawba" ("Mr. Sludge, the Medium," line 9).

31. First published in the *Atlantic Monthly,* January 1858.

32. De Chambrun, *Longworth,* pp. 31–32.

33. *The Cultivator,* 3d ser., 6 (1858): 275.

34. Charles Mackay, *Illustrated London News,* 20 March 1858, p. 297. Catawba has had a singular success among the poets. In addition to the effusions of Longfellow and Mackay, another, by one William Fosdick, appeared in the Cincinnati *Daily Commercial* of 11 December 1855: the poet apostrophizes the grape as, among other things, "the rarest of all vines the fair Catawba."

35. Isabella Trotter, *First Impressions of the New World on Two Travellers from the Old* (London, 1859), p. 207.

36. W. J. Flagg, "Wine in America, and American Wine," *Harper's Magazine* 41 (June 1870): 111. Flagg was Longworth's son-in-law and a former manager of the Longworth Winery.

37. Buchanan, *Culture of the Grape,* 5th ed., p. 59; Paul Cross Morrison, "Viticulture in Ohio," *Economic Geography* 12 (1936): 73; Bureau of the Census, *Agriculture of the United States in 1860* (Washington, D.C., 1864), p. 186.

38. *Cozzens' Wine Press* 1 (20 September 1854): 25.

39. See Von Daacke, "'Sparkling Catawba,'" especially ch. 5.

40. *Report of the Commissioner of Patents, 1853, Part II* (Washington, D.C., 1854), pp. 299, 310; Buchanan, *Culture of the Grape,* 2d ed., pp. 61, 116; *American Farmer,* 4th ser., 14 (December 1858): 198.

41. E.g., Buchanan, *Culture of the Grape,* 5th ed., p. 50.

42. *Harper's Weekly* 2 (24 July 1858): 472.

43. Von Daacke, "'Sparkling Catawba,'" p. 61.

44. *Report of the Commissioner of Patents, 1850, Part II* (Washington, D.C., 1851), pp. 238–41; *Horticulturist* 4 (1849–50): 397.

45. *Horticulturist* 4 (1849–50): 397; Buchanan, *Culture of the Vine,* 5th ed., pp. 28ff.

46. *Report of the Commissioner of Agriculture, 1868* (Washington, D.C., 1869), p. 575.

47. *Report of the Commissioner of Patents, 1850,* p. 241.

48. *Western Horticultural Review* 1 (1850–51): 293.

49. Von Daacke, "'Sparkling Catawba,'" p. 55.

50. But for a rival claim, see p. 000 and the Gasconade Grape Growing Society.

51. *Official Descriptive and Illustrated Catalogue of the Great Exhibition,* 3: 1433.

52. Von Daacke, "'Sparkling Catawba,'" p. 54.

53. Buchanan, *Culture of the Grape,* 5th ed., p. 93.

54. Ibid., p. 32.

55. Ibid., pp. 32, 40, 54.

56. See, e.g., Von Daacke, "'Sparkling Catawba,'" pp. 68–71; 77–80.

57. *Cozzens' Wine Press* 1 (20 August 1854): 18.

58. Buchanan, *Culture of the Vine,* 5th ed., p. iii; *American Farmer,* 4th ser., 14 (December 1858): 198; Von Daacke, "'Sparkling Catawba,'" p. 67.

59. U. P. Hedrick, *The Grapes of New York* (Albany, N.Y., 1908), p. 313; Von Daacke, "'Sparkling Catawba,'" pp. 72–73.

60. James Parton, "Cincinnati," *Atlantic Monthly* 20 (1867): 240.

61. Flagg, "Wine in America," p. 112; De Chambrun, *Longworth,* p. 104, says it was taken over by Moerlein's, a German brewery.

62. Flagg, "Wine in America," p. 112.

63. George C. Huntington, "Historical Sketch of Kelley's Island," *Fire Lands Pioneer* 4 (June 1863): 46.

64. See Huntington, "Historical Sketch of Kelley's Island"; Bert Hudgins, "The South Bass Island Community (Put-in-Bay)," *Economic Geography* 19 (January 1943): 16–36; J. R. McGrew, "A Brief History of Grapes and Wine in Ohio to 1865," *American Wine Society Journal* 16 (1984): 38–41.

65. Morrison, "Viticulture in Ohio," p. 74.

66. Von Daacke, "'Sparkling Catawba,'" p. 45.

67. Harlow Lindley, ed., *Indiana as Seen by Early Travellers* (Indianapolis, 1916), p. 8.

68. John James Dufour, *The American Vine-Dresser's Guide* (Cincinnati, 1826), p. 214.

69. Dufour, for example, repeats the statement: *Vine-Dresser's Guide,* p. 18.

70. Gottfried Duden, *Bericht über eine Reise nach den Westlichen Staaten Nordamerikas* (Elberfeld, 1829).

71. For Duden's influence on German settlement in Missouri, see William G. Bek, "Gottfried Duden's 'Report,' 1824–1827," *Missouri Historical Review* 12 (October 1917): 1–9.

72. William G. Bek, *The German Settlement Society of Philadelphia and Its Colony Hermann, Missouri* (Philadelphia, 1907), p. 1. For the details in the rest of this paragraph, see Bek, pp. 44–45, 55, 59.

73. Charles Van Ravenswaay, *The Arts and Architecture of German Settlements in Missouri* (Columbia, Mo., 1977), p. 48.

74. Ibid., pp. 51–52.

75. Bek, *German Settlement Society,* p. 46.

76. Michael Poeschel, quoted in Henry Lewis, *Valley of the Mississippi Illustrated* (St. Paul, 1967), pp. 262–63.

77. Friedrich Muench, "Vine-Culture in Missouri" (MS, Harvard University, 1867), p. 1.

78. George Husmann, *The Cultivation of the Native Grape, and Manufacture of American Wines* (New York, 1866), p. 18.

79. Bek, *German Settlement Society,* p. 152.

80. Ibid., p. 153.

81. J. T. Scharf, *History of St. Louis* (Philadelphia, 1883), 2: 1329.

82. Husmann, *Cultivation of the Native Grape,* p. 20.

83. George Husmann, *An Essay on the Culture of the Grape in the Great West* (Hermann, Mo., 1863), pp. 36, 40.

84. Muench, "Vine-Culture in Missouri," p. 2; Husmann, *Cultivation of the Native Grape,* p. 18, says that a Mr. Heinrichs brought the Norton to Hermann and that Wiedersprecher first grew it.

85. As early as 1851 Muench was exploring the Ozark region of Missouri hoping to find varieties of grape resistant to the rot: Muench, "Vine-Culture in Missouri," p. 2.

86. W. J. Flagg, *Three Seasons in European Vineyards* (New York, 1869), p. 97.

87. Charles Loring Brace, *The New West, or, California in 1867–68* (New York, 1869), p. 291.

88. George Husmann, for example, made 2,000 gallons of catawba at Hermann in 1857, but in 1858 only 200 gallons from the same acreage (*Cultivation of the Native Grape,* p. 181); Hermann's entire

production of catawba wine in 1857 was 90,000 gallons; in 1858, 15,000 gallons (Muench, "Vine-Culture in Missouri," p. 5).

89. Eight thousand gallons of catawba were consigned from Hermann to Longworth in 1858, at $1.25 a gallon (*DeBow's Review* 24 [1858]: 449). It is only fair to Cincinnati to say that, at the New York Exhibition of 1854, Cincinnati wines took both silver and bronze medals, Missouri wines nothing higher than honorable mentions (*Cozzens' Wine Press* 1 [20 September 1854]: 25).

90. *History of Franklin, Jefferson, Washington, Crawford and Gasconade Counties* (Chicago, 1888), pp. 672–73, 1112, 1119.

91. *American Agriculturist* 20 (December 1862): 368–69.

92. Husmann, *Cultivation of the Native Grape*, pp. 24, 183, 190, 191.

93. Lewis, *Valley of the Mississippi Illustrated*, p. 262.

94. On Muench, see Julius T. Muench, "A Sketch of the Life and Work of Friedrich Muench," *Missouri Historical Society Collections* 3 (1908): 132–44.

95. George Husmann, *American Grape Growing and Wine Making*, 4th ed. (New York, 1895), pp. 263–64.

96. It is based on Husmann's earlier "Essay on the Culture of the Grape in Missouri," published in 1859 as part of the *Report* of the Fourth Annual Fair of the St. Louis Agricultural and Mechanical Association, St. Louis, 1859. The 1859 essay was awarded a prize of $15 by the association.

97. A biographical sketch of Husmann appears in the *Dictionary of American Biography*.

98. Husmann, *Cultivation of the Native Grape*, p. 159.

99. Isidore Bush and Son, *Illustrated Descriptive Catalogue of Grape Vines, Small Fruit, and Potatoes* (St. Louis, 1869).

100. Hedrick, *Grapes of New York*, p. 352; id., *Grapes and Wines from Home Vineyards* (New York, 1945), p. 150.

101. *A Toast to Ontario Wines* (1979), p. 7.

102. William G. Bek, "The Followers of Duden," *Missouri Historical Review* 17 (1922): 333.

103. For a biographical sketch of Engelmann, see the *Dictionary of American Biography*.

104. For Bush, see Jacob Furth, "Sketch of Isidor Bush," *Missouri Historical Society Collections* 4 (1912–23): 303–8.

105. "Biographical Sketch" reprinted from American Academy of Arts and Sciences, *Proceedings* 20, in *The Botanical Works of the Late George Engelmann*, ed. William Trelease and Asa Gray (Cambridge, Mass., 1887), 1: vi.

106. Gustave Koerner, *Memoirs, 1809–1896*, ed. T. J. McCormack (Cedar Rapids, Iowa, 1909), 1: 296–97.

107. Ibid., 2: 633.

108. Oswald Garrison Villard, "The 'Latin Peasants' of Belleville, Illinois," *Journal of the Illinois State Historical Society* 35 (1942): 14; Maynard Amerine, "Hilgard and California Viticulture," *Hilgardia* 33 (July 1962): 2.

109. For Eugene Hilgard's work in California, see below, pp. 351–52. A life of Hilgard appears in the *Dictionary of American Biography*.

110. Leon Adams, *The Wines of America* (Boston, 1973), p. 139.

111. *DeBow's Review* 24 (1858): 550.

112. *Cozzens' Wine Press* 3 (20 January 1857): 57.

113. Guido Rossati, *Relazione di un viaggio d'istruzione negli Stati Uniti d'America* (Rome, 1900), pp. 117–18; Scharf, *History of St. Louis*, 2: 1329–30. Another Missouri enterprise was the St. Louis Vine and Fruit Growers Association, with vineyards of European grapes at Vinelands in 1861: after visiting the association's vineyards, a committee of inspection prophesied that the highlands south and west of St. Louis would "rival France and Germany" (unidentified clipping, 18 September 1861, Hayes Scrapbooks, Bancroft Library).

114. Walter B. Stevens, *St. Louis* (Chicago and St. Louis, 1909), 3: 916–18.

115. Alden Spooner, *The Cultivation of American Grape Vines and Making of Wine* (Brooklyn, 1846), p. 9; Bailey, *Evolution of Our Native Fruits*, p. 94.

116. This very un-Anglo-Saxon effusion sounds better in its native French: "Protège mes faibles écrites . . . protège ma vigne, fais qu'elle prospère et que je puisse bientôt faire des libations sur ta tombe en y pressant le doux Muscat et le suave Malvoisie."

117. *Farmer's Register* 2 (March 1835): 614.

118. Buchanan, *Culture of the Grape* (1852), p. 25.

119. Henry R. Stiles, *A History of the City of Brooklyn* (Albany, N.Y., 1869), 2: 135–36n.

120. Three generations of Princes figure in the *Dictionary of American Biography*.

121. The catalogue is printed as an appendix to William Robert Prince, *Treatise on the Vine* (New York, 1830).

122. Hedrick, *Grapes and Wines from Home Vineyards*, p. 148. Prince's book was written with the assistance of his father, William Prince, and drew largely upon the elder Prince's *Short Treatise on Horticulture* (New York, 1828), which devotes some thirty pages to a description of the Linnaean Garden's stock of vines, both native and foreign.

123. Prince, *Treatise on the Vine*, p. 353.

124. Ibid. Prince names seventy-four correspondents.

125. Ibid., p. vii.

126. The Isabella was widely grown in the Carolinas in the eighteenth century: see Hedrick, *Grapes of New York*, pp. 308–9.

127. Prince, *Treatise on the Vine*, p. 166. The Isabella was one of the varieties most favored in Europe during experimentation with American vines in the phylloxera years; it is now, according to Pierre Galet, the most widely planted grape in the world—from Canada to Africa, from Fiji to the Balkans (*American Wine Society Journal* 13 [Spring 1981]: 19).

128. Prince, *Treatise on the Vine*, p. 166.

129. Ibid., pp. 321–24. Prince had recommended sulfur and lime in an earlier article in the *American Farmer* 11 (10 July 1829): 132.

130. Stiles, *History of Brooklyn*, 2: 135.

131. *American Farmer* 11 (16 October 1829): 243; entry on Parmentier in the *Dictionary of American Biography*.

132. *American Farmer* 11 (26 February 1830): 396.

133. Hedrick, *Grapes of New York*, pp. 23–24.

134. Spooner, *Cultivation of American Grape Vines*, pp. 57–59; Hedrick, *Grapes of New York*, p. 24.

135. *The Cultivator*, 3d ser., 7 (March 1859): 99.

136. *American Agriculturist* 19 (February 1860): 61.

137. Leon Adams, *The Wines of America*, 3d ed. (New York, 1985), p. 149.

138. On Stephen Underhill's work, see Hedrick, *Grapes of New York*, p. 226n.

139. Alexander Jackson Downing in *The Horticulturist* 2 (1847–48): 122.

140. Conway Zirkle, "Beginnings of Plant Hybridization," *Agricultural History* 43 (1969): 33.

141. Adams, *Wines of America*, 3d ed., pp. 151–52. Hedrick, *Grapes of New York*, p. 55, says that Jaques's vineyard was planted in 1837; if so, this makes it unlikely that he could have been producing wine in 1839.

142. Philip Wagner, *American Wines and Wine-Making* (New York, 1956), p. 77.

143. See Hedrick, *Grapes of New York*, pp. 82–83.

144. Goldsmith Denniston, "Grape Culture in Steuben County," *Transactions of the New York State Agricultural Society, 1864* (Albany, N.Y., 1865). For a recent survey of early Finger Lakes wine history, see Dick Sherer, "Finger Lakes Grape Pioneers," *Vineyard View* (Hammondsport, N.Y.), Autumn 1983, p. 14.

145. W. W. Clayton, *History of Steuben County, N.Y.* (Philadelphia, 1879), p. 379.

146. Ibid., p. 380.

147. Ibid., p. 96.

148. Hedrick, *Grapes of New York*, p. 54.

149. Ibid., p. 83.

150. Denniston, "Grape Culture in Steuben County," pp. 133–34; Clayton, *History of Steuben County*, p. 97.

151. Denniston, "Grape Culture in Steuben County," p. 134.

152. *American Wine Press and Mineral Water Review* 1 (1 March 1897): 7; Hedrick, *Grapes and Wines from Home Vineyards*, p. 184.

153. Information from Mr. Charles D. Champlin, who also states that the Massons are not related to the Paul Masson of the California winery.

154. Denniston, "Grape Culture in Steuben County," p. 134.

155. Hedrick, *Grapes and Wines from Home Vineyards*, p. 184.

156. William McMurtrie, *Report upon the Statistics of Grape Culture and Wine Production in the United States for 1880*, U.S. Department of Agriculture Special Report no. 36 (Washington, D.C., 1881), p. 84.

157. George Howell Morris, "Rise of the Grape and Wine Industry in the Naples Valley during the Nineteenth Century" (M.A. thesis, Syracuse University, 1955), pp. 38, 45.

158. *The Cultivator* 6 (November 1858): 338; 7 (May 1859): 143.

159. Lewis Cass Aldrich, *History of Yates County, N.Y.* (Syracuse, N.Y., 1892), p. 241.

160. Raymond Chambers, "The Chautauqua Grape Industry," *New York History* 16 (July 1935): 249–50.

161. John Downs, ed., *History of Chautauqua County* (New York, 1921), 2: 28.

162. Ibid., 2: 28–29; Chambers, "Chautauqua Grape Industry," p. 254, puts this in 1854.

163. Chambers, "Chautauqua Grape Industry," p. 260; Downs, *History of Chautauqua County*, 1: 69; 2: 29; 3: 677–78.

8. Eastern Viticulture Comes of Age

1. An account of experiments with seedlings in the first half of the nineteenth century has been written by J. R. McGrew in "A History of American Grape Varieties before 1900," *American Wine Society Journal* 14 (Spring 1982): 3–5.

2. In 1828 the Bouschets in France developed hybrid grapes for the sake of producing varieties with greater color. But no one seems to have attempted a hybrid that would be a general advance over the varieties already available.

3. Since MacMahon was secretary to the Pennsylvania Vineyard Company founded by Legaux, his recognition that the Alexander is a native hybrid is especially interesting, for it contradicts Legaux's assertion that the Alexander was a vinifera, the "Cape" grape, as he called it. Was MacMahon condoning a fraud when he allowed Legaux to say so? Or did he not recognize the identity of his company's "Cape" with the Alexander?

4. Bernard MacMahon, *The American Gardener's Calendar* (Philadelphia, 1806), p. 235.

5. John James Dufour, *The American Vine-Dresser's Guide* (Cincinnati, 1826), pp. 39, 306.

6. William Robert Prince, *Treatise on the Vine* (New York, 1830), p. 224.

7. Ibid., pp. 252–53.

8. Ibid., p. 254.

9. U.S. Department of Agriculture, *Yearbook, 1899* (Washington, D.C., 1900), p. 475; U. P. Hedrick, *The Grapes of New York* (Albany, N.Y., 1908), p. 501.

10. Liberty Hyde Bailey, *Sketch of the Evolution of Our Native Fruits* (New York, 1898), p. 70.

11. Hedrick, *Grapes of New York*, p. 56.

12. Ibid., p. 166.

13. Ibid., p. 165.

14. The life of Rogers appears in the *Dictionary of American Biography*.

15. George W. Campbell, "The Grape and Its Improvement by Hybridizing, Cross-Breeding, and Seedlings," *Report of the Commissioner of Agriculture, 1862* (Washington, D.C.,'1863), p. 215.

16. Ibid., p. 216.

17. *Dictionary of American Biography*, s.v. "Rogers, Edward Staniford."

18. For Campbell, see the *Dictionary of National Biography;* for Ricketts, see Hedrick, *Grapes of New York*, pp. 318–19; and for Haskell, his autobiography, *A Narrative of the Life, Experience, and Work of an American Citizen* (Ipswich, Mass., 1896).

19. Hedrick, *Grapes of New York*, p. 251; Kansas State Horticultural Society, *Transactions, 1871* (Topeka, 1872), pp. 72–75; id., *Transactions, 1872* (Topeka, 1873), pp. 54–59.

20. Hedrick, *Grapes of New York*, p. 192.

21. Mark Miller, *Wine—A Gentleman's Game* (New York, 1984), pp. 23–24.

22. Hedrick, *Grapes of New York*, p. 231.

23. Ibid., pp. 232–33. One pleasingly romantic notion was that the Delaware was a seedling of the Traminer vines that Joseph Bonaparte had tried to grow in his exile at Bordentown, New Jer-

sey (Friedrich Muench, in George Husmann, *American Grape Growing and Wine Making* [New York, 1880], p. 180).

24. Bailey, *Evolution of Our Native Fruits,* pp. 71-72.

25. For Grant, see Hedrick, *Grapes of New York,* p. 304.

26. *Gardener's Monthly* 7 (1865): 52.

27. Hedrick, *Grapes of New York,* p. 58.

28. *American Agriculturist* 25 (September 1866): 338.

29. See Henry Christman, "Iona Island and the Fruit Growers' Convention of 1864," *New York History* 48 (1967): 332-51.

30. Hedrick, *Grapes of New York,* p. 305.

31. Philip Wagner, *A Wine-Grower's Guide* (New York, 1955), p. 210.

32. U. P. Hedrick, *Grapes and Wines from Home Vineyards* (New York, 1945), p. 167.

33. Ibid., p. 149.

34. For Bull, see the *Dictionary of American Biography* and the series of articles by W. J. Burtscher, "Ephraim Bull and the Concord Grape," *American Fruit Grower* 65 (1945): 12, 24, 26, 28-29, 35.

35. *Fifth Annual Report of the Secretary, Massachusetts Board of Agriculture* (Boston, 1858), p. 197.

36. *American Agriculturist* 12 (1854): 37.

37. Bailey, *Evolution of Our Native Fruits,* p. 72.

38. The dominance of the Concord has also created a confusion in this country about Kosher wines, which are popularly held to be sweet, "grapey" wines. The idea grew up from the accidental circumstance that Kosher winemakers in the East, where the earliest large Jewish communities were located, found that Concord grapes were what they mainly had to work with. Naturally, they, too, had to sugar their Concord wines in order to make them palatable. But any wine—dry, sweet, red, white—may be Kosher. Had the Jewish communities in this country been in California rather than in New York, American Kosher wine would have been a very different thing—as it still may be.

39. *American Agriculturist* 23 (November 1864): 310; 24 (February 1865): 59; 25 (October 1866): 439; Hedrick, *Grapes of New York,* p. 220.

40. This is one of the details that remain obscure: were there three generations, or only two, required to produce the Concord?

41. Wagner, *American Wines and Wine-Making,* p. 35.

42. So Bull stated in an address in 1866, adding: "I will not denounce those as intemperate, who use pure wine without being intoxicated by its use" (quoted in F. Clark, *Regulation versus Prohibition* [Lowell, Mass., 1866], p. 20).

43. William Chazanof, *Welch's Grape Juice* (Syracuse, N.Y., 1977), p. 40.

44. Bailey, *Evolution of Our Native Fruits,* p. 1.

45. Hedrick, *History of Horticulture,* p. 507.

46. J. N. Primm, *Economic Policy in the Development of a Western State: Missouri, 1820-1860* (Cambridge, Mass., 1954), p. 115.

47. *Western Horticultural Review* 1 (1850-51): 293.

48. See *Report of the Commissioner of Agriculture, 1867* (Washington, D.C., 1868), pp. 388, 392; *Southern Cultivator* 16 (1858): 312; Johann Becker, *Der Weinbau* (Evansville, Ind., 1860), Nachtrage; *American Agriculturist* 25 (November 1866); U.S. Department of Agriculture, *List of Agricultural Societies* (Washington, D.C., 1876) (for Nauvoo); *American Agriculturist* 27 (April 1868): 130; *Grape Culturist* 1 (1869): 28.

49. The appeal of Peter Chazotte, in 1822, for example, for a subsidy to undertake the "culture of vines, olives, capers, almonds, etc." in the southern United States (he had Florida in mind) met with no success (*American State Papers, Public Lands* [Washington, D.C. 1834], 3: 460ff). Yet two years later the Marquis de Lafayette was granted lands in Florida for the cultivation of the vine and olive (*Florida Historical Society Quarterly* 1 [July 1908]: 10-11).

50. Henry Leavitt Ellsworth, when commissioner of patents, took a great interest in promoting agriculture, and persuaded Congress in 1839 to give $1,000 towards the cost of distributing seeds, carrying out agricultural experiments, and gathering statistics. This was the beginning of government aid to agriculture in the United States: see the caption to frontispiece, U.S. Department of Agriculture, *Yearbook 1902* (Washington, D.C., 1903).

51. *Report of the Commissioner of Patents, 1859, Part II* (Washington, D.C., 1860), p. 39.

52. Ibid., p. 70.

53. Ibid., p. 17; *Report of the Commissioner of Agriculture, 1863* (Washington, D.C., 1863), pp. 548–49; 1864, p. 10; 1865, pp. 13–16; 1866, pp. 18–19, 97–114.

54. Especially the system devised by William Kniffen: see U. P. Hedrick, *Manual of American Grape-Growing* (New York, 1924), pp. 132–36.

55. U. P. Hedrick, *History of Horticulture in America to 1860* (New York, 1950), p. 286.

56. C. O. Cathey, "Sidney Weller," *North Carolina Historical Review* 31: 1–17.

57. *Cultivator* 8 (September 1841): 151.

58. *American Agriculturist* 7 (1848): 58–60.

59. *Report of the Commissioner of Patents, 1853, Part II* (Washington, D.C., 1854), pp. 306–9.

60. *Cozzens' Wine Press* 4 (20 April 1858): 186.

61. See p. 415 below.

62. According to the sixth U.S. census.

63. *Report of the Commissioner of Patents, 1849, Part II* (Washington, D.C., 1850), pp. 283–86.

64. See Clarence Gohdes, *Scuppernong: North Carolina's Grape and Its Wines* (Durham, N.C., 1982), pp. 19–22.

65. Joseph Togno, *Southern Cultivator* 11 (1853): 298.

66. *Western Horticultural Review* 3 (1852–53): 479.

67. Thomas Ruffin, *Papers of Thomas Ruffin*, ed. J. G. deR. Hamilton (Raleigh, N.C., 1918–20), 3: 98.

68. *Report of the Commissioner of Patents, 1859, Part II*, p. 540.

69. J. C. W. McDonnald's interest went back to 1825, when he had petitioned the state legislature to support a scheme to import Italian vineyard workers: see p. 153 above. He had 110 acres of vines in 1860 (*Southern Cultivator* 18 [1860]: 381).

70. *Horticultural Review* 4 (1854): 59–60.

71. See *The Private Journal of Henry William Ravenel, 1859–1887*, ed. Arney Robinson Childs (Columbia, S.C., 1947), pp. 19, 25, 31, 86, 87.

72. *DeBow's Review*, n.s., 2 (1866): 269.

73. Achille de Caradeuc, *Grape Culture and Winemaking in the South* (Augusta, Ga., 1858), p. 6.

74. *South Carolina Historical Magazine* 49 (1949): 95.

75. For the details of this paragraph and the next, see James C. Bonner, "The Georgia Wine Industry on the Eve of the Civil War," *Georgia Historical Quarterly* 41 (1957): 19–30.

76. *Report of the Commissioner of Patents, 1858, Part II* (Washington, D.C., 1859), p. 372.

77. *American Agriculturist* 19 (June 1860): 186.

78. Ibid., p. 186.

79. *Southern Planter* 20 (June 1860): 383.

80. The names of European wine types were also freely used; no one, however, seems to have thought that they should be permanently used.

81. *Southern Planter* 20: 383.

82. *Proceedings of the Southern Vine Growers' Convention, Aiken, South Carolina, 1860* (Augusta, Ga., 1860), p. 11.

83. Bureau of the Census, *Agriculture of the United States in 1860* (Washington, D.C., 1864), p. 28; *Compendium of the Ninth Census (June 1, 1870)* (Washington, D.C., 1872), p. 704.

84. Bonner, "The Georgia Wine Industry on the Eve of the Civil War," p. 28n.

85. Ben H. McClary and LeRoy P. Graf, "'Vineland' in Tennessee, 1852: The Journal of Rosine Parmentier," *East Tennessee Historical Society Publications*, no. 31 (1959), pp. 95–111. For a contemporary reference, see *American Farmer*, n.s., 14 (November 1858): 152–54.

86. *Horticultural Review* 4 (1854): 311–12. A far earlier pioneer had been Dr. Felix Robertson, who planted ten acres of native vines in Tennessee in 1810 but gave up around 1820 (*Southern Cultivator* 15 [1857]: 96–97).

87. *Cozzens' Wine Press* 3 (20 January 1857): 60.

88. *The Autobiography of Mark Twain*, ed. Charles Neider (New York, 1959), pp. 18, 218.

89. United Kingdom, *Parliamentary Papers* 30 (1859): 203.

90. Ibid., p. 206.

91. The great seal of the state of Connecticut exhibits fruit-laden grapevines under the motto

of "Sustinet Qui Transtulit"—roughly, "Who transplants, sustains." The viticulture in question is wholly symbolic, though real vineyards are now being planted in the state.

9. The Southwest and California

1. E. R. Forrest, *Missions and Pueblos of the Old Southwest* (Cleveland, 1929), p. 159.

2. Maynard Amerine and Brian St. Pierre, "Grapes and Wine in the United States, 1600–1979," in Edward L. and Frederick H. Schapsmeier, eds., *Agriculture in the West* (Manhattan, Kans., 1980), pp. 108–13; A. J. Winkler et al., *General Viticulture* (Berkeley, 1974), pp. 3–4.

3. Josiah Gregg, *The Commerce of the Prairies*, ed. Milo Quaife (Chicago, 1926), pp. 150–51.

4. W. W. H. Davis, *El Gringo, or New Mexico and Her People* (Santa Fe, 1938), p. 193.

5. C. W. Hackett, ed., *Historical Documents Relating to New Mexico, Nueva Vizcaya, and Approaches Thereto, to 1773* (Washington, D.C., 1923–37), 3: 406.

6. Don Pedro Bautista Pino, *Exposición*, in *Three New Mexico Chronicles*, ed. H. B. Carroll and J. V. Haggard (Albuquerque, 1942), pp. 35, 97.

7. John T. Hughes, *Doniphan's Expedition*, reprinted in W. E. Connelly, *Doniphan's Expedition and the Conquest of New Mexico and California* (Topeka, 1907), p. 393.

8. Ibid., p. 393.

9. *Report of the Commissioner of Patents, 1859, Part II* (Washington, D.C., 1860), pp. 38–39.

10. *Cozzens' Wine Press* 5 (20 May 1859): 90.

11. *Report of the Commissioner of Patents, 1859, Part II*, p. 39.

12. William H. Emory, *Report on the United States and Mexican Boundary Survey* (Washington, D.C., 1857), 1: 49.

13. Irving McKee, "The Beginnings of California Winegrowing," *Historical Society of Southern California Quarterly* 29 (1947): 59–60.

14. See, e.g., Junípero Serra, *Writings*, ed. Antonine Tibeser, O.F.M. (Washington, D.C., 1955–66), 1: 263, 281.

15. Ibid., 5: 195.

16. Father Mugartegui to Serra, 15 March 1779, in Edith Buckland Webb, *Indian Life at the Old Missions* (Los Angeles, 1952), p. 95.

17. "Alta California's First Vintage," in Doris Muscatine et al., eds., *The University of California / Sotheby Book of California Wine* (Berkeley and London, 1984), p. 15. This essay derives from Brady's earlier article, "The Swallow That Came from Capistrano," *New West*, 24 September 1979, pp. 55–59.

18. William Heath Davis, *Seventy-Five Years in California*, ed. Harold A. Small (San Francisco, 1967), p. 5.

19. Hugo Reid, *The Indians of Los Angeles County*, ed. R. F. Heizer (Los Angeles, 1968), p. 79; Webb, *Indian Life at the Old Missions*, pp. 96–97.

20. Eugène Duflot de Mofras, *Travels on the Pacific Coast* (Santa Ana, Calif., 1937), 1: 182; Hubert H. Bancroft, *History of California* (San Francisco, 1884–90), 5: 621–22n.; Maynard Geiger, *Franciscan Missionaries in Hispanic California, 1769–1848* (San Marino, Calif., 1969), pp. 266–69.

21. Alfred Robinson, *Life in California* (Santa Barbara, 1970), p. 23.

22. Webb, *Indian Life at the Old Missions*, p. 96.

23. Zephyrin Engelhardt, *Missions and Missionaries of California* (San Francisco, 1908–15), 3: 571–72.

24. Agoston Haraszthy, "Report on Grapes and Wines of California," in *Transactions of the California State Agricultural Society, 1858* (Sacramento, 1859), p. 312.

25. "Duhaut-Cilly's Account of California in the Years 1827–8," *California Historical Society Quarterly* 8 (1929): 228.

26. In 1834 San Luis Obispo, with forty-four acres of vineyard, was second to San Gabriel (Webb, *Indian Life at the Old Missions*, p. 97). The fullest study of the mission statistics bearing on vineyards is by Jacob Bowman, "The Vineyards in Provincial California," *Wine Review* 11 (April–June 1943).

27. Engelhardt, *Missions and Missionaries of California*, 3: 571–72.

28. H. H. Bancroft, *California Pastoral, 1769–1848* (San Francisco, 1888), pp. 371–72; Haraszthy, "Report on Grapes and Wine of California," p. 312.

29. Webb, *Indian Life at the Old Missions,* pp. 98-99.

30. Robert Archibald, *The Economic Aspects of the California Missions* (Washington, D.C., 1978), does not treat wine as a part of the general commerce of the missions.

31. Harrison Clifford Dale, ed., *The Ashley-Smith Explorations,* rev. ed. (Glendale, Calif., 1941), p. 195.

32. Bancroft, *History of California,* 2: 476n.

33. A survey in 1845 showed substantial vineyards at San Fernando, Ventura, Santa Barbara, and San Juan Bautista (Bowman, "Vineyards of Provincial California," *Wine Review* 11 [May 1943]: 24).

34. Geiger, *Franciscan Missionaries in Hispanic California,* p. 80.

35. Ibid.

36. Duflot de Mofras, *Travels on the Pacific Coast,* 1: 172.

37. Antoine Deutschbein, "Warsaw Wine," in Claude Morny, ed., *A Wine and Food Bedside Book* (London, 1972), pp. 68-69.

38. Georg Langsdorff, *Narrative of the Rezanov Voyage to Nueva California in 1806,* trans. Thomas C. Russell (San Francisco, 1927), p. 101.

39. The evidence consists of frequent assertions by Los Angeles winemakers at midcentury that they had vines fifty, sixty, and seventy years old or older in their vineyards. See, e.g., Matthew Keller in *Report of the Commissioner of Patents, 1858, Part II* (Washington, D.C., 1859), p. 345; Ludwig Louis Salvator, *Los Angeles in the Sunny Seventies* (Los Angeles, 1929), p. 139; Ben C. Truman, *Semi-Tropical California* (San Francisco, 1874), p. 59. Admittedly this is likely to be highly inaccurate evidence, but such statements could not be maintained without at least some plausible appearance of truth.

40. Bancroft, *History of California,* 1: 647-48, 659, 665-66, 674, 677, 692-93, 715-16.

41. Herbert Eugene Bolton, *Fray Juan Crespi* (Berkeley, 1927), p. 148. The native grape of southern California, *Vitis girdiana,* is wholly unfit for winemaking.

42. Robert Glass Cleland, *The Cattle on a Thousand Hills* (San Marino, Calif., 1941), p. 19.

43. Ruth Teiser and Catherine Harroun, *Winemaking in California* (New York, 1983), p. 16.

44. Herbert E. Leggett, *Early History of Wine Production in California* (San Francisco, 1941), pp. 37-38.

45. Paul T. Scott, "Why Joseph Chapman Adopted California and Why California Adopted Him," *Historical Society of Southern California Quarterly* 38 (1956): 239-46.

46. J. Gregg Layne, "Annals of Los Angeles," *California Historical Society Quarterly* 13 (1934): 206.

47. In nineteenth-century statistics, the size of vineyards was more often than not reported in number of vines rather than in acres. It is an exasperating practice, since there is no rule as to the spacing of vines, and there is evidence to show that planting densities varied greatly: at one extreme there might be 3,000 vines to an acre; at the other, only 700-800. A rule of thumb in southern California was 1,000 vines to the acre; in northern California it was usually fewer, say 650.

48. Ernest P. Peninou and Sidney S. Greenleaf, *A Directory of California Wine Growers and Wine Makers in 1860* (Berkeley, 1967), p. 15.

49. J. Albert Wilson, *History of Los Angeles County* (Oakland, 1880), p. 33; Bancroft, *History of California,* 2: 526; 4: 717; J. J. Warner, "Reminiscences of Early California—1831 to 1846," *Annual Publications, Historical Society of California* 7 (1908): 190.

50. For Domingo, see Warner, "Reminiscences," pp. 192-93.

51. Inventory dated 4 April 1852 (MS, Huntington Library).

52. Fernand Loyer and Charles Beaudreau, *Le Guide français de Los Angeles et du sud de la Californie* (Los Angeles, 1932), p. 20.

53. Peninou and Greenleaf, *Directory of California Wine Growers and Wine Makers,* pp. 23, 40; Harris Newmark, *Sixty Years in Southern California, 1853-1913,* 4th ed. (Los Angeles, 1970), p. 200; Davis, *Seventy-Five Years in California,* p. 222.

54. Wilson, *History of Los Angeles County,* p. 64.

55. *California Historical Society Quarterly* 8 (1929): 246.

56. Daniel Lévy, *Les Français en Californie* (San Francisco, 1884), p. 64. For the life of Vignes, see especially Léonce Jore, "John Louis Vignes of Bordeaux, Pioneer of California Viticulture," *Southern California Historical Society Quarterly* 45 (1963): 289-303.

57. Idwal Jones says that Vignes made his stake by coopering, but there is no evidence for the

assertion (Jones, *Vines in the Sun* [New York, 1949], p. 212). Vignes did, however, have casks and barrels of his own coopering (Pierre Sainsevain to Arpad Haraszthy, 22 June 1886 [Bancroft Library]).

58. Davis, *Seventy-Five Years in California*, p. 91.

59. Irving McKee, "Jean Paul [*sic*] Vignes, California's First Professional Winegrower," *Agricultural History* 22 (July 1948): 178.

60. Davis, *Seventy-Five Years in California*, p. 91.

61. Ibid.

62. Ibid., p. 92.

63. Duflot de Mofras, *Travels*, 1: 184-85.

64. McKee, "Vignes," p. 179.

65. Davis, *Seventy-Five Years in California*, p. 93.

66. For Wolfskill, see Iris Wilson, *William Wolfskill, 1798-1866: Frontier Trapper to California Ranchero* (Glendale, Calif., 1965).

67. Wilson, *William Wolfskill*, pp. 59, 72, 77, 82-86, 87, 99.

68. Ibid., pp. 157, 174, 176.

69. Edwin Bryant, *What I Saw in California* (1849; reprint, Palo Alto, Calif., 1967), p. 412.

70. Wilson, *William Wolfskill*, p. 158. The Sainsevain brothers anticipated Wolfskill's gift to Buchanan. A letter from the president to the Sainsevains of 14 January 1857 thanks them for their gift of wine and predicts the coming greatness of California as a winegrowing state (Ruth Teiser and Catherine Harroun, *Winemaking in California*, p. 21).

71. W. H. Emory, *Notes of a Military Reconnoissance from Fort Leavenworth, in Missouri, to San Diego, in California*, Senate Executive Documents, no. 7, 30th Cong., 1st sess. (Washington, D.C., 1848), p. 122.

72. "A Doctor Comes to California," *California Historical Society Quarterly* 21 (December 1942): 353.

73. Newmark, *Sixty Years in Southern California*, 4th ed., p. 200.

74. Peninou and Greenleaf, *Directory of California Wine Growers and Wine Makers*, pp. 24, 29.

75. Susanna Bryant Dakin, *A Scotch Paisano in Old Los Angeles: Hugo Reid's Life in California, 1832-1852, Derived from His Correspondence* (Berkeley, 1939), pp. 67, 69-70, 108, 113.

76. For Keller, see J. Gregg Layne, "Annals of Los Angeles," *California Historical Society Quarterly* 13: 315; *Illustrated History of Los Angeles* (Chicago, 1889), pp. 130-31; Peninou and Greenleaf, *Directory of California Wine Growers and Wine Makers*, p. 19. Keller's article is "The Grapes and Wine of Los Angeles," in *Report of the Commissioner of Patents, 1858, Part II*, pp. 344-48.

77. Bill of fare in Keller Papers, Huntington Library.

78. Keller to unidentified recipient, 13 April 1877 (Keller Papers).

79. 13 May 1878 (Keller Papers). Keller's doubtful standards of winemaking are also suggested by a remark in his obituary, that "he often said that there was no better than the ordinary Mission for all the purposes of a vigneron" (copy of unidentified newspaper obituary, 12 April 1881, Keller Papers).

80. J. De Barth Shorb to Mr. Leoser, 21 June 1877 (Shorb Papers, Huntington Library).

81. Walter Lindley and J. P. Widney, *California of the South* (New York, 1888), pp. 115-16.

82. Newmark, *Sixty Years in Southern California*, 4th ed., p. 134.

83. *Transactions of the California State Agricultural Society, 1858* (Sacramento, 1859), p. 285.

84. Peninou and Greenleaf, *Directory of California Wine Growers and Wine Makers*, p. 40.

85. Paul W. Gates, *California Ranchos and Farms, 1846-1862* (Madison, Wis., 1967), pp. 116-17.

86. Peninou and Greenleaf, *Directory of California Wine Growers and Wine Makers*, p. 43.

87. *Report of the Commissioner of Patents, 1858, Part II*, p. 347.

88. Newmark, *Sixty Years in Southern California*, 4th ed., pp. 202-3. The method of crushing by bare-footed Indians was still being used at the Pelanconi Winery in Los Angeles as late as 1876, but the practice was noted by that time as a curiosity (unidentified newspaper clipping [c. September 1876?], Huntington Scrap Books, vol. 1).

89. Newmark, *Sixty Years in Southern California*, 4th ed., p. 25.

90. McKee, "Vignes," p. 179.

91. Ibid. It does not seem to have been the first in California. A letter from the Los Angeles winegrower T. J. White, dated 22 September 1855, states that White had sampled sparkling wine

made by Benjamin D. Wilson (*California Farmer,* 5 October 1855, p. 107). For Wilson and his Lake Vineyard, see p. 294.

92. McKee, "Vignes," p. 179.

93. Charles Kohler, Bancroft dictation, n.d. (MS, Bancroft Library, University of California).

94. Ibid. In 1855 the name was Kohler, Frohling & Scholler, Scholler presumably having furnished the money for the purchase of the Los Angeles vineyard. That partnership was dissolved in 1856. It was next called Kohler, Frohling & Bauck upon the entry of John Henry Bauck, who withdrew in 1860. Frohling died in 1862, but Kohler preserved the title of Kohler & Frohling thereafter (Leo J. Friis, *John Frohling: Vintner and City Founder* [Anaheim, Calif., 1976], pp. 10, 14, 23).

95. Leggett, *Early History of Wine Production,* pp. 47–48.

96. Kohler, Bancroft dictation.

97. *Los Angeles Star,* 24 October 1859, quoted in Wilson, *William Wolfskill,* pp. 173–74.

98. Newmark, *Sixty Years in Southern California,* 4th ed., p. 294; Friis, *John Frohling,* pp. 31–32.

99. Vincent P. Carosso, *The California Wine Industry, 1830–1895* (Berkeley, 1951), p. 33.

100. Ibid., p. 32.

101. Ibid.

102. Leggett, *Early History of Wine Production,* p. 99.

103. *Annual Report of the American Institute, 1862–1863* (Albany, N.Y., 1863), pp. 85–88.

104. To B. D. Wilson, 17 September 1858 (Wilson Papers, Huntington Library).

105. Justin Kaplan, *Mr. Clemens and Mark Twain* (New York, 1966), p. 14.

106. Titus Fey Cronise, *The Natural Wealth of California* (San Francisco, 1868), p. 391.

107. Mechanics' Institute, *Report of the 11th Industrial Exhibition* (San Francisco, 1876), pp. 210–11.

108. Charles Kohler, "Wine Production in California," p. 7 (MS, Bancroft Library).

109. Carosso, *California Wine Industry,* pp. 35–36.

110. Ibid., p. 37.

111. Leggett, *Early History of Wine Production,* p. 85.

112. Irving McKee, "Early California Wine Growers," *California* 37 (September 1947): 16.

113. Otto von Kotzebue, *A New Voyage round the World in the Years 1823, 24, 25, and 26* (London, 1830), 2: 100.

114. Sir George Simpson, *An Overland Voyage round the World* (Philadelphia, 1847), 1: 179–80.

115. Peninou and Greenleaf, *Directory of California Wine Growers and Wine Makers,* p. 37.

116. Ibid., pp. 32, 34, 72–73.

117. Wilson, *William Wolfskill,* p. 129.

118. Marsh is in the *Dictionary of American Biography;* see also Bryant, *What I Saw in California,* pp. 303–4; and George D. Lyman, *John Marsh, Pioneer* (New York, 1930), p. 220.

119. McKee, "Early California Wine Growers," pp. 35–36; id., "Historic Wine Growers of Santa Clara County," *California* 40 (September 1950): 14; Peninou and Greenleaf, *Directory of California Wine Growers and Wine Makers,* pp. 67–68; Teiser and Harroun, *Winemaking in California,* p. 29.

120. Davis, *Seventy-Five Years in California,* p. 54.

121. Bancroft, *History of California,* 5: 643; John Walton Caughey, *California* (New York, 1940), p. 305.

122. Peninou and Greenleaf, *Directory of California Wine Growers and Wine Makers,* pp. 11, 71.

123. *Report of California State Board of Agriculture, 1911* (Sacramento, 1912), p. 184.

124. Bancroft, *History of California,* 7: 47; Peninou and Greenleaf, *Directory of California Wine Growers and Wine Makers,* p. 70.

125. Leggett, *Early History of Wine Production,* p. 86.

126. *Transactions of the California State Agricultural Society, 1860* (Sacramento, 1861), p. 242.

127. Carosso, *California Wine Industry,* pp. 23–24.

128. Leggett, *Early History of Wine Production,* p. 68.

129. *Report of California State Board of Agriculture, 1911,* p. 184.

130. C. A. Menefee, *Historical and Descriptive Sketch Book of Napa, Sonoma, Lake and Mendocino* (Napa, Calif., 1873), p. 203.

131. *Report of California State Board of Agriculture, 1911,* p. 184.

132. Leggett, *Early History of Wine Production,* p. 83.

133. California Horticultural Society, *Report of the First Annual Exhibition* (1857), in San Francisco Mechanics' Institute, *Report of the First Industrial Exhibition* (San Francisco, 1858), p. 148.

134. E.g., *California Farmer*, 7 December 1855, p. 179.

135. "An Act to provide for the better encouragement of the culture of the Vine and the Olive," *Statutes of California*, 10th sess. (Sacramento, 1859), p. 210.

136. Carosso, *California Wine Industry*, p. 50.

137. Julius Jacobs, "California's Pioneer Wine Families," *California Historical Quarterly* 54 (Summer 1975): 151.

138. *Transactions of the California State Agricultural Society, 1858* (Sacramento, 1859), p. 257.

139. Charles L. Sullivan, *Like Modern Edens: Winegrowing in Santa Clara Valley and Santa Cruz Mountains, 1798–1981* (Cupertino, Calif., 1982), pp. 17, 20.

140. *California Farmer*, 19 October 1855, p. 125.

141. *Transactions of the California State Agricultural Society, 1858*, p. 257.

142. Peninou and Greenleaf, *Directory of California Wine Growers and Wine Makers*, p. 50.

143. Ernest P. Peninou, *A History of the Orleans Hill Vineyard and Winery* (Winters, Calif., 1983), pp. 6–7.

144. Peninou and Greenleaf, *Directory of California Wine Growers and Wine Makers*, pp. 55–56. But according to an item in the *California Farmer*, 17 June 1859, Stock imported his vines in 1855: they came from his father's estate near Bingen, on the Rhine.

145. *Transactions of the California State Agricultural Society, 1858*, p. 260; Leggett, *Early History of Wine Production*, p. 64.

146. *Transactions of the California State Agricultural Society, 1858*, pp. 252–53, 256.

147. Irving McKee, "George West: Pioneer Wine Grower of San Joaquin County," *California* 44 (September 1954): 17–18.

148. *Transactions of the California State Agricultural Society, 1858*, p. 241.

149. Louis J. Stellman, *Sam Brannan, Builder of San Francisco* (New York, 1953), pp. 154, 169, 174.

150. Peninou and Greenleaf, *Directory of California Wine Growers and Wine Makers*, p. 68.

151. *California Farmer*, 2 December 1859, p. 133. On the Black St. Peters, see Charles L. Sullivan, "A Viticultural Mystery Solved," *California History* 57 (Summer 1978): 123.

152. MS, 19 November 1886 (Shorb Papers, Huntington Library).

153. Leon Adams, "Historical Note," in *Grapes and Grape Vines of California* (New York, 1981), no pagination.

154. *Report of California State Board of Agriculture, 1911*, p. 197.

155. *Transactions of the California State Agricultural Society, 1860*, p. 244.

156. *Transactions of the California State Agricultural Society, 1859* (Sacramento, 1860), p. 301.

157. Charles Loring Brace, *The New West: or, California in 1867–1868* (New York, 1869), pp. 253–54.

158. John S. Hittell, *The Resources of California* (San Francisco, 1863), p. 207.

10. The Haraszthy Legend

1. The name is pronounced in Hungary as *Hair' as tee*, Hungarian being a language in which the stress uniformly falls on the first syllable; in America the usual pronunciation seems to be *Hair ahz' thee*.

2. What is currently known about Haraszthy is summarized in Theodore Schoenman, *Father of California Wine: Agoston Haraszthy* (Santa Barbara, 1979).

3. Ibid., p. 15.

4. V. S. Pease, "Agoston Haraszthy," in *Proceedings of the State Historical Society of Wisconsin, 1906* (Madison, 1907), p. 227.

5. Schoenman, *Father of California Wine*, p. 17. A very circumstantial account of Haraszthy's political activity and the reasons for his "flight" from Hungary are given in a manuscript entitled "The Haraszthy Family" by Arpad Haraszthy, the colonel's son, now in the Bancroft Library. This document is the basis of many details in the received account of Haraszthy's life and work, but its demonstrable errors make it unreliable in general.

6. Oswald Ragatz, "Memoirs of a Sauk Swiss," *Wisconsin Magazine of History* 19 (December 1935): 204n.

7. Paul Fredericksen, "The Authentic Haraszthy Story" (reprinted from *Wines and Vines* [San

Francisco, 1947?], p. 2. Some notes accompanying Arpad Haraszthy's "The Haraszthy Family" (see n. 5 above), evidently drawn from Agoston Haraszthy's account books, state that Haraszthy did not plant vines in Wisconsin until May 1848, only a few months before he left the state. After Haraszthy's departure the vineyard property was taken over by a German named Peter Kehl, who built a winery in 1867 that operated until 1899; it lay dormant thereafter until 1973, when its present owner bought it and restored it to wine production. What sorts of grapes Haraszthy may have planted is not known; Peter Kehl grew native varieties.

8. It is "The Haraszthy Family" manuscript.

9. Fredericksen, "The Authentic Haraszthy Story," pp. 3–4.

10. See Brian McGinty, *Haraszthy at the Mint,* Famous California Trials, no. 10 (Los Angeles, 1975).

11. Agoston Haraszthy, "Wine-Making in California," *Harper's* 29 (June 1864): 23.

12. *Transactions of the California State Agricultural Society, 1858* (Sacramento, 1859), p. 243; but the figures given for Haraszthy's operations typically show much variation: *The Alta California,* 21 September 1863, reports that there were 34,000 vines at Buena Vista in 1858; in the *First Annual Report* of the Board of State Viticultural Commissioners (San Francisco, 1881), it is stated on the authority of Arpad Haraszthy that 200,000 vines had been put in at Buena Vista in 1857, and another 68,000 in 1858 (2d ed., p. 110).

13. Or so Arpad Haraszthy affirmed in "Early Viticulture in Sonoma," in *Sonoma County and Russian River Valley Illustrated* (San Francisco, 1888), p. 78. The figures in the *State Register* show 170,000 vines for Sonoma and Mendocino Counties in 1857, but only 87,621 in 1858; evidently a mistake has been made. The U.S. Census of 1860 reports only 1,190 gallons of wine from Sonoma County, an impossibly low figure.

14. *Transactions of the California State Agricultural Society, 1858,* p. 242.

15. Agoston Haraszthy, *Grape Culture, Wines, and Wine-Making* (New York, 1862), p. 70.

16. *Transactions of the California State Agricultural Society, 1859* (Sacramento, 1860), pp. 269–70.

17. *Alta California,* 21 September 1863.

18. So Haraszthy himself says: "Thousands were printed by the Legislature and distributed among the people" ("Wine-Making in California," p. 24). I have not succeeded in finding a copy of the essay as a separate pamphlet.

19. *Transactions of the California State Agricultural Society, 1858,* p. 323.

20. Ibid., p. 326.

21. Fredericksen, "The Authentic Haraszthy Story," p. 7.

22. Ibid., p. 5.

23. The other two commissioners were Colonel J. J. Warner of San Diego and Abraham Schell of Knight's Ferry, Stanislaus County. Haraszthy's and Warner's reports are in "Report of Commissioners on the Culture of the Grape-Vine in California," Appendix to Journals of Senate and Assembly, 13th sess., no. 12 (Sacramento, 1862). Abraham Schell was replaced by a Mr. Ramirez of Marysville, who does not seem to have reported.

24. Haraszthy, *Grape Culture, Wines, and Wine-Making,* p. 140.

25. "Report of Commissioners on the Culture of the Grape-Vine in California," pp. 7–10.

26. Haraszthy, *Grape Culture, Wines, and Wine-Making,* p. 142.

27. "Report of Commissioners on the Culture of the Grape-Vine in California," p. 9.

28. Fredericksen, "The Authentic Haraszthy Story," p. 9.

29. A special committee of the state senate visited Haraszthy's Buena Vista property to inspect his imported vines and recommended to the Committee on Agriculture against purchasing them. The Committee on Agriculture recommended that no action be taken (*Journal of the Senate,* 13th sess., 1862 [Sacramento, 1862], pp. 502–3: 7 April 1862). The vote on the recommendation was evenly split. On 15 April a special order was made for Act No. 433, "to purchase certain vines, and provide for the distribution of the same" (ibid., p. 558). On 16 April it was moved and voted by 20 to 9 to "indefinitely postpone" the bill (ibid., p. 570).

30. Advertisement in *California Farmer,* 24 May 1861 and after.

31. *Los Angeles Star,* 22 February 1862.

32. The list of Haraszthy's importations appears in the *First Annual Report* of the Board of State Viticultural Commissioners, 2d ed. (Sacramento, 1881), pp. 184–88.

33. This is substantially the account given by Arpad Haraszthy in "The Haraszthy Family" and

"Early Viticulture in Sonoma" (see nn. 5 and 13 above); his is the basis of most subsequent accounts and may be called the Arpad Haraszthy version of the Haraszthy story. Frona Eunice Wait depended on Arpad's version for the account of Haraszthy in her influential *Wines and Vines of California* (San Francisco, 1889), pp. 91–94. In this she sometimes took over verbatim parts of Arpad's "Early Viticulture in Sonoma."

34. Haraszthy, "Wine-Making in California."

35. For a summary of the evidence for Zinfandel's earlier history in the United States, see Charles L. Sullivan, "A Viticultural Mystery Solved," *California History* 57 (Summer 1978): 115–29; and the same author's "An Historian's Account of Zinfandel in California," *Wines and Vines* 58 (February 1977): 18–20.

36. *Transactions of the California State Agricultural Society, 1858,* p. 98.

37. Sullivan, "Viticultural Mystery Solved," pp. 117–18.

38. Leon Adams, *The Wines of America,* 3d ed. (New York, 1985), p. 548.

39. *Transactions of the California State Agricultural Society, 1879* (Sacramento, 1880), p. 146.

40. California Board of State Viticultural Commissioners, *First Annual Report,* p. 26.

41. Charles Wetmore, *Ampelography of California* (n.d., n.p.; "Reproduced and revised from *San Francisco Merchant* of January 4th and 11th, 1884"), p. 10.

42. Fredericksen, "The Authentic Haraszthy Story," p. 9.

43. Carosso, *California Wine Industry,* p. 68.

44. Ibid. Since the law then forbade a corporation to hold more than 1,440 acres, the California legislature obligingly passed a special exemption for the Buena Vista Vinicultural Society (*Journal of the Senate,* 14th sess., 1863 [Sacramento, 1863], p. 467: 17 April 1863).

45. Of the society's 400 acres of vineyard, 260 were in Mission grapes (*Alta California,* 21 September 1863).

46. Ibid.

47. Carosso, *California Wine Industry,* pp. 70–71. Arpad left the Buena Vista Vinicultural Society in 1864; three years later Buena Vista "Sparkling Sonoma Wine" took a diploma of honorable mention at the Paris Universal Exposition.

48. Carosso, *California Wine Industry,* pp. 71–72.

49. Wilson Flint to Benjamin D. Wilson, 2 November 1865 (Wilson Papers, Huntington Library).

50. See Schoenman, *Father of California Wine,* p. 35.

51. *Alta California,* 26 August 1869.

11. The Fate of Southern California

1. For the general history, see Leo J. Friis, *Campo Aleman: The First Ten Years of Anaheim* (Santa Ana, Calif., 1983); Mildred Yorba MacArthur, *Anaheim: "The Mother Colony"* (Los Angeles, 1959); Hallock F. Raup, *The German Colonization of Anaheim, California* (Berkeley, 1932); and Sister Mary Peter Traviss, O.P., "The Founding of Anaheim, California, 1857–1879" (M.A. thesis, Catholic University of America, 1961).

2. Raup, *German Colonization,* p. 124. Anaheim was still a part of Los Angeles County in 1857; it is now in Orange County, not organized until 1889.

3. MacArthur, *Anaheim,* pp. 22–24.

4. *Alta California,* 21 December 1857.

5. Raup, *German Colonization,* pp. 129–30.

6. Raup, *German Colonization,* p. 124; MacArthur, *Anaheim,* p. 29. One may note here that the Los Angeles formula of 1,000 vines to the acre was still being observed. There were fifty lots of eight acres each to be planted; hence 400,000 vines were required.

7. MacArthur, *Anaheim,* pp. 23, 25.

8. Raup, *German Colonization,* p. 126.

9. Ibid., pp. 123n., 131–32. They were perhaps most like the Hermann settlers, but they did not have even the cultural nationalism of that group.

10. John Hittell, in Raup, *German Colonization,* p. 139.

11. *Alta California,* 28 September 1865.

12. *Alta California,* 26 March 1869; Henry Kroeger, "Early History of Anaheim as Related by a Colonist," *Anaheim Gazette,* 75th Anniversary ed., 1932 (Anaheim Public Library).

13. Charles Loring Brace, *The New West: or, California in 1867–1868* (New York, 1869), p. 295.

14. Traviss, "Founding of Anaheim," p. 40; *Alta California,* 28 September 1865.

15. MacArthur, *Anaheim,* p. 29.

16. Helena Modjeska, *Memories and Impressions* (New York, 1910), pp. 285–305. Sienkiewicz describes a harvest festival in Anaheim in his story "Orso" (*Western Septet: Seven Stories of the American West,* trans. M. M. Coleman [Cheshire, Conn., 1973]); he also reported that in Anaheim the poor drank wine with their meals, "for this is the least expensive drink here" (Marc Pachter and Frances Wein, eds., *Abroad in America: Visitors to the New Nation, 1776–1914* [Reading, Mass., 1976], pp. 180–81).

17. Norton B. Stern and William Kramer, "The Wine Tycoon of Anaheim," *Western States Jewish Historical Quarterly* 9 (1977): 262–78.

18. Benjamin Dreyfus, Biographical Scrapbook, Anaheim Public Library.

19. Stern and Kramer, "Wine Tycoon," p. 267.

20. Undated pamphlet, c. 1869, listing wines offered by J. F. Carr and Co., New York (Anaheim Public Library).

21. See also the list of wines offered in the East by Kohler & Frohling, p. 257 above.

22. Stern and Kramer, "Wine Tycoon," pp. 270–71.

23. This description is drawn from the fullest study of the Anaheim disease yet made: M. W. Gardner and William B. Hewitt, *Pierce's Disease of the Grapevine: The Anaheim Disease and the California Vine Disease* (Berkeley and Davis, 1974), pp. 5–31. See also A. J. Winkler et al., *General Viticulture* (Berkeley, 1962), pp. 468–69.

24. Gardner and Hewitt, *Pierce's Disease,* p. 5.

25. Ibid., p. 13.

26. *Rural Californian* 10 (November 1887): 251. The expert from Washington, F. Lamson Scribner, was accompanied by the eminent French viticultural scientist Pierre Viala.

27. Raup, *German Settlement,* p. 136.

28. Dreyfus, Biographical Scrapbook, Anaheim Public Library.

29. For a summary of current knowledge of Pierce's Disease, see Gardner and Hewitt, *Pierce's Disease,* pp. 164ff.

30. *Wines and Vines* 64 (February 1983): 62.

31. Gardener and Hewitt, *Pierce's Disease,* pp. 192–95.

32. Susanna Bryant Dakin, *A Scotch Paisano in Old Los Angeles: Hugo Reid's Life in California, 1832–1852, Derived from His Correspondence* (Berkeley, 1939), p. 108.

33. Ibid., p. 199. Other authorities give 1854 as the year of purchase.

34. For Wilson, see John Walton Caughey, "Don Benito Wilson: An Average Southern Californian," *Huntington Library Quarterly* 2 (April 1939): 285–300; Midge Sherwood, *Days of Vintage, Years of Vision* (San Marino, Calif., 1982), passim.

35. L. J. Rose, Jr., *L. J. Rose of Sunnyslope, 1827–1899* (San Marino, Calif., 1959), p. 45.

36. Wilson to Mrs. Wilson, 13 July 1856 (Wilson Papers, Huntington Library).

37. See, e.g., Paul W. Gates, *California Ranchos and Farms, 1846–1862* (Madison, Wis., 1967), pp. 102–3.

38. Notes by Edith Shorb Steele, Shorb Papers, Huntington Library; J. De Barth Shorb, "Vines and Vineyards," in A. T. Hawley, ed., *The Present Condition, Growth, Progress and Advantages of Los Angeles City and County* (Los Angeles, 1876), p. 113.

39. Wilson's winemaker sent him a thousand cuttings from General Vallejo's vineyards in 1864. Wilson Flint sent him Muscat of Alexandria in 1866; and Wilson's San Francisco manager sent him 10,000 cuttings of Frontiniac in 1869 (Wilson Papers, 23 February 1864; 16 February 1866; 29 January 1869).

40. See above, p. 481 n91 (on first champagne).

41. H. R. Myles to Wilson, 22 February 1856 (Wilson Papers).

42. Myles to Wilson, 28 January 1857 (Wilson Papers).

43. Eberhart was recommended to Wilson by Kohler & Frohling (Caughey, "Don Benito Wilson," p. 289n).

44. Hobbs, Gilmore & Co. to Wilson, 6 March 1862 (Wilson Papers).

45. Hobbs to Wilson, 20 July 1863 (Wilson Papers). Another problem arose through competi-

tion with the producers of wine from New England's wild grapes: the dealers could not be trusted to refrain from mixing California wine with the native product. New England wild grape wine was produced in substantial quantities in this era. The firm of Paige & Co. in Boston was making 20,000 gallons annually from grapes growing along the Charles River and crushed in "mammoth wine presses" set up under the Boston City reservoir! (*Cozzens' Wine Press* 6 [20 February 1860]: 66; *American Agriculturist* 19 [November 1860]: 340). Another commercial producer of wines from wild grapes was the firm of Glasier & Flint, of Ashburnham, Mass. Ashburnham wine, "for Communion," in barrels at $1 a gallon, is listed for sale by the Massachusetts commissioner for the sale of liquor in 1861.

46. T. Hart Hyatt, *Hyatt's Hand-Book of Grape Culture* (San Francisco, 1867), pp. 218–19.

47. Adolf Eberhart to Wilson, 15 May 1863 (Wilson Papers).

48. Hobbs, Gilmore & Co. to Wilson, 24 September 1863 (Wilson Papers).

49. Wilson, Notebook, 1876–84 (Wilson Papers).

50. The account that follows is drawn from the Shorb Papers in the Huntington Library.

51. Shorb Dictation (MS c. 1888), Bancroft Library.

52. Shorb Papers, Addenda.

53. Shorb to Wilson, 14 March 1868 (Wilson Papers).

54. Shorb to C. C. Spencer, 8 May 1870 (Letterbooks, Shorb Papers). Despite Shorb's statement, some Chinese workers may have been used at Lake Vineyard earlier: "I am coming by next steamer, and bring the Chinese men with me," Adolf Eberhart wrote to Wilson from San Francisco on 6 September 1865 (Wilson Papers).

55. The winegrowing scene in the San Gabriel Valley in the early 1870s is described in some detail by Ben C. Truman, *Semi-Tropical California* (San Francisco, 1874), pp. 121–31.

56. Shorb to Charles Schaur, 29 July 1875 (Letterbooks, Shorb Papers).

57. Shorb to Wilson, 14 June 1869 (Wilson Papers).

58. Shorb to Mr. Lyman, 14 April 1875 (Letterbooks, Shorb Papers).

59. Shorb to Wilson, 19 January 1869 (Wilson Papers).

60. Shorb to Leoser, 31 March, 16 June 1875 (Letterbooks, Shorb Papers).

61. Shorb to George Dietz, 10 November 1872 (Letterbooks, Shorb Papers).

62. Shorb to J. M. Curtis, 13 September 1875 (Letterbooks, Shorb Papers).

63. Sherwood, *Days of Vintage, Years of Vision,* p. 313n.

64. Shorb to S. Lachman & Co., 27 October 1878; to Lachman & Jacobi, 7 June 1879; to B. Dreyfus, 16 June 1880 (Letterbooks, Shorb Papers).

65. The scheme is discussed in several of Shorb's letters during 1881: see, e.g., those of 20 and 25 September and 14 November (Letterbooks, Shorb Papers).

66. The statement, evidently of Shorb's authorship, is quoted on a proofsheet of an article for a new edition of John S. Hittell's *The Resources of California* (San Francisco, 1863) in 1884 (Shorb Papers). The edition does not seem to have been published.

67. In 1881, the year that Shorb had begun to organize his new venture, French wine production was at 38 million hectolitres, only half of what it had been in 1875; in consequence, imports of wine into France, which had been only 292,000 hectolitres in 1875, were at nearly 8 million in 1881, and climbing (George Ordish, *The Great Wine Blight* [London, 1972], p. 214).

68. Evan Coleman to Shorb, 20 January 1885 (Shorb Papers). It is curious that even at this relatively late date in California experience, Shorb and his associates were interested in native as well as in vinifera grapes; they were looking for large quantities of Lenoir and Cynthiana cuttings in 1884: see Charles Wetmore to Shorb, 29 February 1884; William Walsh to Shorb, 20 October 1884 (Shorb Papers). Perhaps they were wanted for rootstocks against phylloxera.

69. Proofsheet for Hittell, *Resources of California,* 1884 (Shorb Papers).

70. Ibid.

71. Coleman to Shorb, 12 October 1884 (Shorb Papers).

72. F. W. Wood to Shorb, 23 January 1886 (Shorb Papers).

73. F. W. Wood to Shorb, 8 February 1886; they were still using "cherry juice" two years later: E. L. Watkins to Shorb, 1 May 1888 (Shorb Papers).

74. F. Pohndorff to Shorb, 5 April 1884 (Shorb Papers).

75. F. W. Wood to Shorb, 10 June 1884 (Shorb Papers).

76. H. Diehl to Shorb, 27 August 1885 (Shorb Papers).

77. C. F. Oldham to Shorb, 8 April 1891 (Shorb Papers).

78. Undated clipping (c. July 1887); Paul Oeker to Shorb, 15 and 28 January 1888 (Shorb Papers).

79. O. S. Howard to Shorb, 5 January 1888 (Shorb Papers).

80. C. W. Howard to Shorb, 27 June 1892 (Shorb Papers).

81. Evan Coleman to Shorb, 19 February 1884 (Shorb Papers).

82. E. L. Watkins to Shorb, 17 April 1888 (Shorb Papers).

83. To Shorb, 10 September 1888 (Shorb Papers).

84. Shorb hired Dowlen in September 1888 (Gardner and Hewitt, *Pierce's Disease*, pp. 16ff).

85. E. L. Watkins to Shorb, 9, 18, and 22 March 1890 (Shorb Papers).

86. Evan Coleman to Shorb, 29 August 1888 (Shorb Papers).

87. Copy, Shorb Papers.

88. Hellman to Evan Coleman, 13 February 1893 (Shorb Papers).

89. E. L. Watkins to Shorb, 5 June 1892 (Shorb Papers).

90. Statement, "San Gabriel Wine Co., Resources and Liabilities January 1st 1893" (Shorb Papers).

91. Lindley Bynum, "San Gabriel," in Joseph Henry Jackson, ed., *The Vine in Early California* ([San Francisco] 1955).

12. California to the End of the Century

1. Frona Eunice Wait, *Wines and Vines of California* (1889; reprint, Berkeley, 1973), p. 180.

2. L. J. Rose, Jr., *L. J. Rose of Sunny Slope, 1827–1889* (San Marino, Calif., 1959), pp. 132–33; 162–64.

3. *Report of the California State Board of Agriculture, 1911* (Sacramento, 1912), p. 197.

4. Leon Adams, *The Wines of America*, 3d ed. (New York, 1985), p. 399.

5. Carey Stanton, *An Island Memoir* (Los Angeles, 1984), p. 16; Helen Caire, "A Brief History of Santa Cruz Island from 1869 to 1937," *Ventura County Historical Society Quarterly* 27 (Summer 1982): 7; Clifford McElrath, *On Santa Cruz Island* (Los Angeles, 1967), pp. 6, 98, 120.

6. *San Francisco Merchant*, 28 December 1883.

7. Guido Rossati, *Relazione di un viaggio d'istruzione negli Stati Uniti d'America* (Rome, 1900), p. 285.

8. U.S. Department of Agriculture, *Yearbook, 1902* (Washington, D.C., 1902), p. 413.

9. Charles Kohler, "Wine Production in California," pp. 9, 11 (MS, Bancroft Library).

10. *Overland Monthly* 7 (May 1872): 398.

11. Writing of a trip made in 1896, the Italian observer Guido Rossati described the winery of William Wehner at Evergreen, Santa Clara County, as typical of California: brick-built, of three floors, it backed up against a hillside; grapes were conveyed to the top floor, where they were crushed; they then descended through chutes to the fermentation vats on the second floor; storage was on the ground floor (*Relazione*, pp. 226–27). An extremely interesting collection of photographs of (mostly) nineteenth-century winery buildings is Irene W. Haynes, *Ghost Wineries of Napa Valley* (San Francisco, 1980).

12. The use of redwood for wine cooperage was one of the innovations for which Haraszthy claimed credit: see *Alta California*, 21 September 1863, and Agoston Haraszthy, "Wine-Making in California," *Harper's* 29 (June 1864): 28.

13. Ernest P. Peninou and Sidney S. Greenleaf, *Winemaking in California: III. The California Wine Association* ([San Francisco?] 1954), 27.

14. California Board of State Viticultural Commissioners, *Directory of the Grape Growers, Wine Makers and Distillers of California* (Sacramento, 1891).

15. *History of San Luis Obispo County, California* (Oakland, 1883), p. 230.

16. *The Diaries of Louis Pasqual Dallidet, 1882–1884*, ed. Patrick and Eleanor Brown (San Luis Obispo, Calif., n.d.).

17. Alexander D. Bell, *Fresno, California* (San Francisco, 1884), p. 4.

18. Ibid.

19. Ibid., pp. 16–17; Wait, *Wines and Vines of California*, p. 188.

20. Bell, *Fresno*, p. 17.

21. Wait, *Wines and Vines of California*, p. 185.

22. Bell, *Fresno*, pp. 9–10; Rossati, *Relazione*, p. 265; California Wine Association, undated brochure, c. 1910? (Huntington Library).

23. Wait, *Wines and Vines of California*, p. 185; Bell, *Fresno*, p. 19.

24. Wait, *Wines and Vines of California*, pp. 185–87; Rossati, *Relazione*, p. 260.

25. Rossati, *Relazione*, p. 265; *American Wine Press and Mineral Water News*, 5 May 1897, p. 5; *California Wine Review*, June 1934, pp. 32–33.

26. Wait, *Wines and Vines of California*, p. 187.

27. Ibid., pp. 189–90; *San Francisco Merchant*, 14 March 1884.

28. U.S. Immigration Commission, *Report*, 24 (Washington, D.C., 1911): 570.

29. David Joseph Gibson, "The Development of the Livermore Valley Wine District" (M.A. thesis, University of California, Davis, 1969), p. 39.

30. Ibid., pp. 40, 47–49.

31. Adolf Eberhart to Benjamin Wilson, 27 May 1863 (Wilson Papers, Huntington Library).

32. Norman E. Tutorow, *Leland Stanford: Man of Many Careers* (Menlo Park, Calif., 1971), p. 186.

33. Joseph A. McConnell, Jr., "The Stanford Vina Ranch" (M.A. thesis, Stanford University, 1961), pp. 5–17.

34. Ibid., pp. 18, 43–49; Tutorow, *Leland Stanford*, p. 187.

35. McConnell, "Stanford Vina Ranch," pp. 29–31, 40, 42, 45–46.

36. Ibid., p. 38; Rose, *L. J. Rose*, p. 105.

37. McConnell, "Stanford Vina Ranch," pp. 38–39.

38. Ibid., pp. 50–51. The Vina Ranch production was 10 percent of the entire California wine crop in that year.

39. George Coes Howell, *The Case of Whiskey* (Altadena, Calif., 1928), p. 120.

40. McConnell, "Stanford Vina Ranch," p. 53.

41. Dorothy F. Regnery, *An Enduring Heritage: Historic Buildings of the San Francisco Peninsula* (Stanford, Calif., 1976), p. 73.

42. McConnell, "Stanford Vina Ranch," p. 33; Elizabeth Gregg, "The History of the Famous Stanford Ranch," *Overland Monthly* 52 (October 1908): 338.

43. Gregg, "History of the Famous Stanford Ranch," p. 338.

44. McConnell, "Stanford Vina Ranch," pp. 56–57; Tutorow, *Leland Stanford*, p. 194.

45. McConnell, "Stanford Vina Ranch," p. 67; F. T. Robson, "The Stanford Vina Ranch," in *The Vine in Early California* ([San Francisco] 1955), no pagination.

46. Irving McKee, "Three Wine-Growing Senators," *California* 37 (September 1947): 15, 28–29.

47. Ruth Teiser and Catherine Harroun, *Winemaking in California* (New York, 1983), p. 85.

48. Wait, *Wines and Vines of California*, pp. 156–57; article on Julius Paul Smith in *Cyclopaedia of American Biography*, 25.

49. Rudyard Kipling, *From Sea to Sea* (London, 1899), 1: 496.

50. Wait, *Wines and Vines of California*, p. 157; Irving McKee, "Historic Alameda County Wine Growers," *California* 43 (September 1953): 22.

51. Teiser and Harroun, *Winemaking in California*, pp. 114, 119; Maynard Amerine, "Hilgard and California Viticulture," *Hilgardia* 33 (July 1962): 4.

52. Ben C. Truman, *Semi-Tropical California* (San Francisco, 1874), pp. 121–22; Teiser and Harroun, *Winemaking in California*, p. 140; Esther Boulton Black, *Rancho Cucamonga and Doña Merced* (Redlands, Calif., 1975), p. 260.

53. George Husmann, *Grape Culture and Wine-Making in California* (San Francisco, 1888), p. 226; Bascom A. Stephens, ed., *Resources of Los Angeles County, California* (Los Angeles, 1887), pp. 91–95.

54. Husmann, *Grape Culture and Wine-Making in California*, pp. 236–37.

55. Ibid., p. 237.

56. *Pacific Wine and Spirit Review*, 23 April 1896, p. 9.

57. Eliot Lord et al., *The Italian in America* (New York, 1906), p. 143.

58. Ibid., pp. 136–37; Italian Swiss Colony, *Italian Swiss Colony, Growers and Producers of Choice California Wines* (undated pamphlet [San Francisco? c. 1910?]), pp. 12–14.

59. Ibid., p. 14.

60. Ibid., pp. 14–16.

61. Ibid., pp. 6, 14–16. See also Italian Swiss Colony, *Sixth Annual Report, 1887* (San Francisco, [1887]).

62. *Italian Swiss Colony,* pp. 40, 42, 52–53.

63. Teiser and Harroun, *Winemaking in California,* p. 151.

64. *Italian Swiss Colony,* pp. 28, 42, 55.

65. Ibid., p. 30; Lord et al., *Italian in America,* p. 138.

66. A start has been made by William F. Heintz, "The Role of Chinese Labor in Viticulture and Wine-Making in 19th Century California" (M.A. thesis, Sonoma State University, 1977). See also Sucheng Chan, *This Bittersweet Soil: The Chinese in California Agriculture, 1860–1910* (Berkeley, 1986).

67. *Transactions of the California State Agricultural Society, 1860* (Sacramento, 1861), p. 78.

68. Rose, *L. J. Rose,* p. 81.

69. *Harper's Weekly* 22 (5 October 1878): 792–93. In 1883 the prominent Santa Rosa wine producer Isaac De Turk, stated that the Chinese are "the principal help in Sonoma County" (De Turk, "Sonoma Wines" [MS, Bancroft Library], 8 September 1883, p. 21).

70. Ernest P. Peninou and Sidney S. Greenleaf, *A Directory of California Wine Growers and Wine Makers in 1860* (Berkeley, 1967), pp. 3, 44.

71. Irving McKee, "The Oldest Names in California Winegrowing," *California* 41 (September 1951): 17.

72. Bob Stuart Barlow, "Historical and Regional Analysis of the Italian Role in California Viticulture and Enology" (M.A. thesis, University of California at Los Angeles, 1964); Adams, *Wines of America,* 3d ed., p. 399.

73. Adams, *Wines of America,* 3d ed., p. 447; Irving McKee, "Historic Fresno County Wine Growers," *California* 42 (September 1952): 13.

74. Irving McKee, "Oldest Names in California Winegrowing," p. 17; C. A. Menefee, *Historical and Descriptive Sketch Book of Napa, Sonoma, Lake and Mendocino* (Napa, Calif., 1873), p. 213.

75. For example, Idwal Jones, *The Vineyard* (New York, 1942); Sidney Howard, *They Knew What They Wanted* (New York, 1924); John Fante, *Dago Red* (New York, 1940); Anita Kornfeld, *Vintage* (New York, 1980); Michael Legat, *Mario's Vineyard* (London, 1980); Jack Bickham, *The Winemakers* (New York, 1977).

76. San Francisco Mechanics' Institute, *Report of the Fifteenth Industrial Exhibition, 1880* (San Francisco, 1880), p. 99.

77. The standard account of Thomas Lake Harris's life and work is Herbert W. Schneider and George Lawton, *A Prophet and a Pilgrim* (New York, 1942).

78. Ibid., p. 160.

79. Harris called his new settlement "Salem-on-Erie" in order to promote the Salem name, but he was soon compelled to accept the original address of Brocton (Ibid., p. 147).

80. Ibid., pp. 149, 160.

81. William Chazanof, *Welch's Grape Juice* (Syracuse, N.Y., 1977), p. 44.

82. Adams, *Wines of America,* 3d ed., p. 152.

83. Schneider and Lawton, *A Prophet and a Pilgrim,* pp. 279–80.

84. *Illustrated History of Sonoma County* (Chicago, 1889), p. 366.

85. Schneider and Lawton, *A Prophet and a Pilgrim,* pp. 223n., 473. I have not found a file of the *Fountain Grove Wine Press.* It would be curious to examine.

86. *Illustrated History of Sonoma County,* p. 367. The Manor House, as it was called, was demolished in 1970. See the excellent photographs in Paul Kagan, *New World Utopias* (New York, 1975).

87. Schneider and Lawton, *A Prophet and a Pilgrim,* pp. 467–68.

88. Ibid., p. 488.

89. Richard Paul Hinkle, "The Wines and the Mystics of Fantastic Fountaingrove," *Redwood Rancher,* July 1979, pp. 20–24.

90. Robert V. Hine, *California's Utopian Colonies* (New Haven, 1966), pp. 63, 72–73.

91. Ibid., pp. 59–61.

92. Ibid., pp. 58, 67–68, 71–72; Kagan, *New World Utopias,* p. 42.

93. Hine, *California's Utopian Colonies,* pp. 74–75.

94. Husmann, *Grape Culture and Wine-Making in California,* p. iii.

95. Wait, *Wines and Vines of California,* p. 147; De Turk, "Sonoma Wines."

96. J. De Barth Shorb, for example: see F. W. Wood to Shorb, 1 March 1886 (Shorb Papers).

97. *Illustrated History of Sonoma County,* pp. 430, 433, 699.

98. Ibid., p. 430; Wait, *Wines and Vines of California,* pp. 139, 142.

99. *Illustrated History of Sonoma County,* p. 499; Wait, *Wines and Vines of California,* pp. 136–37.

100. *Illustrated History of Sonoma County,* p. 402.

101. Ibid., pp. 509, 541, 565.

102. Wait, *Wines and Vines of California,* p. 134.

103. *Illustrated History of Sonoma County,* pp. 587–88, 525–26, 516–17, 551–52.

104. Ibid., pp. 409, 569–70, 714, 732, 427–28, 443–44, 501–2, 538–40, 594–95, 630–32, 665, 452–53.

105. The 118 winemakers produced 1,756,000 gallons in 1891, an average of 14,881 gallons apiece; the 22,863 acres of vineyard in Sonoma County were divided among 728 proprietors, an average of 31⅓ acres.

13. California: Growing Pains and Growing Up

1. Herbert B. Leggett, *Early History of Wine Production in California* (San Francisco, 1941), p. 112; Paul Fredericksen, *The Authentic Haraszthy Story* (San Francisco [1947]), p. 9; Thomas H. Pauly, "J. Ross Browne: Wine Lobbyist and Frontier Opportunist," *California Historical Quarterly* 51 (Summer 1972): 108.

2. Pauly, p. 109.

3. MS resolution of protest, Los Angeles Wine Growers' Association, 9 October 1869 (Wilson Papers, Huntington Library).

4. Vincent P. Carosso, *The California Wine Industry, 1830–1895* (Berkeley, 1951), p. 92; I. N. Hoag to Benjamin Wilson, 4 July 1872 (Wilson Papers).

5. Carosso, *California Wine Industry,* p. 92. The association's first fair was held at Sacramento in September 1872: see the association's *Transactions, 1872,* published in *Transactions of the California State Agricultural Society, 1872* (Sacramento, 1873).

6. Carosso, *California Wine Industry,* pp. 104–5.

7. *Sacramento Daily Union,* 21 March 1872.

8. George Husmann, *American Grape Growing and Wine-Making,* 4th ed. (New York, 1880), p. 173. California itself was then beginning to suffer serious destruction of its vineyards from phylloxera, but it was not yet allowable to admit the fact.

9. For the committee's hearings, see "The Culture of the Grape," in *Appendix to the Journals of the Senate and Assembly,* 23d sess., 5, no. 16 (Sacramento, 1880). For the text of the Act, see California Board of State Viticultural Commissioners, *First Annual Report* (San Francisco, 1881), pp. 5–8.

10. The districts were Sonoma, Napa, San Francisco (including Alameda, San Mateo, and Santa Clara counties), Los Angeles, Sacramento, San Joaquin, and El Dorado.

11. "First Report of the Committee on the Phylloxera, Vine Pests, and the Diseases of the Vine," p. 6, in California Board of State Viticultural Commissioners, *First Annual Report.* This is the earliest established identification of the phylloxera in California, but there was general agreement that the pest had been in the state earlier than that: ibid., pp. 28–29. E. M. Stafford and R. L. Doutt, "Insect Grape Pests of Northern California," University of California, California Agricultural Experiment Station, Extension Service Circular no. 566 (1974), p. 62, state that phylloxera was discovered in California in 1852. Since it is usually supposed that the pest was introduced to California on vines imported from the eastern United States, this date, if correct, is evidence of very early importation indeed. Phylloxera had not even been identified in 1852, so the evidence for so early a date must be indirect.

12. *Southern California Horticulturist* 2 (November 1878): 16.

13. See California Board of State Viticultural Commissioners, *First Annual Report of the Chief Executive Viticultural Officer, 1881* (Sacramento, 1882), pp. ix–xv.

14. Maynard Amerine, "Hilgard and California Viticulture," *Hilgardia* 33 (July 1962): 3. An interesting meeting of Hilgard with the winegrowers of Sonoma is reported in San Francisco Mechanics' Institute, *Report of the Thirteenth Industrial Exhibition, 1878* (San Francisco, 1878), pp. 103–7.

After describing the phylloxera to them, Hilgard concluded that grafting to resistant American root-stocks, as the French were doing, would be necessary for "the vineyards of the future" (p. 106).

15. California Board of State Viticultural Commissioners, *Annual Report, 1887* (Sacramento, 1888), p. 88.

16. George C. Husmann, "Viticulture of Napa County," in Tom Gregory et al., *History of Solano and Napa Counties* (Los Angeles, 1912), pp. 148–49.

17. Charles Wetmore recommends it in, e.g., his *Ampelography of California* (San Francisco, 1884), p. 18; so did Hilgard in a series of bulletins (Amerine, "Hilgard and California Viticulture," p. 4). A. J. Winkler, *General Viticulture* (Berkeley, 1962), p. 18, states succinctly that *V. californica* is "not sufficiently resistant" to phylloxera.

18. International Congress of Viticulture, *Official Report* (San Francisco, 1915), p. 47.

19. California Board of State Viticultural Commissioners, *Second Annual Report of the Chief Executive Viticultural Officer, 1882–3 and 1883–4* (Sacramento, 1884), pp. 103–51.

20. California Board of State Viticultural Commissioners, *Annual Report, 1887* (Sacramento, 1887), pp. 61–62; id., Minutes, 9 March 1887 (MS, Bancroft Library).

21. E.g., California Board of State Viticultural Commissioners, *Second Annual Report of the Chief Executive Viticultural Officer,* pp. 55–68, 103–51.

22. See, e.g., *San Francisco Merchant,* 15 June 1883, p. 201, and 13 July 1883, p. 273.

23. Husmann, *American Grape Growing and Wine-Making,* pp. 166, 169.

24. Charles Wetmore in California Board of State Viticultural Commissioners, *Second Annual Report of the Chief Executive Viticultural Officer,* p. 39.

25. Wetmore, *Ampelography of California,* pp. 9, 10, 15, 16.

26. California Board of State Viticultural Commissioners, *Second Annual Report of the Chief Executive Viticultural Officer,* p. 40. Among the experimenters with new varieties, Wetmore names George West, J. H. Drummond, Charles Lefranc, and L. J. Rose.

27. Ibid., p. 42.

28. California Board of State Viticultural Commissioners, *Annual Report, 1893–94,* appendix B, part 2 (Sacramento, 1894), pp. 46–48.

29. California Board of State Viticultural Commissioners, Minutes, 19 May 1884, 8 June 1885, 15 January 1887, 11 December 1888; minutes of the Executive Committee, 21 March 1895.

30. California Board of State Viticultural Commissioners, *Annual Report, 1893–94,* p. 10.

31. Ibid., pp. 79–89. Among the prize-winners were Paul Masson, Isaac De Turk, Arpad Haraszthy, Charles Wetmore, and H. W. Crabb.

32. *Pacific Wine and Spirit Review,* 30 August 1890.

33. Lilian Whiting, *Kate Field: A Record* (Boston, 1899), pp. 458–59; California Board of State Viticultural Commissioners, Minutes, 11 December 1888.

34. Irving McKee, "Historic Alameda County Wine Growers," *California* 43 (September 1953): 22; Janet Newton, "Cresta Blanca and Charles Wetmore: A Founder of the California Wine Industry" (Livermore, Calif.: Livermore Heritage Guild, 1974).

35. California Board of State Viticultural Commissioners, Minutes, 9 March 1887, 11 June 1888, 20 April 1889, 8 June 1891.

36. Ibid., 8 June 1891.

37. Amerine, "Hilgard and California Viticulture," pp. 9–12.

38. University of California College of Agriculture, *Report of the Viticultural Work during the Seasons 1887–93* (Sacramento, 1896), p. 3.

39. See ibid., passim, for the sources listed for the analyses of specific varieties.

40. Adams, *Wines of America,* p. 300. Despite his name, Bioletti was an Englishman.

41. See Bioletti's summary in University of California College of Agriculture, *Report of the Viticultural Work . . . 1887–93,* pp. 379ff.

42. Ibid., p. 384.

43. Ibid., p. 409.

44. University of California College of Agriculture, *Report of the Viticultural Work during the Seasons 1885 and 1886* (Sacramento, 1886); *Reports of Experiments on Methods of Fermentation and Related Subjects* (Sacramento, 1888); *Report of the Viticultural Work during the Seasons 1887–89* (Sacramento, 1892).

45. Ohio Agricultural Research and Development Center, *Proceedings, Ohio Grape-Wine Short Course, 1973* (Wooster, Ohio, 1973), p. 63.

46. California Board of State Viticultural Commissioners, Minutes of Executive Committee, 20 February 1893; Carosso, *California Wine Industry,* p. 192.

47. The ancestor of the Department of Viticulture and Enology at the University of California, Davis. Many of the records of both the board and the university department went up in smoke when the Agriculture Building at Berkeley burned in 1897.

48. At the beginning of the 1880s, when the California industry began to respond to the possibility of supplying phylloxera-smitten Europe with wine, the total quantity of wine exported from the state was only 154,000 gallons. By 1890 the figure had risen to 393,000 gallons, and would reach a peak of 1,623,000 gallons in 1898. This was a notable increase but made only a small proportion of the total increase in production over those years (*Report of California State Board of Agriculture, 1911* [Sacramento, 1912], p. 203).

49. Charles Wetmore, *Treatise on Wine Production,* appendix B to the *Report of the Board of State Viticultural Commissioners, 1893–94* (Sacramento, 1894), pp. 5–6, 37–38. On this matter, Wetmore and Hilgard were at one. In a letter called "Plain Talk to the Winemen" in the *San Francisco Examiner,* 8 August 1889, Hilgard explained the depressed market in California wine as a simple consequence of "the poor quality of the larger part of the wines made and their immaturity when put on the market." "The foreign guest at our principal hotels might be aghast," Hilgard wrote, "at having the claret cork fly at him, followed by a significant puff of smoke, and a liquid resembling sauce rather than wine and of uncanny odor: the label assured him that it was all right and that such was the nature of California wine." Such deplorable results were the outcome of equally deplorable methods. The California winemaker, "after crushing promiscuously grapes sound, moldy, green and sunburnt . . . allows his fermenting tanks to get so hot as to scald the yeast, and then wonders why the wine has 'stuck'; permits the 'cap' to get white with mold and swarming with vinegar flies and then cheerfully stirs it under so as to thoroughly infect the wine with the germs of destruction."

50. Wetmore, *Treatise on Wine Production,* p. 35.

51. Ibid., p. 36.

52. Adams, *Wines of America,* p. 172; Peninou and Greenleaf, *Winemaking in California* (1954), p. 1.

53. For the history of the California Wine Association, see Ernest P. Peninou and Sidney S. Greenleaf, *Winemaking in California: III. The California Wine Association* ([San Francisco?] 1954); and Ruth Teiser and Catherine Harroun, *Winemaking in California* (New York, 1983), pp. 157–60. The seven firms forming the CWA were Kohler & Frohling, Kohler & Van Bergen, C. Carpy & Company, B. Dreyfus & Company, S. Lachman & Company, the Napa Valley Wine Company, and Arpad Haraszthy & Company.

54. "The California Wine Association," company brochure (n.p., n.d. [San Francisco? c. 1910?]) (Huntington Library).

55. Peninou and Greenleaf, *Winemaking in California: III,* p. 5.

56. Ibid., p. 30.

57. Ibid., p. 31.

58. "The California Wine Association" (brochure cited n. 54 above).

59. Peninou and Greenleaf, *Winemaking in California: III,* pp. 19–20.

60. Ibid., pp. 21–22.

61. Husmann, *Grape Culture and Wine-Making in California,* p. 344.

62. Robert Louis Stevenson, "Napa Wine," in *The Silverado Squatters* (London, 1883).

63. International Congress of Viticulture, *Official Report,* p. 29. Lachman adds: "As California wines began to improve, instead of giving them a half blend of foreign wine the blend was reduced to possibly about 80 per cent California and 20 per cent French. The demand in wine at that time was for a French label, mostly fictitious brands" (ibid.).

64. "California Wine Association" (brochure cited n. 54 above).

65. Ibid.

66. Hiram S. Dewey, in International Congress of Viticulture, *Official Report,* p. 302.

67. Ibid.

68. Peninou and Greenleaf, *Winemaking in California: III,* pp. 28–29; Teiser and Harroun, *Winemaking in California,* pp. 158–59.

69. Adams, *Wines of America,* p. 279; Teiser and Harroun, *Winemaking in California,* p. 150.

70. For the figures on California wine production, see *Report of the State Board of Agriculture, 1911,* p. 191.

71. San Francisco Mechanics' Institute, *Report of the First Industrial Exhibition, 1857* (San Francisco, 1858), p. 58.

72. *Illustrated History of Sonoma County* (Chicago, 1889), p. 571; San Francisco Mechanics' Institute, *Report of the Eleventh Industrial Exhibition* (San Francisco, 1876), p. 162.

73. Agoston Haraszthy, "Wine-Making in California," *Harper's* 29 (June 1864): 28.

74. San Francisco Mechanics' Institute, *Report of the Sixth Annual Industrial Exhibition, 1868* (San Francisco, 1868), pp. 39–40.

75. San Francisco Mechanics' Institute, *Report of the Twenty-Third Industrial Exhibition, 1888* (San Francisco, 1888), p. 121.

76. *California Farmer*, 7 October 1863, p. 69.

77. San Francisco Mechanics' Institute, *Report of the Seventh Industrial Exhibition, 1869* (San Francisco, 1869), p. 39.

78. San Francisco Mechanics' Institute, *Report of the Ninth Industrial Exhibition, 1874* (San Francisco, 1874), p. 55.

79. E. T. Meakin, "The Engineer's Part in the Advancement of the Viticultural Industry," in International Congress of Viticulture, *Official Report*, p. 250.

80. San Francisco Mechanics' Institute, *Report of the Twenty-Third Industrial Exhibition, 1888*, pp. 85–86.

81. San Francisco Mechanics' Institute, *Report of the Twelfth Industrial Exhibition, 1877*, p. 142.

82. San Francisco Mechanics' Institute, *Report of the Ninth Industrial Exhibition, 1874*, p. 54; *Report of the Nineteenth Industrial Exhibition, 1884* (San Francisco, 1885), p. 78.

83. Meakin, "Engineer's Part," in International Congress of Viticulture, *Official Report*, p. 251.

84. *Quercus suber*, the cork oak, grows quite happily in California, but it has never been commercially exploited there so far as I know. No doubt the labor costs of harvesting and processing the bark make the idea unattractive. Spain and Portugal continue to supply the world.

85. *San Francisco Merchant*, 25 May 1883, p. 137.

86. *San Francisco Directory*, 1889; California Board of State Viticultural Commissioners, *Report of the Sixth Annual State Viticultural Convention* (Sacramento, 1888), p. 84; *Illustrated History of Sonoma County*, p. 252.

87. *San Francisco Merchant*, 13 April 1883, p. 3.

88. International Congress of Viticulture, *Official Report*, p. 15. The rest of the description of the congress is drawn from this source.

89. Frank Morton Todd, *The Story of the Exposition* (New York, 1921), 4: 302.

14. The Eastern United States: From the Civil War to Prohibition

1. The actual production figures for New York were: 1870, 82,000 gallons; 1880, 584,000 gallons; 1890, 2,528,000 gallons.

2. *American Agriculturist* 25 (1866): 401.

3. The proportion in 1890 was 60,000 tons sent to market as table grapes and 15,000 tons crushed for wine (11th Census, 1890, *Report on the Statistics of Agriculture in the United States* [Washington, D.C., 1895] p. 602).

4. George Howell Morris, "Rise of the Grape and Wine Industry in the Naples Valley during the Nineteenth Century" (M.A. thesis, Syracuse University, 1955), p. 38n.

5. D. Bauder, "The Grape-Growing District of Central New York," in George Husmann, *American Grape Growing and Wine Making* (New York, 1896), p. 99.

6. U.S. Department of Agriculture, *Yearbook, 1902* (Washington, D.C., 1902), p. 416.

7. Lewis Cass Aldrich, *History of Yates County, N.Y.* (Syracuse, N.Y., 1892), p. 241.

8. *Vineyard View* (Hammondsport, N.Y.) 9, no. 4 (1980): 12; Irvin W. Near, *History of Steuben County, New York* (Chicago, 1911), p. 295.

9. William Chazanof, *Welch's Grape Juice* (Syracuse, N.Y., 1977), p. 46.

10. Chautauqua Grape and Wine Association, "Chautauqua Fruits, Grapes, and Grape Products" (n.p., 1901), unpaginated (Library of Congress).

11. The WCTU was officially founded at Cleveland in 1874, but the organizing committee was

created at the National Sunday School Assembly at Lake Chautauqua in August 1874 (Elizabeth Putnam Gordon, *Women Torch-Bearers* [Evanston, Ill., 1924], p. 13).

12. Chautauqua Grape and Wine Association, "Chautauqua Fruits, Grapes, and Grape Products."

13. Ibid., where they are called "Italian makers of sour wine." See also Guido Rossati, *Relazione di un viaggio d'istruzione negli Stati Uniti d'America* (Rome, 1900), p. 60.

14. See U. P. Hedrick, *The Grapes of New York* (Albany, N.Y., 1908), for accounts of all these.

15. U. P. Hedrick, "Vitis Vinifera in Eastern America," in International Congress of Viticulture, *Official Report* (San Francisco, 1915), p. 79.

16. R. D. Anthony, "Vinifera Grapes in New York," New York Agricultural Experiment Station Bulletin no. 432 (Geneva, N.Y., 1917).

17. *American Agriculturist* 25 (June 1866): 212.

18. *Grape Culturist* 1 (1869): 87–91, 133–35, 235–38.

19. Crisfield Johnson, *History of Cuyahoga County, Ohio* (Cleveland, 1879), pp. 442, 447.

20. Dwight W. Morrow, Jr., "The American Impressions of a French Botanist," *Agricultural History* 34 (1960): 74.

21. H. T. Dewey, "H. T. Dewey and Sons Co., Pure American Wines" (New York, n.d. [c. 1890]) (New York State Library, Albany, N.Y.).

22. John F. Polacsek, "Pop-Pop—Fizz, Fizz: A Glimpse at the Northwest Ohio Wine Industry in Years Gone By," *Northwest Ohio Quarterly* 53 (Spring 1981): 42–46; Rossati, *Relazione,* p. 86.

23. Rossati, *Relazione,* pp. 88–89.

24. Bert Hudgins, "The South Bass Island Community (Put-in-Bay)," *Economic Geography* 19 (1943): 27–28.

25. Paul Cross Morrison, "Viticulture in Ohio," *Economic Geography* 12 (1936): 75, 85; John H. Garber, "Alcoholic Beverages," in 12th Census, 1900, *Census Reports* (Washington, D.C., 1902), 9: 626; Garth A. Cahoon, "The Ohio Wine Industry from 1860 to the Present," *American Wine Society Journal* 16 (Fall 1984): 86.

26. Morrison, "Viticulture in Ohio," pp. 76, 77.

27. George C. Huntington, "Historical Sketch of Kelley's Island," *Fire Lands Pioneer* 4 (June 1863): 48–49.

28. Husmann, *American Grape Growing and Wine Making* (1880), p. 136.

29. *Wine East* 9 (September 1981): 11. After a fire, the winery building was bought by the Lonz family and rebuilt in a different style. It is now owned by Meier's Wine Cellars of Cincinnati.

30. J.-E. Planchon, "Le Phylloxera en Europe et en Amérique, II: La Vigne et le vin aux Etats-Unis," *Revue des Deux Mondes,* 15 February 1874, pp. 931–33.

31. Ibid., p. 933.

32. Ibid., p. 934.

33. Ibid., p. 935.

34. *Report of the Commissioner of Agriculture, 1871* (Washington, D.C., 1872), p. 231.

35. Liberty Hyde Bailey, *Sketch of the Evolution of Our Native Fruits* (New York, 1898), pp. 3–4.

36. Talcott E. Wing, ed., *History of Monroe County, Michigan* (New York, 1890), p. 426.

37. William McMurtrie, *Report upon the Statistics of Grape Culture and Wine Production in the United States for 1880* (Washington, D.C., 1881), p. 22.

38. Garber, "Alcoholic Beverages," pp. 626, 634.

39. Leon Adams, *The Wines of America* (New York, 1985), p. 70; Garber, "Alcoholic Beverages," p. 634; *A Compendium of the Ninth Census (June 1 1870)* (Washington, D.C., 1872), p. 704.

40. *Eastern Grape Grower and Winery News* 8 (June–July 1982): 14. Winegrowing at Reading went back to the 1830s, when John Fehr, George Lauer, William Tibler, and Gottfried Pflieger, among others, planted native vines for winemaking (Robert Buchanan, *The Culture of the Grape, and Wine-Making* [Cincinnati, 1852], p. 61).

41. Alexander Mackay, *The Western World, or Travels in the United States in 1846–1847,* 3d ed. (Philadelphia, 1850), 1: 127.

42. Harry B. Weiss, *The History of Applejack or Apple Brandy in New Jersey from Colonial Times to the Present* (Trenton, N.J., 1954), pp. 76, 133.

43. Carl Raymond Woodward, *The Development of Agriculture in New Jersey* (New Brunswick, N.J., 1927), p. 181.

44. U. P. Hedrick, *Grapes and Wines from Home Vineyards* (New York, 1945), p. 190.

45. *Gardener's Monthly* 7 (1865): 52.

46. "Egg Harbor City Wineries," *Proceedings of the New Jersey Historical Society* 71 (1953): 295, 297; *Wines and Vines* 63 (January 1982): 8.

47. H. T. Dewey, "H. T. Dewey and Sons Co."; Adams, *Wines of America*, p. 65.

48. "Egg Harbor City Wineries," p. 297. In "The Composition and Quality of Certain American Wines," *Report of the Commissioner of Agriculture, 1880* (Washington, D.C., 1881), p. 176, the wine is spelled "Iolhink."

49. Chazanof, *Welch's Grape Juice*, pp. 4–5.

50. U.S. Industrial Commission, *Report* (Washington, D.C., 1901), 15: 499; Rossati, *Relazione*, p. 71.

51. Chazanof, *Welch's Grape Juice*, p. 7.

52. The notion that there are two kinds of wine mentioned in the Bible—one fermented and one unfermented—was first effectively brought forward about 1839 by the Reverend Eliphalet Nott, president of Union College in Schenectady, New York.

53. Chazanof, *Welch's Grape Juice*, p. 9.

54. Ibid., pp. 9–17, 31–34, 68.

55. Ibid., pp. 72–73.

56. Ibid., p. 20.

57. Ibid., p. 77.

58. Ibid., p. 78.

59. Ibid., p. 74.

60. Ibid., pp. 31–32. "The National Drink" appears in *The Story of a Pantry Shelf: An Outline History of Grocery Specialities* (New York, 1925), p. 215.

61. Chazanof, *Welch's Grape Juice*, pp. 89–90, 95.

62. *Story of a Pantry Shelf*, p. 217.

63. Leslie Hewes, "Tontitown: Ozark Vineyard Center," *Economic Geography* 29 (1953): 140, says that there were 5,000 acres of vines in the Springdale region in 1923.

64. *Grape Culturist* 2 (1870): 202–3; 3 (1871): 146.

65. Planchon wrote that Kelley's wines, the whites especially, were superior to the ordinary wines of the Midi (J.-E. Planchon, *Les Vignes américaines* [Montpellier, 1875], p. 70).

66. *Grape Culturist* 1 (1869): 45–47.

67. *Grape Culturist* 1 (1869): 45–47, 86–87, 172.

68. *Report of the Commissioner of Agriculture, 1867* (Washington, D.C., 1868), p. 388.

69. H. D. Hooker, "George Husmann," *Missouri Historical Review* 23 (1929): 357.

70. Husmann, *American Grape Growing and Wine Making*, p. v.

71. Alexis Millardet, "Traitement du mildiou et du rot," *Journal d'Agriculture Pratique* 2 (1885): 513–16, 707–10.

72. U.S. Department of Agriculture, Botanical Division, Circular no. 3 (April 1887); *First Report of the Secretary of Agriculture, 1889* (Washington, D.C., 1889), pp. 399–405.

73. Dr. J. R. McGrew, "A Review of the Origin of Hybrid Grape Varieties," American Wine Society Special Bulletin (Ithaca, N.Y., February 1971), p. 2.

74. *History of Franklin, Jefferson, Washington, Crawford and Gasconade Counties* (Chicago, 1888), p. 1112; Charles G. Van Ravenswaay, *The Arts and Architecture of German Settlements in Missouri* (Columbia, Mo., 1977), p. 256n.; Walter Williams, ed., *The State of Missouri* (Columbia, Mo., 1904), pp. 388–89.

75. *History of Franklin, Jefferson, Washington, Crawford and Gasconade Counties*, p. 1087.

76. *Report of the Commissioner of Agriculture, 1871* (Washington, D.C., 1872), p. 373.

77. George Ordish, *The Great Wine Blight* (London, 1972), pp. 41, 61.

78. Ibid., p. 30.

79. Hooker, "George Husmann," p. 357.

80. Husmann, *American Grape Growing and Wine Making*, p. vii.

81. Ordish, *Great Wine Blight*, pp. 114–15.

82. G. C. Husmann, "Resistant Vines," in International Congress of Viticulture, *Official Report* (San Francisco, 1915), p. 46.

83. Husmann, *American Grape Growing and Wine Making*, pp. 106–7; Hermann Jaeger, in Husmann, *American Grape Growing and Wine Making*, 4th ed., 1896, pp. 110–11; Bush and Son and

Meissner, *Illustrated Descriptive Catalogue of American Grape Vines,* 3d ed. (St. Louis, 1883), pp. 24–26; Ordish, *Great Wine Blight,* ch. 11.

84. Liberty Hyde Bailey, *The Standard Cyclopedia of Horticulture* (New York, 1914–17), 3: 1581.

85. Pierre Viala, *Une Mission viticole en Amérique* (Montpellier, 1889), p. 84.

86. R. E. Subden and A. C. Noble, "How the Hybrids Came to Canada," *Wines and Vines* 59 (December 1978): 42.

87. McMurtrie, *Report upon the Statistics of Grape Culture,* p. 76. Grapes grew on the university farm even before Husmann's arrival, and the undergraduates' raid on the wine made from them in 1871 and stored in a university building is the subject of one of the first published verses of Eugene Field, then a student at Mizzou.

88. Husmann was said to have been among the first to send native stocks to California (*American Wine Press and Mineral Water News,* 5 April 1897, p. 15). Husmann's son recalled that his father had sent 120,000 cuttings of native varieties to Simonton (George C. Husmann, "Viticulture of Napa County," in Tom Gregory et al., *History of Solano and Napa Counties* [Los Angeles, 1912], p. 148).

89. Husmann, *Grape Culture and Wine-Making,* p. 68.

90. *Report of the Commissioner of Agriculture, 1868* (Washington, D.C., 1869), pp. 519–20.

91. Ibid., p. 217.

92. Husmann, *American Grape Growing and Wine Making,* pp. 184–85.

93. Thomas Gregg, *History of Hancock County, Illinois* (Chicago, 1880), p. 960; Adams, *Wines of America,* p. 144.

94. Mildred B. McCormick, "A Land of Corn and Wine," *Springhouse Magazine* 2 (May–June 1985): 38–39.

95. *Grape Culturist* 1 (1869): 228, 300–302; 2 (1870): inside back cover; *Dictionary of American Biography* (for Hecker); Schneiter to Shorb, 16 March 1891 (Shorb Papers); *Past and Present of Rock Island County, Illinois* (Chicago, 1877), p. 374.

96. Adolph Blankenhorn, *Über den Weinbau der Vereinigten Staaten von Nordamerika . . . Briefwechsel zwischen Adolph Blankenhorn und Friedrich Hecker in den Jahren 1872–1880* (Darmstadt, 1883).

97. See the references to their work in Hedrick, *Grapes of New York.*

98. Kansas State Temperance Union, *Prohibition in Kansas: Facts, Not Opinions* (Topeka, 1890), p. 4.

99. "Les Canzes nous apportent du raisin en quantité, dont nous faisons du vin, que nous buvons tous les jours et que nous trouvons fort bien" ("Relation de voyage du Sieur de Bourgmont," in Pierre Margry, ed., *Découvertes et établissements des Français dans l'Amérique septentrionale, 1614–1754* [Paris, 1875–86], 6: 403).

100. Meriwether Lewis and William Clark, *Original Journals of the Lewis and Clark Expedition, 1804–1806,* ed. Reuben Gold Thwaites (New York, 1904–5), 1: 63 (1 July 1804).

101. Kate Stephens, *Life at Laurel Town* (Lawrence, Kans., 1920), p. 3.

102. T. J. Willard, *Log Cabin Days* ([Manhattan? Kans.], 1929), pp. 53–54.

103. A. M. Burns, "The Cultivation of the Grape," introductory essay to catalogue (Manhattan, Kans., 1866), pp. 1, 4 (Kansas State Historical Society).

104. Ibid., p. 4.

105. Alfred T. Andreas, *History of the State of Kansas* (Chicago, 1883), p. 476.

106. Kansas State Board of Agriculture, *Transactions, 1872* (Topeka, 1873), pp. 204–5; Douglas County Bicentennial Commission, *Douglas County Historic Building Survey—A Photo Sampler* (Lawrence, 1976), unpaginated. Vinland is named after the vineyard maintained there by the nurseryman W. E. Barnes from 1857 (Andreas, *History of the State of Kansas,* p. 356).

107. *Grape Culturist* 3 (June 1871): 143.

108. Kansas State Horticultural Society, *Transactions, 1871* (Topeka, 1872), pp. 26–27.

109. Ibid., pp. 72–75; Kansas State Horticultural Society, *Transactions, 1872* (Topeka, 1873), pp. 153–57.

110. Kansas State Board of Agriculture, *Transactions, 1873* (Topeka, 1874), pp. 150–52.

111. Kansas State Board of Agriculture, *Transactions, 1874* (Topeka, 1875), p. 235.

112. Kansas State College, Agricultural Experiment Station, Bulletin no. 14 (Topeka, 1891); no. 28 (Topeka, 1892); no. 44 (Manhattan, 1894).

113. Kansas State Board of Agriculture, *Transactions, 1872,* p. 27.

114. Kansas State Horticultural Society, *How to Grow and Use the Grape in Kansas,* compiled and revised by William H. Barnes ([Topeka], 1901).

115. Ibid., p. 123.

116. *Orange Judd Farmer,* 1 February 1896, p. 109.

117. *Report of the Commissioner of Agriculture, 1866* (Washington, D.C., 1867), pp. 115–18.

118. *San Francisco Merchant,* 21 December 1883, p. 164.

119. Emile Vallet, *An Icarian Communist in Nauvoo,* ed. H. Roger Grant (Springfield, Ill., 1971), p. 25.

120. Adams, *Wines of America,* p. 143.

121. Robert V. Hine, *California's Utopian Colonies* (New Haven, 1965), p. 71.

122. *Report of the Commissioner of Agriculture, 1871,* p. 231.

123. Hine, *California's Utopian Colonies,* p. 71.

124. Garrett R. Carpenter, "Silkville: A Kansas Attempt in the History of Fourierist Utopias, 1869–1892," *Emporia State Research Studies* 3 (1954): 13, 18, 24, 25.

125. Amana Society, "The Amana Colonies" ([Amana Colonies, Iowa], 1969), no pagination. The Prestele family, Joseph and his sons Gottlieb and William Henry, were artists in Amana specializing in horticultural illustration. William Henry became one of the official artists of the Department of Agriculture in Washington. His paintings of native American grape varieties made to illustrate a comprehensive report by T. V. Munson at the end of the century have never been published. They are still preserved in the Department of Agriculture and—who knows?—may yet one day be brought to the light of publication. They would make both a handsome and a historic work.

126. 11th Census, 1890, *Report on the Statistics of Agriculture in the United States* (Washington, D.C., 1895), p. 604.

15. The Southwest; the South; Other States

1. Leon Adams, *The Wines of America* (Boston, 1973), p. 150.

2. U. P. Hedrick, *The Grapes of New York* (Albany, N.Y., 1908), p. 229.

3. According to the list of varietal wines produced in the United States published annually in the September number of *Wines and Vines.*

4. Andrew Rolle, *The Immigrant Upraised* (Norman, Okla., 1968), p. 77.

5. Allessandro Mastro-Valerio, "Italians," in U.S. Industrial Commission, *Reports* (Washington, D.C., 1901), 15: 505.

6. Rolle, *Immigrant Upraised,* p. 79.

7. John L. Mathews, "Tontitown," *Everybody's* 20 (January 1909): 9; Mastro-Valerio, "Italians," pp. 505–6.

8. Mathews, "Tontitown," p. 9.

9. Leslie Hewes, "Tontitown: Ozark Vineyard Center," *Economic Geography* 29 (1953): 139–40.

10. Ibid., p. 140.

11. Mastro-Valerio, "Italians," p. 506; U.S. Immigration Commission, *Report* (Washington, D.C., 1911), 21: 380.

12. The standard discussions of the Sunnyside Italians do not name him; John Stewart says he was A. M. Piazza ("Little Italy of the Ozarks," *Missouri Life* 3 [July–August 1975]: 40).

13. Mastro-Valerio, "Italians," p. 506.

14. *Eastern Grape Grower and Winery News* 10 (August–September 1984): 34.

15. *Report of the Commissioner of Patents, 1859, Part II* (Washington, D.C., 1860), p. 35.

16. Terry G. Jordan, *German Seed in Texas Soil: Immigrant Farmers in Nineteenth-Century Texas* (Austin, 1966), p. 43.

17. Julia Nott Waugh, *Castro-Ville and Henry Castro, Empresario* (San Antonio, 1934), pp. 21, 25, 38–39.

18. Jordan, *German Seed,* p. 48.

19. One of these hopeful Germans was Julius Dresel, a native of the great Rheingau wine town of Geisenheim, who planted Riesling vines on the Guadalupe River in southeast Texas in 1850. Twenty years later he migrated to California to take over the pioneer vineyard in Sonoma that his brother Emil had founded with Jacob Gundlach (*Illustrated History of Sonoma County* [Chicago, 1889], p. 506).

20. Jordan, *German Seed,* p. 78.

21. *Report of the Commissioner of Patents, 1847* (Washington, D.C., 1848), p. 199.

22. Liberty Hyde Bailey, "The Species of Grapes Peculiar to North America," *Gentes Herbarum* 3 (1934): 213.

23. See, e.g., the reports of Gilbert Onderdonk in George Husmann, *American Grape Growing and Wine Making* (New York, 1880), pp. 145–52; and *Report of the Commissioner of Agriculture, 1887* (Washington, D.C., 1888), p. 652.

24. Husmann, *American Grape Growing and Wine Making,* 4th ed. (New York, 1896), p. 123; Guido Rossati, *Relazione di un viaggio d'istruzione negli Stati Uniti d'America* (Rome, 1900), p. 348; Mastro-Valerio, "Italians," p. 500; Virginia H. Taylor, *The Franco-Texan Land Company* (Austin, 1969), p. 291.

25. On the Val Verde Winery, see *American Wine Society Journal* 13 (Summer 1981): 52.

26. *Report of the Commissioner of Agriculture, 1887,* p. 652.

27. See Frank Giordano, *Texas Wines and Wineries* (Austin, 1984), pp. 123–32; *Wines and Vines* 66 (September 1985): 24–34.

28. Pierre Viala, *Une Mission viticole en Amérique* (Montpellier, 1889), p. 206.

29. A sketch of Munson's life is in the *Dictionary of American Biography.*

30. Quoted in *T. V. Munson Memorial Vineyard Report* 2 (April 1982): [2].

31. Munson's major publication is *Foundations of American Grape Culture* (Denison, Tex., 1909). This contains a summary of his work, pp. 5–11.

32. Ibid.

33. LeRoy H. Fischer, "The Fairchild Winery," *Chronicles of Oklahoma* 55 (Summer 1977): 135–56.

34. Munson's pronouncement was on the occasion of a grape exhibit held in 1899 by the Territorial Horticultural Association, Oklahoma City (*American Wine Press,* September 1899, p. 22).

35. Fischer, "Fairchild Winery," p. 155.

36. Carolyn Baker Lewis, "Cultural Conservatism and Pioneer Florida Viticulture," *Agricultural History* 53 (July 1979): 627, 630–31.

37. Ibid., p. 631; Rossati, *Relazione,* p. 363.

38. Lewis, "Cultural Conservatism and Pioneer Florida Viticulture," p. 632.

39. Mastro-Valerio, "Italians," pp. 504–5; U.S. Immigration Commission, *Report,* 21: 301, 303.

40. Alabama Fruit Growing and Winery Association, undated company brochure, California State University Library, Fresno; Rossati, *Relazione,* p. 362; *Birmingham News,* 10 November 1965.

41. *American Wine Press* 3 (15 March 1898): 12; promotional map of Vinemont for Alabama Vineyard and Winery Company, undated (California State University Library, Fresno).

42. *DeBow's Review,* n.s., 2 (1866): 269, reported 300–500 acres of vineyard around Aiken.

43. *First Report of the Secretary of Agriculture, 1889* (Washington, D.C., 1889), p. 401.

44. *San Francisco Merchant,* 18 March 1887.

45. *First Report of the Secretary of Agriculture, 1889,* pp. 401–3.

46. *San Francisco Merchant,* 17 July 1885, pp. 97–98; Hermann Schuricht, *History of the German Element in Virginia* (Baltimore), 2 (1900): 132–33.

47. C. C. Pearson and J. E. Hendricks, *Liquor and Anti-Liquor in Virginia, 1619–1919* (Durham, N.C., 1967), p. 179n.; John Hammond Moore, *Albemarle, Jefferson's County, 1727–1976* (Charlottesville, 1976), p. 250.

48. *San Francisco Merchant,* 17 July 1885; Schuricht, *History of the German Element in Virginia,* 2: 133.

49. S. W. Fletcher, "A History of Fruit Growing in Virginia," *Proceedings of the 37th Annual Meeting of the Virginia Horticultural Society* (Staunton, Va., 1932), pp. 4–6.

50. Moore, *Albemarle,* p. 250.

51. 11th Census, 1890, *Report on the Statistics of Agriculture in the United States* (Washington, D.C., 1895), p. 602; 12th Census, 1900, *Census Reports,* 9 (1902): 634.

52. 13th Census, 1910, *Agriculture 1909 and 1910* (Washington, D.C., 1913), p. 717.

53. According to a note by J.-E. Planchon in the French edition of the Bush & Son & Meissner catalogue, 1876.

54. *San Francisco Merchant,* 8 February 1884.

55. Jules-Emile Planchon, *Les Vignes américaines* (Montpellier, 1875), p. 40n.

56. Clarence Gohdes, *Scuppernong: North Carolina's Grape and Its Wines* (Durham, N.C., 1982), p. 39.

57. Ibid., p. 42; Adams, *Wines of America,* p. 44.

58. Gohdes, *Scuppernong,* pp. 43, 48.

59. Ibid., p. 51.

60. Ibid., p. 49.

61. Ibid., pp. 57–58.

62. Adams, *Wines of America,* p. 45.

63. Gohdes, *Scuppernong,* p. 29.

64. Ibid., p. 32; *American Wine Press,* 5 June 1897.

65. Gohdes, *Scuppernong,* pp. 32–33.

66. North Carolina State Horticultural Society, *Report* (Raleigh, N.C., 1893), p. 16.

67. A few growers from Colorado responded to the Department of Agriculture's survey of national winegrowing in 1880; one gave his opinion that "the foot-hills of the Rocky Mountains are specially adapted to vineyards." In the same survey it was reported that some of the Russian Hutterites in Bon Homme County, Dakota (then still a territory, and undivided) had succeeded in growing grapes (William McMurtrie, *Report upon the Statistics of Grape Culture and Wine Production in the United States for 1880* [Washington, D.C., 1881], p. 48). In the *Directory of the Grape Growers, Wine Makers and Distillers of California* published by the California Board of State Viticultural Commissioners in 1891, a total of two and a half acres were reported for Colorado and Dakota. Montana and Wyoming did not become states until 1889 and 1890 respectively, and neither figures in any of the published reports or surveys after the dates of their statehood. There is now a winery operating in Montana, but it has, I think, no predecessor.

68. The Vergennes grape originated in 1874, the Green Mountain before 1885.

69. See, e.g., Husmann, *American Grape Growing and Wine Making,* 4th ed., pp. 117–18; Rossati, *Relazione,* p. 359.

70. The English traveller Adlard Welby found vineyards at Wheeling, West Virginia, in 1819 (Reuben Gold Thwaites, ed., *Early Western Travels, 1748–1846* [Cleveland, 1904–7], 12: 204). The Friend Winery at Dunbar, West Virginia, was established in the 1850s (*Eastern Grape Grower and Winery News* 8 [1982]: 10).

71. Minnesota Grape Growers Association, *Growing Grapes in Minnesota* (n.p., 1978), p. 1.

72. Hedrick, *Grapes of New York,* pp. 438–39.

73. *Minneapolis Tribune,* 10 September 1978.

74. Adams, *Wines of America,* pp. 348–49; a report by A. B. Ballantyne, "Grape Growing in Utah," appears in the *Official Report* of the International Congress of Viticulture (San Francisco, 1915), pp. 102–6.

75. Reed W. Farnsworth, *The Power of Adversity* (n.p., n.d.), pp. 133–42.

76. Scofield to Shorb, 7 April 1888; H. R. Patrick to Shorb, 6 August 1890 (Shorb Papers, Huntington Library). 11th Census, 1890, *Report on the Statistics of Agriculture,* p. 602.

77. J. R. Cardwell, "The First Fruits of the Land: A Brief History of Early Horticulture in Oregon," *Quarterly of the Oregon Historical Society* 7 (1906): 29.

78. Ibid., p. 34; E. R. Lake, "The Grape in Oregon," Oregon Agricultural Experiment Station Bulletin no. 66 (Corvallis, June 1901), p. 63.

79. *Transactions of the California State Agricultural Society, 1859* (Sacramento, 1860), pp. 180, 270.

80. Cardwell, "First Fruits of the Land," p. 31.

81. *Grape Culturist* 2 (March 1870): 75; Premium list in Catalogue of Oregon State Fair, 1876, 1877.

82. Elizabeth Purser and Lawrence J. Allen, *The Winemakers of the Pacific Northwest* (Vashon Island, Wash., 1977), p. 154.

83. By Richard Sommer, at Hillcrest Vineyard, near Roseburg (Adams, *Wines of America,* p. 341).

84. Lake, "The Grape in Oregon," p. 71.

85. His name was David Hill (Tom Stockley, *Winery Trails of the Pacific Northwest* [Mercer Island, Wash., 1977], p. 5).

86. C. I. Lewis, "The Grape in Oregon," in International Congress of Viticulture, *Official Report,* pp. 91–97.

87. *Grape Culturist* 2 (October 1869): 297; *Northwest Wine Almanac,* November 1985, p. 1.

88. Purser and Allen, *Winemakers of the Pacific Northwest,* p. 66.

89. E. H. Twight, "The Vineyards of the Columbia River Basin," in International Congress of Viticulture, *Official Report,* pp. 89–91.

90. Ibid., p. 90. Robert N. Wing, "Lewiston, Idaho, and Clarkston, Washington: Home of

Northwest's First Wineries?" *Wine Almanac of the Pacific Northwest,* 16 November 1987, pp. 1–2. Robert Schleicher published "Grape Culture in Lewiston-Clarkston Valley" (Lewiston, Idaho, and Clarkston, Wash., 1906).

16. The End of the Beginning: National Prohibition

1. In fact, nearer fifteen years, if one counts the period of "wartime" prohibition in 1919; but that was largely a distraction from the main event. In this chapter, I use "prohibition" for general reference, but "Prohibition" for the period of constitutional prohibition in the United States.

2. The term of all work used by the Drys in their propaganda for any alcoholic drink whatever. It helped inspire this definition by Ambrose Bierce in *The Devil's Dictionary* (1906): "*WINE; n.,* Fermented grape juice known to the Womens' Christian Union as 'liquor', sometimes as 'rum'. Wine, madam, is God's next best gift to man."

3. See the poem excitedly anticipating the production of wine in Georgia written by John Wesley's brother Samuel, quoted on pp. 45–46, above.

4. Herbert Asbury, *The Great Illusion: An Informal History of Prohibition* (Garden City, N.Y., 1950), p. 15.

5. John Kobler, *Ardent Spirits: The Rise and Fall of Prohibition* (New York, 1973), pp. 41–42.

6. In the South, the fear of the combination of alcohol and blacks powerfully aided prohibition (Clarence Gohdes, *Scuppernong: North Carolina's Grape and Its Wines* [Durham, N.C., 1982], p. 52).

7. Kobler, *Ardent Spirits,* pp. 50–51.

8. John Allen Krout, *The Origins of Prohibition* (New York, 1925), p. 90.

9. Ibid., p. 263.

10. Quoted in Alice Felt Tyler, *Freedom's Ferment; Phases of American Social History to 1860* (Minneapolis, 1944), p. 323.

11. Asbury, *Great Illusion,* pp. 12–13.

12. Tyler, *Freedom's Ferment,* p. 372.

13. *Wines and Vines* 67 (July 1986): 22.

14. W. J. Rorabaugh, *The Alcoholic Republic* (New York, 1979), pp. 107–10.

15. Gallus Thomann, *Liquor Laws of the United States* (New York, 1885), pp. 113, 136, 141, 196.

16. Kobler, *Ardent Spirits,* pp. 60, 62.

17. Ibid., pp. 70–73.

18. Virginius Dabney, *Dry Messiah: The Life of Bishop Cannon* (New York, 1949), p. 6.

19. Mark Twain, *Huckleberry Finn* (1884), ch. 5.

20. The word is of disputed etymology, though it is usually attributed to an English workingman named Dicky Turner in 1833; some explanations hold that Turner was a stammerer; others, that the initial "tee" is an intensifier. Yet another holds that it came from putting a *T* before the names of total abstainers on the membership list of a New York temperance society (Ernest H. Cherrington, *The Evolution of Prohibition in the United States of America* [Westerville, Ohio, 1920], p. 83). All seem to agree that "tee" has nothing whatever to do with tea-drinking, though that is an easy and obvious confusion to make (Brian Harrison, *Drink and the Victorians* [London, 1971], pp. 125, 126).

21. Kobler, *Ardent Spirits,* pp. 56–57.

22. Ibid., pp. 84–85.

23. Of the principle of the Maine Law, John Stuart Mill wrote that "there is no violation of liberty which it would not justify" (*On Liberty* [1859], ch. 4).

24. Asbury, *Great Illusion,* p. 60.

25. Kobler, *Ardent Spirits,* p. 356.

26. Ibid., p. 90.

27. Thomann, *Liquor Laws,* p. 211.

28. Alcohol had been untaxed till then except just after the Revolution (when the tax provoked the so-called "Whiskey Rebellion") and, briefly, during and after the War of 1812.

29. Gilman M. Ostrander, *The Prohibition Movement in California, 1848–1933* (Berkeley, 1957), pp. 71–72. I may add that my own grandmother, early in this century, organized a chapter of the Woman's Christian Temperance Union in Anaheim, where once the innocent Germans had made wine without thought of giving offense to any Christian.

30. Ibid., p. 132.

31. Dabney, *Dry Messiah,* pp. 98–99, 102.

32. Kobler, *Ardent Spirits,* p. 157.

33. Dabney, *Dry Messiah,* p. 57.

34. Asbury, *Great Illusion,* pp. 100–101.

35. Ibid., p. 122.

36. Kobler, *Ardent Spirits,* p. 197.

37. Asbury, *Great Illusion,* p. 128.

38. Ibid., p. 136.

39. The National Prohibition Act may be found in *United States Statutes at Large,* 66th Cong., 41 (1919–21): part 1, 305–23; Hoover's phrase is in his speech accepting the presidential nomination in 1928: see Hoover's *Memoirs, 1920–1933* (New York, 1952), p. 201.

40. Thomann, *Liquor Laws,* p. 161.

41. The California Grape Protective Association, formed by Andrea Sbarboro of Italian Swiss Colony and others to fight the prohibition movement, was not organized until 1908 (John R. Meers, "The California Wine and Grape Industry and Prohibition," *California Historical Society Quarterly* 46 [1967]: 21).

42. *United States Statutes at Large,* 41: part 1, 307–23.

43. In the first year there were only 1,512 Prohibition agents for the entire country, and at no time were there more than 3,000 (Kobler, *Ardent Spirits,* p. 270).

44. Ernest H. Cherrington, ed., *Standard Encyclopedia of the Alcohol Problem* (Westerville, Ohio), 6 (1930): 2877.

45. The wine produced in California and stored under the Prohibition agency's bond rose from 17,000,000 gallons in 1920 to 40,000,000 gallons in 1924. Many arrests for illegal sales of wine from this source seem to have been made: see Kenneth D. Rose, "San Francisco and Prohibition in 1924: Wettest in the West," *California History* 65 (1986): 289.

46. Leon Adams, *The Wines of America,* 3d ed. (New York, 1985), p. 25.

47. Ostrander, *Prohibition Movement in California,* p. 179.

48. Ruth Teiser and Catherine Harroun, *Winemaking in California* (New York, 1983), p. 182; Ostrander, *Prohibition Movement in California,* p. 180.

49. Dabney, *Dry Messiah,* p. 304.

50. Adams, *Wines of America, 1st ed.,* p. 27.

51. Alice Tisdale Hobart, *The Cup and the Sword* (Indianapolis, 1942), p. 60.

52. Ruth Teiser and Catherine Harroun, "The Volstead Act, Rebirth, and Boom," in Doris Muscatine, Maynard A. Amerine, and Bob Thompson, eds., *The University of California/Sotheby Book of California Wine* (Berkeley, 1984), p. 57; Ostrander, *Prohibition Movement in California,* p. 181.

53. Philip Wagner, *American Wines and Wine-Making* (New York, 1956), pp. 51–52.

54. Frank Schoonmaker, *Encyclopedia of Wine* (New York, 1964), pp. 358–67.

55. The Concord grape, useless for good winemaking, already dominated in eastern vineyards before Prohibition; but Prohibition greatly confirmed and extended that dominance.

56. *New York Times,* 28 April 1929, sec. 3.

57. The guess of the Wickersham Commission, appointed to inquire into the enforcement of the Prohibition laws, was that home production of wine averaged 111,000,000 gallons annually from 1922 through 1929 (*National Commission on Law Observance and Enforcement* [Washington, D.C., 1931], 1: 128).

58. Thomann, *Liquor Laws,* pp. 187–88.

59. Adams, *Wines of America, 1st ed.,* pp. 30–31.

60. To take one from a vast number of descriptions, here is a passage from D. H. Lawrence's novel, *St. Mawr* (1925); the characters are Americans: "Lou and her mother lunched at the Hotel d'Angleterre [in Havana], and Mrs. Witt watched transfixed while a couple of her countrymen, a stout successful man and his wife, lunched abroad. They had cocktails—then lobster—and a bottle of hock—then a bottle of champagne—then a half-bottle of port—And Mrs. Witt rose in haste as the liqueurs came. For that successful man and his wife had gone on imbibing with a sort of fixed and deliberate will, apparently tasting nothing, but saying to themselves: Now we're drinking Rhine wine! Now we're drinking 1912 Champagne. Yah, Prohibition! Thou canst not put it over me."

Appendix 1. Fox Grapes and Foxiness

1. John Bonoeil, *His Maiesties Gracious Letter to the Earle of South-Hampton . . . commanding the present setting up of Silke works, and planting of Vines in Virginia* (London, 1622), p. 49.

2. These citations may all be found in Mitford Mathews, *A Dictionary of Americanisms* (Chicago, 1951), and Sir William Craigie and James R. Hulbert, eds., *A Dictionary of American English* (Chicago, 1938).

3. Albert C. Myers, ed., *Narratives of Early Pennsylvania, West New Jersey, and Delaware* (New York, 1912), p. 227.

4. This theory is mentioned, only to be dismissed, in Richard R. Nelson, "From Whence Came the Fox?" *Pennsylvania Grape Letter* 5 (October 1977): 3.

5. Liberty Hyde Bailey, *Sketch of the Evolution of Our Native Fruits* (New York, 1898), p. 6.

6. *American Farmer* 10 (20 February 1829): 388.

7. Bailey, *Evolution of Our Native Fruits,* p. 5.

8. Cited in Liberty Hyde Bailey, "The Species of Grapes Peculiar to North America," *Gentes Herbarum* 3 (1934): 187.

9. *Vintage Magazine* 2 (April 1973): 41.

10. William Bartram says that "many have imagined" the name to have arisen because such grapes were "the favourite food of the animal" (Bartram, in James Mease, ed., *Domestic Encyclopaedia* [Philadelphia, 1803–4], 5: 290). Bartram dismisses the idea.

11. U.S. Tariff Commission, *Grapes, Raisins, and Wines,* Report no. 134, 2d ser. (Washington, D.C. [1939]), p. 22.

12. Clarence Gohdes, *Scuppernong: North Carolina's Grape and Its Wines* (Durham, N.C., 1982), p. 25.

13. Myers, ed., *Narratives of Early Pennsylvania,* p. 227.

14. For example, Jules-Emile Planchon, *Les Vignes américaines* (Montpellier, 1875), p. 131.

15. *Revue des Deux Mondes,* 15 February 1874, p. 914.

16. Frank Thorpy, *Wine in New Zealand* (Auckland, 1971), p. 57.

17. Michael Allen, *The Long Holiday* (London, 1974), p. 22.

18. New York State Agricultural Experiment Station, *1972 Wine Meeting for Amateurs,* Special Report no. 12 (Geneva, N.Y., 1973), p. 10.

Appendix 2. The Language of Wine in English

1. See Eero Alanne, "Observations on the Development and Structure of English Wine-Growing Terminology," *Mémoires de la société néophilologique de Helsinki* 20 (1957): 30.

2. Jefferson Peyser, in *Wines and Vines* 64 (March 1983): 24. Leon Adams says that he introduced the term into the language of post-Repeal California winemaking ("Revitalizing the California Wine Industry," California Wine Industry Oral History Project, Regional Oral History Project [Bancroft Library, University of California, Berkeley, 1974]). Both Peyser and Adams were active in the effort to get a California wine marketing order after Repeal.

3. *American Wine Society Journal* 17 (Winter 1985): 107.

Works Cited

Manuscripts

American Philosophical Society Library, Philadelphia
        Benjamin Franklin Papers
        John Leacock, MS commonplace book
        Peter Legaux, Journals
        Rafinesque Papers
Bancroft Library, University of California, Berkeley
        California Board of State Viticultural Commissioners, Minutes of Executive Committee;
            Minutes of Meetings
        Bancroft dictations: Charles Kohler; Isaac De Turk
        Arpad Haraszthy, "The Haraszthy Family"
        Hayes Scrapbooks
        Charles Kohler, "Wine Production"
Harvard University
        Friedrich Muench, "Vine Culture in Missouri"
Historical Society of Pennsylvania
        Edward Antill to Dr. Sonmans, 31 January 1768
Huntington Library
        Robert Bolling, "Pieces Concerning Vineyards"
        Matthew Keller Papers
        J. De Barth Shorb Papers
        Benjamin D. Wilson Papers
Library of Congress
        Thomas Jefferson Papers
        George Morgan Papers
National Agricultural Library
        Prince Family Papers
Royal Society of Arts, London
        Guard Book; Journal Book; Minutes on Colonies and Trade; MS Transactions

Newspapers and Specialized Periodicals

Agricultural History
Alta California
The American Agriculturist
The American Farmer
The American Wine Press and Mineral Water Review
The American Wine Society Journal
California Farmer
California Wine Review
Cozzens' Wine Press

The Cultivator
DeBow's Review
Farmers' Register
Gardener's Monthly
The Grape Culturist
Horticultural Review
The Horticulturist
New England Farmer
Niles' Weekly Register
The Orange Judd Farmer
Pacific Wine and Spirit Review
Rural Californian
San Francisco Merchant (afterwards *Pacific Wine and Spirit Review*)
Southern California Horticulturist
Southern Cultivator
Southern Planter
T. V. Munson Memorial Vineyard Report
Vineyard and Winery Management (formerly *Eastern Grape Grower and Winery News*)
Vineyard View
Vinifera Wine Growers Journal
Western Horticultural Review
Wine Almanac of the Pacific Northwest
Wine East
Wines and Vines

Other Printed Works

Acrelius, Israel. *History of New Sweden.* Memoirs of the Historical Society of Pennsylvania, vol. 11. Philadelphia, 1874.

Adams, John. *Diary and Autobiography of John Adams.* Ed. Lyman Butterfield. 4 vols. Cambridge, Mass.: Harvard University Press, 1961.

Adams, Leon. "Historical Note." In *Grapes and Wines of California.* New York: Harcourt, Brace, & World, 1981.

———. *The Wines of America.* Boston: Houghton Mifflin, 1973.

———. *The Wines of America.* 3d ed. New York: McGraw-Hill, 1985.

Adlum, John. "Adlum on Making Wine." Georgetown, D.C.: J. C. Dunn, 1826.

———. *A Memoir on the Cultivation of the Vine in America, and the Best Mode of Making Wine.* Washington, D.C.: Davis & Force, 1823.

———. *A Memoir on the Cultivation of the Vine.* 2d ed. Washington, D.C.: Printed for the Author, 1828.

Alabama Fruit Growing and Winery Association. Undated company brochure. Copy in the library of California State University, Fresno.

Aldrich, Lewis Cass. *History of Yates County, N.Y.* Syracuse, N.Y.: D. Mason, 1892.

Amana Society. "The Amana Colonies." [Amana Colonies, Iowa], 1969.

American Institute. *Annual Report of the American Institute, 1862–63.* Albany, N.Y.: 1863.

Amerine, Maynard. "Hilgard and California Viticulture." *Hilgardia* 33 (July 1962): 1–23.

Amerine, Maynard, and W. V. Cruess. *The Technology of Wine Making.* Westport, Conn.: Avi Publishing, 1960.

Amerine, Maynard, and B. St. Pierre. "Grapes and Wine in the United States." In Edward L. and Frederick H. Schapsmeier, eds., *Agriculture in the West.* Manhattan, Kans.: Sunflower University Press, 1980.

Andreas, Alfred T. *History of the State of Kansas.* 2 vols. Chicago: A. T. Andreas, 1883.

Anthony, R. D. "Vinifera Grapes in New York." New York Agricultural Experiment Station Bulletin no. 432. Geneva, N.Y., 1917.

Antill, Edward. "An Essay on the Cultivation of the Vine, and the Making and Preserving of Wine, Suited to the Different Climates of North-America." *Transactions of the American Philosophical Society* 1 (2d ed., Philadelphia, 1789): 180–262.

Archibald, Robert. *The Economic Aspects of the California Missions.* Washington, D.C.: Academy of American Franciscan History, 1978.

Arndt, Karl J. R., ed. *A Documentary History of the Indiana Decade of the Harmony Society, 1814–1824.* 2 vols. Indianapolis: Indiana Historical Society, 1975–78.

———. *Economy on the Ohio, 1826–34.* Worcester, Mass.: Harmony Society Press, 1982.

———. *George Rapp's Harmony Society, 1785–1847.* Philadelphia: University of Pennsylvania Press, 1965.

———. *Harmony on the Connoquenessing, 1803–1815.* Worcester, Mass.: Harmony Society Press, 1980.

———. *Harmony on the Wabash in Transition, 1824–1826.* Worcester, Mass.: Harmony Society Press, 1982.

Asbury, Herbert. *The Great Illusion: An Informal History of Prohibition.* Garden City, N.Y.: Doubleday, 1950.

Ashe, Thomas. "Carolina, or a Description of the Present State of that Country" (1682). In Alexander Salley, ed., *Narratives of Early Carolina, 1650–1708.* New York: Charles Scribner's Sons, 1911.

Bailey, Liberty Hyde. *Sketch of the Evolution of Our Native Fruits.* New York: Macmillan, 1898.

———. "The Species of Grapes Peculiar to North America." *Gentes Herbarum* 3 (1934): 149–244.

———. *The Standard Cyclopedia of Horticulture.* 6 vols. New York: Macmillan, 1914–17.

Baird, Charles W. *History of the Huguenot Emigration to America.* 2 vols. New York: Dodd, Mead [1885].

Bancroft, Hubert Howe. *California Pastoral, 1769–1848.* San Francisco: History Company, 1888.

———. *History of California.* 7 vols. San Francisco: History Company, 1884–90.

Barbour, Philip L., ed. *The Jamestown Voyages under the First Charter, 1606–1609.* 2 vols. Cambridge: Cambridge University Press, 1969.

Barlow, Bob Stuart. "Historical and Regional Analysis of the Italian Role in California Viticulture and Enology." M.A. thesis, University of California, Los Angeles, 1964.

Bartram, William. *Travels.* Ed. Francis Harper. New Haven: Yale University Press, 1958.

Bartram's Gardens. *Catalogue.* Philadelphia, 1807.

Becker, Johann. *Der Weinbau.* Evansville, Ind., 1860.

Bek, William G. "Gottfried Duden's 'Report,' 1824–1827." *Missouri Historical Review* 12 (October 1917): 1–21.

———. *The German Settlement Society of Philadelphia and Its Colony Hermann, Missouri.* Philadelphia: Americana Germania Press, 1907.

Bell, Alexander D. *Fresno, California.* San Francisco: Merchant Publishing, 1884.

Betts, Edwin Morris, ed. *Thomas Jefferson's Garden Book, 1766–1824.* Philadelphia: American Philosophical Society, 1944.

Beverley, Robert. *The History and Present State of Virginia.* 1705. Ed. Louis B. Wright. Chapel Hill: University of North Carolina Press, 1947.

———. *History of Virginia.* 1722. Reprint. Richmond, Va.: J. W. Randolph, 1855.

Billings, Warren M., ed. *The Old Dominion in the Seventeenth Century.* Chapel Hill: University of North Carolina Press, 1975.

Bishop, John L. *History of American Manufactures.* 2 vols. Philadelphia: E. Young, 1861–64.

Black, Esther Boulton. *Rancho Cucamonga and Doña Merced.* Redlands, Calif.: San Bernardino County Museum Association, 1975.

Bolton, Herbert Eugene. *Fray Juan Crespi.* Berkeley: University of California Press, 1927.

Bolzius, Johann Martin. "Bolzius Answers a Questionnaire." *William and Mary Quarterly,* 3d ser., 14 (1957): 218–61.

Bonner, James C. "The Georgia Wine Industry on the Eve of the Civil War." *Georgia Historical Quarterly* 41 (1957): 19–30.

Bonoeil, John. *His Maiesties Gracious Letter to the Earle of South-Hampton, Treasurer and to the Councell and Company of Virginia heere; commanding the present setting up of Silke works, and planting of Vines in Virginia.* London: Felix Kyngston, 1622.

Bourgmont, Sieur de. "Relation de voyage du Sieur de Bourgmont." In Pierre Margry, ed., *Découvertes et établissements des Français dans l'Amérique septentrionale, 1614–1754.* 6 vols. Paris: D. Jouaust, 1875–86.

Bowman, Jacob. "The Vineyards in Provincial California." *Wine Review* 11 (April–July 1943).

Brace, Charles Loring. *The New West: or, California in 1867–1868.* New York: G. P. Putnam & Son, 1869.

Brevard, Caroline Mays. "Richard Keith Call." *Florida Historical Society Quarterly* 1 (July 1908): 10–11.

Brissot de Warville, Jacques Pierre. *New Travels in the United States of America.* 1791. Ed. Durand Echeverria. Cambridge, Mass.: Harvard University Press, 1964.

———. "Thoughts on the Cultivation of Vines—and on the Wine Trade between France and America." *American Museum* 3 (December 1788): 568–71.

Brown, Alexander. *The First Republic in America.* Boston: Houghton Mifflin, 1898.

———. *The Genesis of the United States.* 2 vols. Boston: Houghton Mifflin, 1890.

Bryant, Edwin. *What I Saw in California.* 1849. Reprint. Palo Alto, Calif.: L. Osborne, 1967.

Buchanan, Robert. *The Culture of the Grape, and Wine-Making.* Cincinnati: Moore & Anderson, 1852.

———. *The Culture of the Grape.* 5th ed. Cincinnati: Moore, Wilstash, Keys, 1855.

———. *A Treatise on Grape Culture in Vineyards, in the Vicinity of Cincinnati.* Cincinnati: Wright, Ferris, 1850.

Bullock, William. *Virginia Impartially Examined.* London: J. Hammond, 1649.

Burnaby, Andrew. *Travels through the Middle Settlements in North America.* 3d ed. London: T. Payne, 1798.

Burns, A. M. Catalogue. Manhattan, Kans., 1866.

Burtscher, W. J. "Ephraim Bull and the Concord Grape." *American Fruit Grower* 65 (1945): 12, 24, 26, 28–29, 35.

Bush, Isidore, and Son. *Illustrated Descriptive Catalogue of Grape Vines, Small Fruit, and Potatoes.* St. Louis, 1869.

Bush & Son & Meissner. *Illustrated Descriptive Catalogue of American Grape Vines.* 3d ed. St. Louis, 1883.

Bynum, Lindley. "San Gabriel." In Joseph Henry Jackson, ed., *The Vine in Early California.* [San Francisco]: Book Club of California, 1955.

Byrd, William. *Correspondence of the Three William Byrds of Westover, Virginia, 1664–1776.* Ed. Marion Tinling. 2 vols. Charlottesville: University Press of Virginia, 1977.

Cahoon, Garth A. "The Ohio Wine Industry from 1860 to the Present." *American Wine Society Journal* 16 (Fall 1984): 82–86, 94.

Caire, Helen. "A Brief History of Santa Cruz Island from 1869 to 1937." *Ventura County Historical Society Quarterly* 27 (Summer 1982): 3–33.

California. Board of State Viticultural Commissioners. *Annual Reports.* Sacramento: State Office, 1881–94.

———. Board of State Viticultural Commissioners. *Annual Reports of the Chief Executive Viticultural Officer.* Sacramento: State Office, 1882–84.

———. Board of State Viticultural Commissioners. *Directory of the Grape Growers, Wine Makers and Distillers of California.* Sacramento: State Office, 1891.

———. Board of State Viticultural Commissioners. *Report of the Sixth Annual State Viticultural Convention.* [San Francisco], 1888.

———. Legislature. *Journals of the Senate and Assembly.* Sacramento: State Printer, 1862, 1880.

———. Legislature. *Statutes of California.* 10th sess. Sacramento: State Printer, 1859.

———. State Agricultural Society. *Transactions.* Sacramento: State Printer, 1859–80.

———. State Board of Agriculture. *Report of the California State Board of Agriculture, 1911.* Sacramento: Superintendent of State Printing, 1912.

———. University of California. College of Agriculture. *Report of the Viticultural Work during the Seasons 1885 and 1886.* Sacramento: J. J. Ayres, Superintendent of State Printing, 1886.

———. University of California. College of Agriculture. *Report of the Viticultural Work during the Seasons 1887–89.* Sacramento: J. J. Ayres, Superintendent of State Printing, 1892.

———. University of California. College of Agriculture. *Report of the Viticultural Work during the Seasons 1887–93.* Sacramento: A. J. Johnston, Superintendent of State Printing, 1896.

———. University of California. College of Agriculture. *Reports of Experiments on Methods of Fermentation and Related Subjects during the Years 1884–87.* Sacramento: J. D. Young, Superintendent of State Printing, 1888.

California Wine Association. *California Wine Association.* [San Francisco? c. 1910].

California Wine Growers' and Wine and Brandy Manufacturers' Association. *Transactions, 1872.* In

California State Agricultural Society, *Transactions, 1872*. Sacramento: T. A. Springer, State Printer, 1873.

Calvert Papers, Number One. Maryland Historical Society Publications, no. 28. Baltimore, 1889.

Campbell, George W. "The Grape and Its Improvement by Hybridizing, Cross-Breeding, and Seedlings." In *Report of the Commissioner of Agriculture, 1862*. Washington, D.C.: GPO, 1863.

Cardwell, J. R. "The First Fruits of the Land: A Brief History of Early Horticulture in Oregon." *Quarterly of the Oregon Historical Society* 7 (1906): 28–51, 151–61.

Carosso, Vincent P. *The California Wine Industry, 1830–1895*. Berkeley: University of California Press, 1951.

Carpenter, Garrett R. "Silkville: A Kansas Attempt in the History of Fourierist Utopias, 1869–1892." *Emporia State Research Studies* 3 (1954): 3–29.

Carr, John F. *Anaheim: Its People and Its Products*. [New York: John F. Carr & Co., 1869].

Carrier, Lyman. *Agriculture in Virginia, 1607–1699*. Williamsburg, Va.: Virginia 350th Anniversary Celebration Corporation, 1957.

Carroll, B. R., ed. *Historical Collections of South Carolina*. 2 vols. New York: Harper & Brothers, 1836.

Carter, Landon. *The Diary of Colonel Landon Carter of Sabine Hall, 1752–1778*. Ed. Jack P. Greene. 2 vols. Charlottesville: University Press of Virginia, 1965.

Cathey, C. O. *Agricultural Developments in North Carolina, 1783–1860*. Chapel Hill: University of North Carolina Press, 1956.

———. "Sidney Weller: Ante-Bellum Promoter of Agricultural Reform." *North Carolina Historical Review* 30 (January 1954): 1–17.

Caughey, John Walton. *California*. New York: Prentice-Hall, 1940.

———. "Don Benito Wilson: An Average Southern Californian." *Huntington Library Quarterly* 2 (April 1939): 285–300.

Chambers, Raymond. "The Chautauqua Grape Industry." *New York History* 16 (July 1935): 248–65.

Chan, Sucheng. *This Bittersweet Soil: The Chinese in California Agriculture, 1860–1910*. Berkeley: University of California Press, 1986.

Chautauqua Grape and Wine Association. "Chautauqua Fruits, Grapes, and Grape Products." [Dunkirk? N.Y.] 1901.

Chazanof, William. *Welch's Grape Juice*. Syracuse, N.Y.: Syracuse University Press, 1977.

Cherrington, Ernest H. *The Evolution of Prohibition in the United States of America*. Westerville, Ohio: American Issue Press, 1920.

———, ed. *Standard Encyclopedia of the Alcohol Problem*. 6 vols. Westerville, Ohio: American Issue Publishing, 1924–30.

Childs, St. Julien. "The Petit-Guérard Colony." *South Carolina Historical and Genealogical Magazine* 43 (1942): 1–17.

———. *Malaria and Colonization in the Carolina Low Country*. Baltimore: Johns Hopkins University Press, 1940.

Christman, Henry. "Iona Island and the Fruit Growers' Convention of 1864." *New York History* 48 (1967): 332–51.

Clark, F. *Regulation versus Prohibition*. Lowell, Mass., 1866. Copy in the library of California State University, Fresno.

Clayton, W. W. *History of Steuben County, N.Y.* Philadelphia: Lewis, Peck, 1879.

Cleland, Robert Glass. *The Cattle on a Thousand Hills*. San Marino, Calif.: Huntington Library, 1941.

Cobbs, Hamner. "Geography of the Vine and Olive Company." *Alabama Review* 14 (April 1961): 83–97.

Coleman, Kenneth. *Colonial Georgia: A History*. New York: Charles Scribner's Sons, 1976.

Copeland, Pamela C., and Richard K. Macmaster. *The Five George Masons*. Charlottesville: University Press of Virginia, 1975.

Coulter, E. Merton, and Albert B. Saye. *A List of the Early Settlers of Georgia*. Athens, Ga.: University of Georgia Press, 1949.

Cronise, Titus Fey. *The Natural Wealth of California*. San Francisco: H. H. Bancroft, 1868.

Dabney, Virginius. *Dry Messiah: The Life of Bishop Cannon*. New York: Knopf, 1949.

Dakin, Susanna Bryant. *A Scotch Paisano in Old Los Angeles: Hugo Reid's Life in California, 1832–1852, Derived from his Correspondence*. Berkeley: University of California Press, 1939.

Dale, Harrison Clifford, ed. *The Ashley-Smith Explorations.* 1918. Rev. ed. Glendale, Calif.: Arthur H. Clark, 1941.

Dallett, F. J. "John Leacock." *Pennsylvania Magazine of History and Biography* 78 (1954): 456–75.

Dallidet, Louis Pasqual. *The Diaries of Louis Pasqual Dallidet, 1882–1884.* Ed. Patrick and Eleanor Brown. San Luis Obispo, Calif.: San Luis Obispo County Historical Society, n.d.

Danckaerts, Jasper. *Journal, 1679–1680.* Ed. Bartlett Burleigh James and J. Franklin Jameson. 2 vols. New York: Charles Scribner's Sons, 1913.

Davis, Nora Marshall. "The French Settlement at New Bordeaux." *Transactions of the Huguenot Society of South Carolina,* no. 56 (1951): 28–57.

Davis, William Heath. *Seventy-Five Years in California.* 1929. Ed. Harold A. Small. San Francisco: J. Howell Books, 1967.

Davis, W. W. H. *El Gringo, or New Mexico and Her People.* Santa Fe: Rydal Press, 1938.

Dawson, John Charles. *Lakanal the Regicide.* University, Ala.: University of Alabama Press, 1948.

De Brahm, John William. *History of the Province of Georgia.* Wormsloe, Ga. Privately printed: George Wymberley-Jones, 1849.

———. *Report of the General Survey in the Southern District of North America.* Ed. Louis De Vorsey, Jr. Columbia, S.C.: University of South Carolina Press, 1971.

De Caradeuc, Achille. *Grape Culture and Winemaking in the South.* Augusta, Ga.: D. Redmond, 1858.

De Chambrun, Clara Longworth. *The Making of Nicholas Longworth.* New York: R. Long & R. R. Smith, 1933.

Denniston, Goldsmith. "Grape Culture in Steuben County." In *Transactions of the New York State Agricultural Society, 1864.* Albany, N.Y., 1865.

Deutschbein, Antoine. "Warsaw Wine." In Claude Morny, ed., *A Wine and Food Bedside Book.* London: International Wine and Food Publishing Co., 1972.

Dewey, H. T. *H. T. Dewey and Sons Co., Pure American Wines.* New York, n.d. [c. 1890].

Dixon, William Hepworth. *William Penn.* London: Chapman & Hall, 1872.

Doggett, Carita. *Dr. Andrew Turnbull and the New Smyrna Colony.* [Jacksonville, Fla.?]: Drew Press, 1919.

Dossie, Robert. *Memoirs of Agriculture.* 3 vols. London: J. Nourse, 1768–82.

Douglas County Bicentennial Commission. *Douglas County Historic Building Survey—A Photo Sampler.* [Lawrence, Kans., 1976].

Downs, John, ed. *History of Chautauqua County, New York.* 3 vols. New York: American Historical Society, 1921.

Drayton, John. *A View of South-Carolina.* Charleston: W. P. Young, 1802.

Duden, Gottfried. *Bericht über eine Reise nach den Westlichen Staaten Nordamerikas.* Elberfeld: S. Lucas, 1829.

Duflot de Mofras, Eugène. *Travels on the Pacific Coast.* Ed. Marguerite Eyer Wilbur. 2 vols. Santa Ana, Calif.: Fine Art Press, 1937.

Dufour, John James. *The American Vine-Dresser's Guide.* Cincinnati: S. J. Browne, 1826.

Dufour, Perret. *The Swiss Settlement of Switzerland County, Indiana.* Ed. Harlow Lindley. Indianapolis: Indiana Historical Commission, 1925.

Duhaut-Cilly, Auguste Bernard. "Duhaut-Cilly's Account of California in the Years 1827–8." *California Historical Society Quarterly* 8 (1929): 131–66, 214–50, 306–36.

Durand de Dauphiné. *A Huguenot Exile in Virginia.* Ed. Gilbert Chinard. New York: Press of the Pioneers, 1934.

"Egg Harbor City Wineries." *Proceedings of the New Jersey Historical Society* 71 (1953): 295–97.

Egmont, John Perceval, 1st earl of. *Diary.* In *Manuscripts of the Earl of Egmont.* 3 vols. London: Historical Manuscripts Commission, 1920–23.

Eliot, Jared. *Essays upon Field Husbandry in New England.* Ed. Harry Carman and Rexford Tugwell. New York: Columbia University Press, 1934.

Emory, William H. *Notes of a Military Reconnoissance from Fort Leavenworth, in Missouri, to San Diego, in California.* Senate Executive Documents, no. 7. 30th Cong., 1st sess. Washington, D.C.: Wendell & Van Benthuysen, 1848.

———. *Report on the United States and Mexican Boundary Survey.* Executive Documents, no. 108. 34th Cong., 1st sess. 2 vols. Washington, D.C.: A. O. P. Nicholson, 1857.

Engelhardt, Zephyrin. *Missions and Missionaries of California.* 4 vols. San Francisco: James H. Barry, 1908–15.

Engelmann, George. *The Botanical Works of the Late George Engelmann.* Ed. William Trelease and Asa Gray. Cambridge, Mass.: J. Wilson & Son, 1887.

Faust, Albert Bernhardt. *The German Element in the United States.* 2 vols. Boston: Houghton Mifflin, 1909.

Fernald, M. L. "Notes on the Plants of Wineland the Good." *Rhodora* 12 (1910): 17–38.

Field, S. S. *The American Drink Book.* New York: Farrar, Straus & Young, 1953.

Fischer, LeRoy H. "The Fairchild Winery." *Chronicles of Oklahoma* 55 (Summer 1977): 135–56.

Fisher, S. I. *Observations on the Character and Culture of the European Vine, during a Residence of Five Years in the Vine-Growing Districts of France, Italy, and Switzerland.* Philadelphia: Key & Biddle, 1834.

Flagg, William J. *Three Seasons in European Vineyards.* New York: Harper & Brothers, 1869.

———. "Wine in America." *Harper's Magazine* 41 (June 1870): 106–14.

Fletcher, S. W. "A History of Fruit Growing in Virginia." In *Proceedings of the 37th Annual Meeting of the Virginia Horticultural Society.* Staunton, Va., 1932.

Flint, Timothy. *Recollections of the Last Ten Years.* Boston: Cummings, Hilliard, 1826.

Fontaine, John. *The Journal of John Fontaine.* Ed. Edward Porter Alexander. Williamsburg, Va.: Colonial Williamsburg Foundation, 1972.

Force, Peter, ed. *Tracts Relating Principally to the Origin, Settlement, and Progress of the Colonies in North America.* 4 vols. Washington, D.C.: P. Force, 1836–46.

Forrest, Earle R. *Missions and Pueblos of the Old Southwest.* 2 vols. Cleveland: Arthur H. Clark, 1929.

Franklin, Benjamin. *The Papers of Benjamin Franklin.* Ed. Leonard W. Labaree, Whitfield J. Bell, Ralph L. Ketcham, and William B. Willcox. 26 vols. New Haven: Yale University Press, 1959–.

Fredericksen, Paul. *The Authentic Haraszthy Story.* San Francisco [1947]. Reprinted from *Wines and Vines* 28 (1947).

Fries, Adelaide L., Douglas L. Rights, Minnie J. Smith et al., eds. *Records of the Moravians in North Carolina.* 11 vols. Raleigh, N.C.: State Department of History and Archives, 1922–69.

Friis, Leo J. *John Frohling: Vintner and City Founder.* Anaheim, Calif.: Mother Colony Household, 1976.

Furth, Jacob. "Sketch of Isidor Bush." *Missouri Historical Society Collections* 4 (1912–23): 303–8.

Gahn, Bessie Wilmarth. "Major John Adlum of Rock Creek." *Records of the Columbia Historical Society* 39 (1939): 127–39.

Gardien, Kent. "The Splendid Fools: Philadelphia Origins of Alabama's Vine and Olive Colony." *Pennsylvania Magazine of History and Biography* 104 (October 1980): 491–507.

Gardner, M. W., and William B. Hewitt. *Pierce's Disease of the Grapevine: The Anaheim Disease and the California Vine Disease.* Berkeley and Davis: University of California, Department of Plant Pathology, 1974.

Garlick, Richard Cecil. *Philip Mazzei, Friend of Jefferson.* Baltimore: Johns Hopkins University Press, 1933.

Gates, Paul W. *California Ranchos and Farms, 1846–1862.* Madison: State Historical Society of Wisconsin, 1967.

Geiger, Maynard. *Franciscan Missionaries in Hispanic California, 1769–1848.* San Marino, Calif.: Huntington Library, 1969.

Georgia. *Colonial Records of Georgia.* Ed. Alan D. Candler. 26 vols. Atlanta: C. P. Byrd, State Printer, 1904–16.

Gibson, David Joseph. "The Development of the Livermore Valley Wine District." M.A. thesis, University of California, Davis, 1969.

Giordano, Frank. *Texas Wines and Wineries.* Austin: Texas Monthly Press, 1984.

Glover, Thomas. "An Account of Virginia." In *Philosophical Transactions of the Royal Society,* vol. 11. 1676. Reprint. Oxford: B. H. Blackwell, 1904.

Gohdes, Clarence. *Scuppernong: North Carolina's Grape and Its Wines.* Durham, N.C.: Duke University Press, 1982.

Gordon, Elizabeth Putnam. *Women Torch-Bearers.* Evanston, Ill.: National Woman's Christian Temperance Union Publishing House, 1924.

Gray, Lewis Cecil. *History of Agriculture in the Southern United States to 1860.* 2 vols. Washington, D.C.: Carnegie Institution of Washington, 1933.

Grayson, William John. "Autobiography of William John Grayson." *South Carolina Historical Magazine* 49 (1948): 88–103.

Great Exhibition, London. *Official Descriptive and Illustrated Catalogue of the Great Exhibition.* 3 vols. London: Spicer Brothers, 1851.

Gregg, Elizabeth. "The History of the Famous Stanford Ranch." *Overland Monthly* 52 (October 1908): 334–38.

Gregg, Josiah. *The Commerce of the Prairies.* Ed. Milo Quaife. Chicago: R. R. Donnelly & Sons, 1926.

Gregg, Thomas. *History of Hancock County, Illinois.* Chicago: C. C. Chapman, 1880.

Griffin, John. "A Doctor Comes to California." *California Historical Society Quarterly* 21 (December 1942): 193–224.

Hackett, Charles W., ed. *Historical Documents Relating to New Mexico, Nueve Vizcaya, and Approaches Thereto, to 1773.* 3 vols. Washington, D.C.: Carnegie Institution of Washington, 1923–37.

Hakluyt, Richard. *Divers Voyages Touching the Discovery of America and the Islands Adjacent.* 1582. Ed. John Winter Jones. London: Hakluyt Society, 1850.

———. *The Principal Navigations, Voyages, Traffiques, and Discoveries of the English Nation.* 1589. Reprint. 12 vols. Glasgow: J. MacLehose & Sons, 1903–5.

Hamor, Ralph. *A True Discourse of the Present State of Virginia.* 1615. Reprint. Richmond, Va.: Virginia State Library, 1957.

Haraszthy, Agoston. *Grape Culture, Wines, and Wine-Making, with Notes upon Agriculture and Horticulture.* New York: Harper & Brothers, 1862.

———. "Report on Grapes and Wines of California." In *Transactions of the California State Agricultural Society, 1858,* pp. 311–29. Sacramento: State Printer, 1859.

———. "Wine-Making in California." *Harper's Magazine* 29 (June 1864): 22–30.

Haraszthy, Arpad. "Early Viticulture in Sonoma." In *Sonoma County and Russian River Valley Illustrated.* San Francisco: Bell & Heymans, 1888.

———. "Wine-Making in California." *Overland Monthly* 7 (1871): 489–97; 8 (1872): 34–41, 105–9, 393–98.

Harriot, Thomas. *Briefe and True Report of the New Found Land of Virginia.* 1588. In Hakluyt, *Principal Navigations,* 8: 348–74.

Harris, J. McArthur, Jr. "A Wissahickon Anthology, IV." *Germantown Crier* 34 (1982): 80–82.

Harrison, Brian. *Drink and the Victorians.* London: Faber & Faber, 1971.

Harrison, Fairfax. *Landmarks of Old Prince William.* 2 vols. Richmond, Va.: Privately printed, 1924.

Haskell, George. *A Narrative of the Life, Experience, and Work of an American Citizen.* Ipswich, Mass.: Chronicle Publishing, 1896.

Haynes, Irene W. *Ghost Wineries of Napa Valley.* San Francisco: Sally Taylor & Friends, 1980.

Hedrick, Ulysses Prentice. *Grapes and Wines from Home Vineyards.* New York: Oxford University Press, 1945.

———. *The Grapes of New York.* Albany, N.Y.: J. B. Lyon, 1908.

———. *History of Horticulture in America to 1860.* New York: Oxford University Press, 1950.

———. *Manual of American Grape-Growing.* 1919. Rev. ed. New York: Macmillan, 1924.

Heintz, William F. "The Role of Chinese Labor in Viticulture and Wine-Making in Nineteenth-Century California." M.A. thesis, California State University, Sonoma, 1977.

Hening, William Waller, ed. *The Statutes at Large: Being a Collection of All the Laws of Virginia.* 13 vols. Richmond, Va.: Samuel Pleasants, Jr., Printer to the Commonwealth, 1819–23.

Hewes, Leslie. "Tontitown: Ozark Vineyard Center." *Economic Geography* 29 (1953): 125–43.

Hilgard, Eugene. "Plain Talk to the Winemen." *San Francisco Examiner,* 8 August 1889.

Hilldrup, Robert. "A Campaign to Promote the Prosperity of Colonial Virginia." *Virginia Magazine of History and Biography* 67 (1959): 410–28.

Hine, Robert V. *California's Utopian Colonies.* New Haven: Yale University Press, 1965.

Hinkle, Richard Paul. "The Wines and the Mystics of Fantastic Fountaingrove." *Redwood Rancher* 34 (July 1979): 20–24.

Hirsch, Arthur H. *The Huguenots of Colonial South Carolina.* Durham, N.C.: Duke University Press, 1928.

History of Franklin, Jefferson, Washington, Crawford and Gasconade Counties. Chicago: Goodspeed Publishing, 1888.

History of San Luis Obispo County, California. Oakland: Thompson & West, 1883.

Hittell, John S. *The Resources of California.* San Francisco: A. Roman, 1863.

Hobart, Alice Tisdale. *The Cup and the Sword*. Indianapolis: Bobbs-Merrill, 1942.

Holland, James W. "The Beginning of Public Agricultural Experimentation in America: The Trustees' Garden in Georgia." *Agricultural History* 12 (1938): 271–98.

Holmes, A. "Memoir of the French Protestants Who Settled at Oxford, Massachusetts, A.D. 1686." Collections of the Massachusetts Historical Society, 3d ser., vol. 2 (1830): 1–83.

Hooker, H. D. "George Husmann." *Missouri Historical Review* 23 (1929): 353–60.

Hoover, Herbert. *Memoirs, 1920–1933*. New York: Macmillan, 1952.

Howell, George Coes. *The Case of Whiskey*. Altadena, Calif.: G. C. Howell, 1928.

Hubbard, William. *General History of New England from the Discovery to MDCLXXX*. Collections of the Massachusetts Historical Society, 2d ser., vols. 5–6 (1815).

Hudgins, Bert. "The South Bass Island Community (Put-in-Bay)." *Economic Geography* 19 (1943): 16–36.

Hughes, John T. *Doniphan's Expedition*. 1843. Reprinted in W. E. Connelly, *Doniphan's Expedition and the Conquest of New Mexico and California*. Topeka, Kans.: The Author, 1907.

Huntington, George C. "Historical Sketch of Kelley's Island." *Fire Lands Pioneer* 4 (June 1863): 45–49.

Husmann, George. *American Grape Growing and Wine Making*. New York: Orange, Judd, 1880. 4th ed. 1896.

———. *The Cultivation of the Native Grape, and Manufacture of American Wines*. New York: G. E. & F. W. Woodward, 1866.

———. "Essay on the Culture of the Grape in Missouri." In St. Louis Agricultural and Mechanical Association, *Report* of Fourth Annual Fair. St. Louis, 1859.

———. *An Essay on the Culture of the Grape in the Great West*. Hermann, Mo.: C. W. Kielman, 1863.

———. *Grape Culture and Wine-Making in California: A Practical Manual for the Grape-Grower and Wine-Maker*. San Francisco: Payot, Upham, 1888.

Husmann, George C. "Viticulture of Napa County." In Tom Gregory et al., *History of Solano and Napa Counties*, pp. 148–49. Los Angeles: Historic Record Co., 1912.

Hutton, Isaac G. *The Vigneron: An Essay on the Culture of the Grape and the Making of Wine*. Washington, D.C.: The Author, 1827.

Hyatt, Thomas Hart. *Hyatt's Hand-Book of Grape Culture*. San Francisco: H. H. Bancroft, 1867.

Illustrated History of Los Angeles County, California. Chicago: Lewis Publishing, 1889.

Illustrated History of Sonoma County. Chicago: Lewis Publishing, 1889.

International Congress of Viticulture. *Official Report*. San Francisco, 1915.

Italian Swiss Colony. *Italian Swiss Colony, Growers and Producers of Choice California Wines*. [San Francisco? c. 1910?].

———. *Sixth Annual Report, 1887*. San Francisco, 1887.

Jacobs, Julius. "California's Pioneer Wine Families." *California Historical Quarterly* 54 (Summer 1975): 139–74.

Jefferson, Thomas. *The Family Letters of Thomas Jefferson*. Ed. E. M. Betts and J. A. Bear, Jr. Columbia, Mo.: University of Missouri Press, 1966.

———. *The Papers of Thomas Jefferson*. Ed. Julian P. Boyd and Charles T. Cullen. 22 vols. Princeton: Princeton University Press, 1950–.

———. *Writings of Thomas Jefferson*. Ed. Andrew A. Lipscomb and Albert Ellery Bergh. 20 vols. Washington, D.C.: Thomas Jefferson Memorial Association, 1903.

Jessop, George H. *Judge Lynch: A Tale of the California Vineyards*. Chicago: Belford, Clarke, 1889.

Johnson, Cecil. *British West Florida, 1763–1783*. New Haven: Yale University Press, 1943.

Johnson, Crisfield. *History of Cuyahoga County, Ohio*. [Philadelphia]: D. W. Ensign, 1879.

Johnson, Stephen William. *Rural Economy*. New Brunswick, N.J.: W. Elliot for I. Riley, New York, 1806.

Johnston, Edith D. "Dr. William Houston, Botanist." *Georgia Historical Quarterly* 25 (1941): 325–39.

Jones, Charles C. *The Dead Towns of Georgia*. Savannah, Ga.: Savannah Morning News Steam Printing House, 1878.

Jones, Howard Mumford. *America and French Culture, 1750–1848*. Chapel Hill: University of North Carolina Press, 1927.

Jones, Hugh. *The Present State of Virginia*. Ed. Richard L. Morton. Chapel Hill: University of North Carolina Press, 1956.

Jones, Idwal. *Vines in the Sun.* New York: William Morrow, 1949.

Jordan, Terry G. *German Seed in Texas Soil: Immigrant Farmers in Nineteenth-Century Texas.* Austin: University of Texas Press, 1966.

Jore, Léonce. "John Louis Vignes of Bordeaux, Pioneer of California Viticulture." *Southern California Historical Society Quarterly* 45 (1963): 289–303.

Kagan, Paul. *New World Utopias.* New York: Penguin Books, 1975.

Kansas. State Board of Agriculture. *Transactions.* Topeka, 1873–75.

———. Kansas State College Agricultural Experiment Station. Bulletin no. 14, Topeka, 1891; no. 28, Topeka, 1892; no. 44, Manhattan, 1894.

Kansas State Horticultural Society. *How to Grow and Use the Grape in Kansas.* Compiled and revised by William H. Barnes. [Topeka], 1901.

———. *Transactions.* Topeka, 1872–73.

Kansas State Temperance Union. *Prohibition in Kansas: Facts, Not Opinions.* Topeka: C. B. Hamilton & Son, 1890.

Kaplan, Justin. *Mr. Clemens and Mark Twain.* New York: Simon & Schuster, 1966.

Kent, Donald H., and Mearle H. Deardorff. "John Adlum on the Allegheny: Memoirs for the Year 1794." *Pennsylvania Magazine for History and Biography* 84 (1960): 265–324, 435–80.

Kingsbury, Susan M., ed. *The Records of the Virginia Company of London.* 4 vols. Washington, D.C.: GPO, 1906–35.

Kipling, Rudyard. *From Sea to Sea.* 2 vols. London: Macmillan, 1900.

Kobler, John. *Ardent Spirits: The Rise and Fall of Prohibition.* New York: G. P. Putnam's Sons, 1973.

Koerner, Gustave. *Memoirs, 1809–1896.* Ed. T. J. McCormack. 2 vols. Cedar Rapids, Iowa: Torch Press, 1909.

Kotzebue, Otto von. *A New Voyage round the World in the Years 1823, 24, 25, and 26.* 2 vols. London: H. Colburn & R. Bentley, 1830.

Kroeger, Henry. "Early History of Anaheim as Related by a Colonist." *Anaheim Gazette,* 14 September 1932.

Krout, John Allen. *The Origins of Prohibition.* New York: Knopf, 1925.

Lake, Edward R. "The Grape in Oregon." Oregon Agricultural Experiment Station Bulletin no. 66 ([Corvallis], 1901).

Landauer, Bella C. *Some Alcoholic Americana; from the Collection of Bella C. Landauer.* New York: Privately printed, 1932.

Lane, Mills, ed. *General Oglethorpe's Georgia.* 2 vols. Savannah: Beehive Press, 1975.

Langsdorff, Georg. *Narrative of the Rezanov Voyage to Nueva California in 1806.* Trans. Thomas C. Russell. San Francisco: T. C. Russell, 1927.

Laurens, Caroline Olivia. "Journal of a Visit to Greenville from Charleston in the Summer of 1825." *South Carolina Historical Magazine* 72 (1971): 164–73, 220–33.

Laurens, Henry. *The Papers of Henry Laurens.* Ed. Philip M. Hamer, George C. Rogers, David R. Chesnutt et al. 10 vols. Columbia: University of South Carolina Press, 1968–85.

Lawrence, R. de Treville, Sr., ed. *Jefferson and Wine.* The Plains, Va.: Vinifera Wine Growers Association, 1976.

Lawson, John. *A New Voyage to Carolina.* Ed. H. T. Lefler. Chapel Hill: University of North Carolina Press, 1967.

Layne, J. Gregg. "Annals of Los Angeles." *California Historical Society Quarterly* 13 (1934): 195–234, 301–54.

Learned, Marion D. *The Life of Francis Daniel Pastorius.* Philadelphia: W. J. Campbell, 1908.

Leggett, Herbert B. *Early History of Wine Production in California.* San Francisco: Wine Institute, 1941.

Lévy, Daniel. *Les Français en Californie.* San Francisco: Grégoire, Tauzy, 1884.

Lewis, Carolyn Baker. "Cultural Conservatism and Pioneer Florida Viticulture." *Agricultural History* 53 (1979): 622–36.

Lewis, Clifford M., and Albert J. Loomie, eds. *The Spanish Jesuit Mission in Virginia, 1570–1572.* Chapel Hill: University of North Carolina Press, 1953.

Lewis, Henry. *Valley of the Mississippi Illustrated.* 1854. Reprint. St. Paul: Minnesota Historical Society, 1967.

Lewis, Meriwether, and William Clark. *Original Journals of the Lewis and Clark Expedition, 1804–1806.* Ed. Reuben Gold Thwaites. 8 vols. New York: Dodd, Mead, 1904–5.

Lindley, Harlow, ed. *Indiana as Seen by Early Travellers.* Indianapolis: Indiana Historical Commission, 1916.

Lindley, Walter, and J. P. Widney. *California of the South.* New York: D. Appleton, 1888.

Lockwood, Alice B. *Gardens of Colony and State.* 2 vols. New York: Charles Scribner's Sons, 1931–34.

Longworth, Nicholas. "The Grape and Manufacture of Wine." In Hamilton County Agricultural Society, *Western Agriculturist and Practical Farmer's Guide.* Cincinnati: Robinson & Fairbank, 1830.

Longworth's Wine House. Cincinnati: Longworth, n.d. [c. 1864].

Lord, Eliot, John J. D. Trenor, and Samuel J. Barrows. *The Italian in America.* New York: B. F. Buck, 1906.

Loyer, Fernand, and Charles Beaudreau. *Le Guide Français de Los Angeles et du sud de la Californie.* Los Angeles: Franco American Publishing, 1932.

Lyman, George D. *John Marsh, Pioneer.* New York: Charles Scribner's Sons, 1930.

Lyon, Anne Bozeman. "The Buonapartists in Alabama." *Gulf States Historical Magazine* 1 (1902–3): 325–36.

McArthur, Mildred Yorba. *Anaheim: "The Mother Colony."* Los Angeles: Ward Ritchie Press, 1959.

McClary, Ben H., and LeRoy P. Graf. "'Vineland' in Tennessee, 1852: The Journal of Rosine Parmentier." *East Tennessee Historical Society Publications,* no. 31 (1959): 95–111.

McConnell, Joseph A., Jr. "The Stanford Vina Ranch." M.A. thesis, Stanford University, 1961.

McCormick, Mildred B. "A Land of Corn and Wine." *Springhouse Magazine* 2 (May–June 1985): 38–39.

McCormick, R. P. "The Royal Society, the Grape, and New Jersey." *Proceedings of the New Jersey Historical Society* 81 (1963): 75–84.

McElrath, Clifford. *On Santa Cruz Island.* Los Angeles: Dawson's Book Shop, 1967.

McGinty, Brian. *Haraszthy at the Mint.* Famous California Trials, no. 10. Los Angeles: Dawson's Book Shop, 1975.

McGrew, John R. "The 'Alexander' Grape." *American Wine Society Journal* 8 (1976): 19–21.

———. "Black Rot." *American Wine Society Journal* 9 (1977): 3–5.

———. "A Brief History of Grapes and Wine in Ohio to 1865." *American Wine Society Journal* 16 (1984): 38–41.

———. "Brief History of Winemaking in Maryland." *American Wine Society Journal* 9 (1977): 60–62.

———. "An Historical View of Early-Day Winemaking." *Wines and Vines* 57 (1976): 26–28, 43.

———. "A History of American Grape Varieties before 1900." *American Wine Society Journal* 14 (1982): 3–5.

———. *A Review of the Origin of Hybrid Grape Varieties.* [Ithaca, N.Y.: American Wine Society.] Special Bulletin. February 1971.

———. "A Review of the Origin of Interspecific Hybrid Grape Varieties." American Wine Society Manual no. 10. Royal Oak, Mich.: American Wine Society, 1981.

Mackay, Alexander. *The Western World, or Travels in the United States in 1846–1847.* 3d ed. 2 vols. Philadelphia: Lea & Blanchard, 1850.

McKee, Irving. "The Beginnings of California Winegrowing." *Historical Society of Southern California Quarterly* 29 (March 1947): 59–71.

———. "Early California Wine Growers." *California, Magazine of the Pacific* 37 (September 1947): 34–37.

———. "George West: Pioneer Wine Grower of San Joaquin County." *California, Magazine of the Pacific* 44 (September 1954): 17–18.

———. "Historic Alameda County Wine Growers." *California, Magazine of the Pacific* 43 (September 1953): 20–23.

———. "Historic Fresno County Wine Growers." *California, Magazine of the Pacific* 42 (September 1952): 12–13, 23.

———. "Historic Wine Growers of Santa Clara County." *California, Magazine of the Pacific* 40 (September 1950): 14–15, 32–34.

———. "Jean Paul [*sic*] Vignes, California's First Professional Winegrower." *Agricultural History* 22 (July 1948): 176–80.

———. "The Oldest Names in California Winegrowing." *California, Magazine of the Pacific* 41 (September 1951): 17, 34.

————. "Three Wine-Growing Senators." *California, Magazine of the Pacific* 37 (September 1947): 15, 28–29.

MacMahon, Bernard. *The American Gardener's Calendar.* Philadelphia: B. Graves, 1806.

McMurtrie, William. *Report upon the Statistics of Grape Culture and Wine Production in the United States for 1880.* U.S. Department of Agriculture Special Report no. 36. Washington, D.C.: GPO, 1881.

Marambaud, Pierre. *William Byrd of Westover, 1674–1744.* Charlottesville: University Press of Virginia, 1971.

Maryland Historical Society. *Archives of Maryland.* Vol. 14. Ed. William Hand Browne. Baltimore: Maryland Historical Society, 1895.

Massachusetts. State Board of Agriculture. *Fifth Annual Report of the Secretary, Massachusetts Board of Agriculture.* Boston, 1858.

Mastro-Valerio, Allessandro. "Italians." In U.S. Industrial Commission, *Reports,* vol. 15. Washington, D.C.: GPO, 1901.

Mathews, John L. "Tontitown." *Everybody's* 20 (January 1909): 3–13.

Mayo, Bernard. *Henry Clay.* Boston: Houghton Mifflin, 1937.

Mazzei, Philip. *Memoirs, 1730–1816.* Trans. Howard R. Marraro. New York: Columbia University Press, 1942.

————. *My Life and Wanderings.* Trans. S. Eugene Scalia. Ed. Margherita Marchione. Morristown, N.J.: American Institute of Italian Studies, 1980.

————. *Researches on the United States.* Trans. Constance D. Sherman. Charlottesville: University Press of Virginia, 1976.

Mease, James, ed. *Domestic Encyclopaedia.* 1st American ed. 5 vols. Philadelphia: William Young Birch & Abraham Small, 1803–4.

Meers, John. "The California Wine and Grape Industry and Prohibition." *California Historical Quarterly* 46 (1967): 19–32.

Melish, John. *Travels through the United States of America in the Years 1806 and 1807, and 1809, 1810, and 1811.* 2 vols. Philadelphia: The Author, 1812.

A Memorial on the Practicability of Growing Vineyards in the State of South Carolina. Charleston: W. P. Young & T. C. Cox, 1798.

Menefee, C. A. *Historical and Descriptive Sketch Book of Napa, Sonoma, Lake and Mendocino.* Napa, Calif.: Reporter Publishing House, 1873.

Michaux, François André. *Travels to the Westward of the Allegany Mountains.* London: B. Crosby, 1805.

Michel, Francis Louis. "The Journey of Francis Louis Michel." *Virginia Magazine of History and Biography* 24 (1916): 1–43, 113–41, 275–303.

Millardet, Alexis. "Traitement du mildiou et du rot." *Journal d'Agriculture Pratique* 2 (1885): 513–16, 707–10.

Miller, Mark. *Wine—A Gentleman's Game.* New York: Harper & Row, 1984.

Minnesota Grape Growers Association. *Growing Grapes in Minnesota.* [Edina, Minn.?], 1978.

Mittelberger, Gottlieb. *Journey to Pennsylvania.* Ed. and trans. Oscar Handlin and John Clive. Cambridge, Mass.: Harvard University Press, 1960.

Modjeska, Helena. *Memories and Impressions.* New York: Macmillan, 1910.

Montgomery, Sir Robert. "Discourse concerning the Designed Establishment of a New Colony." London, 1717. In Peter Force, ed., *Tracts,* 1, no. 7.

Moore, Francis. *A Voyage to Georgia.* London, 1744. In Trevor R. Reese, *Our First Visit in America: Early Reports from the Colony of Georgia, 1732–1740.* Savannah: Beehive Press, 1974.

Moore, John Hammond. *Albemarle, Jefferson's County, 1727–1976.* Charlottesville: University Press of Virginia, 1976.

Morellet, Abbé André. *Mémoires de l'abbé Morellet . . . sur le dix-huitième siècle et sur la revolution.* 2 vols. Paris: Baudouin frères, 1823.

Morgan, Edmund S. "The First American Boom." *William and Mary Quarterly.* 3d ser. 28 (1971): 169–98.

Morison, Samuel Eliot. *Builders of the Bay Colony.* Boston: Houghton Mifflin, 1930.

————. *The European Discovery of America: The Northern Voyages,* A.D. *500–1600.* New York: Oxford University Press, 1971.

————, ed. *Journals and Other Documents on the Life and Voyages of Christopher Columbus.* New York: Heritage Press, 1963.

Morris, George Howell. "Rise of the Grape and Wine Industry in Naples Valley during the Nineteenth Century." M.A. thesis, Syracuse University, 1955.

Morrison, Paul Cross. "Viticulture in Ohio." *Economic Geography* 12 (1936): 71–85.

Morrow, Dwight W., Jr. "The American Impressions of a French Botanist." *Agricultural History* 34 (1960): 71–76.

Muench, Julius T. "A Sketch of the Life and Work of Friedrich Muench." *Missouri Historical Society Collections* 3 (1908): 132–44.

Munson, T. V. *Foundations of American Grape Culture.* Denison, Tex.: T. V. Munson & Son, 1909.

Muscatine, Doris, Maynard A. Amerine, and Bob Thompson, eds. *The University of California / Sotheby Book of California Wine.* Berkeley: University of California Press; London: Sotheby Publications, 1984.

Myers, Albert C., ed. *Narratives of Early Pennsylvania, West New Jersey, and Delaware.* New York: Charles Scribner's Sons, 1912.

Near, Irvin W. *A History of Steuben County, New York.* Chicago: Lewis Publishing, 1911.

Newmark, Harris. *Sixty Years in Southern California, 1853–1913.* 1916. 4th ed. Los Angeles: Zeitlin & Ver Brugge, 1970.

Newton, Janet. *Cresta Blanca and Charles Wetmore: A Founder of the California Wine Industry.* Livermore, Calif.: Livermore Heritage Guild, 1974.

Nordhoff, Charles. *The Communistic Societies of the United States.* New York: Harper & Brothers, 1875.

North Carolina. *The Colonial Records of North Carolina.* Ed. William L. Saunders. 10 vols. Raleigh, N.C.: P. M. Hale, Printer to the State, 1886–90.

North Carolina State Horticultural Society. *Report of the North Carolina State Horticultural Society.* Raleigh, N.C., 1893.

Ohio Agricultural Research and Development Center. *Proceedings, Ohio Grape-Wine Short Course, 1973.* Horticulture Department Series 401. Wooster, Ohio, 1973.

Oldmixon, John. *The British Empire in America.* 2 vols. London, 1741. Reprint. New York: A. M. Kelley, 1969.

Ordish, George. *The Great Wine Blight.* London: J. M. Dent & Sons, 1972.

Ostrander, Gilman M. *The Prohibition Movement in California, 1848–1933.* Berkeley: University of California Press, 1957.

Pachter, Marc, and Frances Wein, eds. *Abroad in America: Visitors to the New Nation, 1776–1914.* Reading, Mass.: Addison-Wesley, 1976.

Panagopoulos, E. P. "The Background of the Greek Settlers in the New Smyrna Colony." *Florida Historical Quarterly* 35 (1956): 95–115.

———. *New Smyrna: An Eighteenth-Century Greek Odyssey.* Gainesville, Fla.: University of Florida Press, 1966.

Parton, James. "Cincinnati." *Atlantic Monthly* 20 (1867): 229–46.

The Past and Present of Rock Island County, Illinois. Chicago: H. F. Kett, 1877.

Paul, J. G. D. "A Lost Copy-Book of Charles Carroll of Carrollton." *Maryland Historical Magazine* 32 (1937): 193–227.

Pauly, Thomas H. "J. Ross Browne: Wine Lobbyist and Frontier Opportunist." *California Historical Quarterly* 51 (1972): 99–116.

Pearson, C. C., and J. E. Hendricks. *Liquor and Anti-Liquor in Virginia, 1619–1919.* Durham, N.C.: Duke University Press, 1967.

Pease, V. S. "Agoston Haraszthy." In *Proceedings of the State Historical Society of Wisconsin, 1906,* pp. 224–45. Madison, 1907.

Peninou, Ernest P. *A History of the Orleans Hill Vineyard and Winery of Arpad Haraszthy and Company.* Winters, Calif.: Winters Express, 1983.

Peninou, Ernest P., and Sidney S. Greenleaf. *A Directory of California Wine Growers and Wine Makers in 1860.* Berkeley: Tamalpais Press, 1967.

———. *Winemaking in California: III. The California Wine Association.* [San Francisco?]: Porpoise Bookshop, 1954.

Penn, William. *A Letter from William Penn to the Committee of the Free Society of Traders 1683 . . . Containing a General Description of the Said Province. . . . 1683.* In Albert C. Myers, ed. *Narratives of Early Pennsylvania, West New Jersey, and Delaware.* 1912.

Pennsylvania. *Statutes at Large of Pennsylvania from 1682 to 1801.* Ed. J. B. Mitchell and Henry Flanders. 17 vols. Harrisburg: C. M. Busch, State Printer, 1896–1908.

Pickett, Albert James. *History of Alabama*. 3d ed. 2 vols. Charleston: Walker & James, 1851.

Pino, Don Pedro Bautista. *Exposición*. In *Three New Mexico Chronicles*. Trans. and ed. H. B. Carroll and J. V. Haggard. Albuquerque: Quivira Society, 1942.

Planchon, Jules-Émile. "Le Phylloxera en Europe et en Amérique, II: La Vigne et le vin aux États-Unis." *Revue des Deux Mondes*, 15 February 1874, pp. 914–43.

———. *Les Vignes américaines*. Montpellier: Camille Coulet, 1875.

Polacsek, John F. "Pop-Pop—Fizz, Fizz: A Glimpse at the Northwest Ohio Wine Industry in Years Gone By." *Northwest Ohio Quarterly* 53 (Spring 1981): 35–49.

Primm, James N. *Economic Policy in the Development of a Western State: Missouri, 1820–1860*. Cambridge, Mass.: Harvard University Press, 1954.

Prince, William. *A Short Treatise on Horticulture*. New York: T. & J. Swords, 1828.

Prince, William Robert. *A Treatise on the Vine*. New York: T. & J. Swords, 1830.

Purchas, Samuel. *Purchas His Pilgrimes*. 20 vols. Glasgow: J. MacLehose & Sons, 1905–7.

Purser, J. Elizabeth, and Lawrence J. Allen. *The Winemakers of the Pacific Northwest*. Vashon Island, Wash.: Harbor House Publishing, 1977.

Quincy, Josiah. "Journal of Josiah Quincy, Junior, 1773." *Proceedings of the Massachusetts Historical Society* 49 (1915–16): 424–81.

Quinn, D. B. *North America from Earliest Discovery to First Settlements: The Norse Voyages to 1612*. New York: Harper & Row, 1977.

Rafinesque, Constantine. "A Life of Travels." *Chronica Botanica* 8, no. 2 (1944).

———. *Medical Flora, or Manual of the Medical Botany of the United States of America*. 2 vols. Philadelphia: Samuel C. Atkinson, 1830.

Ragatz, Oswald. "Memoirs of a Sauk Swiss." *Wisconsin Magazine of History* 19 (December 1935): 182–227.

Ramsay, David. *The History of South-Carolina*. 2 vols. Charleston: David Longworth, 1809.

Raup, Hallock F. *The German Colonization of Anaheim, California*. Berkeley: University of California Press, 1932.

Ravenel, Henry William. *The Private Journal of Henry William Ravenel, 1859–1887*. Ed. Arney Robinson Childs. Columbia, S.C.: University of South Carolina Press, 1947.

Reeves, J. S. *The Napoleonic Exiles in America*. Johns Hopkins University Studies in History and Political Science, 23d ser. Baltimore, 1905.

Regnery, Dorothy F. *An Enduring Heritage: Historic Buildings of the San Francisco Peninsula*. Stanford, Calif.: Stanford University Press, 1976.

Reid, Hugo. *The Indians of Los Angeles County*. 1852. Ed. R. F. Heizer. Los Angeles: Southwest Museum, 1968.

Robinson, Alfred. *Life in California*. 1846. Reprint. Santa Barbara: Peregrine Publications, 1970.

Robson, F. T. "The Stanford Vina Ranch." In Joseph Henry Jackson, ed., *The Vine in Early California*. [San Francisco]: Book Club of California, 1955.

Rochefoucauld-Liancourt, François, Duc de la. *Travels through the United States of North America*. 2 vols. London: R. Phillips, 1799.

Rorabaugh, W. J. *The Alcoholic Republic*. New York: Oxford University Press, 1979.

Rose, Kenneth D. "San Francisco and Prohibition in 1924: Wettest in the West." *California History* 65 (1986): 285–95.

Rose, L. J., Jr. *L. J. Rose of Sunny Slope, 1827–1899*. San Marino, Calif.: Huntington Library, 1959.

Rossati, Guido. *Relazione di un viaggio d'istruzione negli Stati Uniti d'America*. Rome: Tipografia nazionale di G. Bertero, 1900.

Ruffin, Thomas. *Papers of Thomas Ruffin*. Ed. J. G. deR. Hamilton. 4 vols. Raleigh, N.C.: Edwards & Broughton, 1918–20.

Rush, Benjamin. "An Inquiry into the Effects of Spirituous Liquors on the Human Body." Boston: Thomas & Andrews, 1790.

Russell, Howard S. *Indian New England before the Mayflower*. Hanover, N.H.: University Press of New England, 1980.

St. Pierre, Louis de Mesnil de. *The Art of Planting and Cultivating the Vine*. London: Wilkie & Walter, 1772.

———. *The Great Utility of Establishing the Culture of Vines*. London, 1771.

———. *Plan for the Culture of the Vine etc. at New Bourdeaux*. London, 1771.

———. *A Proposal for the Further Encouragement of the Production of Silk, and Growing of Vines, at the Colony of New Bourdeaux.* [London] 1772.

Salley, Alexander, ed. *Narratives of Early Carolina, 1650–1708.* New York: Charles Scribner's Sons, 1911.

———. *Records in the British Public Record Office Relating to South Carolina, 1663–1690.* Atlanta: Foote & Davies, 1928–29.

Salvator, Ludwig Louis. *Los Angeles in the Sunny Seventies.* Trans. Marguerite Eyer Wilber. Los Angeles: Bruce McCallister & Jake Zeitlin, 1929.

San Francisco Mechanics' Institute. *Reports of the Annual Industrial Exhibition.* San Francisco, 1858–88.

Saul, John A. "Tree Culture, or a Sketch of Nurseries in the District of Columbia." *Records of the Columbia Historical Society* 10 (1907): 38–47.

Savelle, Max. *George Morgan, Colony Builder.* New York: Columbia University Press, 1932.

Scharf, J. T. *History of St. Louis City and County.* 2 vols. Philadelphia: L. H. Everts, 1883.

Schiavo, Giovanni E. *Philip Mazzei.* New York: Vigo Press, 1951.

Schleicher, Robert. "Grape Culture in Lewiston-Clarkston Valley." Lewiston, Idaho, and Clarkston, Wash., 1906.

Schneider, Herbert W., and George Lawton. *A Prophet and a Pilgrim.* New York: Columbia University Press, 1942.

Schoenman, Theodore. *Father of California Wine: Agoston Haraszthy.* Santa Barbara: Capra Press, 1979.

Schoepf, Johann David. *Travels in the Confederation, 1783–1784.* 2 vols. Philadelphia: W. J. Campbell, 1911.

Schoonmaker, Frank. *Frank Schoonmaker's Encyclopedia of Wine.* New York: Hastings House, 1964.

Schoonmaker, Frank, and Tom Marvel. *American Wines.* New York: Duell, Sloan & Pearce, 1941.

Schuricht, Hermann. *History of the German Element in Virginia.* 2 vols. Baltimore: T. Kroh & Sons, 1900.

Scott, Paul T. "Why Joseph Chapman Adopted California and Why California Adopted Him." *Historical Society of Southern California Quarterly* 38 (1956): 239–46.

Scull, G. D. "Biographical Notice of Doctor Daniel Coxe, of London." *Pennsylvania Magazine of History and Biography* 7 (1883): 317–37.

Serra, Junípero. *Writings.* Ed. Antonine Tibesar, O.F.M. 4 vols. Washington, D.C.: Academy of American Franciscan History, 1955–56.

Shand, P. Morton. *A Book of French Wines.* London: Jonathan Cape, 1928.

Sherer, Dick. "Finger Lakes Grape Pioneers." *Vineyard View* [Hammondsport, New York], Autumn 1983, p. 14.

Sherwood, Midge. *Days of Vintage, Years of Vision.* 2 vols. San Marino, Calif.: Orizaba Publications, 1982–87.

Shorb, J. De Barth. "Vines and Vineyards." In A. T. Hawley, ed., *The Present Condition, Growth, Progress and Advantages of Los Angeles City and County.* Los Angeles: Mirror Printing, Ruling and Binding House, 1876.

Sienkiewicz, Henry. *Western Septet: Seven Stories of the American West.* Trans. Marion Moore Coleman. Cheshire, Conn.: Cherry Hill Books, 1973.

Simpson, Sir George. *An Overland Voyage round the World, during the Years 1841 and 1842.* 2 vols. Philadelphia: Lea & Blanchard, 1847.

Smith, Ophia D. "Early Gardens and Orchards." *Bulletin of the Historical and Philosophical Society of Ohio* 7 (April 1949): 67–86.

Smith, Winston. *Days of Exile: The Story of the Vine and Olive Colony in Alabama.* Tuscaloosa, Ala.: W. B. Drake, 1967.

Smyth, S. Gordon. "Peter Legaux." *Historical Sketches* (Historical Society of Montgomery County, Pa.) 2 (1900): 92–125.

South Carolina. *The Colonial Records of South Carolina.* 13 vols. Columbia, S.C.: Historical Commission of South Carolina, 1951–.

———. *The Statutes at Large of South Carolina.* Ed. Thomas Cooper. 8 vols. Columbia, S.C.: A. S. Johnston, 1836–40.

South Carolina Historical Society. *The Shaftesbury Papers and Other Records Relating to Carolina.* Collections of the South Carolina Historical Society, vol. 5. Charleston, 1897.

Southern Vine Growers' Convention. *Proceedings of the Southern Vine Growers' Convention, Aiken, South*

Carolina, 1860. Augusta, Ga.: Steam Power Press Chronicle and Sentinel, 1860.

Spooner, Alden. *The Cultivation of American Grape Vines and Making of Wine.* Brooklyn, N.Y.: A. Spooner, 1846.

Stanton, Carey. *An Island Memoir.* Los Angeles: Santa Cruz Island Co., 1984.

Stellman, Louis J. *Sam Brannan, Builder of San Francisco.* New York: Exposition Press, 1953.

Stephens, Bascom A., ed. *Resources of Los Angeles County, California.* Los Angeles: Sprague & Rodehaver, 1887.

Stephens, Kate. *Life at Laurel Town in Anglo-Saxon Kansas.* Lawrence: Alumni Association of the University of Kansas, 1920.

Stephens, William. *Journal.* Ed. E. Merton Coulter. 2 vols. Athens, Ga.: University of Georgia Press, 1958–59.

———. *A Journal of the Proceedings in Georgia.* In *Colonial Records of Georgia.* Vol. 4 and Supplement. Atlanta: Franklin Printing and Publishing, 1906–8.

———. *A State of the Province of Georgia.* Collections of the Georgia Historical Society, vol. 2. Savannah: Printed for the Society, 1842.

Stern, Malcolm H. "New Light on the Jewish Settlement in Savannah." *American Jewish Historical Quarterly* 52 (1962–63): 169–99.

Stern, Norton B., and William Kramer. "The Wine Tycoon of Anaheim." *Western States Jewish Historical Quarterly* 9 (1977): 262–78.

Stevens, Walter B. *St. Louis.* 3 vols. Chicago and St. Louis: S. J. Clarke, 1909.

Stewart, John. "Little Italy of the Ozarks." *Missouri Life* 3 (July–August 1975): 40–45.

Stiles, Henry R. *A History of the City of Brooklyn.* 3 vols. Albany, N.Y.: J. Munsell, 1869–70.

Stockley, Tom. *Winery Trails of the Pacific Northwest.* Mercer Island, Wash.: Writing Works, 1977.

Stork, William, ed. *A Description of East-Florida with a Journal Kept by John Bartram.* 3d ed. London: W. Nicoll, 1769.

The Story of a Pantry Shelf: An Outline History of Grocery Specialities. New York: Butterick, 1925.

Strachey, William. *The Historie of Travell into Virginia Britania (1612).* Ed. L. B. Wright and Virginia Freund. London: Hakluyt Society, 1953.

Subden, R. E., and A. C. Noble. "How the Hybrids Came to Canada." *Wines and Vines* 59 (December 1978): 42–44.

Sullivan, Charles L. *Like Modern Edens: Winegrowing in Santa Clara Valley and Santa Cruz Mountains, 1798–1891.* Cupertino, Calif.: California History Center, 1982.

———. "An Historian's Account of Zinfandel in California." *Wines and Vines* 58 (February 1977): 18–20.

———. "A Viticultural Mystery Solved." *California History* 57 (Summer 1978): 114–29.

Tailfer, Patrick, Hugh Anderson, David Douglas et al. *A True and Historical Narrative of the Colony of Georgia.* 1741. Ed. Clarence L. Ver Steeg. Athens, Ga.: University of Georgia Press, 1960.

Taylor, Virginia H. *The Franco-Texan Land Company.* Austin: University of Texas Press, 1969.

Teiser, Ruth, and Catherine Harroun. *Winemaking in California.* New York: McGraw-Hill, 1983.

Thomann, Gallus. *Liquor Laws of the United States.* New York: U.S. Brewers' Association, 1885.

Thwaites, Reuben Gold, ed. *Early Western Travels, 1748–1846.* 32 vols. Cleveland: A. H. Clark, 1904–7.

A Toast to Ontario Wines. [Toronto]: Wine Council of Ontario, 1979.

Todd, Frank Morton. *The Story of the Exposition.* 5 vols. New York: G. P. Putnam's Sons, 1921.

Todd, Vincent H., ed. *Christoph von Graffenried's Account of the Founding of New Bern.* Raleigh, N.C.: Edwards & Broughton, 1920.

Traviss, Sister Mary Peter, O.P. "The Founding of Anaheim, California, 1857–1879." M.A. thesis, Catholic University of America, 1961.

Trollope, Frances. *Domestic Manners of the Americans.* 1832. 5th ed. New York: Dodd, Mead, 1927.

Trollope, Thomas Adolphus. *What I Remember.* New York: Harper & Brothers, 1888.

Trotter, Isabella. *First Impressions of the New World on Two Travellers from the Old.* London: Longman, 1859.

True, Rodney. "Early Days of the Albemarle Agricultural Society." *Annual Report of the American Historical Association, 1918,* vol. 1. Washington, D.C.: GPO, 1921.

Truman, Ben C. *Semi-Tropical California.* San Francisco: A. L. Bancroft, 1874.

Tucker, Louis Leonard. "Hiram Powers and Cincinnati." *Bulletin of the Cincinnati Historical Society* 25 (1967): 21–49.

———. "'Old Nick' Longworth: The Paradoxical Maecenas of Cincinnati." *Bulletin of the Cincinnati Historical Society* 25 (1967): 246–59.

Tutorow, Norman E. *Leland Stanford: Man of Many Careers.* Menlo Park, Calif.: Pacific Coast Publishers, 1971.

Twain, Mark. *The Autobiography of Mark Twain.* Ed. Charles Neider. New York: Harper, 1959.

Tyler, Alice Felt. *Freedom's Ferment: Phases of American Social History to 1860.* Minneapolis: University of Minnesota Press, 1944.

United Kingdom. Board of Trade. *Journals of the Commissioners for Trade and Plantations.* 14 vols. London: HMSO, 1920–38.

———. House of Lords. *The Manuscripts of the House of Lords, 1659–1697.* N.s. Vol. 2. London: HMSO, 1903.

———. Parliament. *Acts of Parliament,* 1771.

———. Parliament. *Parliamentary Papers, 1859.* Vol. 30.

———. Public Record Office. *Calendar of State Papers. Colonial Series. America and West Indies.* 44 vols. London: HMSO, 1860–.

United States. *American State Papers: Public Lands.* 8 vols. Washington, D.C.: Gales & Seaton, 1832–61.

———. *Annals of the Congress of the United States.* 42 vols. Washington, D.C.: Gales & Seaton, 1834–56.

———. Bureau of the Census. 8th Census, 1860. *Agriculture of the United States in 1860.* Washington, D.C.: GPO, 1864.

———. Bureau of the Census. 9th Census, 1870. *A Compendium of the Ninth Census (June 1, 1870).* Washington, D.C.: GPO, 1872.

———. Bureau of the Census. 11th Census, 1890. *Report on the Statistics of Agriculture in the United States.* Washington, D.C.: GPO, 1895.

———. Bureau of the Census. 12th Census, 1900. John H. Garber. "Alcoholic Beverages." In *Census Reports,* vol. 9. Washington, D.C.: GPO, 1902.

———. Bureau of the Census. 13th Census, 1910. *Agriculture 1909 and 1910.* Washington, D.C.: GPO, 1913.

———. Department of Agriculture. Botanical Division. Circular no. 3. April 1887.

———. Department of Agriculture. *List of Agricultural Societies.* Washington, D.C.: GPO, 1876.

———. Department of Agriculture. *Report of the Commissioner of Agriculture.* 1862–87. Washington, D.C.: GPO, 1863–88.

———. Department of Agriculture. *First Report of the Secretary of Agriculture, 1889.* Washington, D.C.: GPO, 1889.

———. Department of Agriculture. *Yearbook.* 1899, 1902, 1903. Washington, D.C.: GPO, 1900–1903.

———. Immigration Commission. *Reports: Immigrants in Industries.* Vols. 21, 24. Washington, D.C.: GPO, 1911.

———. Industrial Commission. *Reports.* Vol. 15. Washington, D.C.: GPO, 1901.

———. National Commission on Law Observance and Enforcement. *Reports.* Washington, D.C.: GPO, 1931.

———. Patent Office. *Report of the Commissioner of Patents.* 1845–59. Washington, D.C.: GPO, 1846–60.

———. *Statutes at Large of the United States of America, 1789–1873.* 17 vols. Washington, D.C., 1850–73.

———. Tariff Commission. *Grapes, Raisins, and Wines.* Report no. 134. 2d ser. Washington, D.C.: GPO [1939].

———. *United States Statutes at Large.* 1874–.

Vallet, Emile. *An Icarian Communist in Nauvoo.* Ed. H. Roger Grant. Springfield: Illinois State Historical Society, 1971.

Van Ravenswaay, Charles G. *The Arts and Architecture of German Settlements in Missouri.* Columbia, Mo.: University of Missouri Press, 1977.

Viala, Pierre. *Une Mission viticole en Amérique.* Montpellier: Camille Coulet, 1889.

Villard, Léonie. *La France et les États-Unis: Echanges et rencontres (1524–1800)*. Lyon: Les Editions de Lyon, 1952.

Villard, Oswald Garrison. "The 'Latin Peasants' of Belleville, Illinois." *Journal of the Illinois State Historical Society* 25 (1942): 7–20.

Virginia. General Assembly. House of Burgesses. *Journals of the House of Burgesses of Virginia*. Ed. John Pendleton Kennedy. Vol. 12. Richmond, Va.: [Virginia State Library] 1906.

———. *Legislative Journals of the Council of Colonial Virginia*. Ed. H. R. McIlwaine. 3 vols. Richmond, Va.: [Virginia State Library] 1918–19.

Volney, Constantine F. *View of the Climate and Soil of the United States of America*. London: J. Johnson, 1804.

Von Daacke, John F. "'Sparkling Catawba': Grape Growing and Wine Making in Cincinnati, 1800–1870." M.A. thesis, University of Cincinnati, 1964.

Wagner, Philip M. *American Wines and Wine-Making*. New York: Knopf, 1956.

———. *Grapes into Wine*. New York: Knopf, 1976.

———. "Wine from American Grapes." *American Mercury* 28 (1933): 360–67.

———. *A Wine-Grower's Guide*. New York: Knopf, 1955.

Wait, Frona Eunice. *Wines and Vines of California*. San Francisco, 1889. Reprint. Berkeley: Howell-North Books, 1973.

Wansey, Henry. *Henry Wansey and His American Journal, 1794*. Ed. David John Jeremy. Philadelphia: American Philosophical Society, 1970.

Warner, J. J. "Reminiscences of Early California from 1831 to 1846." *Annual Publications, Historical Society of Southern California* 7 (1907–8): 176–97.

Washington, George. *The Diaries of George Washington*. Ed. Donald Jackson and Dorothy Twohig. 6 vols. Charlottesville: University Press of Virginia, 1976–79.

———. *The Writings of George Washington*. Vol. 27. Ed. John C. Fitzpatrick. Washington, D.C.: GPO, 1938.

Watlington-Linares, Francisco. "The First American Wine." *Eastern Grape Grower and Winery News* 9 (October–November 1983): 50–52.

Waugh, Julia Nott. *Castro-Ville and Henry Castro, Empressario*. San Antonio, Tex.: Standard Printing Co., 1934.

Webb, Edith Buckland. *Indian Life at the Old Missions*. Los Angeles: Warren F. Lewis, 1952.

Weiss, Harry B. *The History of Applejack or Apple Brandy in New Jersey from Colonial Times to the Present*. Trenton: New Jersey Agricultural Society, 1954.

Weld, Charles. *A Vacation Tour in the United States and Canada*. London: Longman, 1855.

Wesley, John. *Journal*. Ed. Nehemiah Curnock. 8 vols., London: R. Culley, 1909–16.

Wetmore, Charles. *Ampelography of California*. Reprinted from *San Francisco Merchant*, 4–11 January 1884. [San Francisco, 1884].

———. *Treatise on Wine Production*. Appendix B to the *Report of the Board of State Viticultural Commissioners, 1893–94*. Sacramento: State Office, 1894.

Whitfield, Gaius, Jr. "The French Grant in Alabama." *Transactions of the Alabama Historical Society, 1899–1903* 6 (1904): 321–55.

Whiting, Lilian. *Kate Field: A Record*. Boston: Little, Brown, 1899.

Willard, T. J. *Log Cabin Days*. [Manhattan, Kans.?] 1929.

Williams, Walter, ed. *The State of Missouri*. [Columbia, Mo.]: E. W. Stephens, 1904.

Wilson, Iris. *William Wolfskill, 1798–1866: Frontier Trapper to California Ranchero*. Glendale, Calif.: Arthur J. Clark, 1965.

Wilson, John Albert. *History of Los Angeles County*. Oakland: Thompson & West, 1880.

Wine Museum of San Francisco. *Thomas Jefferson and Wine in Early America*. San Francisco: Wine Museum, 1976.

Wing, Talcott, ed. *History of Monroe County, Michigan*. New York: Munsell, 1890.

Winkler, A. J. *General Viticulture*. Berkeley: University of California Press, 1962.

Winkler, A. J., J. A. Cook, W. M. Kliewer, and L. A. Lider. *General Viticulture*. Rev. ed. Berkeley: University of California Press, 1974.

Winsor, Justin, ed. *Narrative and Critical History of America*. 8 vols. Boston: Houghton Mifflin, 1884–89.

Woodward, Carl Raymond. *The Development of Agriculture in New Jersey*. New Brunswick, N.J.: New Jersey Agricultural Experiment Station, 1927.

———. *Plantation in Yankeeland.* Chester, Conn.: Pequot Press, 1971.

Young, Alexander. *Chronicles of the First Planters of the Colony of Massachusetts Bay, from 1623 to 1636.* Boston: C. C. Little and J. Brown, 1846.

———. *Chronicles of the Pilgrim Fathers of the Colony of Plymouth from 1602 to 1625.* Boston: C. C. Little and J. Brown, 1841.

Zirkle, Conway. "Plant Hybridization and Plant Breeding in Eighteenth-Century American Agriculture." *Agricultural History* 43 (1969): 25–38.

———. "John Clayton and Our Colonial Botany." *Virginia Magazine of History and Biography* 67 (1959): 284–94.

INDEX